The Encyclopedia of American Independent Filmmaking

The Encyclopedia of American Independent Filmmaking

Vincent LoBrutto

Greenwood Press
Westport, Connecticut • London

Library of Congress Cataloging-in-Publication Data

LoBrutto, Vincent.

The encyclopedia of American independent filmmaking / Vincent LoBrutto.

   p. cm.

Includes bibliographical references and index.

ISBN 0-313-30199-9 (alk. paper)

   1. Motion pictures—Encyclopedias. 2. Independent filmmakers—United

States—Biography—Dictionaries. I. Title.

PN1993.45.L63 2002

791.43'03—dc21   2002023542

British Library Cataloguing in Publication Data is available.

Copyright © 2002 by Vincent LoBrutto

All rights reserved. No portion of this book may be
reproduced, by any process or technique, without the
express written consent of the publisher.

Library of Congress Catalog Card Number: 2002023542

ISBN: 0-313-30199-9

First published in 2002

Greenwood Press, 88 Post Road West, Westport, CT 06881

An imprint of Greenwood Publishing Group, Inc.

www.greenwood.com

Printed in the United States of America

The paper used in this book complies with the
Permanent Paper Standard issued by the National
Information Standards Organization (Z39.48–1984).

10 9 8 7 6 5 4 3 2 1

To my daughter Rebecca Morrison, the most independent person I know

Contents

Acknowledgments

For a project of this scope, there are many to thank. Everett Aison has been a constant source of support and is always there for a lively exchange of information and ideas. Susan Bennett shared her passion and in-depth knowledge of the Beat Generation. Ed Bowes generously communicated his extensive knowledge about New York independent moviemaking and talked about his work with Lizzie Borden. Gary Carey nurtured me as a writer before I had a clue; he grounded me and taught me necessary critical thinking skills to be a filmmaker and to understand the films we see. Director of photography Allen Daviau graciously provided insights and information about Los Angeles independent and experimental filmmaking. The late William K. Everson gave me a solid background in film history during my formative years. Syndicated film critic Marshall Fine presented his invaluable perspective on independent filmmaking at a "914" Film & Video Group forum where we were both participants. Jonathan Kaplan, a dedicated "914" leader, continues to stimulate my thoughts about indie film. Roy Frumkes is a never-ending source of knowledge from the trenches and as editor of *Films in Review* has given me the opportunity to express my views on independent filmmaking.

My thanks to everyone at Greenwood for their support and expertise. Thanks to Andrew Gallagher, independent filmmaker and film historian, who suggested that I was the man for this job to Alicia S. Merritt, former acquisitions editor of Popular Culture. She was the flame that started this particular fire. Thank you to my former editor Pamela Sinclair and to Eric Levy, my current editor, for their patience, good advice and professional contributions. My regards to production editor Nicole Cournoyer and copy editor Susan Badger for their expertise. Manny Kircheimer, the renowned documentarian, explained the often-misunderstood genesis of cinéma vérité filmmaking, Reeves Lehmann, chairman of the School of Visual Arts Department of Film, Video and Animation, and his director of operations Salvatore Petrosino have, as always, given me their unconditional support and guidance and continue their valuable contributions to the education of moviemakers. The professional and helpful staff at the New York Public Library for the Performing Arts Research Collection at Lincoln Center provided a wealth of resources.

My son, Alexander Morrison, is pursuing a film education; his enthusiasm and passion for making movies informed my own study. My wife, Harriet Morrison, was this book's first reader and continues to contribute her impeccable editorial taste and wise counsel to all my work. Her contributions to the entries brought clarity and depth to the manuscript. My appreciation to the entire staff at the Mount Vernon Public Library and their magnificent repository of information. Charles Reynolds schooled me in the world of classic B-movies and titles outside of the traditional film history track. The School of Visual Arts (SVA) has been my filmmaking home for over thirty years both as student and as instructor. SVA is responsible for nurturing inspiration and the opportunity to endlessly explore our art. My eternal thanks to Founder and Chairman of the Board Silas Rhodes, President David Rhodes, and Vice President Anthony Rhodes.

Jack Lorenzo Schwartz proved my theory of how early we are attracted to motion pictures as I joyously observed him watching his first film (*Babe*) when he was just six months old. I also thank little Jack for sharing his ongoing observations on all the "shows" and "videos" he sees and for an intense philosophic discussion about "Who stole Elmo's blanket" in *The Adventures of Elmo in Grouchland*. Gene Stavis, film historian extraordinaire, provided countless insights beyond the official record and answered an onslaught of inquiries with intelligence and grace. As a film student, experimental filmmaker Jud Yalkut taught me the history of experimental filmmaking and was a living example as evidenced by his innovative work with the Bolex camera.

I respectfully acknowledge four persons who passed on during the five years I worked on this project: My father, Anthony LoBrutto, bought me my first tape recorder and let me use the family 8mm camera and projector to become an independent filmmaker. My mother, Rose Lo-Brutto, stimulated my love for movie lore with stacks of *Photoplay* and other movie mags. Film director Stanley Kubrick has been a constant source of inspiration and my definition of a film artist. I respectfully acknowledge the memory of Lawrence Virgilio who perished in the World Trade Center attack on September 11, 2001. Larry was a passionate actor and a member of New York's bravest—he is missed.

I sincerely thank all of my colleagues and students past, present, and future at the School of Visual Arts and Film/Video Arts who prove to me on a daily basis that I am part of a family of filmmakers. Stephen Pizzello, editor of *American Cinematographer*, has provided a forum for me to investigate the wide world of cinematography and filmmaking; my thanks to him and his resourceful staff. My appreciation to all my brothers and sisters at American Cinema Editors and their wonderful publication *Cinemaeditor*—it provides a forum for editors to speak about a critical cinema craft. From my early days as an independent filmmaker I thank friend and actor Robert Elston who served as Harvey Keitel to my Martin Scorsese and David Mittendorf, a fearless cameraman who would do anything to get a shot—the personification of guerrilla filmmakers everywhere. Finally, my thanks to Stephen McGill, who was essential in forming the scope and content of this book and for his many contributions and entries.

Introduction

The purpose of this reference volume is to provide information, perspective, and insight into historical, technical, aesthetic, practical, fiscal, and critical aspects of independent filmmaking over the course of the twentieth century and into the new millennium.

Independent filmmaking has existed since the inception of the medium at the turn of the nineteenth century. Taken literally, an independent film is created, financed, produced, and distributed outside the commercial, corporate conglomerate structure. Using this paradigm, few filmmakers and films can stake claim to independence. The Classical Hollywood Studio System, composed of Metro-Goldwyn-Mayer, Paramount, Universal, and Warner Brothers, historically generated industry-controlled motion pictures manufactured in a factory mode from the 1920s through the 1950s. The studios employed writers, directors, producers, actors, cinematographers, designers, and sound and music personnel who contributed to the art and craft of American film. All these employees worked under a central authority that determined what films were made and how they were created. The studios funded, supervised, and distributed films that were the principal property of the moguls who owned and ran them.

Films made before the emergence of the Studio System and after its corporate transformation during the 1960s were to a great degree independent. The creation, and exhibition, of an independent motion picture often intersects with the corporate sector. Raising money to finance a film through private investors, grants, credit cards, loans, or personal savings guarantees artistic independence, but it is the rare filmmaker such as John Cassavetes or documentarian Frederick Wiseman who approaches total control over his or her work. Many have had an autonomous production company but release through a major studio. Miramax was the model of an independent company during the 1980s until they were bought by Disney in 1993. The true independents throughout film history have been the nontraditional avant-garde/experimental and non-fiction filmmakers, many who operate as self-governing artists.

The public reference point for the modern era of independent film-making is generally identified with the release of Steven Soderbergh's *sex, lies, and videotape* in 1989. This low-budget film provided an alternate, content-driven production devoid of the professional slickness and ho-mogenized presentation that previously condemned general audiences. As audiences responded to the personal, stylized, daring, inclusive, and more socially probing alternatives, the industry at large took note, and in short notice, every major studio opened an indie boutique. Eventually the independent film became a genre as much as a mode of production. Studios imitated the narrative themes and look of the independent film, in many cases spending a great deal of money to mimic the results.

At the dawn of the twenty-first century, independent film faces new challenges. Grant money has dwindled due to attacks from religious and political forces that have slashed the National Endowment for the Arts and other funds at national and local levels.

In the 1990s the star system resurfaced, and audiences went to see movie stars. The corporate industry catered to please a frighteningly younger and younger demographic. The independent film is alive and well but back on the fringes where it belongs, so it can thrive, grow, and evolve into its own mode of communication, not mutate in mainstream film. We are currently in the midst of an electronic cinema revolution. The new digital technology offers unprecedented opportunities. Short and feature films can be made at a fraction of the cost of film production. The film purist's argument about the look of film gets weaker with the advent of better DV (digital video) cameras, improving digital postprod-uction platforms, and software that can replicate film stocks; texture and properties are supported by high-definition television, DVD (digital video disk), and improving video products.

This new technology presents the independent filmmaker with a man-date to search for new ground. Just when we think we've seen it all, a visionary comes along and finds a new path. John Cassavetes, John Say-les, and Lars von Trier have proven that; others will also.

HOW TO READ AND USE THIS BOOK

In its encyclopedic format, this sourcebook can be used to inform the reader generally or to look up a particular topic of interest. It was created to cover the canvas of film history to enlighten readers to the notion that there was independent life before *sex, lies, and videotape*. The approach is not purist. With a subject of this scope the perimeters will invariably create both omissions and expansions of any definition. The intention is to examine films and filmmakers who complement the tenets of independent filmmaking. The volume is selective. Within its selectivity exist diversity and an overview. If there is a bias, it is toward the New York independent film community. New York City has long been a mecca for indie filmmakers. Whereas the mainstream industry burgeoned in Hollywood, New York has represented the training ground for the practice and philosophy of independent filmmaking. The reader is advised that venues, educational facilities, film festivals, newsletters, Web sites, and publications concerning independent filmmaking exist throughout the United States and internationally. It is the intention of this book to provide information and to inspire the reader to explore other avenues that lead from this volume.

This encyclopedia does not address the subject of electronic cinema, which requires its own space to do it justice adequately.

The Internet was indispensable in researching this book; the reader is also encouraged to explore the opportunities and valuable sources available on the Net by searching and following the plethora of organized and well-referenced links. Cyberspace has also become a viable venue for the presentation of short films and has created exhibition and distribution possibilities that deliver the indie short around the globe with relative ease. The independent film community is an extended family.

A few words about text organization. Boldface names and terms within each entry refer to entries found elsewhere in the book. Topics of primary interest to the specific entry are indicated in the *See also* suggestions immediately following the entry. At the end of many entries, selected bibliographical material in the form of books and articles is included for the interested reader. At the book's end, three appendixes—"100 Significant Independent Films"; "Winners of the Sundance Film Festival and Independent Spirit Awards"; and "Distributors of Independent Films"—provide the reader with valuable information. And finally, the bibliography contains publications of broad interest to the study of independent filmmaking.

An encyclopedia is a reference work that presents history, fact, technical and aesthetic information, and critical perspective. *The Encyclopedia of American Independent Filmmaking* is a celebration of independent film created to inspire and encourage filmmakers, aspiring, established, doers, and viewers everywhere. Independent filmmaking is an alternative to commercial entertainment and is no longer on the fringe or underground. In the information age of the twenty-first century, the dream of the pioneers has arrived—let all cinematic voices be heard.

A

above-the-line deferrals. Postponement of salary negotiated with individuals involved in above-the-line costs such as story acquisition, property rights, script development, and hiring of the producer, director and principal cast members.

Ackerman, Forrest J. Publisher, archivist. *b.* November 11, 1916. "Forry" Forrest Ackerman's enormous contribution to independent filmmaking is as publisher of *Famous Monsters of Filmland* (1958–). The magazine was standard reading for prepubescent and teenage boys in the 1950s. It featured black-and-white photos of classic horror and monster films and ran ads for a makeup kit that allowed any kid to transform into Frankenstein, Dracula, the Wolfman, or a ghoul of his or her own creation. *Famous Monsters of Filmland* influenced a generation of sci-fi and horror film directors including Steven Spielberg, **Joe Dante,** and John Landis and makeup master Rick Baker. The magazine captured the imagination of thousands, inspiring them to read classic science fiction and to see the best and worst horror and fantasy movies from the silent era to the genres' heyday during the 1950s and 1960s. Ackerman is the godfather of gore and fantastical alien creatures that found their way into independent and Hollywood filmmaking during the resurgence of horror and science fiction in the 1960s and 1970s. His home, the Ackermansion, a museum of horror and sci-fi memorabilia, is considered the largest collection of such artifacts in the world. In November 1995, Ackerman resigned his position of editor at *Famous Monsters of Filmland* complaining that the current publisher, Ray Ferry, was not meeting his financial obligations. He claimed Forry's work had become incompetent and not fit to print. A lawsuit ensued. Currently a judgment is held in favor of Ackerman, and Ferry has suspended use of the name *Famous*

Monsters of Filmland. He is now using the monikers *Classic Monsters* and *Filmland Classics Filmbooks,* promising to be back in business by summer of 2002. Both Forry and Ferry continue to fight and hype their positions from separate Web sites. Old issues are available by order. Fans await the future and fate of the elite horror magazine.

actor-hyphenates. The low production and distribution costs of independent filmmaking have offered actors the opportunity to write, direct, produce and star in personal projects. Actors who have stepped behind the camera include **John Cassavetes, Clint Eastwood, Lee Grant** and **Ida Lupino.** Films directed by actors are generally well received by audiences and critics because of the culture of celebrity. The industry finds name recognition appealing, increasing box office potential. Directing, writing, and producing represent power for the actor and often are payback for starring in commercial studio projects. Some of the many actors who have directed, produced, or written screenplays for personal projects, most often independent or low-budget productions, include Robert Duvall, *We're Not the Jet Set* (1975), *Angelo My Love* (1983), *The Apostle* (1997); Bob Balaban, *Parents* (1989); Danny DeVito, *Throw Momma From the Train* (1987), *The War of the Roses* (1989), *Hoffa* (1992), *Jack the Bear* (1993), *Matilda* (1996); John Turturro, *Mac* (1992), *Illuminata* (1999); Jodie Foster, *Little Man Tate* (1991), *Home for the Holidays* (1995); Edward James Olmos, *American Me* (1992); **Steve Buscemi,** *Trees Lounge* (1996), *Animal Factory* (2000); Anne Bancroft, *The August* (1976, not released), *Fatso* (1980); Tim Robbins, *Bob Roberts* (1992), *Dead Man Walking* (1995), *The Cradle Will Rock* (1999); Richard Benjamin, *My Favorite Year* (1982), *Racing with the Moon, City Heat* (both 1984), *The Money Pit* (1986), *Little Nikita, My Stepmother Is an Alien* (both 1988), *Downtown, Mermaids* (both 1990), *Made in America* (1993), *Milk Money* (1994), *Mrs. Winterbourne* (1996); Stanley Tucci, *Big Night* (1996; codirected by Campbell Scott), *The Imposters* (1998), *Joe Gould's Secret* (2000); Sean Penn, *The Indian Runner* (1991), *The Crossing Guard* (1995), *The Pledge* (2000); Ben Stiller, *Reality Bites* (1994), *The Cable Guy* (1996), *Zoolander* (2001); Sylvester Stallone, *Paradise Alley* (1978), *Rocky II* (1979), *Rocky III* (1982), *Staying Alive* (1983), *Rocky IV* (1985); Keith Gordon, *The Chocolate War* (1988), *A Midnight Clear* (1991), *Mother Night* (1996), *Waking the Dead* (2000); Sondra Locke, *Rat Boy* (1986), *Impulse* (1990), *Do Me a Favor* (1997); and Tim Roth, *The War Zone* (1999).

BIBLIOGRAPHY

Stevens, John. *Actors Turned Directors: On Eliciting the Best Performances from an Actor and Other Secrets of Successful Directing.* Los Angeles: Silman-James Press, 1997.

actors. In the Classical Hollywood Studio System, movie stars were central to financial and popular success. Independent films can be a platform for actors largely unknown in commercial filmmaking or those no longer bankable in the mainstream. A-list actors tend to work in an independent film when the characters and story compel them. Working for scale, for a back-end deal, or for no pay, actors find independent films keep them in the public eye and are a venue for roles that develop their art. A commitment by a name actor can be instrumental to critical and box office success. The independent film movement has created its own star system and schools of acting.

adult film industry. From inception, **hard-core** pornographic **films** were independently produced and distributed outside of the larger movie industry. Until the 1970s films depicting sex acts and featuring nonexistent or loose narratives were shot and distributed on **8mm**, **Super 8mm**, and **16mm** film. The 1970s saw the rise of the **porno chic** movement when a new generation of product gained attention in neighborhood adult theaters. The genre has its own star and auteur systems and narrative and aesthetic conventions. During the 1980s the industry switched from film to video, theaters were closed, and the local video store became the principal outlet. Currently the adult video production industry is in California and is thriving. *See also* hard-core films; porno chic; soft-core films

BIBLIOGRAPHY

Butler, Jerry, as told to Robert Rimmert and Catherine Tavel. *Raw Talent: The Adult Film Industry as Seen by Its Most Popular Male Star.* Amherst, NY: Prometheus Books, 1990.

Ford, Luke. *A History of X: 100 Years of Sex in Film.* Amherst, NY: Prometheus Books, 1999.

Williams, Linda. *Hard Core: Power, Pleasure, and the "Frenzy of the Visible."* Berkeley: University of California Press, 1999.

African American cinema. From the inauguration of the medium until the 1960s, African Americans struggled for equality in the film industry. They had little control or power over their portrayals on screen or representation in the workforce. The civil rights movement of the 1960s helped expand on screen black images and themes, but they were not always positive or reflective. In the 1970s the **blaxploitation** movement emerged as the dominant representation of African Americans in film. By the late 1980s and throughout the 1990s black filmmakers began developing a real voice and presence in the power structure of filmmaking, in large measure in independent films. *See also* blaxploitation; Burnett, Charles; Chenzira, Ayoka; Dash, Julie; Hudlin, Reginald; Hudlin, Warrington; Hughes, Albert and Allen; Lee, Spike

BIBLIOGRAPHY

Marker, Reid. *Redefining Black Film.* Berkeley: University of California Press, 1993.

Agee, James. Film critic, screenwriter. *b.* November 11, 1909, Knoxville, Tennessee. *d.* May 16, 1955. *ed.* Harvard University. Renowned film critic, as a participant in the independent filmmaking movement, Agee helped formulate the aesthetic philosophy of the New York school of the period where fiction and nonfiction were combined in poetic documentaries. In 1948, Agee, **Helen Levitt,** and Janice Loeb began work on *In the Street,* an experimental documentary about the children of Harlem. The film was shot by Levitt and Agee on a borrowed **16mm** camera. Agee wrote the commentary for the project.

BIBLIOGRAPHY

Agee, James. *Agee on Film Volume 1: Essay and Reviews by James Agee.* New York: Grosset and Dunlap, 1969.

Bergreen, Laurence. *James Agee: A Life.* New York: E.P. Dutton, 1984.

Moreau, Genevieve. *The Restless Journey of James Agee.* New York: William Morrow, 1977.

Ahearn, Charles. Screenwriter, producer, director. *Wild Style* (1982) is the first full-length film to feature the music, breakdancing, DJs (disc jockeys), and graffiti artists of hip-hop culture. Ahearn, a member of New York's avant-garde art scene since 1973, produced art films presented at the Museum of Modern Art and the Collective for Living Cinema. By the end of the decade, Ahearn shifted his pursuits to life in lower Manhattan's public housing projects, which led to *The Deadly Art of Survival* (1979), a **Super 8mm,** self-distributed film about martial arts as dance, choreography, and lifestyle. It was shown at local art houses and on public access cable.

In 1980, Ahearn met Fred Brathwaite (later FAB 5 Freddy of *Yo! MTV Raps* fame), who introduced him to South Bronx hip-hop Bronx where the culture was emerging. Ahearn and Brathwaite conceived *Wild Style* as a hybrid documentary/narrative to present a positive alternative to gang rituals. "I wanted to make an art movie that would play to a ghetto audience," Ahearn declared. The film was produced in color on **16mm** and framed for an eventual 35mm blow up for $250,000. The budget came from ZDF German television and England's Channel Four and a small completion grant from the New York State Council on the Arts (NYSCA); the balance came from private sources. Members of the hip-hop community were employed as actors and performers, paid $50 a day. Production assistants received less, and camera personnel were paid $100 a day. The cast and crew all believed in the project and received points. *Wild Style* was shot on location in seven weeks. Often scenes were filmed in front of the Bronx apartment buildings where the performers, costumed in their own clothes, lived. Several scenes were reshot due to sound problems, and new sequences were created. A three-hour rough cut was compressed to eighty-two minutes. Most of the improvisation and sociological material was cut, focusing the film on the music and art house plot.

Wild Style was screened at the 1982 Independent Feature Film Market and premiered at the New Directors/New Films festival. Films Around the World represented the project, paying for the 35mm blowup and one release print. Although there was a lot of interest, First Run Features made the only solid offer, a $25,000 cash advance with a 30/70 gross deal, 30/70 split to the distributor. They also paid for additional prints. Flyers went out to high schools and hip-hop clubs. A graffiti mural of the title was spray-painted on Riverside Drive. *Wild Style* opened at Embassy 3 in Times Square on Thanksgiving weekend in 1983 and ran thirteen weeks. It opened at twenty-one theaters the next year, shown at midnight screenings and as a second feature in **drive-ins**. It became a New York phenomenon. *Wild Style* has been inducted into the Rock 'n' Roll Hall of Fame as one of the ten best rock 'n' roll movies of all time.

In 1999 Ahearn released *Fear of Fiction*, a **road movie** about possession, ghosts, and supernatural coincidences the director claims are autobiographical.

Alberti, Maryse. Director of photography. *b.* 1953, France. In 1972 Alberti traveled to the United States to see a Jimi Hendrix concert, unaware the legendary musician had died two years earlier. A tip from a boyfriend landed her a job as unit still photographer on porn films. In 1982 she assisted cinematographer Steven Fierberg on *Vortex*, directed by **Beth and Scott B**. Alberti purchased a **16mm** Aaton camera and began to work in documentaries and narrative feature films. In 1988, Alberti garnered her first cinematography credit on *Way of the Wicked*, directed by **Christine Vachon**. She has worked with **Todd Haynes** photographing his short film *Dotty Gets Spanked* (1993) and the features *Poison* (1991) and *Velvet Goldmine* (1998); with **Todd Solondz** on *Happiness* (1998); with Anthony Drazen on *Zebrahead* (1992); and with Raul Ruiz on *The Golden Boat* (1990). In documentaries Alberti photographed *When We Were Kings* (1996) and *Paris Is Burning* (1990) and twice received the best cinematography prize at Sundance for *H-2 Worker* (1989) and *Crumb* (1994). Recent credits for Maryse Alberti include: *Joe Gould's Secret* (2000), directed by Stanley Tucci; *Twilight: Los Angeles* (2000), featuring Anna Deavere Smith, directed by Marc Levin; **Richard Linklater**'s *Tape* (2001); and *Inspirations* (1997), directed by Michael Apted.

Aldrich, Robert. Producer, director. *b.* August 9, 1918, Cranston, Rhode Island. *d.* 1983. *ed.* University of Virginia, law and economics. Aldrich was born into the politically powerful Rockefeller family but rejected his pedigree and made a pilgrimage to Hollywood in 1941, where he started as a production clerk at RKO. Aldrich's apprenticeship as a director began as a script clerk and developed by observing and assisting **Charles Chaplin**, Edward Dmytryk, Richard Fleischer, Joseph Losey, Louis Milestone, Abraham Polonsky, Jean Renoir and William Wellman. Aldrich became a production manager, then associate producer in the Classical Hollywood Studio System. In 1953 he directed his first feature, *The Big Leaguer*, and in 1954 Aldrich established himself as an independent with Associates and Aldrich Company. In 1967 after the financial success of his landmark black comedy/action war movie *The Dirty Dozen*, he formed Aldrich Studios and produced and directed *The Legend of Lylah Clare* (1968), *The Killing of Sister George* (1969), *Too Late the Hero* (1971), *The Grissom Gang* (1972), and the cult classic revisionist western *Ulzana's Raid* (1973). Poor box office forced Aldrich to sell his studio in 1973, but he reorganized as the Aldrich Company in 1976.

Audiences responded to the ensemble mayhem of *The Dirty Dozen* and the irreverent humor of *The Longest Yard* (1974), but over the course of his twenty-eight-year career, Aldrich was largely ignored and misunderstood. Aldrich's work sustained the stylistic rigor and consistency of theme of a Hollywood auteur. His view was ironic and cynical, his cinema style audacious, his intent to undermine the Classical Hollywood Studio System product. Republican by birth, he rebelled as a radical. Aldrich's principal contribution to independent film is his iconoclastic spirit and glee in reinventing and smashing genre conventions. Two of his greatest achievements are *The Flight of the Phoenix* (1965), where he disassembled the adventure film, and *Kiss Me Deadly* (1955), a penultimate film noir.

BIBLIOGRAPHY

Arnold, Edwin T. and Eugene L. Miller. *The Films and Career of Robert Aldrich.* Knoxville: University of Tennessee Press, 1986.

Allen, Woody. Director, actor, screenwriter. *b.* Allan Stewart Konigsberg, December 1, 1935, Bronx, New York. A distinctive narrative voice, a rigorous cinematic style, artistic and fiscal control, and recurring themes of neurosis in New York have earned Woody Allen a significant place in independent filmmaking. Allen's film career has gone through incarnations from the schtick of *Take the Money and Run* (1969) and *Bananas* (1971), to the comic artistry of *Annie Hall* (1977) and the Jewish angst of *Oedipus Wrecks* (1989) and *Crimes and Misdemeanors* (1989), to his Bergmanesque *Interiors* (1978) and *Another Woman* (1988). *Husbands and Wives* (1992) is reminiscent of **John Cassavetes**; *Manhattan Murder Mystery* (1993) evokes Bob Hope. Audiences and critics perceive each film as uniquely Woody Allen. Allen's narratives are personal and largely autobiographical. He has a cinematic vision and style that is both his own

and supported by long collaborations with cinematographers Gordon Willis and Carlo Di Palma; production designers Mel Bourne, Stuart Wurtzel, and Santo Loquasto; editors Ralph Rosenblum and Susan E. Morse; and costume designer Jeffrey Kurland. Allen maintained creative control by entering into long-term commitments with United Artists and Orion Pictures, who enjoyed the prestige of having him on their roster. Recent studio reversals and upheavals in his personal life have required Allen to regroup more than once in order to mainstream his creative independence.

BIBLIOGRAPHY

Lax, Eric. *Woody Allen: A Biography.* New York: Knopf, 1991.
Meade, Marion. *The Unruly Life of Woody Allen: A Biography.* New York: Scribner, 2000.

Altman, Robert. Director, screenwriter, producer. *b.* February 20, 1925, Kansas City, Missouri. Along with **John Cassavetes,** Altman was one of the leading maverick filmmakers to emerge in the 1960s. Like Cassavetes, Altman did not bow to studio pressure and became influential for his innovative cinematic devices, most notably the use of overlapping dialogue, the zoom lens, large ensemble casts and multiple story lines. After cutting his teeth on industrials, television shows like *Bonanza* and *Alfred Hitchcock Presents,* and *Countdown* (1968) and *That Cold Day in the Park* (1969), Altman directed his breakthrough film *M*A*S*H** in 1970. It opened to critical and commercial success and earned the Palme d'Or at Cannes as well as six Academy Award nominations. Flooded with offers from Hollywood, Altman rejected them all and made the whimsical and quirky *Brewster McCloud* (1970) for his newly formed production company, Lion's Gate Films. The film did not equal its predecessor's success (Altman never had another commercial success the size of *M*A*S*H*), but his work over the next several years amounted to one of the most critically successful strings of films in American movie history. Following *Brewster McCloud,* Altman directed *McCabe & Mrs. Miller* (1971); *The Long Goodbye* (1973), and *Thieves Like Us* (1974). He hit his career apex with *Nashville* (1975), which garnered another Oscar nomination. The wildly ambitious three-hour film is generally considered among the best of the 1970s. In 1980 his partnership with Hollywood producer Robert Evans resulted in the woeful *Popeye* (1980), and Altman immediately lost his status as a critical darling. Ever resourceful, Altman switched his focus to theater, television, and filmed adaptations of stage plays for most of the 1980s. Notable during this period are *Come Back to the Five and Dime, Jimmy Dean, Jimmy Dean* (1982), which Altman directed on Broadway and on film, *Secret Honor* (1984), an imaginary look at Richard Nixon's nonexistent Watergate confession, and *Tanner '88* (1988), a politically satirical

Robert Altman directing *Kansas City* (1996). Courtesy of The Del Valle Archive

miniseries commissioned by HBO. Altman regained his footing in 1992 with *The Player*, a savage look at Hollywood, and the Raymond Carver–inspired *Short Cuts* (1993), which gave him his fourth and fifth Academy Award nominations. In the 1990s, *The Gingerbread Man* (1998) and *Cookie's Fortune* (1999) have met with critical, if not commercial, success. In 2000 *Dr. T. and the Women* met a similar fate but *Gosford Park*, featuring an all-star British cast, met with critical and box office success topped off with Oscar nominations that included Best Picture and Best Director. Altman's next project was *Voltage* (2002).

BIBLIOGRAPHY

McGilligan, Patrick. *Robert Altman: Jumping Off the Cliff: A Biography of the Great American Director.* New York: St. Martin's Press, 1989.

American International Pictures. American International Pictures (AIP) was formed in 1954 by James H. Nicholson and Samuel Z. Arkoff as American Releasing Corporation (ARC) to appeal to the burgeoning youth market and as rebellion against the Classical Hollywood Studio System, then in its declining decades. In 1956, ARC was renamed American International Pictures and captured the attention of the rock 'n' roll, surfer, juvenile delinquent, and hippie movements with low-budget exploitation flicks in the sci-fi, western, and horror genres. AIP was largely responsible for creating the **beach party** and **biker** genres (which led to the creation of the seminal *Easy Rider* [1969]) and graduated a generation of actors and filmmakers ready to become the new establishment. The overwhelming majority of AIP films, featured in **drive-ins**, were delivered by independent producer/director **Roger Corman**, proclaimed king of **B-movies** who could shoot a complete feature in five days for next to no budget. AIP broke the rigidity of conventional Hollywood by sometimes paying Corman a fee plus participation points or putting up partial financing or paying him a straight fee for a project. Ideas were often generated by a title or poster design. AIP's prolific output in its first two decades include: *Five Guns West* (1955), *It Conquered the World* (1956), *The Undead* (1957), *Rock All Night* (1957), *Sorority Girl* (1957), *Machine Gun Kelly* (1958), *Teenage Caveman* (1958), *A Bucket of Blood* (1959), *X: The Man with the X-Ray Eyes* (1963), *The Wild Angels* (1966), and *The Trip* (1967). In 1960, AIP began their color, CinemaScope, Poe cycle with *The House of Usher* starring Vincent Price, which scored good box office and nurtured future generations of horror aficionados. In 1972, Nicholson left the company, and Arkoff remained as president. AIP's later period, which included *The Island of Dr. Moreau* (1977) and *The Amityville Horror* (1979), was not as profitable as its earlier product. In 1979 the company experienced its first losses and merged with Filmways, which later became Orion Pictures.

BIBLIOGRAPHY

McGee, Mark Thomas. *Fast and Furious: The Story of American International Pictures.* Jefferson, NC: McFarland, 1984.

American New Wave. Also called the Movie Brat Generation, The Film School Generation. U.S. film movement comparable to the French New

Wave. During the 1960s the Classical Hollywood Studio System was in decline and divesting its interests to television, real estate, and finance. The moguls were gone, stars were aging, and directors were in their twilight. Hollywood professionals John Ford, Howard Hawks, William Wellman, and Raoul Walsh were lauded as artists, poets, and auteurs. While other baby-boomers were reinventing medicine, law and business, a group of film students, mavericks, and movie fanatics raised on the Golden Age of Hollywood, rock 'n' roll, and emerging Aquarian culture fought to enter the still-standing Hollywood empire. After breaking ground with **Francis Ford Coppola**'s *You're a Big Boy Now* (1966) and the **Peter Fonda/Dennis Hopper** production of *Easy Rider* (1969), the wavers managed to take over the town during the 1970s. Significant participants include **Robert Altman**, *M*A*S*H* (1970), *McCabe & Mrs. Miller* (1970), Hal Ashby, *Harold and Maude* (1972), *Shampoo* (1975); Peter Bogdanovich, *The Last Picture Show* (1971), *Paper Moon* (1973); Michael Cimino, *The Deer Hunter* (1978), *Heaven's Gate* (1980); **Brian De Palma**, *Greetings* (1968), *Carrie* (1976); William Friedkin, *The French Connection* (1971), *The Exorcist*, (1973); John Hancock, *Bang the Drum Slowly* (1973); **Henry Jaglom**, *A Safe Place* (1971), *Tracks* (1976); Jeremy Paul Kagan, *Heroes* (1977), *The Big Fix* (1978); **Jonathan Kaplan**, *Truck Turner* (1974), *Over the Edge* (1979); George Lucas, *THX 1138* (1971); Terrence Malick, *Badlands* (1973), *Days of Heaven* (1978); John Milius, *Dillinger* (1971), *Big Wednesday* (1978); Bob Rafelson, *Five Easy Pieces* (1970), *The King of Marvin Gardens* (1972); Michael Ritchie, *Downhill Racer* (1969), *Smile* (1975); **Richard Rush**, *Getting Straight* (1970), *The Stunt Man* (1980); Paul Schrader, *Blue Collar* (1978), *Hardcore* (1979); **Martin Scorsese**, *Mean Streets* (1973), *Taxi Driver* (1976); Jerry Schatzberg, *Panic in Needle Park* (1971), *Scarecrow* (1973); Steven Spielberg, *The Sugarland Express* (1974), *Jaws* (1975); James Toback, *Fingers* (1977), *Love and Money* (1980); and Howard Zieff, *Hearts of the West* (1971), *Slither* (1976). Many came out of the **Roger Corman** school of fast, cheap exploitation films, others from television and academic study. The films were outgrowths of personal experiences and excesses of the era. The movement broke ground tackling provocative content, pushing the envelope in social, political, and sexual arenas. The American New Wave attempted to and largely succeeded in rewriting and reinventing the grammar, production methods, and financing of the Hollywood narrative film. It developed a new breed of screenwriters, producers, cinematographers, editors, production designers, and creators of film sound. Other landmark films include *The Godfather* (Coppola, 1972), *Nashville* (Altman, 1975), *Close Encounters of the Third Kind* (Spielberg, 1977), *Star Wars* (Lucas, 1977), *Apocalypse Now* (Coppola, 1979), and *Raging Bull* (Scorsese, 1980).

BIBLIOGRAPHY

Biskind, Peter. *Easy Riders, Raging Bulls: How the Sex-Drugs-and-Rock 'n' Roll Generation Saved Hollywood.* New York: Simon and Schuster, 1998.

Pye, Michael, and Lynda Myles. *The Movie Brats: How the Film Generation Took Over Hollywood.* New York: Holt, Rinehart and Winston, 1979.

American Playhouse. Public Broadcasting System television series that began on January 12, 1982 dedicated to showcasing independent films. Under the original executive director, **Lindsay Law,** *American Playhouse* developed, funded and bought independent films and created original programming in the genre, style and method of theatrical indie features by employing low-budget financing techniques. Notable films shown on the series include: *Stacking* (Martin Rosen, 1997), *The Ballad of Gregory Cortez* (**Robert M. Young,** 1982), *Thin Blue Line* (**Errol Morris,** 1988), *Stand and Deliver* (**Ramón Menéndez,** 1988), *Longtime Companion* (**Norman René,** 1990), *All the Vermeers in New York* (**Jon Jost,** 1992), and *Brother's Keeper* (**Joe Berlinger** and Bruce Sinofsky, 1992). The series is best known for "granola movies," often based on Horton Foote material about rural life presented in a conventional three-act screenplay structure. *See also* Law, Lindsay

American Zoetrope. A production facility founded by **Francis Ford Coppola** in 1969 with primary financing from Warner Bros./Seven Arts. Created for the director's personal film work, it evolved into a home for independent filmmaking. It was housed in a San Francisco warehouse with production and postproduction facilities. American Zoetrope has recently experimented with merging high-tech video and digital technologies with traditional filmmaking and over the years supported projects involving Carroll Ballard, Scott Bartlett, Willard Huyck and Gloria Katz, George Lucas, Walter Murch, and other second-generation filmmakers. Zoetrope's emphasis was on the development of personal content, new production techniques, a redefinition of Classical Hollywood Studio System aesthetics, and the creation of new financing and distribution methods. The Zoetrope warehouse was converted into Harry Caul's warehouse office for *The Conversation* (1974) and also supported *Apocalypse Now* (1979) and *One from the Heart* (1982). The company was forced to file for bankruptcy in 1990 before reorganizing as Zoetrope Studios. *See also* Coppola, Francis Ford

Anders, Allison. Screenwriter, director. *b.* November 16, 1954, Ashland, Kentucky. Anders lived a frustrated and tragic youth of odd jobs, stays in mental hospitals, and a horrifying gang rape when she was twelve years old. Somehow (Anders herself does not know how) she was allowed to enter the University of California at Los Angeles (UCLA) without a high school diploma. At UCLA she read a lengthy article about Wim Wenders and began a correspondence with the German director that eventually resulted in a job as production assistant on *Paris, Texas* (1984). Inspired, Anders entered UCLA's film program where she co-wrote and directed *Border Radio* (1988), about the Los Angeles punk scene, with future collaborator Steve Voss. Her first feature-length screenplay, *Lost Highway*, about a man searching for a rockabilly music legend, earned Anders the Nicholl Fellowship. When a college friend told Anders her production company, Cineville, had acquired rights to Scott M. Peck's novel *Don't Look and It Won't Hurt*, Anders expressed interest in directing the film adaptation. One year later she was offered the job on the film now titled *Gas Food Lodging* (1992). Although the story originated with Peck, Anders rewrote much of it to reflect her life experiences. *Premiere* magazine editor Chris Connelly called it "nearly as courageous and moving as the life of its creator." The film drew on Anders's experiences as a fatherless child and rape victim. Focusing on the efforts of two teenage girls to find life and love for themselves and their mother, *Gas Food Lodging* was praised for its honesty at the Berlin and **Sundance** film festivals, and Anders was quickly regarded as a major talent.

Next Anders drew on her experiences for *Mi vida loca/My Crazy Life* (1994), a risky film about a group of Latina gang members. Set in Anders's former neighborhood of Echo Park in Los Angeles, the film features many real-life gang members. In 1995, Anders teamed up with friends and fellow independent directors **Quentin Tarantino**, Alexandre Rockwell, and **Robert Rodriguez** to direct the anthology film *Four Rooms*. The film, particularly the Anders segment, "The Missing Ingredient," and the one directed by Rockwell were fiercely panned, and the film quickly vanished. In 1997 *Grace of My Heart* was released, a film loosely based on the life of singer Carole King and produced by **Martin Scorsese.**

Allison Anders is the recipient of a MacArthur Foundation Genius Award. In 1998 Allison Anders was a director on the successful cable television series *Sex and the City*, 1999 saw the release of *Sugar Town*.

BIBLIOGRAPHY

Barker, Nicola. "Lust, Lies and Lipstick." *London Observer*, March 1995.

Benson, Laurie Halperin. "A Director's Life Fuels Her Film." *New York*, July 27, 1992.

Breslauer, Jan. "Hangin' with the Homegirls." *Los Angeles Times*, July 26, 1992. Connelly, Christopher. "Allison Anders." *Premiere* (August 1992).

Anderson, Paul Thomas. Director, screenwriter. *b.* January 1, 1970, Studio City, California. When Paul Thomas Anderson emerged from the independent film world in 1996, he was hailed as one of the best new voices in American cinema. Borrowing from his heroes **Robert Altman** and **Martin Scorsese**, Anderson avoids being labeled as simply derivative by skillfully weaving classic filmmaking approaches with bravura touches and a 1990s POV (point of view). After dropping out of Emerson College, Anderson enrolled in New York University's film program. He never attended the school, deciding instead to pursue work as a production assistant on independent films. Anderson wrote and directed *Cigarettes and Coffee*, a short that debuted at the 1993 Sundance Film Festival and won him an invitation to the **Sundance Institute**, where he developed his first feature, *Hard Eight* (1996). The film contained a stirring performance by veteran actor Philip Baker Hall and landed on many year-end top-ten lists, giving Anderson the clout to make a three-hour period piece set against the backdrop of the Los Angeles porn industry. *Boogie Nights* was released in 1997 to much acclaim. The film uses the 1970s **adult film** culture as a metaphor for family and the coming video/digital age. Anderson won an Academy Award nomination for its screenplay's deeply developed characters and expansive plot. Julianne Moore and Burt Reynolds were nominated for their supporting work. The success of *Boogie Nights* gave Anderson carte blanche for his next project, *Magnolia* (1999). The film starred many of Anderson's stock company including Moore, Philip Seymour Hoffman, and William H. Macy. It delved into the lives of several Los Angelenos, crosscut in the manner of Altman's *Nashville* and *Short Cuts*. *Magnolia* received high praise for successfully attempting to sum up the emotional climate of the last decade of the twentieth century. In 2002, Anderson surprised critics and admirers by directing *Saturday Night Live* alumni and dumb comedy king Adam Sandler in *Punchdrunk Knuckle Love*.

Anderson, Wes. Director, screenwriter *b.* 1970, Houston, Texas. *ed.* University of Texas. Wes Anderson studied philosophy and wrote plays in which he cast himself as a hero. As a child he made **Super 8mm** films, and in 1994 Anderson directed a short film, *Bottle Rocket*, that led to his feature debut in 1996. The short was produced by Polly Platt and executive produced by Barbara Boyle and James L. Brooks. The expanded story concerned two friends in crisis who make a sorry attempt at a life. Anderson's original comic vision received a welcoming reception from critics and audiences. In 1998 *Rushmore*, starring Jason Schwartzman, Bill Murray, Seymour Cassel, and Brian Cox, brought Anderson greater attention as a writer/director with an off-center voice and an ear for quirky characters and unusual narratives. *Rushmore* is a Houston, Texas, high school where a student falls in love with a first-grade teacher and befriends a local tycoon with a penchant for iconoclasts. Schwartzman, the son of Talia Shire (**Francis Coppola**'s sister), gives a fresh and dimensional performance in the lead role. *The Royal Tenenbaums* (2001) was cowritten by Owen Wilson, who has collaborated with Anderson on all of his films. It is about a family of five geniuses in New York and is in the vein of Orson Welles's 1942 adaptation of Booth Tarkington's *The Magnificent Ambersons.*

Angelika Film Center. New York City's Angelika Film Center has long been an unofficial home for the New York independent film community who regularly gather there to chat in the theater complex's trendy café before seeing the latest indie film on one of the theater's six screens. When the theater opened its doors in 1989, it was one of the nation's first to showcase independent films. While Angelika-type features are now shown on screens throughout the city, the theater continues to sell out shows each weekend. Privately owned for years, City Cinemas bought the theater in 1997 after talks with **Miramax** Films fell through. An Angelika Film Center has since opened in Houston, with more planned in coming years.

Anger, Kenneth. Filmmaker. *b.* Kenneth Wilbur Anglemyer, February 3, 1927, Santa Monica, California. Anger is an **underground/avant-garde/experimental** filmmaker who explores the dark side of Classical Hollywood as a film historian/archivist and gay and satanic cultures as an independent filmmaker. As film historian, Anger wrote the notorious book *Hollywood Babylon* that depicted the excesses and private lives of the star system. It had a major influence on celebrity and tabloid cultures of the 1980s and 1990s. Anger was raised in Hollywood and is imbued in its history and lifestyle. He was a child actor who appeared in *A Midsummer Night's Dream* (1935) and graduated from Beverly Hills High School. In France, he met Henri Langlois of the Cinémathèque Française and later became the master archivist's personal assistant. With a birthday gift of a sturdy **16mm** Bell and Howell camera from his grandmother and a supply of Kodachrome and Ektachrome film stocks, Anger conceived and executed his own movies. His first film *Who Has Been Rocking My Dreamboat?* is a seven-minute, silent, black-and-white film. Later he experimented with color and sound and expressed his obsessions about homosexuality and underworld lifestyles. *Fireworks* (1947) was a celebration and examination of gay life in the 1940s and featured an infamous shot of a sailor's penis transforming into an exploding Roman candle. *Scorpio Rising* (1963) glorified motorcycle, death, and sexual fetish cults. *Invocation of My Demon Brother* (1969) and *Lucifer Rising* (1970–1980) plunged into the core of satanic evil. Stylistically Anger admired the gloss of Hollywood and the poetry of Cocteau. The gay subculture he was so long a part of shaped his worldview. Kenneth Anger made films for himself and kindred spirits in the world of bikers, satanists, and gays,

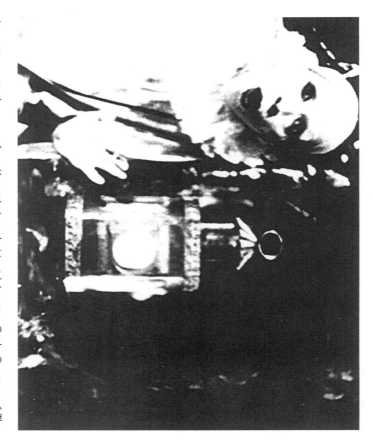

A poetic, magical moment from Kenneth Anger's *Magick Lantern Cycle*. Courtesy of The Del Valle Archive

but the stylistic and thematic influence of his work on the independent moving image during the second half of the twentieth century is staggering. Just a few of the people and movements Anger influenced are **Martin Scorsese, queer cinema** of the 1990s, **exploitation films** starting in the 1950s, **Dennis Hopper,** music videos and decades of experimental works of all kinds. Anger's experiments with the relationship of rock music to narrative and nonnarrative visual storytelling may be his greatest and longest-lasting achievement, stronger than ever after fifty years. Anger's use of rock music in his films directly inspired the soundtrack of *Easy Rider* (1969), in turn, a major influence on rock film soundtracks and the music video industries.

BIBLIOGRAPHY

Frumkes, Roy. "Look Back with Anger." *Films in Review* (January–February 1997): 16–25.

Lands, Bill. *Anger: The Unauthorized Biography of Kenneth Anger.* New York: HarperCollins, 1995.

animation. The moving image can be live action, the recording of humans in real physical space or animation, drawings, objects, photographs, pup-

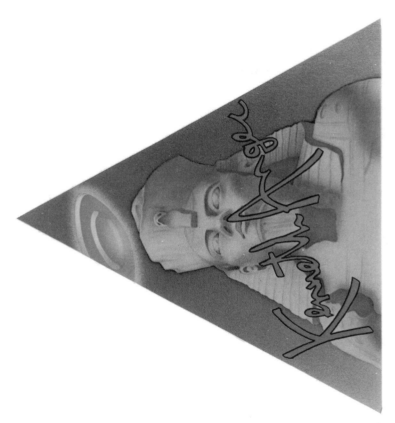

Lobby card for Kenneth Anger's *Lucifer Rising*. Courtesy of The Del Valle Archive

pets, silhouettes, figures, places, and images registered a frame at a time to create the illusion of movement. Over the course of the history of animation, which began in 1832, long before the development of the motion picture, creators of animation have used a wide range of techniques connected to their philosophy, aesthetics, style, politics, methods, content issues, and economic goals. Animation techniques include direct painting on celluloid, cel animation, stop motion, claymation, and computer imaging. Tools range from the pencil to the digital chip. Commercial feature and television animation has dominated the concerns of general audiences, but a vital independent community and spirit have made its impact throughout the twentieth century. The major Classical Hollywood Studios and their contemporary counterparts controlled the commerce of animation geared to the children's market, then to adults who are still kids, and finally to adult animation.

The indie animation movement has set its main focus on the art of animation. Key figures in independent animation include **Ralph Bakshi,** the politically incorrect creator of *Fritz the Cat* (1972) and *Heavy Traffic* (1973); Jordan Belson, the visionary experimental filmmaker whose films

Mandala (1953) and *Re Entry* (1964) influenced **Stanley Kubrick**'s seminal *2001: A Space Odyssey* (1968); Don Bluth, former Disney animator who formed his own company in 1979 and is best known for *An American Tail* (1986); and Robert Breer, an experimental animator whose ground-breaking work combines traditional artist materials with **16mm** film stock and a camera and whose films include *Eyewash* (1959) and *70* (1970). **Walt Disney**, the man responsible for the assembly-line, mass-produced studio cartoon and feature film, was the independent of the Classical Hollywood Studio System that dominated movies when he began the Walt Disney Company with his brother Roy in 1923. Max and Dave Fleischer, Disney's competition in the 1930s, created *Out of the Ink-well* (1938), *Betty Boop* (various years), and *Popeye the Sailor* (various years). John Hubley, former Disney animator, later United Productions of America (UPA) member, was one of the creators of *Mr. Magoo* (1948) and owner of Storyboard Productions, an animation company that produced intelligent and educational work. He worked along with his wife Faith Hubley on *Moonbird* (1959), *Windy Day* (1968), and *Everybody Rides the Carousel* (1975). She also created her own work and collaborated with their daughter Emily, who independently created *Delivery Man* (1982) and *One Self: Fish/Girl* (1997), a ten-minute short. Walter Lantz owned and operated his production company and is most notable as creator of *Woody Woodpecker*. John Lassiter, of Pixar, directed the computer-generated *Toy Story* (1995) with his creative team Len Lye and Norman McLaren, whose work in painting directly on celluloid influenced a generation of experimental animators. Other major influences are Windsor McCay, creator of *Gertie the Dinosaur* in 1909; Hans Richter, Fernand Leger and Walter Ruttmann for their avant-garde cinematic creations in the early 1920s; Steven Spielberg and Jeffrey Katzenberg of DreamWorks, great investors and believers in the storytelling of animation; Jay Ward, creator of *Crusader Rabbit* and the anarchistic *Rocky and His Friends*; and the Whitney brothers, pioneers in computer-generated **experimental films** such as *Lapis* (1963–1966) and *Permutations* (1967).

Significant events in indie animation history include the 1941 artist and worker strike against the Walt Disney Studio, which led to the creation of the United Productions of America in 1943. The UPA protested against the conservatism and sentimentality of the Disney style and fought for a less commercial and more artistic and socially oriented view of popular animation. UPA work includes *Mr. Magoo, Gerald McBoing Boing* (1951), *Christopher Crumpet* (1953), and *Howdy Doody*. In the 1990s digital technology empowered independents like Pixar and other high-tech companies to compete with the studios while offering alternative style and content. In the new millenium animation began a new era with the popular acceptance of digital animation in feature films such as *Shrek, Monsters Inc., Waking Life* (directed by **Richard Linklater**), and the **Farrelly**

Gertie the Dinosaur (1914, Winsor McCay). Courtesy of The Kobol Collection

brothers' *Osmosis Jones*, all released in 2001. Two thousand and two saw the first Oscar for animated feature film, the historic honor was given to the green giant starrer *Shrek*.

BIBLIOGRAPHY

Barrie, Michael. *Hollywood Cartoons: American Animation in Its Golden Age*. New York: Oxford University Press, 1999.

Lutz, Edwin George. *Animated Cartoons: How They Are Made; Their Origin and Development*. Applewood Books, 1998.

Anthology Film Archives. In 1968, the vision and generosity of filmmaker and philanthropist Jerome Hill made it possible for a Film Selection Committee consisting of **Jonas Mekas, P. Adams Sitney,** Peter Kubelka, James Broughton, Ken Kelman, and **Stan Brakhage** to select a repertory collection of essential **avant-garde films.** The Essential Cinema Repertory collection of around 330 titles made its original home in the Public Theater building on Lafayette Street in New York City. Plans for a film museum, library, and theater moved forward, and a special Invisible Cinema Theater specializing in avant-garde and independent films from around the world was designed by Peter Kubelka. The theater featured partitions to the left and right of each seat so the viewer could direct complete attention to the screen and not be distracted or aware of the audience around them. The concept supported the notion of the viewer/image relationship so important to Mekas, the **experimental film** community, and the personal cinema movement. When Anthology Film Archives opened a few years later in New York City's Public Theater, filmmakers, theoreticians, and film enthusiasts alike greeted it with excitement. After Jerome Hill's passing in 1974, Anthology relocated to 80 Wooster Street. Since its inception, Anthology has served as a crucial repository for little-known independent and experimental films. It currently holds some 4,000 titles. Through its Essential Cinema program the library holds the world's largest collection of documentation on the history and practice of independent film and video. Financial troubles have caused cutbacks in the Anthology's screenings, but the nonprofit theater continues to thrive as a center of the personal film.

In the 1990s programmer Fabiano Canosa joined Mekas at Anthology at its current location at 32 Second Avenue at Second Street. The site, the Second Avenue Courthouse building, was acquired in 1979 and renovated into a space with two theaters, a reference library, film preservation department, offices and gallery for $1,450 million. The Courthouse Theater has 200 seats, and the **Maya Deren** Theater holds 66.

anthropological filmmaking. A nonfiction form that joins anthropologists and filmmakers who utilize film and video to record the environmental, cultural, racial, and social aspects of human beings. Anthropologists were at first uncomfortable with filmmakers who used the camera and cinematic technique in what they considered a manipulation of data. Anthropologists gradually accepted visual anthropology, what they considered a direct recording of their findings and not the edited, subjective results of the ethnographologist. To the anthropologist the film and video cameras are a visual way of recording their findings. The ethnographologist is a **documentary** filmmaker who employs cinematic devices to organize and give the material a point of view and allows the subject to interplay with the camera, while the anthropologist tries to remain objective in approach. *See also* ethnographic filmmaking

Arnold, Jack. Director, producer. *b.* October 14, 1916, New Haven, Connecticut. *d.* March 17, 1992. *ed.* Ohio State. Arnold worked as a stage and screen actor and was producer/director on numerous documentaries for government agencies and private industry before turning to the **B-movie** business in the early 1950s. His most famous works—*It Came From Outer*

Space (1953), *Creature from the Black Lagoon* (1954, originally released in black-and-white 3D), and *The Incredible Shrinking Man* (1957)—are classics of sci-fi and horror and have influenced B-movie and **exploitation films** and expanded the genre. Arnold was a genre specialist and professional craftsman who could turn entertainment into a philosophical meditation. *The Incredible Shrinking Man*, based on a novel and screenplay by Richard Matheson, can be interpreted both as a conventional sci-fi narrative and as a metaphor for man's acceptance of his place in the cosmos.

Aronofsky, Darren. Screenwriter, director. *b.* February 12, 1969, Brooklyn, New York. *ed.* Harvard University, American Film Institute. Aronofsky's thesis film *Supermarket Sweep* won international awards for the director and was a finalist at the 1991 Student Academy Awards. After receiving an M.F.A. from the American Film Institute (AFI) and being inspired by a trip to the Sundance Film Festival, Aronofsky began writing his first feature film *Pi* (1998), a paranoia-filled exploration into the nature of mathematics and madness. Aronofsky raised much of the film's $60,000 budget by soliciting $100 donations from an assortment of friends and acquaintances, then began workshopping the screenplay with producer Eric Watson and the film's star, Sean Gullette. Matthew Libatique's distinct cinematography (Aronofsky describes it as "black or white"), rapid-fire editing, subjective sound design, and a narrative POV inside the head of a genius mind going mad won a cult following and the renown of many critics. *Pi* was entered into the Sundance Film Festival in 1998, where it garnered the director's prize and a $1 million distribution deal from Artisan Entertainment.

In 2000 Aronofsky released *Requiem for a Dream*, a breakthrough screen adaptation of Hubert Selby Jr.'s harrowing novel about codependence. The film is a sophomore achievement that makes food addiction as scary as a junkie's habit. All the main characters swirl in a hurricane of insanity and loss of dignity and humanity. With just two films, Aronofsky has already proven himself a daring visualist and dark storyteller with a fixation on the theme of mental stability. In 2001 at thirty-one, Aronofsky became the youngest recipient of the AFI's Franklin J. Schaffner Alumni Medal. In 2003, Aronofsky enters the blockbuster sweepstakes with *Batman—Year One*.

Arthur, Karen. Director. *b.* August 24, 1941, Omaha, Nebraska. Karen Arthur moved to New York from Palm Beach, Florida, and developed her talents in choreography, acting, and directing for the theater. In 1971 Arthur signed up for a six-week crash course in filmmaking at UCLA. There she wrote, directed, photographed, recorded sound, edited, and actually cut the negative on her first film *Hers*, a fifteen-minute short.

Arthur was accepted for the first American Film Institute woman's workshop along with Anne Bancroft, Margot Kidder, Lynne Littman, and Susan Oliver. At AFI she interned with directors Arthur Penn and Peter Hyams and learned the craft of feature filmmaking.

Arthur is a pioneering woman's filmmaker. In the early 1970s when she was trying to break into the industry's boy's club, **Ida Lupino**, who began directing in 1949, was the last woman to hold a Director's Guild of America (DGA) card. It took Arthur six years to raise the $70,000 necessary to make her 35mm feature film debut *Legacy*, released in 1975. The script was written by Joan Hotchkis, who adapted her play for the screen and focuses on an upper-class woman trying to break out of the monotony of her privileged lifestyle. *Legacy* was shown at the Director's Fortnight at Cannes. Arthur's second film, *The Mafu Cage* (1978), featured **Lee Grant**, Carol Kane, Will Geer, and James Olson. This melodrama concerns incest, jealousy, and murder. Mafu, a pet orangutan, is a metaphor for the caged victimization of two sisters played by Kane and Grant. The film received good reviews but fared poorly at the box office. *Lady Beware* (1987) took eight years for Arthur to finance. The feminist **exploitation film** about psychological rape was set and shot in Pittsburgh, where the window displays of the Diane Lane character arouse a psychotic who progresses from phone calls to breaking into the woman's loft. Arthur did not get final cut on the low-budget thriller, and the studio softened her original intentions.

Arthur has had a very successful television career. *Rich Man, Poor Man* (1976) earned her a DGA card and the distinction as the first woman to direct an American television miniseries. She has directed many socially conscious television movies including *Victims for Victims: The Theresa Saldana Story* (1984).

Asian American cinema. Asian Americans were heavily stereotyped from the beginning of film throughout the Classical Hollywood era as cooks, houseboys, coolies, and Chinatown gang members. Charlie Chan, the popular screen detective, typified the caricature of the ingratiating, humble detective and was portrayed only by Caucasian actors. Females were either lotus blossoms or dragon ladies. The Fu Manchu character was a popular Hollywood villain. Asian Americans were not empowered to present the scope of their lives or to make their own films until the 1980s. **Wayne Wang**, born in Hong Kong and educated in the United States, became the first Asian-American to break through with *Chan Is Missing* (1982), a detective story that provides an insider's look into the inner workings of New York's Chinatown. Wang continued to work independently on *Dim Sum: A Little Bit of Heart* (1984), *Eat a Bowl of Tea* (1989) and *Life Is Cheap ... But Toilet Paper Is Expensive* (1990). He went on to

The Wedding Banquet (1993), directed by Ang Lee. *Left to right:* Winston Chao, May Chin, Sihung Lung, and Ah-Leh Gua. Kobol Collection/Central Motion Picture Corp./ Good Machine

adapt the bestselling Amy Tan novel *The Joy Luck Club* as a studio production before returning to the indie scene.

Ang Lee was born in Taiwan and arrived on the scene with the gay comedy *The Wedding Banquet* (1994) and *Pushing Hands* (1992). As a director Lee examined cross-cultural and generational issues important to the Asian American community. Lee also directed *Eat, Drink, Man, Woman* (1994) in the Chinese language before moving beyond Asian themes with *Sense and Sensibility* (1995) and *The Ice Storm* (1997).

Tony Bui's *Three Seasons* (1999) was the first American-financed movie to be filmed entirely on location in Vietnam and went on to win three awards at Sundance including the Grand Jury Prize. Tony Chan's 1993 *Combination Platter*, shot on location in his parents' Chinese restaurant in Queens, New York, studies a young immigrant waiter struggling with the predicament of marrying an American woman to become a U.S. citizen. Asian American actors have made substantial strides in television drama and comedy but generally are still ghettoized in motion pictures both independent and studio financed.

Association of Independent Video and Filmmakers. The Association of Independent Video and Filmmakers (AIVF) is a media arts organization that began when AFI board member John Culkin became disillusioned with the Hollywood direction of the institute. In 1973 Culkin set out to create an alternative. He obtained a Department of Education grant, then met cinematographer Ed Lynch and chose him to organize the project. **Martha Coolidge** and experimental filmmaker Ed Enshwiller became founding members. The original members were documentary filmmakers interested in fictional feature film forms. Meetings, events, screenings, and workshops were all part of the AIVF's development. In 1974 screenings held at the Fifth Avenue Cinema were called Independent Cinema Lives! Documentary and fictional films began to emerge from the organization that spread from the East to West Coast. Funding became a challenge and an issue among the board members. A deal was struck with HBO for short films. In 1975 they incorporated. The board resisted monies from AFI, the Ford Foundation, and the **National Endowment for the Arts** (NEA). In 1977 Lynch stepped down and documentarian Ting Barrow took over. The AIVF transitioned to a national executive-directed operation. By 1980 every founding member save one had departed. Barrow's involvement with radical politics caused dissension over the association's purpose, and Barrow left in 1979. The government-sponsored CETA (Comprehensive Employment and Training Act) program helped stabilize the growing organization. Today there are 5,000 members internationally. The AIVF supports artists throughout their careers and in many media advocacy efforts.

Avakian, Aram. Film editor, director. b. April 4, 1926, New York City. d. January 17, 1987. ed. Yale University, the Sorbonne. Leading New York film editor in the 1950s and 1960s, Avakian edited the landmark music documentary *Jazz on a Summer's Day* (1959). The intercutting of the concert, audience, and surroundings created the editorial structure for big rock documentaries like *Monterey Pop* (1969) and *Woodstock* (1970). From 1955 to 1958 Avakian cut the Edward R. Murrow television series *See It Now*. His work for director Arthur Penn on *The Miracle Worker* (1962) gave cinematic shape to the play Penn had directed on Broadway. Avakian also collaborated with Penn on *Mickey One* (1965), where the editor brought the French New Wave school of jump-cutting to American fictional feature films. In 1964 Avakian edited Robert Rossen's last film *Lilith* (1964) and in 1966 **Francis Ford Coppola**'s official directorial debut *You're a Big Boy Now*. Avakian's work on both films reflected a distinct departure from the formulaic Hollywood studio style of editing and inspired many independent filmmakers and film editors with his daring sense of structure and pace. In 1962, Avakian made his directorial debut with *Lad: A Dog*, a conventional boy and his dog story. In 1970 he directed an adaptation of John Barth's novel *End of the Road*, which placed Avakian in the company of the American New Wave that was changing the style and content of U.S. filmmaking. The film also has the distinction of being Gordon Willis's first feature as a director of photography.

BIBLIOGRAPHY

Baker, Fred, with Ross Firestone. *Movie People: At Work in the Business of Film.* New York: Lancer Books, 1973.

avant-garde cinema. Throughout the first century of cinema, many terms have been used to describe films whose goal is pure art and not commercial narrative storytelling. *Avant-garde cinema* is the first term to describe the movement that moved away from and rebelled against the Hollywood product in content, theme, style, and approach. The avant-garde was a larger movement that included painters, writers, musicians, and dancers working in the first decades of the twentieth century. In the 1950s and 1960s filmmakers working in this idiom were more commonly known as **underground** filmmakers or **experimental** filmmakers. Many movements and factions formed, and often the politics of the art determined what term defined a non-narrative filmmaker's work. There has always been an alternate, independent cinema fascinated with the structural, surreal, expressionistic, abstract, and formalistic aspects of film and later video and digital imagery. Movements come and go. Preference determines whether a current artist is working in the area of avant-garde, experimental, underground, or recent micromovements like the **cinema of transgression**. The films are always independently created and reach a limited audience who attend specialty theater screenings. Many of these filmmakers are teachers and artists-in-residence in universities across America and distribute their films through co-ops and their own resources. The avant-garde cinema has made its contribution to mainstream filmmaking in films like **Stanley Kubrick's** *2001: A Space Odyssey* (1968) and the work of **David Lynch, Tim Burton,** and **David Cronenberg.** The general film community applies the various avant-garde terms interchangeably, but scholars, critics, archivists, and historians including **Jonas Mekas, P. Adam Sitney,** Amy Taubin, J. Hoberman, and **Howard Guttenplan** have dedicated their artistic and working lives to explaining, chronicling, understanding, and celebrating these alternative cinematic forms.

BIBLIOGRAPHY

Peterson, James. *Dreams of Chaos, Visions of Order: Understanding the American Avant-Garde Cinema.* Detroit, MI: Wayne State University Press, 1994.
Sitney, P. Adams, ed. *Visionary Film: The American Avant-Garde 1943–1978.* Oxford: Oxford University Press, 1979.

Avildsen, John. Director, editor, cinematographer. *b.* December 21, 1935, Oak Park, Illinois. *ed.* New York University. Catapulted to directorial prominence with the colossal success of the Academy Award-winning *Rocky* (1976), Avildsen spent his early career as an advertising copy-writer, then worked in below-the-line capacities in the mid-1960s on *Black Like Me* (1964), Arthur Penn's *Mickey One* (1965) and *Hurry Sundown* (1967), directed by **Otto Preminger.** As director, his earliest features were **soft-core** films including *Guess What We Learned in School Today?* (1970), which he also photographed and edited. In 1970, Avildsen also shot and directed *Joe*, a low-budget surprise hit that became a cult favorite starring Peter Boyle as a prole bigot and a nascent Susan Sarandon in her film debut. With his direction of Jack Lemmon's Academy Award perform-ance in *Save the Tiger* (1973), Avildsen gained legitimacy in the Holly-wood community. Avildsen won the Academy Award for Best Director of *Rocky* and returned to the series to coedit and direct the fourth sequel, *Rocky V* (1990). In the 1980s Avildsen directed and edited the commer-cially popular *The Karate Kid* (1984) and its sequels.

B

B, Beth and Scott. Beth B. *ed.* The Institute of Chicago, School of Visual Arts. Scott B. *b.* Scott Billingsly. *ed.* University of Wisconsin, St. Cloud State College. Former husband and wife filmmaking team known as the Bs, best known for their **Super 8mm** films screened at rock clubs, art theater venues, and on college campuses. They collaborated for five years during the late 1970s and early 1980s and with **punk** and **no-wave** artists of the era. The Bs opposed conventional commercial movies they considered too safe. They found leading **experimental** and **avant-garde** films and their venues too arty, so they set out to create their own films and philosophy from the emerging punk culture. *G-Men* (1978) was screened in rock halls and other venues at varying running times until it reached its final thirty-seven-minute duration. The Bs featured sound design and music in their films, insisting on special sound systems when appearing at colleges. *G-Men* features Max Karl, a law enforcement man dedicated to stopping terrorist acts. In his private life Karl hires a dominatrix to brutalize him, creating a conflicting metaphor. *G-Men* was based partly on Beth's experiences as a brothel receptionist and on a video interview the Bs conducted with a real-life bomb squad commander. The Super 8mm medium was an aesthetic choice to undermine slick Hollywood images of law enforcement. *Letters to Dad* (1979) featured nineteen men and women speaking directly into the camera that became "Dad." At the end of the film it is revealed they had been reciting portions of letters written to the infamous Jim Jones just hours before the mass suicide at Jonestown. The chilling revelation changes the way we perceive the entire film and the notion of a father. In 1979 the Bs created *The Offenders*, a weekly Super 8mm punk, comic book–like serial about New York street toughs trying to survive. The serial was programmed by **John Pierson** and shown at the Bleeker Street Cinema, where it became an event. In

1980 the Bs created *The Trap Door*, a Super 8mm film later blown up to **16mm**, about a man manipulated by his boss, women, and salesmen. Veteran experimental filmmaker **Jack Smith** plays Dr. Shrinkenstein, a mad psychiatrist and hypnotist who tells the man he has to be a bigger ogre than the next guy or he will fall through a trap door. At the conclusion, Jeremy, the main character, does fall through the trap door that is the bottom of the film frame itself.

After two years of reconsidering careers, the Bs made their first film shot in 16mm. *Vortex* (1983), starring punk diva **Lydia Lunch** as a noir detective, is loosely based on the life of Howard Hughes. The Bs wanted a more conventional film to play in more traditional venues. *Vortex* played the New York Film Festival and had a modest success in the art house circuit. **Jim Jarmusch** was a member of the *Vortex* crew, and musician **John Lurie** contributed to the soundtrack. After *Vortex* the Bs split up. Beth went on to make music videos for Dominatrix, Joan Jett and Taka Boom and directed the 35mm feature *Salvation!* (1987). Scott made two Super 8mm short films, *The Specialist* (1984) and *Last Rights* (1985). Recent credits for Beth B include: *Too Small Bodies* (1993), *Visiting Desire* (1996), *Belladonna* (1989), and the documentary *Breathe in Breathe out* (2000).

back-end deal. Agreement to compensate cast, crew, or investors when a producer receives gross receipts equal to negative costs. Payment can be in many forms—gross participation, net profit participation, or bonuses.

Baillie, Bruce. Filmmaker. *b.* September 24, 1931, Aberdeen, South Dakota. *ed.* University of Minnesota, University of California at Berkeley, London School of Film Technique. One of the most important **experimental film** artists of his time, Bruce Baillie used homespun camera technology to layer and combine beautiful images that are poetic and lyrical and illustrate themes that challenged the established social order. His most famous works include *Quixote* (1965), *Castro Street* (1966), and *Quick Billy* (1970). Baillie is a significant artist and organizer. He was the catalyst for the **Canyon Cinema** exhibition programs that became Canyon Cinema Distribution, which as a circulating program of experimental films ranks next to the Museum of Modern Art. *See also* Canyon Cinema

Bakshi, Ralph. Animator, director, fine artist. *b.* October 26, 1938, Haifa, Palestine (now Israel). When Bakshi graduated from the High School of Industrial Arts in Manhattan, he began work as an animator for Terrytoons Studio inking Hekyll and Jekyll and Mighty Mouse. He became the studio's creative director in 1965. In 1966 Bakshi became president of Paramount's New York cartoon division. When it disbanded he became an independent animation director. As an indie Bakshi concentrated exclusively on adult animated material that was controversial and often offensive. He created the X-rated *Fritz the Cat* (1972), *Heavy Traffic* (1973), *Coonskin* (1975), *Wizards* (1977), and the epic *Lord of the Rings* (1978). An outspoken rebel, Ralph Bakshi's characters were often based on outlandish racial stereotypes and spoke vile and profane street language. Bakshi wrote most of his own films, often out of his own experience. His masterpiece *American Pop* (1981) follows several generations of musicians through turbulent musical and cultural changes. *Hey Good Lookin'* was completed in 1975 but was not released until 1982, followed by *Fire and Ice* (1983) and *Cool World* (1992). Ralph Bakshi's work blends live action with animation and utilizes rotoscoping, a technique whereby live-action footage is literally traced and translated into animated realism and nontraditional techniques such as live-action backgrounds. Bakshi's work gained acceptance with cutting-edge critics and audiences but not always within the mainstream animation community.

Baltimore Pictures. Beginning with *Avalon* in 1990, director Barry Levinson formed Baltimore Pictures with producer Mark Johnson. They secured a deal with Tri-Star to make films without studio interference. The company went on to make feature films and branched out to television.

BIBLIOGRAPHY

Thompson, David, ed. *Levinson on Levinson*. London: Faber and Faber, 1992.

Barenholtz, Ben. Motion picture theater entrepreneur, distributor. Barenholtz operated the legendary repertory house The Elgin in Chelsea, New York—home for cineasts, cultists, film students, and aficionados during the 1970s. Barenholtz helped create the **midnight movie** concept by showing *El Topo* (1970) and *Pink Flamingos* (1972) at the Elgin at the witching hour. When the Elgin closed its doors in 1978 it marked the end of the repertory era in New York. Barenholtz continued to foster the indie movement. He was instrumental in the careers of the **Coen** brothers and started Libra Films, which released **David Lynch**'s *Eraserhead* (1978) and **John Sayles**'s *The Return of the Secaucus Seven* (1980).

Bartel, Paul. Director, screenwriter, actor. *b.* August 6, 1938, Brooklyn, New York. *d.* May 13, 2000. *ed.* UCLA. Paul Bartel directed bizarre comedies like the paranoia send-up *The Secret Cinema* (1969) and **exploitation films** *Death Race 2000* (1975) and *Cannonball* (1976) for **Roger Corman**'s New World Pictures. After trying and failing to entice Corman with his next script, Bartel was forced to make his breakthrough film *Eating Raoul* (1982), a satirical and sometimes gruesome look at modern-day life and work, on his own. With the lure of **Andy Warhol** favorite Mary Waronov in the lead role and inspiration from **John Waters** movies, the film became an instant underground classic. With the exception of the upper-class satire *Scenes from the Class Struggle in Beverly Hills* (1989), Bartel films did not have widespread releases. But *Lust in the Dust* (1985), starring Divine in her first non-John Waters lead role, and the failed Andy Kaufman vehicle *Heartbeeps* (1981) secured Bartel's position in the independent film pantheon.

BBS. Independent production company, cofounded by director Bob Rafelson, producer Bert Schneider, and Schneider's friend Steve Blauner. BBS was an offshoot of Rafelson's and Schneider's Raybert production company after they became New Hollywood millionaires with the television and recording phenomenon *The Monkees*. BBS was formed in response to what Rafelson saw as a critical moment in American filmmaking. The decline of the Classical Hollywood Studio System had left American film without direction or leaders, and while Rafelson acknowledged that young, talented filmmakers existed, there were no producers, studios, or production companies to offer financial and creative support. BBS was created in 1969 after embarking on a tenuous relationship with Columbia Pictures. Under an agreement reached between the upstart company and one of the majors, the studios agreed to greenlight six films and exert no influence over production, as long as BBS kept the budgets under $1 million.

During their brief reign in Hollywood, BBS produced some of the most significant films of the time including **Dennis Hopper's** *Easy Rider* (1969), Rafelson's own **Five Easy Pieces** (1971), and Peter Bogdanovich's *The Last Picture Show* (1971). The anti-Vietnam War documentary *Hearts and Minds* won the Oscar for best documentary in 1974. The New York Film Festival that anointed *The Last Picture Show* and *The King of Marvin Gardens* (1972) as American art films embraced BBS.

The company was conceived as a collaborative collective, but Schneider made all of the business decisions. He came to the realization this utopian ideal was impossible without the powerful distribution arm of the feudal studio system. Schneider eventually became disillusioned, and the company lost its way. As the 1970s progressed and Steven Spielberg's *Jaws* (1975), and George Lucas's *Star Wars* (1977) steered Hollywood filmmaking toward blockbusters, the BBS building on La Brea was no longer the hip and happening capital of youth-driven Los Angeles. The building was sold to comedian Red Foxx. BBS disintegrated under the weight of the new system and disbanded. *See also* American New Wave

beach party films. By the 1950s, Hollywood was searching for genres to lure hordes of teenagers into the theaters. Films for the teenage audience were usually low budget, often independent. In the early 1960s teenagers

Poster for *Bikini Beach* (1964), starring Frankie Avalon and Annette Funicello, directed by William Asher, released by American International Pictures. Courtesy of The Del Valle Archive

were in between rebellions. The juvenile delinquents of the 1950s personified by Marlon Brando in *The Wild One* (1954) and James Dean in *Rebel without a Cause* (1955) and the proto-gang punks of *The Blackboard Jungle* (1955) were retired, dead, or had gone straight. The new 1960s teens were well scrubbed and ready to take their place in society before partying down. With statehood, Hawaiian culture became the rage in 1959. California blondes, surfing, and hanging at the beach took the country by storm. *Gidget* (1959), starring Sandra Dee, started the wave. In 1960, MGM exploited spring break fever with *Where the Boys Are* with Connie Francis, Paula Prentiss, Yvette Mimieux, and Dolores Hart. Music was part of the genre, but in 1963 **American International Pictures** fully developed it by putting Annette Funicello and Frankie Avalon in *Beach Party*. Girls in bikinis, surfer music, and California characters like Animal, Deadhead, and a motorcycle group called The Rats defined the rules of beach party films with plenty of water, surfing, and good clean fun. In 1964 seven beach party films were released including *Beach Party* sequels *Pajama Party* and *Horror at Party Beach*, already creating a subgenre. AIP was king, and the imitators like *Ride the Wild Surf* (1964) and United Artists's *For Those Who Think Young* (1964) with James Darren, Bob Denver, and Nancy Sinatra were abundant. *Beach Ball* (1965) featured an all-guy band posing as an all-girl band with pop star appearances including a young incarnation of Diana Ross and the Supremes. *Surf Party* (1964) and *Wild on the Beach* (1965) tried to bring social relevance to the genre, but the kids wanted fun. William Asher directed most of AIP beach movie cycle of the 1960s starring Funicello and Avalon. Asher directed *Beach Party* (1963), *Muscle Beach Party* and *Bikini Beach* (both 1964), and *Beach Blanket Bingo* and *How to Stuff a Wild Bikini* (both 1965). Mario Bava directed *Dr. Goldfoot and the Girl Bombs* (1966), sleazemeister Stephanie Rothman directed *It's a Bikini World* (1967), **B-movie** old-timer Norman Taurog came out with *Dr. Goldfoot and the Bikini Machine* (1965), and studio professional Don Weis helmed *Pajama Party* (1964) and *The Ghost in the Invisible Bikini* (1966). Alan Rafkin, who led Don Knotts through his screen paces, came out with *Ski Party* (1965), but Asher remains the auteur of the genre.

The films were fun for most teens; traumatic for others who couldn't swim or get a date or who looked like ninety-nine-pound weaklings. Beach party films are now part of American pop culture and document Hollywood's regressive movie aesthetic and processed image of the youth of the period. *See also* American International Pictures

Beat cinema. A cinematic attempt to create films in the tradition of the Beat Generation: **Jack Kerouac**, Allen Ginsberg, William S. Burroughs, Gregory Corso and others. Robert Frank and Alfred Leslie directed the definitive beat film *Pull My Daisy* (1958), written and narrated by Kerouac. Beat cinema embraces Ron Rice's *The Flower Thief* (1960) with **Taylor Meade**, where the childlike characters achieve Kerouac's state of beatitude, and the magical animated films of Harry Smith, a filmmaker, painter, folklorist, anthropologist, music historian and member of the occult. Other beat films include **Jack Smith**'s notorious *Flaming Creatures* (1963); Peter Whitehead's *Wholly Communion* (1965), a record of the International Poetry incarnation at London's Albert Hall held on June 11, 1965, with performances by Ginsberg, Corso, Burroughs, Lawrence Ferlinghetti, and other beat poets; and **Conrad Rooks**'s *Chappaqua* (1966), photographed by **Robert Frank** and featuring Burroughs. Beat films inspired the punk film movement. Hollywood tried to exploit the cultural phenomenon but failed miserably with *The Beat Generation* (1959), *The Rebel Set* (1959), and a pathetic adaptation of Kerouac's *The Subterraneans* (1960). **David Cronenberg** finally filmed Burroughs's *Naked Lunch* (1991) after others gave up. The characters in **Gus Van Sant**'s *Drugstore Cowboy* (1989) and *My Own Private Idaho* (1991) personify the beat hero. *See also* Frank, Robert; Kerouac, Jack

BIBLIOGRAPHY

Sargeant, Jack. *The Naked Lens: An Illustrated History of Beat Cinema.* London: Creation Books, 1997.

Beaudine, William. Director. *b.* January 15, 1892, New York City. *d.* March 18, 1970. William Beaudine came to Hollywood in 1909 and worked as a handyman and prop boy for director **D.W. Griffith**. After moving through many studio jobs, in 1915, Beaudine became a director of short subjects and then feature films in 1922. Beaudine directed hundreds of films at various Hollywood **poverty row** studios including PRC, Monogram, and Allied Artists over a fifty-year period ending in the late 1960s. Beaudine worked in a wide range of genres including many Westerns, with low to medium budgets. Known as William "One Shot" Beaudine, the director avoided retakes, a practice that resulted in many mistakes including mike booms dropping into frame and cowboys falling to their death before they were even shot. Beaudine was not attracted to complex subject matter and gravitated to light formulaic narratives. The prolific filmmaker also directed many of the popular East Side Kid comedies that starred Leo Gorcey and Huntz Hall. In 1944, Beaudine directed the sex education **exploitation film** *Mom and Dad* that featured footage of the actual birth of a baby. The controversial picture met with legal action from community groups that attempted to ban the film. After many brief, clandestine bookings, *Mom and Dad* had a solid release in 1957 with some deleted and added scenes. Beaudine also directed many religious dramas for the Protestant Film Commission. When Beaudine died at seventy-eight, he was the oldest working director of his time.

Beckett, Samuel. *See Film*

Behind the Green Door. **Hard-core** feature film released in 1972 that launched Marilyn Chambers, the former Ivory Soap model, into a career as an **adult film** performer. The film was codirected by San Franciscan filmmakers **Art** and **Jim Mitchell**. The Mitchells envisioned themselves as artists, and in fact the gauzy cinematography by Jon Fontana, production values, and creative direction by the brothers advanced *Behind the Green Door* beyond the usual technical crudeness of an adult film. The plot features Chambers as a kidnapped woman to be used as a star attraction at a private sex club. The proceedings develop into an orgy. Chambers is bewildered but not unwilling to engage in various explicit sex acts including an infamous scene on a trapeze with four men. The Mitchells distributed the 35mm seventy-two-minute color film. It was a solid success at the box office, enticing couples to share an erotic experience, and thus was a trendsetter during the **porno chic** era of the 1970s. The Mitchells bypassed screening the film for the Motion Picture Association of America (MPAA) and self-assigned an X rating. *Behind the Green Door* was banned in New York in 1973, Colorado in 1975, California in 1979, and Texas from 1974 to 1981. Upon release the film was reviewed by *Variety* and *The New Yorker* and over the decades has reached legendary cult celebrity. *See also* Mitchell, Jim and Artie; porno chic

BIBLIOGRAPHY

De Grazia, Edward, and Roger K. Newman. *Banned Films: Movies, Censors & the First Amendment.* New York: R.R. Bowker, 1982.

McCumber, David. *X-Rated: A True Story of Sex, Money, and Death.* New York: Simon and Schuster, 1992.

Bender, Lawrence. Producer, actor. *b.* 1958, Bronx, New York. *ed.* American Film Institute. On moving to Los Angeles Bender studied at the American Film Institute and produced his first film in 1988. *Intruder* was a low-budget thriller starring *The Evil Dead* director **Sam Raimi** and was made for $125,000. It soon disappeared, but **Quentin Tarantino** approached Bender with the script for *Reservoir Dogs.* Bender showed the script to his acting class tutor, who gave it to an enthusiastic **Harvey Keitel.** With Keitel attached, the film attracted more attention and the $30,000 budget shot up to $1.5 million with commitments from Tim Roth, **Steve Buscemi,** and others. *Reservoir Dogs* (1992) was a critical smash, immediately making Bender one of the most desirable American independent producers. Boaz Yakin's debut *Fresh* (1994) was Bender's next project, followed by friend Roger Avary's 1994 debut (and *Reservoir Dogs*–inspired) *Killing Zoe.* Bender teamed up with Tarantino for *Pulp*

Marilyn Chambers, star of *Behind the Green Door* (1972) in the 1980s. Courtesy of The Del Valle Archive

Fiction in 1994. Made for $8 million, *Pulp Fiction* went on to gross over $100 million and became one of the most influential films of the 1990s. Bender produced the 1995 anthology film *Four Rooms* and 1997's *Jackie Brown* and was executive producer for **Robert Rodriguez's** *From Dusk Till Dawn* (1996). In addition to Boaz Yakin's *Price above Rubies* (1998), Bender has recently produced decidedly more genteel fare including **Gus Van Sant's** *Good Will Hunting* in 1997 and the big-budget Jodie Foster film *Anna and the King* in 1999. In 2001 Bender produced *The Mexican* and *Knockaround Guys.*

Berlinger, Joe. Director, producer, editor. *b.* October 30, 1961. Berlinger and his partner Bruce Sinofsky, who had worked as an editor for the **Maysles** brothers, burst onto the documentary scene with *Brother's Keeper* (1992), which chronicles a man accused of killing his sickly brother. The filmmakers captured the rural backcountry of America and investigated media exploitation of controversial legal matters. After *Brother's Keeper,* HBO gave the documentarians a huge budget to make the epic *Paradise Lost: The Child Murders at Robin Hood Hill* (1996). The nonfiction film examined a murder case that delved into heavy metal music and the devil karma of the young men accused of the heinous child murders. *Paradise Lost 2: Revelations* (2000) also aired on HBO. The two critically acclaimed original **documentaries** attracted the producers of **The Blair Witch Project,** who hired Berlinger to direct the sequel *Book of Shadows: Blair Witch 2* (2000) to lend credibility to the pseudo-documentary hype of the original box office phenomenon. The sequel had none of the original film's narrative and aesthetic audacity and failed miserably at the box office.

bicycling. Exploitation filmmakers would play a print of their low-budget genre film in one city, then pack up and go to the next city until they covered the country. The practice avoided the cost of manufacturing numerous prints for a multiple territory release on the same play dates.

Bigelow, Kathryn. Director, screenwriter. *b.* November 27, 1951, San Carlos, California. *ed.* San Francisco Art Institute, Independent Study Program at the Whitney Museum, Columbia University. While female directors coming of age in the 1980s filled a gap in "women's" pictures, Bigelow took the opposite route and made inroads in traditionally male-dominated genres. *The Set-Up* (1978) is a short about a back-alley street fight. Bigelow made her first feature, the **juvenile delinquent/biker** film deconstruction *The Loveless,* in 1983, featuring the screen debut of Willem Dafoe. The fledgling director first made a name for herself with the intellectual vampire film *Near Dark,* about a midwestern boy who becomes a reluctant bloodsucker. Released in 1987, the film was largely ignored by mainstream audiences in favor of that year's much more commercial

The Lost Boys, but *Near Dark* has since gained cult recognition. The female cop film *Blue Steel,* the heist picture *Point Break,* and sci-fi *Strange Days* followed in 1990, 1991, and 1995, respectively. In 2000 Kathryn Bigelow directed *The Weight of Water* followed by *K-19: The Widowmaker* (2002), which she also produced. Bigelow bends the genres she works in and tends to elevate social outcasts in her films. Perhaps as a consequence, her features have not gained wide audience acceptance, and she has yet to break into the Hollywood mainstream.

biker movies. **Exploitation films** that feature motorcycle gangs cruising and causing mayhem across America. The biker film was born of *The Wild One,* released in 1954 and directed by Laszlo Benedek with a badboy defining performance by Marlon Brando. *The Wild One* was based on an actual incident in Hollister, California. The biker is a rebel without a cause. When Brando's Johnny is asked what he's rebelling against, he retorts, "Whattaya got!" Starting in the late 1940s and especially during the 1950s and 1960s, motorcycle clubs became motorcycle gangs. The most notorious, the Hell's Angels, were a family, a cultist band of unfashionably long-haired, bearded, unwashed hooligans, a postwar metaphor for the desperados who terrorized the Old West. The Angels lifestyle was tailor-made for exploitationists, plenty of sex, drugs, and rock 'n' roll, outlaw behavior, exterior landscapes for stunning visuals, and psychotic personalities to mine for characters. Although the Angels had a strict code and militarylike protocol, bikers represented the ultimate nonconformist life—the freedom to go and do as one pleased. The biker became a substitute icon—an American cowboy with a chrome horse. By the mid-1960s there was a proliferation of biker movies. *All the Fallen Angels* was a **Roger Corman** production starring **Peter Fonda**, who later produced *Easy Rider* (1969), a biker movie that changed the film industry. Fonda was given the lead because he could ride a Harley. Members of the Venice chapter of the Hell's Angels played extras. Corman changed the title of *All the Fallen Angels* to *The Wild Angels* (1966), which played Cannes and established itself as the most stylistically accomplished of the genre. When the Hell's Angels saw the completed film they felt betrayed by their portrayal, and they slapped Corman with a $5 million slander and defamation suit that was settled out of court for $300,000.

Corman and **American International Pictures** followed with *Devil's Angels* (1967) with actor **John Cassavetes**. The producer was exploitation specialist Joe Soloman, publicist for the infamous *Mom and Dad,* who brought in the film for $200,000. Ultimately it grossed several million. Soloman invested in *Angels from Hell* (1968) and *Run Angel Run* (1969), which were under the Fanfare Productions banner and endorsed by Angels chieftain Sonny Barger. The film was directed by **Richard Rush** and photographed by **László Kovács**, the Hungarian émigré who shot *The Savage Seven* (1968) for Rush and *The Rebel Rousers* (1970) and *Hell's Bloody Devils* (1967). Kovacs almost turned down *Easy Rider*, telling Hopper and Fonda he was burned out on biker movies. Kovacs's work on *Easy Rider* helped launch American cinematography into a new era. Along with fellow émigré **Vilmos Zsigmond**, they cornered the photography of the biker movie market. *Born Losers* (1967) featured a character named Billy Jack and led to director **Tom Laughlin**'s legend-creating smash hit. The years 1967 to 1970 were benchmark years for biker films and helped establish the careers of Harry Dean Stanton, Jack Nicholson, Bruce Dern, and Diane Ladd.

As with every successful genre, biker movies morphed and mutated. Horror films boasted *Werewolves on Wheels* (1971), *Psychomania* (1972), *Northville Cemetery Massacre* (1977), *Chopper Chicks in Zombie Town* (1988), and goremeister **Herschell Gordon Lewis**'s *She-Devils on Wheels* (1968) and *Bury Me an Angel* (1971), directed by Barbara Peeters, who made *Humanoids from the Deep* (1980). Sex was always an element in biker films, especially in **Russ Meyer**'s *Motor Psycho* (1965) and *Faster, Pussycat!/Kill! Kill!* (1966), *The Mini-skirt Mob* (1968), and *Sisters in Leather* (1969). **Hard-core** films were attracted to the sadistic possibilities that produced *The Cheater* (1971), *Revenge of the Motorcycle Mama* (1972), the inevitable *Sleazy Rider* (1976), *Little Orphan Dusty* (1976), *Biker Chicks in Love* (1971), *Motorcycle Mistress Mamas* (1991), and *Butt-Ganged Sluts* (1995).

In **blaxploitation** there were *The Black Angels* (1970), *The Black Six* (1974), and *Darktown Strutters* (1975). Footballer "Broadway" Joe Namath got into the trend with *C.C. and Company* (1970). The documentary *Gimmie Shelter* (1970) became the penultimate biker film when it captured an Angel murdering a man at the Altamont Speedway Rolling Stones concert that figuratively and literally ended the 1960s. *The Losers* (1970) exploited the Vietnam War in which the president hires a biker gang to rescue soldiers in Cambodia. For the diehard aficionado the genre offers *Satan's Sadist* (1968), *Hell's Chosen Few* (1968), *The Cycle Savages* (1969), *Naked Angels* (1969), *Hell's Angel's '69* (1970), *Angels Die Hard* (1970), *The Undertaker and His Pals* (1967), *The Leather Boys* (1963), *Angels Hard as They Come* (1971), *The Hard Ride* (1971), *Hellriders* (1974), and **Kenneth Anger**'s underground classic *Scorpio's Rising* (1964).

Billy Jack. *See* Laughlin, Tom

Biograph. The American Mutoscope and Biograph Company was founded by Elias Koopman, Henry Marvin, Herman Casler, and William K.L. Dickson, who owned an early camera and projector known as The American Biograph that used nonperforated film. At first, the **Thomas Edison** Company refused to supply the founders with products. The embittered competition ended when they joined forces to form the Motion Picture Patents Company, which contrived to block all independent producers trying to break into the burgeoning film business. Located on East 14th Street in New York, **D.W. Griffith** directed hundreds of films there. It was also the training ground for Mack Sennett, Mary Pickford, Lillian and Dorothy Gish, and Florence Lawrence, who was known as "The Biograph Girl." In 1915 Biograph was forced to close when the federal government won an antitrust action against the company. *See also* Griffith, D.W.

Black Filmmakers Foundation. Founded in 1978, this not-for-profit national organization supports up-and-coming black filmmakers and attracts audiences to their work. Located in the **Tribeca Film Center,** the BFF is a forum for networking and the exchange of ideas. The foundation develops new talents by providing showcases and exhibitions. *See also* Hudlin, Warrington

Blair Witch Project, The. After a debut before an unsuspecting audience at a midnight screening at **Sundance** in 1999, *The Blair Witch Project* emerged as the film sensation of the year, eventually grossing over $140 million and becoming one of the most successful films ever made. Based on an idea by University of Central Florida film school grads Daniel Myrick and Eduardo Sanchez, the $35,000-budgeted horror film was shot without a script in the Maryland woods by its main players—Heather Donahue, Michael Williams, and Joshua Leonard. Myrick and Sanchez developed the story with the actors, then guided the film's progress with a series of notes; as a result, much of the actors' frustration and terror is real. After spending the majority of the budget editing the film (the lack of professional actors, sets, lights, etc., kept the production costs virtually nonexistent), Myrick and Sanchez sold the distribution rights to Artisan Entertainment after the Sundance screening. A phenomenally effective advertising campaign commenced, largely relying on word-of-mouth and the film's Web site. The initial art house opening drew record crowds (some who camped out overnight to be the first to see the film). *The Blair Witch Project* appeared simultaneously on the covers of *Time* and *Newsweek* when it opened in wide release. Although the film failed to excite critics in the way it excited the public, its maverick style and production methods ushered in a new wave of digital **guerrilla filmmaking.**

Blank, Les. Documentary filmmaker. *b.* November 27, 1935, Tampa, Florida. *ed.* Tulane University, USC Film School. Les Blank is a documentary filmmaker with a humanist vision who explores ethnic and regional life in America with a penchant for Cajun culture, blues music, and a down-

Richard Roundtree in *Shaft in Africa* (1973), directed by John Guillerman. Courtesy of The Del Valle Archive

home sense of humor. His films include *God Respects Us When We Work, But Loves Us When We Dance* (1968), *The Blues Accordin' to Lightnin' Hopkins* (1969), *Hot Pepper* (1973), and *Garlic Is as Good as 10 Mothers* (1980). His best-known work is *Burden of Dreams* (1982) that documented the making of Werner Herzog's maddening obsession *Fitzicarraldo*. In 1990 Les Blank won the AFI **Maya Deren** award for lifetime achievement in independent filmmaking. Recent films by Les Blank include: *My Old Fiddle: A Visit with Tommy Jarrell in the Blue Ridge* and *Sworn to the Drum: A Tribute to Francisco Agubella* (both 1995).

blaxploitation. Low-budget **exploitation films** made in the 1970s that starred African American performers as urban heroes and crime figures and featured action, sex, and violence. Although the genre that includes *Shaft* (1971), *Superfly* (1972), *The Mack* (1973), *Cleopatra Jones* (1973), and *Truck Turner* (1974) had black casts, many of the filmmakers and crews were not. The films tapped a market heretofore ignored by the Hollywood establishment. Blaxploitation entertained ethnic, urban audiences but perpetuated racial stereotypes. Primarily, they were black versions of tried and true exploitation themes and formats. The blaxploitation

Scream, Blacula, Scream! (1973) directed by Bob Kelijan. Courtesy of The Del Valle Archive

movement failed to empower black filmmakers, and a solid black cinema did not emerge until **Spike Lee**, John Singleton and other young black directors began forging the way in the late 1980s.

Bloom, John. Investigative reporter, essayist. *b.* January 27, 1953, Dallas, Texas. The brainchild behind redneck scholar of the **drive-in** Joe Bob Briggs, John Bloom is a satirist and Gonzo film journalist who celebrates lowbrow American culture by writing about the underbelly of the American cinema. Briggs/Bloom reviewed the cinema that "real Americans" consider down-home entertainment while eating nachos and swilling beer straight out of the can at the local drive-in.

BIBLIOGRAPHY

Briggs, Joe Bob. *Joe Bob Goes to the Drive-in.* New York: Delacorte, 1987.

B-movies. A much-maligned term often implying a low-budget movie that is short, sloppy, exploitative, and cheesy. The reality is far from the case. The B-movie is an important cinematic art form that has

B-movie poster from 1965. Courtesy of The Del Valle Archive

produced entertaining and thoughtful films. B-movies came into existence in the mid-1930s when the Hollywood Studio System began programming double features for movie houses. The studios produced low-cost films designated for exhibition with a main big-budget, glossy, star vehicle, then called an A-picture. Studio moguls intended to fill out their packages as economically as possible. They were not intending to create a new form of cinema, although eventually—with the acceptance of audiences and critics—they did just that. As the studio system collapsed during the 1950s and 1960s, so did the B-movie. In the early 1960s **American International Pictures** and **Roger Corman** reclaimed the B-movie concept on its own merits. Since the 1970s, the B-movie, with offbeat subjects and treatments in low-budget productions, has become the domain of the independent filmmaking community.

BIBLIOGRAPHY

McCarthy, Todd and Charles Flynn, eds. *Kings of the Bs: Working within the Hollywood System: An Anthology of Film History and Criticism.* New York: E.P. Dutton, 1975.

Miller, Don. *B Movies.* New York: Ballantine Books, 1988.

Bolex camera. 16mm movie camera developed by the Paillard S.A. Company of Switzerland in the early 1930s. It revolutionized the film industry by affording access to both amateur and professional filmmakers to this versatile and high-quality motion picture camera. The Bolex has been the camera of choice for **avant-garde** and **experimental** filmmakers since the 1940s. Historically, film students have shot their early works on the Bolex, then moved up to the Arriflex or other more sophisticated and more cumbersome 16mm cameras. Many of the original H-16 Bolex cameras are still in use, a testament to their durability and craftsmanship. The Bolex can be operated by a built-in hand-cranked spring-driven power or by accessing an electric motor. It is easily handheld or mounted on a tripod, shoots from eight to sixty-four frames per second, can photograph a single frame at a time, and performs in-camera fades, dissolves, and superimposition. The most serious competition to the Bolex began with the consumer camcorder in the late 1960s and 1970s and continues with current digital video technology.

Borden, Lizzie. Director, writer. *b.* February 3, 1950, Detroit, Michigan. *ed.* Wellesley College. Borden's debut feature, the science fiction film *Born in Flames* (1983), was made for $30,000 and has become a critical piece of modern feminist theory. Its portrayal of a disparate group of women battling to save what's left of a dying cultural revolution won Borden intense praise, though the film was barely seen and remains largely out of circulation. Borden's follow-up, 1986's *Working Girls*, portrays a day in the life of a group of prostitutes working in a Manhattan brothel and acknowledges sex for money as a viable form of work. It is Borden's best-known film, but she was not able to parlay its critical success into another film and began to work largely in television. In 1991 *Love Crimes* was released. The film stars Sean Young and Patrick Bergin and concerns a female district attorney who investigates a man who photographs women then physically and financially harasses them.

Brakhage, Stan. Filmmaker. *b.* January 14, 1933, Kansas City, Missouri. *ed.* Dartmouth University. Stan Brakhage is the most celebrated and well-known **experimental** filmmaker working in the United States. In 1952 Stan Brakhage completed *Interim*, his first film. In 1954 he married Jane Collum; they had five children and settled in Boulder, Colorado, in Lump Gulch, 9,000 feet up in the Rockies. Brakhage's family life became the exploration of a series of films including *Wedlock House: An Intercourse* and *Window Water Baby Moving*, both completed in 1959. From the outset, Brakhage's films were difficult viewing. He photographed with a hand-held camera searching for what he would later call "closed eye vision." Although he had been raised watching Hollywood movies, Brakhage was fascinated with how the human eye really sees and not the camera eye of a professional cameraman. Most of his early work is silent to give the image prominence. Brakhage has created many films without a camera by scratching directly on celluloid, applying color paints and dyes, even gluing moths to film and then printing the result for *Mothlight* (1963). The plasticity of cinema is Brakhage's principal concern as a filmmaker. Brakhage's most celebrated work is the epic mythopoetic film *Dog Star Man*, filmed from 1961 to 1964. *Dog Star Man* includes a prelude and four separate parts. The **16mm** color film features Brakhage and his dog in their quest to climb a mountain. Upon completion of *Dog Star Man* Brakhage published his manifesto *Metaphors on Vision* in *Film Culture* magazine.

Brakhage is a film poet whose films experiment with light, shape, and form explored in a non-narrative search for "the art of vision," the title of his 270-minute film actualized from 1961 to 1965. In 1964 his 16mm filmmaking equipment was stolen, and Brakhage worked in **8mm** until 1969. Brakhage has never been able to completely support himself by his personal filmmaking. Over the course of his career he has worked on television commercials and industrials, has lectured as a film historian and theorist, and has been a teacher at the School of the Art Institute in Chicago and the University at Boulder, Colorado. He is the author of several books on filmmaking including *A Moving Picture Giving and Taking Book*, published in 1971, a sixty-five page, pocket-sized, black leather volume that is a poetic and technical guide to the art of experimental filmmaking. Brakhage has also sustained himself financially by receiving grants and money from fund-raisers and by selling prints of his films. His most recent work has been described as a tender and prayerful cinema that plays on the viewer's metabolism.

For decades Brakhage developed his films at Western Cine Lab in suburban Denver, working with technician Sam Bush who was sometimes credited as a collaborator. The lab eventually had to cut back on expenses due to competition from the video and digital revolution, dismissing Bush and selling their elaborate **optical printer** used to create countless images in Brakhage's films. Determined, Brakhage turned to a less sophisticated printer at the University of Colorado and announced that if the manufacturing of film stock ever ceased, he would scratch on rocks at the beach and line them up like dominos, creating a primitive flip book when they fell. Stan Brakhage has created over 300 films ranging in length from nine seconds to four hours and has won numerous honors and awards including Film Culture's Fourth Independent Film Award in 1962, a Rockefeller Fellowship from 1967 to 1969, and three retrospectives at the Museum of Modern Art. In 1986 he received the first AFI **Maya Deren** award for independent film and video artists. Recent films from the prolific Stan Brakhage include: *The Persian Series* (2000), *Jesus Wept* (2000), and *Love Song 6* (2001). *See also* avant-garde cinema; experimental film; optical printer

BIBLIOGRAPHY

Brakhage, Stan. *Brakhage Scrapbook: Collected Writings 1964-1980.* New York: Documentext, 1982.

———. *Metaphors on Vision.* Ed. P. Adams Sitney. New York: Film Culture No. 30, 1963.

Elder, Bruce R. *The Films of Stan Brakhage in the American Tradition of Ezra Pound, Gertrude Stein and Charles Olsen.* Waterloo, Ontario: Wilfrid Laurier University Press, 1999.

Brooks, Mel. Actor, director, screenwriter, producer. *b.* Melvin Kaminsky, June 28, 1926, Brooklyn, New York. Best known for outrageous film parodies, Brooks's irreverent directorial debut *The Producers* (1968) is based on his own screenplay. The story, now a Broadway smash, concerns one professional, a neophyte producer mounting a musical named *Springtime for Hitler* by raising oodles of money from little old ladies so they can finagle an instant windfall when the show flops in one night. To Mel Brooks it was just Borsch-belt schtick, but this low-budget classic turned American comedy on its head. Taboo subjects were now fodder for a new kind of joke mill. *The Producers* was more than a series of pungent one-liners; its concept created a brilliant plot that Brooks and his leads Gene Wilder and an unleashed Zero Mostel exploited to push the limits of good taste. This comedy classic led to a renaissance in film comedy

in the 1980s and 1990s. The originality of his brave debut may have been too difficult for Brooks to top. His next film *The Twelve Chairs* (1970) reworked the tale of a man searching for one of twelve dining room chairs that has jewels sewn into the seat. The tried-and-true plot had been filmed in Hollywood, Germany, England, Argentina, and Cuba. When it failed at the box office and did little to grow Brooks's reputation as an inventive comic maverick, he settled into a long string of parodies and satires beginning with the hilariously successful *Blazing Saddles* (1974), which ripped apart America's sacred western genre. Although funny and impudent, Brooks began to rely on bathroom and "tits and ass" humor. Throughout the 1970s Brooks and **Woody Allen** dominated American film comedy. While Allen continued to break new ground, Brooks took the "if it ain't broke, don't fix it" attitude, directing genre send-ups—the sidesplitting *Young Frankenstein* (1974), *Silent Movie* (1976), and a Hitchcock spoof, *High Anxiety* (1977). In the 1980s he formed Brooksfilms and produced serious works that expanded his professional profile. Critics and audiences rejected *The Elephant Man* (1980), directed by **David Lynch**, and the screen adaptation of *84 Charing Cross Road* (1986). In his directorial career Brooks continued to find subjects to satirize in *History of the World: Part I* (1981) and *Spaceballs* (1987), a silly take on *Star Wars*. Brooks returned to original comedy in 1991 with *Life Stinks*, which tried to make a significant social statement about homelessness. When the film fared poorly, Brooks returned to spoofs. *Robin Hood: Men in Tights* (1993) and *Dracula: Dead and Loving It* (1995) stuck to his formula of zingers and sight gags. Since *The Producers*, Brooks has maintained his independence and significant control over his product. He pushed comic limits and influenced the commercial market for comedy films of all stripes.

Broomfield, Nick. Director, producer. b. January 30, 1948. Veteran British documentarian closely identified with a **cinéma vérité** style exemplified in his in-your-face examination of a Nevada brothel in *Chicken Ranch* (1983). Broomfield's intrusive work method is captured on film when the brothel's owner ultimately shows him the door. Broomfield's career began in England in the early 1970s when he directed a short entitled *Proud to Be British* (1973). His next film, *Juvenile Liaison* (1975), marked his first collaboration with fellow Brit Joan Churchill, who codirected and shot several of his films. Broomfield and Churchill made *Soldier Girls* (1981), an edgy profile of females in the military undergoing basic training. *Lily Tomlin* (1986) is largely a performance profile of Tomlin's in-development one-woman show. In 1989 Broomfield directed his first dramatic feature, *Diamond Skulls* (aka *Dark Obsession*) about a hit-and-run accident caused by drunken carousing. The film was received poorly. Returning to documentaries, Broomfield's next projects were the base

Aileen Wuornos: The Selling of a Serial Killer (1992) and *Tracking Down Maggie: The Unofficial Biography of Margaret Thatcher* (1994), an irreverent portrait of the British prime minister. For the BBC, Nick Broomfield directed an exposé of the notorious Heidi Fleiss—*Heidi Fleiss: Hollywood Madam* (1995), initially released as a TV movie before it gained theatrical distribution. Broomfield's *Kurt & Courtney* (1998), a controversial tabloid depiction of the life and death of Kurt Cobain and the exploits of Courtney Love, caught significant media attention when Love tried to block its release, prompting the **Sundance** Film Festival to pull its screening. *Biggie and Tupac* (2002) is a documentary on the deaths of Tupac Shakur and Biggie Smalls chronicling the east coast-west coast Rap rivalries.

Brown, Bruce. *See Endless Summer, The*

Bui, Tony. Director, producer, writer. *b.* 1973, Saigon, Vietnam. *ed.* Loyola Marymount University. The Bui family left their homeland just before the fall of Saigon when Tony was two years old and settled in Sunnyvale, California. As a teenager Bui was fascinated with storytelling, creating his own **Super 8mm** and video movies. In 1992 Bui began a series of expeditions to Vietnam. As a child, his country was torn and ravaged by war; upon return, Bui found a Vietnam in continuing stages of rebuilding and moving away from tradition toward Westernization. The conflict of East and West cultures fascinated him. In 1995 Bui took a student crew of ten and $9,000 to Vietnam to direct *Yellow Lotus*, a thirty-minute short he had written to explore the humanity and spirit of the Vietnamese people. The film was shot in a studio with little money and ancient Russian dollies left over from the years when the former Soviet Union helped finance the North Vietnamese. *Yellow Lotus* premiered at the Telluride Film Festival, aired on PBS, was screened at **Sundance**, and won awards at the Hampton, San Francisco, and Chicago film festivals. The showing at Sundance led to an invitation to a month-long lab to develop four scenes for his first feature *Three Seasons* (1999). All the major and indie studios wanted Bui's feature debut but demanded the film be shot in English for box office insurance. Bui insisted that his film, which presented the changing seasons as a metaphor for the social, economic, and architectural reconstruction of Vietnam, be shot in-country and in its native language, making it a foreign film with limited box office potential. **Harvey Keitel** became connected to the project, and producers Jason Kliot and Joanna Vicente of Open City films committed to Bui's vision. October Films agreed to distribute *Three Seasons*, which became the first American-financed film to be shot entirely on location in Vietnam. Bui and cinematographer **Lisa Rinzler** worked with Keitel, as a returning Vietnam vet, and a Vietnamese cast to create a film of tradition, change, pain and beauty. *Three Seasons* continues in the tradition of neorealism and contemporary nonlinear storytelling, weaving the principal stories into a single tapestry. The film won the audience award and the Grand Jury Prize at Sundance, and Lisa Rinzler won the cinematography prize for her artful yet realistic photography. Tony Bui contributed the story and produced *Green Dragon* (2001) for his brother Timothy Linh Bui. *See also* Rinzler, Lisa

BIBLIOGRAPHY

LoBrutto, Vincent. "Culture Clash: In Shooting the Film Three Seasons, Cinematographer Lisa Rinzler Joins Writer/Director Tony Bui on a Trip to Changing Homeland of Vietnam." *American Cinematographer* 80.2 (February, 1999).

Burnett, Charles. Director. *b.* April 13, 1944, Vicksburg, Mississippi. *ed.* UCLA. Drawing on Italian neorealism, Burnett's penetrating looks into black family life have won many admirers but little commercial attention. Fueled by increasing frustration with the American film community's portrayal of blacks, Burnett made his thesis film *Killer of Sheep* in 1977. The film, about a working-class Los Angeles couple, received awards at the Berlin and **Sundance** film festivals several years after its release and was one of the first films entered in the Library of Congress Historic Film Registry. *Killer of Sheep* was poorly distributed and remains out of circulation. A Guggenheim Fellowship allowed Burnett to make his second feature *My Brother's Wedding* in 1984, but that film also suffered from poor distribution. With the 1990s *To Sleep with Anger*, Burnett finally found wider acclaim. Funded by a MacArthur Foundation grant and starring Danny Glover, the film follows the mysterious arrival of a stranger at the home of a stable family. *To Sleep with Anger* won an award at Sundance and appeared on several year-end "best of" lists. *The Glass Shield* in 1994 and his 1996 film *Nightjohns*, though favorably reviewed, received little attention. Since 1996 Charles Burnett has primarily directed television and episodic series. In 1999 *Olivia's Story*, a short film and *The Annihilation of Fish*, a feature, were released.

Burns, Edward. Director, screenwriter, actor. *b.* January 29, 1968, Valley Stream, Long Island, New York. *ed.* SUNY–Albany, Hunter College. Few films have had a greater impact on the independent film world than Edward Burns's 1995 comedy *The Brothers McMullen*. After studying film at Hunter College in Manhattan, Burns worked as a production assistant on the syndicated showbiz television show *Entertainment Tonight* (*ET*). He began work on *The Brothers McMullen* while at *ET*, using several fellow staffers on the crew and a group of unknowns, including him, for the cast. The film was made for $25,000 and debuted at the 1995 **Sundance** Film Festival, where it won the festival's Grand Jury Prize. It became the most successful independent film of 1995, Burns used his newfound influence to cast Cameron Diaz and Jennifer Aniston in his follow-up feature *She's the One* (1996), but neither this film nor 1998's *No Looking Back* or *Sidewalks or New York* (2001) received the critical or audience response that greeted his debut. Burns created the network television series *The Fighting Fitzgeralds* featuring Brian Dennehy and has appeared as an actor in *Saving Private Ryan* (1998), *15 Minutes* (2001), and *Confidence Man* (2002).

Burton, Tim. Director, screenwriter, producer. *b.* August 25, 1958, Burbank, California. *ed.* California Institute of the Arts. Tim Burton is a unique filmmaker who has been financed exclusively by major studios but whose work is stylistically daring and narratively unconventional. After studying animation, Burton was hired by Disney and worked on *The Fox and the Hound*. His personal visual style and macabre sense of storytelling was way out of Mickey's mainstream. Somehow Disney bankrolled two short films, *Vincent* (1982), a stop-motion animation tribute to Vincent Price who Burton persuaded to narrate, and *Frankenweenie* (1984), a live-action retelling of the Mary Shelly gothic horror classic, in which a young boy brings his deceased dog back to life. Neither film was released nationally, but Burton began laying down his imagery like a cinematic Edward Gorey and Gahan Wilson. In the shorts, Burton expressed his own childhood anxieties and fears in a gentle but scary manner that was a cross between a campfire fright tale and the classic children's book *Where the Wild Things Are*. Burton had grown up on comic books, cartoons, and horror movies all filtered through a personally sad childhood. He might have been relegated to the experimental or cult cinematic ghettos, but Paul Rubens, the then-popular television star, hired Burton to direct *Pee-Wee's Big Adventure* (1985). Burton's imaginative sensibilities were a perfect complement for the modern-day Pinky Lee, and the collaboration produced a magical comedy, *Beetlejuice* (1988), that features a brilliant madcap performance by Michael Keaton in a delightfully wicked story of a dead couple coping with the afterlife.

Although Burton was not making any significant money for the studios, he was developing a singular stylistic voice and an obsession with dark but playful macabre. On his artistic merit alone, Burton was entrusted with a megaproject, and in 1989 Tim Burton reinvented *Batman* with an interpretation that fused the Bob Kane caped crusader with Frank Miller's Dark Knight. Burton's love of comics and his boyish point of view resulted in a major blockbuster followed by his sequel *Batman Returns* (1992). Burton capitalized on his *Batman* clout with his most personal project, *Edward Scissorhands* (1990), a fable about a young man with scissors for hands who is a gardener artiste. The film was a satire on suburban life and a metaphor for the plight of the iconoclastic artistic

Director Tim Burton on the set of *Edward Scissorhands* (1990). Courtesy of *The Del Valle Archive*

creator. It dumbfounded general audiences but developed a loyal following. After his second *Batman* blockbuster, Burton directed another deeply personal project, *Ed Wood* (1994), a black-and-white biopic of the director often tagged as the world's worst. Burton emphasized Wood's passion for moviemaking and his cracked sensibility toward the material he chose to film. Burton saw his relationship with Vincent Price in Wood's affection for Bela Lugosi, making the film a valentine for low-rent, out-of-the-mainstream filmmaking. The subject was just too inside for general audiences, but it pleased many critics and the legion of Tim Burton fans.

Returning to a large canvas, Burton had a major failure with *Mars Attacks!* (1996), an outrageous satirical take on 1950s hysteria based on a series of sci-fi trading cards. Like Steven Spielberg's *1941*, the film's broad satire and outlandish style failed to engage the audience. In 2001 Burton reimagined the cult classic *Planet of the Apes*. In addition to producing many of his own films, Tim Burton has produced the animated features *The Nightmare before Christmas* (1993), *James and the Giant Peach* (1996), and *Cabin Boy* (1994). Tim Burton is that rare filmmaker who makes personal films bought and paid for as entertainment product on his own independent-minded terms.

BIBLIOGRAPHY

Hanke, Ken. *Tim Burton: An Unauthorized Biography of the Filmmaker.* Los Angeles, CA: Renaissance Books, 1999.

Salisbury, Mark, ed. *Burton on Burton.* London: Faber and Faber, 1995.

Buscemi, Steve. Actor, producer, director. *b.* December 13, 1957, Brooklyn, New York. Among actors in the independent film world, Buscemi has distinguished himself in acclaimed often-risky performances in some of the most notable independent films of the era. Although he gained his widest critical attention as the artist dying of AIDS in Bill Sherwood's seminal 1986 film *Parting Glances*, Buscemi is more familiar for his later work with some of the preeminent names in the independent world. Since coming into prominence in the later 1980s, Buscemi has appeared in films by **Abel Ferrara** (*The King of New York*, 1990), Alexandre Rockwell (*In the Soup*, 1992), **Robert Rodriguez** (*Desperado*, 1995), and **Robert Altman** (*Kansas City*, 1996). His most fruitful (and popular) collaboration has been with the **Coen** brothers who have cast him in *Miller's Crossing* (1990), *Barton Fink* (1991), *The Hudsucker Proxy* (1994), *Fargo* (1996), and *The Big Lebowski* (1998). His gravitation toward quirky parts in quirky films has gained Buscemi a loyal following, and in 1996 he wrote, directed, and starred in another—the highly praised *Trees Lounge*. Buscemi's story is highly autobiographical, focusing on the working class on Long Island and their slim prospects for a better life. In 2000 Steve Buscemi directed *Animal Factory*, an edgy and original prison drama. Recent acting appearances include: *Ghost World* (2001), the voice of Randall in *Monsters Inc.* (2001), *The Laramie Project* (2002), and *Voltage*, directed by **Robert Altman.**

C

Cammell, Donald. Screenwriter, director. *b.* Donald Seton Cammell, January 17, 1934, Edinburgh, Scotland. *d.* April 24, 1996, Hollywood, California. *ed.* Royal College of Art. Donald Cammell is best known for codirecting *Performance* (1970) along with Nicholas Roeg, starring Mick Jagger and James Fox. Roeg went on to establish a substantial body of work as a director, but Cammell only completed four films in forty years, leading most critics and historians to conclude *Performance* was more Roeg's work than Cammell's. After Donald Cammell's death, scholars uncovered compelling markers of a unique independent voice and distinct vision. Cammell studied painting at the Annigoni school of classical painting, named after the artist known for hosting parties that celebrated disguise, role-play, and adoration of the beautiful. Cammell's father wrote biographies of Annigoni and Aleister Crowley, the lord of black magick. There were unfounded rumors that Donald was Crowley's godson. To further a connection with Satanism, Cammell played Osiris, the Egyptian god of agriculture, who was ripped into four pieces, then reborn to reign as the lord of the underworld, in **Kenneth Anger**'s notorious *Lucifer Rising* (1968). Before *Performance*, Cammell cowrote *The Touchables* (1973) with his brother David, about four female fans that kidnap a rock star and tease and torture him for attention. The influences of magick, sex, duality, and drugs surfaced when Cammell worked on *Performance*, a complex narrative about exchanging identities and obsessions with sex, drugs and rock 'n' roll. When *Performance* was shown to Warner Bros. the studio was horrified by the display of degradation as the characters played by Fox, Jagger, Anita Pallenberg, and Michele Breton formed and reformed into druggy, sex groupings. There was a two-year battle with Warner's, who finally released the film.

Marlon Brando approached Cammell to collaborate as a writer/director on *Fan-Tan*, an unrealized 1920s period project about female pirates. In 1977 Donald Cammell directed *Demon Seed* with Julie Christie as a woman impregnated by a supercomputer with a psychedelic consciousness. Cammell envisioned the film as a warped comedy, but the studio demanded serious sci-fi and hampered the director's sardonic sensibilities. In 1978 Cammell was scheduled to direct *Tilt*, the story of a female pinball wizard, but he left the project when the producer vetoed Jodie Foster and turned the project into a Brooke Shields vehicle. Cammell directed David Keith and Cathy Moriarty in *White of the Eye* (1987), where a young passionate couple falls under the spell of a serial killer. Disturbing sexual encounters and a flashcut structure that psychically divides the characters clearly identified Cammell as an auteur with a style and theme. *3000* (the amount of money to procure a call girl for the night) made the studio rounds and after a reincarnation was released as *Pretty Woman* (1990), directed by Garry Marshall, launching the superstar career of Julia Roberts. Cammell's last screenplay was written in collaboration with former wife China Kong and Drew Hammond in which a journalist in 1933 is dispatched to Istanbul to investigate a heroin kingpin but is ensnared in a Cammellian web of identity confusion and dark deeds.

BIBLIOGRAPHY

Chang, Chris. "Cinema, Sex, Magick: The Films of Donald Cammell." *Film Comment* 32.4 (July–August 1996): 14–19, 83.

Cannon Group. Throughout the 1980s the U.S.-based Cannon Group formed by Israelis Menahem Golan and Yoram Globus dominated the independent film market, producing and distributing sex and violent action films along with artistic endeavors by **John Cassavetes, Robert Altman,** Andre Konchalovsky, and Jean-Luc Godard. Menahem Golan, a leading figure of the Israeli film industry, began as an assistant director at the Habrimah Theater in Tel Aviv. After studying at London's Old Vic, Golan returned to Israel to direct stage productions. The Israeli film industry was developing, so Golan studied filmmaking at New York University and did his "graduate" work at **Roger Corman** University as Corman's assistant. Returning home, Golan produced and directed his first feature, *El Dorado* (1963). Golan formed Noah Films and then Golan-Globus Productions in partnership with Yoram Globus. They produced low-budget Israeli films financed and released through a subsidiary, Amer-Euro Pictures International. In 1979 Golan-Globus bought the controlling shares of New York's Cannon films, and Golan was installed as chairman.

Through expansion that consisted of low-budget productions and the development of an aggressive advertising and promotion machine, Cannon quickly became a leading force in American and international independent film production. Before **Miramax**, Cannon dominated the marketplace, challenging the major studios with a huge production slate including *Lady Chatterley's Lover* (1981), *Enter the Ninja* (1981), *Death Wish II* (1982), *Breakin'* (1984), *Missing in Action*, *Grace Quigley*, *Exterminator 2*, *Bolero* (all 1984), *Love Streams*, *American Ninja*, *Runaway Train*, *King Solomon's Mines*, *Rappin*, *Fool for Love* (all 1985), *The Delta Force*, *Cobra*, *Murphy's Law*, *52 Pick-up* (all 1986), *Over the Top*, *Superman IV: The Quest for Peace*, *Barfly*, *Tough Guys Don't Dance*, *Shy People*, *Allan Quartermain and the Lost City of Gold*, *King Lear* (all 1987), *A Cry in the Dark*, *Salsa* (both 1988), and the Cannon Movie Tales that were retellings of classic fairy tales.

In addition to running the company, Menahem Golan directed many Cannon programmers. Overexpansion through acquiring production, distribution, and exhibition assets brought Cannon to the verge of collapse by the end of the 1980s. The troubles led to Giancarlo Paretti's Pathé Communications gaining control over Cannon Entertainment. In 1989 Golan resigned and formed 21st Century Distribution, and Globus stayed with Pathé. Throughout the 1990s Golan continued to direct and produce low-budget genre films including *Lambada* (1990), *Desert Kickboxer* (1992), *Street Knight*, *The Mummy Lives*, *Teenage Bonnie and Klepto Clyde* (all 1993), *American Cyborg: Steel Warrior* (1994) and *Delta Force One: The Lost Patrol* (1999).

Canyon Cinema. Berkeley, California, co-op founded by filmmaker **Bruce Baillie** in 1960. Baillie screened films informally on a sheet in his backyard. By 1961 the Canyon Cinematheque was formed, had regular screenings, and produced a newsletter, *The Canyon Cinemanews*. In 1966, the Cinematheque moved to San Francisco and began distribution of co-op films. Dependent on funding, Canyon moved to various Bay Area locations. In the early 1970s, an activist group from Canyon occupied the projection booth at the Cinematheque at the San Francisco Art Institute to protest for more local filmmaker screenings. The splinter group became the **No-Nothing Cinema** and later reemerged as the New-Nothing Cinema, a free venue where any film could be shown.

Canyon Cinema publishes a catalog and sporadically holds public screenings of co-op members' works. Canyon has over 35,000 films and videos tracing **avant-garde** and **experimental films** from as early as 1930. They service universities worldwide. Canyon filmmakers include James Broughton, Sidney Petterson, Bruce Conner, Robert Nelson, Gunver Nelson, Warren Sonbert, **Kenneth Anger, George Kuchar**, and **Les Blank**. Any filmmaker can join by paying a yearly fee and submitting their films for review. The filmmakers set their own rental fees, own their prints, and get the majority of the generated income.

A haunting image from *Carnival of Souls* (1962), directed by Herk Harvey. Courtesy of The Del Valle Archive

Carnival of Souls. Independently produced low-budget horror film written by John Clifford and directed by Herk Harvey on location in Lawrence, Kansas, and Utah, released in 1962. A highly original work, *Carnival of Souls* broke ground by presenting living-dead zombies and surrealistic creepiness years before **George Romero, David Lynch, David Cronenberg,** and **Wes Craven.** Herk Harvey entered the industry as an actor in educational and industrial films for the Centron Corporation in Lawrence, Kansas. He eventually became a director of the company. In 1961, he decided to make his own independent feature film. Harvey teamed up with John Clifford, a joke writer for radio comedian Ken Murray, to write the script for the creepy horror film. *Carnival of Souls* was shot in black and white for $30,000.

It is the story of a young woman who plunges off a bridge with her friends during a drag race. They all appear to have drowned, but the young woman emerges from the deep. The distant and disturbed woman becomes a church organist and is drawn to a closed and run-down carnival. Throughout the film, she is stalked by a phantom-like figure, perhaps her soul seeking salvation. *Carnival of Souls* is truly creepy and unnerving, never campy or weird like Romero's *Night of the Living Dead* (1968). *Carnival of Souls* developed a large following and inspired a 1998 remake directed by Adam Grossman and executive produced by Wes Craven. Working with originality, passion, no-name actors, and a local crew, Harvey and Clifford entered independent film history with a chiller that doesn't just scare but goes deeper to explore spirituality and speculate about the pain of a tormented soul.

Carolco Pictures. Founded by Mario Kassar and Andrew Vajna in 1976 as Carolco Services Inc. specializing in foreign sales. They became Carolco Pictures, independent movie producers who attained great financial and popular success with *First Blood* (1982), starring Sylvester Stallone, and scored even higher with its sequels *Rambo: First Blood Part II* (1985) and *Rambo III* (1988). Carolco built itself into the paradigm of a successful independent producer and then chose to put its money into big-budget action films. *Basic Instinct* (1992) was also a major hit for Carolco, but a series of flops, like *Chaplin* (1992), sent Carolco into restructuring in 1993.

Carpenter, John. Director, producer, screenwriter, composer. *b.* January 16, 1948, Carthage, New York. *ed.* Kentucky University, University of Southern California (USC). Carpenter began making films as a teenager in 1962 and followed his ambitions to the USC film school, where he created at least a dozen shorts. He was cowriter, cocameraman, composer, and assistant director on *The Resurrection of Bronco Billy* (1970), which won the Oscar for best live-action short. Carpenter and Dan O'Bannon, the future screenwriter of *Alien* (1979) and *Blue Thunder* (1983), cowrote a short film they expanded into a feature-length screenplay. With $1,000 from USC, Carpenter began work on his first feature, *Dark Star*, released in 1974. Completed at a final cost of $60,000 with O'Bannon creating the special effects, *Dark Star* is a sci-fi satire about astronauts charged with blowing up unstable planets. In 1976 Carpenter directed *Assault on Precinct 13*, an update of Howard Hawks's western *Rio Bravo* transposed to a nearly deserted LA police station under siege by a youth gang. The low-budget thriller contains a lot of action sequences and kinetic shoot-em-ups that display Carpenter's keen sense of editing and cinematic tension.

In 1978 Carpenter hit it big with *Halloween,* a $300,000 horror classic that grossed over $60 million worldwide and was the most profitable independent film of its day. The film launched the career of scream-queen Jamie Lee Curtis and is the tale of Mike Myers, an escaped mental patient out to create mayhem. *Halloween* spawned five sequels over a twenty-year period. Working with director of photography **Dean Cundey,** Carpenter keeps the audience constantly on edge by clever use of composition and staging. By using every inch of the film frame, Carpen-

A classic scare moment from John Carpenter's *The Fog* (1980). Courtesy of The Del Valle Archive

ter creates a scary atmosphere where Myers can jump out at any moment. Thematically, Carpenter employed genres as a metaphor for the dark side of American culture. In entertainment films like *The Fog* (1980), *Escape from New York* (1981), and *Big Trouble in Little China* (1986), he was able to inject feelings of isolation and mistrust for mass communications and comment on the ills of urban decay.

Carpenter composed the scores for most of his films working with a synthesizer in a minimalist musical style. He was in the vanguard of producing simple, but highly effective, tension-heightening music that has influenced hundreds of low-budget horror films. Toward the end of the century, Carpenter's career began to wane. Although *Vampires* (1998) was a critical and box office failure domestically, John Carpenter remains in the firmament of horror enthusiasts worldwide. As he attests, "In France I'm an auteur, in Germany a filmmaker, in England, a genre film director, in the USA, bum." *Ghosts of Mars* (2001), did little, if any to change this assessment. *See also* Cundey, Dean; *Halloween*

Carson, L.M. Kit. Screenwriter, actor, producer, director. *b.* 1947, Dallas, Texas. *ed.* New York University Film School. Kit Carson was an actor in **Sidney Lumet**'s *Running on Empty* (1988), wrote *Paris, Texas* (1984) for director Wim Wenders, and was coproducer of **Wes Anderson**'s *Bottle Rocket* (1996), but he achieved independent film immortality for his participation in **Jim McBride**'s landmark directorial debut *David Holzman's Diary* (1967). Carson wrote the screenplay and plays the lead role in this **self-referential, diary film** produced for only $2,500. The faux **cinéma vérité** film launched Carson's career, but his work in the industry since then has been sporadic. He directed and wrote *The American Dreamer* (1971), a portrait of **Dennis Hopper,** wrote the screenplay for Jim Mc-Bride's *Breathless* (1983), and was the associate producer of *The Texas Chainsaw Massacre Part II* (1986). Like many 1960s and 1970s generation film freaks, he did not reach his potential. In 1996 Carson was an independent producer for Mike Medavoy's Phoenix Pictures, a New York–based company. Carson cowrote, coproduced, and played a role in *Bullfighter* (2001). In 2001 Carson wrote and produced *Perfume and Bullfighter,* directed by his son Hunter Carson. He also wrote the screenplay for *Tempo* (2002). *See also David Holzman's Diary;* diary film; McBride, Jim; self-referential filmmaking

BIBLIOGRAPHY

Carson, L.M. Kit. *David Holzman's Diary: A Screenplay by L.M. Kit Carson from a Film by Jim McBride.* New York: Farrar, Straus and Giroux, 1970.

Cassavetes, John. Actor, director, screenwriter. *b.* December 9, 1929, New York City. *d.* February 3, 1989. *ed.* Colgate University. American Academy of Dramatic Arts. John Cassavetes began his acting career in a Providence, Rhode Island, stock company and worked steadily in the Golden Age of Television in dramas and the detective series *Johnny Staccato.* In the movies Cassavetes appeared in *Crime in the Streets* (1956) and *Edge of the City* (1957). In 1959, Cassavetes pooled his personal earnings and with a group of actors created *Shadows,* the first of many totally independent films made in his lifetime. He used his own money and often self-distributed his work through his personal production company. *Shadows* was shot in grainy, handheld black-and-white **16mm** and deals with the lives of a young white man and his black girlfriend. Much of the film was improvised or based on improvisations. Cassavetes immediately renounced the aesthetics of the Hollywood film and adapted the raw, direct cinema style of **cinéma vérité** and the **underground film**. His lifelong theme emerged at the outset—love in all its permutations—without happy endings or the predictable narratives he despised. Like all his films, *Shadows* is grueling for an audience programmed by the Classical Hollywood mold. A Cassavetes film is intense, tedious, boring, self-indulgent, amateurish, brutally honest and always very much alive with humanity in all its conflicted glory.

In 1963 Cassavetes directed *A Child Is Waiting* for Paramount but felt confined by the Hollywood conventions imposed on him and was at constant odds with producer **Stanley Kramer**. The film starred Burt Lancaster and Judy Garland and featured his wife Gena Rowlands. This story about mentally challenged children gave Cassavetes the chance to explore another of his career themes—the nature of sanity, insanity, and the acceptance of human behavior. Like another cinematic maverick, Orson Welles, Cassavetes worked as an actor in commercial films such as *The Killers* (1964), *The Dirty Dozen* (1967), *Rosemary's Baby* (1968), *Two Minute Warning* (1976), *The Fury* (1978), and *Whose Life Is It Anyway?* (1981) in order to finance his own films so he could direct with complete artistic autonomy.

Cassavetes was a dangerous and adventurous actor who always brought an intense edge to his work even in Hollywood films. His personal works allowed him to peel off layers of artifice from all his actors. Over the years he developed a stock troupe of performers who included his muse Gena Rowlands, Peter Falk, Ben Gazzara, Seymour Cassell, and a number of character actors as well as his mother, family and friends. *Faces* (1968) was a breakthrough personal film. Shot in black and white, with a handheld camera often in uncomfortably close close-ups held longer than conventional audiences could endure, Cassavetes explored the raw emotions of his characters as they struggled with relationships, marriage, and fidelity. Cassavetes's working method has been widely misunderstood by critics and audiences. His films were not total freeform performances improvised on camera. A script was written, the actors improvised the script in rehearsal workshop sessions, the improvs were transcribed word for word, and the transcript served to develop a final shooting script that was adhered to. In this manner Cassavetes was able to achieve improvisation with control. His rambling sense of story was also misread and criticized. Cassavetes was trying to capture the rhythm of life on the screen. Life is filled with both boredom and excitement; people don't talk and behave in short movielike scenes; conversations ramble with moments of insight and confusion. Cassavetes didn't match shots or use optical effects for transitions, utilizing jump cuts and discontinuity in favor of order and structure in editing. Many of the Cassavetes films are long by the standards of his day and with his stylistic rigor played out even longer.

In 1970, Cassavetes directed *Husbands* (1970), released by Columbia Pictures, which followed three suburban friends catapulted into a midlife crisis when a friend dies, desperately trying to break away from their constricted lives. With *A Woman under the Influence* (1974), Cassavetes arrived at a new maturity as an artist and began to cultivate his own audience. The film, independently produced and distributed by Cassavetes's Faces International, features Gena Rowlands as a housewife struggling with her sanity and the constraints of her marriage. Brutally harrowing, *A Woman under the Influence* earned the attention of critics and audiences. Rowlands received an Oscar nomination for her work and Cassavetes for his direction. *The Killing of a Chinese Bookie*, released in two different versions, originally in 1976 and again in 1978 in another form, was a film noir about the fringes of the entertainment industry and the consequences of dealing with organized crime. The dark, convoluted film didn't find an audience but has since developed a following. *Opening Night* (1977), which follows a troupe of stage actors, also produced and self-distributed by Cassavetes, never really had a theatrical run when it was completed and was eventually shown in art theaters and museums. For *Gloria* (1980) Cassavetes returned to the studio system; the film was marketed and widely distributed by Columbia. The film about a woman who finds herself running from the mob with a small boy who has a price on his head did well at the box office but is not considered by the director or his followers to be a true Cassavetes film. Although Cassavetes felt he was pandering to a commercial audience, the film is far from a Hollywood production, still carrying his imprint as a filmmaker. *Love Streams* (1984) was another Cassavetes meditation on the difficulties of love and relationships, released by Cannon who wanted to associate the company with an artist of Cassavetes's stature. Back in full artistic control, *Love Streams* was really only seen by Cassavetes's enthusiasts in a very limited release. *Big Trouble* (1986), an offbeat comedy reteaming the screenwriter and cast of *The In-Laws*, suffered from studio interference and barely resembles the director's signature style. The film received a shoddy release and passed by with little notice—it was the last film directed by Cassavetes.

Although he was often dismissed during his lifetime, Cassavetes is now considered one of the founding fathers of American independent film. *See also* Cassavetes, Nick

BIBLIOGRAPHY

Carney, Raymond. *American Dreaming: The Films of John Cassavetes and the American Experience.* Berkeley: University of California Press, 1985.

Charity, Tom. *John Cassavetes: Lifeworks.* London: Omnibus Press, 2001.

LoBrutto, Vincent. "John Cassavetes." *Films in Review* (January–February 1997): 6–10.

Cassavetes, Nick. Actor, director. *b.* May 21, 1959. Son of **John Cassavetes** and Gena Rowlands, Nick began as an actor in his father's *A Woman under the Influence* (1974) and developed his craft in a series of low-budget films: *The Wraith* (1986), *Assault of the Killer Bimbos* (1987), *Delta Force 3: The Killing Game* (1991), and *Class of 1999 II: The Substitute* (1994). Cassavetes made his directorial debut in 1996 with *Unhook the Stars,* starring his mother Gena Rowlands, and established himself as a low-budget independent filmmaker in the humanist tradition of his father. His second film, *She's So Lovely* (1997), was based on a script by his late father and starred Sean Penn and John Travolta. Nick continues in the Cassavetes tradition, exploring love and relationships and moving his actors through the gamut of genuine emotions. Nick Cassavetes co-wrote the screenplay for *Blow* (2001) and directed a mainstream hit, *John Q* (2002) starring Denzel Washington. *See also* Cassavetes, John

Castle, William. Director, producer. *b.* William Schloss, April 24, 1914, New York, New York. *d.* May 31, 1977. William Castle broke into show business at age fifteen by falsely representing himself as **Samuel Goldwyn**'s nephew in order to get a small part on Broadway. As a young theatrical producer he painted swastikas on a Connecticut theater to convince the press fascists were trying to stop the public from seeing his play—the result was an audience of proud antifascists who filled the seats in support of Castle's bogus cause. After a variety of acting, producing, and writing assignments for Hollywood studios, Castle landed a position as acting coach for Columbia Pictures. His directing career began in 1943 with two films, *Klondike Kate* and *The Chance of a Lifetime.*

After directing over thirty **B-movies,** Castle began to produce and direct chillers and horror films that would establish his reputation as a promoter and master showman. Modeling his career on P.T. Barnum, Castle created a series of outlandish stunts to lure audiences to his movies. For *Macabre* (1958) he insured audience members with a $1,000 life insurance policy from Lloyds of London if anyone died of fright during the running of the picture. *The House on Haunted Hill* (1958) featured "Emergo"; during a key sequence when a woman is shoved into a vat of acid by a walking skeleton, Castle rigged a plastic skeleton on a guide wire to fly over the heads of the crowd. *The Tingler* (1959) billed "Percepto." A jumbo joy buzzer was attached to the bottom of a few seats in each of the theaters running *The Tingler* so patrons could be given a mild electric shock punctuating scary moments in the film. For *Mr. Sardonicus* (1961) audiences were given a cardboard fist with a thumbs up/thumbs

Consummate showman and horror film producer William Castle in a publicity shot with Vincent Price and a makeup artist. *Courtesy of The Del Valle Archive*

down. Castle called this gimmick the "Punishment Poll." As they voted, an on-screen Castle counted the results, sporting a $5 cigar. He appeared at the opening of many of his films to warn the audience about the terror they were to experience. For *13 Ghosts* in 1960 Castle cashed in on the 3-D craze by inventing a variation of the process he called "Illusion-O," a handheld viewer with two strips of cellophane that made the on-screen spooks visible to the viewer. *Homicidal* (1961) sported a "fright break" when terrified members of the audience could leave and get their money back. The caveat was they had to follow a yellow streak that marked the aisle and led to "coward's corner" in the lobby where an audiotaped announcement bellowed, "Look at the coward. See him quiver in the coward's corner!" There were few takers. In 1964, Castle featured Joan Crawford in *Strait-Jacket*. Everyone buying a ticket was given a souvenir axe fashioned out of cardboard—it was the last of his legendary gimmicks.

The films of Castle were competently crafted, but the stories were pure schlock that chilled and delighted his fans. Castle was considered by many to be the poor man's Hitchcock. Known as the "Earl of Deferral" because of all the **deferred payments** he offered to cast and crew to get a picture started with little cash, he made his films fast and cheap. In 1968 Castle went legit and produced a true horror classic, *Rosemary's Baby*, directed by Roman Polanski. He created the tag line "Pray for Rosemary's Baby," which at the time caused controversy among the religious. Castle's work as a producer and director pleased audiences and inspired many young filmmakers who entered the horror genre in the 1970s and 1980s. **Joe Dante**'s *Matinee* (1993) is a tribute to Castle starring John Goodman as a schlockmeister movie-showman modeled on Castle. As a teenager, iconoclast **John Waters** religiously attended each new Castle extravaganza.

BIBLIOGRAPHY

Castle, William. *Step Right Up!:...I'm Gonna Scare the Pants Off America.* New York: Putnam, 1976.

Castle Rock Entertainment. Motion picture and television production company founded in 1987 by Alan Horn, Glenn Paddick, Rob Reiner, Andrew Scheinman and Martin Shafer. Castle Rock has released over fifty feature films including *Absolute Power* (1997), *City Slickers* (1991), *In the Line of Fire* (1993), *Honeymoon in Vegas* (1992), and *Misery* (1990). The company has been the home of director Rob Reiner's films, acquired production deals with Hugh Grant and Elizabeth Hurley's Simian Films and Billy Crystal's Face Productions, and first-look deals with Frank Darabont, Christopher Guest and William Goldman. Other Castle Rock releases include *Miss Congeniality* (2000), *Best in Show* (2000), *Mickey Blue Eyes* (1999), *The Last Days of Disco* (1998), *SubUrbia* (1996), *The Spitfire Grill* (1996), *Lone Star* (1996) and *Before Sunrise* (1995). Castle Rock was purchased by Turner Broadcasting in 1993 and in 1996 became part of the Time/Warner merger and subsequently Time/Warner-America Online, thus making it part of the largest media company in history.

Celebration, The. (*Festen*, aka *Dogme 1*). Danish film directed by Thomas Vinterberg in 1998. *The Celebration* holds the distinction of being the first feature project created under the **Dogme 95** manifesto written by Vinterberg and **Lars von Trier** in 1995. *The Celebration* is the story of a Danish patriarch celebrating his sixtieth birthday at his estate surrounded by his children for a family reunion. Christian, the prodigal son, returns to deliver the speech of honor that turns out to reveal the father's abuse of his children and his responsibility for his daughter's suicide. *The Celebration* received enormous global attention, heralded as launching a new movement of pure cinema where actors and story are the main focus. Mogens Rukov, a professor of screenwriting at the National Film School of Denmark, responsible for training a diverse and respected group of screenwriters in Denmark and Europe, created the story.

The Celebration was shot on location in six weeks using available light, daylight, and low-level tungsten light. No standard movie lighting equipment was utilized. Cinematographer Anthony Dod Mantle even mixed daylight and tungsten light, a technique often looked down upon by professional Hollywood directors of photography. *The Celebration* was completed for just under $1 million. The sound was mixed live on digital audiotape (DAT) in sync with the Sony PC7 E digital video camera during the shooting. The film was edited on an Avid nonlinear computer system. No sound editing was done to the production track. The digibeta was transferred to a waveform using the edit decision list (EDL) from the picture editing and then was mixed to one-track Beta that became the final master.

A collective produced *The Celebration*, and Vinterberg's name does not appear on the film. The original intention of Dogme 95 was to shoot on 35mm film in standard Academy format, but Vinterberg worked in color digital video for mobility and economic concerns. This established that a Dogme 95 project could be shot on video as long as the distribution format was film. Vinterberg transferred the video master to film for worldwide distribution. Vinterberg found that Dogme's strict rules were an emancipation that encouraged his imagination. Purists were attracted to the idea of making feature films without artifice, but Vinterberg's decision to shoot on digital video made a greater impact on independent filmmakers who began to take the medium more seriously. *See also* Dogme 95; von Trier, Lars

Chaplin, Charles. Actor, director, producer, composer. *b.* Charles Spencer Chaplin, April 16, 1899, Lambeth, London, England. *d.* December 25, 1977, Vevey, Switzerland. Charlie Chaplin was a fiercely independent artist in total control of his work. He first stepped on stage at age five. His father died when he was a child, and his mother, a stage performer, suffered a nervous breakdown. Charles and his brother Sidney danced on the streets for pennies and were placed in an orphanage for destitute children. At seventeen, after playing many children's roles in London stage plays, Chaplin joined the Fred Carno Company. In 1913 he joined Mack Sennett's Keystone Company and appeared in a staggering thirty-five comedy shorts in his first year. Chaplin moved to Mutual in 1916 and First National in 1918. In 1919, looking for even more independence, he became a founder of the **United Artists Corporation** with **Douglas Fairbanks, D.W. Griffith**, and Mary Pickford.

Although known as a sentimentalist, Chaplin did have a dark side. *Monsieur Verdoux* (1947) is an early black comedy about a Bluebeard who murders wives for their money. *A King in New York* (1957), produced in England, bitterly jabbed at the American way of life. His leftist leanings were clearly demonstrated not only in the brilliant *Modern Times* (1936), but in *The Great Dictator* (1940) in which he used his comic skills to make one of the most powerful statements against fascism in film history.

As a director Chaplin concentrated on story and performances more than cinematic craft. He was a perfectionist whose take ratio rivaled **Stanley Kubrick** and Polanski (both admirers of the pioneering film-maker). Among Chaplin's greatest achievements are *The Kid* (1921), *The*

Martha Raye and Charlie Chaplin in *Monsieur Verdoux* (1947), directed by Chaplin. Kobol Collection/United Artists

Circus (1928), *The Gold Rush* (1925), and *City Lights* (1931). Every film comedy and comedic actor owes something to Charlie Chaplin. Indie filmmakers can look to his body of work as an example of what passion, vision, and iron will can do for the integrity of a filmmaker. *See also* United Artists Corporation

BIBLIOGRAPHY

Robinson, David. *Chaplin: His Life and Art.* New York: McGraw-Hill, 1985.

Chappaqua. A 1966 watershed psychedelic film created by **Conrad Rooks.** After his father's sudden death in 1962, Rooks abandoned a life of drug and alcohol addiction and traveled to Switzerland to engage in a rest cure. He emerged drug free and enlightened. His plan was to make a movie—the process would be therapeutic and keep him from relapsing. In January 1964, Rooks began work on *Chappaqua,* the title referring to the upstate New York community where he resided since age nine. *Chappaqua* is the Indian word for sacred place of Running Water where tribes buried the dead who disappeared and transitioned into a spiritual state. The project was an adaptation of Rooks's poem *Chappaqua* that probed the profound sadness one experiences after the death of a loved one. The film took almost three years to complete. *Chappaqua* was financed with Rooks's inheritance and money borrowed from family and friends totaling nearly $450,000. Largely improvised, Rooks whipped himself into frenzy and panic contrived to get him in contact with his psyche and his creative powers. The director filmed when inspired, often shooting twenty-four hours nonstop when the muse was in the house. *Chappaqua* was photographed in France, Mexico, India, Ceylon, England, and forty-eight of the United States.

The cinematographer was renowned still photographer **Robert Frank.** *Chappaqua* was photographed in black and white and color with sequences of superimposed imagery representing a hallucinatory state. Rooks had met William Burroughs in 1963 to purchase the screen rights to his novel *Naked Lunch* but abandoned the film idea as impossible (later **David Cronenberg** proved otherwise). He asked Burroughs to play Opium Jones, a man who personified heroin addiction—the decision was inspired typecasting. Burroughs also influenced the experimental narrative mode of storytelling in *Chappaqua* by exposing Rooks to the literary concept of "lines of association" to develop stories that could be applied to film aesthetics. Burroughs introduced Rooks to Ian Sommerville, who meticulously worked on the sound design for *Chappaqua,* creating over fifty separate tracks that corresponded narratively to the complexity of the imagery. Eugene Shuftan, a veteran cinematographer who invented the Schufftan Process, a method of combining full-scale studio sets with artwork or a miniature component, was project consultant and introduced Rooks to Jean-Louis Barrault, who joined the cast. In Ceylon, Rooks met Swami Satchidananda, credited as "The Guru, a disciple of Siva Ananda, founder of the Divine Life Society," and became a devotee. Indian sitarist Ravi Shankar wrote the score and gave the film an aural spirituality and a divine sense of Eastern religion. Allen Ginsberg appeared as "The Messiah," bringing in another layer of Eastern thought. The eclectic casting included musicians Ornette Coleman, The Fugs, and Moondog.

Rooks played the central autobiographical role of Russell Harwick, an alcoholic who escalates to hallucinogenic drugs and peyote while suffering from memories that plagued him. As he struggles through the withdrawal process in a sanatorium, the story flashes back to Harwick's New York life in Chappaqua as a biker, followed by a series of hallucinations of rituals in India, a guru meditation on a druid at the mystery of Stonehenge, shooting Opium Jones during the St. Valentine's Day massacre, and fantasies of a gorgeous woman and a demonic figure surrounding him. Harwick leaves the sanatorium in a helicopter in a state of detox. Rooks's conclusion is that expanded consciousness from hallucinates and exorcism of evil spirits can achieve spiritual enlightenment. In *Chappaqua* addiction is a metaphor for the absence of spirituality in the Western Hemisphere.

Producing the film wiped out Rooks's financial legacy, but he was philosophical about the loss, reasoning that if the money had been applied to substance abuse, it would have ended his life. The spiritual awareness gained from therapy and religious practice kept Rooks sober for ten years. For Rooks, substance addiction was replaced by an obsessional addiction to filmmaking. *Chappaqua* won the Silver Lion at the 1966 Venice Film Festival. Universal Studios purchased the distribution rights but decided against releasing the controversial counterculture film. Eventually Rooks bought back the rights for as much money as the film cost to produce.

Chappaqua was banned in England due to a rule against films depicting drug use. The film was finally released in 1968 when Rooks provided backup evidence that the content was accurate, making *Chappaqua* the first film about drugs to receive the British certificate necessary for public exhibition. *Chappaqua* received a mixed reaction in the United States. Although it was commercially distributed, an **underground** film crew independently produced the project. **Parker Tyler**, a dominant voice in experimental cinema, tore *Chappaqua* apart, dismissing it as lacking ideas and cinematic imagination. Many felt the reliance on optical effects to create the narcotic consciousness was as exploitative as **Roger Corman's** *The Trip* (1967). *Chappaqua* is a strange hybrid funded with more money and industry power behind it than any **experimental film** ever made. Largely rejected by both sides of the cinematic fence, it remains an oddity—a sign of its times, a celebration of independent production, and a record of a counterculture now revered, reviled and commercialized. *See also* Rooks, Conrad; trip movies

Chenzira, Ayoka. Filmmaker, video artist. *b.* 1956, Philadelphia, Pennsylvania. *ed.* New York University film school: Columbia University Teachers College, M.A., education. Ayoka Chenzira is a noted African American female filmmaker, professor of communications, film, and video at the City College of New York and chief executive officer and founder of Red Carnelian Films, a Brooklyn-based production company with a mission statement that places black people at the center of their own stories. Chenzira was trained in dance, painting, still photography, music, film, and video. Dance and movement are especially influential in her cinematic work. Chenzira is considered the first African American female animator and one of the first to write, produce, and direct a 35mm feature film. The film *Alma's Rainbow* (1994) deals with the problems of women talking to their children about sexuality. Other films include *Zajota and the Boogie Spirit* (1989) and *Hair Piece: A Film for Nappyheaded People* (1985).

Chronicle of a Summer. (*Chronique d'un été*). Influential 1961 independent French **cinéma vérité** documentary directed by Jean Rouch and Edgar Morin. Rouch, an anthropologist, was approached by Morin, a sociologist, long interested in the cinema. He was impressed by an article he read on the cinéma vérité movement and wanted to create a film about Paris featuring nonprofessionals. The **16mm** black-and-white film was shot during the summer of 1960 when Morin, a member of the French resistance expelled from the Communist Party for his opposition to Stalin, anticipated that the Algerian War was nearing an end. Morin conceived the project as a sociological fresco to capture the views of his leftist friends who had left the Party over Communist occupation of Hungary. Rouch had done extensive ethnographic research in Africa utilizing a motion picture camera to document life on the continent. Morin was ebullient, working with Rouch during the planning stages of the project, promising the anthropologist complete artistic freedom, but Morin's enthusiasm turned to annoyance over Rouch's idiosyncratic working methods during production.

Chronicle of a Summer is subtitled *Une Expérience de Cinéma-Vérité* as an homage to Dziga Vertov, the great Russian experimental filmmaker who celebrated the freedom of camera movement to capture his artistic, political, and social vision. Rouch continued the grand experiment by first dealing with the cumbersome camera and sound technology that hampered sync-sound documentarians. He engaged the services of four French cameramen, Roger Morilliere, Jean-Jacques Tarbes, Michel Brault, and the New Wave's Raoul Coutard, who had already shot *The 400 Blows* (1959) for Truffaut and *Breathless* (1960) for Godard. They began shooting with a lightweight Arriflex, but the camera was too noisy for shooting on the Paris streets without attracting attention. It also wreaked havoc on the quality of the soundtrack. Rouch had met Brault at the **Flaherty Seminar** and learned the cameraman had conducted experiments shooting a handheld Arriflex that was blimped to muffle the camera noise. Coutard contacted Andre Coutant of the Éclair Company who was instrumental in the development of the Cameflex, a lightweight motion picture camera created for space satellite military surveillance. The camera was quiet, dependable, and equipped with a magazine that held three minutes of film stock. Coutant worked every night at the Éclair factory to extend the magazine so cameramen could shoot longer before the interruption of changing magazines. A prototype of the KMT Coutant-Mathot Éclair, the first light, silent, portable 16mm sync-sound camera, was utilized on the production. Sync-sound was recorded with the portable Nagra tape recorder invented by Stefan Kudelski. The Nagra revolutionized the industry, allowing filmmakers to work on location and move freely with the synchronized camera and sound recorder.

Rouch believed that the camera was a "catalyst," an "accelerator" that allowed a subject to be revealed on film, but he found the French to be more reticent than the Africans he was familiar with documenting. For some of the street interviews Rouch conducted and for sequences inside a Renault factory, Coutard shot from a long distance with a handheld camera without the subjects being aware. For a memorable and emotional scene where a woman walks through Halles reminiscing about her wartime deportation, the KMT Coutant-Mathot Éclair was on the backseat of a vehicle moving away from her, and a Nagra hidden in her handbag recorded the recollections. When Rouch and his team were finished they had twenty-one hours of material that had to be organized, structured, and compressed by the director and his editors, Jean Ravel, Nena Baratier, and Françoise Colin. *Chronicle of a Summer* was not a commercial success; however, it was well received by critics and won prizes at the Manaheim, Cannes and Venice film festivals. Rouch had made a major influence on the cinéma vérité movement that was gaining momentum, especially in the United States. *See also* cinéma vérité

BIBLIOGRAPHY

Eaton, Mick, ed. *Anthropology-Reality-Cinema: The Films of Jean Rouch.* London: BFI, 1979.

cinema of transgression. Lower East Side New York **underground** film movement of the late 1970s and early 1980s named by **Nick Zedd** after making *They Eat Scum* (1979). The movement includes filmmakers Richard Kern, **Beth B**, Manuel Delanda, and Kembra Pfahler and was inspired by the downtown **punk** and no-wave music scenes. The no-budget films, many shot on **Super 8mm**, were influenced by **exploitation** movies and the work of early underground filmmakers **Kenneth Anger, Jack Smith**, and **Andy Warhol** and dealt with drugs, sexual brutality, poverty, and nihilism. Zedd edited *The Underground Film Bulletin* using the pseudonym Orion Jeiko to celebrate the movement and in 1985 wrote a manifesto to define its goals. The manifesto rejects academic snobbery, the **structural** film movement, film schools, media art centers, and film **critics** for creating boring films and promises a new cinema of shock, blood, shame, pain, and ecstasy that breaks every cinematic and social rule possible. The filmmakers attempted to transgress the boundaries of the socially acceptable to—in Zedd's words—"convert, transfigure and transmute a higher plane of existence in order to approach freedom in a world full of unknowing slaves" (*The Cinema of Transgression Manifesto*). *See also* Zedd, Nick

BIBLIOGRAPHY

Sargeant, Jack. *Deathtripping: The Cinema of Transgression*. London: Creation Books, 1995.

Cinema 16. *See* Vogel, Amos

Cinema V. Now regarded as a precursor to **Miramax** and October Films, Cinema V was the first film distributor to specialize in independent film. The company began as a movie theater chain with prestigious venues including the Paris and Sutton in New York. In 1963, the company began distributing independent films including **Shirley Clarke's** *The Cool World* (1963), François Truffaut's *The Soft Skin* (1964), and Bruce Brown's surfing documentary *The Endless Summer* (1966).

cinéma vérité. French term translated as "cinema truth." A documentary film form developed in France and the United States during the 1950s and 1960s. Cinéma vérité was a reaction to **documentaries** staged and overmanipulated by the filmmaker who utilized narration to present a nonobjective point of view. Lightweight camera and sound recording equipment allowed filmmakers to attempt filming life as it was. French cinéma vérité filmmakers like Jean Rouch, whose pioneering *Chronique d'un été* (1961) defined the philosophy, involved the subjects in the process. American filmmakers such as **Albert and David Maysles, Robert Drew, D.A. Pennebaker,** and **Richard Leacock** preferred to call their objective approach **direct cinema.** *See also Chronicle of a Summer*

BIBLIOGRAPHY

Eaton, Mick, ed. *Anthropology-Reality-Cinema: The Films of Jean Rouch*. London: BFI, 1979.

Cineprobe. On-going forum of independent and experimental filmmakers held at the Museum of Modern Art, which began in 1968. Cineprobe features screenings where filmmakers introduce their work and answer questions afterward.

Clark, Larry. Director, photographer. *b.* 1943, Tulsa, Oklahoma. *ed.* Layton School of Art. Larry Clark became a junkie and self-described outlaw at age fifteen. As a young man, Clark was a violent burglar convicted of armed robbery. He served time in a penitentiary and throughout his life shot, inhaled, and injected every drug he could find. In 1963 Clark began to photograph the miserable and violent lives of speed freaks in his native Tulsa. The result was the collection *Tulsa*, photographed from 1962 to 1971. The graphic nature of the subject and Clark's direct, nonjudgmental approach shocked many. Clark received a **National Endowment for the Arts** grant for his second photo collection *Teenage Lust* (1983). The semiautobiographical project investigated the world of teenage runaways. Publication had been delayed by nineteen months when Clark served a jail sentence in 1976 for parole violation. Clark is considered by critics to be one of the most important photographers in the last twenty-five years with over fifty solo exhibitions at major art galleries.

In 1990, he made the transition from photography to video installations. Filmmaking became a natural extension. For his controversial directorial debut *Kids* (1995), Clark began research by hanging out with the troubled young teens who inspired the semidocumentary-style film written by **Harmony Korine**. The graphic sex, drugs, and violence of *Kids* caused a critical and public uproar. Clark became the center of attention and was called everything from a major new cinematic talent to a pedophile. The notoriety brought in a stream of offers, but only for clones of *Kids*.

It took Clark three years to get the money for his second film, *Another Day in Paradise* (1998). He eventually financed the project by getting a $5 million personal loan from a bank, and although he knew the material was NC-17, he promised Trimark he would deliver an R-rated film. When the film was released in 1998, the fifty-nine-year-old Clark had just checked himself into a Los Angeles treatment center, suffering another relapse from his longtime addiction to heroin. Clark's sophomore film was not as shocking or as independently daring in its storytelling and stylistic aesthetics as *Kids*. In his own way and on his own terms Clark had gone Hollywood. *Kids* featured unknowns and nonactors; *An-*

other Day in Paradise starred James Woods, who also coproduced, and Melanie Griffith. Clark based the film on the book by Eddie Little but incorporated his life experience to portray people who casually shoot drugs as part of what they perceive as a pedestrian routine—just something to do. The violence in the film happens and ends suddenly. Clark's unconventional filmmaking methods caused stress on the set. On *Kids* he was working in his own style, functioning more like an artist than conforming to the process of making a feature film. Melanie Griffith went along with Clark's unorthodox methods and accepted his deglamorized image of her character. James Woods and Clark battled throughout production. Clark was obsessed with getting what he perceived as the real Jimmy Woods to blend with the role he played on screen by forcing the veteran actor to stay in character. Clark was resentful when Woods and the crew lectured him about how films were made. The rebel in Clark announced he was free from rules and rejected them on principle. Clark's point of view was to make what he described as an outlaw/road/crime genre picture. The film is set in 1971, but the period was not clearly defined. A scene depicting rough sex was cut in order to get the promised R-rating. Clark admits he sold out, knowing all along that he wouldn't have the full artistic control he had on *Kids*. *Bully* (2001) another uncompromising film about disenfranchised youth, this time based on a true story, was released. *Ken Park* co-directed with **Ed Lachman** and a screenplay by **Harmony Korrine** is Clark's next feature film project. In 2002 Clark brought his personal brand of controversy to the Showtime Cable television network who boldly stand behind their "No Limits" slogan. A two-hour television film or pilot for a potential series will be executive produced and directed by Clark who is co-writing the project with Christopher Shinn and Don Murphy of *Natural Born Killers* (1994) notoriety. The subject: Clark's take on older teenagers in New York City. *See also Kids*; Korine, Harmony

Clarke, Shirley. Director. *b.* Shirley Brimberg, October 2, 1919, New York. *d.* September 23, 1997. After spending her youth pursuing a career as a dancer, Shirley Clarke's inclinations toward choreography transitioned into a film career. Several dance-related documentary shorts followed, then two non-dance shorts including the Oscar-nominated *Skyscraper* in 1959. Clarke's first feature came in the form of **cinéma vérité** narrative. *The Connection* (1961), based on a play by Jack Gelber, was a drama about junkies. The film's use of vulgar language led New York State to ban it for a year. *The Connection* was written off by many but hailed by others for its unflinching portrait of heroin addiction. Clarke's next film was made under the auspices of **The Film-Makers Cooperative**, which she cofounded with **Jonas Mekas**. *Robert Frost: A Lover's Quarrel with the World* (1963) won an Academy Award and is still shown in college literature classes. Clarke's best-known film is *The Cool World* (1963), a drama about a Harlem street gang shot on location in upper Manhattan. Following *Portrait of Jason* (1967), a controversial film about a black male prostitute, Clarke became disenchanted with filmmaking and worked largely out of the spotlight in video and as a teacher of moving images at UCLA until her death in 1997.

classroom films. For almost twenty-five years during the 1940s to the 1970s American schoolchildren were indoctrinated by **16mm** films that attempted to influence their behavior toward sex, recreational substances, driving safety, and social activities. These films were shown in classrooms and school auditoriums across the country and were often received with howls of laughter and clever repartee hurled back at the screen. However, like all propaganda, they still made an impression on many baby-boomers exposed to them. The films were part of the "Mental Hygiene" program begun during World War II by the progressive education movement and were engineered to create a civilized society free from rebellion and teenage angst. The model for classroom films was the training film made under the supervision of sociologists, psychologists, and academics during the war to motivate the country during a time of crisis. After the war, educators felt the need to have visual aids to tame and guide teenagers traumatized by the global conflict. The films were usually ten minutes long, and teachers were supposed to run discussion groups on the sensitive topics—they often didn't. The 16mm prints were run through badly maintained school projectors and were often scratched, full of splices with jumps in continuity. They were archived in school libraries until 1980 and were eventually replaced by video. Mental Hygiene films were part of the budgeted curriculum. In the 1990s classroom films became part of postmodern culture and were distributed as entertainment to a generation that perceived them as camp artifacts of the America that raised their parents.

Independent production companies produced classroom films. On the East Coast, McGraw-Hill, Caravel, Sound Masters, Knickerbocker, and Audio Productions supplied the educators with product. The Midwest had Encyclopedia Britannica, Centron, Cornet, and Portafilms. The West Coast companies functioned independent of the Hollywood studio industry and included Simmel-Meservey, Churchill-Wexler, Gateway, Charles Cahill & Associates, Avis, Bailey Films, Jerry Fairbanks Productions, and John Sutherland Studios. Classroom films were created and organized in genres: Drugs, Sex Education, Fitting In, Cautionary Tales, Girls Only, Driving Safety, and Social Guidance. Some of the classic titles need little explanation: *Keep off the Grass, Soapy the Germ Fighter, The Bottle and the Throttle*, and the infamous *Duck and Cover*, which depicted young schoolchildren hiding under their wooden desks to protect themselves in the event of a nuclear attack.

Scholars of this independent film industry like Ken Smith and **Richard Prelinger** have applied Andrew Sarris's Americanized auteur theory to identify the masters of classroom films. Sid Davis has worked on and off in Hollywood since he was four years old. Once a stand-in for John Wayne, the Duke loaned him $1,000 to make *The Dangerous Stranger* (1950), a cautionary tale about child molesters. Davis was interested in aberrant behavior and dedicated his career in the field to stamping it out. David Smart visited Germany in the 1930s and studied how the Nazis shaped youth behavior with propaganda films. He returned to the United States to start Cornet Films using this new Nazi instructional tool to make social guidance films for a democratic nation. In a postmodern context, classroom films are perceived as funny, but for all their good intentions and mostly bad writing, acting, and production values, their instructional value is dubious.

BIBLIOGRAPHY

Smith, Ken. *Mental Hygiene: Classroom Films 1945–1970*. New York: Blast Books, 1999.

Clerks. *See* Smith, Kevin

Coen, Joel and Ethan. Joel Coen: director, writer. *b.* November 29, 1954, St. Louis Park, Minnesota. *ed.* New York University, University of Texas. Ethan Coen: producer, writer. *b.* September 21, 1957, St. Louis Park, Minnesota. *ed.* Princeton University. The Coen brothers became interested in film early in their lives, claiming the harsh Minnesota weather kept them primarily indoors watching television and reading. Soon they evolved to making films on **Super 8mm**. After high school, Joel and Ethan went their separate ways. After an undistinguished career as a film student, Joel graduated the New York University film school and briefly attended the University of Texas Graduate film program. He left after a semester and traveled back to New York, briefly toiling on the set of a Barry Sonnenfeld–directed industrial film. Joel's first break in film was as assistant editor on *The Evil Dead* (1983), beginning a long and fruitful alliance with the film's director **Sam Raimi**. When Ethan graduated from Princeton as a philosophy major, he also came to New York and worked odd jobs, most significantly as a statistical typist at Macy's.

In 1980, the Coen brothers decided to collaborate on a screenplay and draw from their love of film noir, horror, and pulp fiction. The result was *Blood Simple* (1984), a film that cannily recalls all three influences in a story that evolved with the recurring question, as Ethan told a *Washington Post* reporter, "Okay, we've got these characters in a bad situation—how can we make it worse?" In the film, the husband of an adulterous wife hires a hit man to kill his wife and her lover, but the hit man decides to take the money and run, leading up to a violent and heart-stopping finale. Joel and Ethan shot a two-minute trailer for the film as a tool to lure studios and possible investors, but when no one stepped forward, they spent nearly all of 1981 raising the necessary $750,000 from friends, family, and businesses around their hometown. With a precept to "shoot stylish," thereby giving the film an expensive look, friend and future director Barry Sonnenfeld photographed *Blood Simple* in a forty-day period in Texas. Unable to afford an editor, Joel and Ethan decided to cut the film themselves using the pseudonym Roderick Jaynes, a name they have used for all of their efforts as editors. Soon, the film that no one would finance was receiving a glut of film festival invitations, including one to **Sundance** in 1985. In the first of many festival awards, *Blood Simple* won for Best Dramatic Feature and secured a long-term distribution deal for the Coens with Circle Releasing Corporation. New York critic David Denby called *Blood Simple* "one of the most brazenly self-assured directorial debuts in American film history." The film went on to gross more than $5 million.

To avoid being pigeonholed as the makers of only crime films, the Coens turned to comedy for their second film. *Raising Arizona* (1987) blends their trademark wit with occasionally zany moments to create their first genuine hit with the story of an infertile couple that kidnap the son of a local furniture tycoon who has just fathered quintuplets. *Raising Arizona* starred relative unknowns Nicholas Cage and Holly Hunter and was financed in large part by Circle Releasing, who put up $4 million of the eventual $5 million budget. While the film advanced the Coen brothers' standing within the independent film community and made more than $22 million, *Raising Arizona* divided critics. The film was called "as chatty as *Bringing Up Baby*, as kitsch as a powder blue leisure suit and as adorable as a Pampers ad" by Walter Thomas of *Scene* magazine, but others didn't accept the film's tone or style. Pauline Kael, in her *New Yorker* review, wrote, "The reason the camera whoop-de-do is so noticeable is that there's nothing else going on."

Following the success of *Raising Arizona*, the Coens again switched genres to make the gangster film *Miller's Crossing* (1990), featuring their first widely recognizable star (Albert Finney); with a budget of $10 million, Joel and Ethan graduated to the next strata of filmmaking. The film performed modestly and was generally well received by critics, but it was *Barton Fink* (1991) that made the Hollywood community stand up and take notice. In the title role, John Turturro plays an idealistic young playwright (loosely based on Clifford Odets) who arrives in Hollywood with a severe case of writer's block. The Coens wrote the screenplay about their own case of writer's block on *Miller's Crossing*. The film won an unprecedented three awards at the 1991 Cannes Film Festival, for best actor (Turturro), director (Joel Coen), and the festival's top prize, the Palme d'Or for best film. *Barton Fink* also represented the Coens' first showing at the Academy Awards, with a best supporting actor nomination for Michael Lerner as studio chief Jack Lipnick.

With *Barton Fink*'s appearance on several critics' year-end top-ten lists and its strong showing at Cannes, the Coen brothers were lured to Hollywood filmmaking for their next film, *The Hudsucker Proxy* (1991). Produced by Joel Silver and cowritten by old friend Sam Raimi, the film was a critical and commercial disaster, earning back just $3 million of its $25 million cost. Wisely opting to return to small budgets, the Coens made what is regarded as one of the great films of the 1990s, *Fargo* (1996). The film was made for $6.5 million and is loosely based on a real incident, although Joel and Ethan claim most of the story is their own. Centering on a car salesman who pays to have his wife kidnapped so he can collect the ransom, *Fargo* represented what became known as "the year of the independent film" in 1996. The film became the Coens' biggest success to date and was widely praised, most notably by Gene Siskel and Roger Ebert, who each named *Fargo* the best film of the year and fiercely promoted it when the film was nominated for six Academy Awards. It was nominated for best actress (Francis McDormand), supporting actor (William H. Macy), screenplay (Joel and Ethan Coen), editing (Roderick Jaynes), directing (Joel Coen), and best picture of the year. The Coens captured their first Oscar (for screenwriting), as did Joel's wife, Francis McDormand, who won the award for her performance as the pregnant local police chief who solves the mystery. *Fargo* put the Coens' names on the lips of every film lover and was later named by the American Film Institute as one of the 100 best American films ever made.

Following the overwhelming success of *Fargo*, almost anything would have been a disappointment. With *The Big Lebowski* (1998), the Coens returned to the type of comedy that made *Raising Arizona* such a hit. Using the classic formula of mistaken identity, *The Big Lebowski* failed to engender the same type of box office or critical support as *Fargo*. Although Joel and Ethan Coen each have separate credits at the end of their films, writing, producing, and directing are always a joint effort, Joel claiming he gets the directing credit because he is older. They are symbiotic both on and off the set, finishing each other's sentences and generally sharing the same sensibilities. Although they do not allow for much input (Nicolas Cage has called them "autocratic"), actors clamor to work with the Coens because of their originality, visual audacity, and the respect they engender. *O Brother, Where Art Thou?* (2000) also received a tepid reaction even from many Coenheads. The film, named after the movie within the movie of Preston Sturges's *Sullivan's Travels*

(1941), is a chain-gang comedy based on Homer's *The Odyssey*. In 2001, the Coens received great acclaim for *The Man Who Wasn't There*, featuring a haunting performance by Billy Bob Thornton and meticulously textured black-and-white cinematography by Roger Deakins. Their next project is *Intolerable Cruelty* (2003). *See also* Raimi, Sam

BIBLIOGRAPHY

Bergan, Ronald. *The Coen Brothers*. New York: Thunder's Mouth Press, 2000.

Biskind, Peter. "The Filmmaker Series: Joel and Ethan Coen." *Premiere* (March 1996).

Woods, Paul A. *Joel & Ethan Coen: Blood Siblings*. London: Plexus, 2000.

Cohen, Larry. Director, screenwriter, producer. *b.* Lawrence G. Cohen, July 15, 1938, New York, New York. *ed.* City College of New York, New York University. As a child Larry Cohen often attended two double bills a week and used an overhead projector to put comic book images on his wall. Later, Cohen's father bought an **8mm** camera that Larry borrowed. He conned his friends into acting for films he shot in Fort Tryon Park. Shortly after beginning his career at age twenty-two as an NBC-TV page in New York, Cohen sold two teleplays to *Kraft Mystery Theater* and went on to write a slew of TV fare. In 1966 Cohen sold his first screenplay, *Return of the Seven*, and then *The American Success Company* (1979), *I, the Jury* (1982), *Best Seller* (1987), and *Maniac Cop* in 1988. In 1972 he directed *Bone*, a low-budget **blaxploitation** picture with Yaphet Kotto that Cohen shot in his home. He established himself as a science fiction/fantasy/ horror genre specialist on such films as the box office hit *It's Alive!* (1974), the sequels *It Lives Again* (1978) and *It's Alive III: Island of the Alive* (1987), and *Q* (1982). Larry Cohen is a professional filmmaker with fine business acumen and a twisted sense of narrative loaded with more social/ political metaphors than can be deciphered by your average **B-movie** audience. Now Larry Cohen mostly works as a screenwriter for television movies and feature films. In 1996 he directed *Original Gangstas*, a **Blaxploitation** film starring Fred Williamson, Jim Brown and Pam Grier.

BIBLIOGRAPHY

Vale, V., and Andrea June, eds. *Incredibly Strange Films*. San Francisco, CA: Re/ Search #10, 1986.

Collective for Living Cinema. When students of filmmakers **Ken Jacobs** and Larry Gottheim at SUNY Binghamton became dissatisfied with the direction of **Jonas Mekas's Anthology Film Archives**, they formed their own venue for **experimental films**. The Collective for Living Cinema didn't have the staying power of Anthology but created an option for the presentation of alternative cinema. The collective was located on New York's Upper West Side in an upstairs screening room that was 100 feet long and 50 feet wide with a high ceiling and around 120 seats. Their mission was to present personal filmmakers and their work. Among the leading filmmakers working in the experimental mode who appeared at the Collective for Living Cinema are Michael Snow, Marjorie Keller, Vivienne Dick, **Beth and Scott B,** and **Yvonne Rainer.** *See also* Jacobs, Ken

Coming Apart. See Ginsberg, Milton Moses; self-referential filmmaking

Conner, Bruce. Filmmaker, artist, sculptor. *b.* 1933, McPherson, Kansas. *ed.* University of Wichita, University of Nebraska, University of Colorado, Brooklyn Museum Art School. Bruce Conner first became known as a sculptor and artist. Fame brought him a New York gallery contract, but Conner felt restricted by a lack of control over his work and methods. In the late 1950s he moved to San Francisco and became involved in filmmaking. In 1958 he completed his first film, *A Movie.* Conner couldn't afford to buy a camera, so he bought condensations of old movies at a local supply store, which led him to his collage/montage editing style. The twelve-minute black-and-white film is a creative compilation of stock footage from old newsreels, **documentaries,** and narrative films described by experimental film historian Scott MacDonald as "the Bosch-like vision of modern progress." This highly influential film has been studied by television commercial directors and ad agencies and inspired the art of contextual montage for generations of filmmakers. *A Movie* intercuts images of a submarine periscope with a 1940 **nudie cutie** film of Hollywood icon Marilyn Monroe. The sub fires a torpedo that through Conner's adroit editing becomes an atomic bomb blast, shifting the viewer quickly through the emotions of laughter, then dread. Black leader, Academy leader, and titles that read "End of Part Four" and "The End" are intercut between shots throughout the film's duration. *A Movie* concludes with footage of a Jacques Cousteau underwater documentary montaged with pauses of black leader, so the viewers ultimately transcend the fact they are watching stock footage or "junk film." Many filmmakers, both **experimental** and traditional, have tried to imitate the mystery, humor, and magic of *A Movie,* but Conner truly understands the alchemy that occurs when seemingly random images are intercut and sequenced in a montage that creates its own original narrative.

Cosmic Ray (1962) was constructed in three different versions numbered 1, 2 and 3, created to be projected simultaneously but also to work as individual films. Here Conner deals with the theme of censorship utilizing images of **sexploitation,** television shows and advertising. From 1963 to 1967 Conner made various versions of *Report,* a film reflecting his obsession with the assassination of President John F. Kennedy. The film is a metaphor on death, repeating images taken during the tragedy and intercutting television commercial footage to make the montage even more menacing. Conner struggled with the project, concerned that if he, like others, had exploited the martyred president and that if he completed the film, Kennedy would then truly be dead. The process and multiversions of *Report*, funded by a Ford Foundation grant, were completed when Conner finally accepted JFK was gone.

Throughout his work Conner experiments with repetition and slight variations of a particular image. He often uses a well-known piece of music on the soundtrack without manipulation. The feeling and meaning of the music are transformed by the editing of Conner's images. Conner works in black and white to create a consistency of images. Intercutting random color footage would distract the viewer eye caught by shifts in hue and intensity. The films are tape-spliced so the viewer can see the mechanics of putting two shots together. An exception is *The White Rose* (1967), which Conner printed with standard A and B rolls to create a spliceless work. Over the years Conner's collection of found footage has grown. He hates to throw away a piece of film and always finds a place in his work for each shot. Conner has made less than one short film a year but has remained a distinguished figure in **avant-garde** filmmaking. Recent films include: *Television Assassination* (1995) and *Looking for Mushrooms* (1996).

BIBLIOGRAPHY

Brakhage, Stan. *Film at Wit's End: Eight Avant-Garde Filmmakers*. New York: Documentext, McPherson and Company, 1989.

Coolidge, Martha. Director. *b.* August 17, 1946, New Haven, Connecticut. *ed.* School of Visual Arts, Columbia University, Rhode Island School of Design, New York University, American Film Institute. Martha Coolidge was one of a small group of pioneering women who tried to break into the male-dominated film industry in the 1970s. In the late 1960s she produced a children's show for Canadian television. Coolidge began making films in college and spent ten years as a New York independent filmmaker. She learned her craft by recording sound, working as a cinematographer, and on commercials. Martha Coolidge was a founding member of the **Association of Independent Video and Filmmakers.** Coolidge directed several documentary shorts including *More Than a School* (1973) and *Old Fashioned Woman* (1974) about her grandmother, which was funded by a **National Endowment for the Arts** grant and private investors, mainly family members, and ultimately sold to PBS. *David Off and On* (1975), a candid portrait of her brother as he struggled with drug addiction, was shot for $9,000. In 1976 Coolidge made the courageous autobiographical feature documentary *Not a Pretty Picture* for which she received $46,500 from the NEA. The film premiered at the Kennedy Center and contains a dramatized recreation of her own rape during high school, merging nonfiction with emotional analysis. The film is remarkably objective, intercutting a fictional depiction of the rape and the events that followed. Using the documentary camera and a Brechtian distancing aesthetic, Coolidge and the men portraying the attackers are seen in rehearsal discussing their feelings in recreating the heinous act. The repetition and candor of the rehearsal process strips away the action and male arousal devices that Hollywood features often employed to depict this serious crime. The critical attention from *Not a Pretty Picture* encouraged Coolidge to move to Hollywood to direct dramatic feature films. She received an AFI Academy internship and was mentored by Hollywood veteran editor and director Robert Wise. Coolidge spent five years working on feature projects that never made it into production. One of her screenplays featured two female characters; another was a dramatic film about a character going insane. There was little support from other women in the business. Coolidge's boyfriend left her because he couldn't take the career frustrations. Her house was almost totally destroyed after a series of floods, her car blew up, and a studio president chased Coolidge around his office rather than listen to her project pitch.

Returning to her indie roots Coolidge formed a partnership with friends and directed *Bimbo* (1978), a comedy about a reunion of three male college roommates, written and produced with an all-male crew. Coolidge made the film just to prove to the Hollywood community that she could do it—it was the only film Coolidge directed in the five years she lived in Los Angeles. **Francis Ford Coppola** put Coolidge on his **American Zoetrope** payroll to develop a girl empowerment, coming-of-age story set in a Pennsylvania mining town. The woman who had written the original screenplay refused to let Coolidge direct and decided to make it her directorial debut instead. Coolidge took out a $5,000 bank loan against her Zoetrope salary in order to pay the bills. She then developed *Photoplay*, a rock 'n' roll musical love story for Coppola, writing many drafts of the screenplay in the two and a half years she worked on the project. The film was canceled when Zoetrope ran into its legendary financial difficulties.

Then producers Wayne Crawford and Andrew Lane offered Coolidge *Valley Girl* (1983) because they wanted her to bring a feminist sensibility to the teen comedy genre; still they made her agree to show naked breasts four times to guarantee pubescent boys would pay to see it. The director vowed to include the nudity in her own way. In one of the inclusions she shows the despair of a well-endowed woman who realizes a guy trying to get back at a girl who dumped him has just used her.

Coolidge received a $5,000 fee to direct *Valley Girl*, which cost the producers $350,000 and grossed $17 million.

She was offered a slew of teen flicks without substance, so Coolidge decided to go independent again with *The City Girl* (1984), a film that directly reflected her feminist sensibilities. Laura Harrington plays a young woman who tries to advance her career as a photographer and relationships with men that continue to be unsuccessful. The project was initiated by the producer of *Not a Pretty Picture* who recommended Coolidge to a tax shelter producer who had an incoherent script, essentially a **soft-core** porn film. The announced cash flow of $400,000 turned out to be $40,000. In desperation, the producer allowed Coolidge to do whatever she could to save the film. The rewritten, revamped production was shot in Toronto to maintain the low budget, but Coolidge ran out of money in the third week of production. Actress Colleen Camp who had a role in the production suggested that Coolidge go back to Los Angeles, where she introduced Coolidge to Peter Bogdanovich, who bought the film and became executive producer.

In 1984 Coolidge made her first studio film for Paramount, *The Joy of Sex*, which borrowed only the title of Alex Comfort's bestselling artsy, touchy-feely sex manual. The film is the story of a virgin who believes she has only weeks to live. She decides to run the A to Z of sexual experience before it's too late. The high school comedy was a disaster at the box office and with critics. *Real Genius* (1985), bankrolled by Tristar, tells the tale of a self-styled college genius who recruits a whiz kid to his think tank. The youth revenge comedy cost $10 million and involved special effects that helped to capture its target audience.

Producers and studio executives continued to send Coolidge stacks of silly teen comedy scripts that she turned down and turned to television to keep working. In 1986 Coolidge redefined her career with the kind of feminist independent film she wanted to be known for. She found the screenplay adaptation of Calder Willingham's autobiographical novel *Rambling Rose* in a dead script pile. Coolidge learned that Edgar Scherick had an option on the material for seventeen years as he doggedly tried to get the coming-of-age story of a young woman in the South, but the studios and financiers always rejected him. Director Renny Harlan read the script and wanted to produce it as a vehicle for Laura Dern, his girlfriend at the time. Harlan took the package to Mario Kassar, with Coolidge attached as director, and *Rambling Rose* finally was made. The film resonated with audiences and received Oscar nominations for Dern and her mother Diana Ladd. At the 1992 Independent Spirit Awards *Rambling Rose* won honors for directing, Ladd as supporting actress and best film.

Throughout the 1990s Coolidge continued to work steadily in theatrical features and television films. One of a handful of woman directors who works steadily, Coolidge has been vocal in the media press about the widespread sexual harassment in her industry. She's taken the boy's club on and has not just survived but prospered. In 2000, Martha Coolidge directed Halle Berry in *Introducing Dorothy Dandridge*. In 2002 she became the first woman president of the Directors Guild of America. Her next directorial project is *Adventures in Darkness* (2003).

co-op. A group of independent filmmakers who form a cooperative where their films can be rented or purchased. In a co-op, the filmmakers control the fees and decide which of their films are made available. The filmmakers receive all the revenue from their work except for a small percentage necessary to keep the co-op running. Co-ops are an alternative to commercial distribution where the distributor buys films outright or gets a high percentage of the profits. **The Film-Makers' Cooperative** and the **Canyon Cinema** Co-op are two of the most successful cooperative endeavors.

Cooper, Karen. *See* Film Forum

Coppola, Francis Ford. Director, screenwriter, producer. *b.* April 7, 1939, Detroit. *ed.* Hofstra College, University College of Los Angeles. Francis Ford Coppola was the first of his generation to go to cinema school and crack the closed ranks of the Hollywood film industry. Coppola rang the blockbuster bell with *The Godfather* (1972) and *The Godfather Part II* (1974). Coppola positioned himself by writing screenplays for big-budget studio productions *Is Paris Burning?* (1966), *Patton* (1970), and *The Great Gatsby* (1974) and by directing low-budget **B-movies** for **Roger Corman** including *Dementia 13* (1963), an artsy horror movie. He even made a **nudie cutie,** *Tonight for Sure!* (1961). Paramount did not hire Coppola to direct the screen adaptation of Mario Puzo's bestseller *The Godfather* because they were impressed with his work on his UCLA thesis *You're a Big Boy Now* (1966). The musical *Finian's Rainbow* (1968) was a box office failure; his personal film *The Rain People* (1969) attracted some good reviews but did not make money. Primarily Paramount wanted Coppola because his last name ended in a vowel, and they felt his ethnic background would lend authenticity to their Mafia movie. Coppola turned the organized crime potboiler into an epic about family and the dark side of American enterprise.

Coppola used his fame and success to create **American Zoetrope,** an environment where young filmmakers could experiment and make films that mattered. *The Conversation* (1974) was an art film made under the banner of **The Directors Company,** his business venture with Peter Bogdanovich and William Friedkin. The deeply personal character study of an electronic spy who slowly convinces himself that technology has

Francis Ford Coppola on the set of *Bram Stoker's Dracula* (1992). Courtesy of The Del Valle Archive

turned on him is considered one of Coppola's greatest accomplishments, but it was not recognized in its time. The power and ambition that drove the original Hollywood moguls obsessed Coppola's soul. He made decisions driven by passion, money, and ego. Coppola was always willing to risk going for broke. He was reckless and staked everything on *Apocalypse Now* (1979), which nearly drove him mad and broke. After years of indecision, and endless production and postproduction, Coppola made a flawed but important film about America. His fixation with total artistic control and disregard for fiscal responsibility sent out warning signs to the powers-that-be that the era of the excessive young American director as superstar, an artist with total control over his work, was nearing its end.

Coppola leaped off the precipice with *One from the Heart* (1982). The project began as what he called a small Neil Simonesque comedy, but the megalomania of the former film student who now owned his own studio and created a counterculture roster of actors and filmmakers brought Coppola's fever dream to a crash. The high-budget/high-style/low-content disaster lost Coppola his studio, his money, and his stature and ended the 1970s hope for a New American Cinema. With *One from the Heart*, the leader and champion of the movement had self-destructed from too much of too much. Coppola regrouped and reassessed his situation and made two films for a young audience who idolized novelist S.E. Hinton. *The Outsiders* and *Rumblefish* (both 1983) were shot back to back on location in Tulsa, Oklahoma, with modest budgets, a small crew, and a group of exciting little-known young actors including Tom Cruise, Patrick Swazye, Ralph Macchio, Emilio Estevez, Rob Lowe, Matt Dillon, and Diane Lane, who would eventually all become stars. Money was tight, but Coppola's stylistic flamboyance survived. He anointed *The Outsiders* a *Gone With the Wind* for kids applying an epic cinematic approach and pulled out all of the poetic stops for *Rumblefish*, turning Hinton's teen tale into an existential mediation that unspools as if Albert Camus wrote the screenplay.

In 1984 extravagance overtook Coppola's artistic spirit once again with the disastrous megabuck production of *The Cotton Club*. More like *The Godfather* meets *That's Entertainment* than a historic account of the legendary Harlem nightspot, the film went wildly over budget and narratively astray. The miserable box office failure gave Coppola gallons of bad ink in the press as the excessive megalomaniacal out-of-control director of *Apocalypse Now* and *One from the Heart*. He was seen as a man who could never resolve the conflict between his artistic nature and his Cecil B. DeMille bombast. *Peggy Sue Got Married* (1986) was a critical and financial success that pulled off the combination. Coppola revisited Vietnam with *Gardens of Stone* (1987), a moderately budgeted sensitive drama that unfortunately never found its audience. Coppola was back to trying to define the American experience with *Tucker: The Man and His Dream* (1988), another big production personal labor of love that failed to capture a mainstream audience. His contribution to *New York Stories* (1989) was a self-indulgent gift to his daughter Sophia who wrote the screenplay. The long anticipated *The Godfather Part III* (1990) made Coppola a laughing stock when he gave Sophia the pivotal role of Michael Correleone's daughter after Winona Ryder dropped out due to nervous exhaustion. In 1992 Coppola turned the Dracula legend into a phantasmagoric, expressionistic grand opera, then directed *Jack* (1996), starring Robin Williams as a little boy who is rapidly aging. The film fared poorly and was barely stylistically recognizable as a Coppola production but remains a poignant tribute to his son Gian-Carlo who was killed in a boating accident.

Coppola became more interested in lording over his winery, hotel, and restaurant acquisitions than regaining his position at the forefront of his generation of filmmakers. In 1997 he took on an assignment as a hired hand with John Grisham's *The Rainmaker*, mounting a handsome, well-acted, coherently told production, but the cries of sell-out stung Coppola. The film was a box office winner, but it severely hurt his image as a rebellious dreamer who taught boomer directors that they should make personal films and fight for independence from the movie power elite. Coppola was the executive producer on *The Virgin Suicides*, directed by his daughter, Sofia Coppola, *Dr. Jekyll and Mr. Hyde* (both 1999), and *Jeepers Creepers* (2001). His next film as director is the long-planned pet project *Megalopolis*. Currently Coppola is not revered like **Martin Scorsese** or consistently successful in capturing the imagination of the masses like George Lucas or Steven Spielberg. But Coppola will always be the man who made *The Godfather*, one of the great American classics, and a maverick film director willing to risk it all for his independent spirit and vision.

BIBLIOGRAPHY

Goodwin, Michael, and Naomi Wise. *On the Edge: The Life and Times of Francis Coppola.* New York: William Morrow, 1989.

Schumacher, Michael. *Francis Ford Coppola: A Filmmaker's Life.* New York: Crown Publishers, 1999.

Corman, Roger. Director, producer. *b.* April 5, 1926, Detroit, Michigan. *ed.* Stanford University, Oxford University. When the man known as the king of **B-movies** and head of the school of fast and cheap **exploitation films** got his first industry job as a messenger for the A-list studio Twentieth-Century-Fox, he had already studied engineering at Stanford and completed graduate work in English literature at Oxford. After a brief stint as a literary agent, Corman began his prolific career. By 1950

Roger Corman directing House of Usher (1960). Courtesy of The Del Valle Archive

Corman had seventy-five films on his resume. Corman directed and produced low-budget exploitation films for **American International Pictures** in many genres, traditional and nontraditional to the American film, the Western, science fiction, horror, hot rod, rock 'n' roll and **biker** flicks, all geared to the teenage **drive-in** crowd. In 1957 alone Corman completed nine films, some shot in a record two to three days. In the early 1960s he achieved box office and cult success with a cycle of films based on the stories of Gothic horror master Edgar Allan Poe. The films, which include *House of Usher* (1960), *Pit and the Pendulum* (1961), and *The Raven* (1963), benefited from screen adaptations penned by Richard Matheson, polished production values, and their star, the elegant and sardonic Vincent Price.

In 1970 Corman and his brother Gene formed New World Pictures. Roger's wife Julie produced for the company, and Corman shifted away from directing toward producing and presiding as an executive. New World became a leader in distributing new films of important European directors such as Federico Fellini and Ingmar Bergman. Corman remained at the forefront of B-movie quickies with films like *Bloody Mama*

(1970), *Private Duty Nurses* (1971), *Death Race 2000* (1975), *Jackson County Jail* (1976), *Piranha* (1978), and *Rock 'n' Roll High School* (1979).

In 1983 Corman sold New World to a group of investors for $17 million. He founded New Horizons in 1984 to produce his product, and in 1985 he created the Concorde Company to distribute his wares. Corman created the model, format, and formula for successful low-budget movies shot as quickly and inexpensively as humanly possible. Corman insisted on a catchy, sexy title to start a new project like *The Little Shop of Horrors* (1960), *Viking Women* (1958), *The She Gods of Shark Reef* (1958), *A Bucket of Blood* (1959), *The Wild Angels* (1966) and *Deathsport* (1978). Corman demanded the right balance of sex, violence, action, and rock 'n' roll in a movie before shipping it out to the nation's drive-ins and local theaters. He often ordered more car crashes, explosions, and sex to a director's cut even if the new material was taken from the Corman stock film archive.

Corman created the paradigm for low-budget filming: detailed preplanning; completing many, many quick set-ups in a day's work; and maintaining a low-shooting ratio (sometimes one take) to get a film out under budget and ahead of schedule. Roger Corman's legacy is an enormous stable of screenwriters, directors, actors, producers, cinematographers, and film editors who were trained under his tutelage. The film school generation and others shut out of mainstream Hollywood were eager to work on any film for any price. Corman got them cheap but paid them back with invaluable experience in real moviemaking. The list of Corman graduates speak for itself; Jack Nicholson, **Francis Ford Coppola, Jonathan Demme, Dean Cundey, Joe Dante,** Peter Bogdanovich, **Tina Hirsch, László Kovács, John Sayles, Vilmos Zsigmond, Robert De Niro,** Robert Towne, **Paul Bartel, Martin Scorsese,** Ron Howard, and many other famous and working filmmakers. Roger Corman is a passionate filmmaker with a keen business sense who proudly proclaims he made "a hundred movies in Hollywood and never lost a dime." He helped launch a generation of filmmakers and has created a body of work that for better and worse reflects the youth culture of postwar America. In 2001 Roger Corman was credited as executive producer on *Avalanche Alley, The Arena,* and *Raptor.* He is also the executive producer of *The Haunting of Slaughter Studios.* The films were all distributed by one of Corman's companies, New Horizons, Concorde or New Concorde.

BIBLIOGRAPHY

Corman, Roger, with Jim Jerome. *How I Made a Hundred Movies in Hollywood and Never Lost a Dime.* New York: Random House, 1990.

Gray, Beverly. *Roger Corman: An Unauthorized Biography of the Godfather of Indie Filmmaking.* Los Angeles, CA: Renaissance Books, 2000.

Cox, Alex. Director, writer. *b.* December 15, 1954, Liverpool, England. *ed.* Oxford Law School, Bristol University, University College of Los Angeles. Alex Cox couldn't find work in Los Angeles, so he settled for the lowest common denominator, taking a job with a car repossession outfit. The on-the-job experience of living the life of a repo man and Cox's affinity with the punk movement led to instant cult success with *Repo Man* in 1984. The $1.5 million film that mixed punk with science fiction is a wacky satire inhabited by CIA (Central Intelligence Agency) types, nuclear scientists without their gray matter intact, UFO zealots, and a pair of rebellious brothers searching for a 1964 Chevy containing a deadly cargo. The European vision of America as seen through the perceptive lens of German cinematographer Robby Muller, the zonked-out take on the thriller genre, and a killer punk soundtrack made Alex Cox a hot young director to watch in the 1980s. In 1986 Cox released *Sid and Nancy*, a biopic about the late Sid Vicious, member of the infamous and nihilistic pioneer punk band The Sex Pistols and his girlfriend Nancy Spungen. The film premiered at the New York Film Festival and starred Gary Oldman and Chloe Webb in a doomed and depraved love story. By focusing on their self-destructive relationship and punk lifestyle, Cox made a film that went beyond a rock genre movie into an examination of the extremes and thresholds of love in the 1980s. *Walker* (1987) is a historical political film about a nineteenth-century American explorer who invades Nicaragua, overthrows the country's corrupt leader, and takes the president's chair himself. Cox circumvented the period by inserting Zippo lighters, tape recorders, and a Mercedes limo.

Always the punk anarchist, Cox makes his political statement by turning the historic event into a sham. *Straight to Hell* (1987) is a parody of spaghetti westerns starring punk musicians Joe Strummer and Courtney Love. *Highway Patrolman* (1993) was shot in Mexico with a Spanish-speaking cast and pits an idealistic young patrolman against the corruption of his police force. Cox's loopy sense of narrative and truly wacky characters bring irony to an off-hand political statement about the authoritarian greed for money and power over the lower class. In 2002 Alex Cox directed *A Revenger's Tragedy.* Cox still believes in the 1980s philosophy and aesthetic of punk nihilism. He uses a camera rather than a screeching guitar and always was a kinder, gentler, more stable sort of bloke when compared to, say, Johnny Rotten or Iggy Pop.

BIBLIOGRAPHY

Davies, Steven Paul. *Alex Cox: Film Anarchist.* London: B.T. Batsford, 2000.

Craven, Wes. Writer, director, producer. *b.* Wesley Earl Craven, August 2, 1939, Cleveland, Ohio. *ed.* Wheaton College, John Hopkins University. The depraved mind of low-budget horror specialist Wes Craven resides inside a man who looks like and was actually a college professor. Quiet, highly intelligent, and civil, Craven is responsible for inflicting evil Freddy Krueger into the nightmares of our collective unconscious in *A Nightmare on Elm Street* (1984), which became a successful **franchise** now totaling six sequels. *Scream* (1996), a self-referential, thinking person's fright flick, became a trilogy with integrity. When they make Halloween masks of your screen characters, you've made more than a movie; you've entered the pop iconography of America.

Craven took his B.A. and M.A. degrees and began to teach humanities, but like many of his generation raised on movies and pop culture, he entered the film business through the low-budget back door. Craven began as a production assistant in 1970 and graduated to film editor on low-budget productions like *You've Got to Walk It Like You Talk It or You'll Lose That Beat* (1971). His first feature as director, *The Last House on the Left* (1972), produced by **Sean S. Cunningham** of **Friday the 13th** fame, is a brutal and cruel film about a suburban family who gets revenge on the lowlifes who raped and murdered a young girl. Uncompromising and offensive to many, the film was a metaphor for the once innocent American boys who were perceived as committing violent atrocities in Vietnam and develops the theme violence can come from a civilized middle-class white-bread culture where you would least expect it. Even Craven, the creator of the grisly film, found it so difficult to watch he turned down producer Peter Locke's offer to make a sequel.

Craven couldn't get any of his personal projects produced, so he worked as a screenwriter and film editor for other directors. In 1977 Wes Craven wrote, directed, and edited *The Hills Have Eyes*, another attack on an American family who are rampaged by cannibalistic mutants while on a camping trip. The film became an instant cult event; a sequel was made in 1985, but the project did little to raise Craven's stature as a filmmaker. In 1981 Craven wrote and directed *Deadly Blessing* featuring Sharon Stone and Ernest Borgnine, but the film was not his concept, rather a rewrite of a failed script that the eight producers controlling the project saw as *Charlie's Angels* in jeopardy. The story of a young woman who is confronted with a bizarre religious cult began to break Craven's spirit, but he needed the money. *Swamp Thing* (1982) was based on a popular comic and was a difficult production for the director when Swampy's costume constantly needed repair and demanded a three-man crew to maintain it. The delays forced the film off schedule, and Craven had to throw out handfuls of script pages to avoid takeover by completion bondsmen.

After a long struggle Craven hit popular box office success and franchise heaven with the 1984 *A Nightmare on Elm Street*. Craven began with the premise of the evil Freddy Krueger who stalked and murderously violated a town of young people by invading their dream space. Craven wrote by day and dreamed scenes and solved story problems by night in his own dream world. Craven was directly involved in the creation of the first three Freddy films and then the seventh, which he directed. *The Serpent and the Rainbow* (1988) was an anthropological chiller about black magic. *Shocker* (1989) concerned the spirit of a serial killer that inhabits his victims after he is executed. *The People under the Stairs* (1991) was another dysfunctional family horror movie, this time with creatures living in stairwells. The film displayed Craven's flair for weird characters and narrative invention, telling the story as a twisted fable. In 1996 Wes Craven returned to ingenious horror storytelling, again, as with the *Nightmare* series, turning the genre on its head. *Scream* is both a straight-forward horror film filled with terror, murder, tension, and release but transformed by a **self-referential** concept. The complex narrative is filled with classic horror conventions that the characters play out to solve a real murder happening in their community. *Scream*, written by **Kevin Williamson** is hip, funny, and very scary and keeps the audience guessing until the very end. Rather than entering in a franchise like *Nightmare* where producers can dilute the original concept, making sequel after sequel, Craven took the blockbuster success and made it into a self-contained trilogy promising not to return.

Integrity is not often a word used about exploitation horror directors, but Craven has plenty. He directed *Music of the Heart* (1999) starring Meryl Streep, who was nominated for her role as a passionate teacher who brings the joy and motivation of music to an urban school plagued with budget cuts. Craven's association with the successful, mainstream, feel-good movie may be the greatest shocker of his career. As a film-maker and canny careerist Wes Craven likes to keep 'em guessing. He is a filmmaker who has done what was necessary to stay true to his independent spirit. Craven's next project *Alice* (2003), is based on the computer game, *American McGee's Alice* that features an older Alice revisiting a Wonderland gone mad. *See also* Cunningham, Sean S.

critics. All film critics review or write about independent film, but there are specialists who have in-depth knowledge about the nature and history of independent filmmaking. Amy Taubin writes regularly on indies and experimental films for the *Village Voice* and in film journals with extensive knowledge about the **feminist, avant-garde** and **experimental** genres as well as the mainstream and **underground** indie scene. Jonathan Rosenbaum, a reviewer for the *Chicago Reader* and contributor to *Film Comment* and *Cineaste*, is a brilliant scholar, theorist, and critic with a deep understanding of film history and the independent film in all of its facets. J. Hoberman, a *Village Voice* regular reviewer with a filmmaker's understanding of experimental and independent films, writes with an intelligent and critical eye of the highest standards. B. Ruby Rich has written insightfully about independent film with a feminist focus for *The Village Voice*, *Elle*, *Sight and Sound*, *The Advocate*, and *The San Francisco Bay Guardian*. In addition to his duties on *Entertainment Tonight*, the erudite and prolific Leonard Maltin is a scholar on **B-movies** and independent filmmaking. Roger Ebert, the first film critic to become a millionaire, has long been a total indie supporter of and has championed many young filmmakers. He is a regular at **Sundance** and other festivals, on the lookout for the next big indie thing. Michael Medved is public enemy number one as a film critic whose rhetoric about the content of independent and all American films continues to call for censorship in the name of so-called good taste and morality.

Cronenberg, David. Director, writer. *b.* March 15, 1943, Toronto, Ontario. One of the most distinctive voices in film, Cronenberg's work both celebrates and defies the horror genre conventions upon which his films rest. Originally a biochemistry major, Cronenberg switched to the English Department before making two short films that utilized his science background. His 1969 debut feature, *Stereo*, gained Cronenberg a small cadre of fans, but it was his work throughout the 1970s and 1980s that cemented his reputation. *Shivers* (1975), *The Brood* (1979), and *Scanners* (1981) synthesized his science and English backgrounds to produce these gruesome, highly allegorical and intelligent films. The National Film Board of Canada provided the funding, and a parliamentary debate ensued over the appropriateness of the government funding horror films.

In the mid-1980s Cronenberg shifted away from the horror to make the hybrid films *The Fly* (1986), *Dead Ringers* (1988), and *Naked Lunch* (1991). Cronenberg's adaptation of the play *M. Butterfly* seemed like a stretch, but the director was fascinated with the notion of a man's obsession with another male who transformed himself into women. The theme of transformation, the evolution of the body, and the emotionless mechanics of sexual function have been the focus of all his work. *Crash* (1996) was an adaptation of the J.G Ballard novel correlating sex with the violence of car crashes. Cronenberg's film was explicit but cold and disturbing. *eXistenZ* (1999) is about a virtual reality game that involves direct alteration of the brain and is structured in many levels of consciousness. In 2001, David Cronenberg wrote and directed the short film *Camera*. *Spider* (2002) is a feature thriller.

BIBLIOGRAPHY

Cronenberg, David. *Cronenberg on Cronenberg*. Ed. Chris Rodley. London: Faber and Faber, 1993.

Handling, Piers, ed. *The Shape of Rage: The Films of David Cronenberg*. New York: New York Zoetrope, 1983.

Director David Cronenberg in 1990. Courtesy of The Del Valle Archive

Cundey, Dean. Director of photography. *b.* 1945. *ed.* California State University at Los Angeles, University College of Los Angeles, Dean Cundey is a cinematographer who learned his craft shooting low-budget indies he calls "projector fodder for the drive-in circuit" and graduated to megabudget and special effects–driven films that brought him recognition as an A-list Hollywood director of photography. Cundey studied design and film history and then was accepted to UCLA, where he studied with legendary Hollywood master cinematographer James Wong Howe. After film school Cundey photographed over twenty **exploitation** features including *Ilsa, Harem Keeper of the Oil Sheiks* (1975) and *The Charge of the Model T's* (1976). In 1978 he began a long and fertile collaboration with director **John Carpenter**, shooting the landmark horror classic *Halloween*. Cundey and Carpenter continued as a team into the 1980s on *The Fog* (1980), *Escape from New York* (1981), *The Thing* (1982), and *Big Trouble in Little China* (1986).

Cundey's profile as a low-budget B-movie genre specialist changed dramatically when he first began a relationship with Robert Zemeckis. Cundey shot the Zemeckis blockbusters *Romancing the Stone* (1984) and the *Back to the Future* trilogy (1985, 1989, 1990) and was nominated for his work on *Who Framed Roger Rabbit?* (1988), a film that became state-of-the-art for combining live action with animation. This led to his association with Steven Spielberg on *Hook* (1991) and *Jurassic Park* (1993), one of the highest-grossing giants of all time. The man who photographed *The Flintstones* (1994), *Apollo 13*, and *Casper* (both 1995) is also an indie at heart with credits like *Roller Boogie* and *Rock 'n' Roll High School* (both 1979), which features punk royalty, The Ramones. *See also* Carpenter, John; *Halloween*

BIBLIOGRAPHY

LoBrutto, Vincent. *Principal Photography: Interviews with Feature Film Cinematographers*. Westport, CT: Praeger, 1999.

Cunningham, Sean S. Producer, director. *b.* December 31, 1941, New York. *ed.* Franklin and Marshall, Stanford University, studied Shakespeare for a year in Ashland, Oregon. Raised in Connecticut, the young Sean briefly contemplated becoming a doctor, then went on the road with the Lincoln Center production of *The Merry Widow* and learned the craft of stage management. He became the youngest stage manager ever hired by City Center Theater. In 1971 he realized that theater was a bad investment and formed a film production company that made commercials, **industrials, documentaries,** and eventually feature films. He found his natural abilities as a producer but dreamed of becoming a feature film director. Cunningham's first two features as a director, *The Art of Marriage* (1970) and *Together* (1971), were **soft-core, white coaters.** *Together* played the Rialto Theater in Times Square and ran for thirty-one weeks.

In 1974 Cunningham coproduced a sex comedy, *The Case of the Smiling Stiffs*, shot on location in Florida. The film was a minor hit in Australia. In that year Cunningham found himself working sixteen hours a day, seven days a week, just to keep his company together, but he was not making features himself. He shut down the company, traveled to Spain, and made a tax shelter film *Planeta Ciega (Blind Planet)* (1976). In 1978 he directed *Here Come the Tigers*, a copycat of the successful studio film *The Bad News Bears* (1978) that he produced for only $200,000. In 1979 he directed and produced *Kick*, aka *Manny's Orphans*, a Disneyoid film optioned by United Artists who were interested in it for a television pilot.

Cunningham had met **Wes Craven** on *Together* and produced Craven's first feature, *Last House on the Left* (1972). Looking for a way to make money with a low-budget horror film, Cunningham came up with the title ***Friday the 13th***, envisioned a television commercial, and devised the tag line "*Friday the 13th*, the most terrifying film ever made!" Without a script, Cunningham began to attract investors with just the title. The film was made with investor money and from producing *Last House on the Left*. *Friday the 13th* was a big box office hit, receiving massive buzz and interest from teenagers hungry for a good horror film. The story concerns a group of teens in a summer camp that are slaughtered in gory fashion. *Friday the 13th* became a **franchise** and sported eight sequels. Cunningham had little to do with the series after creating it; he claims not to have even seen some of them. In 1993, he regained the rights to produce *Jason Goes to Hell: The Final Friday*. Cunningham directed *A Stranger Is Watching* (1982), a psychological thriller that fared poorly at the box office. In 1983 he produced and directed *Spring Break* with $10,000 from Columbia Pictures. Again there was no script—only a title. Columbia promised to release it the following year during spring break. The film is basically about teenagers getting drunk and having sexual liaisons in Fort Lauderdale, Florida.

Cunningham desperately wanted to make serious films but felt stuck with his success as a producer. The studios would only talk to him about sequels to *Friday the 13th* or *Spring Break*—he was trapped in his own stereotype. In 1985 he got a call from studio chief Guy McElwaine, offering a lot of money for a May 25 release date that needed to be filled. The film, *The New Kids*, was described as *Walking Tall* in high school. Cunningham directed and produced. His literary idol Harry Crews contributed additional dialogue to the script. In 1986 Cunningham produced *House* for New World Pictures, the biggest hit for them at that time. *House* is another variation on the old haunted house theme that franchised with four sequels. In 1989 Cunningham produced and directed *DeepStar Six* but he didn't make another film until *XCU: Extreme Close*

Up (2001) which he produced and directed. His cherished project remains an unmade adaptation of the Harry Crews novel *The Gypsy's Curse. See also* Craven, Wes; *Friday the 13th*

BIBLIOGRAPHY

McDonagh, Maitland. *Filmmaking on the Fringe: The Good, the Bad, and the Deviant Directors.* New York: Citadel Press, 1995.

D

Dahl, John. Director. *b.* 1956, Billings, Montana. *ed.* Montana State University, AFI. While John Dahl was a student at AFI, he became enamored with film noir classics like *Sunset Blvd.* (1950). Following graduation, Dahl was a storyboard artist and music video director before cowriting and directing *Kill Me Again* (1989), a fine neo-noir set in the Nevada desert, starring Val Kilmer as a PI hired to help a femme fatale (his real-life wife Joanne Whalley Kilmer) fake her own death. While the film did not make a theatrical impression, it did gain a devoted following, enticing Propaganda Films to finance Dahl's second feature, the highly praised *Red Rock West* (1992). This film, also set in the western wastelands and starring Nicolas Cage as a wanderer who stumbles into a precarious situation not of his own making, was a critical smash, although it almost didn't reach the theaters. *Red Rock West* premiered on HBO, where it attracted considerable attention. In a rare move, the film was then rushed into theaters to capitalize on its word of mouth, where it earned nearly $2 million. *Red Rock West* was a critical and commercial hit, making Dahl's third feature, *The Last Seduction*, a highly anticipated film.

Dahl again focused on a femme fatale duping innocent men, and while it embraced more noir stereotypes than it eschewed, the film shared an unfortunate fate similar to *Red Rock West*. *The Last Seduction* debuted on pay cable in 1994, and when critics discovered it, the film was put into theaters. Unfortunately, due to an outdated quirk in the Academy Awards rule book, this prevented the film (or, most notably, star Linda Fiorentino) from Oscar recognition. The Oscar-season debate was furious, but ultimately it was not considered. After an unsuccessful studio picture, *Unforgettable* (1996) with Fiorentino, Dahl returned to more humble moviemaking with *Rounders* (1998), a gambling noir that featured Matt Damon who was cast based on a few scenes in *Courage under Fire*

(1996) and the dailies of *Good Will Hunting* (1997). *Rounders* did not encounter the same level of critical praise as *Red Rock West* and *The Last Seduction*, but with over-the-top performances by John Turturro and John Malkovich, and a release after Damon's big splash, the film became the biggest hit of Dahl's career, earning more than $22 million. In 2001 John Dahl directed *Joy Ride*.

Damiano, Gerald. Director. *b.* Gerald Rocco Damiano, 1928. In 1969, Gerald Damiano, a Queens, New York, hairdresser, made the transition to independent filmmaking and quickly cashed in on the liberated sense of sexuality sweeping the country. Blue or pornographic movies had been around since the dawn of the medium, and Damiano, who saw himself as part businessman, part artist, decided to reinvent the subterranean genre that had been confined to male stag parties and sleazy theatrical screenings frequented by men in raincoats. His first two productions, *We All Go Down* (1969) and *Teenie Tulip* (1970) got him started but with little notice. *Deep Throat* (1972), a **hard-core** production directed under the name Jerry Gerard, became a landmark film that changed America's perception of adult entertainment and launched the 1970s **porno chic** era. Linda Lovelace starred as a sexually dissatisfied woman who learns from her doctor that her clitoris is actually in her throat. Damiano followed up his mega-hit with *The Devil in Miss Jones* (1973), a hard-core sex fantasy starring Georgina Spelvin as a suicide who chooses to save herself from going to hell by performing myriad sex acts. The film was more "artistic" and had more sophisticated production values than *Deep Throat*. Audiences responded, and respectable couples began to attend trendy showings at legitimate and quasi-legitimate adult emporiums. Damiano continued to make adult films into the 1980s when the industry made the aesthetic, economic decision to shoot on video rather than film. Damiano reluctantly made the switch. His latest foray into the home adult market was *Naked Goddess* (1993) and its sequel in 1994. *See also Deep Throat*

dance films. A film form honed in the 1950s and 1960s by **avant-garde** and **experimental** filmmakers who used dance and choreography as a mode of artistic expression and interpretation. The most significant of these artists was **Maya Deren** whose *A Study in Choreography for Camera* (1945), a two-and-a-half-minute film, was an early inspirational example. Deren's *The Very Eye of Night* (1958) is considered to be the high mark of the art. Other dance film pioneers include **Shirley Clarke**, *Dance in the Sun* (1953), *Bullfight* (1955), and *Moment in Love* (1957); Ed Emshwiller, *Dance Chromatic* (1959), *Lifelines* (1960), *Totem* (1963), and *Fusion* (1963); and Stan Vanderbeek, *Sight* (1965) and *Spherical Space* (1966). Over the decades, filmmakers, choreographers, and dance companies have turned the dance film into a varied creative mode. Dance films now include narrative and nonnarrative works, records of performances, reinterpretations of classic work, presentations of new work, and objective, subjective, and abstract projects.

BIBLIOGRAPHY

Clark, VeVe A., with Millicent Hodson and Catrina Neiman. *The Legend of Maya Deren: A Documentary Biography and Collected Works.* New York: Anthology Film Archives/Film Culture, 1984.

Dante, Joe. Director. *b.* November 28, 1946, Morristown, New Jersey. Joe Dante's training as a low-budget filmmaker who made it to the big leagues is a model of the American film fanatic raised in the 1950s and 1960s—a kid who had no choice but to make the movies his profession. Dante was a movie-mad youngster who read the horror movie bible *Famous Monsters of Filmland* magazine religiously. As a teenager, Dante wrote for *Castle of Frankenstein* magazine and later was movie reviewer for the trade publication *Film Bulletin,* where he wrote in a style cribbed from British reviews. Dante's college had a film society, and he began to book dates, changing the steady diet of postwar Italian films to everything from *It's a Gift* (1934), starring W.C. Fields, to Tod Browning's grotesque masterpiece *Freaks* (1932).

Dante and his friends began collecting **16mm** prints. Later, he gained possession of discarded films from a rental company, adding old television shows and commercials to his private archive. Dante and boyhood friend Jon Davison, the future producer of *RoboCop* (1987), decided to assemble what they called *The 7 Hour All Night Once in a Lifetime Atomic Movie Orgy,* a cinematic collage of Bela Lugosi movies, cartoons, commercials, TV intros, and other archival finds. Response to the format was wildly successful; so they created a sequel the next year, featuring *College Confidential* (1960) with Steve Allen and the **Roger Corman** classic *Little Shop of Horrors* (1960) and made actor Morris Ankrum, who played a general in *Rocketship X-M* (1950), *Invaders from Mars* (1953), and *Earth vs the Flying Saucers* (1956), a main character in the marathon. When Ankrum looked up, Dante would cut to a flying saucer or a giant claw from other movies. Also included were familiar baby-boomer images from *Howdy Doody, Tales of the Texas Rangers,* old commercials, and Hollywood actors plugging products now seen in a new funny context. Dante and Davison's movie orgy was even screened at rock palace Filmore East. A Schlitz beer rep was in the audience and convinced the company to take the film on the college circuit where they could run it for free and sell a lot of brew. The intense film editing experience would influence Dante's work as a trailer editor and his feature work as a director, giving him what he calls an "absurdist world view."

Director Joe Dante posing with one of the stars of *Gremlins* (1984). Courtesy of The Del Valle Archive

Dante's encyclopedic knowledge of the horror, fantasy and science fiction genres got him an audition at Roger Corman's New World Pictures. Dante was locked into the trailer department with a 35mm print of **Jonathan Demme's** directorial debut *Caged Heat* and challenged to exit with a preview trailer that would sell the 1974 babes-behind-bars **sexploitation** flick to Corman's target youth audience. Dante applied his **B-movie** instincts and cut a sexy trailer. *Caged Heat* made money, and Dante received a staff position, joined in the trailer department by fellow future director Alan Arkush.

After cutting trailers for everything from *Last Days of Man on Earth* (1974) to Ingmar Bergman's *Cries and Whispers* (1972) and a slew of Filipino cheapies that barely had enough money shots to make a decent trailer, Davison, Dante, and Arkush convinced Corman they could make the cheapest feature ever at New World—a film for $60,000 to be shot in ten days. The result, *Hollywood Boulevard* (1976), is a behind-the-scenes look at B-moviemaking that can be read as a primer on how movies were made in the Corman system. Arkush and Dante built the film around house footage of action scenes, explosions, and other key B elements. The shoestring narrative took Mary Woronov, **Paul Bartel**, and Dick Miller through a series of episodes of sex, violence, mockumentary, action, and plenty of comic one-liners shot for the film. He intercut this new footage with archival B schlock classics. The method was a step up from the movie orgy and got *Hollywood Boulevard* in on schedule and on budget. Its movie-junkie aesthetic made it a hit at the box office.

In 1980 Dante put himself on the horror map with *The Howling*, written by **John Sayles.** This contemporary take on the werewolf legend featured startling special effects by Rob Botkin. The low-budget horror movie always relied on editing and opticals to metamorphose a man into a werewolf, but Botkin was able to make the frightening transformations on camera without a cut by developing prosthetic makeup that could be animated with a series of air pumps. Dante deftly handled the contrast of comedy and mayhem and gave the audience a good laugh while scaring them stiff. Dante graduated to Spielberg protégé status directing *Gremlins* (1984) and an episode of *The Twilight Zone* feature (1985), while *The Howling* **franchise** racked up five sequels without him.

Dante has never abandoned his allegiance to B-movies that were responsible for his Hollywood success, but the scale and budgets of his projects reached A-movie proportions with *Explorers* (1985), *Innerspace* (1987), and *The 'Burbs* (1989), and he was criticized for selling out. *Matinee* (1993) was a tribute to the showmanship of **William Castle** and a boomer nostalgia piece to the good-ole days of trashy double bills. *Small Soldiers* (1998) is a boy's fantasy of toy soldiers coming to life. *Haunted Lighthouse* (2002) features a screenplay written by Sam Hamm. Like his hero Steven Spielberg, Dante has never let his inner child die, and with his recurring use of animation techniques and the casting of pop culture icons like Dick Miller, he may celebrate childhood forever, bringing others along for the romp. *See also* Corman, Roger

Dash, Julie. Director. *b.* October 22, 1952, Long Island City, New York. *ed.* City College, New York; AFI. Julie Dash holds the distinction of being the first African American woman to achieve a major theatrical release for an independent dramatic feature film. The journey from idea to screen took seventeen years. Dash was introduced to filmmaking at an after-school workshop at the Studio Museum of Harlem in 1969. After college, Dash moved to Los Angeles and took a course at the AFI, where in 1975 she created *Four Women*, an award-winning experimental **dance film**. In 1982 she directed *Illusions*, a thirty-four-minute film shot for $28,000, set in 1942. It concerns a black movie executive who passes for white.

Learning her craft through short films including *Working Models of Success* (1973) and *Diary of an African Nun* (1977), Dash developed the idea for her breakthrough feature *Daughters of the Dust* at New York's Film Forum in 1991. Armed with the themes of sexual culture and racial domination, Dash conducted intensive research at the National Archives, The Library of Congress, The Smithsonian, The Schomburg Center for Research in Black Culture, and the Penn Cultural Center on St. Helena Island off the South Carolina coast. She wrote an original screenplay chronicling the turn-of-the-century story of a Gullah sea island family. Dash created a ten-minute promotional trailer as a fund-raising tool and eventually received an $800,000 working budget from **American Playhouse.** *Daughters of the Dust* was filmed on location at the U.S. Carolina Islands of the South where African captives were brought to be sold into slavery. Working in an impressionistic, nontraditional tableau narrative style and told from the point of view of an African American woman, Dash crafted a powerful portrait of the struggle to maintain tradition in the face of change. Set in 1902, *Daughters of the Dust* tells the story of the Gullah women, descendants of slaves, as they celebrate before traveling to the mainland. Dash bravely created a difficult film. The characters speak in their islander Gullah dialect and events are not explained, but the yield for the patient and compassionate viewer is a greater understanding of African and American history.

The visionary film won the cinematography prize at its **Sundance** premiere in 1991 for Arthur Jafa's poetic images, but generally *Daughters of the Dust* was not well received at the festival, and its release was set back for a year. Kino International picked up the distribution, and flyers were handed out in black churches to reach the film's target audience—educated black women. *Daughters of the Dust* opened at New York's **Film Forum** and eventually grossed $2 million. The critical and box office success brought Dash a lot of "Let's Do Lunch" invitations, but no one believed she could tell a linear narrative. The powers that be were unable to see the potential in her body of short films. Dash's career has been difficult to date. Recently Julie Dash has been directing television movies that include: *Incognito* (1999), *Love Story* (2000), and *Rosa Parks* (2002). *See also American Playhouse*

BIBLIOGRAPHY

Dash, Julie, with Toni Cade Bambara and Bell Hooks. *Daughters of the Dust: Making of an African American Woman's Film*. New York: New Press, 1992.

dated film stock. Very low-budget indies often purchase out-of-date film stock at a much lower price to save money. If the stock is not too long out of date, results will not be very different. Film that is long past expiration can produce interesting or startling aesthetic results that enhance the visual style of a project, as in the ghostly, otherworldly look **Jack Smith** achieved in his cult classic *Flaming Creatures* (1963).

David Holzman's Diary. After filmmaker **Jim McBride** graduated New York University film school and struggled to find a place in the industry, he was encouraged by cinematographer Michael Wadleigh (who would go on as Michael Wadleigh to direct *Woodstock* [1970]) to make a personal film. McBride had been thinking about making a film that would document the life of a filmmaker in a faux **cinéma vérité** style. In 1967, McBride found the ideal David Holzman in **L.M. Kit Carson**, a Texas-born actor who also attended NYU. The twenty-five-year-old McBride began writing pages of notes for scenes and monologues to give the film a direction; no formal script was ever created. McBride and Carson spent hours dictating ideas into a tape recorder. The tapes were not transcribed; the two men just listened to them repeatedly, soaking up the themes they wanted to capture in the film. They came up with a **self-referential** point of view. David would address the camera and talk directly to the audience. We observe David filming a diary of his life. McBride and Carson decided that David was a West Side Manhattanite obsessed with movies and surrounded by film equipment. He didn't have a job, his draft status had been reclassified, and the relationship with his girlfriend was at an impasse. It is David's hope that this cinematic diary of his life will help explain his existence.

David Holzman's Diary was shot over a three-month period including a four-day weekend when all the scenes that take place in David's apartment were filmed. Waldley shot with a used **16mm** Éclair camera with a 9.5 to 95 Mersault zoom lens for flexibility and one lighting instrument. Sound was recorded on a Nagra tape recorder. McBride never shot more than two takes of one shot. The seventy-four-minute black-and-white film cost $2,500. The budget included a rented policeman's uniform and fees for film stock and laboratory work.

McBride edited the film (uncredited) at night over a period of several months, then set out to find a distributor, a torturous one and a half-year search, during which he was unable to work on any new projects. Deals were made with French and British distributors, but McBride did not have a lawyer. He didn't receive any money, and the film was not picked up. Grove Press was interested, but only in distributing the film directly to college campuses. McBride wanted a theatrical release and said no. **Richard Leacock** and **D.A. Pennebaker** signed a contract with McBride. They offered to blow the film up to 35mm, give it a New York theatrical opening, and pay an advance for the filmmaker—nothing happened and the contract dissolved. *David Holzman's Diary* played the Mannheim Film Festival in Germany where it won the Grand Prize. The film still hadn't earned any money, and to make matters worse, an actress sued McBride for nonpayment. Even though McBride didn't have a theatrical release, prints of the film got around, and he developed a reputation as a hot young film director. The film's cult status remains high. For many filmmakers like McBride who began their careers in the 1960s and 1970s, *David Holzman's Diary* is much more than a historical footnote; it represents the culmination of a dream for the personal filmmaker. *See also* Carson, L.M. Kit; McBride, Jim

BIBLIOGRAPHY

Carson, L.M. Kit. *David Holzman's Diary; A Screenplay by L.M. Kit Carson from a Film by Jim McBride*. New York: Farrar, Straus and Giroux, 1970. (Note: this is a direct transcription from the finished film, no script was completed.)

de Antonio, Emile. Documentary filmmaker. *b.* 1920, Scranton, Pennsylvania. *d.* 1989. *ed.* Harvard University, Columbia University. Emile de Antonio was a New York independent documentary filmmaker known to his friends simply as D, a man who took on controversial subjects from an antiestablishment point of view. The son of a doctor, de Antonio rebelled against his upper-class background by living the life of a blue-collar worker as a longshoreman, barge captain, peddler, and war surplus broker and then pursued more intellectual concerns as a book editor and instructor at William and Mary College.

In the 1960s while others marched, protested, and were arrested for their political beliefs, de Antonio, who embraced Marxism, began creating documentary films that took on the power elite directly. The ninety-minute *Point of Order* (1964) presents footage from 180 hours of archival documentation of the U.S. Army-McCarthy hearings edited to allow the demonic, alcoholic, anti-Communist senator Joseph McCarthy to expose the government's evil motives through his own words—without a line of commentary or narration. The powerful, self-explanatory political statement was the first independent documentary made after World War II not produced for television. It was released theatrically to successful box office returns. *Rush to Judgment* (1966) attacked the validity of the Warren Commission's conclusion that Lee Harvey Oswald was the sole assassin of President John F. Kennedy. *In the Year of the Pig* (1969) is a historical and intellectual overview of the Vietnam War beginning before World War II, through the French involvement, then U.S. intervention until the Tet Offensive. De Antonio intercut European, Soviet, East German, and Czechoslovakian footage with original interviews he conducted. De Antonio made Ho Chi Minh the hero of the film, supporting the director's belief that the Vietnamese should defeat the United States for interfering in their governmental affairs. Film critic Pauline Kael accused de Antonio of demonizing America with his editorial choices. The radical filmmaker agreed that he found Western civilization to be rotten. De Antonio created films out of rage and opportunity. He had been angry with Richard Nixon since his career was launched with the Alger Hiss case in 1946. The opportunity to record his feelings on film came when de Antonio received a phone call from a man who had stolen all the footage on Nixon from one of the three television networks. De Antonio took the footage given to him for free and made the devastating portrait *Milhouse: A White Comedy* (1971). De Antonio became the only filmmaker to land on Nixon's infamous enemies list for making a film.

For *Painters Painting* (1972), de Antonio turned away from politics to art, documenting the creative process he understood from his bohemian life in New York. De Antonio was actually instrumental in motivating **Andy Warhol** to experiment with filmmaking. *Painters Painting* was a forum for New York artists, **critics**, and patrons to illuminate the process of abstract expressionism. De Antonio interviewed Warhol, Robert Rauschenberg, Henry Geldzahler, and others and structured it with footage from the Metropolitan Museum of Art exhibition *New York Painting and Sculpture 1940–1970*. De Antonio was the only filmmaker given permission to document this seminal cultural event.

Underground (1976) became de Antonio's most subversive documentary. It began with his interest in the Radical Left group the Weathermen. The film was shot in May 1975 when the movement had essentially broken up after bombing a townhouse and the U.S. Capitol building. The radicals were living underground. De Antonio was attracted to the concept of filming under difficult conditions and enjoyed the challenge of being unable to show the faces of his subjects. De Antonio gained access to the now-named Weather Underground and brought in filmmakers Mary Lampson and **Haskell Wexler**, a director and longtime cinematographer sympathetic to radical causes. Questions were limited in scope, and the filmmakers had worked sub rosa. The Federal Bureau of Investigation (FBI) still managed to find out about the secret filming and served de Antonio with a warrant to turn over his materials. The Hollywood community rallied behind de Antonio's First Amendment protection rights, and the film was finally completed by Lampson and de Antonio, who blacked out by hand a section of any frame that might have revealed the identity of their outlaw interview subjects. The filmmakers worked without assistants and destroyed all backup paperwork and film elements so it wouldn't fall in the hands of the government.

In the King of Prussia (1982), de Antonio reconstructed a trial against the General Electric corporation nuclear weapons facility. Daniel and Philip Berrigan portray their saintly selves, and activist actor Martin Sheen plays the judge deciding the case. Mr. Hoover and I (1989) was completed just months before de Antonio's death and is D's personal look at his life and his central enemy, J. Edgar Hoover, founder and first director of the FBI. The swan song cinematic memoir from the left-wing radical, art patron, womanizer and all-around carouser gives a personal account of Hoover, a man de Antonio and many Americans saw as an evil enemy of personal freedom. It was more than just an independent documentation of D's life and political philosophy—it was a celebration of emancipation.

BIBLIOGRAPHY

Kellner, Douglas, and Dan Streible, eds. *Emile de Antonio: A Reader.* Minneapolis: University of Minnesota Press, 2000.

Lewis, Randolph. *Emile de Antonio: Radical Filmmaker in Cold War America.* Madison: University of Wisconsin Press, 2000.

death films. *See* snuff films

Deep Throat. Adult **hard-core film** released in 1972, directed by **Gerald Damiano,** initiated the **porno chic** trend in the early 1970s. The notorious XXX film starred Linda Lovelace as a woman who learns she has a clitoris in her throat from Doctor Young, played by Harry Reems, really Herbert Streicher, a minor actor who had bit roles in the National Shakespeare Company and Off-Off Broadway. Damiano shot the film in Florida with Reems assigned to behind-the-camera duties. When the director ran into trouble casting the role of the doctor, Reems volunteered and performed in two explicit sex scenes. During the editing process Damiano structured the material so it appeared that Reems was in several sexual encounters.

Aquarius Films released the seventy-three-minute *Deep Throat* in 35mm color prints in seventy-three U.S. cities. It was an instant hit, word spread by advertising and buzz. *Deep Throat* was even reviewed by *Variety*, *Newsweek*, and *The Hollywood Reporter*. The film was labeled obscene in a number of states and in federal cases. With the exception of **D.W. Griffith**'s *Birth of a Nation* (1915), *Deep Throat* had more legal action against it than any film in history. Everyone associated with the creation and selling of *Deep Throat* was prosecuted in Memphis, Tennessee. The case cost taxpayers $4 million. In July 1974 Harry Reems was arrested by the FBI while he was sleeping, becoming the first performer in history to be indicted on the federal level for work in a motion picture. Eleven other people were charged, and ninety-eight unindicted coconspirators were named including a projectionist, publicist, and a ticket taker. The judge's charge to the jury directed that First Amendment rights granting freedom of speech did not protect Reems. After the jury screened the film, Reems was found guilty. The appeal was handled by Alan Dershowitz, whose defense contended his client had no way of knowing what the final film would look like when he participated in the shooting. Reems's lawyers motioned for a new trial, the government declined, and Reems was freed. He became a household name as a porno star in countless productions.

Deep Throat ultimately grossed over $25 million. Later a New York distributor cut several scenes from the film, and no new legal action occurred in New York City. In her autobiography, Lovelace claims her then-boyfriend Chuck Traynor drugged and abused her into working in adult films and that Damiano was aware but did nothing. *See also* Damiano, Gerard

BIBLIOGRAPHY

De Grazia, Edward, and Roger K. Newman. *Banned Films: Movies, Censors & the First Amendment*. New York: R.R. Bowker, 1982.

Lovelace, Linda, with Mike McGrady. *Out of Bondage*. Secaucus, NJ: Lyle Stuart, 1986.

deferred payments. Cast, crew, or vendor fees set and promised at the beginning of production but paid out after completion. Independent filmmakers defer payments to lower out-of-pocket costs during production and postproduction.

Demme, Jonathan. Director, producer, screenwriter. *b.* February 22, 1944, Baldwin, New York. After an early career as a film and music journalist, Jonathan Demme began working for **Roger Corman**'s New World Pictures. In 1971, his first credits appeared as producer and writer on *Angels Hard as They Come*, but he did not direct until 1974 on the Corman picture *Caged Heat*. Demme also made *Crazy Mama* (1975) and *Fighting Mad* (1976) for Corman. The young director's first major film was the low-

Jodie Foster and cast members of *The Silence of the Lambs* (1991), take direction from Jonathan Demme. Courtesy of The Del Valle Archive

budget *Handle with Care* (1977), an energetic exploration of the American CB radio trend. While it is largely forgotten as a 1970s relic, it laid the groundwork for the everyman motif Demme developed in later studio films like *Melvin and Howard* (1980) and *Married to the Mob* (1988), Following the overwhelming critical success of the whimsical *Melvin and Howard*, Demme used his newly established clout to make what appeared to be a standard World War II film, *Swing Shift* (1984), for Warner Bros. except it presented a clear feminist point of view. *Stop Making Sense* (1994), a compilation of a three-night stand at L.A.'s Pantages Theater by the avant-garde rock group Talking Heads, is a significant concert film. The film is as much performance art as it is a rock concert showcasing David Byrne's manic stage presence, coupled with Demme's restrained style where quick cuts and ecstatic fan shots are virtually nonexistent. Despite opening in limited release by Cinecom, the film made $2 million. Demme later worked with Cinecom on *Swimming to Cambodia* with postmodern monologist Spalding Gray in 1987. *Something Wild* (1986), a yuppie angst film about an uptight Manhattan businessman who gets mixed up with an eccentric Jersey girl for a freewheeling trip back to her hometown, grossed over $8 million, a healthy return for Orion Pictures.

Known for his gentle sensibilities, Demme seemed an unlikely choice to direct the infamous *The Silence of the Lambs* (1991). It was a huge smash, grossing over $130 million and won all five of the major Oscars that year, including Demme's first for best director. The success of *The Silence of the Lambs* is all the more surprising because Orion was on the verge of bankruptcy and had little money to promote the film, especially during its Oscar campaign. Since this career epoch, Demme, recognized for his consistently honest portrayals of women, has divided his time between making big-budget films like *Philadelphia* (1993) and *Beloved* (1998) and producing independent films such as Nancy Savoca's *Household Saints* (1993) and Carl Franklin's acclaimed *Devil in a Blue Dress* (1995).

BIBLIOGRAPHY

Bliss, Michael, with Christina Banks. *What Goes Around Comes Around: The Films of Jonathan Demme.* Carbondale: Southern Illinois University Press, 1996.

De Niro, Robert. Actor, producer. *b.* August 17, 1943, New York City. De Niro's debut film performance was a small speaking role in *The Wedding Party* (completed in 1967, released in 1969), codirected by **Brian De Palma** who befriended the young actor and cast him in the $58,000–budgeted antiwar comedy *Greetings* (1968), where he is credited as "Robert De Nero," then in the equally low-budget *Hi, Mom!* (1970). Also in 1970 De Niro appeared in the **Roger Corman** production *Bloody Mama.*

Considered one of America's finest actors, De Niro's long and celebrated career spans many challenging and diverse roles in both studio and independent productions. He has long been associated with **Martin Scorsese,** for whom he has executed some of his most intense and ferocious performances including roles in *Mean Streets* (1973), *Taxi Driver* (1976), and *Raging Bull* (1980), for which he won the Oscar. With his Tribeca Productions and its accompanying **Tribeca Film Center,** De Niro helped reinvigorate the independent film movement in New York City in the early 1990s, a trend that continues in earnest today. The company's first film was Scorsese's *Cape Fear* (1991), but it was with De Niro's insightful, low-budgeted directorial effort *A Bronx Tale* (1993) that Tribeca Productions began to make a name. Other independent films followed including *Marvin's Room* and *Faithful* (both in 1996). As an actor, De Niro continues to work in both high- and low-budget films. The year 1997 saw the actor appear in the independent films *Wag the Dog, Cop Land,* and *Jackie Brown. See also* Tribeca Film Center

BIBLIOGRAPHY

Dougan, Andy. *Untouchable: A Biography of Robert De Niro.* New York: Thunder's Mouth Press, 1996.
McKay, Keith. *Robert De Niro: The Hero behind the Masks.* New York: St. Martin's Press, 1986.

De Palma, Brian. Director. *b.* September 11, 1940, Newark, New Jersey. *ed.* Columbia University, Sarah Lawrence College. The purchase of a secondhand **16mm, Bolex camera** led Brian De Palma to the world of independent filmmaking. He created three short films. *Icarus* (1960) is a self-professed, pretentious, adolescent exercise De Palma was only supposed to photograph. He graduated to creator when the director quit because of too many arguments with De Palma over the visualization of the project. De Palma invested the money he received from academic science awards and made his second short, *660124: The Story of an IBM Card* (1961), where a painter loses his life for the sake of his art. In 1962, De Palma continued investigating the plight of the committed artist with *Woton's Wake* in which a crazed sculptor falls in love with one of his sculptures. The statue transforms into a live woman and escapes as the artist chases her in desperation. *Woton's Wake* won the Rosenthal Foundation Award for best short film.

De Palma then won a Music Corporation of America writing fellowship to the predominantly female Sarah Lawrence College, where he was mentored by noted theater director Wilford Leach. In 1964 Cynthia Mun-

Robert De Niro as the devilish Louis Cyphre in *Angel Heart* (1987), directed by Alan Parker. Courtesy of The Del Valle Archive

Nancy Allen and an in-drag, razor-wielding Michael Caine in Brian De Palma's *Dressed to Kill* (1980). Courtesy of The Del Valle Archive

roe, a wealthy film student, invested $100,000 in *The Wedding Party*, a feature film she cowrote with Leach and De Palma. Munroe preferred the experienced Leach direct, but he worked only with the actors, while De Palma designed, photographed, and edited the film. The story follows a young man who runs from his upcoming wedding when he discovers his fiancée and her family have the couple's future planned for a conservative and conventional life. The film starred Sarah Lawrence students Jill Clayburgh and **Robert De Niro**. De Palma found the story, limited by the low budget, to be dull, so he imposed a visual style that included slow-motion and high-speed photography, while the actors improvised in the tradition of the French New Wave. *The Wedding Party* took two years to complete. De Palma was constantly at odds with Munroe over the budget and with Leach over the lead actor.

During the long production of *The Wedding Party*, De Palma returned to the short form, making *Jennifer* (1964), featuring actress Jennifer Salt who was also in the feature. In 1965 De Palma traveled to New Orleans and other southern cities for *Bridge that Gap*, sponsored by the National Association for the Advancement of Colored People (NAACP). In 1966, he directed *Show Me a Strong Town and I'll Show You a Strong Bank* for the U.S. Treasury Department and a **documentary**, *The Responsive Eye*, about an exhibit at the Museum of Modern Art. By concentrating his documentary camera on the patrons attending the event, he was able to make a statement about how the public and the New York intelligentsia related to art.

In 1966, to solicit backing, De Palma arranged a multitude of screenings of the finally completed *The Wedding Party* (1969), but in the end, the trio had to finance the release themselves. The student film proved to De Palma that he could make a feature without going to Hollywood. De Palma's second feature *Murder à la Mod* (1968) was another student collaboration. De Palma's screenplay was an erotic thriller about an actress stabbed in the eyes with an icepick, shown from three distinct points of view; a soap opera, the inevitable Hitchcock treatment, and a burlesque comedy. The plot was confused, the acting unconvincing, the film a stylistic display of camera pyrotechnics without substance. The exercise in cinematic technique played for two weeks only in New York City.

Greetings (1968) was an indie success for De Palma. Robert De Niro plays a voyeur who tries to beat the draft and avoid Vietnam. De Palma met **Charles Hirsch** when their paths crossed through the Universal Pictures search for talented young directors. Hirsch was frustrated with the negative attitude toward young filmmakers growing at the studio. De Palma, who had already proved films could be made outside the system, struck up a partnership with the twenty-six-year-old wanna-be producer. The story for *Greetings* by Hirsch gave the characters an autobiographical DNA. The voyeur was based on De Palma with like tendencies of his own and those inherited through the voyeuristic fantasies of his idol, Alfred Hitchcock. The sexual obsessions and out-of-control behavior of another character were transposed from Hirsch, a man more often interested in womanizing and partying than filmmaking.

Greetings was shot with a nonunion crew of eight, composed of friends of the producer and director and film students hungry to work on a feature film. Completion costs totaled $43,100. Only $15,000 in cash was spent to get the film in the can; salaries and vendor costs were **deferred.** Four thousand dollars went up in smoke when the filmmakers began to shoot in 16mm before they came to the conclusion the format would limit distribution to a handful of art houses. They began reshooting the satire on the Vietnam draft, sex, and the counterculture that also featured De Niro, from scratch in 35mm. Thankfully postproduction was swift due to the lack of editorial choices created by De Palma's decision to shoot the majority of the scenes in master shots without coverage.

Hirsch self-financed the film with a $20,000 credit line from a lab backed by $1,000 in cash. To meet expenses Hirsch borrowed from his parents, sold his Bolex camera and $1,500 in stock he acquired, and promised large gross percentages to two unwitting investors, one who brought first $7,000, then an additional $5,000 to the production. Another investor was offered a large percentage of any profits, something Hirsch didn't lavish on his parents. Fund-raising continued while De Palma directed the film on location in New York's Greenwich Village. Thirty percent of the profits were set to go to the investors (who never saw any return on their investments), and 28 percent of the profits had been promised to the cast and crew. *Greetings* earned $130,000 in its New York run. Again De Palma infused his work with cinematic wizardry to dress up a bland narrative. The director, who would soon be known for his gratuitous use of sex and violence to attract excitement to his films, put in erotic sequences that landed *Greetings* an X rating. *Greetings* was distributed by Sigma III, whose deal demanded 80 percent of the grosses. *Greetings* went on to earn three times its budget, but Hirsch and his parents never made a dime on their investment. The film found its under-thirty audience and enjoyed a solid run at New York's 34th Street Theater.

Success brought interest from the money barons in the film industry. Martin Ransohoff of Filmways, a parent company of Sigma III, offered De Palma and Hirsch a deal to make a sequel entitled *Son of Greetings*, which later became *Hi, Mom!*, the further exploits of the voyeur Jon Rubin, representing De Palma's inner life. Before embarking on the sequel, De Palma directed the documentary *Dionysus in '69* (1970), a triptych split-screen presentation of the Performance Group's radical erotic adaptation of the ancient Greek play *The Bacchae*. The troupe and members of the audience took off their clothes, writhed, and groped to participate in the death ritual of King Penteus. The film didn't get much attention—the actual performance received all that—but the split-screen technique, rarely used as a narrative device in features up to that time, should have. Historically the **documentary** was De Palma's first major experiment with a multiscreen technique he would use in fictional storytelling throughout his career.

Hi, Mom! (1970), made nonunion on location for $95,000, continued De Palma's interest in 1960s political and social changes with the voyeur of *Greetings* turning his Peeping Tom tendencies into a profession by becoming a filmmaker who is derailed by a treacherous porn producer, then joins a radical group who embraces black militancy and who create *Be Black Baby*, a performance art event designed to allow white people to experience racial oppression. Hirsch felt *Hi, Mom!* was an offbeat take on the box office smash *The Graduate* (1967) and convinced exhibitors to run the film in big commercial theaters rather than smaller art theaters. De Palma disagreed with his producer and saw *Hi, Mom!* as an **underground** film. The brutal but very funny underground comedy, also produced by Hirsch, marked the end of De Palma's independent filmmaking.

Hollywood called for the Warner Bros. film *Get to Know Your Rabbit* (1972) concerning a would-be magician played by Tom Smothers and a tyrant of a boss portrayed by John Astin. Orson Welles was brought in to help the troubled production, but the legendary actor/director's assistance was to no avail. De Palma was unhappy living and working on the West Coast. He was a New York filmmaker. Even as De Palma became the new master of suspense he continued to return to New York. Later, De Palma permanently located himself in Hollywood. De Palma was headed toward his fate for a long time, ever since he first identified with a Hollywood legend, Alfred Hitchcock, an iconoclast who was successful at the box office. De Palma achieved financial prosperity with *Carrie* (1976), *The Untouchables* (1987), *Dressed to Kill* (1980), *Scarface* (1983), and *Mission Impossible* (1996). Recently De Palma has directed *Snake Eyes* (1998), *Mission to Mars* (2000), and *Femme Fatale* (2002).

BIBLIOGRAPHY

Bouzereau, Laurent. *The De Palma Cut: The Films of America's Most Controversial Director.* New York: Dembner Books, 1988.

Deren, Maya. Avant-garde filmmaker. *b.* Eleanora Derenkowsky, April 29, 1917, Kiev, Ukraine. *d.* October 13, 1961. *ed.* University of Syracuse, New York University, Smith College. A committed socialist, the highly educated Deren dedicated herself to the creative life writing short stories and poetry. After working as a secretary and editorial assistant for several writers, cowriting a detective novel, Deren worked as a secretary for Katherine Dunham, a dancer-anthropologist who incorporated her interest in the traditions of African dance into work as a Broadway theater dancer and choreographer. Dunham's influence inspired Deren to investigate dance, psychology, and Vodoun, a Haitian religion.

Deren channeled her poetic, cultural, and choreographic sensibilities to filmmaking. Deren's second husband Sasha Hammid taught her the technical aspects of the new medium. Together Deren and Hammid, a cinematographer for *The March of Time*, made *Meshes of the Afternoon* (1943), a classic of **avant-garde cinema.** Hammid photographed the film in a European tradition of polished craftsmanship and presents psychological symbology from within Deren's personal existence to deal with issues of her past. Deren, who became a champion and theorist of avant-garde cinema, wrote in her program notes that the film "does not record an event that could be witnessed by other persons. Rather, it reproduced the way in which the subconscious of an individual will develop, interpret and elaborate an apparently simple and casual incident into a critical emotional experience." The poetic imagery and mesmerizing performance by Deren symbolically illustrates a woman who finds a flower on the street. She arrives at a house, but the door is locked. A key falls from her hand and down the stairs. She enters and tours the rooms in search of someone. A phonograph turns, the telephone is off the hook, but the house is empty. She waits, looking out the window, in one of the film's most memorable and enduring images. Asleep, she repeats the experience in a dream, but reality is now altered. A woman in black with a mirror face carries the flower. The dreamer can't catch her. Objects change place. She enters the house three times and multiplies into a trio. A state of emotional complexity becomes a force transformed into reality for the woman. *Meshes of the Afternoon* was widely shown and influenced and encouraged a stream of personal cinema.

Hammid left to work for the Overseas Motion Picture Division of the Office of War Information (OWI), and Deren embarked on her second film, *The Witch's Cradle*, in 1944. The project was photographed in the surrealist "Art of This Century" gallery featuring dadaist Marcel Duchamp and Chilean surrealist Pajarito Matta in a parallel between feudal witches and the surrealists who both desired to investigate the subconscious drives that underlie events. The film was never completed.

Throughout the 1940s and 1950s Deren was a visual poet who explored the altered time and space inherent in the power of cinema. She became a dedicated advocate of the independent film and founded the Creative Film Foundation, a support organization for personal filmmakers. In 1945 Deren and Talley Beatty created *A Study in Choreography for Camera*, a **dance film** that, in Deren's words, was "a duet between space and dancer. A duet in which the camera is not merely an observant sensitive eye, but is itself creatively responsible for the performance."

Deren was the first person to receive a prestigious Guggenheim fellowship for motion picture creation. She was the first woman to win the Grand Prix Internationale in the avant-garde category at the Cannes Film Festival. She used the Guggenheim grant to sponsor trips to Haiti in 1947, 1949, and 1954, shooting 20,000 feet of film interpreting Vodoun rituals. Deren left the film that would mythologize Vodoun incomplete when she died suddenly in 1961 of a brain hemorrhage. The footage is preserved at the **Anthology Film Archives.** In her short but vibrant artistic life, Deren inspired women to become directors and left a poetic legacy for the art of film to everyone.

BIBLIOGRAPHY

Brakhage, Stan. *Film at Wit's End: Eight Avant-Garde Filmmakers: Broughton, Conner, Deren, Hill, Jacobs, MacLaine, Menken, Peterson.* New York: Documentext, McPherson and Company, 1989. *The Legend of Maya Deren, Volume One.* New York: Anthology Film Archives.

de Rochemont, Louis. Producer, director. *b.* January 13, 1899, Boston, Massachusetts. *d.* December 23, 1978, Newington, New Hampshire. *ed.* Massachusetts Institute of Technology. Louis de Rochemont worked for several newsreel companies and learned the business in various capacities from cameraman to executive. The newsreel was a cinematic form that delivered the news to the public on the big screen before television completely took over the job. The black-and-white segments of news items explained by a deep-voiced, male narrator and graphic headline text were exhibited along with cartoons, A- and B-feature films, and various short subjects like **industrial** and wildlife films.

By 1934 de Rochemont had become disenchanted with the shallow content of American newsreels and had a vision for a dynamic in-depth presentation of national and international news events. In partnership with Roy E. Larsen of Time Inc., de Rochemont created the popular *The March of Time* newsreel unit. Utilizing documentary and cinematic recreation techniques to present news and entertainment items, de Rochemont brought content and style together to inform and delight the moviegoing public. *The March of Time* released a new edition once a month for sixteen years, beginning in the spring of 1935 through the fall of 1951. The influential cinema series shaped political views, editorializing on impacting events such as the Great Depression and controversial figures of World War II, Adolf Hitler, Benito Mussolini, and Japan's Tojo.

The March of Time presented journalism with bravado showmanship. The confident golden-throated narrator led the viewer quickly through the news illustrated with maps, diagrams, and text. *The March of Time* was not within the model of the classic newsreel; it was closer to the contemporary television magazine format filtered through a tabloid prism. De Rochemont recreated scenes involving popular celebrities, a forerunner of the television docudrama format. The twenty-minute *The March of Time* installments did not report up-to-the-minute news like the newsreels; its content was limited to the personal interests of the producers who controlled the content much like cable television's *Larry King Live* and *Rivera Live*.

Early on, de Rochemont learned how to find and dramatize news events. In 1915 as a sixteen-year-old reporter, de Rochemont covered the arrest of a German saboteur charged with blowing up a bridge in Vancebro, Maine. When de Rochemont and his competitors rushed to Portland where the suspect was imprisoned, the arrest had already occurred. De Rochemont had the savvy to convince the sheriff to recreate the arrest with the suspect as they performed for the camera. The footage was widely distributed by film companies and perceived as reality. The incident taught de Rochemont a valuable lesson about media manipulation that is evidenced on tabloid television shows such as *A Current Affair* and *Extra*.

In 1940 de Rochemont produced and directed the first *March of Time* theatrical feature, *The Ramparts We Watch*, a dramatization of the impact of World War II on a small American town. In 1943 de Rochemont became a Twentieth-Century-Fox Studios producer where he pioneered a trend toward realism by bringing semidocumentary, fictionalized dramas based on real-life experiences, exemplified in *The House on 92nd Street* (1945) and *Boomerang!* (1947). In 1944 de Rochemont produced the Oscar-winning documentary *The Fighting Lady* in association with the U.S. Navy. Later he became an independent producer, forming Louis de Rochemont Associates with former colleagues from *The March of Time*. The showman in de Rochemont resurfaced when he produced theatrical films in Cinerama and other wide-screen formats such as *Cinerama Holiday* and *The Miracle of Todd-AO* (both 1955), to lure back audiences lost to television.

de Rochemont, Richard. Producer, director. *b.* December 13, 1903, Boston, Massachusetts. *d.* August 4, 1982, Flemington, New Jersey. The younger brother of **Louis de Rochemont,** Richard worked with his sibling on *The March of Time* series and took over as executive producer in 1943. As a New York independent producer with his Vavin Inc., de Rochemont was always looking for young directorial talent. He became a mentor and benefactor for the young **Stanley Kubrick,** then a struggling New York independent filmmaker trying to get his first feature film made.

Deutchman, Ira. Producer. *b.* March 24, 1953. *ed.* Northwestern University. While still in college, Ira Deutchman organized and led the marketing campaign for the Midwest premiere of **John Cassavetes**'s *A Woman under the Influence* (1974). Deutchman has devoted his substantial career to the advancement of independent films. He worked at United Artist Classics, Films Incorporated, and **Cinema V** Ltd. and was a founding partner and president of marketing and distribution for Cinecom Entertainment Group, which released Merchant and Ivory's *A Room with a View* (1986); *Stop Making Sense* (1984), directed by **Jonathan Demme; Gregory Nava**'s *El Norte* (1983); and the **John Sayles** film *The Brother from Another Planet* (1984). As president of the Deutchman Company he was a marketing consultant for *sex, lies and videotape* (1989), directed by **Steven Soderbergh;** *To Sleep with Anger* (1990), directed by **Charles Burnett;** and **Whit Stillman**'s *Metropolitan* (1990). Deutchman was the founder and president of Fine Line Features and senior vice president of the parent company New Line Cinema. Deutchman acquired and released over sixty films at Fine Line including **Gus Van Sant**'s *My Own Private Idaho* (1991); *Night on Earth* (1991), directed by **Jim Jarmusch; Robert Altman**'s *The Player* (1992) and *Short Cuts* (1993); and **Alan Rudolph**'s *Mrs. Parker and the Vicious Circle* (1994) and the **documentary** *Hoop Dreams* (1994). Deutchman is a partner in Redermaple Features, an indie production company, and the CEO (chief executive officer) of Studio Next—a New

York digital media solutions provider. In over twenty-five years, Deutchman has been involved in over 130 independent feature films.

diary film. **Avant-garde, experimental film** form where the filmmaker carries a camera, often a **Bolex** or a digital video camera, and records personal observations, impressions, and events as a diarist would with pen and notebook. **Edward Pincus**'s *Diaries* (1976) is a five-year portrait of his marriage. Andrew Noren's *Kodak Ghost Poems* are short, one- to two-minute segments of daily realism, romantic episodes filled with texture, and lovingly rendered female nudity. Howard Guttenplan, director of **The Millennium**, is also an accomplished diary filmmaker. The best-known diarist is **Jonas Mekas** whose *Diaries, Notes and Sketches* is a model of the form. The epic work is in several parts, *Walden* (1969), *Lost, Lost, Lost* (1975), *In Between* (1978), *Notes for Jerome* (1978) and other films. Mekas helped define the style by utilizing single-frame shooting, bursts of frames, handheld camera movement, and over- and underexposure. Diary films, often unedited, are direct impressions of the diarist. This most personal cinema is **documentary** and artistic and shares the innermost emotions and feelings of the "writer."

DiCillo, Tom. Cinematographer, director, screenwriter. *b.* 1954, Jacksonville, Florida. *ed.* New York University. During the 1980s, Tom DiCillo was the premier indie director of photography. In 1982 he shot **Jim Jarmusch**'s first feature *Permanent Vacation* and his breakthrough project *Stranger Than Paradise* (1984). In 1984 DiCillo was one of four cinematographers on *Burroughs*, a **documentary** of the *Naked Lunch* author and Beat Generation legend William S. Burroughs, directed by Howard Brookner. In 1985 DiCillo shot *The Beat* (1988), about a new kid who moves into the turf of a tough gang and teaches them poetry. In 1990, DiCillo photographed Keith McNally's *End of the Night* featuring **Eric Mitchell** as a father-to-be who becomes unglued. In 1991 DiCillo became a writer/director. His debut *Johnny Suede* featured Brad Pitt wearing a pompadour as Suede who dreams of becoming a Ricky Nelson/Fabianesque rock star. *Living in Oblivion* (1995) was a knowing and very funny peek into the world of independent filmmaking, with DiCillo poking fun at his experiences in the low-budget film world. *Box of Moonlight* (1996) starred John Turturro, Sam Rockwell, Catherine Keener, and Dermot Mulroney in a whimsical tale of an engineer who falls in love with a free spirit and is liberated from his constricted life. *The Real Blonde* (1998), with Matthew Modine, Catherine Keener, Daryl Hannah, Kathleen Turner, Christopher Lloyd, Buck Henry, Denis Leary, and **Steve Buscemi**, is a New York story about an "aspiring" actor and his girlfriend, a makeup artist for a supermodel. *Double Whammy* (2001) features Denis Leary, Elizabeth Hurley, and Steve Buscemi in a comedy/drama about a tired police detective who is unable to stop a fast-food restaurant massacre and deals with his reputation and self-esteem.

Dickerson, Ernest. Cinematographer, director. *b.* 1952, Newark, New Jersey. *ed.* Howard University, New York University Film School. Ernest Dickerson was the first African American cinematographer inducted into the American Society of Cinematographers (ASC). Dickerson was **Spike Lee**'s director of photography (DP) on his short film *Joe's Bed-Stuy Barbershop: We Cut Heads* (1983) and Lee's feature films *She's Gotta Have It* (1986), *School Daze* (1988), *Do the Right Thing* (1989), *Mo' Better Blues* (1990), *Jungle Fever* (1991), and the epic biopic *Malcolm X* (1992).

In 1992 Dickerson surprised—fair to say, shocked—the indie world when he began a directorial career. He has yet to photograph another film. Ironically, the transition from DP to director came with *Juice* in 1992, the same year as the release of *Malcolm X*, Dickerson's most challenging and impressive work as a cinematographer. *Juice* is an urban drama about four African American teenagers whose lives take a violent turn when a robbery spins out of control. It featured Omar Epps, Cindy Herron of En Vogue and the late rapper Tupac Shakur. Dickerson's sophomore effort *Surviving the Game* (1994) recycled the 1932 film *The Most Dangerous Game*, based on a Richard Connell story of a megalomaniacal count who hunts down humans on his desolate island. Dickerson's puts a racial twist on the often-filmed tale by casting rapper Ice-T in the role of a black man hunted down by white hunters. Next, Dickerson directed *Tales from the Crypt Presents Demon Knight* (1995), based on the popular HBO horror series. The big-screen version was dominated by gross-out gore and plenty of nudity. In 1996 Dickerson directed *Bulletproof*, starring Adam Sandler and Damon Wayans, in a racially inverted version of *48 Hrs.* (1982). In *Blind Faith* (1998), a film that premiered on cable before its theatrical release, Dickerson explored the racial divide in the U.S. justice system. *Ambushed* (1998) is an action movie starring Courtney B. Vance in a story of explosive racial tension caused by the murder of a Klan leader. Recent directorial credits for Ernest Dickerson include: *Bones* (2001) and *Monday Night Mayhem* (2002), a cable feature about Howard Cosell and his *Monday Night Football* exploits at the ABC television network. As a cinematographer Dickerson brought a vivid color and lighting sense that enhanced the production design of **Wynn Thomas** and served the theatrical vision of director Spike Lee. His treatment of black-themed films brought clarity and sensitivity to the photographic conception of the content and characters. Working with **John Sayles** on *Brother from Another Planet* (1984), Dickerson heightened the metaphor of the black male as an alien in his own country with his vivid camera and cinematic color treatment. *See also* Lee, Spike; Thomas, Wynn

direct cinema. The American interpretation of *cinéma vérité* as practiced by **Richard Leacock, D.A. Pennebaker** and the **Maysles** brothers. Cinéma vérité filmmakers in France used the camera subjectively and maintained the natural form of the material during the postproduction process. The direct cinema group was nonobjective and as invisible as possible during production and tightly structured their films during the editing. *See also* cinéma vérité; Leacock, Richard (Ricky); Pennebaker, D.A.; Maysles, Albert and David

Directors Company, The. An outgrowth of an idea by then–Gulf & Western president Charles Bluhdorn, The Directors Company was a filmmaker's cooperative formed by three preeminent American directors of the 1970s—Peter Bogdanovich, **Francis Ford Coppola**, and William Friedkin. The idea, as Bluhdorn envisioned it, was to bring top directors to the company, where they could make feature films that would be released by Paramount Pictures, sight unseen, so long as the films' budgets remained under $3 million. The company was launched as the three directors were coming off huge box office smashes (Bogdanovich's *The Last Picture Show* [1971], Coppola's first two *Godfather* [1972, 1974] films, and Friedkin's *The French Connection* [1971]); thus, all involved had reason to be excited. The company's first film, Bogdanovich's *Paper Moon* (1973), was a financial and critical hit, netting each of the players a sizable cut of the profits. *Daisy Miller* (1974) followed, starring Bogdanovich's then-girlfriend Cybil Shepard, and it opened to bad reviews, the first of the young director's career. Burdened by healthy egos and a desire for money, The Directors Company disbanded soon after *Daisy Miller's* release. Although William Friedkin had not yet made a picture for the company, he could sense the group's inner turmoil and felt that any film he made would ultimately be sabotaged. He left, followed quickly by Bogdanovich and Coppola whose *The Conversation* (1974) was also released under The Director's Company banner. Founded on similar principles as **BBS**, The Directors Company ultimately suffered a similar demise.

direct-to-cable. Feature films produced to be sold to the cable television market or intended for theatrical release but sold to cable because they are unable to find a theatrical distributor.

direct-to-video. Feature films produced to be distributed solely for the video market or intended for theatrical release but sold to video because they are unable to find a theatrical distributor.

Disney, Walt. Animator, executive. *b.* Walter Elias Disney, December 5, 1901, Chicago, Illinois. *d.* December 15, 1966, Los Angeles, California. *ed.*

Kansas City Art Institute. Walt Disney, one of the major cultural figures of the American century, was responsible for creating the classical aesthetics and production methods of the Hollywood animated feature film and for building a company that is now a controlling media empire. Disney began as a small independent while the major studios reigned, and he died as head of an independently controlled conglomerate composed of motion picture, television, and publishing enterprises and product franchises and theme park divisions. The Disney name and logo represented a pure, traditionally American, politically correct entertainment that totally rejected a changing, more diverse worldview.

In 1919 while working at a commercial art studio in Kansas City, Walt Disney met animator Ub Iwerks, who became a lifelong collaborator. Disney and Iwerks joined a Kansas City advertising firm where they created animated commercials. Independently they produced a series of satirical animated cartoons they sold to local movie theaters. Disney then formed Laugh-O-Gram, a cartoon production company that quickly went bankrupt. Walt Disney headed for Hollywood and in 1923 formed a partnership with his brother Roy with the creative input of Iwerks to produce an animation and live-action cartoon series *Alice in Cartoonland*. In 1927, Disney and Iwerks launched a new animated series, *Oswald the Rabbit*.

In 1927 Walt Disney picked up his pencil and brought to life his seminal character, the jovial, good-natured Mickey Mouse he featured in a silent cartoon *The Gallopin' Gaucho*. He was given a voice in *Steamboat Willie*. Disney called his cartoons *Silly Symphonies*. Stalwarts of the Disney family, Donald Duck, Goofy, and Pluto, followed. Disney and his growing staff pioneered the multiplane animation camera that brought perspective and depth to the one-dimensional cartoon. Walt Disney built an animation factory employing hundreds of workers.

In 1934 the Disney Company created *Snow White and the Seven Dwarfs*, a feature animation that premiered in 1937. The Disney product was perceived as entertainment, but the landmark experimental animated feature *Fantasia*, first released in 1940, proved that animation was an art form. When first released, its visual, at times abstract, images orchestrated by Leopold Stokowski's classical accompaniment moved beyond traditional narrative and overwhelmed and confounded general audiences. In the late 1960s *Fantasia*, a film that stands as prehistory to psychedelic cinema, reemerged to delight and influence a generation of turned-on and tuned-out baby-boomers.

Ironically, while Disney sent Donald Duck and fellow toons to the front to fight the fascists during World War II, the voice of dissent was heard within the Disney Studio. In 1941 a contentious strike tore the home of Mickey Mouse apart. Many of the workers rebelled against Disney's authoritarian rule and his reigning philosophy of a naturalistic

Walt Disney, 1935. Courtesy of The Kobol Collection

drawing style and traditional content. The conflict resulted in mass resignations and the creation of the UPA (United Productions of America), an alternate to the apple pie–white bread world of Disney.

In 1950 Disney began to produce family-oriented live-action entertainment with the release of *Treasure Island*. A true-life adventure series was also very popular with the American public. Walt Disney formed the Buena-Vista Company to distribute the studio's releases. This venture made Disney totally independent of the Hollywood studio system. Walt Disney expanded to the medium of television in 1954 and in 1955 to the theme park, Disneyland. The Disney Studio floundered after the death of its founder in 1966 until Michael Eisner and Jeffrey Katzenberg rebuilt the company to a greater empire than even its independent architect ever imagined.

BIBLIOGRAPHY

Eliot, Marc. *Walt Disney: Hollywood's Dark Prince.* New York: HarperCollins, 1993.
Maltin, Leonard. *The Disney Films.* New York: Popular Library, 1973.
Schickel, Richard. *The Disney Version.* New York: Simon and Schuster, 1985.

distributors. *See* "Appendix C: Distributors of Independent Films"

documentaries. Nonfiction filmmaking has gone through an evolution from the purest recording of real-life events to a merging of fiction and reality. Foundations, grants, and personal investors support documentaries as well as corporations and television networks. The first major technological and aesthetic landmark in nonfiction films was the advent of lightweight cameras and sound equipment. Prior, documentarians were limited to title cards, narration, and musical scores to express information over the visuals. Lightweight sync-sound equipment in the 1960s led to the **cinéma vérité** and direct sound era when filmmakers sought to capture real life. In the 1970s video began to be utilized to lower the tremendous shooting costs of nonfiction film with its massive take ratios. In the 1980s and 1990s the docudrama emerged. These reenactments of true-life events employed production values and techniques similar to fictional films. The range of nonfiction subject matter is limitless; distribution, however, is difficult. Fewer and fewer feature-length documentaries receive theatrical runs, and television has become a prime venue. The nonfiction film with its hallowed history of capturing seminal events and discussing important social, historical, and political themes is not without subjectivity and cinematic manipulation in its process. This does not disparage its integrity, but all information is vulnerable to subjectivity. Documentarians are now liberated to use any means necessary to document and impart the truth as they see it, and the audience, no less subjective, can assess it in kind.

BIBLIOGRAPHY

Rotha, Paul (in collaboration with Sinclair Road and Richard Griffith). *Documentary Film.* New York: Communication Arts Books, 1935.

Dogme 95. A manifesto created by **Lars von Trier** and Thomas Vinterberg in 1995 when they wrote the ten rules and took a Vow of Chastity to make less manipulated films centered on the characters and natural environment. Like the Ten Commandments, von Trier and Vinterberg immediately knew that the rules could never be rigidly held to and that the perfect Dogme film would never be made. The rules were written in Copenhagen on Monday, March 13, 1995, in twenty-five minutes, amidst what von Trier describes as "continuous bursts of merry laughter."

The movement is a serious one, but practiced in the spirit of play and duplicity. The rules dictate that the production of a Dogme film include shooting only on location with no sets or props. Only direct synchronous sound can be used, including music, and no postsound. The camera must be handheld at all times. The camera is there for the characters, story, and environment. The point of view must be where the film takes place, not where the camera is standing. All films must be in color and shot with no special lighting. A single lamp can be attached to the camera if the light is too low to gain a decent exposure. No filters or optical effects can be used. No superficial action and no murders or weapons are allowed in a Dogme film. No temporal and geographical alienation; the film must place in the here and now. No genre films. The format is to be Academy standard 35mm. The director is not to be credited; a collective makes Dogme films.

The first Dogme film released was *The Celebration* (1998), directed by Vinterberg. Other Dogme films include von Trier's *The Idiots* (1998) and *Mifune*, directed by Søren Kragh-Jacobsen (1999). The movement has spread globally. **Harmony Korine**'s *Julien Donkey-Boy* (1999) was the first American film to be officially certified by Dogme 95; *Chetzemoka's Curse* (2001), created by **Rick Schmidt**'s workshop, was the second.

Filmmakers must submit their project on VHS to the Dogme Secretariat. If the film meets the rules as stated by the Vow of Chastity and various interpretations of the four original "priests/brethren," the film receives, for a fee, a Dogme certificate containing a solemn declaration that the filmmaker must sign. The tape is then filed in the Dogme library. The Brethren were originally the supreme judges, but now more Dogme followers have been given that power. Because the perfect Dogme film can never be made, many rules have either been broken or loosely interpreted by the original practitioners. The name of the director can be used in marketing, so everyone knows who directed the film.

The original intention was to shoot on 35mm color film stock in standard Academy ratio, but *The Celebration* and other Dogme films were photographed on video and later transferred to 35mm standard Academy ratio, and the rule was applied only to the distribution format and not to the medium used during shooting. Vinterberg found video cheaper and easier to shoot handheld. An agreement was made to transfer to video by setting the white balance to automatic so as not to alter or manipulate the original color in any way. On *The Idiots*, von Trier allowed the actors to bring in props to the empty house used as a location. He has also given actors money to buy food to be cooked and eaten during the production, but Vinterberg insists the food must be at the location before filming begins. Post music scoring is not allowed; musicians must appear on camera and be recorded in sync, but many Dogme films have utilized live musicians playing in sync during the shooting but sequestered behind the camera to create an aesthetic similar to conventional post music scoring.

Von Trier does not raise or lower the sound level in postproduction, but others do. Although filters are not allowed during shooting, they were used during the lab processing for *The Idiots*. Von Trier has moved a chair five centimeters to get a better shot of an actor, and Kragh-Jacobsen moved a painter's loft 200 meters to get a shot of a field that was a principal image in the film—von Trier found this a grave transgression. Von Trier has used stand-ins for sex scenes, claiming that it was an essential effect but that it clearly violates the principle of creating a pure cinema cleansed of all artifice and manipulation by the director. Candles have been moved to achieve more effective lighting. Premeditated rationalized actions by the director seem to be considered worse sins than acts of passion that occur during filming without much thought. Dogme 95 brethren are all sinners, but each truly answers to his or her own cinematic God. *See also Celebration, The*; Vinterberg, Thomas; von Trier, Lars

BIBLIOGRAPHY

Dogme's official Web site: http://www.tvropa.com/tvropa1.2/film/dogme95/index.htm

Kelly, Richard. *The Name of This Book Is Dogme 95*. London: Faber and Faber, 2000.

Downney, Robert. Director, screenwriter. *b.* June 1936, Tennessee. In the 1960s and 1970s Robert Downey was a pioneering independent filmmaker making outrageous and irreverent satires years before comedy's bad boys of the 1980s. In 1961 Downey met his wife Elsie on *The Comeuppance*, an Off-Off Broadway play he had written. The theater production was about dogs in a pound waiting to be adopted or gassed and was inspired by the rebellious Downey's experiences in the stockade during his stint in the army. Elsie played a mutt. When a German shepherd tries to come on to a French poodle, the reply is, "Not after what your country did to mine." A penguin cries out in frustration, "What the hell am I doing here, I'm a penguin."

When Downey was a Civil War extra in *The Anderson Trial* on Broadway, he got the idea it would be funny to create a film about a Civil War veteran walking through the streets of New York. Downey bought film stock out of his waiter's salary and without any formal training directed the short *Ball's Buff* (1961), shot on weekends for $2,000. Downey proceeded to create four more weekend shorts including one concerning the New York singles bar scene from outtakes of a freelance job he landed for ABC-TV. The five **16mm** shorts were intercut and released in 1968 as *No More Excuses* at a personal cost of around $12,000. In 1963 Downey made the 16mm short *Babo 73*. He took the next two years to make his next short *Chafed Elbows* (1965) in 35mm. Downey raised $3,500 from an ad he placed in the *Village Voice* with the copy, "Walk softly and carry a blank check." *Chafed Elbows* cost $25,000. In one scene a criminal fires two warning shots into a policeman's shoulder. Another shows a man on welfare having a sexual relationship with his mother, and a visual gag presents a man drawing a line down the middle of a street proclaiming, "You've got to draw the line somewhere!" Downey had to dub in almost every actor's lines in postproduction—a costly lesson. Downey's wife Elsie played all thirteen female roles in *Chafed Elbows*.

After seven years of domestic sacrifice, Downey's breakthrough was *Putney Swope* (1969). The outrageous black-and-white low-budget Madison Avenue satire begins with the takeover of an advertising agency by black militants. Downey worked on the story and characterizations for a year. He had been a resident eccentric at an ad agency where his outlandish ideas were never used. Downey worked many of his not-ready-for-prime-time commercials into the script. Downey's agent at William Morris put him in touch with an American silk and rubber tycoon who put up $200,000 on the condition he remain anonymous. Downey's salary as writer/director was originally established at $18,000, but when the budget increased because of his inexperience, he put back $9,000 of his fee. The script demanded a cast of 200—with 120 speaking roles; 30 were key characters. Many of the cast members were nonactors plucked off the street. For one scene Downey had African Americans rounded up to fill the frame and satisfy the premise. Method actors desperately searching for their motivation instead of just delivering the hysterically impudent jokes blew some of Downey's one-liners. Shooting was so hectic that Downey was only able to set the frame for six shots; the rest were left to the serviceable hands of the director of photography (DP) Jerry Cotts of National Educational Television's (NET) *Black Journal*. Neither director nor DP was familiar with the 35mm Mitchell camera, the Hollywood standard at the time. The Mitchell was a heavy and cumbersome camera, so little handheld work was incorporated into the visual style. Downey didn't encourage his actors to improvise except for one ten-minute take, compressed to six minutes in the final cut, in which a Secret Service man jokes with the president of the United States, portrayed by a midget. Downey had only shot one or two takes on his short films. On *Putney Swope* his **shooting ratio** was as high as 5 or 6 to 1. A lot of footage was not usable because Downey was learning on his first outing how to make a feature.

Putney Swope was shot on location in ten weeks. Fifty business offices were approached for the principal location. After reading the script only four or five agreed. Downey's backer was a friend of David Rockefeller, who gave permission to shoot in a Chase Manhattan Bank. Cast and crew shot nights and slept days. There was no time for rehearsals. The opening shot was accomplished in a bank's boardroom after thirty-six straight hours over the course of a weekend. An eighty-three-year-old actor played the owner of the agency who dies in the scene. During the fourteen-minute sequence he had to fall over repeatedly. The green marble conference table suffered scratches, and a $15,000 insurance claim covered the damages.

Putney Swope's theme is corruption in power structures against which Downey had a lifelong rebellion. Downey's biting wit was a defense mechanism and a weapon he used often and well. Cinematographer and filmmaker **Haskell Wexler** screened a rough cut of *Putney Swope* and urged Grove Press to pick up the film. When the postproduction was complete, Don Rugoff of **Cinema V** screened *Putney Swope* and made a handshake deal to distribute the film. *Putney Swope* was the talk of the town. Audiences responded to the outrageous premise and outre commercials. After years of struggle Downey had finally established himself as a major independent filmmaker.

In 1970 Downey adapted his allegorical play about dogs into the film *Pound*. The large cast portrayed a wide range of canines including Antonio Fargas as a greyhound, Marshall Efron as a dachshund, Elsie Downey as a mutt bitch, and their young son Robert Jr. as a puppy. The Floyd L. Peterson production company financed the film, and because of Downey's success with *Putney Swope*, a major studio, United Artists, distributed *Pound*. The satire and social content eluded most critics and all but the most selectively sophisticated audiences.

In 1972, Don Rugoff's Cinema V distributed Downey's next feature, *Greaser's Palace*—a parody of the life of Jesus transposed to the old American West. Downey's big statement film was a total disaster at the box office. In 1980 Robert Downey finally got another chance to direct but only as a hired hand on *Up the Academy*, a military school comedy financed and distributed by Warner Bros. In 1982 Downey filmed his screenplay *America*, a satire featuring a wacky television cable station that achieves worldwide fame when its broadcast signal is accidentally bounced off the moon. The independent production was not released until 1986 when it crashed and burned at the box office.

Downey directed *Rented Lips*, released in 1988, from a script by comic actor Martin Mull. The film featured Mull, Dick Shawn, Jennifer Tilly,

Eileen Brennan, and Pat McCormick and is the story of a veteran documentary filmmaker whose résumé includes *Aluminum Our Shiny Friend*. He finally receives an offer to make a wish-list project on Indian farming but must make a porno at the same time. The adult film becomes a musical, *Halloween in the Barracks*, paralleling Downey's experience when he was hired to direct a porno he hoped would pay the bills. *Rented Lips* and Downey's next comedy *Too Much Sun* did little to resurrect his career. The 1991 farce written by Downey, Laura Ernst, and Al Schwartz is the story of a brother and sister in competition to be first to have a child in order to inherit their father's fortune. The plan is complicated by the fact that they are both gay.

In 1997 Downey cowrote and directed *Hugo Pool*, about a Los Angeles pool cleaner who falls in love with a man dying of Lou Gehrig's disease. The story was developed after Downey's wife Laura, who nursed him through his addiction to drugs, was diagnosed with amyotrophic lateral sclerosis (ALS). She died at age thirty-six after collaborating on the script. *Hugo Pool* premiered at **Sundance.** It featured Malcolm McDowell, Sean Penn, Cathy Moriarty, Patrick Dempsey and Robert Downey Jr. In 2001 Downey directed the dark comedy *Forrest Hills Bob.* Although Robert Downey may always be known for one film, his politically incorrect *Putney Swope,* he is an American independent film original.

Drew, Robert. Documentary producer and director. *b.* February 15, 1924, Toledo, Ohio. *ed.* Harvard University. In the late 1950s, Robert Drew took a leave from his staff job at *Life* magazine and was given financial backing by NBC to create an on-air magazine. *Life* magazine photographer Alan Grant was the principal cameraman, forced to work with cumbersome equipment and narration rather than sync sound. The show was delivered to NBC under two titles—*Key Picture* and *Magazine* X. Drew returned to *Time-Life* and became obsessed with the challenge of finding portable production equipment to take into the field so filmmakers could record life directly. They began raising money for research, development, and production of lightweight camera and sound recording equipment. When he returned to *Life* Drew assembled production teams and commissioned equipment to be engineered. He needed $1 million to put his plan into action. Henry Luce at *Life* looked at *Key Picture* and passed. Networks offered him jobs, but Drew persisted with his vérité vision. Drew was inspired and assisted by **Ricky Leacock,** Arthur Zegart, CBS documentary producer Bill McClure, cameramen **Morris Engel,** and Fons Ianelli, who both experimented with lightweight equipment.

After five more years Drew had all the elements he required. In 1960 Wes Tullien, vice president in charge of *Time*'s television operations, asked Drew to teach local station affiliates how to produce **documentaries** and provided the funds to finance the mission. Sound pioneer Loren

Ryder was commissioned to design and build a portable machine that could be used to edit and mix multiple sound tracks on location. **D.A. Pennebaker** translated Leacock's camera specs to an equipment modifier Mitch Bogdanovich, Peter's father. They proceeded with *Primary* (1960), a **cinéma vérité** documentary about the 1960 Democratic primary between Hubert Humphrey and John Kennedy. ABC made *Yanki No!*, another documentary exploration in the new form, broadcast in 1960. The vice president of news resigned because management had contracted an independent producer.

The camera company Bell and Howell wanted more documentary programs and made a deal with Drew for a show on Latin America. Drew Associates, owned by Creative Associates, was set up, and Drew hired a research staff for the project. Drew Associates produced six close-ups for Bell and Howell. *Time* and ABC fought over the documentaries. *Time* had ordered the programs produced, but ABC did not air them. The documentaries were screened at film festivals. Eventually *Time Inc.* released Drew Associates from its exclusive contract.

Drew then made a direct network deal to create a documentary on President Kennedy and George Wallace. ABC bought the show *Crisis* sponsored by Xerox. The new ABC president would only allow Drew to work on staff; he could not be an indie. Drew did work as an independent producer for two years and made films on Vietnam, bullfighting in Malaysia, and the death of John F. Kennedy. In 1974 Drew produced and directed the television documentary *On the Road with Duke Ellington*. In 1975 Xerox wanted Drew to make films on subjects too controversial for the networks and sent him a two-page list of ideas. Drew chose the topic of drugs and made *Storm Signal* (1967). Robert Drew is a relentless pioneer. His struggles led to the development of an independent form of nonfiction that gave life and inspiration to the American vérité movement and the next generation of nonfiction filmmakers **Barbara Kopple, Michael Moore, Errol Morris,** and **Ross McElwee.** *See also* Leacock, Richard; Pennebaker, D.A.

BIBLIOGRAPHY

White, Thomas. "Take the IDA-Train to Drew's Duke Doc." *International Documentary* 19.6 (July–August 2000).

drive-in theaters. Outdoor movie theaters that first arrived on the American entertainment scene on June 6, 1933. By 1939 drive-ins were located across the country. During the 1940s, the number of drive-ins grew, and by 1948 there were 820 venues. By the 1950s, the drive-in hit its pinnacle with 5,000 locations as the number of indoor theaters declined from 17,000 to 12,000. At their inception, drive-in theaters screened any available product from Hollywood studios, but by the 1950s and 1960s, films

The title character in producer David F. Friedman's *She Freak* (1966), an example of 1960s drive-in projector fodder. Courtesy of the Del Valle Archive

were being produced specifically for drive-in devotees. The demographics initially were families with young children and ultimately teenagers who came to make out and watch **beach party films**, **biker movies**, horror, sci-fi **B-movies**, and plenty of **exploitation films**. **American International Pictures**, **Roger Corman**, and other independent companies and filmmakers were making what they called drive-in fodder. Supply and demand kept indies busy, and the phenomenon was a training ground for a generation of filmmakers who bloomed in the 1970s, when the drive-in boom was over. As a new American cinema appeared at the dawn of the 1970s, the under-thirty audience was looking for more serious films in a more serious setting. In the 1980s cable television and VCRs led to the drive-in's demise. But at the end of the century drive-ins began to reopen as part of a retro cycle—the everything that goes around comes around theory.

Driver, Sara. Director, producer, writer, actress. *b.* 1955, New York. *ed.* New York University graduate film school. After three short films, *Dream Gone Bad* (1979), *Death in Hoboken*, and *Sir Orpheo* (both 1980), Driver created *You Are Not I* (1982), a fifty-minute, black-and-white film that gained critical attention. The film was photographed by **Jim Jarmusch** who Driver worked for as production manager on *Permanent Vacation* (1982) and *Stranger Than Paradise* (1984), which she also produced. *You Are Not I* was adapted from a 1940s Paul Bowles short story concerning a woman who escapes from a mental hospital during a chaotic car accident. She places a stone in the mouth of a woman who dies of shock and is mistaken for the lead character. She arrives at her sister's house. Confused and angered the sister has two neighbors come over. They call the hospital; the escaped sister puts a stone in her sibling's mouth. The screen goes black, and then the sister is taken away while the mental patient stays in the house. *You Are Not I* ends like Hitchcock's *Psycho* (1960), but with the schizophrenic sister explaining everything offscreen. Driver's principal inspiration was the **John Cassavetes** film *A Woman under the Influence* (1974), which challenged society's notion of female sanity. Driver also directed *Sleepwalk* (1986), which received a $7,000 advance from First Run Features, the television series *Monsters* (1988), and *Wenn Schweine fliegen* (*When Pigs Fly*, 1993) in Germany. Driver was a story consultant on Jim Jarmusch's *Ghost Dog: The Way of the Samurai* (1999). *See also* Jarmusch, Jim

BIBLIOGRAPHY

Rosenbaum, Jonathan. *Film: The Front Line.* Denver, CO: Arden Press, 1983.

DuArt Laboratories. *See* Young, Irwin

Dunne, Griffin. Actor, producer. *b.* June 8, 1955, New York City. *ed.* Neighborhood Playhouse. Son of writer/producer Dominick Dunne, Griffin Dunne has balanced a duo career as an actor and producer for two decades. Most notable for his performances in *An American Werewolf in London* (1981) and *After Hours* (1985), he had a successful producing partnership with **Amy Robinson:** Double Play Productions produced several successful midsized indies in the 1980s. In 1995 Dunne directed the television short *Duke of Groove*. He continues to work as an actor. Dunne's recent directing credits include: *Addicted to Love* (1997), *Practical Magic* (1998), *Lisa Picard Is Famous* (2000), and *Nailed Right In* (2002). *See also* Robinson, Amy

E

Eastwood, Clint. Actor, director, producer. *b.* May 31, 1930, San Francisco. *ed.* Los Angeles City College. Consummate filmmaker known first as an actor in several forgettable films of the mid-1950s, Eastwood was noticed on the popular TV series *Rawhide*, where he became comfortable in the saddle. He was able to exploit this image and develop a portrait of a taciturn, trammeled hero for Italian director Sergio Leone in three wildly successful "spaghetti westerns"—*A Fistful of Dollars* (1964), *For a Few Dollars More* (1965), and *The Good, the Bad and the Ugly* (1966).

Eastwood established an indelible persona as a larger-than-life, close-mouthed superhero and transformed this character into an urban law and order hero in a series of roles for director **Don Siegel**, beginning with *Dirty Harry* (1971). With Siegel as his mentor, Eastwood branched out and began directing and producing as the head of his own company, Malpaso Productions. Starting with *Play Misty for Me* (1971) Eastwood's projects have cut across genres. He amassed a significant body of work noted for its economical style and production method, and proficiency. Eastwood surrounds himself with a technical support system that has included cinematographers Bruce Surtees and Jack Green, editor Joel Cox, and production designer Henry Bumstead, and his productions are known for equanimity and diversity on the set. He is at home directing hard action as in *The Eiger Sanction* (1975), *The Gauntlet* (1977), *Firefox* (1982), *Sudden Impact* (1983), *Heartbreak Ridge* (1986), and *The Rookie* (1990). A substantial number of his productions have been Westerns: *High Plains Drifter* (1972), *The Outlaw Josie Wales* (1976), *Bronco Billy* (1980), and *Pale Rider* (1985).

His career reached its pinnacle in 1992 when he produced, directed, and starred in a somber western elegy *Unforgiven*, which won an Academy Award as best picture. Eastwood was also named best director by

Clint Eastwood
Dirty Harry

Detective
Harry Callahan.
He doesn't
break
murder cases.
He smashes
them.

Original poster art depicting Clint Eastwood as his defining urban character Harry Callahan in *Dirty Harry* (1972), directed by Don Siegel. Courtesy of the Del Valle Archive the Academy. Eastwood has pursued his passion for jazz as director of *Bird* (1988) and as executive producer of *Thelonius Monk: Straight, No Chaser* (1989) and has injected jazz into many of his productions. Clint Eastwood is also the director of *The Bridges of Madison County* (1995), *Absolute Power* (1997), *True Crime* (1999), *Space Cowboys* (2000), and *Blood Work* (2002). In the last decades of the twentieth century, Clint Eastwood took his place as a master of American independent filmmaking. *See also* Siegel, Don

BIBLIOGRAPHY

Kaminsky, Stuart M. *Clint Eastwood*. New York: Signet, 1974.
Schickel, Richard. *Clint Eastwood: A Biography*. New York: Knopf, 1996.

Easy Rider. A 1969 film directed by **Dennis Hopper,** produced by **Peter Fonda,** written by Hopper, Fonda, and Terry Southern, and photographed by **László Kovács.** This vanguard **BBS** production single-handedly launched a youth revolution signaling the beginning of the New Hollywood known as the **American New Wave.** Fonda and Hopper star as Captain America and Billy who score a cocaine deal and set off on choppers to find America. Jack Nicholson gives a career-making performance as George Hanson, an alcoholic, liberal lawyer who befriends them. *Easy Rider* examined prejudice, drug experimentation, communal living, and America's unwillingness to accept social change. It pioneered the use of rock music in segments that were the prehistory of music videos, resulting in a chart-busting soundtrack album. For more than thirty years Hopper and Fonda have argued and fought legally over the authorship of *Easy Rider* but remain in denial that much of the narrative invention came from Terry Southern, who shaped their concepts and ideas into a structured screenplay. Kovács's visualization utilized a handheld and often on-the-road camera as the Hungarian émigré showed the beauty of America through the virgin eyes of an immigrant. *See also* BBS; Fonda, Peter; Hopper, Dennis

Edison, Thomas Alva. Inventor, producer. *b.* February 11, 1847, Milan, Ohio. *d.* October 18, 1931, West Orange, New Jersey. With little formal education and heady ambition, Thomas Edison, best known as the inventor of the electric light bulb, was a ruthless businessman who strove to dominate and eliminate all competitors. Edison put W.K.L. Dickson in charge of construction of a motion picture apparatus. The Edison Kinetophonograph, capable of running the 4 perf 35mm celluloid film stock just invented by George Eastman, made its appearance in 1889. In 1891 the Edison Company demonstrated the Kinetograph camera and Kinetoscope viewer.

Dickson constructed the first movie studio, The Black Maria, in 1893.

Director Dennis Hopper as Billy and producer Peter Fonda as Captain America in the American New Wave landmark film *Easy Rider* (1969). Courtesy of The Del Valle Archive.

The Edison films were entertainment and not explorations of a new art. At first Edison didn't produce films for theater exhibition. The Kinetoscope was a peepshow novelty viewed one customer at a time. Eventually Edison was convinced of the new medium's potential, and he purchased the rights to the Jenkins-Armat Vitascope projector, an advancement of Edison's original invention. On April 23, 1896, The Edison Vitascope was publicly displayed at a vaudeville show produced at the Koster and Bial Music Hall in New York City. Twelve short films were projected on a screen to the audience; one of the films was hand-tinted in color. The historic showing was the birth of a new industry in the United States.

In 1909, Edison and other growing motion picture companies bonded to form the Motion Pictures Patents Company, a trust designed to block independent film producers anxious to get into the market. The power play by "The Wizard of Menlo Park" was ultimately challenged by an antitrust legal action and found by the courts to be an illegal monopoly. The dissolution of Edison and his partners' stranglehold over the film industry in 1917 dissipated the inventor's interest in a medium he saw mainly as commerce, not art, and his company dropped out of the film industry. With the powerful entrepreneur out of the way, major and independent studios grew and flourished.

BIBLIOGRAPHY

Rawlence, Christopher. *The Missing Reel: The Untold Story of the Lost Inventor of Moving Pictures.* New York: Atheneum, 1990.

educational filmmaking. A genre of films produced and distributed for use in elementary, junior high, and high school settings. Originally these projects were created on **16mm** film and projected in classrooms and school auditoriums. They were intended as a visual method of teaching science, history, and other curriculum subjects. Encyclopedia Britannica, McGraw-Hill, and The Learning Corporation of America were the principal producers and distributors. A solid group of filmmakers committed to the education film produced the vast majority of the work. Individuals and smaller companies also were part of the educational film community. Like other areas of motion picture production, educational films switched to video as a medium.

Norman Bean (*b.* November 12, 1925) was a key 16mm educational filmmaker. Bean taught high school biology for twelve years in Los Angeles. His specialty was insect films for young children, and he contributed to the *Backyard Science* series. Bean began his career as an educational filmmaker in 1953 and completed a staggering 100 films including 6 travel films and 18 on the English language. His filmography includes *Farm Babies and Their Mothers* (1954), *Amazon: Life along the River in Brazil* (1962), *Turtle: Care of a Turtle* (1963), *Animals Hear in Many Ways* (1968) and *What Do Plants Do?: A First Film* (1971).

William F. Deneen was founder of the New York–based Learning Corporation of America that was sold in 1987 to New World Pictures. In the 1950s he formed William Deneen Productions, later bought by Encylopedia Britannica Educational Corporation. In the 1950s and 1960s Deneen was screenwriter, director, and cinematographer on many films including *Life in Ancient Rome, Frontier Boy* (1962), *Japan—Miracle in Asia* (1963), *The Nile Valley and Its People* (1962) and *Arts and Crafts of Mexico Parts 1 & 2* (1961).

Bruce Hoffman (*b.* 1955) was raised in Chicago and studied communication arts at the University of Wisconsin. In 1980, he was hired as an apprentice at the Encylopedia Britannica Educational Corporation in Chicago where his father was on the board of directors. Hoffman specializes in films concerning the human body, which include *Skin: Its Structure and Function* (1983), *Blood: The Microscopic Miracle* (1983), *The Human Brain* (1983), *Human Reproduction* (1985), and *Your Ears* (1989).

Bruce J. Russell, a former high school biology teacher, formed Bio-MEDIA, a company that produced biology films. He is coinventor of the

DiscoveryScope, a handheld microscope he used to locate tiny objects, invisible to the naked eye. His work for the Cornet Company's Biological Sciences series includes *Life in Lost Creek* (1978), *Cell Biology* (1981), *Genetic Biology* (1981), *Inquiring into Life* (1987), and *Cell Biology—Plasma Membrane* (1987).

In the 1970s Bert Salzman made films about ethnic awareness and diversity. In 1975 he made *Angel and Big Joe*, starring Paul Sorvino, about a Puerto Rican migrant youngster. Salzman's filmography includes *Geronimo Jones* (1970), *Joshua: Black Boy in Harlem* (1969), *Lee Suzuki: Home in Hawaii* (1973), and *Matthew Alvik: Eskimo in Two Worlds* (1973).

Bert Van Ronk (*b.* 1928, Augustuburg, Germany) studied art and photography. *The Seventeen Year Locust* (1957) was his first film. Van Ronk has made over 200 films and is best known for adventurous geological studies films. They include *Cave Community* (1960), *Heartbeat of a Volcano* (1970), and *Erosion and Weathering: Looking at the Land* (1976).

Between 1958 and 1981 Clifford B. West made over twenty-five films on artists and art history. They include *The Basilica of San Lorenzo* (1964), *Michelangelo: The Medici Chapel* (1964), *The Cantoria of Luca della Robbia* (1965), *Eduard Munch: Paintings* (1968), and *The Fountains of Carmilles*.

Bernard Wiltes (*b.* March 19, 1928, Milwaukee, Wisconsin) has made films for his *Man and the State* series, playwriting, and music. A sampling of his more than eighty films includes *The Trial of Socrates* (1971), *Machiavelli on Political Power* (1972), *Marx and Rockefeller on Capitalism* (1977), *Discovering the Music of Middle Ages* (1968), and *Discovering Electronic Music* (1983).

Larry Yust made dramatic films based on literary works for Encyclopedia Britannica: *Bartleby* (1969), *The Lottery* (1969), *Doctor Heidegger's Experiment* (1969), *The Secret Sharer* (1973), and *The Lady or the Tiger?* (1969).

On the whole, educational films were finely crafted short films intended to further educate students in subjects they were studying. They were well researched and contained serious scholarship by passionate independent filmmakers.

BIBLIOGRAPHY

http://Cine16.com. Web site dedicated to the educational film featuring the dedicated scholarship of Geoff Alexander.

8mm filmmaking. The 8mm film gauge was originally created for the home market and was packaged on fifty-foot spools. The stock was actually **16mm**. The home user shooting a birthday, wedding, or family event threaded the film in the camera, shot for twenty-five feet, then reversed the roll to shoot the remaining twenty-five feet. From the 1940s through the 1970s, 8mm practitioners brought their exposed film to a local drugstore or camera shop that sent it to a lab, usually Kodak in Rochester, New York. The roll was processed, split down the middle, and connected so the customer got back a continuous fifty feet of 8mm print on a gray or white reel. There was one splice in the roll, where the two strips were joined. Eight millimeter cameras were accessible and easy to operate. In the 1940s aspiring independent filmmakers began using the medium to create artistic works. Many of the **American New Wave** directors of the 1970s created their early work in 8mm, editing their productions on a viewer, then adding a soundtrack with a separate tape recorder or by playing records or tapes. The medium was the principal training ground for film students until the appearance of the camcorder in the late 1970s. Many **experimental** filmmakers like **Stan Brakhage** have worked in 8mm. *See also* Super 8mm filmmaking

El Mariachi. See Rodriguez, Robert

El Topo. This notorious independent feature film, which translates as *The Mole*, directed by **Alejandro Jodorowsky**, is considered the first **midnight movie**. In 1971, *El Topo* began a long run at New York's Elgin Theater, a popular rep-house for cinematically adventurous and voracious film buffs, where it instantly developed a cult following. There was no other place or time to see the movie. By word of mouth, *El Topo* drew the nocturnal at heart and those who craved the bizarre and verboten. Jodorowsky wrote the screenplay, designed the production and costumes, and composed the musical score in addition to directing and starring as El Topo. The story concerns a mysterious gunfighter dressed in black and his young son. He tries to defeat four master gunmen who have slaughtered locals in a village outside a desert. El Topo and his son, played by Jodorowsky's son Brontis, encounter a dwarf woman, a sadistic sheriff, and a religious cult in this bloody surrealistic epic. A Spanish-language film, *El Topo* was produced in Mexico. Jodorowsky filled the narrative with Eastern fables, Catholic symbolism, and a mythology that comes from his love and practice of comic book art.

Admirers saw the film repeatedly, heralding *El Topo* as a mystical, spiritual allegory. Some fled the theater after a sequence where hundreds of rabbits are slaughtered. In addition to starting a midnight movie trend that would launch *The Rocky Horror Picture Show* (1975), *Eraserhead* (1978), and other cult features, *El Topo* incited animal activists to demand supervised humanitarian treatment of animals in motion pictures. *El Topo* separated the hip from the square, the brave from the timid, and the nocturnal from the early-to-bed set. After a successful run at the Elgin, *El Topo* appropriately opened on Times Square decades before its Giuliani Disneyfication. *See also* midnight movies

Endless Summer, The. This 1966 independent **documentary** written, directed, and narrated by Bruce Brown is one of the most successful low-budget indies of all time. Brown's genius was to cash in on the surfing craze of the 1960s by making a film that was not a **beach party** movie. There is no imposed plot, docudrama, or fabricated drama—just surfing and more surfing. *The Endless Summer* follows surf bums Robert August and Mike Hynson as they travel around the world surfing in California, Hawaii, Tahiti, Australia, New Zealand, and Africa. For Mike and Robert it is always summer. The film is photographed in color in a style not much more sophisticated than an amateur home movie. Brown's narration is tongue-in-cheek—informative at times, unenlightening to all but surfing aficionados at other times. *The Endless Summer* enjoyed extended runs at theaters like the Kips Bay in New York City and was supported by word of mouth and repeated viewings from rabid fans.

The Endless Summer, distributed by Don Rugoff's **Cinema V,** is not a traditional documentary. It used many conventions of the home movie, especially the show-and-tell relationship of the narration and images, although it was made for commercial distribution. The film doesn't have the slickness of an *ABC Wide World of Sports* segment, but Brown understood that surfers and wannabes would sit transfixed watching their iconic heroes who had been immortalized by Brian Wilson and The Beach Boys in their American rock 'n' roll classic recording "Surfin' U.S.A." Twenty-eight years later in 1974, Bruce Brown directed a sequel, *The Endless Summer 2,* a big-budget, sleekly photographed surfing extravaganza that features Robert August and a large cast of surfers catching waves from Alaska to Java. The charm of the American original was lost to professionalism and proved once again that the innocence of the 1960s was long over.

Engel, Morris. Director, producer, screenwriter. *b.* April 8, 1918, New York City. Engel and his wife Ruth Orkin were both successful still photographers. In 1953 they collaborated on an independent film, *Little Fugitive,* the story of a seven-year-old boy who believes he has killed his brother and then goes to Coney Island and enjoys the day with no remorse. The lyrical low-budget, black-and-white film made for $50,000 is considered a classic independent film credited with facilitating the distribution of other indies because of its exposure at international film festivals. On viewing the *Little Fugitive,* **Jonas Mekas** announced the **avant-garde** film movement of the 1940s and 1950s had reached its end and proclaimed Morris Engel a filmmaker of the 9th Wave that began with **Stan Brakhage** and **James Agee** and Sidney Myers's *In the Street* (1951). Engel and Orkin codirected *Lovers and Lollipops* in 1956 with a screenplay they wrote with Mary Lamphier. Again, a child's point of view drove the narrative; a young widow's romance is disrupted by her six-year-old daughter. Engel handled the cinematography and Orkin edited. The film was shown at the Venice Film Festival in 1955.

Wedding and Babies (1958) was one of the first films shot on location with a portable sync camera designed by Engel and **Richard Leacock.** In the film, a wedding and baby photographer dreams of making real movies while his girlfriend assistant is looking for a wedding and babies of her own. *Wedding and Babies* won the Critic's Prize at the 1958 Venice Film Festival. Engel was mostly behind the camera for the project; Orkin was not credited. Engel and Orkin returned to still photography, and Engel completed one more film, *I Need a Ride to California* (1983), but it was never released. *See also Little Fugitive*

Epstein, Rob. Documentary filmmaker. Collaborating with Jeffrey Friedman, Rob Epstein has made topical films about homosexuality. Epstein was an apprentice sound editor on *Never Cry Wolf* (1983). Jeffrey Friedman was an associate editor on the film and also was the assistant editor on **Martin Scorsese's** *Raging Bull* (1980). In the 1970s Epstein was a member of **The Maripose Group** responsible for *Word Is Out* (1978), a benchmark film that presented the real lives of gay men and women. In 1984 Epstein directed and edited the Oscar-winning *The Times of Harvey Milk.* Friedman was an animator on the documentary that detailed the murder of San Francisco Mayor George Mosconi and supervisor Harvey Milk, an openly gay politician with deep roots in the San Francisco gay community. The film put Milk's life and the gay liberation movement into perspective, and the Oscar helped give the film mainstream acceptance. In 1989, Epstein and Friedman cowrote and directed *Common Threads: Stories from the Quilt.* The **documentary** focused on the project where loved ones created a quilt in memory of someone who died of AIDS. The individual quilts were all assembled, providing a poignant and powerful symbol for the enormity of the AIDS crisis. The film covers the lives of five people represented on the quilt and ends with its display in Washington, D.C. Again, the Oscar brought needed attention to the subject.

Epstein was an AFI intern in 1991 and worked on **Martha Coolidge's** *Rambling Rose.* In 1992, Epstein and Friedman coproduced and directed *Where Are We?: Our Trip through America,* in which the filmmakers travel through the South and encounter both homophobia and compassion. They discover abuse but hope that goes beyond ideology and stereotypes. *The Celluloid Closet* (1995), cowritten, produced, and directed by Epstein and Friedman is a documentary adaptation of Vito Russo's landmark critical study about how Hollywood has treated homosexuals. Through narrator Lily Tomlin, other celebrities, and numerous examples from the studio system, the film reveals the overt and hidden references that reflect gay life throughout the history of film. In 1999, Epstein and Friedman directed and produced *Paragraph 175,* a documentary about the Nazi persecution of homosexuals. In 2000 the team released *Save Me.*

Eraserhead. See Lynch, David

ethnographic filmmaking. The study and systematic recording of human cultures on film. To the academic anthropologist their work was science, not art, aesthetic, cinematic style, or technique. From 1910 through the 1920s the major approaches to ethnographic film were a single aspect of a culture or inventory, a cultural romanticization and fiction. Edward S. Curtis's *In the Land of Head Hunters* (1914) was a love story filmed among the Kwakiutl of British Columbia that mixed fact and fiction, a style that later became reflected in **Robert Flaherty's** *Moana* (1926), featuring the Savai people of Western Samoa. Flaherty was one of the innovators of reconstruction of reality and the participatory camera. The personal eye directs the viewer inside an action. *Nanook of the North* (1922) developed these principles. Flaherty used montage editing and expressed his point of view through intertitles in the silent film. *Nanook of the North* was a staged ethnographic narrative based on Flaherty's extensive research of Inuit life. Prior to World War II, a few anthropologists consulted with professional filmmakers who made theatrical shorts about exotic cultures. Anthropologists largely ignored Flaherty's directed cinematic approach, but it was embraced by documentarians and those interested in the merging of nonfiction and fiction filmmaking.

In 1958, John Marshall made *The Hunters of the !Kung Bushmen of the Kalahari,* an important ethnographic film that documented the culture but was also considered overproduced. He remained an influential figure in the field, producing *A Joking Relationship* (1962). Robert Gardner's *Dead Birds* (1961) was a narrated and dramatic film about the Dani people created with a subjective viewpoint aimed toward Western viewers. In the 1960s and 1970s, Herman Schlenk made nonnarrated films working out of Germany, distributed by an international film foundation. A prolific ethnographic filmmaker, Schlenk made fourteen films about the Afghan cultures, Venezuelan films about the Orinoco Indians, five Melanesian films, and twelve Mallan films about the Bozo people.

In the late 1960s, Robert Gardner, John Marshall, and Tim Asch created films to be used as a teaching tool for anthropology. Their films about far-off cultures were widely shown in classrooms. Karl G. Heider and Timothy Asch developed a scientific approach. Heider created a fourteen-point list that included "minimal, inadvertent or intentional distortion of behavior or time" and photographing "whole bodies, whole acts and whole people." Asch produced several films on the Yanomano and developed a "utilization chart" that divided cultural research into ten categories including socialization, women, field work, ecology and subsistence, cosmology, religion, and acculturation, emphasizing spontaneous, not staged, events. Those included *Building a House* (1967) and *Daily Life of the Bozo People* (1967). In 1972 he made *Indian Village Life: Two Villages in Orissa Province* (1972), a popular title on the educational circuit.

The renowned anthropologist Margaret Mead was instrumental in the development of ethnographic filmmaking. In 1977 the **Margaret Meade Film & Video Festival** was founded to celebrate and educate through the ethnographic film and its ever-changing approaches. For over twenty-five years public television has supported ethnographic filmmaking, which has shifted from film to video and digital production. *See also* anthropological filmmaking

BIBLIOGRAPHY

Barbash, Ilisa, and Lucien Taylor, contributor. *Cross-Cultural Filmmaking: A Handbook for Making Documentary and Ethnographic Films and Videos.* Berkeley: University of California Press, 1997.

Crawford, Peter, and David Turton, eds. *Film as Ethnography.* Manchester: Manchester University Press, 1992.

expanded cinema. Term used by moving-image philosopher, seer, and historian **Gene Youngblood** in his 1970 landmark book of the same name. Expanded cinema is the extension of filmmaking into the evolution of computer films, video, laser movies, and multiple projection environments. Youngblood was thirty years ahead of his time in detailing the way technology would develop and change the nature of filmmaking into electronic moving image making, which is still in its infancy at the dawn of the twenty-first century. *See also* Youngblood, Gene

experimental film. Nonnarrative filmmaking created in opposition to the commercial nature of the Hollywood studio film has been identified with many terms including **avant-garde, underground,** and **New American Cinema.** Each has meaning to various filmmakers, **critics,** theorists, and schools of thought. *Experimental film* is the most frequently used term to describe a motion picture, usually created by an individual who has artistic intentions and uses nontraditional, often abstract concepts and techniques. The term came into fashion to distinguish the beginning of a new era first initiated by artists, writers, and others in the avant-garde tradition. Filmmakers **Stan Brakhage,** Hollis Frampton, **Bruce Baillie,** Jordon Belson, **Bruce Conner, Kenneth Anger,** and others were established as experimental filmmakers whose work ranged from expressionistic to nonnarrative to nonrepresentational works of film art. The period continued into the 1970s when the **structural** film divided practitioners and lost its most widespread interest by the end of the decade. The 1980s

Mom and Dad (1945), an exploitation film that featured footage of an actual child-birth, was a shocking sensation which drew massive audiences and big box office. Courtesy of The Del Valle Archive

experimentalists have been more confined to academia, and the advent of consumer video infused the discipline. Experimental films are supported by grants and foundations, but they are a truly independent concern. They are created totally outside of commercial cinema and are distributed by the filmmakers, **co-ops**, and small specialty distributors and exhibited at museums, film societies, and independent venues that champion the art of film. *See also* avant-garde cinema; New American Cinema Group

BIBLIOGRAPHY

Curtis, David. *Experimental Cinema: A Fifty-Year Evolution.* New York: Universe Books, 1971.

Rees, A.L. *A History of Experimental Film and Video.* London: BFI, 1999.

exploitation films. Low-budget independent films that exploit sex, violence, drug and alcohol abuse, and a cornucopia of human vices going where the mainstream film wouldn't dare to wander. The films often have poor production values, less-than-respectable performers, and little narrative interest past their singular base concerns. The titles of exploitation films are designed to announce their intentions without any social-redeeming values. Over eighty years of exploitation have brought forth: *The Drug Monster* (1923), *The Greatest Menace* (1923), *White Slave Traffic* (1928), *Unguarded Girls* (1929), *Girls of Loma Loma* (1930), *Birth* (1931), *The Blonde Captive* (1932), *Sins of Love* (1934), *Gambling with Souls* (1936), *Hell-A-Vision* (1936), *Marijuana* (1936), *Narcotic* (1936), *Reefer Madness* (1936), *The Wages of Sin* (1938), *Mad Youth* (1939), *Child Bride* (1941), *Confessions of a Vice Baron* (1942), *Mom and Dad* (1944), *Youth Aflame* (1944), *Burlesque for Wolves* (1948–1952), *I Married a Savage* (1949), *Chained for Life* (1950), *Wild Rapture* (1950), *The Story of a Teenage Drug Addict* (1951), *Night at the Zomba Club in Hollywood* (1951), *Racket Girls* (1951), *Teenage Menace* (1951), *Violated!* (1953), *Tijuana after Midnight* (1954), *The Flesh Merchant* (1955), *Atrocities of the Orient* (1959), *Naughty New York* (1959), and *Young Sinners* (1959).

BIBLIOGRAPHY

McCarty, John, ed. *The Sleaze Merchants: Adventures in Exploitation Filmmaking.* New York: St. Martin's Griffin, 1995.

Schaefer, Eric. "*Bold! Daring! Shocking! True!*": *A History of Exploitation Films, 1919–1959.* Durham, NC: Duke University Press, 1999.

F

Fairbanks, Douglas. Actor, producer. *b.* Douglas Elton Ulman, May 23, 1883, Denver, Colorado. *d.* December 12, 1939, Santa Monica, California. By 1910, Douglas Fairbanks was an established Broadway star, the definition of the devil-may-care American hero and perfection of the male physique. In 1915 Fairbanks signed a lucrative contract with the Triangle Corporation and began his popular career in films. In 1916 he had his own production company, The Fairbanks Film Corporation, affiliated with Artcraft-Paramount that released his productions. Fairbanks had total artistic and fiscal control and installed family members in key corporate positions. In 1919, Fairbanks, Mary Pickford, **Charles Chaplin,** and **D.W. Griffith** formed the **United Artists Corporation** to distribute all their productions. Fairbanks, the prototype of the swashbuckling action hero, broke ground with performances in *The Mark of Zorro* (1920), *Robin Hood* (1922), and *The Thief of Bagdad* (1924) validating the sex appeal = box office equation for success and power on the silver screen. *See also* Chaplin, Charles; Griffith, D.W.; United Artists Corporation

Famous Monsters of Filmland. See Ackerman, Forrest J.

Farrelly, Peter and Bobby. Peter, *b.* December 15, 1956, Phoenixville, Pennsylvania. Bobby, *b.* 1958, Cumberland, Rhode Island. *ed.* Providence College. The Farrelly brothers write, produce, and direct outrageous, naughty comedies in hilariously bad taste. The Farrellys are below lowbrow, yet they have captured the public's imagination and have been propelled into A-list blockbuster status. *Dumb and Dumber* (1994), starring Jim Carrey and Jeff Daniels, is about two brainless chums who drive cross country to return a briefcase filled with ransom money. The Farrellys encouraged over-the-top performances to punctuate every gross-out gag, making the stupid comedy a surprising smash. *Kingpin* (1996), starring Woody Harrelson and Randy Quaid, is a story about a former bowling champ who seeks redemption in an Amish pin-clobberer. It is a dumb and dumbest comedy, but it is impossible to ignore the side-splitting bad-taste gags and lines. *There's Something about Mary* (1998), with Cameron Diaz, Matt Dillon, and Ben Stiller, is the penultimate adolescent, sophomoric comedy about a geek who is prevented from going to the prom by a bathroom zipper accident. The film contains many hysterical and equally notorious scenes like the dog attack and the pièce de résistance, "hair gel" sequence. The film was a blockbuster and gave the easygoing brothers, who laugh at their own jokes in front of the video playback monitor, status in Hollywood. *Me, Myself and Irene* (2000) was a Jim Carrey vehicle written and directed by the Farrellys. The film was a natural for Carrey, who plays a man with multiple personalities who all fall in love with the same woman. Same bad taste, grossed-out approach but a less-than-favorable response from the audience. *Osmosis Jones* (2001), which the Farrellys produced, is an animated film about a

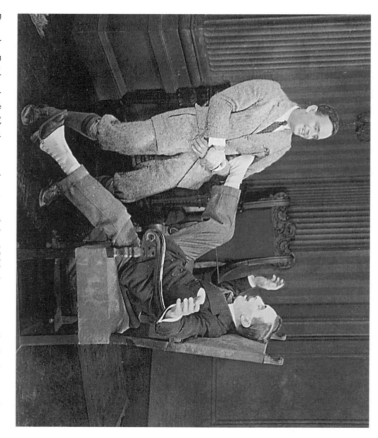

Douglas Fairbanks (left), the popular star of the 1920s known equally for his swash-buckling roles as well as social comedies like *His Majesty the American* (1919), shown here. Courtesy of the Del Valle Archive

construction worker with a cold who is inhabited by two cops, Osmosis Jones and Drixoral, who fight an invading virus taking over his body. *Shallow Hal* (2001) is a live-action comedy starring Jack Black, Gwyneth Paltrow, and Jason Alexander, about a man who falls in love with the "inner beauty" of a 300-pound woman.

Feature Filmmaking at Used-Car Prices. *See* Schmidt, Rick

feminist filmmaking. An outgrowth of the woman's movement in the early 1970s when women began making films that directly addressed gender, social, sexual, and political issues that concerned them. As the liberation process and struggle for equality took shape in all areas of society, the feminist influence made a major impact on independent cinema. The movement was a conduit for women's expression before the old-boy studio-controlled industry began to accept women as directors, screenwriters, and craft arts. Feminist filmmakers also began to change the portrayal of women on screen, expanding it from a limited male gaze and point of view. The **avant-garde** and **experimental** world of filmmaking was not any more liberated—consciousness raising was the only way women made their cinematic voices heard in independent fiction and nonfiction films. Central figures include **Jill Godmilow**, Claudia Weill, Chantal Akerman, Yvonne Rainer, Sally Potter, Vera Chytilova, Marguerite Von Trotta, **Ayoka Chenzira**, **Julie Dash**, Leslie Harris, Jackie Renal, **Lizzie Borden**, Carolee Schneemann, Majorie Keller, Nelly Kaplan, **Bette Gordon**, and Michelle Citron. Along with the films came feminist film theory, a serious critical movement that supported the films and began analysis of the cinema through the feminist prism. B. Ruby Rich, Amy Taubin, Annette Michaelson, and Laura Mulvey were pioneering scholars in the field. Feminist filmmaking continued to thrive in independent film in the 1980s and 1990s, and the trickle-down effect slowly began to make an impact on mainstream cinema as well.

BIBLIOGRAPHY

Mulvey, Laura. *Visual and Other Pleasures.* Bloomington: Indiana University Press, 1989.
Rabinovitz, Lauren. *Points of Resistance: Women, Power & Politics in the New York Avant-garde Cinema, 1943–71.* Urbana: University of Illinois Press, 1991.
Rich, B. Ruby. *Chick Flicks: Theories and Memories of the Feminist Film Movement.* Durham, NC: Duke University Press, 1998.

Ferrara, Abel. Director. *b.* July 11, 1952, Bronx, New York. Hard-hitting, urban, edgy filmmaker who creates provocative, violent, and sexually tense movies with characters who live in the margins. After a childhood spent in proximity to an **8mm** camera, Ferrara and frequent collaborators

Nicholas St. John and John McIntyre founded Navaron Films. Soon after, the young director made his first film, *Nine Lives of a Wet Pussy*, in 1976. Four years later, Ferrara wrote, directed, edited, and starred (under the pseudonym Jimmie Laine) in *The Driller Killer* (1979), a gruesome low-budget film about an unstable man who takes out his frustrations, first on a group of homeless people, and later on friends and family, with a power drill. *Ms. 45* was released in 1981 and established Ferrara as one of independent film's most fearless directors. The film follows a waifish New York woman as she brutally kills all comers (dismembering one of them). It received harsh treatment from **critics** when it first arrived on screens but has since established a sizable following.

Low-budget **slasher films** followed until 1990, when Ferrara hit his stride in his first collaboration with Christopher Walken, a director/actor relationship frequently likened to **Martin Scorsese** and **Robert De Niro**. *King of New York* (1990) follows Walken, an ex-con drug lord, as he and his partners unceremoniously eliminate their competition. It premiered at the New York Film Festival and was greeted by a number of walkouts (including a noticeable early exit by Ferrara's wife) but gained the director a fair number of admirers as well. The Walken character was one of many charismatic central figures in Ferrara's movies, as is **Harvey Keitel** in the stunning *Bad Lieutenant* (1992). As the drug-addicted and morally bankrupt cop investigating the rape of a nun, Keitel delivers what is widely regarded as his most ferocious performance. The existential vampire film *The Addiction* (1995) and the mobster thriller *The Funeral* (1996) followed, adding to Ferrara's vision of New York as a sinister city full of miscreants and, like their director, perpetually dark. *New Rose Hotel* (1999) was dark but muddled, with an almost incomprehensible narrative based on a William Gibson story in which industrial spies hire a prostitute to lure a brilliant geneticist to their company.

The Blackout (1997), featuring Matthew Modine and **Dennis Hopper,** again explores the hell of drug addiction, this time through the making of an experimental digital movie. *See also* Keitel, Harvey

BIBLIOGRAPHY

Johnstone, Nick. *Abel Ferrara: The King of New York.* London: Omnibus Press, 1999.

Film. Samuel Beckett's only foray in the film medium is the enigmatic *Film*, written in 1963 and directed by his longtime collaborator Alan Schneider. The project was produced by Barney Rosset for Evergreen Theatre, a subsidiary of Beckett's publisher Grove Press. The twenty-two-minute film, photographed in 35mm black and white, stars silent screen comedy legend **Buster Keaton.** The story is told without dialogue and is visually presented in two points of view—a subjective camera Beckett identifies as E, the perceiving eye, and an objective camera named O that observes the character's environment. The six-page outline even baffled Schneider, who had directed premieres of the playwright's most challenging work and had established a firm communication and working method with Beckett. Preparation took one year, involving a battery of letters from director to screenwriter to clarify the content and intention. Keaton's deadpan personality and weathered face were ideal for the role of O. Keaton wore his trademark flattop hat and was costumed in a rumpled trenchcoat and scarf to hide his face, which, when revealed, features a startling black eye patch.

Schneider assembled a seasoned New York independent film crew for his film debut. It was shot by **Boris Kaufman,** cinematographer for **Elia Kazan's** *On the Waterfront* (1954) and **Sidney Lumet's** *12 Angry Men* (1957). The editor, Sidney Meyers, was a noted **documentary** film editor who codirected *The Savage Eye* (1960) and a film adaptation of Henry Miller's *Tropic of Cancer* (1970).

Keaton, who had seen his glory days as a great silent screen comic performer pass, took on the mystifying role, understanding little of Beckett's purpose or Schneider's direction. The comic constantly suggested comedy bits to liven the obscure narrative, but Beckett, who was on set in New York with Schneider, kept him firmly in the emotionally desolate landscape of the existentialist conception. The New York independent film has been seen rarely since its initial release. It continues to perplex audiences looking to make narrative sense of Beckett's exploration of loneliness and a search for self in the absurdist tradition. *See also* Kaufman, Boris; Keaton, Buster

BIBLIOGRAPHY

Beckett, Samuel. *Film: Complete Scenario / Illustrations / Production Shots with an Essay on Directing Film by Alan Schneider.* New York: Grove Press, 1969.

***Film Culture* magazine.** Publication known to cineastes as "America's Independent Motion Picture Magazine." Under the guiding stewardship of **Jonas Mekas,** *Film Culture* began its first incarnation in 1955 as a general intellectual review of filmmaking. The magazine presented a catholic interest in film history, sociology, and economics. At first, *Film Culture* had no polemic thrust but championed mature filmmaking and socially relevant themes over innovative technique. Mekas attacked the **avant-garde,** calling the movement "a conspiracy of homosexuality," and dismissed **Kenneth Anger** and **Stan Brakhage** as adolescents. The nonprofit magazine advertised itself as a quarterly, but finances and Mekas's many activities made publication dates erratic at times.

As editor in chief Mekas surrounded himself with writers full of passion for the cinema, his brother Adolphas, **P. Adams Sitney, Parker Tyler,** Andrew Sarris, and others. In the 1960s *Film Culture* embraced the work of **John Cassavetes, Lionel Rogosin**, Gregory Markopolous, and Robert Breer. Changing his earlier position, Mekas defended the avant-gardists, proclaiming they created "the proper vocabulary and syntax to express the true and beautiful . . . the psychological and visual reading of modern man."

In 1959, the magazine began giving out the Independent Film Award, which reflected changes in editorial perspective from the improvisations of Cassavetes's *Shadows* (1959) to the **beat cinema** manifesto *Pull My Daisy* (1959), to the **cinéma vérité documentary** *Primary* (1960), then to Brakhage's *The Dead* (1960) and *Prelude Dog Star Man* (1961) and **Jack Smith**'s notorious *Flaming Creatures* (1963). In 1962 Andrew Sarris published his "Notes on the Auteur Theory," launching a heated debate over cinema authorship that continues today. In recent decades *Film Culture* has not continued to search for new cinematic astronauts but has become the home for archiving the achievement of established avant-garde, **experimental**, and **structural** film masters like Harry Smith, Hollis Frampton, and **Maya Deren**. *Film Culture* has always been a forum of conflicting passions, radical claims, and manifestos. Jonas Mekas has catalogued and preserved precious interviews and daring essays few would publish. *See also* Mekas, Jonas

Film Forum. Founded in 1970 by Karen Cooper in a West Side, New York, screening room with fifty folding chairs, Film Forum is a showcase for independent filmmaking. Cooper's dream and humble beginnings have been transformed to a three-screen, not-for-profit cinema in Lower Manhattan opened every day of the year. This third location (the second bordered the Chinatown district) is a leading venue for independent features, nonfiction, European art films, and **experimental** works. Karen Cooper is the director of Film Forum and director of independent premier programming. Its prestigious board of directors includes **Mira Nair, Sheila Nevins**, and David Salle. Film Forum has premiered important films over the last thirty years, and its repertory program, directed by Bruce Goldstein, has presented retrospectives that have showcased rarely seen films.

Filmmakers' Cooperative, The. Formed by the **New American Cinema Group** in 1961 on Park Avenue South in New York City to create a noncommercial distribution venue run by and for filmmakers. The office was a resting place for visiting filmmakers and was where *Film Culture* magazine was edited. To join, a filmmaker gave a print to the **co-op** with a synopsis of the film. Filmmakers set the rental fee. Sixty percent of all income went to the filmmaker, and 40 percent helped to support the co-op's operation. *See also Film Culture* magazine; Mekas, Jonas; New American Cinema Group

Filmmaker's Newsletter. Magazine popular in the 1970s dedicated to independent filmmaking that featured interviews with filmmakers and craftspeople, technical articles, product reports, Film Nut News, and film festival reports. *Filmmaker's Newsletter* was written by specialists in **16mm**, **8mm**, and video production, animation, and the business of indie film. The magazine was must reading for film students, filmmakers, educators, and those interested in making independent films. Publication ceased in September 1978.

film market. A gathering of producers and distributors to buy, sell, or license motion pictures. The best-known film markets include the American Film Market, MIFED, the Cannes Film Festival, and the Independent Feature Film Market (IFFM).

Film Threat. Magazine, Web site, and distributor that specializes in independent and **underground** films. In 1985 Chris Gore founded *Film Threat* as a college fanzine that developed into a national magazine and relocated to Los Angeles. The magazine covered cult films, **midnight movies**, underground short films, and indie features. Gore self-published *Film Threat* until 1991 when Larry Flynt purchased it. Gore developed publications for Flynt while remaining as *Film Threat*'s editor in chief. Gore left Flynt, formed Gore Group Productions, and bought back the rights to the magazine. *Film Threat* was an irreverent alternative to the mainstream *Premiere* magazine. The success of *Film Threat* was proof that the public wanted an alternative to Hollywood product.

Film/Video Arts. Largest nonprofit media arts center in the New York region. Founded in 1968 when educators **Rodger Larson** and Lynne Hofer and filmmaker Jaime Barrios worked with Latino youth on the Lower East Side, introducing them to **16mm filmmaking**. Originally called Film Club, they opened up in a Bowery storefront and encouraged teenagers to make personal films. They incorporated as The Young Filmmakers Foundation. In 1971, in collaboration with the New York State Council on the Arts, they established the first public access center, serving film and video makers of all age groups with production and postproduction services, charging no fees. They operated out of a basement on West 53rd Street. In 1973, the foundation moved to a loft at 4 Rivington Street and in 1978 started a modest fee structure for adults interested in motion pictures. In 1985, the foundation became Film/Video Arts (FVA) relocated at 817 Broadway with an established curriculum. In 1997, FVA introduced a digital cinema program, and in 2000 they relocated to the Wall Street area. After September 11, 2001, FVA just relocated to the Wall Street area. After September 11, 2001, FVA just blocks from ground zero, relocated and is currently sharing space with **Women Make Movies** in Soho. FVA continues to embrace emerging media technology. FVA encourages diversity, collaboration, and non-traditional film and video works. *See also* Larson, Rodger

Flaherty, Robert. Documentary filmmaker. *b.* February 16, 1884, Iron Mountain, Michigan. *d.* July 23, 1951, Brattleboro, Vermont. Robert Flaherty is widely accepted as a founding father of the **documentary** film. *Nanook of the North* (1922) is a landmark silent study of the life of Eskimos. Flaherty was one of the first filmmakers to bring a camera to remote parts of the world to capture life and culture. Flaherty was not an unobtrusive filmmaker; he recreated what he saw and encouraged Nanook to play to the camera. The popular success of *Nanook of the North* brought Hollywood courting with two studio-financed collaborations that caused Flaherty to quit because the method violated his philosophy.

Before *White Shadows in the South Seas* (1928), codirected with W.S. Van Dyke, and *Tabu* (1931), with F.W. Murnau, Jesse L. Lasky of Paramount financed Flaherty's trip to the South Seas. The result, *Moana* (1926), was attacked as being too prettified, not true to historical fact and over-manipulated in production and postproduction. The film failed at the box office. In 1934, Flaherty returned to the serious documentary with *Man of Aran*, the study of a fisherman living off the coast of Ireland. In 1937, with his credibility intact in the nonfiction community, Flaherty misstepped again with *Elephant Boy*, codirected with Zoltan Korda, a fiction film that captured the reality of India. Robert Flaherty's last work, a commission for the Standard Oil Company, *Louisiana Story* (1948), contained reenactments later known as docudrama, telling the story of a Bayou family distressed by an oil-drilling company. The film retained and captured the honesty of time and place. Flaherty made us understand that the creator and the cinematic process itself manipulate all documentary filmmaking. Flaherty was a serious lay anthropologist who was a film artist. The combination produced beautiful, powerful, well-crafted films that didn't pretend to search for the truth—they are one man's vision that reached out with a humanist, compassionate desire to capture the way we live on film. *See also* Robert Flaherty Film Seminar, The

BIBLIOGRAPHY

Rotha, Paul *Robert J. Flaherty: A Biography.* Ed. Jay Ruby. Philadelphia: University of Pennsylvania Press, 1983.

Flaming Creatures. *See* Smith, Jack

Florey, Robert. Filmmaker, assistant director, actor, screenwriter. *b.* September 14, 1900, Paris. *d.* May 16, 1979, Santa Monica, California. Robert Florey worked in the Hollywood studio system as a technical director, a gag writer, publicist, director of two-reel comedies, and assistant director and wrote eight books on Hollywood history. In 1950 France awarded Florey with the Legion d'Honor for his longtime contribution to film.

From 1927 to 1928 Florey directed four independently produced **experimental** short films. The best known, *The Life and Death of 9413—A Hollywood Extra* (1928), was in the style of a German expressionist fantasy in which an extra climbs the stairs to success, electric lights fall, he rides a bike to heaven, and his number is rubbed away. The film was a radical indictment of the totalitarianism of the studio system, orchestrated to Gershwin's *Rhapsody in Blue*. A young Gregg Toland, who later revolutionized the art of cinematography on *Citizen Kane* (1941), was one of three cameramen on the project. The expressionistic sets were designed by art designer/coeditor/cocinematographer and montage innovator **Slavko Vorkapich.** The film cost $97.50 to produce.

Florey completed three other shorts in his year underground: *The Loves of Zero* (1928), *Johann the Coffin Maker* (1928) and *Sky Scraper Symphony* (1929). The films were screened privately and well received by the Hollywood community, who liked being in the company of artists, although they rarely supported those like Florey and Vorkapich who merged the film art of Europe with the technology of commercial Hollywood. *See also* Vorkapich, Slavko

Fluxus. Art movement founded by artist George Maciunas dedicated to the fusion of forty years of avant-garde developments including Dada, Zen, Bauhaus, and the work of Marcel Duchamp and John Cage. In 1966, Maciunas coordinated the Fluxfilm program that included the work of **Yoko Ono, Bruce Baillie,** and other independent **experimental** and **avant-garde** filmmakers. *See also* Ono, Yoko; structural filmmaking

Fonda, Peter. Actor, producer, director. *b.* February 23, 1939, New York. Son of Henry, brother of Jane, member of America's acting dynasty that includes his daughter Bridget. Peter began his career in conventional studio films *The Victors* (1963), *Tammy and the Doctor* (1963), Robert Rossen's *Lilith* (1964), and *The Young Lovers* (1964). Working in **Roger Corman** productions gave Peter Fonda an education in low-budget filmmaking and shaped his persona as a handsome, hippie-rebel prince of cool. *The Wild Angels* (1966) is one of the most accomplished **biker films.** *The Trip* (1967) was an Aquarian celebration of LSD drug culture and counterculture. In 1969, Fonda became a part of independent film history as producer and star of *Easy Rider*, which spearheaded the New Hollywood by achieving big box office and inviting a new under-thirty audience brought up on John Wayne movies to see their world reflected on screen. The revolution was over as soon as it began.

Peter Fonda under the influence in *The Trip* (1967), an American International Pictures LSD film, directed by Roger Corman. Courtesy of The Del Valle Archive

Fonda made his directorial debut with the exquisite cosmic western *The Hired Hand* (1971), which received critical recognition for its fine performances by Fonda, Warren Oates, and Verna Bloom. The cinematography by **Vilmos Zsigmond** is an amalgam of light, desaturated color, texture, and a European sensibility opposed to the gloss and artificiality of the studio system factory style. The offbeat, revisionist western ran approximately two weeks and disappeared.

Fonda returned to acting with a long series of failed projects: *Two People* (1973), *Dirty Mary, Crazy Larry* (1974), *Open Season* (1974), *Race with the Devil* (1975), *Killer Force* (1975), *Futureworld* (1976), *Fighting Mad* (1976), *Outlaw Blues* (1977), and *High-Ballin'* (1978). Fonda ended the decade of American film mavericks with his third directorial outing, *Wanda Nevada* (1979), starring Fonda, Brooke Shields, and his legendary dad. The gold prospecting western was so antigenre, so LA laid back, it became a relic for an industry moving into a blockbuster mode. *Idaho Transfer* (1973), Fonda's second film as a director, takes place in 2044 and is a muddled attempt at a social message—the dangers of environmental hazards—but the film was seen by few.

In the 1980s Peter Fonda struggled to find good acting roles and appeared in films less distinguished than before: *Split Image* (1982), *Spasms*

(1983), *Dance of the Dwarfs* (1983), and *Mercenary Fighters* (1987), as well as many television projects. The 1990s were a slow climb to acceptance in the new independent American cinema. Fonda gained attention as Dracula and Dr. Van Helsing in *Naja* (1994), a trendy reworking of the Bram Stoker creation. But his career was resurrected in *Ulee's Gold* (1997) with his portrayal of an emotionally contained beekeeper. The maturing Fonda won a Golden Globe for his understated performance, an Oscar nomination and a new prestige. Recent work as an actor includes: *The Passion of Ayn Rand*, *The Limey* (both 1999), Dwight Yoakam's *South of Heaven, West of Hell*, *Thomas and the Magic Railroad*, *Second Skin* (all 2000), and *The Laramie Project*, a telling of the Matthew Shepard story for HBO.

40 Acres & A Mule Filmworks. *See* Lee, Spike

franchise. A single film so successful at the box office that it spawns sequels and becomes a series of films. *Friday the 13th, Halloween, Police Academy*, and *Rocky* all became lucrative franchises. The original creator may or may not have much involvement in the sequels or installments in a franchise. Actors change, directors often change, but the audience comes back for the characters and story. Early franchises of the 1970s and 1980s grew out of public interest, but by the 1990s cynical money-driven distributors and exhibitors tried or forced sequels on the public for any film that fared decently. Greed inspired them to look for franchise gold by making money in an easier way than starting with an original idea. As ticket prices rose and a director-driven cinema once again became dominated by actors, franchises offered characters like Jason, Freddy Krueger, and Rocky Balboa as a comforting guarantee for audiences who needed to know they would be pleased with the product. The *James Bond* and *Star Wars* films rank among the most successful, but the low-budget horror and action franchises provide a wide profit margin for little investment. *See also* sequel

Frank, Robert. Still photographer, filmmaker. *b.* 1924, Zurich, Switzerland. Robert Frank immigrated to the United States in his twenties and became part of the Beat Generation. In 1955, he received a Guggenheim Fellowship for a photographic project that became the 1958 book *The Americans.* Frank spent two years traveling the country photographing the visual equivalent of a **Jack Kerouac** novel or an Allen Ginsberg poem. The beats had plenty of poets and writers; Robert Frank was their official photographer—a man who understood alienation and shared the beat ideal to expose hypocrisy and conformity. In 1958, Frank, along with Alfred Leslie, directed *Pull My Daisy,* the only film created by the core beat writers themselves. *Me and My Brother* (1968) was about Peter and Julius Orlovsky. Peter was the companion of Allen Ginsberg; Julius was a catatonic who got lost and later came back home. In 1966 Frank was the cinematographer of *Chappaqua* for director **Conrad Rooks**.

In 1972 Frank directed the notorious feature-length **documentary** *Cocksucker Blues* that followed the Rolling Stones on tour and has barely been screened due to the sex, drugs, and rock 'n' roll exploits of Mick, Keith, and the boys. Frank was hired and paid for the film that is still bogged down in litigation. Frank codirected three film projects with novelist and screenwriter Rudy Wurlitzer. Two are **16mm** shorts, *Keep Busy* (1975) and *Energy and How to Get It* (1981), that feature cameos by beat writer William Burroughs, New York poet John Giorno, and New Orleans musician Dr. John known as "The Night Tripper." Wurlitzer and Frank also collaborated on *Candy Mountain* (1987), a **road movie**. In recent years Frank has worked in video and remains an independent filmmaker outside the system. His latest credits include: *Run* (1989), *It's Real* (1990), *Last Supper* (1992), *Sanyu* (2000), and the short films *The Present*, *Summer Cannibals* (both 1996) and *Hunter* (1989). For Frank the movie camera is an extension of his still camera, a tool for personal, subversive, artistic expression. *See also* beat cinema; Kerouac, Jack; Rooks, Conrad

Friday the 13th. Landmark low-budget horror film directed by **Sean S. Cunningham** in 1980. The film featured a group of young actors including Kevin Bacon and veteran actress Betsy Palmer in a tale of teenagers at a summer camp slaughtered in a gory fashion. After knocking around in theater and film production for years, Cunningham sat down one day and was struck by an idea for a film title. Not a story, script, or characters, just a title—*Friday the 13th*. Then images for a TV commercial came to him and finally the tag line, "Friday the 13th: The most terrifying film ever made!"

Cunningham was living in Connecticut at the time and had no money in the bank but asked a local commercial artist to design a poster on which he added the copy, "From the producer of *Last House on the Left* comes the most terrifying film ever made!—Available in December." It was July; Cunningham began getting calls and telexes from around the world clamoring for the film. Cunningham approached Victor Miller, who had written his last two projects. Neither man had written a horror film before, but working together, they fleshed out the story. Cunningham assembled a crew even before he raised $500,000 to shoot the film. The production was filmed on location using a Boy Scout camp in New Jersey for the doomed summer camp. Cunningham designed every detail of *Friday the 13th* for a twelve-year-old audience. His son was a fan of the horror magazine *Fangoria* that gave him insight into the market.

When it was complete, Paramount, **United Artists**, and Warner Bros. engaged in a bidding war for its distribution; they even offered an advance to Cunningham. Paramount offered a May release, a $3 million

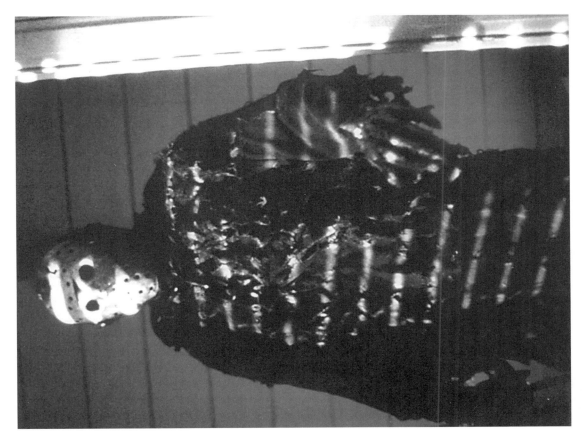

The face that launched the successful gore franchise of the 1980s, Jason in *Friday the 13th* (1980). Courtesy of the Del Valle Archive

print and advertising budget, plus a $1.5 million advance. Warner's gave Cunningham $1 million against the foreign rights. Cunningham had $2.5 million in his pocket before *Friday the 13th* even opened. The film immediately hit it big with audiences; box office went through the roof, and the buzz swept across the country. The film became a lucrative **franchise** with eight sequels.

Cunningham has had little involvement in the series. He claims not to have even seen many of the films. Eventually, Cunningham bought the rights back so he could produce *Jason Goes to Hell: The Final Friday* (1993) and executive produce *Jason X: Friday the 13th Part 10* (2001).

In its time *Friday the 13th* became a lightning rod for the national debate against violence in films, although there had been horror and gore before; in fact, *Friday the 13th* was so tame Cunningham had to remove only fourteen seconds of footage for the television release. Cunningham explains the phenomenon in hindsight by stating that the low-budget film was distributed by a major studio who gave it high visibility, and, of course, Jason, the killer was unstoppable for reasons more having to do with making sequel money than mortality. *See also* Cunningham, Sean S.

Friedman, Jeffrey. *See* Epstein, Rob

Frumkes, Roy. Screenwriter, director, editor in chief, historian, educator. The grandson of Bernard Burke, the leading Keith Circuit booking agent of the 1920s whose clients included Houdini, Roy Frumkes has been an independent filmmaker for over thirty years. His first credit was assistant director and associate producer on the cult classic *The Projectionist* (1971), directed by **Harry Hurwitz** and starring Chuck McCann. Frumkes wrote and produced *Street Trash* (1987), directed by James Muro who later became one of the country's leading Steadicam operators. The low-budget film takes place in Brooklyn, New York, where poisonous liquor is sold to bums, which makes them melt and explode. Critics called *Street Trash* gross and cheap. *The Videohound* and *Leonard Maltin* film and video guides both gave the film their lowest ratings—Woof! and BOMB—but the film has a rabid cult following and won several foreign festival awards.

Frumkes spent over ten years as the writer, producer, director, and on-camera subject of *Document of the Dead* (1989), a **documentary** study of U.S. independent filmmakers centering on low-budget horror master **George Romero.** Frumkes and his screenwriting partner Rocco Simonelli hit **franchise** gold with their screenplay for *The Substitute* (1996), the story of a CIA agent who substitutes for his teacher-girlfriend when a gang member breaks her leg. The tough disciplinarian uses his undercover position to fight the school's drug smugglers. *The Substitute* spawned three sequels and may become a television series. Frumkes produced *The Sweet Life* (2002), which he cowrote with Rocco Simonelli, who also directed.

Frumkes has been a member of The National Board of Review of Motion Pictures since 1966. He has written for *Films in Review* for over thirty years and in 1996 copurchased the magazine. Frumkes has conducted extensive interviews with hundreds of independent filmmakers and mainstream Hollywood figures. Frumkes has a long association with the School of Visual Arts as an instructor of screenwriting, film studies, and filmmaking, where he has helped to train independent filmmakers.

Fuller, Samuel. Director, producer, screenwriter. *b.* August 12, 1911, Worcester, Massachusetts. *d.* October 30, 1997, Hollywood, California. Sam Fuller, the quintessential maverick **B-movie** director, began as a newspaperman. After several assignments as a screenwriter, Fuller made his directorial debut on *I Shot Jesse James* in 1949. Fuller wrote, produced, and directed the majority of his films—B-movies with direct, brutal violence. Fuller promulgated coarse political views that alienated both Right and Left political philosophies and delighted audiences who drank their movie coffee, black, no sugar. Fuller worked in a graphic visual style. He often wore a Civil War hat and sunglasses and smoked a big cigar on the set, where he fired a gun to signal when he wanted a scene to end. Fuller was revered in France, where he eventually relocated.

His films *Pickup on South Street* (1953), *Forty Guns* (1957), and *The Naked Kiss* (1964) have influenced and inspired independent filmmakers to be bold and fight in the face of cinematic conformity. The French and **American New Waves** saw him as a patron saint. Jean Luc Godard, Wim Wenders, and **Dennis Hopper** featured him as an actor in their films. Fuller was employed by the studio system to produce lower bill fare to support their A-list product. Fuller took advantage of the lack of supervision or interest in the B division and, within the system and with company money, forged a body of work worthy of the most independent of filmmakers.

His masterpiece *Shock Corridor* (1963) is a model of cutting-edge narrative. In the film a reporter poses as a mental patient to investigate a murder. The characters include a black student modeled on Medgar Evers who is transformed into an N-word shouting bigot, a military coward who now believes he's a great Civil War general and a brilliant scientist reduced to the behavior of a child. The stress causes the reporter to hallucinate and imagine a major lightning and thunder storm is flooding the institution's endless hallway. Fuller shot this scene in the studio without proper drainage. At the end of the scene, he fired his gun; yelled, "Forget it!" (a phrase meaning "get this scene behind us and let's move on,"); and jumped into his car and drove away from the flooded-out building. He never returned to the studio.

BIBLIOGRAPHY

Hardy, Phil. *Samuel Fuller*. New York: Praeger, 1970.

G

gay cinema. During the era of the Classical Hollywood Studio System homosexuality was treated as a codified negative stereotype, and few films with positive portrayals of gay life were evident in mainstream filmmaking. **Avant-garde** and **experimental** filmmakers presented openly gay imagery, usually with content embracing underground gay life. In the 1960s the sexual revolution opened investigation into the scope of human sexuality. Frank Simon's **documentary** *The Queen* (1967) examined a male transvestite beauty contest. **Shirley Clarke**'s *A Portrait of Jason* (1967) featured an interview with a black male hustler. In the 1970s the gay liberation movement emerged. *Some of Your Best Friends* (1971) is a **cinéma vérité** documentary by Ken Robinson that examines the oppression of gays in New York and Los Angeles. In 1977 Arthur Bressan was part of the collective Artists United for Gay Rights. Filmmakers in San Francisco, San Diego, Chicago, Houston, Los Angeles, and New York documented gay rights parades on a single day, June 26, to show a burgeoning gay consciousness. *Word Is Out: Stories of Some of Our Lives* (1978) was created by **The Mariipose Group** and was a breakthrough in depicting gay men and women in positive portraits as part of mainstream America with identity and pride.

In the 1980s the exploration of gay characters began appearing in fictional films, most notably in Donna Deitch's *Desert Hearts* and Bill Sherwood's *Parting Glances* (both 1986), which featured a powerful and complex performance by **Steve Buscemi**. Noted stage director Christopher Ashley made his film debut in 1995 with *Jeffrey* (1995), an adaptation of Paul Rudnick's highly successful play. The sex comedy focused on a gay man's vow of chastity in the wake of the AIDS epidemic, tested when he meets and falls in love with an HIV-positive man. By casting Steven Weber (then on NBC's *Wings*) in the film's title role and Sigourney Weaver, Patrick Stewart, and Olympia Dukakis in the supporting ensemble, Ashley gained wider distribution and exposure than most predominantly gay films. As a result, *Jeffrey* became the first widely seen American gay sex comedy, paving the way for 1997's *Kiss Me, Guido*, among others.

A series of documentaries by **Rob Epstein** and Jeffrey Friedman were well received by general audiences and helped enlighten mainstream audiences to gay life. *Longtime Companion* (1990) was a critical and box office success. The poignant drama showed the devastating effect the AIDS epidemic had on a group of gay men. Just a few of the many independent films with honest portrayals of the lives and loves of gay men and lesbians include *Claire of the Moon* (Nicole Conn, 1993), *Go Fish* (Rose Troche, 1994), *The Incredibly True Adventures of Two Girls in Love* (Maria Maggenti, 1995), *Watermelon Woman* (Cheryl Dunye, 1997), *Relax, It's Just Sex* (P.J. Castellaneta, 1998), *Billy's Hollywood Screen Kiss* (Tommy O'Haver, 1998), *I Think I Do* (Brain Sloan, 1998), *The Opposite of Sex* (Don Roos, 1998), and *High Art* (Lisa Cholodenko, 1998).

Radha Mitchell and Ally Sheedy in *High Art* (1998), directed by Lisa Cholodenko. Kobol Collection/October Films

BIBLIOGRAPHY

Creekmur, Corey K., and Alexander Doty, eds. *Out in Culture: Gay, Lesbian, and Queer Essays on Popular Culture.* Durham, NC: Duke University Press, 1995.

Ehrenstein, David. *Open Secret: Gay Hollywood 1928–2000.* New York: Perennial, 2000.

Russo, Vito. *The Celluloid Closet: Homosexuality in the Movies.* Rev. ed. New York: Harper and Row, 1986.

Gilroy, Frank D. Playwright, screenwriter, director, producer. *b.* October 13, 1925, New York City. *ed.* Dartmouth College, Yale School of Drama. A respected New York writer, Frank Gilroy's first Broadway play *The Subject Was Roses* won the 1964 Tony Award and Pulitzer Prize for Drama. After writing several screenplays, Gilroy directed a number of films in the 1970s and 1980s. He made his debut with *Desperate Characters* (1971), starring Shirley MacLaine, Kenneth Mars, Sada Thompson, Rose Gregorio, and Carol Kane, an exploration of the day-to-day struggle of living in New York City. *From Noon Till Three* (1976) was Gilroy's adaptation of his novel featuring Charles Bronson and his wife Jill Ireland. *Once in Paris . . .* (1978), released by Atlantic Releasing Corporation, was Gilroy's first collaboration with actor/entrepreneur Wayne Rogers and is the story of a Hollywood screenwriter who goes to Paris to work and falls in love instead. The independent film captured the attention of critics and audiences. *The Gig* (1985), released by Castle Hill Productions, about a group of friends who play in a jazz group on the side, found a cult following. The low-budget indie featured Wayne Rogers and touched audiences with its fully realized characters and theme of midlife crisis. *The Luckiest Man in the World* (1989) starred Philip Bosco as a Scrooge-like businessman who escapes death in a plane crash and experiences a metamorphosis. In 1997 Gilroy wrote the television movie *Money Plays.*

Ginsberg, Milton Moses. Editor, director, screenwriter. *b.* 1935, Bronx, New York. In 1969 the winds of social change began to blow on American movie screens. Independent feature films were rare, and those that existed struggled for distribution and attention. *Coming Apart* (1969), starring Rip Torn, was shot in just three weeks for $60,000. Ginsberg wrote the screenplay to take place in one room so the film could be produced quickly and cheaply. Although *Coming Apart* is filled with sexual situations, it is not an **exploitation film.** Ginsberg was making a serious art drama. Created in a **self-referential faux diary film** style, *Coming Apart* is a fictional documentation of a womanizing psychiatrist who rents an apartment under an assumed name and using a hidden camera records his life coming apart. The rigorous aesthetic of what appears to be a single camera position, grainy black-and-white cinematography, jump cuts, leaders, and moments between action creates the illusion that the entire film has come from the doctor's camera. In reality it was carefully scripted, photographed, and edited. *Coming Apart* has daring sexual content played out by Viveca Lindfors, Sally Kirkland, and an ensemble of complex female characters. The apartment wall is covered with a mirror that allows an interesting visual perspective and maximum coverage. The design also functioned as a metaphor suggesting the doctor's life was as fragile as glass. *Coming Apart* attracted interest from the film community and a strong positive review from Richard Schickel. Andrew Sarris panned the film in his then-powerful *Village Voice* column, a death-blow Ginsberg claims quieted his phone and prevented audiences from discovering the film.

In 1973, Ginsberg directed *The Werewolf of Washington*, a political satire inspired by the Nixon/Watergate scandal. Dean Stockwell plays a character modeled on John Dean who turns into a werewolf at night. The low-budget film was harmed by the downmarket production values that failed to convince audiences it was taking place in the seat of government. Ginsberg then turned to **documentary** film editing and cut two Oscar winners, *Down and Out in America* (1986) and *Educating Peter* (1992) and a cutting-edge documentary *Listen Up: The Lives of Quincy Jones* (1990). Ginsberg is an in-demand New York documentary film editor and has had a long association with director **Lee Grant**. He continued to write and receive options on his feature scripts, but no productions came to fruition. In 1999 Ginsberg returned as a director with a sixty-minute video *The City Below the Line*, a new take on Dostoevsky's *Notes from the Underground*. In Ginsberg's version, a film editor pursues a woman and then abandons her. It was produced for $2,000 with Ginsberg and his wife, the painter Nina Polansky, and friends in the cast. The video was shown at the Hamptons Film Festival. Recent editing credits for Milton Moses Ginsberg include: the documentary short film *The Personals* (1999), *Meatloaf to Hell and Back* (2000), a TV movie directed by **Jim McBride**, and the cable television miniseries *Fidel* (2001).

Coming Apart was shown at the Museum of Modern Art in the early 1970s as a prime example of the self-referential film and rescreened there in 1997 and 1998. *See also* self-referential filmmaking

Giovinazzo, Buddy. Director, screenwriter. *b.* Carmine Giovinazzo, May 5, 1957, Staten Island, New York. Giovinazzo learned his craft while still in college, where he directed a string of short films. His feature debut began as *American Nightmares*, a screenplay written by Giovinazzo while he was a student haunted by the Vietnam War. Giovinazzo raised $40,000 and shot the film with a small crew of film students. **Troma** bought it and reedited it when the MPAA forced their hand. It was released under the title *Combat Shock* (1986). *She's Back* (1989) was produced by the now-defunct Vestron Pictures. The film starred Carrie Fisher as the victim of a brutal homicide who comes back to life and forces her husband to avenge her death. The original title *Dead and Married* was changed by the producers.

In 1991 Giovinazzo vowed to gain more control over his work. He began to write the screenplay for *No Way Home*, the story of an ex-con who returns home after a six-year prison term, which was eventually produced and then released in 1997. He is reunited with his brother and his wife, now an emotionally drained stripper. Several deals to greenlight the project fell apart. Giovinazzo got actor Tim Roth attached to the project, and eventually the London-based Company Goldcrest came on board. The film had a controversial third act that exploded into explicit violence. To protect his vision, Giovinazzo shot the sequence without coverage, making it difficult, if not impossible, to reedit. In 1999 Giovinazzo directed *The Unscarred*. The determined East Coast independent filmmaker refuses to compromise or play the Hollywood game, telling *Films in Review*, "I'm never gonna wear a pastel shirt. I'm not gonna smoke cigars. I'll tell you the truth, my watch is still on New York time."

BIBLIOGRAPHY

Esposito, John. "Buddy G. Still on New York Time." *Films in Review* (January–February 1997): 35–37.

Globus, Yoram. *See* Cannon Group

Godmilow, Jill. Editor, director. *b.* 1943. Godmilow is a pioneer member of the New York independent **documentary** film community where she was in demand as a film editor. In 1974 Godmilow codirected *Antonia: A Portrait of a Woman* with folk singer Judy Collins. The story of symphony conductor Antonia Brico was nominated for an Academy Award for best documentary. The landmark feature-length documentary portrait inspired women in two ways: The film was crafted from the dreams of two women, and the documentary's subject motivated women to follow their passions and break barriers in nontraditional fields for females. After a series of short films, *The Popovich Brothers of South Chicago* (1977), *Nevelson in Process* (1977), and *The Odyssey Tapes* (1978), both codirected with Susan Fanshel, Godmilow directed *The Vigil* (1980) and *At Nienadawka with Grotowski* (1981), documentary portraits of people who embraced creativity with courage and strength. *Far From Poland* (1984) presented a filmmaker as the central character and broke ground in its use of both fictional and nonfictional material.

In 1987 Skouras Pictures released *Waiting for the Moon*, a film based on the relationship between Gertrude Stein and Alice B. Toklas. Because there was little documentation available, the **Sundance Institute** accepted Godmilow as a screenwriter to develop a reconstruction of history. At Sundance they workshopped scenes from the screenplay with actors. *American Playhouse* committed partial funding, and then producer Sandra Schulberg found the rest of the budget. Linda Hunt played Toklas, and Linda Bassette portrayed Gertrude Stein. In 1994 Godmilow adapted the one-man show Roy Cohn/**Jack Smith**, starring Ron Vawter, who had created the Off-Broadway production. In 1997 Godmilow directed *What Farocki Taught*, which contained a shot-for-shot color English-language recreation of the 1969 black-and-white German film *In Extinguishable Fire*, directed by Harun Farocki. Farocki's film examined the production of napalm, human labor abuses, and filmmaking. Godmilow's intent was to question the significance of secondhand material by avoiding any new historical insights on the political activities Farocki criticized in his original film. Godmilow continues to make radical waves, remaining truthful to the vital New York film community from whence she came.

Golan, Menahem. *See* Cannon Group

Goldwyn, Samuel. Producer. *b.* Schmuel Gelbfisz, July 1879, Warsaw, Poland. *d.* January 31, 1974, Los Angeles, California. Samuel Goldwyn immigrated to England at eleven years old, making the trip alone. He lived with relatives and worked as a blacksmith's helper. Coming to America, he was an apprentice glovemaker in New York and earned $3 a week; by age fifteen Goldwyn was an expert glove cutter and was soon considered the best glove salesman in the business. In 1910 Goldwyn married into the film industry with the sister of producer Jesse L. Lasky. An economic depression hit the glove business, and Goldwyn persuaded his brother-in-law to form the Jesse L. Lasky Feature Play Company with Lasky as president, Goldwyn as treasurer and salesman, and Cecil B. DeMille as director. The company produced *The Squaw Man* (1914), which was a resounding success and gave them the capital to produce twenty-one films in their first year. In 1916, they merged with Adolph Zukor's Famous Players. Goldwyn was installed as chairman, Zukor was president, and Lasky was vice president. The partners fought with their chairman and bought him out for $900,000. Next Goldwyn forged a partnership with Edgar Selwyn. The new company combined Goldfish (Sam's Americanized name) with Selwyn and called itself Goldwyn. In 1922 the company was failing, and Goldwyn was edged out. The Goldwyn Company merged with Metro Pictures and Louis B. Mayer Productions to form MGM. Samuel Goldwyn was not part of the deal to create a major studio.

The experience motivated Goldwyn to go it alone as an independent.

He formed Samuel Goldwyn Productions with no partners—he had total artistic and fiscal control. Goldwyn acquired a stable of movie stars that included Ronald Coleman, Gary Cooper, Teresa Wright, Danny Kaye, David Niven, Farley Granger, Will Rogers, Lucille Ball, Susan Hayward, and Merle Oberon. He sought and contracted superior literary talent: Robert Sherwood, Sinclair Lewis, Ben Hecht, Lillian Hellman, and Sidney Kingsley. Some of his finest productions include *Wuthering Heights* (1939), *The Westerner* (1940), *The Little Foxes* (1941), *The Pride of the Yankees* (1942), *The Best Years of Our Lives* (1946), *The Secret Life of Walter Mitty* (1947), *Guys and Dolls* (1955), and *Porgy and Bess* (1959). In 1946 Samuel Goldwyn was given the Irving Thalberg Award. Goldwyn didn't make low-budget films, but he was a true independent filmmaker who understood the importance of artistic and financial control over his work.

BIBLIOGRAPHY

Berg, A. Scott. *Goldwyn: A Biography.* New York: Knopf, 1989.

Gomez, Nick. Director, screenwriter. *b.* 1963, Somerville, Massachusetts. *ed.* SUNY Purchase. A sixth-grade dropout living on the edge in Cambridge, Massachusetts, Nick Gomez was brought up on assault charges and put on probation. His life was at a dead end until he formed a punk band. A passion for music motivated Gomez to get his high school equivalency diploma and attend the State University of New York (SUNY) at Purchase, where he met **Hal Hartley** and other aspiring filmmakers. In 1990 Gomez edited Hartley's *Trust*, which gave him the opportunity to direct his own project. The filmmaking collective **The Shooting Gallery,** headed by SUNY alumni Bob Gosse and his partner Larry Meistrich, told Gomez he could direct if he could make a feature for $38,000. Gomez was an ardent admirer of **Martin Scorsese**'s *Mean Streets* (1973). He wrote *Laws of Gravity* (1992) using his personal experiences as a lynchpin for the story of petty criminals who try to break out of their doomed, dead-end lives. The film was shot on location in Greenpoint, Brooklyn, in just twelve days. Cinematographer Jean De Sejonzc photographed the film in an immediate, controlled, shaky handheld style as the cast performed semiimprovised dialogue and action. Gomez was hailed as a third-generation New York indie following the tradition of **Elia Kazan, John Cassavetes,** and Martin Scorsese.

He wanted to follow up his impressive debut with *Animals,* a screenplay about carjackers he had already cannibalized to complete *Laws of Gravity.* **Spike Lee** screened Gomez's film and was enthusiastic about working with the street auteur. Lee was against *Animals,* feeling it was too much like *Laws of Gravity.* After the script *New Jersey Drive* (1995) was completed, Lee landed Gomez a deal with Universal. The project was originally budgeted at $8 million, but the studio didn't like many of the plot points and character scenes and pushed Gomez to center in on action. They forced his hand by lowering the budget to $5 million. Gomez considered walking out but persevered. He lost control of the project, a realistic look at black teenage carjackers in Newark, New Jersey. It did little to advance his career.

Next, Gomez wanted to make a Hong Kong–style thriller in Florida, but lack of budget revised his plans. *Illtown* (1996) is a drug film with a hallucinatory dreamlike atmosphere. Gomez developed a transcendental style for the untouchable world of drug lords, where the luxurious lifestyle is contrasted with the misery and degradation in the outside world affected by their destructive merchandise. Gomez was obsessed with men who couldn't escape their past, and in *Illtown* he was able to evolve his raw, direct visual style into an expressive approach with studied compositions in place of the unleashed camera of his earlier work.

Drowning Mona (2000) is a black comedy about a small town's reaction when its most hated citizen drowns. There are many suspects and oddball characters. The film succeeds in capturing the ambiance, but Gomez doesn't really understand these people as well as **Joel and Ethan Coen** demonstrated in *Fargo* (1996).

Good Machine. New York–based production company founded by Ted Hope, David Linde, and James Schamus in 1991. The company secured a respected position in independent film by producing or coproducing projects by key emerging filmmakers of the 1990s: Ang Lee, **Todd Solondz**, Nicole Holofcener, **Edward Burns**, Cheryl Dunye, and their crown jewel **Hal Hartley**. As a distributor of international films, Good Machine has supported cutting-edge films such as **Lars von Trier**'s *Dancer in the Dark* (2000) and prestige projects like Joan Chen's *Xiu Xiu* (1998). Films nurtured by Good Machine include *Happiness* (1998), *Walking and Talking* (1996), *Ride with the Devil* (1999), *The Golden Boat* (1990), and *The Myth of Fingerprints* (1997). Ted Hope has produced over forty-five films including *The Brothers McMullen* (1995), *Flirt* (1995), *The Ice Storm* (1997), *Wonderland* (1997), *Simple Men* (1992), *Trust* (1990), and *Safe* (1995). Good Machine fell on bad times in the late nineties and, by 2001, after being sold to Itemus, was near death. In 2002 Good Machine continues to survive. Only time, luck and managerial judgment will see them grow and prosper once again.

Gordon, Bette. Director. *b.* 1950. The independent filmmaker of *Michigan Avenue* (1973), *I-94* (1974), and *The United States of America* (1975), Bette Gordon's most celebrated work is *Variety* (1985). Photographed by **Tom DiCillo**, this feminist feature is the story of Christine who works in a porn theater and becomes obsessed with a male customer, secretly following him to the Fulton Fish Market, Yankee Stadium, and the Staten

Island Ferry, reversing the voyeur/object male-to-female relationship. Gordon never shows the porn that plays in the theater, only letting us hear Christine's depiction of what she sees in the films.

In 1998 Gordon directed a screen adaptation of Scott Bradfield's novel *The History of Luminous Motion*, which features an eight-year-old boy's first-person account as he and his mother, who have no permanent home, take to the road and survive off stolen credit cards. The screenplay was written by Bradfield and Robert Roth, independently produced by Fiona Films and **Good Machine**, and distributed by Artistic License.

Gordon, Stuart. Director, screenwriter, producer. *b.* August 11, 1947, Chicago, Illinois. *ed.* University of Wisconsin. In 1985 Stuart Gordon directed *Re-Animator*, which he adapted from a H.P. Lovecraft story. The explicit horror/comedy is about a scientist who develops a serum that brings the dead back to life. A severed head and sexual content caused trouble for Gordon with the MPAA. The director wanted an R-rating and was informed this could be achieved if he cut out everything after the second reel. *Re-Animator* was released uncut and unrated. The intelligent dark-humored Gordon had a sensibility often out of touch with authorities. *Re-Animator* was mean-spirited, funny, and gross. Gordon planned to do a Lovecraft series in the tradition of the **Roger Corman** Poe cycle, but the project didn't fly.

Dolls (1987) was a horror film featuring murderous playthings. *Robot Jox* (1989) was threatened with a lawsuit from Orion because it delayed *Robocop* by three years. *Robot Jox* did poorly in release, but like many genre films, it flourished in video. *From Beyond* (1986), also based on a Lovecraft story, was submitted four times to the MPAA before the X-rating was changed to R. The film features scientists searching for the sixth sense, but experiments cause the subjects to go berserk—another gross-out for the fans of *Re-Animator*.

Gordon wrote a screenplay *The Teenie Weenies* that landed him a nonexclusive deal to develop family films at Disney, a bizarre turn of events. Gordon wanted to direct the project, but Disney protected themselves by assigning the film to director Joe Johnson. Gordon was credited with the story and given an executive title for the 1989 hit film *Honey, I Shrunk the Kids*. In 1997 Stuart Gordon was the writer, producer and director of *Space Truckers*. In 1998 he produced and directed an adaptation of the play *The Wonderful Ice Cream Suit* by Ray Bradbury. In 2001, Gordon returned to the writings of H.P. Lovecraft and directed *Dagon*.

Grant, Lee. Actress, director. *b.* Lyova Haskell Rosenthal, October 31, 1927, New York City. *ed.* Julliard. After her screen debut in *Detective Story* (1951) and roles in *The Balcony* (1963), *In the Heat of the Night* (1967), *Marooned* (1969), *The Landlord* (1970), for which she received an Oscar nomination, and *Shampoo* (1975), for which she won the statuette for best supporting actress. Lee Grant made the difficult transition to directing. Her 1980 feature film *Tell Me a Riddle* received critical acclaim. Grant gained a solid reputation as a documentarian, with HBO supporting many of her projects. *Down and Out in America* (1986), a study of the homeless, tied for the Best Documentary Feature Oscar. During the 1980s and 1990s Lee Grant flourished as an actress and director. From 1998 to 2001 Grant directed a series of documentaries on prominent women for the Lifetime Cable network called *Intimate Portrait*. Among her subjects were, Tipper Gore, Marlo Thomas, Jasmine Guy, Gloria Steinem, Laura Dern, Bella Abzug, Lela Rochon and Christine Lahti. Along with Claudia Weill and **Joan Micklin Silver**, Lee Grant is a pioneer. Her triumph is reflective of the continuing accomplishments of women filmmakers who look to her as a mentor.

grants. Many independent filmmakers, especially nonfiction and experimental artists, rely on grants to help fund their motion picture projects. Grant monies come from government agencies, foundations, special interest groups, educational organizations, and media outlets. Each grant source has its own requirements, restrictions, and dollar amounts available. With each year, grants become more competitive for a larger group of submissions, and government grants continue to be slashed by the enemies of free expression and from the political Right. Just a sampling of the many grant sources available include: The Film Arts Foundation, **The National Endowment for the Arts (NEA)**, The New York Foundation for the Arts and The All Media Arts Center. Specialized grant sources include: The National Foundation for Jewish Culture's Fund for Jewish Documentary Filmmaking, The Astraea National Lesbian Action Foundation, The Funders Directory of Gay, Lesbian, Bisexual and Transgendered Programs, Black Collegian Organizations Assisting People of Color. *See also* New York Foundation for the Arts (NYFA); National Endowment for the Arts (NEA)

Graver, Gary. Cinematographer, director, producer, screenwriter, actor. Gary Graver has photographed over 200 independent and studio films, the overwhelming majority **exploitation** and **hard-core adult films** where he is credited under the pseudonym Robert McCallum. Graver also photographed Ron Howard's low-budget directorial debut *Grand Theft Auto* in 1977 and worked with **John Cassavetes** as an additional cameraman and camera operator on *A Woman under the Influence* (1976). In his publicity materials, Graver claims to have worked with Steven Spielberg, Frank Marshall, and **Samuel Fuller**. In the early 1970s Graver made a cold call to Orson Welles, telling the legendary director he wanted to work with him. Welles replied the only other person who called him in this manner was Gregg Toland who photographed *Citizen Kane* (1941). Graver and Welles remained friends until Welles's death in 1985. Graver photographed Welles's last feature, *The Other Side of the Wind* (1972), still unseen because of a legal conflict in Iran, and *F Is for Fake* (1975). Graver has made a documentary *Working with Orson Welles* (1993) and has presented the films of the director in many parts of the world. Recent credits for Gary Graver as a cinematographer include: *The Prophet* (1999), the documentary *A Lord Portrait* (2000), and *The Long Ride Home* (2001).

Griffith, D.W. Director. *b*. David Llewelyn Wark Griffith, January 22, 1875, LaGrange, Kentucky. *d.* July 21, 1948, Hollywood, California. D.W. Griffith may be the single-most important film director of the twentieth century. He is widely credited with the establishment of cinematic grammar with direct narrative use of textbook editorial devices such as intercutting, parallel storytelling, optical time altering devices such as the fade, the iris, and a sophisticated camera vocabulary including close-ups, moving shots, and panoramic views, all for the sake of visually expressing a story. Griffith was a giant of early Hollywood, an independent who personified the artist/auteur/showman in the industry.

Griffith began as an actor in 1897. He toured with stock companies and tried to establish himself as a writer of short stories and poems but had little success. Eventually Griffith sold a number of stories to **Biograph** Studios and acted in several of their film productions. He became involved in many aspects of film production at Biograph and learned the craft thoroughly. Griffith made his directorial debut in 1908 with *The Adventures of Dollie*. For the next eighteen months Griffith directed Biograph's entire product, becoming the New York studio's general director through 1913. Griffith directed a staggering 450 films at Biograph and supervised all of the studio's productions. Griffith, along with his brilliant and inventive cameraman Billy Bitzer, explored and experimented with cinematic grammar and the art of visual storytelling. In 1910 Griffith began transporting his Biograph troupe of actors and crew to California during the winter to benefit from the warm climate and the greater variety of backgrounds to film his stories. Griffith joined the Triangle Corporation in 1915 with Thomas Ince and Mack Sennett. In 1917 Griffith joined Adolph Zuckor's Artcraft Company.

In 1919 Griffith set up his own studio complex in Mamaroneck, New York. In that same year Mary Pickford, **Charles Chaplin, Douglas Fairbanks,** and Griffith formed the **United Artists Corporation** as a means of controlling the artistic and financial destiny of their films. In 1920, the D.W. Griffith Corporation was formed. Griffith's mammoth production *Intolerance* (1916), which featured the largest set ever built in Hollywood at that time, was the director's apologia for the racial hatred displayed in *Birth of a Nation* (1915). The landmark epic features several stories of the evils of man's intolerance in a parallel storytelling structure that created a dramatic vortex of emotion.

Griffith's last years were sad. He directed less than 20 films from 1920 until his final work *The Struggle* in 1931. From 1908 to 1919 he had directed over 500 motion pictures. The man who helped create the film industry and wrote the cinematic language for the narrative feature film was shunned as old-fashioned. With little personal wealth and an addiction to alcohol, Griffith was forgotten in his own time. His legacy is the vision of the individual and the ability to harness technology to create moving images that are pure cinematic expression. *See also* Biography; Chaplin, Charles; Fairbanks, Douglas; United Artists Corporation

BIBLIOGRAPHY

Schickel, Richard. *D.W. Griffith: An American Life.* New York: Simon and Schuster, 1984.

guerrilla filmmaking. Term used to describe low-budget, independent films made quickly without permits for locations, a union crew, or elaborate equipment. It is filmmaking on the fly, on the cheap, a bare-bones production. Guerrilla filmmakers function on a by-any-means-necessary basis.

Guttenplan, Howard. Filmmaker, educator. Guttenplan is an independent filmmaker who works in the **diary film** style. His **16mm** film work in the 1970s includes *European Diary '71, Haiti Diary '72, Laporte Diary '72, Middle East Diary '76, N.Y.C. Diary '74, San Francisco Diary '79 (Shadow Trail),* and *Western Diary '75.* Guttenplan has been the able and dedicated director of **The Millenium** Film Workshop in Lower Manhattan since the founder **Ken Jacobs** stepped down in the 1970s. He oversees publication of *The Millennium Film Journal,* a magazine covering the **experimental film** scene. Guttenplan is dedicated to the art of film and has kept this vital institution afloat and thriving through budget cuts, changing film tastes, and the general hostility toward the experimental film. He has nurtured a new generation of filmmakers and preserved the lessons and history of every important **avant-garde** and experimental film artist. *See also* diary film; The Millenium

H

Haas, Belinda. Editor, screenwriter, producer. Partner with husband director **Philip Haas**, Belinda Haas has edited four fictional independent feature films he directed: *The Music of Chance* (1993) and *Angels and Insects* (1995), for which she wrote the screenplay adaptations, *The Blood Oranges* (1997), which she adapted and produced, and *Up at the Villa* (2000). Haas has adapted and edited complex literary works and nurtured the productions through the difficult maze of film financing and distribution pitfalls. *See also* Haas, Philip

Haas, Philip. Director. Specialist in adapting complex literary material to the screen, Philip Haas's feature film debut was a faithful adaptation of Paul Auster's transcendental novel *The Music of Chance*. The film was a surprise to critics and audiences. Haas was generally unknown and had the courage to take on the challenging literary work. The existential story features a high-stakes poker game between two eccentric millionaires and two men they meet on the road. The film showcases excellent performances by James Spader, Mandy Patinkin, M. Emmett Walsh, Charles Durning, Joel Grey, Samantha Mathis, and Christopher Penn. Haas displays a delicate visual and narrative adaptation style that captures the novel's off-center reality. Next, Haas took on A.S. Byatt's sexually provocative novella *Morpho Eugenia* in a PBS *American Playhouse* production retitled *Angels and Insects* (1995). The art film reached its intended sophisticated audience and established Haas as adept at transferring difficult and elusive novels to the screen. For his third feature, *The Blood Oranges* (1997), Haas faced an even greater adaptation challenge in the John Hawkes story of a long-married couple who travel to a tropical coastal town to follow their sexual fantasies and engage in partner swapping with a couple who have three children. In 2000 Philip Haas directed

Kristin Scott Thomas, Sean Penn, Anne Bancroft, James Fox, and Derek Jacobi in *Up at the Villa* based on a Sommerset Maughn novel. This romantic thriller is set in fascist Italy and again explores the consequences of sexual behavior and the dangers of class warfare. The latest literary adaptation for Philip Haas is *The Lathe of Heaven* (2002), a television movie based on the novel by Ursula Le Guin. Haas is a welcome literate voice in independent filmmaking dedicated to making serious mature films that intellectually stimulate the audience. *See also* Haas, Belinda

Hall, Arch. Actor, screenwriter, producer, director. *b.* William Waters, December 21, 1908, Missouri. *d.* April 28, 1978, Los Angeles, California. William Waters was an **exploitation** filmmaker who began as an actor in **B-movie** westerns. Waters found his stage name sitting in his den one night in an easy chair looking down the hall at an arch in a doorway—he became Arch Hall! Throughout his career he used the monikers Archie Hall, Nicholas Merriwether, and William Waters. In the 1960s he formed Fairway-International Productions. Hall began in independent filmmaking as a screenwriter and producer of *The Choppers* (1961), a black-and-white **drive-in** product that featured his son Arch Hall Jr. who had a burning ambition to be a teen idol in the image of Frankie Avalon and Fabian. Junior plays the leader of a car-stripping gang who avoids the police while singing his original compositions "Konga Joe" and "Monkey in My Hatband." *Magic Spectacles* (1961) was a **sexploitation** flick Hall produced to help bankroll his son's screen career. Arch Hall's best-known film, *Eegah!* (1962), featured sixteen-year-old Arch Jr. as the boyfriend of a girl who discovers a giant, played by Richard Kiel who later achieved international fame as "Jaws," the toothy James Bond villain. *Wild Guitar* (1962) is another vehicle for Jr, who this time goes to Hollywood and is ripped-off by a crooked agent played by Sr.—another chance for Jr. to sing, play his guitar, and sell his songs. *The Nasty Rabbit* (1965) stars Sr. and Jr. in the improbable story of foreign agents who descend on a dude ranch where a Soviet spy is about to release a contaminated rabbit on the Continental Divide. Arch Jr. and the Archers perform classics like "The Jackrabbit Shuffle," "The Robot Walk," and "The Spy Waltz." *Deadwood '76* (1965) was the next-to-last production of Hall's Fairway International and was photographed by William **Zigmond**, now known as Vilmos. Junior plays a cowboy mistaken for Billy the Kid, is captured by Indians, runs into Arch Sr, and falls in love. He escapes and has a showdown with Wild Bill Hickcock. The indie world has a caste system divided by the esthetes and the old Times Square crowd who truly loved movies, those deliberately bad, accidentally bad, and just bad, and those producers, like Arch Hall Sr, who dared to go beyond acceptability into the cosmos of the outrageous.

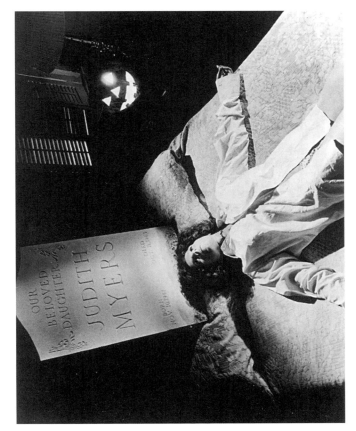

Moments of horror like this one from John Carpenter's *Halloween* (1978), helped to launch a new era for the genre. Courtesy of The Del Valle Archive

Halloween. A 1978 landmark low-budget independent horror film cowritten and directed by **John Carpenter**, coproduced and cowritten by Debra Hill, and photographed by **Dean Cundey.** Carpenter's third feature was brought in for $300,000 and grossed over $60 million worldwide, crowning it the most profitable independently made film of its day. Prior to production, Carpenter studied the films of his idol Howard Hawks to learn to maximize the use of the film frame itself to engender fear and fright in his audience. *Halloween*'s story centered on Michael Myers who had brutally murdered his sister on Halloween when the six-year-old discovered her having sex with her boyfriend. The main action occurs in October 1978 when the adult Myers escapes from a sanitarium and heads for his hometown, bent on a killing spree. His psychiatrist races to stop the psychotic killer before he again strikes on Halloween night. Three teenage girls are Michael's prey. The frightfest ends with the possibility of future mayhem. *Halloween* featured Jamie Lee Curtis in her acting debut, and she was christened "The Teen Queen of Scream," and Donald Pleasance as Dr. Loomis. Carpenter learned the Hawksian lessons from *The Thing* (1982) by keeping Myers at the edge of the frame with occasional shocking surprise entrances. Throughout the film the viewer never knows when Michael will appear or precisely what he looks like. Carpenter composed the effective, minimalist musical score. Good performances and Dean Cundey's meticulous compositional control make *Halloween* a tension-filled, scared-out-of-your-wits experience audiences craved but hadn't experienced in many a year. *Halloween* spawned seven sequels and sent low-budget genre filmmakers scrambling in search of the next big **franchise**. *See also* Carpenter, John; Cundey, Dean

hard-core films. Motion pictures that contain explicit sex acts. Blue movies had been produced and distributed underground from the early days of the cinema. Poorly made **16mm** and later **8mm** and **Super 8mm** films were produced independently and shown at clandestine locations and male smokers. Originally unorganized and later produced in an alternate distribution system to the legitimate studio film, hard-core sex films were marketed to males, presented in a male gaze with limited story lines, generated to stimulate and satisfy every fantasy. The genre became codified with predictable narrative and action patterns screened in low-rent theaters on the seedier end of neighborhoods across American cities. In the 1970s films such as *Deep Throat* (1972), *Behind the Green Door* (1972), and *The Devil in Miss Jones* (1973) brought hard-core films into the mainstream. **Porno chic,** as it was known, was a short-lived era when women and couples attended screenings of **adult films** at legitimate venues. With the advent of multiplex theaters, many neighborhood establishments devoted one screen to hard-core fare. Community pressure and home video drove the adult film onto tape and into the home. The primary audience continues to be male, although repeated attempts have been made to market adult films to women. Attacked by feminist groups, civic associations, and moral arbiters, ironically hard-core films have become the subject of academic study and interest. DVD technology is quickly becoming the delivery system of choice. The adult film industry, centrally located in California, thrives with its own conventions and award ceremonies. Numerous guides and bibliographic tomes are also available. Currently hard-core films are again low on production values with little or no plot and plenty of explicit sex, and the days of chic and art achieved by **Gerard Damiano, Jim and Artie Mitchell,** and **Chuck Vincent** are long gone. *See also* adult film industry; porno chic; soft-core films

BIBLIOGRAPHY

Flint, David. *Babylon Blue: An Illustrated History of Adult Cinema.* London: Creation Books, 1999.

Ford, Luke. *A History of X: 100 Years of Sex in Film.* Amherst, NY: Prometheus Books, 1999.

Williams, Linda. *Hard Core: Power, Pleasure, and the "Frenzy of the Visible."* Berkeley: University of California Press, 1999.

Harlan County U.S.A. See Kopple, Barbara.

Harrington, Curtis. Director, screenwriter. *b.* September 17, 1928, Los Angeles. *ed.* University of Southern California. In his teens and twenties, Curtis Harrington directed **8mm** and **16mm** films including *The Fall of the House of Usher* (1942), *Fragment of Seeking* (1946), *Picnic* (1948), *On the Edge* (1949), *Dangerous House* (1952), and *The Assignation and the Wormwood Star* (1955). Harrington became an executive assistant to producer Jerry Wald and in 1955 was an associate producer at Twentieth-Century Fox. *Night Tide* (1963) was Harrington's first feature. The film starring **Dennis Hopper** and Luanna Anders is the tale of a sailor involved with a woman who may be a killer and an ancestor to the Sirens. The strange, dreamlike narrative is often mistaken for a horror film. Harrington had deep roots in the **avant-garde** and **experimental film** communities. He designed **Kenneth Anger's** *Puce Moment* (1949) and played a somnambulist in *Inauguration of the Pleasure Dome* (1954). The two emerging young filmmakers bonded in their admiration for the silent cinema of Rudolph Valentino, **D.W. Griffith**, and Lillian Gish. As teenagers, the shy and brooding Harrington and the intense Anger founded The Creative Film Associates Company, distributors of independent films by the Whitney Brothers, **Maya Deren**, and many East Coast filmmakers interested in myth, mysticism, personal sexuality, and the unconscious mind. Harrington embarked on beach excursions with Anaïs Nin and was part of the Boho, coffeehouse, gallery, and underground scenes.

In 1965 he directed *Voyage to the Prehistoric Planet* under the pseudonym John Sebastian, an **American International Pictures** production for which **Roger Corman** purchased a Leningrad studio film called *Planeta Bura* featuring cosmonauts exploring Venus. Corman was impressed by its excellent special effects and hired Harrington to shoot new scenes to intercut with the Russian film so it could be released to television as a new movie. *Queen of Blood* (1966) was also an AIP production, and again Corman acquired Russian footage, this time spectacular shots of spaceships. Harrington wrote a screenplay and shot the film in seven and a half days for $65,000. Basil Rathbone commands an expedition to Mars to rescue a spacecraft in distress. The sole survivor, a green alien woman, drains the blood from crew members played by John Saxton, Dennis Hopper, and **Forrest J. Ackerman**. *Games* (1967) starred Simone Signoret, James Caan, Katherine Ross, and Don Stroud. The plot involves a mysterious woman who triggers a double-cross conspiracy. *Who Slew Auntie Roo?*, a sick take on *Hansel and Gretel*, was released in 1971, about an old woman who lures children into her lair. In that same year *What's the Matter with Helen?* hit theaters featuring Debbie Reynolds, Shelly Winters, Dennis Weaver, Agnes Moorhead, and Michael MacLiammoir in a campy 1930s Hollywood murder story. *The Killing Kind* (1973) is a re-

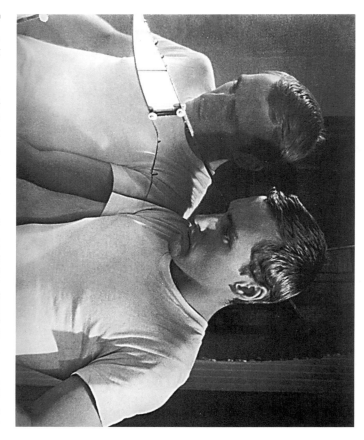

Dennis Hopper in Curtis Harrington's dreamlike *Night Tide* (1963). Courtesy of The Del Valle Archive

venge story about a man released from prison obsessed with getting back at his lawyer and accuser. Four years later Harrington directed *Ruby* (1977) with Piper Laurie and Stuart Whitman in which a gangster's spirit inhabits a deaf-mute woman who goes on a killing spree at a **drive-in theater** that specializes in horror movies. An epilogue was added to the film, and Harrington asked the DGA to allow the Allen Smithee credit as the film no longer represented his vision. In 1985, Harrington directed *Mata Hari* with Sylvia Kristel playing the World War I femme fatale. Frequent nudity was the film's main attraction.

Harris, James B. Producer, director. *b.* August 3, 1928, New York City. *ed.* Julliard. Producing partner of producer/director team James B. Harris and **Stanley Kubrick.** Harris-Kubrick Pictures made three films in a ten-year partnership: *The Killing* (1956), *Paths of Glory* (1957), and *Lolita* (1962). In 1964 Kubrick, yearning for more control, moved on to produce and direct *Dr. Strangelove*, and Harris pursued his ambition to direct, debuting with *The Bedford Incident* (1965) and continuing with *Some Call It Loving* (1973), *Fast-Walking* (1982), *Cop* (aka *Blood on the Moon*, 1987) and *Boiling Point* (1993). In 1977 Harris produced *Telefon*, directed by Don Siegel and starring Charles Bronson. Harris cut deals with studios, raised money, and handled all producing chores for Harris-Kubrick Pictures. He provided artistic input and collaborated on screenplays and production matters. The team remained friends and fans of each other's work until Kubrick's death in 1999.

BIBLIOGRAPHY

Baxter, John. *Stanley Kubrick: A Biography*. New York: Carrol and Graf, 1997.
LoBrutto, Vincent. *Stanley Kubrick: A Biography*. New York: Donald I. Fine, 1997.

Harris–Kubrick Pictures. *See* Harris, James B.

Harron, Mary. Director, screenwriter. *b.* Canada. *ed.* Oxford University. Harron worked as a rock journalist and **documentary** filmmaker for the BBC where she created shows on **Andy Warhol** and Jackson Pollack for *The South Bank Show* and the documentaries *Campaign!* and *Winds of Change.* For her debut as a fictional feature director, Harron chose the true story of Valerie Solanas, the woman who wrote the SCUM (Society for the Cutting Up of Men) Manifesto and expressed her hatred for men by shooting Andy Warhol. As Solanas, Lili Taylor gives a dangerous performance that inhabits the disturbed woman who confused her sexuality with her lack of self-identity to disastrous results. Harron never tries to understand why Solanas shot Warhol, and her objectivity creates an eerie platform for the life and times of Solanas and Warhol. An impeccable period production understated and knowing, *I Shot Andy Warhol* (1996) received an Independent Spirit Award nomination for best film, and Lili Taylor won a special jury award at **Sundance**. The film, produced by **Christine Vachon**, was a valuable contribution to **gay cinema**.

For her sophomore film, Harron took on Brett Easton Ellis's incendiary novel *American Psycho* (2000). The book was considered an impossible adaptation. The story of a misogynist serial killer by night who is a Wall Street player by day is told in first person. The book's violence toward women even broke the content barriers of **splatter films;** many scenes of torture and murder could not be filmed for a commercially distributed movie. Harron originally wanted Leonardo DiCaprio for the controversial role. DiCaprio eventually declined, and Christian Bale got the part and played it full out. The screenplay by Harron successfully captured Ellis's satiric intent and plays the horrific details for their black humor. Harron's film was a triumph for a female director—a no-holds-barred look into hatred toward women driven by the anger resulting from the mania to succeed in the upscale yuppified 1980s. Where the book nau-

Hartley, Hal. Director, screenwriter, producer, composer. *b.* November 3, 1959, Lindenhurst, Long Island, New York. New York. *ed.* Massachusetts Institute of Art, State University of New York (SUNY) at Purchase. Hartley graduated from the film program at SUNY/Purchase in 1984, moved to New York, and worked in and around the local film community until 1988. His first feature *The Unbelievable Truth* (1990) was bankrolled by his boss at the Industrial Video Company, where Hartley answered phones, and from TVT, a local bank that was offering $10,000 low-interest loans. The deadpan black comedy was about a mysterious man who returns home after a prison term. It was shot in eleven days for $75,000.

Hartley has a select audience who relate to his impersonal and precise sense of black humor and consider him a genius. Hartley knows the size of his audience is small but large enough to break even, supporting his lean production methods. This allows him to make many films, seven in one ten-year period, a feat equaled only by **Woody Allen**, who has a similar equation. Like his idol Jean-Luc Godard, Hartley executes precision timing, creates stylized visuals, and distances his narratives from reality while making social and political statements. Hartley's characters are out of sync and collide, producing surprising results. All of Hartley's characters are concerned with difficult ethical and moral decisions. Hartley has a loyal crew—director of photography Michael Spiller, production designer Steve Rosenzweig, and editor Steve Hamilton, who have worked on virtually all of his films, and has composed the musical scores for nine, sometimes using the pseudonym Ned Rifle. Often his own producer, Hartley is able to track the spending of every dollar, making sure it gets on the screen. Ironically, although Hartley films are uniquely American in theme, their sensibilities are decidedly European. They stress the importance of loyalty, the hatred of betrayal, the search for passion, the lack of love in marriage, the ordinary semblance of life, and the power of transcendence. Nothing is ever resolved in a Hartley film; his characters are on an endless search fueled by fear and hope.

In *Trust* (1991), a pregnant high school girl is abandoned by a football star that fears the loss of his pending scholarship. Her father dies hearing the news, and she finds a savior in a nerdish young man who doesn't live up to his father's expectations. *Simple Men* (1992) concerns two brothers as they search for their father who played shortstop for the Brooklyn Dodgers and has become a bomb-loving revolutionary. *Amateur* (1994) is about an ex-nun who writes pornographic fiction and a man with a disturbing past suffering from amnesia. *Flirt* (1995) is a three-part drama with the story told from three perspectives, straight, gay, and with roles

seates, the film elicits maniacal comedy and a clear satirized vision of the greed-is-good decade.

reversed. In *Henry Fool* (1997), the title character encourages a shy garbageman to write poetry. Recent work from Hal Hartley includes: *The Book of Life* (1998), the short film *Kimono* (2000), and *No Such Thing* (2001).

Hartley's characters rarely smile and display a **Buster Keaton/Samuel Beckett** deadpan attitude. Hartley, who has been hailed an American Harold Pinter, is a postmodernist who works in a spare, minimalist style. A student of Bertold Brecht, Hartley uses melodrama and ironic parables to deconstruct and satirize the working class of his Long Island upbringing. Hartley is detached from his presentation and applies a didactic approach to storytelling. Like Beckett and Pinter, Hartley's humor comes out of a worldview, not traditional comic situations or one-liners. He maintains control by shooting and editing his low-budget films quickly. Clearly Hartley is an auteur, the poet laureate of Long Island, and the voice of his generation.

Hauser, Wings. Actor, director, screenwriter. *b.* Gerald Dwight Hauser, December 12, 1947, Hollywood, California. An actor who belongs in the **psychotronic film** hall of fame, Wings Hauser has appeared in over eighty-five theatrical, **direct-to-video**, and television shows. Hauser is known to his rabid fans as the primo psychotic, often playing villains in low-budget films such as *Vice Squad* (1982), *Tough Guys Don't Dance* (1987), and *L.A. Bounty* (1989). *Vice Squad* launched his **B-movie** career where he gained a reputation as the hardest-working man in the low-rent film business. Hauser made his directorial debut with *Living to Die* (1990), where he also plays Nick Carpenter, a tapped-out Vegas P.I. who delves into blackmail and murder. *Coldfire* (1991) features Hauser assigned to stop distribution of a designer drug that offers the ultimate high–death, spread by enemies of the United States whose mission is to dismantle the superpower. Also in 1991 Hauser released *The Art of Dying,* the story of an evil cameraman who kills aspiring actors. *Skins* (1994) starred Hauser and *The Exorcist's* Linda Blair. His son Cole Hauser is an actor who first met his famous dad at age eleven. Cole also has an impressive indie résumé, appearing in *Dazed and Confused* (1993), *Higher Learning* (1995), and *The Hi-Lo Country* (1998). Recent credits for Wings Hauser include: *Clean and Narrow* (1999), *Savage Season* and *Irish Eyes Are Crying* (both 2001). Wings Hauser may not have the prestige of many significant independent film figures, but he is prolific, off center, ambitious, and committed. Hauser has directed and created dangerous, over-the-top characters rejected by mainstream commercial cinema. *See also* direct-to-video

Haynes, Todd. Director, producer, writer, editor. *b.* January 2, 1961, Encino, California. *ed.* Brown University. While attending Brown University Todd Haynes made *Assassins: A Film Concerning Rimbaud* (1985), a stylish reconstruction of the poet's relationship with Paul Verlaine. When he arrived in New York, he formed Apparatus Productions with Barry Ellsworth and **Christine Vachon**, a company they envisioned would help fund, produce, and distribute the work of emerging short film directors who did not see the form only as a way into feature films. While listening to a lite FM radio station, Haynes happened upon The Carpenters' song "Yesterday Once More." He began to recall the early 1970s, an era Haynes considered the last time of true American innocence. He resolved to make a film about the life and eventual death of Karen Carpenter from anorexia. Haynes recalled an episode of *The Mickey Mouse Club* that featured a Barbie doll in a promotional film. It struck him that this icon of bodily perfection was being forced upon young children, and he decided to cast his film exclusively with Barbie dolls. Haynes released the forty-three-minute short film *Superstar: The Karen Carpenter Story* in 1987 to immediate acclaim and controversy. After successful bookings and enthusiastic reviews, the film won the award for Best Experimental Short at the USA Film Festival. In October 1989, A&M Records, The Carpenters' former label, filed a cease and desist order against Haynes, citing his use of unapproved copyrighted music in the film as reason to halt further distribution. *Superstar* was pulled from release and has not been screened theatrically since.

In 1991 Haynes again courted controversy with his first feature, *Poison*, a blend of three distinct and interwoven stories written by Haynes. The film's distinguishing characteristic, as with all of Haynes's work, is its visual style. Each of the three stories, termed by writer Chuck Stephens as "body fluid–drenched tales of transgression and punishment," is presented in a different way. The first, *Hero*, about a homicidal young boy, was shot in the style of a television news report, complete with booming narration. *Horror*, which tells the story of a doctor who has isolated the human sex drive into a liquid, is shot in an appropriately kitschy **B-movie** tone. *Homo*, inspired by the prison writings of Jean Genet, appears alternately colorful and bleak as it tells the story of a gay prisoner's love affair with a fellow prisoner. *Poison*'s $250,000 budget was partially funded by the **National Endowment for the Arts** at a time when it was under constant conservative attack. The American Family Association, led by the fanatical Reverend Donald Wildmon, condemned the film as pornography based on a misleading review in *Variety*. But it hardly mattered. *Poison* won the **Sundance** Film Festival's Grand Prize Award before David Ehrenstein, film critic for *The Advocate*, wrote, "*Poison* is the most important gay American film since *Mala Noche*," referring to **Gus Van Sant**'s debut film.

In 1995, Haynes broke new ground again with the ultraminimalist *Safe*, a response to New Age healing in which he used his largest budget ($1 million) and first recognizable star (Julianne Moore). The film is set in the 1980s and follows a housewife and mother (Moore) who falls victim to what is known as "environmental sickness," an illness caused by the presence of certain fumes. Inspired by **Stanley Kubrick's** *2001: A Space Odyssey*, *Safe* is presented mostly in ultrawide shots with very few close-ups so as to focus on the environment surrounding her. In addition to the visual element, Haynes added a unique aural quality to the film in the form of a low buzz heard on the soundtrack. The film polarized **critics** and audiences, but *Time* magazine critic Richard Corliss spoke for the majority when he called the film "scarily confident and beautifully acted.... It will also seize any viewer who dares to surrender to its spell."

In 1998 Haynes released *Velvet Goldmine*, an ode to the glam rock days of David Bowie and T. Rex, set in 1970s-era London. The film won Haynes a rarely given award for Best Artistic Contribution at the 1998 Cannes Film Festival. *See also* National Endowment for the Arts; queer cinema

BIBLIOGRAPHY

Gross, Larry. "Antibodies." *Film Comment* (Summer 1995): 76-81.
Stephens, Chuck. "Gentlemen Prefer Haynes." *Film Comment* (July–August 1995): 2-3.
Wyatt, Justin. "Cinematic/Sexual Transgression." *Film Quarterly* (Spring 1993).

Hecht, Harold. Producer. *b.* June 1, 1907, New York City. *d.* May 26, 1985, Beverly Hills, California. In the 1930s Harold Hecht was a dance director and applied his trade to the Marx Brothers vehicle *Horse Feathers* (1932) and *She Done Him Wrong* (1933) with Mae West and Cary Grant. Later Hecht made the pilgrimage from New York to California and put up a shingle as a Hollywood agent. During this time he discovered actor **Burt Lancaster**, which changed the lives and careers of both men. In 1947 Hecht and Lancaster formed Norma Productions, an independent film production company, part of a new movement breaking away from the Hollywood studio factory approach to film production. In 1952, the Hecht-Lancaster Company was formed and released productions through **United Artists**. Later they were joined by James Hill and changed their name to the Hecht-Hill-Lancaster Company. The final evolution of the indie force dissolved in the early 1960s. Hecht continued as a solo producer until his death in 1985. His producing credits include *Apache*, *Vera Cruz* (both 1954), *The Kentuckian*, *Marty* (both 1955), *Run Silent, Run Deep* (1958), *The Devil's Disciple* (1959), *The Young Savages* (1961), *Taras Bulba* (1962), and *Cat Ballou* (1965). *See also* Lancaster, Burt

Hecht-Hill-Lancaster Company. *See* Hecht, Harold; Lancaster, Burt

Hell, Richard. Poet, actor, musician. *b.* Richard Meyers, October 2, 1949, Lexington, Kentucky. With spiky hair and ripped clothes, Richard Hell helped create the archetypal punk fashion style and is credited with inventing the defining term, Blank Generation. Hell was the singer and bass player of Neon Boys that evolved into the seminal punk band Television. He was also the singer and bass player for The Heartbreakers with Johnny Thunders and the former lead singer for the self-named Richard Hell and the Voidoids. Hell became involved in the **punk cinema** scene when he appeared in *Blank Generation* (1979), directed by Ulli Lommel. He played Eric in **Susan Seidelman's** directorial debut *Smithereens* (1982), the first major film to examine the punk social phenomenon. Hell played The Rawhide Kid in **Nick Zedd's** *Geek Maggot Bingo* (1983). His most prominent film role was as Madonna's boyfriend in Seidelman's *Desperately Seeking Susan* in 1985. Hell retired from the music scene in 1996 to concentrate on writing. He is the author of the novel *Go Now*.

Hellman, Monte. Director, editor. *b.* July 12, 1932, Greenpoint, New York. *ed.* Stanford, University College of Los Angeles. Monte Hellman is the director of the existential cult Westerns *Ride in the Whirlwind* (1965), starring screenwriter and coproducer Jack Nicholson and Cameron Mitchell, and *The Shooting*, starring Nicholson, Warren Oates, Will Hutchins, and Millie Perkins, released in 1967, but shot back-to-back. Hellman is virtually unknown in the United States but ranks with **John Cassavetes** in auteur worship by no less an authority than *Cahier du Cinema*.

Hellman's reputation rests largely on *Two-Lane Blacktop* (1971), a much-anticipated **road movie** in its time. Hellman had the perfect package, a screenplay by Rudy Wurlitzer, Zen Master of 1960s and 1970s cool, and a cast that featured the popular Warren Oates and rock stars James Taylor and Dennis Wilson, drummer of the Beach Boys. A working film editor who had cut **Roger Corman's** *The Wild Angels* (1966), Hellman's directorial work included *Beast from Haunted Cave* (1959), *Back Door to Hell* (1964), and *Flight to Fury* (1966). He was given free rein on *Two-Lane Blacktop*. Hellman explained his directorial methods to journalists observing that work as an editor taught him to cover every scene thoroughly on location to avoid problems in the cutting room. He reportedly shot many dialogue scenes by setting the camera and shooting as many takes as necessary to get what he wanted. He then moved the camera 15 degrees to the right and repeated the process until the imaginary 360-degree circle enclosing the actors was completely covered. The audience expected action and an overload of sex, drugs, and rock 'n' roll, but the film Hellman made played poorly for two weeks in its initial 1971 release and then vanished. The characters were named The Driver, The Mechanic, The Girl, and GTO. Hellman applied the existential philosophy of the Westerns to the hardtop road. There was no traditional action—the two young men drive and race, but the result is meaningless, aimless, and disenfranchised characters. The pace is deliberate and slow; many scenes (including those shot from all possible angles) were played in a single long take with little, if any, interscene editing. Hellman was thrown off the A-list and never recovered. Thirty years later *Two-Lane Blacktop* was rediscovered, and the revisionist view positions it as a significant film of the 1970s.

After *Two-Lane Blacktop*'s failure and with his stature diminished, Hellman found himself down and out. He began directing a Hammer production of the Kung Fu film *Call Him Mr. Shatter* (1974) in the United Kingdom but was replaced by Michael Carreras. Also in 1974, Hellman directed *Cockfighter* starring Warren Oates. The film about the illegal world of cockfighting has been seen by a handful of Hellman loyalists but has yet to qualify for official cult status. Later Hellman took over for two feature directors who died during filming, Tom Gries on *The Greatest* (1977) and Mark Robson on *Avalanche Express* (1979). In 1978 the mythical western *China 9, Liberty 37* was released to little attention and no box office. In 1988 Hellman directed *Iguana* in Spain about a misfit seaman who gets revenge on society by holding castaways hostage. The action/horror/drama confused the distributor and video stores who didn't know how to categorize it. The year 1989 saw the release of *Silent Night, Deadly Night III: Better Watch Out*, the second remake of the Christmas horror franchise that Hellman directed because he needed a paycheck.

Over the years Hellman has used his editing skills to stay afloat financially. He edited Sam Peckinpah's *The Killer Elite* (1975) and was uncredited on *Harry and Walter Go to New York* (1976), directed by Mark Rydell. Hellman is another definition of the independent filmmaker, revered by critics and cult fans, his work largely unseen by the masses. Hellman has a reputation and legend bigger than the maverick filmmaker's reality.

Henenlotter, Frank. Director. *b.* 1950, Lyndbrook, Long Island, New York. Frank Henenlotter is a horror movie specialist who found his calling as a child raised on Forty-Second Street fare. As a teen Henenlotter began to make sleazy **8mm** and **16mm films.** His short *Slash of the Knife* played with the notorious **John Waters** film *Pink Flamingos* (1972) at **midnight movie** screenings in New York City. An East Coast independent, who shoots on the streets of New York City at every opportunity he can afford, Henenlotter was thirty-one years old when he caused a sensation with *Basket Case* (1982). The creepy and twisted story followed the adventures of a twin and his mutant brother carried in a basket. It was shot for $35,000 with a total cost after postproduction of $150,000 to $160,000. After the success of *Basket Case*, Henenlotter didn't make a film for six years. He was offered many genre projects that he rejected out of hand. It was the 1980s and producers clamored for **slasher films.**

For the release of *Brain Damage* (1988), Henenlotter acquired a deal memo from Embassy pictures that liked the script. The story, that Henenlotter describes as *The Tingler* (1959) meets *The Trip* (1967), concerned a man who has a monster parasite that injects fluid into his brain and causes a psychedelic altering of his mind. Elmer, the killer slug, was voiced by an uncredited John Zachele, the legendary vampire television horror host and rock 'n' roll disc jockey. The Coca-Cola Company acquired *Brain Damage*, then sold the film to The Cinema Group, who wanted to get a fast rating from the MPAA and get it to the marketplace. They cut the film for an R, but after four submissions and many imposed deletions, *Brain Damage* still received an X rating.

In 1990 Henenlotter directed *Frankenhooker*, an outrageous horror/comedy about a mad scientist desperate for body parts to complete a severed head he keeps on ice. His solution is to sell mega-crack to Forty-second Street hookers. When ingested it causes them to explode, thus supplying all the organs he needs. The film went beyond the standard offenses piled on by slasher genre fare and also received an X rating. Henenlotter could only get a greenlight to produce *Frankenhooker* by agreeing to *Basket Case* 2 and 3 (1990, 1992), thereby creating a successful **franchise** for the distributor. Eventually Henenlotter decided to make low-budget **direct-to-video** and **direct-to-cable** horror films to avoid the struggles he'd encountered. Henenlotter continues to protest, with much merit, the argument that the MPAA has a double standard for sex and nudity over graphic horror violence. *See also* direct-to-video; direct-to-cable

Henkel, Kim. Screenwriter, director. Kim Henkel has been associated with two disparate filmmakers, horror specialist **Tobe Hooper** and Texas lowdown auteur **Eagle Pennell**. Henkel's screenplay created the characters and outrageous violent mayhem of *The Texas Chainsaw Massacre* (1974). Henkel is also the writer, producer, and director of *The Return of the Texas Chainsaw Massacre* (1994). Henkel also wrote *Eaten Alive* (1976) for Tobe Hooper; scripted, edited, and acted in Pennell's *Last Night at the Alamo* (1983); and wrote *Doc's Full Service* (1994). *See also* Pennell, Eagle

Herz, Michael. *See* Troma Studios

Hickenlooper, George. Director, author. *b.* May 25, 1965, St. Louis, Missouri. *ed.* Yale, B.A., Film Studies. In 1988 two years after graduating Yale, George Hickenlooper directed the short film *Newark Needs Insurance*. He wrote on film subjects for *Billboard*, *L.A. Style*, and *Cineaste*. In 1991, Hickenlooper published *Reel Conversations: Candid Interviews with*

Film's Foremost Directors and Critics, which contains interviews with indies and American new wavers including Peter Bogdanovich, **John Carpenter**, Michael Cimino, **Dennis Hopper, Martin Scorsese, John Sayles,** and Oliver Stone.

Hickenlooper has directed a series of **documentaries** on filmmakers including *Art, Acting and the Suicide Chair: Dennis Hopper* (1988), *Picture This: The Times of Peter Bogdanovich in Archer City, Texas* (1991), and *Monte Hellman: American Auteur* (1997). His best-known movie documentary is *Hearts of Darkness: A Filmmaker's Apocalypse* (1991), the harrowing making of *Apocalypse Now* codirected with Fax Bahr. *Some Folks Call It a Sling Blade* is a 1993 short directed by Hickenlooper that became the basis for the landmark indie film *Sling Blade* (1996). In 1997 Hickenlooper directed *Dogtown*, a fictional film about a beauty queen and her truck-driving boyfriend. In 1999 a cineaste's dream came true, when Hickenlooper directed the Orson Welles screenplay *The Big Brass Ring* for the Showtime cable network, merging his love for the movies with the work of one of its greatest mavericks. *The Man from Elysian Field* and *The Mayor of Sunset Strip* (both 2001) and 2.2. are recent directorial efforts from George Hickenlooper.

Hirsch, Charles (Chuck). Producer, writer. *b.* December 1942, New York. Chuck Hirsch made several short films before he came to the realization he was an efficient producer and a so-so director. He entered the film industry as a booker and theater manager. Hirsch founded the Huntington Hartford Film Center at the Gallery of Modern Art with filmmaker **Jim McBride.** They were fired after six months because their eclectic programming choices weren't bringing in enough patrons. Hirsch was manager and booker for the Garrick Cinema revival house and in January 1967 became director of new talent for **Universal Studio's Young Filmmaker's Program.** The position was created to subsidize the making of short films by young filmmakers. Hirsch discovered seven or eight promising talents, but the studio didn't support them. At twenty-six, Hirsch was disillusioned with Universal's attitude towards young filmmakers.

At Universal he met **Brian De Palma,** who had completed two feature films. He convinced De Palma to move on from the dead-end studio route. They began to write personal projects together on Universal's dime. De Palma had gotten paid for a treatment about a mass murder—the seed money motivated him to go independent. Working with De Palma, Hirsch produced *Greetings* (1968), *The Wedding Party* (1969), and *Hi, Mom!* (1970). Hirsch directed *Utterly Without Redeeming Social Value* (1969), which he cowrote with **Paul Bartel** who starred in the comedy that featured the tag line "It was group sex . . . therapy!" and was edited by Hirsch's wife at the time, **Tina Hirsch.** In 1975 Chuck Hirsch was an associate producer of *The Money*, codirected by Rodney Amateaur and Chuck Workman; the drama follows a businessman whose children become the target of an unemployed man who identifies them as a ticket to his personal wealth. Hirsch was also chairman of the School of Visual Arts film department for a time during the 1980s. *See also* Bartel, Paul; De Palma, Brian; Hirsch, Paul; Hirsch, Tina; McBride, Jim

Hirsch, Paul. Editor. Brother of producer **Chuck Hirsch** and most widely known as **Brian De Palma**'s longtime editor and member of the Oscar-winning postproduction team on *Star Wars* (1977), Paul Hirsch began with De Palma on *Hi, Mom!* (1970) and became a devoted collaborator editing *Sisters* (1973), *Phantom of the Paradise* (1974), *Obsession, Carrie* (both 1976), *The Fury* (1978), *Blow Out* (1981), *Raising Cain* (1992), *Mission Impossible* (1996), and *Mission to Mars* (2000). Other independent filmmaking editorial credits include *Creepshow* (1982), *Footloose* (1984), the **John Hughes** productions *Ferris Bueller's Day Off* (1986) and *Planes, Trains & Automobiles* (1987), *Steel Magnolias* (1989), and *Coupe de Ville* (1990). In 1999 Paul Hirsch edited *Lake Placid* and then once again collaborated with De Palma on *Mission to Mars* (2000). *See also* De Palma, Brian; Hirsch, Chuck

Hirsch, Tina. Editor. The first female president of the American Cinema Editors (ACE), an editor on the award-winning television series *The West Wing*, Tina Hirsch began cutting low-budget feature films for **Roger Corman**. She edited **Paul Bartel**'s *Death Race 2000* (1974) and Ron Howard's directorial debut *Eat My Dust!* (1976). Other indies edited by Hirsch include *Macon County Line* and *Big Bad Mama* (both 1974). Her collaborations with **Joe Dante** include his episode for *Twilight Zone: The Movie* (1983), *Gremlins* (1984), and *Explorers* (1985). In 1998 Tina Hirsch edited the miniseries *A Will of Their Own*.

Hollywood Film Institute, The. *See* Simens, Dov S-S

Honeymoon Killers, The. *See* Kastle, Leonard; Scorsese, Martin

Hooper, Tobe. Director. *b.* January 25, 1943, Austin, Texas. Horror specialist Tobe Hooper began his career directing **documentaries, industrials**, and commercials in his native Texas. Later Hooper was appointed assistant director of film programming at the University of Texas where he continued making films with assistance from his students. In 1974, Tobe Hooper made his fictional feature debut with ***The Texas Chainsaw Massacre***, a low-budget cult classic that developed a reputation as the defining **splatter film** of the era and spawned two sequels, a video game and its greatest recognition—an onslaught of imitators. The landmark

The results of terror and gore from *The Texas Chain Saw Massacre* (1974), directed by Tobe Hooper. Courtesy of *The Del Valle Archive*

film pushed the envelope with unthinkable violence, gore, bones, sex, and that chainsaw. Although challenged by some connected to the ragtag production made up of friends, recent graduates, and young performers, director Hooper claims the story came to him one Christmas season while he waited in frustration in line in the hardware section of a department store. He was pondering how to get out of his situation when his eyes fell upon the chainsaw rack. Lurid fantasy took over, and Hooper and friend **Kim Henkel** wrote the screenplay in two or three weeks. The budget of around $140,000 was raised through private investors. Henkel's sister invested $1,000, and the largest amount came from Texas legislator Bill Parsley. The story was borrowed from the Brothers Grimm and serial murderer Ed Gein, whose notorious deeds had already been mined for *Psycho* (1960). Working titles for the project included *Leatherface, Head Cheese*, and *Scum of the Earth*.

The story followed five teenagers en route via van to visit a grandfather's grave that had been ritualistically desecrated. They pick up and quickly get rid of a sinister hitchhiker and are plunged into a nightmare when they arrive at the residence now inhabited by a family of cannibals armed with a chainsaw, cutlery, and sledgehammers. The film was shot in five weeks over a six-week period. Cameras were taken from the University of Texas during the summer when the film school was closed. The unknown cast featured carpenter, Gunnar Hansen, a veteran of college productions who was cast as Leatherface, the murderous chainsaw-wielding human monster. The Texas heat averaged 95 to 100 degrees during production. Scenes taking place inside the van were unbearably uncomfortable and produced performances of real physical discomfort and emotion. Hooper and Henkel constantly revised the screenplay during the shooting. The dictatorial Hooper was often impatient with his cinematographer, at times grabbing the camera and shooting scenes himself.

Real bones and carcasses from dead dogs and cats and even a human skeleton were procured for the gore effects. Every member of the cast was injured as some point. Actress Teri McMinn was hung on a meat hook with an unsafe, homemade rig that caused her great pain. Another actress was accidentally injected with formaldehyde when an exhausted crew member was preserving the dead animals and shot the needle through the deceased animal and into the actress's body. Another actor was hit with a crowbar on camera protected only by the foam rubber that lined the blunt instrument. The production could only afford one chainsaw. It was in disrepair and ripped into wood inches from the actors, who were pelted with splinters. The final day of shooting lasted twenty-seven hours and ended with the crew burning the animal carcasses in a gasoline fire to dispose of the remains. Actor John Larroquette was engaged to speak to narrate in a Wellesian oratory.

The Texas Chainsaw Massacre was screened for distributors, and both AIP and Bryanston, who also owned **Deep Throat**, were interested. Bryanston picked up the film for around $280,000; investors were paid back and actually made a profit. The distributor proved to be less than honorable in paying dividends, while the film grossed over $20 million. A lawsuit settled out of court for $400,000, but none of the money was ever returned to the participants.

General audiences were disgusted by the film, but the subculture of gore and splatter fans were obsessed with *The Texas Chainsaw Massacre*, finding it horrifically funny entertainment in the post-Manson age. A **franchise** was created following the original with *The Texas Chainsaw Massacre 2* (1986), *Leatherface: Texas Chainsaw Massacre III* (1990), and *The Return of the Texas Chainsaw Massacre* (1994). Hooper directed *Eaten Alive* (1976) featuring Neville Brand, Mel Ferrer, Carolyn Jones, and Stuart Whitman in a twisted horror film about a man who feeds guests of his hotel to his pet alligator. In 1979 Hooper had the bad luck of being replaced on *The Dark* (1979) by director John Cardos. In 1981 Hooper directed the theatrical feature *The Funhouse*, a low-budget horror flick that didn't live up to the expectations of his fans.

Then it happened; actually, it happened once before on *The Thing* (1951), produced by Howard Hawks with direction credited to Christian Nyby. No one believed Nyby, a minor figure, could have created the sci-fi classic. Historians later discovered Hawks was on the set influencing the making of the film with his advice. In 1982 *Poltergeist,* a megahit commercial horror film, gained enormous attention. The producer was Steven Spielberg, and the direction was credited to Tobe Hooper. No one believed the man who made the raw bargain basement *The Texas Chainsaw Massacre* could have directed the slick, Spielbergian, very commercial *Poltergeist.* Then reports Spielberg was often on the set giving his director "advice" appeared. In 1986 Hooper directed a remake of *Invaders from Mars* and several forgettable horror films and currently concentrates his career in television. In 1995 Hooper directed *The Mangler* and in 2000 *Crocodile.* Recently he has worked extensively in episodic television on *The Others* (2000), *Night Visions* (2001) and the miniseries *Taken* (2002). *See also* Henkel, Kim

Hope, Ted. *See* Good Machine

Hopper, Dennis. Actor, director. *b.* May 17, 1936, Dodge City, Kansas. In 1969 Dennis Hopper made independent film history as the director of *Easy Rider.* The **biker film** with lofty intentions burst the narrative, aesthetic, content, and moral rules of old Hollywood wide open, launched Jack Nicholson to superstardom, and put Hopper and his producer/costar **Peter Fonda** at the top of the New Hollywood heap. The low-budget counterculture film about two hippies out to discover America after a big cocaine score was a box office smash. It opened the youth market with sex, drugs, and real rock 'n' roll on the soundtrack and began a new era in film soundtracks. After *Easy Rider,* Hopper moved to Taos, Mexico. The drugging, boozing, and carousing that began on *Easy Rider* reached out-of-control proportions.

His next project, *The Last Movie* (1971), almost ended Hopper's career as a director and destroyed the momentum and power base gathered with *Easy Rider. The Last Movie* was released by Universal, and few had a clue as to what was going on in Taos as Hopper's ego and excess ran rampant. The story followed a stunt actor played by Hopper working on a Hollywood western shot on location in Mexico. When the crew leaves, the Mexicans shoot their own movie using a camera and lights made out of bamboo. *The Last Movie* is a daring autobiographical experiment contrasting the thin line between existence and movie reality. The narrative structure, as edited by Hopper, is convoluted, confused, and layered with "scene missing" cards and other **self-referential** devices to blur the viewer's perceptions of fiction and the illusion of the filmmaking process. When Hopper proudly returned from the Venice Film Festival

Dennis Hopper as Billy with sixties hat and mustache laying down a rap, "man," in *Easy Rider* (1969). Courtesy of The Del Valle Archive

clutching an award for his film, he was devastated to learn the domestic reviews were horrific. Audiences left the theater angry, feeling cheated. Hopper didn't give them *Easy Rider: Part II. The Last Movie* died quickly.

Eight years later Hopper got another opportunity to direct with *Out of the Blue* (1980). Hopper plays an ex-biker, Linda Mantz, his daughter, Sharon Farrell, her junkie mother. The depressing, meandering drama received some critical attention but little in box office returns. Eight more years went by before *Colors* (1989) was released, starring Sean Penn and Robert Duvall as street cops assigned to the LA gang detail. The distributor deleted seven minutes from Hopper's director's cut. The project was edgy, but more coherent and professional than the previous two films.

In 1989, *Catchfire* was released in Europe; Hopper disowned it and removed his name from the credits when the producers reedited his cut. In 1991 Hopper's version titled *Backtrack*, which was eighteen minutes longer, was released on cable television and video. The impressive cast included Hopper, Jodie Foster, Dean Stockwell, Vincent Price, John Turturro, Fred Ward, Charlie Sheen, Joe Pesci, and Bob Dylan. The story, set in the art world, tracked a hit man that falls in love with his target. In 1990, Hopper finally got positive critical and audience attention for his neo-noir *The Hot Spot* featuring Don Johnson and Jennifer Connelly. The film was stylish, entertaining, and narratively sound. Hopper had cleaned up, gotten off drugs and alcohol, settled down, began watching a lot of pro football, and even became a Newt Gingrich Republican. Hopper got embroiled in legal disputes with Peter Fonda concerning ownership of *Easy Rider* and desperately tried to claim credit for his contribution on the film during those drug-induced days. In 1994 Hopper directed the disappointing comedy *Chasers* with Tom Berenger, Crispin Glover, Gary Busey, Frederic Forrest, and Marilu Henner about two navy men escorting a prisoner who turns out to be a gorgeous babe.

Dennis Hopper cannot be easily dismissed as a 1960s burnout or a counterculture Judas who sold out. A portrait of his life reveals a complex man deeply committed to the arts. His work as an actor began in the mid-1950s. Hopper appeared in many classic television westerns and dramatic series and has appeared in over 125 feature films including *Rebel without a Cause* (1955), where he became friends with James Dean, an actor who had an indelible influence on him. Other Hollywood roles prior to *Easy Rider* include *Giant* (1956), *Gunfight at the O.K. Corral* (1957), *From Hell to Texas* (1958), *Night Tide* (1961), *The Sons of Katie Elder* (1965), *Hang 'em High* (1967), *Cool Hand Luke* (1967), and *True Grit* (1969). Hopper was exposed to low-budget independent counterculture filmmaking on *The Glory Stompers* (1967), *Head* (1968), and *The Trip* (1967), which influenced his transition from New York TV actor to rebellious studio contract player to let-it-all-hang-out hippie thesbian.

Hopper has been a longtime art collector and friend of **Andy Warhol** and other late-twentieth-century artists and **experimental** filmmakers. After *Easy Rider* Hopper floundered with directing projects but managed to give outstanding, if quirky, performances in *Tracks* (1976), directed by **Henry Jaglom**, Wim Wenders's *The American Friend* (1977), and **Francis Ford Coppola**'s *Apocalypse Now* (1979). In the 1980s Hopper made a major comeback as an actor in *The Osterman Weekend* (1983) for Sam Peckinpah; *Rumble Fish* (1983) for Coppola; *Blue Velvet* (1986), directed by **David Lynch**; *Hoosiers* (1986); and *River's Edge* (1987), directed by **Tim Hunter**. Hopper was clean and sober and revisited his distinctive method-based, iconoclastic acting style steeped in Strasberg, Brando, and Dean. Throughout the 1990s Hopper worked regularly as an actor, well accepted back in the fold by the film community and audiences. Dennis Hopper continues to work steadily as an actor in films that include: *Unspeakable* (2001), *Firecracker*, and *The Piano Player* (both 2002).

BIBLIOGRAPHY

Rodriguez, Elena. *Dennis Hopper: A Madness to His Method.* New York: St. Martin's Press, 1988.

Hudlin, Reginald. Director, producer, writer. *b.* December 15, 1961, East St. Louis, Missouri. *ed.* Harvard University. Industrious younger brother of filmmaker **Warrington Hudlin**, Reginald Hudlin exhibited a distinct comic flair as writer/director of the enormously popular hip-hop comedy *House Party* (1990) that began as a student thesis project at Harvard. *Boomerang* followed in 1992 and was a commercially successful romantic comedy starring Eddie Murphy. His brother and their production company produced both films. Hudlin wrote *Bebe's Kids* (1992), credited as the first African American animated feature film, on which he also served as a coexecutive producer. In 1996 he directed *The Great White Hype*, which featured a soundtrack released on the newly formed Hudlin Bros.Record./Iepic Soundtrax label. Hudlin handpicks his projects and while continuing to direct movies has expanded into music videos and children's television programs. In 1996 Reginald Hudlin directed *The Great White Hype*. Recent credits include producing *Ride* (1998), directing *Saturday Night Live's* Tim Meadows in *The Ladies Man* (2000), and *Serving Sam* (2002), which he also directed. *See also* Hudlin, Warrington

Hudlin, Warrington. Director, producer. *b.* 1953, East St. Louis, Illinois. *ed.* Yale University. Older brother of filmmaker **Reginald Hudlin**. Warrington Hudlin is the cofounder of the **Black Filmmakers Foundation**. Hudlin collaborated with his brother as producer on the immensely popular *House Party* (1990) and *Boomerang* (1992), both directed by Reginald. Warrington Hudlin is a pioneering black filmmaker who began his career as a documentarian as the director of *Black at Yale* (1974) and *Streetcorner Stories* (1977). Hudlin has provided valuable support to independent black filmmakers by showcasing their work at the annual Acapulco Black Film Festival, of which he is executive director. Warrington Hudlin was the screenwriter and executive producer of *Bebe's Kids* (1992), and co-produced *Ride* (1998) with his brother Reginald. *See also* Hudlin, Reginald

Hughes, Albert and Allen. Directors, screenwriters. *b.* April 1, 1972, Detroit, Michigan. These African American fraternal twin brothers began making music videos when they were twelve years old, already rabid movie fans from watching every behind-the-scenes program they could. Their prestigious talents emerged growing up in Pomona, California. The boys repeatedly petitioned their mother to rent a video camera. The patient and supportive woman took her sons to town and rented a magic box for them for a twenty-four-hour period. Albert and Allen took the rental time period literally, not sleeping so they could shoot video for the complete duration of the agreement. They made a movie outside their home. After shooting each take, they took out the video cassette and ran back inside, shoved it into their VCR so they could see what they had done, and flew back out to reshoot or find another exciting visual way to tell a story. Later working on **Super 8mm** film they made *The Drive-By*, a short film about urban street life.

The brothers were highly motivated to make movies and music videos. They became friends with music video director Tamra Davis, who was about to direct her feature debut *Guncrazy* (1992). Davis screened *The Drive-By* for her director of photography **Lisa Rinzler**. The women had worked before on rap videos. Rinzler was so impressed with the short she asked to meet the moving image prodigies and offered to shoot their next film for free. Some time passed, Albert attended film school, and the brothers collaborated with Tyger Williams on a script for their directorial debut *Menace II Society* (1993). When New Line greenlighted the project, Albert and Allen remembered Rinzler. They originally thought the rising star cinematographer was kidding, but when they talked again, Rinzler agreed to photograph the film. *Menace II Society*, made before their twentieth birthday, starred Tyrin Turner, Larenz Tate, Jana Pinkett, Samuel L. Jackson, and Charles Dutton in a harrowing, realistic story of the violent urban life in LA's Watts district. The story rings with **documentary** truth; the visual style is raw and unrelenting, as the camera is an active participant in expressing the dire circumstances of the inhabitants of a world without hope. The film received laudatory reviews and instant recognition for the new talents. The brothers were candid about their admiration for **Martin Scorsese** and Oliver Stone as well as the secret to their working method. Albert, the spokesman for the team, worked with Rinzler and on the technical aspects. Allen, the quieter of the two, but an equal voice in their vision, worked with the actors.

Their highly anticipated sophomore effort *Dead Presidents* (1995), also photographed by Rinzler, starred Larenz Tate, Keith David, Chris Tucker, and N'Bushe Wright in an epic and violent odyssey of a young man from his urban neighborhood to Vietnam, then to a life of desolation and crime. The film was a quantum challenge for the Hughes brothers in narrative, characterization, and cinematic techniques. Reviews criticized the film that premiered at the New York Film Festival, generally feeling the brothers had overreached.

Box office was tepid, but the Hughes brothers built up their production company and branched out to rap music and video projects. Their dream project, a biopic of Jimi Hendrix starring Lawrence Fishburne, didn't get out of developmental hell. Next the Hughes brothers moved to nonfiction filmmaking, striking a deal with HBO cable to make a documentary on pimps. HBO reneged, and the Hughes made their own film on the subject. The brothers plunged on with Albert as director of photography. The result, *American Pimp* (1999), featured interviews with black male procurers intercut with clips from **blaxploitation** films and music by Isaac Hayes and Marvin Gaye. It explored the life and iconography of this urban underground profession. In 2001 they released *From Hell*, a new take on the Jack the Ripper legend with Johnny Depp and Heather Graham. The Hughes brothers are major talents; they are filmmakers who happen to be black. They have explored the urban landscape they know, but their ambition and enormous talent can take them wherever they want to go.

BIBLIOGRAPHY

LoBrutto, Vincent. "Three Moods Prevail in *Dead Presidents*." *American Cinematographer* 76.9 (September 1995): 58–66.

Hughes, John. Screenwriter, producer, director. *b.* February 18, 1950, Lansing, Michigan. *ed.* University of Arizona. John Hughes dropped out of college in junior year, married, and worked as an advertising copywriter. He developed as a writer, creating short stories, articles, novels, and material for stand-up comics. In 1979, Hughes became an editor for *National Lampoon* magazine and early in the decade was screenwriter on their movie projects *National Lampoon's Class Reunion* (1982) and *National Lampoon's Summer Vacation* (1983). In 1984 Hughes wrote and directed *Sixteen Candles*, a major box office hit aimed at the teen market, starring their instant queen, Molly Ringwald.

In 1985 Hughes made a multipicture deal with Paramount that allowed him to produce films for his own independent John Hughes Company. Working out of Chicago, Hughes dominated the 1980s, becoming a teenflick mogul with *The Breakfast Club* (1985), the defining teen angst film of the decade, *Weird Science* (1985), *Ferris Bueller's Day Off* (1986), *Pretty in Pink* (1986), which he produced and wrote, *Some Kind of Wonderful* (1987), *The Great Outdoors* (1988), and *Uncle Buck* (1989). In 1988 Hughes Entertainment became part of Universal.

After a tremendously successful decade, Hughes climbed to greater popular success as writer and producer of *Home Alone* (1990), making a star out of young Macaulay Culkin that led to two sequels, *Home Alone 2: Lost in New York* (1992) and *Home Alone 3* (1997). John Hughes became a one-man family entertainment conglomerate, concentrating on writing and producing films that include *Beethoven* (1992), *Beethoven's 2nd* (1993), *Dennis the Menace* (1993), *Miracle on 34th Street* (1994), *101 Dalmatians* (1996), and *Flubber* (1997).

After the 1991 hit *Curly Sue*, Hughes wrote and produced *The Chambermaid* (2003), directed by **Wayne Wang**, a present-day Cinderella story set in Chicago starring Sandra Bullock and Hillary Swank. In content and style Hughes is a commercial filmmaker whose goal is to entertain and create product geared for substantial financial returns. His independence and artistic control as a producer and the larger and rarer feat of creative freedom as a writer and director make him a unique figure in the industry.

Hunter, Tim. Director, screenwriter. Hunter first gained prominence in 1982 with the release of *Tex* that starred Matt Dillon, Emilio Estevez, and

Molly Ringwald and Michael Schoeffling in *Sixteen Candles* (1984), directed by John Hughes. Kobol Collection/Universal

Meg Tilly. The low-budget Disney film was the first S.E. Hinton novel to make it to the screen (**Francis Ford Coppola**'s productions of *The Outsiders* [1983] and *Rumble Fish* [1983] followed). The understated drama tells the story of a boy trying to raise his brother after their mother has died and father has left. *Tex* premiered at the New York Film Festival. Next, Hunter directed *Sylvester* (1985), a girl and her horse story with Melissa Gilbert, Richard Farnsworth, Arliss Howard, and Constance Towers.

River's Edge (1987) was a breakthrough for Hunter. The edgy teen film explored the dark side of disaffected youth and a senseless murder of a young girl. The recurring image of the dead girl's pale, naked body had a chilling effect portraying the teens as dehumanized and emotionless. The true life story was well acted by Keanu Reeves, Ione Skye, Roxanna Zal, Leo Rossi, and effectively crazed performances by Crispin Glover and **Dennis Hopper.** Hunter's next film *Paint it Black* (1989), with Rick Rossovich, Sally Kirkland, and Martin Landau, is a thriller that was never released theatrically.

Hunter didn't work in features for four years and turned to television. In 1993 he got the opportunity to direct *The Saint of Fort Washington* starring Matt Dillon and Danny Glover in a portrait of a New York City homeless man. The film was barely released, receiving little support from the distributor. Hunter returned to television and has not made another theatrical feature. Hunter's work in television includes the TV movies: *Mean Streak* (1999), *Anatomy of a Hate Crime* (2000), and *Video Voyeur: The Susan Wilson Story* (2001). In episodic television he has directed on the *Soul Food* series in 2000. His sensitive and, at times, disturbing films are the result of a director committed to quiet human stories and not over-blown Hollywood melodrama. Box office rules in the film marketplace. In the case of Hunter, that reality denies the audience quality dramas and in its place are more remakes, **franchises**, star vehicles, mindless action films, and superficial teen fare.

Hurd, Gale Anne. Producer. *b.* October, 25, 1955, Los Angeles. *ed.* Stanford University, Phi Beta Kappa. Gale Anne Hurd is an active member of the Hollywood Women's Political Committee. The American Film Institute offers a grant in her name to encourage female directors. Hurd, the producer of blockbusters *The Terminator* (1984), *Aliens* (1986), *The Abyss* (1989), *Terminator 2: Judgment Day* (1991), and *Armageddon* (1998) has her roots in the independent, low-budget film community. Upon graduation Hurd was hired as executive assistant to **Roger Corman**, president of New World Pictures. She was a production assistant on *Humanoids from the Deep* and *Alligator* and assistant production manager on *Battle beyond the Stars*, all released in 1980. In 1982 Hurd formed her own independent film company, Pacific Western Productions. Recent producing credits for Gale Anne Hurd include: *Armageddon* (1998), *Clockstoppers* (2002), and *The Hulk* (2000). The characters she helped create along with James Cameron for the terminator movies will appear again in *Terminator 3: Rise of the Machines* (2003), for which Arnold Schwartznegger is reportedly receiving thirty million dollars, a figure that could produce at least thirty independent films. Hurd's training in the Corman trenches taught her the movie business. She may have chosen to play with the power brokers, but her support of young women filmmakers succeeds in bringing new talent into all walks of cinematic life.

Hurwitz, Harry. Director, screenwriter, producer. *b.* January 27, 1938, New York City. *d.* September 21, 1995, Los Angeles, California. Harry Hurwitz wrote, produced, and edited *The Projectionist* (1971), an independent, **self-referential** comedy about the movie-driven fantasy life of a lonely projectionist poignantly portrayed by Chuck McCann. The projectionist works in a local movie theater, harassed by a mean manager played to the hilt by Rodney Dangerfield, and lives an uneventful, drab existence. Caught up in the world of movies, the projectionist transforms himself into the superhero Captain Flash in vivid fantasies that fill his days. The captain is a nice-guy hero who protects the world from evil personified by The Bat played by Dangerfield and an army of Nazis visualized with World War II stock footage. The world of silent movie serials allowed the talented McCann to showcase his adroit sense of physical comedy and impressions honed from his many years as the host of a popular children's show on which he displayed his own reverence for the Golden Age of filmmaking, especially his beloved Laurel and Hardy. *The Projectionist* didn't find an audience in its initial release. While **American New Wave** filmmakers were examining contemporary American life, Hurwitz was looking back, alienating the youth market that was revitalizing the film industry. *The Projectionist* was not a traditional comedy; Hurwitz was exploring a lonely, insignificant man encased in pop culture. *The Projectionist* steadily has become a cult film especially embraced by cineastes and filmmakers.

In 1972 Hurwitz codirected *Richard* with Lorees Yerby, featuring Hollywood veterans John Carradine, Paul Ford, Kevin McCarthy, and Mickey Rooney. Hurwitz wrote and directed a documentary homage to his idol **Charlie Chaplin**, *Chaplinesque: My Life and Hard Times* (1972), narrated by Gloria Swanson. *Fairy Tales* (1978) was a soft porn/comedy/musical about a prince who searches for the one woman who sexually excites him—the princess Sleeping Beauty. For *Auditions* (1978), Hurwitz used a pseudonym Harry Tampa. Next Hurwitz directed *Nocturna*, aka *Granddaughter of Dracula* (1979), a disco comedy horror film with John Carradine as Dracula, Yvonne De Carlo as Jugula, and the exotic, but talentless, Nai Bonet who played Scherezade in *Fairy Tales*. Bonet cowrote the script and plays the title vamp. Legendary performance artist Brother Theodore does his usual bizarre turn. The plot concerns the count turning his castle into a disco when tax troubles arrive.

Safari 3000 (1982) follows an ex-Hollywood stuntman up against a multitude of adversaries in an international race. It stars Hamilton Camp, David Carradine, Stockard Channing, and horror legend Christopher Lee. The 1982 comedy *The Comeback Trail* is about a Grade Z movie czar who features an old cowboy star to salvage his studio. The typically Hurwitzian bizarre cast includes Chuck McCann, Buster Crabbe, Ina Balin, Henny Youngman, Professor Irwin Corey, Hugh Heffner, Joe Franklin, and Monti Rock III. **Roy Frumkes**, who worked with Hurwitz on *The Projectionist*, wrote the screenplay for the seventy-six-minute feature. *The Rosebud Beach Hotel* (1984) is a bargain basement sex comedy about a resort hotel with hookers as bell girls. The eclectic cast featured Colleen Camp, Hamilton Camp, Fran Drescher, Chuck McCann, and Peter Scolari. *That's Adequate* (1989) is a mockumentary about a fictional movie studio featuring Hurwitz's oddest cast yet: Ina Balin, screenwriter Marshall Brickman, James Coco, Professor Irwin Corey, Susan Dey, Robert Downey Jr. as Albert Einstein, Joe Franklin, Chuck McCann, Anne Meara, Tony Randall, Peter Riegert, Rita Rudner, Jerry Stiller, Renee Taylor, and Bruce Willis and the comedian Sinbad as themselves, another

Brother Theodore happening, Robert Townsend, and the distinguished Robert Vaughn as Adolf Hitler. Hurwitz's last film, *Fleshtone* (1994), was a change in direction, an unknown cast in a complex plot concerning the murder of a painter's phone-sex partner.

Hurwitz was an independent filmmaker with a passion for old movies and aging movie stars. His major theme was the ever-blurring line between reality and fantasy. In the clutter of a career filled with just trying to survive, Hurwitz's *The Projectionist* will sustain its integrity and wait patiently for rediscovery. *See also* Frumkes, Roy

Hurwitz, Leo. Filmmaker. *b.* June 23, 1909, Brooklyn, New York. *d.* January 18, 1991. *ed.* Harvard University. American **documentary** filmmaker who began his career in the early 1930s. In 1937, Hurwitz participated in the Film and Photo League. That same year he was cofounder of Pioneer Films, the first U.S. company to independently produce documentaries. Hurwitz collaborated with the most important documentarians of his time: **Pare Lorentz, Willard Van Dyke, Ralph Steiner,** and **Paul Strand.** During World War II, Hurwitz made nonfiction films for the American Office of War and the British Information Service. He was also a producer, director, and chief of news and special events in the early days of the CBS television network. In 1948, Hurwitz created the documentary *Strange Victory,* which explored postwar racism in America. The film was branded left wing by a government obsessed with red-baiting. Throughout the 1950s and into the early 1960s Hurwitz was blacklisted for his political and social views.

Hurwitz continued to work as an independent. He contributed to the landmark television series *Omnibus* without credit because of his blacklisted status. In 1961 Hurwitz's *Verdict for Tomorrow,* a television documentary, examined the Adolf Eichman Nazi war crime trial. From 1969 to 1974 Hurwitz was a professor of film and chairman of the New York University Graduate Institute of Film and Television. In 1980, Hurwitz filmed *Dialogue with a Woman Departed,* a four-hour visual poem to Peggy Larson, his second wife, who died in 1971. Some of the landmark documentaries benefiting from Hurwitz's participation are: *The Plow That Broke the Plains* (1936), *Native Land* (1942), *Scottsboro* (1934), *Heart of Spain* (1937), *The Museum and the Fury* (1956), and *Here at Water's Edge* (1960).

Hurwitz, Tom. Cinematographer. Tom, the son of **documentary** pioneer **Leo Hurwitz,** has photographed many important nonfiction films including *Harlan County U.S.A.* (1976) and *American Dream* (1990) for **Barbara Kopple,** both winners of the Oscar for Best Feature Documentary. He also shot *The Weavers: Wasn't That a Time* (1982); *Down and Out in America* (1986), directed by **Lee Grant,** also an Oscar winner; and *The Source* (1999), Chuck Workman's documentary on **Jack Kerouac** and the

Beat Generation. In fiction Hurwitz was lighting director on *Between the Lines* (1977), directed by **Joan Micklin Silver,** and *Enormous Changes at the Last Minute* (1983), directed by Mirra Bank with a screenplay by **John Sayles.** Hurwitz was the director of photography on the horror feature *Creepshow 2* (1987) and continues to be in demand as a documentary cameraman. Recent non-fiction cinematography credits for Tom Hurwitz include: *The Turandot Project* (2000), *My Generation* (2000), **Barbara Kopple'**s documentary about the Woodstock concerts, and the television documentary *Middle School Confessions* (2001).

Independent Feature Film Market (IFFM). *See* Independent Feature Project (IFP)

Independent Feature Project (IFP). In 1979 Sandra Schulberg curated a sidebar at the New York Film Festival called American Independents where classic and new independent features were screened. *Passing Through* (1977) by **Larry Clark, Warrington Hudlin'**s *Streetcorner Stories* (1977), and **Martha Coolidge'**s *Not a Pretty Picture* (1975) were among the selections. Out of American Independents grew the Independent Feature Project. The IFP now has over 10,000 members and sponsors many programs. The Resource Consultants Program members meet with industry experts and hold networking sessions, quarterly gatherings of filmmakers and industry members. The Producer's POV Workshop is held monthly. An industry expert offers fifteen-minute consultations with IFP members over a two-hour session. The Legal Consultants Workshop offers legal advice to members. Music in Film Roundtable brings composers and filmmakers together. The IFP Market Conference Marathon is seven days of workshops on indie distribution, international sales, financing, digital distribution, and film music. The Independent Producers Series presents information on financing and distributing films under $3 million and how to work with agents and managers. The IFP expanded into branches in New York, Los Angeles, Chicago, Miami, and Minneapolis. IFP West, a nonprofit organization, was founded by a group of LA filmmakers in 1980 to serve the needs of the West Coast indie. Their mission is to provide education in producing, financing, and screenwriting and to promote filmmakers by showcasing films seeking distribution. They run screenwriting and directing labs; Independent Focus presents film directors such as **John Waters, David Lynch, Richard Link-**

later, Michael Moore, and Wes Craven talking to members about their work.

Festival Buzz presents the best of the LA Film Festival circuit. Preview Screenings show new indies before they are released. The Cinema Lounge screens shorts, works in progress, trailers, and music videos. The Independent Producers Series, sponsored by Kodak, FotoKem Film and Video, and the Screen Actors Guild, introduces the major elements of producing indie films. Master Workshops focus on publicity, the Panavision Camera, producer's reps, **Super 16mm**, blocking actors, composition, self-distribution, and the ins and outs of film festivals. The Resident Line Producers Program offers consults and conferences on screenwriting, film music, and financing. The IFP has a newsletter, a store, job bank, and classifieds.

This premiere venue for emerging indies draws in buyers worldwide to screen features, documentaries, works in progress, and screenplays. A sampling of films that found distributors at the Independent Feature Film Market (IFFM) includes *Return of the Secaucus 7* (1980), *My Dinner with André* (1981), *El Norte* (1983), *Blood Simple* (1984), *Sherman's March* (1986), *Down By Law* (1986), *Paris Is Burning* (1990), *Roger & Me* (1989), *Slacker* (1991), *Clerks* (1994), *The Brothers McMullen* (1995), *Welcome to the Dollhouse* (1995), and *Star Maps* (1997). The IFP West also sponsors the annual Independent Spirit Awards that started at a North Hollywood restaurant and now is a seaside event televised on the Bravo cable network. Held each year on Oscar weekend, this alternative award ceremony celebrates the best of independent cinema. The IFP has grown considerably over the last twenty years and is a well-supported organization that insures the independent spirit will remain vital and survive the mega industry of commercial filmmaking.

Independent Film Channel. Cable television channel dedicated to presentation and support of independent films. Managed and operated by Bravo Networks, it is commercial free, 24/7, and uncut. The advisory board is made up of **Martin Scorsese, Robert Altman,** Tim Robbins, **Joel and Ethan Coen, Martha Coolidge, Jim Jarmusch, Spike Lee, Steven Soderberg,** Ed Saxon and Jodie Foster. The Independent Film Channel (IFC) also sponsors support programs including a $10,000 cash award to a student filmmaker to produce their next film.

independent producer. An individual producer or production company not connected to a major studio. Since 1971 independent producers have been responsible for more than 50 percent of the films created in the United States. Not all get a theatrical release; not all make a profit. There are some independent producers who enter into contractual relationships with major studios to provide financing for their projects.

independent production. A motion picture project not financed by a major studio. As independent films become more profitable, major studios often finance a producer's overhead and have created boutique companies under their corporate umbrella.

independent production company. A company that produces motion pictures without an association to a major studio providing preproduction, production, and postproduction services. Indie production companies may at times contract with a major studio for partial financing, assistance, or distribution.

Independent Spirit Awards. *See* Independent Feature Project (IFP)

industrial films. Films commissioned by corporations, businesses, and organizations to inform, educate, and promote their concerns. Industrials, as they are known, are produced by independent production companies and filmmakers for in-house or personal use of the client. Industrials are often narrated and project the point of view determined by the customer.

International Documentary Association. The International Documentary Association (IDA) is a nonprofit organization founded in 1982 to raise public consciousness of the importance of nonfiction films. With an office in Los Angeles, the IDA has over 2,500 members in fifty countries. The governing board includes documentarian **Frederick Wiseman**, Michael Rabiger, and Steven Poster. The board of trustees includes cable network A&E, Kodak, David L. Wolper, HBO, and The Discovery Channel. Members include producers, directors, writers, editors, camera operators, musicians, researchers, technicians, journalists, broadcast and cable TV executives, academics distributors, and interested members of the general public. The IDA publishes a monthly international **documentary** magazine, a survival guide, a list of funding and grant resources without deadlines, and a guide to fiscal sponsorship.

Since 1997 the IDA has supported Doctober, a weeklong documentary showcase for domestic and international productions. They offer The David L. Wolper Student Documentary Award and support the Kodak project, Access Grant Program. The mission of the cultural/educational arm of the IDA is to spread the importance of film, video, and interactive media in a free society and to encourage understanding throughout the world. The IDA runs screenings, is an advocacy group speaking out on government regulations, marketing, and distribution practices, runs workshops and seminars, supports DocuDay honoring the Academy

Awards, and is a fiscal sponsor that enables members to apply for nonprofit status grants and tax-deductible donations for nonfiction projects. They also have a credit union and offer health benefits.

Ivory, James. *See* Merchant-Ivory Productions

J

Jackness, Andrew. Production designer. Trained as a theater designer, Andrew Jackness designed many Broadway, Off-Broadway, regional, and opera productions. In 1990, Jackness made the transition to designing for film on *Longtime Companion.* He continued the collaboration with the director **Norman René** on *Prelude to a Kiss* (1992) and *Reckless* (1995). Jackness also has a long relationship designing directorial projects for actor Stanley Tucci. They include *Big Night* (1996), *The Impostors* (1998), and *Joe Gould's Secret* (2000). Jackness was production designer on *In the Gloaming* (1997), directed by Christopher Reeve, and two films for director John Madden, *Ethan Frome* (1993) and *Golden Gate* (1994). Jackness demonstrates that low-budget independent films with short schedules and limited resources can enjoy a production design that enhances the director's vision of a project. Working simultaneously on stage and film production design, Jackness brings artistic discipline, literary intelligence, craft, the fine hand of the artist, a wealth of pictorial and historic research, a sharp visual eye, the tradition of the theater, and the understanding that stories and characters count to every film he designs. *See also* René, Norman

Jacobs, Ken. Experimental filmmaker. *b.* May 25, 1933, Brooklyn, New York. A pioneer **experimental** filmmaker for over forty years, his landmark film *Tom, Tom, the Piper's Son* (1969, revised 1971) took a silent black-and-white **Biograph** Studios film made in 1905 and analyzed the image by exploring the temporal space, the grain, and the chemical properties within it. With this 115-minute **16mm film,** Jacobs created an understanding of the nature, properties, and possibilities of film in a way no theorist had achieved in print or lecture. Jacobs's early films were often collaborations with **Jack Smith,** work that in **Andy Warhol** and

John Waters's time would have been identified as trash cinema. The gender-bending preperformance art, melodramatic shenanigans filmed in Lower Manhattan include *Saturday Afternoon Blood Sacrifice* (1964), *Star Spangled to Death* (incomplete 1958–1960), and *Blonde Cobra*, screened in many different versions from 1958 to 1963. In 1963 Jacobs, his wife Florence, and **Jonas Mekas** were arrested for a public screening they organized of Jack Smith's *Flaming Creatures*, a legal battle that helped end New York State's intolerable censorship laws. In 1996, Jacobs established **The Millennium** Film Workshop at St. Mark's Church in Washington Square, where he held Friday-night open screenings that led to the discovery of many new talents in experimental filmmaking.

In 1969, Jacobs began to teach at the State University of New York at Binghamton. Along with Larry Gottheim, he turned the school into a force for cutting-edge filmmaking that inspired a generation of students, many of whom have made their own impact including Alan Berliner and Jim Hoberman. His students were responsible for creating The **Collective for Living Cinema** in opposition to Jonas Mekas and **Anthology Film Archives.** Since the early 1970s, Jacobs has evolved new cinematic terrain from found filmstrips in presentations he called "The Nervous System." They involve two 16mm analytic projectors that can run film forward or back at 1, 2, 4, 6, 8, 12, 16, and 24 frames per second with a propeller spinning in front of the lens to create 3D and other visual effects. Among Jacobs's over fifty films are *Little Stabs at Happiness* (1960), *Soft Rain* (1968), and *The Impossible* (1979–1980). Recent films by Ken Jacobs include the short film *Opening the Nineteenth Century: 1886* (1990). Jacobs continues to explore unmined possibilities even as digiheads claim the medium is dead. *See also* Collective for Living Cinema; Millennium, The; Smith, Jack

Jaglom, Henry. Director, screenwriter, editor, actor. *b.* January 26, 1941, London. *ed.* University of Pennsylvania, Actor's Studio. Jaglom's first feature, *A Safe Place* (1971), was a **BBS** production, but few saw it even though it starred Jack Nicholson, Orson Welles, and Tuesday Weld. Jaglom is not interested in commercial viability; his is a cinema of narcissism and self-discovery, exploring facets of his own life that helped define the Me Decade of the 1970s. Jaglom is a filmmaker in love with the sound of his own voice, both on screen as an actor essentially playing himself and as an inner voice presenting characters, often female, pontificating on his favorite subjects: relationships and love, usually in trouble or lost. Jaglom began as an actor appearing in Off-Broadway plays and on the popular television shows *Gidget* and *The Flying Nun.* In the late 1960s and early 1970s Jaglom buddied with **American New wavers Dennis Hopper, Peter Fonda,** Jack Nicholson, and their patron saint Orson Welles.

Jaglom performed in a series of cutting-edge films: *Psych-out* (1968), which also featured his debut as a screenwriter; Nicholson's *Drive, He Said* (1971); and Welles's last and still unseen film as a director, *The Other Side of the Wind* (1972). *A Safe Place* was engineered to launch Jaglom into movie brat generation firmament—it did not. The story of a spaced-out young woman who is stuck in a dream world where she remains forever young was so filled with disjointed narrative techniques that audiences stayed away.

Like **John Cassavetes**, Jaglom's films defy classical Hollywood conventions. *Tracks* (1976) starred Dennis Hopper as a Vietnam soldier bringing back fallen comrades on a long train ride home. The narrative is told through his shell-shocked point of view, making *Tracks* an anomaly in antiwar cinema. *Sitting Ducks* (1980) featured Jaglom's brother Michael Emil and Zack Norman as a syndicate accountant and womanizer. Patrice Townsend, then married to Jaglom, is a babe they pick up. An American New Wave comedy, *Sitting Ducks* is a twisted Hope/Crosby **road movie** run through a post-hippie sensibility and the jump-cut mill. *Can She Bake a Cherry Pie?* (1983) featured Michael Emil and Karen Black as an unbalanced neurotic woman whose husband has left her; she takes up with a nonstop babbling and rambling man. It is a tedious and distracting film that further emphasizes Jaglom's compulsion to probe the female consciousness. *Always* (1985) is a stream-of-consciousness self-indulgent essay on three marriages; Jaglom and his then-ex-wife Patrice Townsend play one couple. The film received critical attention, and the core of Jaglom aficionados grew. In *Someone to Love* (1987), Jaglom plays Danny, a filmmaker looking for love. Orson Welles is featured in a touching and fitting last screen appearance as a sage with insights from a life of love and love lost. (Jaglom was devoted to Welles and spent years nursing the aging enfant terrible, trying to get him work and recognition.) The film alternates as a self-indulgent exercise and an opportunity to explore the truth about the need to love and be loved. In *New Year's Day* (1989), Jaglom plays a writer trying to reclaim his New York City apartment who is confronted by three women who have sublet it. This situation is an excuse for another talk marathon on relationships and sex.

During *Eating* (1990), a group of women at a birthday party sit and discuss food and life. In *Venice/Venice* (1992), Jaglom satirized himself, playing a maverick filmmaker attending the Venice Film Festival where he falls in love with a beautiful French journalist. The title refers to the other Venice in California—where the director also has an entourage of admirers who see him as a visionary and original artist. *Babyfever* (1994) is a companion to *Eating*, where career women at a baby shower in Malibu talk, incessantly, about their ticking biological clocks. Jaglom's usual quasi **cinéma vérité** approach makes the film simultaneously real, exasperating, boring, and insightful. *Last Summer in the Hamptons* (1995) is about an insecure movie star who summers in trendy East Hampton, Long Island, and gets embroiled with friends, lovers, and colleagues in another Jaglom talk fest about jealousy and feelings. Jaglom, a functioning neurotic, is driven to psychoanalyze his small piece of the world using film and his roving analyst's couch. His films are pretentious and unbearable for those outside Jaglom's influence. In 1997 Jaglom released *Déjà Vu*, a romance between an American woman abroad, played by his wife and co-scenarist Victoria Foyt, and a London painter who continue to have a cosmic confirmation they should be together. Henry Jaglom's most recent films are *Festival in Cannes*, and *Shopping* (both 2002).

Jaglom has total control of his idiosyncratic films including self-distribution. His work is not readily accessible to general audiences in style, content, or even availability in theaters or home entertainment. Jaglom is stubborn and self-involved, but his work is adventurous and sincerely attempts to probe the current human condition. The truth lies within the endless talk of his characters. Even though Jaglom is independently wealthy, he has funded his work as an independent filmmaker for over thirty years on income generated by his production company.

Jarmusch, Jim. Director, producer, actor, editor. *b.* January 22, 1953, Akron, Ohio. *ed.* Columbia University, New York University. When Jim Jarmusch graduated from Columbia University and left for Paris, he intended to stay only a few months. Once there, however, he discovered the famed Cinematheque Française and began to see the work of Robert Bresson, Yasujiro Ozu, and Carl Dreyer, transcendental filmmakers who all had a profound impact on his work. In 1976, one year after arriving in Paris, Jarmusch returned to the United States and entered the New York University graduate film program, where he became a teacher's assistant to **Nicholas Ray** and later made his thesis film, *Permanent Vacation* (1980). Once out of school, Jarmusch made his first feature, *Stranger Than Paradise* (1984), about two losers and a teenage Hungarian immigrant who travel across America. The film, which he described to a writer for the *New York Native* as "a semi-realistic comedy in the style of an imaginary Eastern European film director obsessed with Ozu and familiar with the Honeymooners," announced the arrival of a major new talent. Japanese influences are evident in his use of wide, static shots extending throughout entire scenes, photographed by future director **Tom DiCillo.** As with all of Jarmusch's early films, there is an emphasis on dialogue but not on "acting," reminding many of two of his heroes, Dreyer and Bresson. This deadpan approach became Jarmusch's trademark and distinguished him from other directors arriving in the early 1980s. Made on a budget of $125,000, part of which was donated by filmmaker **Paul Bartel,** *Stranger Than Paradise* was an instant success. The film won Jarmusch the coveted Camera d'Or for best first film at the

Jim Jarmusch directing *Dead Man* (1995). Kobol Collection/12-Gauge Productions/Pandora

1984 Cannes Film Festival and the National Society of Film Critics award for best film of the year (1986).

Given $1 million by Island Pictures for his next film, Jarmusch made *Down By Law* (1986), photographed in black and white by Robby Muller and starring Italian comedian Roberto Benigni and Jarmusch stalwart Tom Waits. The film follows three escaped prisoners through the Louisiana swamps. *Down By Law* is the second in a trilogy of Jarmusch films on the American landscape. It won a best artistic achievement award at the 1986 Cannes Film Festival. The final picture in the trilogy was *Mystery Train* (1989), an ambitious film set in Memphis composed of three interwoven stories. It was Jarmusch's third straight success and caused *New York Times* writer Vincent Canby to call Jarmusch "the most adventurous and arresting filmmaker to surface in the American cinema in this decade."

Continuing to experiment with a multiple story form, Jarmusch made *Night on Earth* (1991). With a budget of $3.5 million, Jarmusch increased the number of stories he told to five, each taking place in a different city on the same night. The film follows five taxi cab drivers in five different cities (New York, Los Angeles, Paris, Rome, and Helsinki) as they cruise the streets picking up fares. It was Jarmusch's most difficult shoot, and he did not direct another feature film until *Dead Man*, released in 1996, which starred Johnny Depp. The existential western follows a man named William Blake (not the poet) as he evades the law. This was Jarmusch's first critical flop, though it has ardent admirers. Following *Dead Man*, Jarmusch directed a music video for one of his music heroes, Neil Young. Young liked Jarmusch's style so much that the musician asked the director to follow his band, Crazy Horse, on a European tour. The result was Jarmusch's first **documentary,** *Year of the Horse* (1997), which, he tells the audience, was "proudly shot in **Super-8.**" Jarmusch's ability to remain commercially viable in the independent film world without sacrificing his European film sensibility has made him a role model in the independent film community and has allowed him to form a unique body of work. The year 1999 saw the release of *Ghost Dog: The Way of the Samurai* where martial arts and Zen meet *Goodfellas* and *The Sopranos*. In 2002, Jarmusch contributed to *Ten Minutes Older* a compilation film with short films by Bernardo Bertolucci, Jean-Luc Godard, Werner Herzog, Spike Lee, Wim Wenders and others. An independent's independent, Jim Jarmusch owns the negatives to the majority of his work.

Jazz on a Summer's Day. This 1959 **documentary** of the 1958 Newport Jazz Festival, directed by Bert Stern, written by Albert D'Annibale and Arnold Perl, and edited by **Aram Avakian,** is a landmark concert film that influenced *Monterey Pop* (1969) and *Woodstock* (1970). The musicians performing that year are a who's who of modern jazz. They include Thelonius Monk, Sonny Stitt, Dinah Washington, Gerry Mulligan, Chico Hamilton, Louis Armstrong, Jack Teagarden, Bob Brookmeyer, Art Farmer, and Philly Joe Jones. The color documentary broke ground by intercutting the musical performances with images of the audience experiencing peace and leisure and the America's Cup Race. Concentrating equally on the music and the audience's joyful interaction, *Jazz on a Summer's Day* presents an optimistic America enjoying a postwar boom. Bert Stern was a member of the **New American Cinema Group,** and his film was celebrated by **Jonas Mekas** and the New York **underground** film community. In 1960, *Jazz on a Summer's Day* opened at New York City's Fifth Avenue Cinema, where it was enjoyed as a new documentary genre—a concert film that makes the viewer part of the experience.

Jhabvala, Ruth Prawer. *See* Merchant-Ivory Productions

Jodorowsky, Alejandro. Director, screenwriter, actor, comic book creator. *b.* February 7, 1930, Iquique, Chile. The man known as El Topo, Alejandro Jodorowsky is a quintessential independent film artist who answers to no commercial force, only his own mix of mysticism, violence, myth, and pre–New Age spirituality. The flamboyant and ultra-egocentrical Jodorowsky studied the art of pantomime with its greatest practitioner, Marcel Marceau, in Paris. In the early 1950s Jodorowsky made a mime performance film, *The Severed Head,* believed to be lost.

In the 1960s Jodorowsky became a prolific theater writer and director exploring **avant-garde** regions, creating **experimental** performance art pieces. He wrote books and created a long-running comic strip *Fabulas Panicas.* Jodorowsky made a pilgrimage to Mexico, attracted by the culture of native mysticism and consciousness-altering experiences. Jodorowsky directed *Fando y Lis* (1967), then masterminded and created *El Topo* (1970), one of the first **midnight movies** drawing hordes of disciples to its bloody, mystical cinematic journey. Although **critics** dismissed *El Topo* as a pretentious self-indulgent mishmash, Jodorowsky became a legend with just one film release. Loyal followers waited for three years until *The Holy Mountain* arrived in 1973. Jodorowsky apostles weren't disappointed, though the critics and general audiences were bewildered. *The Holy Mountain* follows a Christlike figure who moves through surreal, spiritual, and sacrilegious situations. A mystic introduces him to six individuals who represent a planet in our solar system. They all seek the Holy Mountain to unseat the Gods who preside there and achieve immortality. The film didn't achieve the success of *El Topo,* and Jodorowsky abandoned his production company, Producciones Panicas, and announced he was withdrawing from filmmaking.

In 1978 Jodorowsky returned to the cinema with *Tusk,* a French-language film concerning an English girl and an elephant born on the same day. The film quickly disappeared. In the mid-1970s Jodorowsky contracted to adapt Frank Herbert's science fiction classic novel *Dune.* The production was to star his son Brontis, Orson Welles, fellow surrealist Salvador Dali, and legendary screen star Gloria Swanson. Jodorowsky's screenplay would have produced a twelve- to sixteen-hour film. It was no surprise when backers pulled out financing in 1976. In 1989, *Santa Sangre* was released. The film concerned a young man in a mental institution. Flashbacks reveal the boy and his family were circus performers. He witnessed his father sever the arms of his mother, leader of the heretical church of Santa Sangre, which translates as Holy Blood. The father then commits suicide. The man escapes the institution and rejoins his mother. She forces him to become her arms as they seek murder and revenge. The film delighted Jodorowsky's followers, but critics continued to ridicule him. His work received limited release, and many of the films were drastically altered before release.

In 1990 *The Rainbow Thief* was released. Jodorowsky directed a cast that included Peter O'Toole, Omar Sharif, and Christopher Lee in the story of a low-level crook searching for the mythical pot of gold. The fable involves the crook's dream to cash in by befriending a prince who lives underground and is heir to a fortune. Even Jodorowsky's cult agreed with critics on this one. The film was a **straight-to-video** release. Currently Jodorowsky is planning a new project with a screenplay by **Roy Frumkes.** Jodorowsky is also the writer and director of *Abelcain* (2002), featuring the infamous Marilyn Manson.

Jones, Amy Holden. Screenwriter, director, editor, producer. *b.* September 17, 1953, Philadelphia. In 1975 Amy Holden Jones won top prize at the American Film Institute's National Film Student Film Festival. One of the judges, **Martin Scorsese,** offered Jones an assistant position on his next film, *Taxi Driver* (1976). He also introduced Jones to **Roger Corman,** a man always interested in young talent for his New World Pictures **B-movie** studio. Jones went to work for New World as an editor on *Hollywood Boulevard* (1976), directed by **Joe Dante** and Allan Arkush. She also edited *Corvette Summer* (1978), directed by Mathew Robbins, and Hal Ashby's troubled *Second-Hand Hearts* (1981). Jones worked as Martin Scorsese's editor on *American Boy: A Profile of Steven Prince* (1978), a **documentary** portrait of his friend who worked in the music business and played the fast-talking gun runner in *Taxi Driver.*

Jones made her directorial debut with *Slumber Party Massacre* (1982) from a screenplay by lesbian novelist Rita Mae Brown. The project began when Jones invested $1,000 in a seven-minute segment of the first seven pages of the proposed horror film. Jones shot on **short ends** with UCLA students as actors and a crew of four and edited on Joe Dante's Moviola at New World where he was editing *The Howling* (1980). Jones put music to the short, and Dante showed it to Corman. Jones asked for $250,000, but the ever-frugal Corman offered her $10,000 to direct the film in 35mm in six weeks for a budget of $500,000 to $600,000. Corman financed the completion for *Slumber Party Massacre.* The low-budget **exploitation film** is true to its title. The combination of sex and violence scored once again. The film was popular at **drive-ins** and local theaters, with enough success to spawn two sequels directed by two other female directors.

As a screenwriter Jones made her debut with her second directorial outing *Love Letters* (1983). The film starred Jamie Lee Curtis, James Keach, Amy Madigan, Bud Cort, and Sally Kirkland. Corman offered Jamie Lee Curtis $25,000 at a time she was netting a million dollars a film as the teen scream queen of *Halloween* (1978) and *Prom Night* (1980). Actually, Meg Tilly was Jones's first choice, but her agent wanted $30,000, and Corman stood pat. The story, which established Jones's potential as a director who could honestly probe the inner life of female lead characters, dramatized a young woman who uncovers her deceased mother's love letters to her lover. The experience moves her to get romantically involved with a married man. Curtis's sensitive portrayal and Jones's abilities were well received by **critics.** The film attracted an audience, but was no blockbuster or career lynchpin. Next, Jones wrote and directed *Maid to Order* (1987) starring Ally Sheedy, Beverly D'Angelo, Michael Ontkean, Valerie Perrine, Dick Shawn, and Tom Skerritt. The film is a comic fairy tale about a rich girl forced to work as a maid for a Malibu couple.

Jones hit indie gold with the screenplay for *Mystic Pizza* (1988), directed by Daniel Petrie and a cast that featured Julia Roberts in a career-launching role, Lili Taylor, Conchita Ferrell, and a young Matt Damon. The story of the romantic desires of three women working in a pizzeria located in Mystic, Connecticut, was an indie sleeper that attracted a large female audience. Jones wrote another low-budget box office hit *Beethoven* (1992), directed by Brian Levant, about a family and their St. Bernard. A sequel *Beethoven's 2nd* (1993) and a **direct-to-video** return followed. In 1997 Holden-Jones was the screenwriter of *The Relic*. She continues to write for the *Beethoven* franchise. *Beethoven's 3rd* was released in 2000, followed by *Beethoven's 4th* in 2001.

Jost, Jon. Filmmaker. *b.* May 16, 1943. The early life of Jon Jost, an **experimental** filmmaker who came to prominence in the early 1970s, reads like a textbook definition of Aquarian baby-boomer radicalism. Although the majority of his generation practiced more chic than radical action, Jost was the real thing. Jost was born into a strict military family, part of the occupation troops stationed in Japan, Germany, and Italy.

Not only didn't he follow tradition; he slammed up against it. In 1963, Jost was expelled from college and taught himself filmmaking. When he refused to comply with registration at his local draft board, Jost was arrested for resistance and served two years in federal prison. In 1968, Jost, as a member of the militant filmmaking cooperative **Newsreel**, was in the center of the confrontation in the streets outside Chicago's Democratic Party Convention. He documented the clash on **16mm** film. Again Jost was arrested for crimes against the state for wielding a camera while Mayor Daley's police force beat protesters with billy clubs. Newsreel was composed of two factions, the political and the artistic. Jost, whose passions were somewhere in between, was distrusted by both. Jost grew tired of political demonstrations that were more like a be-in than political commitment.

He left Newsreel, perceiving its activities interfered with his cinematic development. Jost went deeper underground, living with a woman who was a major SDS (Students for a Democratic Society) member who ran in rad circles including the Weather Underground. Jost began talking of assassinations as a political act. Jost and his comrade were armed and ready for the revolutionary cause, but Jost shot film frames instead of bullets to express himself. Jost developed a jaundiced eye for politics and began making films that criticized both the American Right and the New Left.

He made his first film while hitchhiking in Europe. Without funds he lived under a bridge. Jost was taken in by an Italian family and lived in their home for three months. During this time he made a portrait of their twelve-year-old daughter, which he later realized had subconscious sexual overtones. Jost created a film portrait of his first girlfriend in Salzburg, Austria. This time his sexual desires were more overt as the camera observed her naked body. Jost continued to make short films in Europe and Mexico.

Difficult to categorize, Jost is a totally independent film artist doing what he calls A to Z on every project including distribution. A keen observer of trends and technical innovation, Jost has entered the brave new world of electronic cinema but maintains his cynicism concerning capitalism's body politic. Jost has taken on academics, contrasting theory with the science and mechanics of moving imagemaking. His feature films have few critical champions and a loyal audience aboard. Jost's films, honored by a Museum of Modern Art retrospective in 1991, range from essays to neonarratives that confront trained actors with nonactors who make them work harder. *Angel City* (1976) is a narrative, essay/documentary about Los Angeles. *Last Chants for a Slow Dance* (1977) is a straight experimental narrative that contains elements of **structural** film philosophy. *Stage Fright* (1981) was made for German television in which Jost locked actors in a black room for four days to see what would happen.

Jost's films are miracles of no-budget filmmaking. Working outside any organized independent film community, he managed to finish feature films in the 1970s for under $3,000. Jost's most screened film is *All the Vermeers in New York* (1990), about a Wall Streeter who meets a mysterious woman resembling a Vermeer subject at the Metropolitan Museum. Jost uses the narrative thread to explore art, commerce, and the connective politics of the art and financial worlds. Recent films from Jon Jost include: *Frame Up* (1995), *London Brief* (1999), and *Roman Walls* (2000). Jost may be an anarchistic loner and disaffected soul, but he is truly an American phenomenon. He is a stubborn explorer, a tireless adventurer, and a man who fights hypocrisy with his self-taught dedication to the only thing Jost really has besides his cranky self-determination: his work.

juvenile delinquent films, aka J.D. films. Movies about troubled teenagers involved in crime have been around since the 1920s. There were those lovable scalawags the Dead End Kids who became The Bowery Boys, but that was before rock 'n' roll. The prehistory of the J.D. film came in the form of Marlon Brando as Johnny, the biker rebel, in *The Wild One* (1954). The Richard Brooks production of *Blackboard Jungle* exploded onto U.S. screens with Billy Haley's *Rock Around the Clock* (1956), blaring out of the theater speakers. It featured a motley crew of juvenile delinquents

The icon of troubled youth, James Dean from the JD classic, *Rebel Without a Cause* (1955), directed by Nicholas Ray. Courtesy of The Del Valle Archive

who were out of control, angry, and raging against authority. *Rebel without a Cause* (1955), directed by **Nicholas Ray** and starring James Dean, Sal Mineo, and Natalie Wood, is the masterpiece of the genre. Dean's personal and deep-rooted psychological pain communicated alienation to millions of teenagers who were disassociated from their parents' Greatest Generation. Sam Katzman, a low-budget producer known for his uncanny sense for box office gold, quickly pounded out *Teen-Age Crime Wave* (1955) and later cashed in with *Rock Around the Clock*, *Don't Knock the Rock* (1956), and *Calypso Heat Wave* (1957). **American International Pictures** became the studio of choice for J.D. films. Their logo was synonymous with youth culture. Teens flocked to *The Cool and the Crazy* (1958), *Reform School Girl* (1957), and *Hot Rod Girl* (1956). Other J.D. films include *The Delinquents* (1957), *The Explosive Generation* (1961), *High School Hellcats* (1958), *The Hoodlum Priest* (1961), *Hot Rod Gang* (1958), *The Incident* (1967), *This Rebel Breed* (1960), *Riot in Juvenile Prison* (1959), *Riot on Sunset Strip* (1967), *Running Wild* (1955), *Shake, Rattle and Rock* (1956), *Speed Crazy* (1959), *Stakeout on Dope Street* (1958), *Teenage Bad Girl* (1957), *Teenage Rebel* (1956), *Untamed Youth* (1957), *Wild Youth* (1959), *Young and Wild* (1958), and *The Young Savages* (1961).

BIBLIOGRAPHY

McGee, Mark Thomas, and R.J. Robertson. *The J.D. Films: Juvenile Delinquency in the Movies.* Jefferson, NC: McFarland, 1982.

Kalin, Tom. Director, screenwriter, producer. After writing and directing short films and videos and working as a producer of educational films about the AIDS crisis, Tom Kalin cowrote, coproduced, edited, and directed *Swoon* (1992), a benchmark in **queer cinema**. Photographed in a daring camera style in black and white by **Ellen Kuras**, *Swoon* is a revisionist presentation of Chicago's 1924 Leopold and Loeb thrill-kill murder trial. The story of the homicidal homosexual lovers had been filmed twice. In *Rope* (1948), Alfred Hitchcock was more interested in the no-editing challenge he set for himself than in exploring the lives and motivations of the murderous gay men. Richard Fleischer's *Compulsion* (1959) wasn't more than a compelling courtroom drama; the repressive times made it impossible to present the subject of homosexuality directly. *Swoon* is an experimental narrative that enters the underground of gay life in the 1920s and frames Leopold and Loeb's fate within an exploration of the intense homophobia of their times. Kalin was less interested in making a period film than in stating his social/sexual/political views on the treatment of gay men through the paradigm of this historic case. *Swoon* is a film created to instruct and incite, not entertain. *Swoon* is didactic and engineered to provoke its audience into action.

Kalin, who dedicated himself to raising consciousness through queer cinema, formed a partnership with producer **Christine Vachon** to shepherd two important lesbian films. *Go Fish* (1994), directed by Rose Troche, is a lesbian comedy about finding a soul mate. Kalin and Vachon shared director **Mary Harron**'s fascination for Valerine Solanas, a member of SCUM (Society for the Cutting Up of Men) who shot **Andy Warhol** in the 1960s and produced the aptly titled *I Shot Andy Warhol* (1996). In 1996, Kalin's second film produced by Vachon, *Plain Pleasures*, was released and starred Frances McDormand, Will Paton, and Lili Taylor.

Kalin cowrote the screenplay for the 1997 film *Office Killer,* a low-budget horror film, the directorial debut of photographer Cindy Sherman. The plot concerns a magazine proofreader who is downsized into a home office position and discovers murder can cure her loneliness. In 1998 Tom Kalin was the postproduction supervisor for the short film *Tree Shade.* He directed *Plain Pleasures* in 1996. *See also* Kuras, Ellen; queer cinema; Vachon, Christine

Kaplan, Jonathan. Director. *b.* November 25, 1947, Paris, France. *ed.* University of Chicago, New York University. A student of **Martin Scorsese**'s, Jonathan Kaplan graduated from New York University Film School in 1970, the year he won first prize at the National Student Film Festival. At NYU Kaplan had worked on *Street Scenes* (1970), a Scorsese antiwar project, with fellow student Oliver Stone. Kaplan waited by the phone; Hollywood didn't call, but Julie Corman, wife of **Roger Corman,** head of New World Pictures, **B-movie** mogul, did. Scorsese recommended Kaplan to direct *Night Call Nurses* (1972), part of a Corman cycle that came with one of his airtight formulas for box office success—nudity, action, violence, actually not much violence. The tag was "It's always hardest at night for the *Night Call Nurses.*" The nurse series had a sense of social consciousness usually embodied in the character of an ethnic nurse. Corman taught Kaplan to always know whose point of view each scene should be shot from, and the novice director was able to shoot the film in thirteen days. Corman never screened any of the dailies; five days after shooting, Kaplan screened the first cut for his boss. When the screening was over, Corman read his charge thirty specific notes suggesting how to speed up the pace by techniques such as double cutting in two-character dialogue scenes. Some notes were as specific as telling Kaplan where to cut three frames. Kaplan enjoyed the nurturing at New World where Corman created a noncompetitive, familylike atmosphere. Corman's comments were the last notes anyone ever gave him on a film. *Night Call Nurses* was a B-movie hit, breaking the house record in a theater in Chattanooga, Tennessee.

Corman was pleased and hired Kaplan for *The Student Teachers* (1973), a **sexploitation** flick that took place at a school with an alternate and feminist lifestyle curriculum. In 1975 Kaplan directed *White Line Fever* starring Jan-Michael Vincent, Kay Lenz, Slim Pickens, and L.Q. Jones, featuring a trucker who battles corruption with his diesel truck. The low-budget film grossed $35 million. In 1974, Kaplan directed the **blaxploitation** film *Truck Turner* with Isaac Hayes, who also composed the score, as a detective who hunts down bail jumpers. The film was violent and action packed in the Corman tradition. In 1977 Kaplan directed *Mr. Billion* with Terrence Hill, Valerie Perrine, Jackie Gleason, Slim Pickens, and

Chill Willis, a comedy about a mechanic who goes cross country to claim a billion-dollar legacy while fighting off those trying to swindle him.

In 1979 Kaplan was through paying dues with **exploitation.** *Over the Edge* is a disturbing examination of teens in a planned suburban community. The script by **Tim Hunter** and Charlie Haas reveals the drugs, alcohol, and guns that plummet alienated youths into a dead-end lifestyle. The cast included Matt Dillon in his screen debut, Vincent Spano, Lane Smith, Harry Northup, and Ellen Geer. The relentlessly honest film brought attention to its talented director and the truth about disaffected youth in America's suburbs. *Heart Like a Wheel* (1983) was a biopic of racecar driver Shirley Muldowney with Bonnie Bedelia in a spectacular character-probing performance. Kaplan captured the pro-feminist spirit of the project with sensitivity and insight. In 1987, Kaplan directed *Project X,* a serious film exposé of animal testing made on a B-movie budget. Jodie Foster won an Oscar for her role as a rape victim who bravely testifies against her attackers in Kaplan's *The Accused* (1988). *Immediate Family* (1989), featured Glenn Close, James Woods, Mary Stuart Masterson, Kevin Dillon, and Jane Greer in the story of a professional married couple who are introduced to a pregnant teenager by an adoption agency. Again, Kaplan elicited fine performances and deftly handled the serious subject matter.

Love Field (1992) starred Michelle Pfeiffer and Dennis Haysbert in a dramatic and honest portrayal of race relations. *Unlawful Entry* (1992) featured Kurt Russell, Ray Liotta, and Madeline Stowe in a professional and tautly directed urban thriller of a disturbed cop who develops a dangerous fixation on a neighbor's wife. In the 1994 film *Bad Girls,* Kaplan again attempted a feminist statement with the story of prostitutes on the lam after a brothel shooting, but the film failed to find an audience. *Brokedown Palace* (1999) suffered the same fate. Clare Danes and Kate Beckinsdale play high school friends set up by drug smugglers who are locked up in a repressive Thailand prison. Kaplan is also a regular member of the production team for the television series *ER,* directing and producing the popular medical drama. In 1996 Kaplan directed a television movie remake of Truman Capote's *In Cold Blood.* He also has directed for the episodic series *The Court* (2001).

Karlson, Phil. Director. *b.* Philip N. Karlstein, July 2, 1908, Chicago, Illinois. *d.* December 12, 1985. *ed.* Chicago Art Institute, Loyola Marymount University. Before Phil Karlson became a hard-nosed, **B-movie** director, he studied painting and law and he was a prop man, assistant director, first assistant film editor, associate producer, and a director of short subjects. Karlson became a feature director in the early 1940s and spent the decade grinding out B-movie fare. In the 1950s Karlson turned out hardhitting crime dramas that placed him in the good favor of auteurists and cultists. Films like *Kansas City Confidential* (1952), *99 River Street* (1953), *The Phoenix City Story* (1955), *5 Against the House* (1955), and *The Brothers Rico* (1957) nurtured a young **Martin Scorsese** and later influenced crime culture throughout the indie scene in the 1980s and 1990s.

After directing the Dean Martin movies *The Silencers* (1966) and *The Wrecking Crew* (1969) and *Ben* (1972), the sequel to the boy and his rat movie *Willard* (1971), Karlson hit the jackpot. In 1973, Karlson, considered over the hill by the youth audience that drove the film industry economy, made independent film history. *Walking Tall* was the true story of Buford Pusser, a southern lawman who fought corruption by carrying a big stick—literally. The revenge-fueled action movie was bloody, ultraviolent, and totally politically incorrect. Joe Don Baker gave a powerful performance as Pusser, dangerous yet heroic. The film was an instant box office phenomenon. Critics both condemned and hailed *Walking Tall* as a fascist classic in the mode of Sam Peckinpah's *Straw Dogs* (1971) and **Don Siegel**'s *Dirty Harry* (1971). Karlson took his final screen bow with *Framed* (1975), another revenge tale in which Joe Don Baker gets back on corrupt cops who railroaded him into prison. *Walking Tall* became a small, but lucrative, **franchise** with two sequels and a television series as Karlson moved into retirement and independent firmament. *See also Walking Tall*

Kassar, Mario. *See* Carolco Pictures

Kastle, Leonard. Director, screenwriter. *b.* February 11, 1929, New York City. In the late 1960s a young Italian American film director, hungry to advance his feature film career, was hired to direct *The Honeymoon Killers,* based on the true story of Martha Beck, a large-sized nurse, and Raymond Fernandez, a swarthy gigolo who murdered a lonely wealthy woman. The director had a 200-page screenplay and, playing the role of artiste, shot everything in masters with little coverage or change in angle. The producers had a $150,000 budget for the black-and-white film. They told the director they needed close-ups and that the way the novice director was proceeding the film would be four hours long, so they fired him—that director was **Martin Scorsese.** Ultimately, Scorsese was replaced by the film's screenwriter, Leonard Kastle. Warren Steibel, an English teacher at Syracuse University and City College and producer of television's *Firing Line,* was on board as a first-time feature producer. Steibel originally came up with the idea to turn the true-life tale into a film and was supportive of his new director. Kastle studied the court records of Beck and Fernandez's Bronx trial. "The Lonely Heart Murders" trial lasted three months and resulted in a conviction. Beck and Fernandez were given the death penalty and electrocuted at Sing Sing. Kastle's background was steeped in the tradition of classical music as a composer. His work in music poem cycles and operatic narrative was his only related preparation to direct a film. The story of *The Honeymoon Killers* (1970) may be the stuff of opera, but Kastle made a tough, uncompromising realistic film that was ahead of its time. The low-budget, true-crime, gritty drama became an indie classic in the decades that followed. Shirley Stoller and Tony Lo Bianco give chilling and detailed performances. Kastle and his cast shocked the small cadre of viewers who discovered the film.

Kaufman, Boris. Cinematographer. *b.* August 24, 1897, Bialystock, Poland. *d.* June 24, 1980, New York City. *ed.* The Sorbonne. The legendary New York–based cinematographer, known for his painstaking black-and-white cinematography on **Elia Kazan**'s *On the Waterfront* (1954) and **Sidney Lumet**'s directorial debut *Twelve Angry Men* (1957), was the brother of Russian directors Dziga Vertov and Mikhail Kaufman. Boris Kaufman emigrated from Poland to France in 1927. There he became friends with director Jean Vigo and photographed all four of the master filmmaker's works: *À propos de Nice* (1930), *Taris, champion de natation* (1931), *Zéro du conduite* (1933) and *L'Atalante* (1934). In 1942 Kaufman emigrated to the United States where he worked on propaganda documentaries and shorts for the prestigious National Film Board of Canada. After winning the Academy Award for his naturalistic location photography for *On the Waterfront*, Kaufman shot *Patterns* (1956), directed by Fielder Cook. Twilight Zone creator Rod Serling wrote this indictment of abusive corporate power in America.

In 1956, Kaufman worked again with Kazan on Tennessee Williams's *Baby Doll* (1957) and shot *Splendor in the Grass* (1961) in colors that psychologically defined the troubled character portrayed by Natalie Wood. Kaufman collaborated with Sidney Lumet again on *That Kind of Woman* and *The Fugitive Kind* (both 1959), *Long Day's Journey into Night* (1962), *The Pawnbroker* (1965), and *The Group* (1966). In 1966 Kaufman was selected by theater director Alan Schneider to photograph his directorial debut and the only film script written by Samuel Beckett, the experimental *Film* (1968). *Up Tight!* (1968) was a Jules Dassin remake of *The Informer* (1935) with the Irish rebellion replaced by black revolutionaries betrayed by one of their own. Kaufman worked with Martin Ritt on *The Brotherhood* (1968), a Mafia film that explored the conflicts of changing times four years before *The Godfather*.

Kaufman remained in New York working with the best directors the small but vital community had to offer. By all accounts he was a slow, methodical man, painstaking with lighting and camera preparations. His work method was often at odds with the tireless energy of Kazan and Lumet, but their collaborations with Kaufman set the standard for the New York school where art and message were more important than Hollywood efficiency and entertainment. Kaufman was first in a lineage of master New York cinematographers who rewrote the Hollywood cinematographic rules about prettifying back and eye lights, diffusion filters, and violation of source light for glamour over reality. *See also* Kazan, Elia; Lumet, Sidney

Kaufman, Lloyd. *See* Troma Studios

Kazan, Elia. Director. *b.* Elia Kazanjoglou, September 7, 1909, Constantinople. *ed.* Williams College, Yale University Drama Department. One of the most respected stage directors of his time, Elia Kazan mounted legendary productions of *The Skin of Our Teeth, All My Sons, A Streetcar Named Desire,* and Arthur Miller's masterpiece *Death of a Salesman.* His interest in filmmaking dated back to the early 1930s, and he was especially impassioned by the work of Russian filmmakers. In 1934 Kazan worked as an actor in **Ralph Steiner**'s independent short film *Pie in the Sky.* In 1937 Kazan directed the short documentary *The People of the Cumberland,* which concerned the plight of Tennessee miners, photographed by Steiner. Kazan's feature-length **documentary** *It's Up to You* (1941), about food rationing, was made under the auspices of the U.S. Department of Agriculture. Kazan made his Hollywood debut as a feature film director with *A Tree Grows in Brooklyn* (1945). Although much of Kazan's work was made under the Classical Hollywood Studio System, he took on controversial social issues such as anti-Semitism in *Gentleman's Agreement* (1947) and racial politics in *Pinky* (1949).

Kazan's contribution to screen acting has left a lasting mark on American filmmaking. He was the cofounder of the Actor's Studio and responsible for a new kind of film acting based on a search for truth and raw emotion. Kazan's work with Marlon Brando in *On the Waterfront* (1954) and James Dean in *East of Eden* (1955) influenced a generation of actors that came of age in the 1970s including **Robert De Niro**, Meryl Streep, Al Pacino, and Dustin Hoffman. Breaking away from the Hollywood Studio System, Kazan constantly returned to the New York stage and set up Newtown Productions to direct the film *Baby Doll* (1956), written by Tennessee Williams, which broke new ground in exploring raw sexuality on the screen. In 1957 Kazan directed *A Face in the Crowd* (1957) that was prophetic in exploring the dangerous power of television in the hands of a man with political ambitions. *Splendor in the Grass* (1961) with Warren Beatty and Natalie Wood was a Newtown Production shot on location in Long Island and on New York sound stages. Kazan's most independent and personal film *America, America* (1963) deals with his Greek ancestry and the immigrant struggle to assimilate in the new world. The expressive black-and-white cinematography of **Haskell Wexler** and the dynamic editing of Dede Allen take the film on an adventurous, independent cinematic exploration of the narrative. *The Arrangement* (1969), produced by Kazan's Athena Enterprises and starring Kirk Douglas and Faye Dunaway, tried to capture the excitement and immediacy of the emerging **American New Wave.** But the exploration of a man's midlife crisis is bogged down with flashy, self-conscious technique that tries too hard to imitate the new youth-driven cinema.

In 1971 Kazan set out with his son Chris and producer/cameraman Nick Proferes to make a totally independent film. *The Visitors*, a powerful film about Vietnam veterans starring Steven Railsback and James Woods, shot in **16mm** with a small crew in a raw, direct style at Kazan's Connecticut home, succeeded in bringing the director back to the roots of his early days in filmmaking. Kazan returned to Hollywood one more time for *The Last Tycoon* (1976), starring Robert De Niro, but the film was a critical and box office failure. Since then Kazan has developed many film projects including a sequel to *America, America.* None have made it into production. He has spent the last thirty years primarily concentrating on his work as a novelist and has had several bestsellers and an autobiography.

Kazan's single most significant contribution to independent filmmaking is *On the Waterfront*, a tough and brutally honest look at union corruption on the New York docks. The black-and-white film shot by the legendary New York cameraman **Boris Kaufman** makes its bid along with *Citizen Kane* (1941) for the great American movie. It is emotional, highly realistic, immediate in acting, narrative, and cinematic technique and achieves the raw human power that personal filmmakers strive for. *On the Waterfront* won eight Academy Awards including best picture and best director and has influenced countless actors and directors including **Dennis Hopper, Martin Scorsese, Abel Ferrara, Francis Ford Coppola,** and Oliver Stone. *See also* Kaufman, Boris

BIBLIOGRAPHY

Ciment, Michel. *Kazan on Kazan.* New York: Viking Press, 1974.
Kazan, Elia. *Elia Kazan: A Life.* New York: Knopf, 1988.
Young, Jeff. *Kazan: The Master Director Discusses His Films.* New York: Newmarket Press, 1999.

Keaton, Buster. (Actor, director, screenwriter. *b.* Joseph Frances Keaton VI, October 4, 1885, Piqua, Kansas. *d.* February 1, 1966, Los Angeles, California. Legendary comedic/tragic figure, young Joseph Frances auditioned for his unique role in show business when at six months he survived his first pratfall down a flight of stairs at a boarding house for show people. The great Harry Houdini admired the lad and nicknamed him Buster. At three Buster joined the family's acrobatic act. Billed as the Human Mop, his father swept the floor with the boy. Buster's acrobatic skills were so refined audiences swore he was a midget. Keaton got into comedy shorts directed by "Fatty" Arbuckle. After working on film stages in New York and Long Beach, California, having his films released through Paramount Famous Players–Lasky and Metro, Joseph M. Schenck and Keaton purchased First National, the former Chaplin Studios, and renamed it The Buster Keaton Studios. By mid-1921 Schenck's production company was renamed Buster Keaton Productions.

In 1923 Keaton and Schenck switched from production of short films to feature-length comedies. Keaton quickly emerged as an innovative film director. In the 1920s, Keaton directed and starred in some of his most notable work: *The Three Ages* (1923), *Sherlock, Jr., The Navigator* (both 1924), *Seven Chances, Go West* (both 1925), *Battling Butler* (1926), *The General, College* (both 1927), and *Steamboat Bill, Jr.* (1928) Keaton gave up his studio and signed with MGM, where he had no control over his films, when he had previously maintained total artistic authority. In 1928 Keaton made *The Cameraman* and in 1929 *Spite Marriage*; then he began to decompensate. Keaton's wife divorced him; his physical and mental state deteriorated until he was forced to enter a psychiatric clinic in 1937.

He eventually returned to films as an actor and uncredited gag writer and assistant director. Old and barely remembered as the giant he had been, Keaton appeared in *Li'l Abner* (1940) and *Sunset Blvd.* (1950), where he played himself as a has-been silent star in a new Hollywood. In 1952 Keaton's greatness shone again in *Limelight*, appearing with **Charles Chaplin**. In 1960 Keaton appeared in *The Adventures of Huckleberry Finn* and in 1963 in *It's a Mad, Mad, Mad, Mad World*. Keaton went further downhill, paying bills by working in *Beach Blanket Bingo* and *How to Stuff a Wild Bikini* (both 1965). Richard Lester cast him in *A Funny Thing Happened on the Way to the Forum* (1966). But Keaton's most unusual and bizarre role came when Samuel Beckett cast him in the playwright's only cinematic venture *Film* (1966). Keaton had little idea what Beckett and director Alan Schneider were up to and tried to add old silent movie touches to the silent role in which he was disguised from the camera. *Film* is a haunting memory of the experimental genius of the 1920s, his body nimble and his ideas cutting-edge.

Keaton was way ahead of his time. It was long after his death before young filmmakers realized Keaton had plowed the road less traveled, creating endless possibilities for postmodernists like **Jim Jarmusch** to follow. Keaton was the old stone face, master of deadpan, a humor and behavior trend that wouldn't catch the public consciousness until the 1990s. Keaton was a surreal, magical, acrobatic, kinetic performer and director whose films were experiments in cinematic pyrotechnics. Keaton's narrative invention, superhuman physical feats, cinematic visuals, and abstract concepts searched for pure cinema. Keaton was an absurdist, an existentialist—a postmodern figure before the modern era. *See also Film*

BIBLIOGRAPHY

Dardis, Tom. *Keaton: The Man Who Wouldn't Lie Down.* New York: Penguin Books, 1980.

Keitel, Harvey. Independent filmmaker, actor. *b.* May 13, 1939, Brooklyn, New York. Harvey Keitel is a patron saint of independent filmmaking. No single actor has godfathered more films into existence or has committed to edgy, dangerous, and adventurous roles for as many maverick filmmakers. Keitel is a working actor who is in it for the art. He has never sold out, never sought to move up the ladder from low and modest budget films to the $20 million club. Keitel is a character actor who lives for the work. A private man, who moves from film to film, he has generated almost ninety performances in thirty-three years in the profession.

In the 1970s Keitel worked with **Martin Scorsese,** *Mean Streets* (1973), *Alice Doesn't Live Here Anymore* (1974), *Taxi Driver* (1976); Paul Schrader, *Blue Collar* (1978); Peter Yates, *Mother, Jugs & Speed* (1976); **Alan Rudolph,** *Welcome to L.A.* (1977); Ridley Scott, *The Duellists* (1978; **Robert Altman,** *Buffalo Bill and the Indians* (1976); and James Toback, *Fingers* (1978).

In the 1990s, when many actors of his generation were unable to work steadily, or at all, let alone be directed by the young mavericks and indies of the time, Keitel collaborated with **Spike Lee,** *Clockers* (1995); **Quentin Tarantino,** *Reservoir Dogs* (1992), *Pulp Fiction* (1994); **Wayne Wang,** *Smoke* (1995), *Blue in the Face* (1995); **Tony Bui,** *Three Seasons* (1999); James Mangold, *Cop Land* (1997); **Abel Ferrara,** *Bad Lieutenant* (1992); *Dangerous Game* (1993); Jane Campion, *The Piano* (1993); Alexandre Rockwell, *Somebody to Love* (1994); and Theo Angelopoulos, *Ulysses' Gaze* (1995). The prolific actor continues to work in many projects including: *Dreaming of Julia,* which he also produced, *Beeper* (both 2001), and *Red Dragon* (2002).

Keitel's commitment to independent filmmaking and daring roles may have kept him from becoming a superstar, but it has made him a vital and positive force in low-budget filmmaking. Some of his groundbreaking roles include Charlie in *Mean Streets,* George Banes in *The Piano,* Jimmy Fingers in *Fingers,* and the junkie cop in *Bad Lieutenant.*

BIBLIOGRAPHY

Fine, Marshall. *Harvey Keitel: The Art of Darkness.* London: HarperCollins, 1997.

Kerouac, Jack. Writer. *b.* March 12, 1922, Lowell, Massachusetts. *d.* October 21, 1969, St. Petersburg, Florida. Jack Kerouac was the heart, soul, and conscience of the Beat Generation. His writings and lifestyle set the

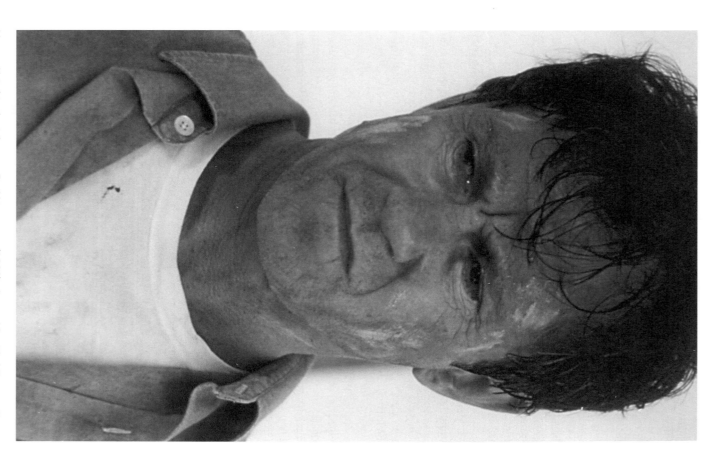

Harvey Keitel in the infamous *Bad Lieutenant* (1992), directed by Abel Ferrara. Courtesy of The Del Valle Archive

standard for the movement, and his legend has influenced generations of youth to drop out and explore the underground media culture. Kerouac's novels, especially the seminal *On the Road*, affected independent filmmakers in a manner that no film historian can accurately record. Kerouac narrated the **Robert Frank**/Alfred Leslie film *Pull My Daisy* (1958), and his novel *The Subterraneans* was made into a film released in 1960, directed by Randall MacDougall and starring Leslie Caron, George Peppard, Janice Rule, and Roddy McDowell. On- and offscreen music was provided by André Previn, Gerry Mulligan, Carmen McRae, Art Pepper, Art Farmer, and Shelly Manne. Once again Hollywood made superficial mush out of a literary work, one that helped define a changing America. **Francis Ford Coppola** has come close to filming *On the Road* but has not realized the project. The imagination quivers at the notion of Kerouac collaborating with **Darren Aronofsky, Kevin Smith, Richard Linklater, Alex Cox,** or **Jim Jarmusch** or hanging out with Johnny Depp, Brad Pitt, Ed Harris, Nicholas Cage, Mickey Rourke, Matt Dillon, Robert Downey Jr., or Ethan Hawke. Cool. *See also* Beat cinema; Frank, Robert

Kerrigan, Lodge. Director, screenwriter. *b.* 1964, New York. Little is known about the mysterious Mr. Kerrigan who has written and directed two disturbing, original films about the inner life of characters in the margins of society. Even the editor of Kerrigan's remarkable feature film debut *Clean, Shaven* (1995) knows nothing about his background. The film about a schizophrenic man trying to connect enters the mind of this deeply alienated man through a penetrating and chilling performance by Peter Greene. Kerrigan creates a disturbing atmosphere with an expressive visual style and a sound design that gives the viewer insight into the psychic pain of mental illness. Kerrigan's second feature, *Claire Dolan* (1998), captures the inner life of his female protagonist with uncomfortable intimacy, as well as he understood his male subject in *Clean, Shaven*. Claire Dolan is an Irish call girl in New York who shows little emotion even as violence surrounds her life and her pimp. Claire escapes to Newark, New Jersey, to find a life after her mother dies but must return to the prison waiting for her in New York. *Claire Dolan* is hypnotically disturbing and quiet, where *Clean, Shaven* was loud and agitating; both are equally troubling in their proximity to the raw edge of a life.

Kids. A 1995 film directed by **Larry Clark**, written by a then-nineteen-year-old **Harmony Korine**, coproduced by **Christine Vachon**, and executive produced by **Gus Van Sant**. *Kids* was entered into **Sundance** by **Miramax**, where it was screened unannounced at midnight, making it the buzz of the event. *Kids* won the Gold Palme at Cannes and became the most controversial film of the year. Larry Clark was a noted still photographer drawn to edgy and lurid subject matter. Clark and his director of photography Eric Edwards, who had worked with Gus Van Sant, created a polished **cinéma vérité** documentary visual style to the scripted fictional film.

Kids is a shocking, honest, unvarnished look at aimless New York City teens absent any guidance from their disinterested parents. They have unprotected sex, engage in senseless violence, and abuse and drug themselves into submission. The film created a national scandal because of its nonjudgmental point of view toward the subject and its direct approach to a nihilistic lifestyle. It is up to the audience to deal with the cold, amoral behavior presented as realism, not dramatic recreation.

Clark achieved a believability with his cast of real kids that blurred the line between fiction and nonfiction filmmaking. From the opening graphic sex scene, the viewer is thrown into a world of the next generation, uncensored and without apologies. Clark's affinity for subcultures and behavior without a traditional moral code gave *Kids* a wallop especially to "enlightened audiences" who thought they "understood" today's youth until *Kids* showed them the real thing. *Kids* is at once a cautionary tale and an **exploitation film**. Clark wanted real teenagers for *Kids*, so he spent two summers hanging out with his cast in Washington Square Park. One year was spent raising money for the daring project.

Clark, who was fifty when he directed this first feature, had difficulty accepting collaboration from his under-thirty crew, although it was necessary because the still photographer didn't fully understand the filmmaking process. Only a few members of the cast were minors. No pot smoking or beer drinking occurred on the set, but the cast often went off and came back in an altered consciousness. Casting director Katie Roumel was young and able to go into clubs with flyers for the project and approach kids to appear in *Kids*. The film was produced nonunion, the only way for Clark to direct and use actors not in the Screen Actor's Guild. Skateboard designers gave the production free clothes and were pleased by the baggy fashion look in the film. *Kids* was distributed by Excalibur, a company specially created by Miramax for its release because Miramax's parent company Disney would not release an NC-17 film. Miramax paid $3 million for *Kids* and launched an aggressive marketing campaign that resulted in a $7 million gross. *See also* Clark, Larry; Korine, Harmony; Miramax; Vachon, Christine

King, Stephen. Author, screenwriter, actor, director. *b.* September 21, 1947, Portland, Maine. The bestselling author of horror novels has supplied the story, novel, or screenplay for over fifty feature films. King's massive output has been adapted by many maverick filmmakers including **Brian De Palma** (*Carrie*, 1976), **Tobe Hooper** (*Salem's Lot*, TV mini-

Sissy Spacek as the bloody prom queen with telekinetic powers in *Carrie* (1976), directed by Brian De Palma. Courtesy of The Del Valle Archive

series, 1979; *The Mangler*, 1995), **Stanley Kubrick** (*The Shining*, 1980), **George Romero** (*Creepshow*, 1982; *The Dark Half*, 1993), **John Carpenter** (*Christine*, 1983), Rob Reiner (*Stand by Me*, 1986; *Misery*, 1990), and **David Cronenberg** (*The Dead Zone*, 1983).

Stephen King's extraordinary marketability has given lesser-name, low-budget filmmakers significant opportunities. Beneficiaries include Lewis Teague (*Cujo*, 1983; *Cat's Eye*, 1985), **Mark L. Lester** (*Firestarter*, 1984), **Larry Cohen** (*A Return to Salem's Lot*, 1987), **Mary Lambert** (*Pet Sematary*, 1989; *Pet Sematary II*, 1992), Paul Michael Glasser (*The Running Man*, 1987), and Ralph S. Singleton (*Graveyard Shift*, 1990). King, who grew up on low-budget horror and **exploitation films**, has directed one low-budget movie himself, *Maximum Overdrive* (1986), starring Emilio Estevez and Pat Hingle. King had fun making what he called a "junk movie" where a truck stop is terrorized by the vehicles themselves as part of a global machine rebellion. King was just having fun—writing novels is his profession. The latest King tales to come to the screen include: *Dolan's Cadillac*, produced by Tom Cruise, *Dreamcatcher*, directed by Lawrence Kasdan (both 2002), and *Desperation* (2003).

King, Zalman. Actor, director, screenwriter, producer. *b.* Zalman King Lefkowitz, 1941, Trenton, New Jersey. Zalman King began as an actor in episodic television. King also played villains and psychopaths in television movies but was less successful on the big screen. *The Ski Bum* (1971) and the role of Christ in *The Passover Plot* (1975) did little to launch his career as a major film actor. King produced two films for **Robert Altman**'s protégé **Alan Rudolph**, *Roadie* (1980), for which he also contributed the story, and *Endangered Species* (1982). King began making a living acting in indies. In 1973 he appeared in *Trip with the Teacher*, in which bikers terrorized stranded, nubile schoolgirls. In *Blue Sunshine* (1976) good kids are transformed into bald glassy-eyed murderers when they take LSD. King also was in **Lee Grant**'s *Tell Me a Riddle* (1980) and **Roger Corman**'s *Galaxy of Terror* (1981).

In 1988, King made the transition to directing, with *Wildfire*, but it was a disastrous beginning. The story concerned two teenagers in an orphanage who fall in love. The girl becomes pregnant and has a miscarriage; they rob a bank and go to prison. King was not allowed final cut and still feels *Wildfire* was his best work but that audiences only saw a bastardized version. One week after being dismissed on *Wildfire*, King was in preproduction on *Two Moon Junction* (1988), an old script he had written as a parody of Sandra Dee films. Theatrically, *Two Moon Junction* was a flop, but it made money in video and foreign markets.

It was *Wild Orchid* in 1990 that crowned King as *the* erotic filmmaker of the moment. In 1986, King had written and coproduced *9 ½ Weeks* directed by Adrian Lyne. King originally wanted to direct the film. His friends raised the money to move into production, and the studios were interested, but then backed away, frightened by the deviant sexual subject matter. Tristar became interested when King signed Lyne, hot off of *Flashdance* (1983), but the studio pulled out at the last minute—*9 ½ Weeks* was then produced independently. The scandalous film starred Kim Basinger and Mickey Rourke in what could be called sadism and masochism lite. King learned on *9 ½ Weeks* that soft, kinky sex with a theme, not a plot, was the key to box office success. So he applied the theme of a character who pushes people away to *Wild Orchid*, starring Mickey Rourke, Jaqueline Bisset, and Carrie Otis. The film takes place in sultry, sexy Rio de Janeiro and features a hot simulated sex scene. The MPAA helped in softening the sex. They rated the originally submitted cut X, and the film was heavily reedited to get the R they needed for a wide commercial audience. *Wild Orchard* took in big box office returns, and King had his formula. The simulated nongraphic sex, romantic setting, and erotic situations tapped into a market larger than the raincoat crowd. Women and couples were patrons for the naughty film, and King didn't look back. With his wife, sculptor and writer Patricia Knop, as a collaborator, King built an empire out of the *Red Shoes Diaries*, exploiting the same paradigm of sex, romance, and exotica, creating a successful cable series with a lucrative by-product of huge video sales. King has been labeled the King of Kink and a classy smutmonger. Recent work by Zalman King includes: *Girl on a Bike: Red Shoes Diaries, Radio Silence* (both 2000), and the television movie *ChromiumBlue.Com* (2001).

Klaw, Irving. Photographer, filmmaker. Irving Klaw was the pin-up king of New York City. Strippers would come to his loft to be photographed nude and seminude in provocative poses. Klaw ran a photography store in Manhattan where the pictures were distributed subrosa. Klaw began making black-and-white films for the home market. The blue movies were made of ten to twelve separate segments of strippers performing their acts. Klaw would structure the segments into different movies that were sold under the table. The photos he took of model **Bettie Page** were Klaw's contribution to underground pop culture. The dark-haired, Amazonian beauty dominated the sexual-fantasy life of American men in the 1940s and 1950s. In the late 1940s, Klaw went beyond the playful innocent pin-up into sadism and masochism and bondage photographs featuring Bettie Page in domination over other women who were tied, spanked, had their hair pulled, gagged and taunted with whips while they appeared nonchalant and indifferent. In 1954 Klaw directed *Varietease* featuring legendary stripper Lilli St. Cyr. *Teaserama* (1955) featured the popular ecdysiast Tempest Storm. Klaw also directed *Buxom Beautease* (1956), *Nature's Sweethearts* (1963) and *Girls Come Too* (1968). When threatened with a jail sentence, he burned his archive of original negatives and prints in 1963, and part of adult entertainment history was lost. Klaw was an underground adult filmmaker who influenced such films as **Russ Meyer's** *Faster, Pussycat, Kill! Kill!* (1965) and Roger Vadim's *Barbarella* (1968) and was a bad boy who fathered a movement that grew far beyond his quaint fantasies of women being naughty. *See also* Page, Bettie

Kopple, Barbara. Documentary filmmaker. *b.* July 30, 1946, New York City, *ed.* Northeastern University. Barbara Kopple was raised in the suburb of Scarsdale in Westchester County. She earned a degree in psychology and used filmmaking for clinical studies. Kopple learned her craft by assisting **documentary** filmmakers as an editor, sound technician, and cinematographer. In 1976, Kopple burst onto the American documentary film scene with *Harlan County, U.S.A.,* a powerful feature-length record of struggling nonunion coal miners in Harlan County, Kentucky. The film struck an immediate chord with the American people and had a rousing premiere at the New York Film Festival, where Kopple, members of the now-unionized coal workers, and union organizers sang folk songs as the audience joined in rejoicing. Kopple also won the Oscar for best feature-length documentary for a film that was both militant and steeped in American core values. Kopple received instant recognition for her accomplishment—she was the documentarian of the moment. Kopple had started the project in 1972. She spent four years recording every event in Kentucky as it unfolded, capturing the coal miners and the labor organizers as they fought the corporate structure that oppressed them.

In 1981 *Keeping On* aired on PBS's **American Playhouse.** The prestigious series funded Kopple's foray into fictional filmmaking, but she kept close to her political commitment to unionism. The screenplay by Horton Foote, which starred Rosalind Cash and Carol Kando, is the story of a preacher-worker trying to unionize a mill. Fourteen years after *Harlan Country, U.S.A.,* Kopple completed *American Dream* (1990), a documentary about striking union workers at a Hormel meatpacking plant in Austin, Minnesota, in the mid-1980s. Kopple's cameras were everywhere, at union meetings, at press conferences, and in the homes of the workers. Again, Kopple's fervent political beliefs in the power of union activism resulted in a New York Film Festival premiere and her second Oscar for best feature documentary.

In 1992, Kopple collaborated with Danny Schechter on *Beyond JFK: The Question of Conspiracy,* a documentary reexamining the assassination of President John F. Kennedy. In 1993, a made-for-television documentary *Fallen Champ: The Untold Story of Mike Tyson,* produced and directed by Kopple, aired. Kopple collaborated with directors Judy Korin, Sylvia Morales, and Christen Harty Schaefer for the television miniseries *A Century of Women* (1994). The project examined the role of American women during the twentieth century in documentary and dramatic form, framed by a story of a fictional family tracing their women from every generation. *A Century of Women* featured Jane Fonda as narrator and an all-star female cast, photographed by **Ellen Kuras.** Kopple chronicled the twenty-fifth anniversary celebration of the Woodstock Music and Art Festival in *Woodstock '94* (1998). The same year Kopple released *Wild Man Blues,* a documentary that follows **Woody Allen** on tour with his jazz group. In 2000, Kopple directed *My Generation,* a documentary about three generations of Woodstock concerts and an adaptation of David Rabe's play *In the Boom Boom Room.* In 2002 Barbara Kopple was the producer of the documentary *American Standoff,* and director of the television movie *The Hamptons Project.*

Korine, Harmony. Screenwriter, director. *b.* 1974, Bolinas, California. At just nineteen years old Korine wrote the script for *Kids,* a too-close-for-adult-comfort look at a group of nihilistic teenagers who express no responsible morality as they engage in destructive sexual, physical, and psychological behavior. Korine's remarkable achievement is the documentarylike detachment he brings to his characters and situations. As the creator of *Kids,* Korine was lauded for his honesty and pelted for what some felt was exaggeration and exploitation. Korine made his directorial debut with *Gummo* (1997), a disturbing film about two teenage boys in a midwestern suburb who kill stray cats, sniff glue, have sex with prostitutes, and tamper with the life-support systems of patients. Again, Korine doesn't judge the behavior of his subjects. As a director, Korine propels the film into a dangerous combination of **cinéma vérité** and scripted moments. In 1999 Korine made *Julien Donkey-Boy,* aka *Dogme #6,* with Chloe Sevigny of *Kids* and German New Wave director Werner Herzog, in the first American film created under the **Dogme 95** manifesto. Korine continued to explore depravity in this story of a family headed by a sadistic father, a schizophrenic son, and pregnant sister. In 2002 Harmony Korine once again collaborated with director **Larry Clark,** this time writing the screenplay for *Ken Park.*

Korty, John. Filmmaker. *b.* June 22, 1936, LaFayette, Indiana. *ed.* Antioch College. John Korty began making amateur films when he was sixteen years old. He worked his way through college making animated television commercials. In the mid-1960s Korty began making independent films. He was earning a decent living in the San Francisco Bay area and had a fully equipped but modest and functional film studio setup in a gray barn on Stinson Beach. In 1964, he completed *Breaking the Habit,* a **documentary** short. Korty's first feature, *The Crazy-Quilt* (1966), gained the attention of critics and the film community. The story follows an idealistic young woman who marries an exterminator with no illusions about life. She has numerous affairs but returns to her husband. They have a daughter and live a life balanced between her idealism and his realism. The cast was composed of unknowns. Korty cowrote the screenplay, photographed, and edited the seventy-five-minute film. *The Crazy-Quilt* was shot silent, and Korty postsynched the dialogue with mixed results, so he got Burgess Meredith to record a narration. The music by Peter Schickele of PDQ Bach fame was considered unusual for its time. *Funnyman* (1967) was cowritten by Korty and Peter Bonerz as an improvisational comic who feels he should be doing something more with his life. The improvisational comedy troupe The Committee performed hilarious skits in the film, and Korty created animated spoofs and was the director of photography. *Riverrun* (1968) concerns an unmarried couple expecting a baby whose life is shadowed when the woman's sea captain father unexpectedly arrives.

While **Francis Ford Coppola** was making *The Rain People* (1969), Korty met George Lucas. Coppola convinced Korty to rent an office at **American Zoetrope**, and Korty became the first tenant. He finished *Riverrun* at Zoetrope and was making plans for television projects when Coppola raised his rent from $200 to $1,000 a month. Korty headed back to the Stinson Beach studio. Director Michael Ritchie was impressed with Korty's work as a cinematographer and hired him to shoot *The Candidate* (1972). In 1977, John Korty shared an Oscar for the feature documentary *Who Are the DeBolts and Where Did They Get Nineteen Kids?* In 1978, Korty directed *Oliver's Story*, the sequel to *Love Story* (1970), but most of his career has been in television movies including the acclaimed *The Autobiography of Miss Jane Pittman* (1974) and *The Ewok Adventure* (1984), produced by friend George Lucas. Recent television credits for John Korty include: *Ms. Scrooge* (1997), *Oklahoma City: A Survivor's Story* (1998), and *A Gift of Love: The Daniel Hoffman Story.*

Kovács, László. Cinematographer. *b.* May 14, 1933, Hungary. Along with his countryman **Vilmos Zsigmond,** László Kovács reinvented the cinematographic look of American films in the 1960s and 1970s. He worked with many young **American New Wave** directors: **Richard Rush,** *A Man Called Digger, Hell's Angels on Wheels* (both 1967), *Psych-Out, The Savage Seven* (both 1968); *Getting Straight* (1970), *Freebie and the Bean* (1974); **Dennis Hopper, Easy Rider** (1969), *The Last Movie* (1971); **Robert Altman,** *That Cold Day in the Park* (1969); Paul Mazursky, *Alex in Wonderland* (1970); Peter Bogdanovich, *Targets* (1968), *What's Up, Doc?* (1972), *Paper Moon* (1973), *At Long Last Love* (1975), *Nickelodeon* (1976); Hal Ashby, *Shampoo* (1975); Bob Rafelson, *Five Easy Pieces* (1970), *The King of Marvin Gardens* (1972); and **Martin Scorsese,** *New York, New York* (1977), *The Last Waltz* (1978).

Kovács broke all the old Hollywood rules, shooting into the sun to produce glorious light flares, handholding his camera, experimenting with film stocks to interpret the changing narrative and stylistic visions of a new generation of American filmmakers. Kovács graduated from the famed Budapest Academy of Drama and Film Art where he met Vilmos Zsigmond. The men became lifelong friends. During the 1956 Hungarian revolution against the Soviets, the young cameramen shot 30,000 feet of 35mm film and smuggled it into Vienna. At their peril they had documented the revolution day by day from October 23 to November when they escaped. Unfortunately for Kovács and Zsigmond, the news agencies weren't interested—the story was over for them. Finally, they sold off their archive to a man interested in making a documentary. On the first anniversary of the revolution, CBS contacted Zsigmond, desperate for the footage. He explained it had been sold, and the network bought all the footage for $100,000 from its new owner.

Kovács, who was not yet able to speak English, lived in Upstate New York and then Seattle. He got a job in a lab where he worked for a year, then contacted Zsigmond, who was also working in a lab in New York. Although they were educated with the Russian films of Eisenstein, Dovshevko, and Pudovkin and had not been able to see many American films living in a Communist-occupied country, they decided to try their luck in Hollywood. The cameraman's union sent them on their heels to learn English. When they returned, conversant in the language, they found the industry impenetrable. Kovács worked in the home photography business for four years printing microfilm documents for an insurance company. Kovács became friendly with UCLA cinema students and worked on their films. He met **Francis Ford Coppola** and other aspiring American New Wavers. Zsigmond also made contacts; they worked for free and at times comprised the entire camera crew on no-budget films.

This led them to low-budget **biker films** that were the rage of the **drive-ins**. Many of the features Kovács shot were made for only $60,000 to $80,000. *Blood of Dracula's Castle* (1967) was made for $30,000. The films were shot in ten to twelve days with minimal camera equipment, usually a blimped Arriflex with no more than three lenses. Kovács matriculated to the **Roger Corman** University of **B-movies**. Corman got around the union roadblock by shooting for one or two weeks with a union-sanctioned crew, then telling them shooting was complete. Corman then brought in Kovács and Zsigmond, who would finish the film, giving it an exciting new look cultivated from their Eastern European training.

Kovács was so burned out on low-budget motorcycle movies, having shot *The Savage Seven, Hells Angels on Wheels,* and *Rebel Rousers* (1967), that he turned down production manager Paul Lewis when offered *Easy Rider,* a project the cinematographer thought was just another biker movie. Kovács eventually agreed to meet with Dennis Hopper, who dressed as he would appear in the film as Billy. Hopper threw the script across the room and told Kovács the story from his head. Kovács agreed and drove from LA to New Orleans with Hopper scouting locations and planning the film. There are many apocryphal stories about the making of the landmark 1969 film, but undeniably Kovács gave *Easy Rider* the freewheeling, premusic video, artistic documentary look. Kovács photographed the film while traveling across the country shooting from the hip, mostly handheld, capturing America and the two underground outlaws who encountered a country entering a time of social and political upheaval. Kovács and his small crew lived on the road with the performers but abstained from the mind-altering substances that may have given the characters a realistic authority. The stoned-out Hopper and **Peter Fonda** would have returned with an unreleasable psychedelic mish-mosh were it not for the steady and artistically adventurous Kovács.

Kovács was just beginning his cinematographic revolution with *Easy Rider*. Kovács and Zsigmond are responsible for the look of the New American Cinema of the 1970s. In the 1980s and 1990s Kovács continued to innovate working on large budget productions like *Ghostbusters* (1984) and *My Best Friend's Wedding* (1997). He continued to shoot independent films such as *Inside Moves* (1980), *Heart Beat* (1980), *Frances* (1982), *Mask* (1985), *Say Anything* (1989), and *Radio Flyer* (1992). Recent credits for Lázslo Kovács as director of photography include: *Jack Frost* (1998), *Return to Me*, and *Miss Congeniality* (both 2000).

Kowalski, Lech. Filmmaker. Kowalski's four films *D.O.A.* (1980), *Story of a Junkie*, aka *Gringo* (1984) *Rock Soup* (1991), and *Born to Lose: The Last Rock and Roll Movie* (1999) are a record of the punk aesthetic as music and social consciousness. *D.O.A.* is a historical record of The Sex Pistols' infamous 1981 American tour and of New York's Lower East Side presented through the eyes of the denizens of the underground community held in the long shadow of Wall Street. Crude handmade shelters, trash-littered streets, and garbage-jammed gutters are some of the urban details Kowalski captured on film. The neighborhood, historically known as a home for immigrants, was banished from tourists by those power brokers that believe its residents were rotting in the Apple's "melting pot." In the 1980s New York's Lower East Side had become pure punk.

Kramer, Robert. Director, screenwriter. *b.* June 22, 1936, New York City. *d.* November 10, 1999. *ed.* Swarthmore College, Stanford University. The education of Radical Left filmmaker Robert Kramer began with the study of philosophy and Western and European history at Swarthmore and a radicalization at Stanford. In 1965, Kramer was the organizing force behind a community project in an African American neighborhood in Newark, New Jersey. Kramer was one of the founders of the **Newsreel** movement that produced short films on radical political subjects and the anti–Vietnam War movement from 1967 to 1971.

During the Newsreel period Kramer directed *The Edge* (1967) and *Ice* (1969). *The Edge* portrayed disillusionment in the Radical Left movement and a doomed assassination plot. Kramer received critical and political attention for *Ice* that portrayed an imminent urban guerrilla warfare in the United States fighting against an American regime repressively intervening in Mexico. *Ice* was widely reviewed and taken seriously both as a political statement and as an engaging cinematic work. Kramer quickly emerged as a filmmaker with an impassioned Radical Left political view. Unlike many politicos who used the medium as a means to deliver their message without a sense of craft and narrative invention, Kramer was equally passionate about the medium and the message.

In 1975 Kramer's most important and best-known film *Milestones* was released. The three and a half hour political epic, codirected, photographed, and edited with John Douglas, features the lives of fifty survivors of the Radical Left in the mid-1970s. The characters are fictionalized versions of the people who play them. In Kramer's screenplay some are much less fictionalized than others. The community of 1960s political activists are seen now as army deserters, commune members, hitchhikers, couples about to split up; their children, who have more sense than their parents, moved from parent to parent. Kramer repeatedly makes the point that political diatribe and jargon brought down the once vital movement. Now the social and political movers and shakers of their generation could barely communicate. The writer Grace Paley plays the role of a filmmaker and *Milestones*' producers David and Barbara Stone play fatigued saloonkeepers committed to radical causes. John Douglas portrays a blind pottery-maker whose studio becomes the refuge of old friends searching for a new life. The long and narratively chaotic film angered many from the Radical Left. *Milestones* was criticized but became a record of broken dreams as the time to "seize the moment" and change the world had passed.

Kramer's films never appealed to or reached a wide audience. His loyal followers were rooted in the **avant-garde** and **experimental film** communities. His work was frequently screened at film festivals. In 1980 Kramer relocated to Paris, where he was accepted as an important political filmmaker and original cinema artist. *Guns* (1980) was shown at the New York Film Festival, but Kramer could only find financing in France. In 1982, *À toute allure* was an official selection from France for the Cannes Film Festival. *Doc's Kingdom* (1987), about a burned-out radical living in Portugal, and *Route1/USA* (1989) were both released in America. In 1996 Robert Kramer directed *Le Manteau.* In 1997 *The Ghosts of Electricity* was released followed by the documentary *Cities of the Plain* in 2000. Kramer may have felt like a failed 1960s radical, but his films were more than protests, political rhetoric, or just another cause against the military industrial complex. He was a filmmaker who proved that film could speak loud and clear with a lasting impression for future generations. *See also* Newsreel

Kramer, Stanley. Producer, director. *b.* September 29, 1913, Brooklyn, New York. *d.* February 19, 2001. *ed.* New York University. Stanley Kramer was dismissed by **critics** as a well-meaning bleeding-heart liberal who as a producer and director took on the big themes of his time but wasn't a legitimate, serious filmmaker. They questioned his integrity as an artist and refused to let him into the Hollywood pantheon of auteurs. Kramer was not subtle about his social/political point of view. He didn't direct with visual style, textural metaphors, or narrative experimentation. Kramer started in the film industry as a researcher, film editor, and writer. He worked his way up to associate producer by the early 1940s and during World War II was a member of the Army Signal Corps. Later, Kramer formed an independent film company, Screen Plays Inc., where he produced modestly budgeted message films. By 1951 the harsh economical reality of being an indie forced him to become an autonomous producer under the Columbia Studios banner. The deal was not beneficial to the studio. Only Kramer's production of *The Caine Mutiny* made money. In 1954, the year of its release, Columbia and Kramer mutually terminated the arrangement.

In 1955 Kramer gambled with bigger budgets backed by star power. *The Defiant Ones* (1958), featuring Tony Curtis and Sidney Poitier as two escaped criminals handcuffed together, was a metaphor for the strain of race relations in America. *On the Beach* (1959) took on nuclear annihilation and starred Gregory Peck, Ava Gardner, Anthony Perkins, and Fred Astaire. *Inherit the Wind* (1960) dramatized the Scopes Monkey Trial, which pitted the Bible against Darwin's theory of evolution. Spencer Tracy played Clarence Darrow, and Frederic March portrayed William Jennings Bryan. *Judgement at Nuremberg* (1961) bravely exposed Nazi atrocities revealed at the German War Crime Tribunals, supported by an all-star cast, Spencer Tracy, Burt Lancaster, Richard Widmark, Marlene Dietrich, Judy Garland, Maximilian Schell, and Montgomery Clift. *Pressure Point* (1962) is adapted from a true psychiatric case from Dr. Robert M. Linder's bestselling *The Fifty-Minute Hour* about a prison psychiatrist who tries to analyze a Nazi patient. It features Sidney Poitier, Bobby Darin, and Peter Falk. *A Child Is Waiting* (1963), directed by **John Cassavetes**, goes inside a private pediatric institution for the mentally ill and stars Burt Lancaster, Judy Garland, and Gena Rowlands. *Ship of Fools* (1965) presented an international cast, Vivian Leigh, Oscar Werner, Simone Signoret, José Ferrer, Lee Marvin, José Greco, George Segal, Elizabeth Ashley, Michael Dunn, and Lilia Skala, in an adaptation of Katherine Anne Porter's novel set at sea before World War II.

Guess Who's Coming to Dinner (1967) single-handedly gave Kramer the stereotype of a bleeding heart dishing out social issues palatably to the masses. Casting Sidney Poitier as an impeccably groomed and mannered doctor softened the story of an interracial relationship with strong support from Tracy and Hepburn as the girl's liberal but concerned parents. *Bless the Beasts & Children* (1971) protested the killing of buffalo with the story of six boys who work to free the animals who personify the tradition of the American West. In 1973 *Oklahoma Crude* with George C. Scott and Faye Dunaway barely upheld the theme of corporate abuse in a comedy about a woman defending a lone oil well from an oil trust. *The Domino Principle* (1977) is a conspiracy thriller about a covert organization whose mission is political assassination. The failure of *The Runner Stumbles* (1979), the true story of a priest accused of killing a nun the authorities believe he was inappropriately attracted to, forced the independent big budget producer/director to retire.

During his career Kramer was a dedicated believer that filmmakers had a responsibility to take a stand on the pressing social/political issues of the day. If his films are liberal, bourgeoise, and simplistic to the critical elite, so be it, but Kramer was a lone independent voice fighting the Hollywood maxim "If you want to send a message, go to Western Union." There is a kinship between Kramer's message movies and contemporary indies like *Boys Don't Cry* (1999), *Matewan* (1987), and *Longtime Companion* (1990), films that compassionately deal with serious social and political issues and speak with the point of view of their makers. Kramer's films have received some eighty nominations and sixteen Oscars. The prevailing wisdom that financial success and public acceptance breeds mediocrity doesn't apply to Stanley Kramer. As an independent filmmaker working during the days when the studios ruled, he made a difference. Just take a look at *The Men* (1950), *High Noon* (1952), and *The Wild One* (1954), films produced by Kramer that represent a conscience and reflection of the American scene the moguls tried to avoid.

BIBLIOGRAPHY

Kramer, Stanley, with Thomas M. Coffey. *A Mad, Mad, Mad, Mad World: A Life in Hollywood.* New York: Harcourt Brace, 1997.
Spoto, Donald. *Stanley Kramer Film Maker.* Hollywood, CA: Samuel French, 1978.

Kubrick, Stanley. Filmmaker. *b.* July 26, 1928, Bronx, New York. *d.* March 7, 1999, Harpenden, Hertfordshire, England. Kubrick began his career as a wunderkind still photographer for *Look* magazine while he was still attending high school. As the youngest *Look* staff photographer Kubrick learned the craft of photography by shooting hundreds of assignments.

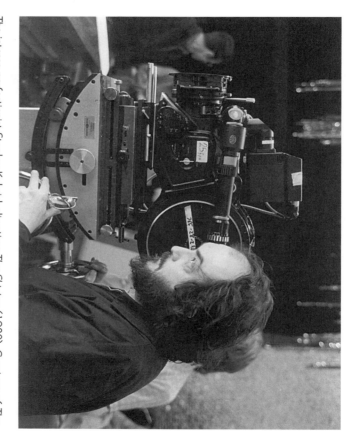

The intense perfectionist Stanley Kubrick directing *The Shining* (1980). Courtesy of The Del Valle Archive

He developed a classic compositional sense, learned the art of lighting, and shot many photo stories that prepared him to be a filmmaker. In 1951 Kubrick independently produced, then sold his first short *Day of the Fight*. Kubrick did not go to film school. An autodidact, he taught himself how to operate a motion picture camera and postproduction equipment by receiving brief instruction from the staff of film rental houses in New York's Film Center building in Times Square and learned through hands-on experience. He went on to direct another short, *Flying Padre* (1951), and was commissioned by the Seafarers International Union to create an **industrial film** *The Seafarers* (1953). Kubrick was a New York independent, **guerrilla** filmmaker before the terms were defined and trendy.

Kubrick independently produced and sold his first two features *Fear and Desire* (1953) and *Killer's Kiss* (1955). The black-and-white efforts are amateurish when compared with the Hollywood product at the time. But Kubrick was already establishing himself as a serious filmmaker, working in a film noir style and expressing a misanthropic view of the world, exploring the dark side of war, then the underbelly of the life led by a professional boxer. The films are existential in philosophy, experimental in narrative structure, and display a burgeoning cinematic vision.

Kubrick and producer **James B. Harris** formed Harris-Kubrick Pictures, a New York–based independent film company. Their first production was *The Killing* (1956), a racetrack caper film based on Lionel White's novel *Clean Break*. The film incorporated the book's constant time-shifting structure, presenting the action from the point of view of many characters. *The Killing* was not a box office success but attracted the attention of the Hollywood community with his examination of time and space that gave the **B-movie** story depth and meaning. Harris-Kubrick's second production was the antiwar classic *Paths of Glory* (1957), made in conjunction with Kirk Douglas's Bryna Productions. Douglas starred in the gritty drama. Kubrick created one of the most harrowing battle scenes put on film using his signature dolly shots and handheld camera to cinematically express the horror of war. Kubrick's bold use of camera and design emphasized the moral corruption of the military leaders who sacrificed innocent men for their egos and reputation.

Douglas had Kubrick under contract so he asked him to take over the direction of *Spartacus* (1960) when Anthony Mann was fired early on in the production. Kubrick took over with two days of preparation and had, to his standards, no real control over the film. Kubrick would never again make a film without total artistic control. In 1962, Harris-Kubrick adapted Nabokov's scandalous novel *Lolita* for the screen. The film pushed the sex-on-the-screen envelope for its time and managed to survive the scrutiny of both the Catholic Church and the Motion Picture Code board due to Harris's diplomatic skills and Kubrick's clever use of innuendo. The film was produced in England to save money and to be far away from the Hollywood machine.

Douglas let Harris-Kubrick out of their contract, and the team decided to go their separate ways. Harris wanted to direct, and Kubrick chose to produce his work in England to insure the artistic control he desired. In 1964, Kubrick directed the landmark black comedy *Dr. Strangelove or: How I Learned to Stop Worrying and Love the Bomb*. He eventually moved his family to an estate outside of London where Kubrick set up his production company and began to buy his own camera, lighting, and post-production equipment to work out of his home, just minutes away from first-class soundstages. MGM financed and distributed Kubrick's visionary science fiction epic *2001: A Space Odyssey* (1968) that pioneered a new era in special effects and cinematic storytelling structure. Kubrick had reached an artistic summit and achieved the power he needed to remain independent.

He struck a deal with Warner Bros. who, starting with the controversial *A Clockwork Orange* in 1971, financed and distributed Kubrick's films for the rest of his life. Kubrick was given complete artistic control over his films. Under the relationship with Warner's, Kubrick directed *Barry Lyndon* (1975), *The Shining* (1980), *Full Metal Jacket* (1987), and his final film *Eyes Wide Shut* in 1999. Kubrick's dedication to his craft and insight into the dark side of human nature have inspired generations of filmmakers. To many, Kubrick is an icon of the independent filmmaker. He may have needed the financial assistance of the Hollywood studio complex, but his vision was never corrupted by commercial concerns. *See also* Harris, James B.

BIBLIOGRAPHY

Ciment, Michel. *Kubrick.* New York: Holt, Rinehart and Winston, 1984.

LoBrutto, Vincent. *Stanley Kubrick: A Biography.* New York: Donald I. Fine, 1997.

Walker, Alexander. *Stanley Kubrick Directs.* 1972. New York: Norton, 1999.

Kuchar Brothers. Experimental filmmakers. *b.* 1942, Bronx, New York. Twin brothers George and Mike Kuchar were teenage movie moguls producing, directing, and performing in regular **8mm** melodramas with their friends dressing in their parents' clothes, shot on the Kuchar studio lot—the roof of their Bronx apartment building where they lived with their family in the 1950s. The Kuchars were autodidacts who loved Hollywood movies and were determined to make real, if not demented, studio productions with little to no money. The titles of the early Kuchar films explain: *The Naked and the Nude* (1957), *The Slasher* (1958), *The Thief and the Stripper* (1959), *I Was a Teenage Rumpot* (1960), *Pussy on a Hot Tin Roof* (1961), and *Lust for Ecstasy* (1963). The 8mm originals were stored in their mother's closet; there was no money for prints. During the 1960s the Kuchar brothers screened their films in downtown Manhattan art houses where they were considered landmarks in the **underground cinema** movement.

In 1965, George and Mike Kuchar began to work independent of each other. George made the transition from 8mm to **16mm** with *Corruption of the Damned* (1967) and his first work in color, *Hold Me While I'm Naked* (1966), a seventeen-minute autobiographical film. George Kuchar made or appeared in sixty films including *Knocturne* (1968), *The Sunshine Sisters* (1972), *Back to Nature* (1976), *A Reason to Live* (1976), *The Mongreloid* (1978), *The Oneers* (1982), and *Cattle Mutilations* (1983). The 1968 film *Encyclopedia of the Blessed* is a forty-two-minute black-and-white and color, sound documentary on the artists Red Grooms and Mimi Gross. *House of the White People* (1968) is a documentary of sculptor George Segal. Recent films directed by George Kuchar include: *Motel Capri* (1985), and *La Noche d' Amour* (1986). He has appeared as an actor in *Mary Jane's Not a Virgin Anymore* (1997), directed by Sarah Jacobson, and *3 Days of Rain* (2000), directed by Michael Meredith.

Solo, Mike Kuchar directed *The Pervert* (1963), *Born of the Wind* (1964), *Sins of the Fleshapoids* (1965), *The Secret of Wendel Samson* (1966), *Green Desire* (1966), *Fragments* (1967), *The Craven Sluck* (1967), *Variations* (1968), and *Cycles* (1968). Mike Kuchar was a cinematographer on many projects including: *March on Paris 1914 of Generaloberst Alexander von Kluck and His Memory of Jessie Holladay* (1977), directed by Walter Gutman, *Rote Liebe* (1982) and *Silence = Death* directed by Rosa von Praunheim.

The Kuchars developed a cult following in San Francisco and New York and have an official fan club in Madison, Wisconsin. The early Kuchar films had a wide-reaching influence on underground and commercial filmmaking. The Kuchars were camp humorists whose films featured zaftig leading ladies and geeky men. The narratives inspired by Hollywood melodramas were cheap and raucous. The Kuchars adored old Hollywood aesthetics. They borrowed musical scores from classic movies and used miniatures and homegrown special effects to create remarkable scenes like the tornado sequence in *A Town Called Tempest* (1963). Bad taste ruled in Hollywood-on-the-Bronx. There were bathroom and turd scenes. At twelve, the Kuchars made a film with a transvestite cast because they couldn't find real girls to work with them.

The Kuchars helped develop what became known as trash cinema, and they directly inspired **John Waters**. The Kuchars are also an early example of what eventually became the **punk** and New-Wave and **No-Wave** film movements. *Devil's Cleavage*, made in 1973, is a 16mm feature-length black-and-white sound film that was revived and celebrated by the punk movement. Hollywood-in-the-Bronx did not lead to tinseltown for the Kuchars, but it did lead to landmark independent films.

Kuras, Ellen. Cinematographer. *ed.* Brown University. Kuras was studying anthropology at Brown when in her second year she became interested in still photography and then studied film theory. For one interested in anthropology, photography, and film it was a natural transition for Kuras to work in **documentary** filmmaking. For several years she apprenticed as a production assistant, associate producer, and assistant cameraman on many nonfiction projects. In 1989 Kuras was given the opportunity to be the director of photography on *Samsara*, a documentary shot on location in Cambodia. Kuras's first narrative feature as a director of photography was **Tom Kalin**'s audacious *Swoon* (1992). Kuras's adventurous and unconventional black-and-white cinematography won the **Sundance** Best Feature Cinematography award. In 1994 Kuras was director of photography for the miniseries *A Century of Women*, an examination of the role of American women over the twentieth century. The film starred an A-list of actresses and combined both documentary and narrative film styles. Kuras worked with four directors, **Barbara Kopple**, Judy Korn, Sylvia Morales, and Christin Harty Schaefer. The challenging project demanded a consistent and textured style.

Postcards from America (1994) was a British production, the directorial debut of Steve McLean based on the autobiographical writings of multimedia artist and gay activist David Wojnarowicz who died of AIDS in 1992 and was critically acclaimed for the adventurous cinematic vision achieved by the director and cinematographer. In 1994, Kuras also shot *Roy Cohn/Jack Smith*, adapted from the stage production in which Ron Vawter plays both the former McCarthy henchman and the experimental filmmaker of the notorious *Flaming Creatures* (1963), directed by **Jill Godmilow**. *Unzipped* (1995) is a raucous documentary following the exploits of outrageous fashion designer Isaac Mizrahi. Kuras photographed *Angela* (1995), directed by Rebecca Miller, the story of a ten-year-old girl who conducts purification rituals with her six-year-old sister to rid them of evil, which Angela believes brought on their mother's mental illness. Again Kuras won the Sundance cinematography award for her work.

In 1996 Kuras shot **Mary Harron**'s *I Shot Andy Warhol*, the story of Valerie Solanas who did shoot **Andy Warhol**. The project involved recreations of Warhol's grainy, black-and-white screen tests and the psychedelic color of Andy's swinging 1960s. Kuras went back to documentaries in 1997 as one of the cinematographers of *Poverty Outlaw*, directed by Peter Kinoy, Pamela Yates, and on **Spike Lee**'s *4 Little Girls*.

In 1999 Kuras worked with Spike Lee again, this time on *Summer of Sam*, a hyperdramatic fictionalized story of the season in 1997 when serial killer David Berkowitz stalked New York and its boroughs for unsuspecting couples he could murder. Kuras gave the film a visual metaphor for the confluence of events including the rise of punk, disco, and sex clubs by cross-processing reversal film stocks to create torrid and garish reds and greens to capture the conflict and decadence of the times. Kuras went deeper into moving picture experimentation on Lee's *Bamboozled* (2000), shot with consumer digital video cameras for budgetary and aesthetic reasons and to render the raw look of the project that brutally examines the sad and demeaning legacy of blackface performing. In 2002 *Jim Brown All-American* (2002), a documentary about the legendary football player and actor, directed by Spike Lee, and *Personal Velocity: Three Portraits*, directed by Rebecca Miller, both photographed by Ellen Kuras were released.

BIBLIOGRAPHY

Pizzello, Stephen. "*I Shot Andy Warhol*, Sundance '96: Of Cell Phones and Celluloid." *American Cinematographer* 77.4 (April 1996): 74–76, 78–79, 82, 84, 86, 88–99.

———. "Spike Lee's Seventies Flashback: The Maverick Director Discusses His Modus Operandi for *Summer of Sam*." *American Cinematographer* 80.6 (June 1999): 50–52.

Thompson, Andrew. "Psycho Killer: Director of Photography Ellen Kuras, ASC, Helps Spike Lee Explore a Serial Killer's Impact on New York in *Summer of Sam*." *American Cinematographer* 80.6 (June 1999): 38–42, 44, 46, 48–49.

L

laboratory deferments. When a film, sound, video, or digital house performs work on a project first and receives a contractual payment after the film is completed or distributed. This allows the independent filmmaker to lower out-of-pocket expenses during production and postproduction phases of a project.

LaBute, Neil. Director, screenwriter. *b.* March 19, 1963, Detroit, Michigan. *ed.* Brigham Young University, University of Kansas theater master's program, New York University writing program. Button-pushing and provocative writer/director, Neil LaBute made a stunning, directorial debut with *In the Company of Men* in 1997. The low-budget indie is a disturbing and misogynist tale of two yuppie office workers who plan to get revenge against women by both dating the same woman and dumping her just for personal kicks. LaBute won the **Sundance** Filmmaker's Trophy, and the film created an uncanny reaction from **critics** and audiences taken aback by its hateful attitude toward women. The heartless plot presented such a convincing point of view there was concern that LaBute harbored the sexist feelings of his characters. Initially the reaction of women was negative; but eventually attitudes changed, and many perceived the film as a revealing analysis of misogyny. Stylistically, *In the Company of Men* is bare-bones filmmaking—LaBute was all story and character.

His second film, *Your Friends & Neighbors* (1998), was a major leap, as it combined a distinctive visual style with a Mamet-like ability to write about base emotions and create music within the language that drives relationships and personal motivation. LaBute gets stunning and brutally honest performances from Amy Brenneman, Jason Patric, Ben Stiller, Aaron Eckhart, Catherine Keener, and Natassja Kinski. The film centers on two couples and their friends, driven by a sexually charged atmosphere and dysfunctional behavior. The accomplished film drew attention for its frank examination of destructive contemporary relationships.

Nurse Betty (2000) was a departure for LaBute, who was establishing himself as a writer/director known for searing commentaries on the state of male/female relationships. *Nurse Betty* was written by John C. Richards and James Flamberg and stars Renée Zellweger as a delusional woman who believes her favorite soap opera is real. The black comedy turns serious when her husband is murdered and she is stalked by two men played by Morgan Freeman and Chris Rock. LaBute demonstrates he can interpret material, bring a visual style to the narrative, and elicit great performances. *Nurse Betty* received great critical acclaim. LaBute wrote and directed *Bash: Latterday Plays*, which aired on the Showtime cable network. In 2002 he wrote, directed, and produced *The Shape of Things* and wrote and directed *Possession*, based on the novel by A.S. Byatt.

Lachman, Ed. Cinematographer. New York–based director of photography who has worked all over the globe for almost thirty years. Lachman is a true indie who owns all his camera equipment. Although he is incredibly prolific, he has carefully chosen projects with artistic, political, social, or aesthetic meaning to him. Lachman is a veteran of **documentary** and nonfiction films. His work includes *Christo's Valley Curtain* (1973), *Say Amen, Somebody*, *Passion: The Script* (1983), *Stripper*, *Tokyo-ga*, *Ornette: Made in America* (all 1985), *The World of Mother Teresa* (1986), *Chuck Berry, Hail! Hail! Rock 'n' Roll* (1987), and *Songs for Drella* (1990). Lachman was in the forefront of postmodern film style in feature films: *Desperately Seeking Susan* (1985), *Making Mr. Right*, *Less Than Zero* (both 1987), and *True Stories* (1986), directed by Talking Heads' brainiac David Byrne. Lachman's long list of independent features includes *Backtrack* (1989), *Light Sleeper* (1992), *Selena* (1997), *Why Do Fools Fall in Love?* (1998), and *The Virgin Suicides* (2000).

He has worked with directors **Gregory Nava**, Paul Schrader, **Mira Nair**, Hanif Kureishi, **Dennis Hopper, Susan Seidelman**, Sophia Coppola, **Shirley Clarke, Nicholas Ray**, and **Albert and David Maysles**. Recent works with Ed Lachman as director of photography include: *Far From Heaven* (2002), directed by **Todd Haynes**, and *Simone* (2002). Lachman also codirected *Ken Park* with **Larry Clark**, based on a screenplay by **Harmony Korine**. Lachman is a self-styled film historian and theorist who inhales and absorbs the work of an eclectic group of aesthetic space travelers. Lachman, a member of the American Society of Cinematographers (ASC), calls himself "a visual gypsy."

Laemmle, Carl. Production executive, producer. *b.* January 17, 1867, Laupheim, Württemburg, Germany. *d.* September 24, 1939, Los Angeles, Cal-

Carl Laemmle, the founder of the company that became Universal, one of the major studios (center, with glasses), smiles while surrounded by admirers. Courtesy of The Del Valle Archive

ifornia. Carl Laemmle created Universal Studios, one of the original Hollywood studios. From 1906 to 1912 Laemmle was an independent filmmaker fighting against the power consortium that tried to dominate the industry and shut down all outsiders. Laemmle had emigrated in 1884 and worked as an errand boy in a New York drugstore. He moved to Chicago, where he delivered newspapers and was a bookkeeper. In Oshkosh, Wisconsin, Laemmle became a clothing store manager and married the boss's daughter.

After acquiring some savings Laemmle invested in a Chicago nickelodeon, a new American business he felt had exciting potential. It opened to a rousing success in January 1906, and he launched a second nickelodeon emporium just two months later. Laemmle was dissatisfied with the local film exchange that supplied nickelodeon films, so in 1909 he set up the Laemmle Film Service. He quickly opened Laemmle exchanges in American and Canadian cities, becoming the leading distributor in the business. The all-powerful Motion Picture Patents Company started putting up film exchanges, but Laemmle refused to go under; instead he went into direct competition by founding the Independent Motion Picture Company of America (IMP).

In 1909 Laemmle launched a massive publicity campaign to discredit the Patents Company and started creating his own movie studio. The **Biograph** Company and the Patents Company did not name their stars because they were concerned that if the actors became identified by name, they would become popular and demand more money. In 1910, Laemmle lured Florence Lawrence, then known only as the Biograph Girl, to his studio and publicized her name. The popular Mary Pickford followed. Laemmle's actions helped start the star system that eventually propelled the Hollywood Studio System into a mega-industry. Laemmle produced short films glamorizing his stars while continuing to block the Patents Company's repeated attempts to destroy him. In 1912 Laemmle finally won a court battle that led to the Patents Company's demise. The Independent Motion Picture Company of America merged with a smaller company to form The Universal Film Manufacturing Company, later Universal, one of Hollywood's major studios, thus ending Laemmle's career as an independent production executive. Just some of the many of almost 400 films associated with Carl Laemmle during his career include: *All Quiet on the Western Front* (1930), *The Phantom of the Opera* (1931), *Dracula*, *Frankenstein* (both 1931) and *Flash Gordon* (1936), which he produced.

Lambert, Mary. Director. *b.* 1951, Helena, Arkansas. *ed.* University of Denver, Rhode Island School of Design. Lambert was experienced in a multitude of production capacities when she headed to Los Angeles to become a music video director. She made it to the top of the profession directing clips for Madonna (*Material Girl*, *Like a Virgin*, *Borderline*, and *Like a Prayer*), Sting, Mick Jagger, Janet Jackson, The B52s, Motley Crue, The Pretenders, Chris Isaak, and The Tom Tom Club.

In 1987 she made the difficult transition from music videos to features with *Siesta*. The reality-bending story concerned a woman who mysteriously ends up in Spain surrounded by sexual danger and murder. *Siesta* was not the film late 1980s audiences wanted to see. Lambert's phantasmagoric vision would have been more readily embraced in the adventurous 1960s and 1970s. Lambert did hit big box office with her next feature *Pet Sematary* (1989), the **Stephen King** novel adapted for the screen by the horrormeister himself. The novel, one of King's scariest, became a nasty, pure contemporary horror film with Lambert taking no prisoners. She also directed the 1992 sequel. In 1991 Lambert was chosen to direct *Grand Isle*, an adaptation of the classic Kate Chopin feminist novel *The Awakening*, coproduced and starring Kelly McGillis. Songwriter and record producer Glen Ballard wrote *Clubland* (1999). The film is a sex, drugs, and rock 'n' roll cautionary tale aimed at those who live the "Music is my life" trip that takes down many young dreamers. In 2000 Lambert's *The In Crowd* was released, the story of a girl who is befriended by the leader of a clique of wealthy college students hiding dark secrets.

Lancaster, Burt. Actor, producer, director. *b.* Burton Stephen Lancaster, November 2, 1913, New York City. *d.* October 20, 1994, Century City, California. *ed.* New York University. The circus athlete who made his debut as Ernest Hemingway's "The Swede" in *The Killers* (1946) became one of the most enduring and accomplished Hollywood actors of the postwar era. Burt Lancaster was among the first actors working within the studio contract system to break out as an independent. Lancaster formed the Hecht-Lancaster Company with his agent **Harold Hecht**; later they were joined by producer James Hill and became Hecht-Hill-Lancaster. They produced many important films including *Apache* (1954), *Vera Cruz* (1954), Oscar-winning *Marty* (1955), *The Catered Affair* (1956), directed by Richard Brooks from a teleplay by *Marty* author Paddy Chayefsky, *Trapeze* (1956), *Sweet Smell of Success* (1957), *Run Silent, Run Deep* (1958), *Separate Tables* (1958), *The Devil's Disciple* (1959), and *The Unforgiven* (1960). In 1955 Lancaster directed, starred in, and coproduced *The Kentuckian* through his partnership. Throughout his career Lancaster worked with maverick directors of independent spirit. They include John Frankenheimer, **Robert Aldrich**, Sam Peckinpah, Bernardo Bertolucci, Luchino Visconti, **Robert Altman**, Bill Forsyth, and Richard Brooks. *See also* Hecht, Harold

BIBLIOGRAPHY

Fishgall, Gary. *Against Type: The Biography of Burt Lancaster*. New York: Scribner, 1995.

Larson, Rodger. Educator, author. In 1963, Rodger Larson began making films with a few students at the Summer Theater Arts Program at the

Burt Lancaster with a prone Michael York in *The Island of Dr. Moreau* (1977), a remake of the 1933 film *Island of Lost Souls. Courtesy of The Del Valle Archive*

Mosholu-Montefiore Community Center in the Bronx, New York. Larson quit his job as an art teacher and was unemployed for six months while he fervently tried to convince any organization that filmmaking impacted on teens more than any other creative arts program. After tireless fundraising, Larson set up a temporary base for his youth program at New York's 92nd Street YM-YWHA. In 1966 Larson wanted to create a permanent film workshop where young people could learn how to express their creativity and unique points of view by making films. Larson gave a voice to a generation shut out of the media. He called his brainchild Film Club, starting in the kitchen pantry of the University Settlement on New York's Lower East Side. In 1969, the Young Filmmaker's Foundation supported the program, and today it continues empowering young people, corporate clients, documentarians, and **experimental** filmmakers as Film/Video Arts. Larson's humble, passionate experiment with a few teens has developed into a hub of digital and traditional filmmaking, offering courses on filmmaking and a certificate and internship program.

See also Film/Video Arts

BIBLIOGRAPHY

Larson, Rodger, with Ellen Meade. *Young Filmmakers*. New York: E.P. Dutton, 1969.

Latino cinema. People of Hispanic culture have had poor representation in Hollywood cinema. Historically, they have been portrayed as criminals or as poor, ignorant, and without resources. More positive roles often went to non-Hispanic actors. Few Latino performers had the opportunity to develop careers. Independent filmmaking helped Latinos break studio system constraints. Important directorial figures in Latino independent cinema are **Robert Young**, a non-Hispanic, who directed *Alambrista!* (1978) and *The Ballad of Gregorio Cortez* (1983); **Gregory Nava**; **Robert Rodriguez**; Luis Valdez, who directed *Zoot Suit* (1981) and *La Bamba* (1987); and Ramón Menéndez, the director of ***Stand and Deliver*** (1987). Miguel Arteta went beyond heritage with *Star Maps* (1997), a film about the cultural divide in Los Angeles. The independents brought Latino life to film audiences, and its impact has now spread to mainstream cinema where roles for Hispanic actors are developing and more diversity is evident in the portrayal of Latinos.

BIBLIOGRAPHY

Fregoso, Rosa Linda. *The Bronze Screen: Chicana and Chicano Film Culture*. London: University of Minnesota Press, 1993.

Laughlin, Tom. Actor, director, screenwriter, producer. *b.* August 10, 1938, Minneapolis, Minnesota. *ed.* University of Indiana, University of Minnesota. Known as T.C. Frank, Frank Christina, Frank Laughlin, and his given name, Tom Laughlin, he is most familiar to the moviegoing public as Billy Jack. Laughlin began in films in the late 1950s as an actor playing secondary juvenile roles in such Hollywood films as *The Delinquents* (1957), *South Pacific* (1958), and *Gidget* (1959). As if in preparation for his most famous role as Billy Jack, Laughlin ran a Montessori school in Santa Monica, California. In the mid-1960s he worked as an actor, director, producer, and writer on low-budget independent films including *The Proper Time* (1960), *Among the Thorns* (1960), *Like Father, Like Son* (1961), *The Young Sinner* (1965), and *Born Losers* (1967), a **biker film** that created the theme and model for *Billy Jack*. Laughlin survived on the fringes of the industry, going through his slew of pseudonyms as he worked in front of and behind the camera. In 1971, *Billy Jack* was released, and the independent film was more than a box office smash; it became a cultural phenomenon and the launching pad for Laughlin's media empire, Billy Jack Enterprises, an office complex in the center of Hollywood. *Billy Jack* starred Laughlin and his wife Delores Taylor and was made and distributed outside the studio system for $800,000 and grossing tens of millions of dollars. *Billy Jack* is the story of a half-breed, martial arts master who becomes the protector of a progressive free school under physical threat by local yahoos and bigots who focus their venom and hatred on the diverse students and the school's mission of peace and creativity. *Billy Jack*'s mega success was not principally because of its message of peace. Laughlin's genius was in his real agenda, a belief that violence cannot be stopped with nonviolence but only with a return of force. Mainstream audiences relished the sight of bad guys getting whooped as they had since the beginning of film narratives. This time the hero was associated with counterculture types, and the violence wasn't conventional fisticuffs but martial arts. Many Americans were fascinated with the self-defense tool not only for its philosophy or Eastern cultural ties but also for its reinvention of the classic fight scene and action film. Laughlin turned *Billy Jack* into a trilogy—*The Trial of Billy Jack* (1974) and *Billy Jack Goes to Washington* (1977) followed. The films were savaged by the critical establishment, but audiences embraced the character as a hero for their times.

In 1975, Laughlin directed *The Master Gunfighter* starring Laughlin and Ron O'Neal of *Superfly* fame, a western based on the Japanese Samurai film *Goyokin* (1969). The story of a gunfighter who dislikes killing but is driven to do so continued to deliver Laughlin's conflicting message of peace through violence.

In 1975 Laughlin announced plans for Billy Jack Enterprises to become an entertainment conglomerate with record and book subsidiaries. Laughlin's mega plan included acquiring the CBS West Coast Production Center, but overexposure of the *Billy Jack* persona, a dwindling cash flow, and the complete failure of *The Master Gunfighter* brought the Laughlin empire to the verge of bankruptcy in 1976. In 1985 Laughlin resurfaced to announce plans to direct and star in *The Return of Billy Jack* and the creation of a Laughlin School of Filmmaking in Houston, Texas. Neither materialized. Since the 1980s Tom Laughlin has created a series of videos and online Jungian seminars concerning such topics as Love, Sex, Cancer and Health, and Politics and Political Change. He still claims there will be another Billy Jack movie but his web site billyjack.com hawks the old movies on DVD, tee shirts and caps with the Billy Jack logo and books he has written such as "Tom Laughlin's 9 Secrets to Writing a Hit Movie, TV Show, Play or Novel." The filmmaker who played a rough and tumble philosopher on screen has come full circle in life.

Laurel Productions. *See* Romero, George A.

Law, Lindsay. Producer, executive. *b.* February 21, 1949. Former executive director of the Public Broadcasting series *American Playhouse*, Lindsay Law was responsible for bringing independent film projects to life and air on national television. By funding projects the studios were not initially interested in, many filmmakers were later able to get a theatrical release for their work. Some of the independent films Law supported include *Smooth Talk* (1985), ***Stand and Deliver*** (1987), *Stacking* (1987), *The Thin Blue Line* (1988), *Eat a Bowl of Tea* (1989), *All the Vermeers in New York* (1990), *Straight Out of Brooklyn* (1991), *The Music of Chance* (1993), *Ethan Frome* (1993), and *Amateur* (1994). Later, Law became chief of Fox Searchlight. He also executive produced *Mi Familia/My Family* (1995), *Safe* (1995), *Angels and Insects* (1995), *Reckless* (1995), *I Shot Andy Warhol* (1996) and *Fast Cheap & Out of Control* (1997). As the *American Playhouse* chief, Law was criticized for his parochial film taste, nicknamed Granola Movies because of his admiration and relationship with Horton Foote and his tendency to be attracted to traditional three-act structures. Law is one of the godfathers of independent filmmaking. Without his insight and determination, countless films might never have been produced and completed. That fact makes quibbles over personal taste seem petty.

Leacock, Richard (Ricky). Documentary filmmaker. *b.* July 18, 1921, Canary Islands. *ed.* Harvard University. When Ricky Leacock was fourteen, he was given a movie camera to record a school camping trip. He spent most of his shooting time filming the terrain and environment. He only shot images of people if they were doing an interesting action or exhibiting revealing behavior—A documentarian was being born. As a combat cameraman during World War II, Leacock photographed many battles and traveled cinematically to the Alaska Highway, India, Burma, and China, turning in his exposed footage without seeing the result. After the army brass screened Leacock's work, he received angry telegrams complaining he was shooting too many local festivals—not part of the military objective.

Robert Flaherty had seen a **documentary** Leacock made about bananas on the Canary Islands. Impressed with the young man's work, Flaherty brought Leacock on location when he was making *Louisiana Story* (1948). Leacock carried the equipment and watched the master documentary filmmaker; he eventually became an associate producer and cameraman on the project and witnessed Flaherty creating one of his most significant works. Leacock had come of age admiring the traditional documentaries of Flaherty and John Grieson. He was aware that sound presented new possibilities to the documentary experience, but the heavy and encumbered tools available made it impossible to capture actual sound. After much experimentation, Leacock developed a quiet sync-sound camera and portable tape recorder in 1960, just as American society was about to undergo a social and political transformation. *Primary* (1960) followed the presidential Democratic primary campaigns of Hubert Humphrey and John F. Kennedy; Leacock filmed the two men on the campaign trail. *Primary* captures the charismatic young senator and the less-than-glamorous sincere challenger from Minnesota. The contrast between the two politicians is clearly delineated by the direct use of camera and editing. *Primary* documents the cult of celebrity that is now the operating principle in presidential politics.

Leacock was the director and cinematographer on his films, and a second person ran the sound recorder. No cables or lights were necessary. If the two-man crew missed any of the action, Leacock would never interject and ask the subjects to repeat themselves. No interviews were conducted; subjects were never questioned. Leacock stuck to his documentary scriptures and always regretted the result if he broke a commandment.

Leacock had substantive collaborations with **Robert Drew** Associates as part of a team producing documentaries intended for CBS-TV. He partnered with **D.A. Pennebaker** and worked with **Louis de Rochemont**, **Willard Van Dyke**, and other renowned documentarians. His association with Drew, Pennebaker, and **Albert Maysles** pioneered the American **cinéma vérité** style known as **direct cinema**, less rigorous and more eclectic in execution. It still thrives today on digital video.

After creating *Happy Mother's Day* (1963), about the birth of quintuplets in the Midwest, and *Chiefs* (1969), chronicling a convention of 3,000 police chiefs and their wives in Waikiki Beach, Leacock founded and chaired the Department of Film at Massachusetts Institute of Technology. Leacock's reputation as a consummate cinematographer made him attractive to figures as diverse as Jean-Luc Godard and **Norman Mailer**. As a filmmaker, educator, theorist, and essayist, Leacock is a defender of artists' rights and is committed to revealing life as it is—on a low budget and with total independence. Recent credits for Richard Leacock includes three films that he directed: *Félix et Josephine*, the short film *A Celebration of Saint Silas* (both 1993), and *A Hole in the Sea* (1994). *See also* documentaries; Pennebaker, D.A.

BIBLIOGRAPHY

Levin, G. Roy. *Documentary Explorations: 15 Interviews with Film-Makers.* Garden City, NY: Anchor Press, 1971.

Lee, Spike. Director, producer, screenwriter, actor. *b.* Shelton Jackson Lee, March 20, 1957, Atlanta, Georgia. *ed.* Morehouse College, New York University. Spike Lee's thesis film *Joe's Bed-Stuy Barbershop: We Cut Heads* (1983) won the Motion Picture Academy Student Award. Lee tried to capitalize on the attention to launch his feature film career. Lee crafted a screenplay he was confident would start him on the path to success. *Messenger* was a semiautobiographical script ready to shoot. Lee cast the project, put together a crew, and struggled to get financing. Then disaster

Director Spike Lee proudly wears his Malcolm X tee shirt. Courtesy of The Del Valle Archive

struck—the independent filmmaker's very worst nightmare. The money fell through and the production was forced to shut down. The news quickly spread throughout the New York film community.

Fighting off humiliation and anger, Lee's determination kept him going. He began writing a new feature script for his directorial debut *She's Gotta Have It* (1986), the story of Nola Darling, a black female in search of her identity and her three lovers. Raising the money was slow and difficult, but Lee persevered. From the start Lee surrounded himself with talented craftspeople. Cinematographer **Ernest Dickerson** and production designer **Wynn Thomas** were young African American filmmakers equally dedicated to breaking into features, an area that had been just about locked off to people of color. *She's Gotta Have It* garnered accolades from the **critics** and a wide enough release to generate an intense buzz. Black audiences laughed out loud and thrilled at being able to identify with the screen characters. General audiences found Lee's film hilarious, while it smashed all the contrived Hollywood images of African Americans. *She's Gotta Have It* did strong box office and put Spike Lee out there.

Everyone wanted a piece of the first major black filmmaker. After being courted, Lee signed a deal with Columbia Pictures. His first studio project, *School Daze* (1988), was a big-budget production (compared to a typical indie project at the time) and dealt with the caste system based on skin color at an all-black college. The film was a box office disaster. The style was overproduced and film school amateurish. For his next film Lee switched to Universal Pictures. *Do the Right Thing* (1989), an incendiary film about the volatile state of race relations in America, presented Lee's beloved Brooklyn as the center of the universe on the hottest day of the year. Back on track, armed with his production company 40 Acres & A Mule Filmworks and his personal tag line "A Spike Lee Joint," Spike Lee was here to stay.

A consummate businessman, Lee made studio deals for daunting projects extremely difficult to finance independently, specifically the epic biography *Malcolm X* (1992) and the handsomely mounted productions *Mo' Better Blues* (1990), *Jungle Fever* (1991), and *Clockers* (1995). Only *Girl 6* (1996), *Get on the Bus* (1996), and *Bamboozled* (2000) were independently funded projects.

Many of Lee's films have divided critics and alienated even African American audiences with their Afrocentrist views, perhaps more angry than insightful on being black in America. Tackling interracial relationships, drugs in the urban community, phone sex, the corruption of the black athlete, Italian American/African American conflicts, Jewish dominance over black jazz musicians, and Muslim conversions, Lee has taken on controversy at almost every cinematic turn. Stylistically, Lee takes realistic, serious content and treats it visually with theatrical flamboyance. As he has grown more sophisticated in his craft, Lee retains the curiosity and the willing-to-try-anything approach of the student filmmaker, sometimes at the price of excess that prevents films like *He Got Game* (1998) and *Summer of Sam* (1999) from becoming the mature works they set out to be. Spike Lee directed *A Huey P. Newton Story* (2001), for television's Black Starz! In 2002 he contributed a short film to the compilation project *Ten Minutes Older*, and was the director and producer of *Jim Brown All-American*.

Lee is a pioneer; he carved the way for the explosion of black talent that followed his stunning debut. John Singleton, the **Hudlin** brothers, **Robert Townsend**, and Keenan Ivory Wayans are all in his debt. Lee gave actors Laurence Fishburne, Giancarlo Esposito, Samuel L. Jackson, Delroy Lindo, and superstars Denzel Washington and Wesley Snipes a platform for their talents. Still angry after all these years, Spike Lee will continue to speak out as a celebrity and on screen as a filmmaker whose independent spirit continues to grow. *See also* Dickerson, Ernest; Thomas, Wynn

BIBLIOGRAPHY

Lee, Spike. *Spike Lee's Gotta Have It: Inside Guerrilla Filmmaking*. New York: Fireside, 1987.
Lee, Spike, with Lisa Jones. *Do The Right Thing*. New York: Fireside, 1989.
———. *Mo' Better Blues*. New York: Fireside, 1990.
———. *Uplift the Race: The Construction of School Daze*. New York: Fireside, 1988.

Lennon, John. Musician, filmmaker. *b.* October 9, 1940, Liverpool, England. *d.* December 8, 1980, New York City, murdered by Mark David Chapman. Lennon collaborated with **Yoko Ono** on many nonnarrative independent **16mm** films including *Two Virgins* (1968), *Bed-In* (1969), *Rape* (1969), *Apotheosis* (1970), *Erection* (1971), *Imagine* (1971), and *Ten for Two: Sisters, O Sisters* (1972). Chapman's bullets didn't just take the life of a twentieth-century musical icon; they also took down a serious **experimental** filmmaker. *See also* Ono, Yoko

BIBLIOGRAPHY

Goldman, Albert. *The Lives of John Lennon*. New York: William Morrow, 1988.

Lerner, Irving. Director, editor. *b.* March 7, 1909, New York City. *d.* December 25, 1976, Los Angeles, California. Irving Lerner produced and directed **anthropological** short films for Columbia Pictures, the prestigious Rockefeller Foundation, and other organizations. In 1939, Lerner was film editor and second unit director on the **documentary** *One Third of a Nation* and worked with **Willard Van Dyke** on *Valley Town* and *The Children Must Learn* (both 1940). Lerner was one of four cinematographers on **Robert Flaherty**'s *The Land* (1941). Later Lerner was in charge of the Educational Film Institute at New York University. In 1948 Lerner codirected the documentary short *Muscle Beach* with **Joseph Strick**. In 1951, he directed the World War II documentary *Suicide Attack*. In the 1950s Lerner directed low-budget **B-movies,** many shot in just one week. The black-and-white film *Man Crazy* (1953) is the sordid story of three wayward, aimless teenage girls, who hang out at their local drugstore, find $28,000, and head straight to Hollywood in search of stardom. Instead they encounter... Well, the tabloid ads said it best: "It's Bold! Blunt! Brutal! Today's Most Searching Story of Youth... Written in Shame and Shock, Tears and Tragedy, Truth and Terror!" *Edge of Fury* (1958) was another black-and-white B about a deranged beachcomber who slaughters a family after renting them a summer cottage.

Lerner's best-known film *Murder by Contract* (1958) examines the making and undoing of a professional hit man. *City of Fear* (1959) tracked an escaped convict who mistakenly robs a container filled with radioactive material instead of loot and is hunted down by both the police and frantic health officials. In 1960 Lerner took on the classic James T. Farrell trilogy *Studs Lonigan.* In 1963 Lerner directed *Cry of Battle,* an action film about the son of a rich businessman who joins a partisan cause in the Philippines. *The Royal Hunt of the Sun* (1969) was an uncharacteristically large-scale big-budget production for Lerner based on Peter Shaffer's play about the Spanish explorer Pizzaro.

In the 1970s Lerner returned to editing, cutting *Executive Action* (1973), a fictional investigation of the JFK assassination, an adaptation of Herman Hesse's novel *Steppenwolf* (1974), and *The River Niger* (1976), based on the Tony Award–winning play. Lerner was supervising editor on **Martin Scorsese**'s musical epic *New York, New York* (1977), released after his death.

lesbian cinema. The Hollywood Studio System historically portrayed lesbians in negative stereotypical roles. It wasn't until the late 1980s that independent film finally gave gay women a truer voice. *Desert Hearts* (1985), a 1950s love affair, took director Donna Deitch four years to bring to the screen. *Claire of the Moon* (1992), directed by Nicole Conn, featured steamy sex scenes but a conventional plot concerning two opposites who attract—here they both happen to be female. Rose Troche's *Go Fish!* (1994) was the most successful lesbian film to date and was a breakthrough. The comedy showed lesbians thriving in exclusive communities, living their lives happily. *The Incredibly True Adventures of Two Girls in Love* (1995), directed by Maria Maggenti, celebrated love between women. *The Watermelon Woman* (1996), directed by Cheryl Dunye, is a semiautobiographical film about a black lesbian filmmaker researching a 1930s actress known as the Watermelon Woman. *High Art* (1998), directed by

Lisa Cholodenko, is an acclaimed film about a photographer who has given up her career before her time, a heroin-addicted woman, and a young ambitious editor working her way to the top.

BIBLIOGRAPHY

Creekmur, Corey K., and Alexander Doty, eds. *Out in Culture: Gay, Lesbian and Queer Essays on Popular Culture.* Durham, NC: Duke University Press, 1995.

Darren, Alison. *Lesbian Film Guide.* London: Cassell. 2000.

Rich, B. Ruby. *Chick Flicks: Theories and Memories of the Feminist Film Movement.* Durham, NC: Duke University Press, 1998.

Lester, Mark L. Director, screenwriter, producer. *b.* November 26, 1946, Cleveland, Ohio. *ed.* University of California, Northridge. Low-budget action/violence specialist best known for *Class of 1984* (1982) and *Class of 1999* (1990), which camp up mayhem and revenge in high school. The ultraviolent students make the boys from *Blackboard Jungle* (1955) look like Peace Corps volunteers. Mark L. Lester, not to be confused with the sweet-faced child actor in *Oliver!* (1968), spent 1971 living in the Yucatan and Guatemala making his first feature, *Twilight of the Mayas,* that documented the culture and natural phenomena of the countries. Although Lester solidified his career in **exploitation films** like *Truck Stop Women* (1974), *Extreme Justice* (1993), and *Blowback* (1999), he continues to make **documentaries** and films with political content. His dream projects were a biopic of political activist Mother Jones and *Death in Washington,* which he feels would elevate him to the stature of Costa Gravas's *Z* (1969); but films like 1979's *Roller Boogie* dampened hopes for their realization. Lester's best fictional works are his cinematic adaptation of **Stephen King**'s *Firestarter* (1984), starring a young Drew Barrymore, and the Schwartzenegger fan club favorite *Commando* (1985). Recent films directed and produced by Mark L. Lester include: *Blowback* (1999), the television movie *Guilty as Charged* and *Betrayal* (both 2001).

Levin, Marc. Director, producer, screenwriter. Marc Levin is a **documentary** and fictional filmmaker interested in politics, crime, and urban, racial, and cultural issues and is obsessed and committed to films about prisons and the American criminal justice system. In 1993 Levin codirected *The Last Party* with Mark Benjamin. It was cowritten by Robert Downey Jr. and Donovan Leitch. The documentary takes place during the 1992 Democratic National Convention. Downey interviews a bevy of politicians and celebrities including Bill Clinton, Curtis Sliwa, **Spike Lee,** Jerry Brown, Roger Clinton, Oliver Stone, the Reverend Al Sharpton, G. Gordon Liddy, Senator John Kerry, Peter Jennings, Jerry Falwell, Oliver North, and Mary Stuart Masterson. *Slam* (1998) is a low-budget fictional feature concerning a gifted African American poet jailed for possession of marijuana. In prison he uses his power of words to stop violence. He later meets a young woman who enters him in a Slam Poetry event that transforms his life. Levin utilizes a documentary, **Cassavetes**-like style to bring a sense of reality to the film and to connect it to his nonfiction work. *Thug Life in D.C.* (1999) is a crime and prison documentary. *White Boys* (1999) is a fictional film about a young white man who wants to be a rap star. He speaks in black slang, dresses in hip-hop fashions, and sells flour as cocaine. In 2000, Levin filmed Anna Deavere Smith in her award-winning one-woman theater piece *Twilight: Los Angeles*. For *Brooklyn Babylon* (2001), Levin returns to fiction with the story of a rapper who falls in love with a young Jewish girl from a religious family. In 2001 Marc Levin directed *Street Time*.

Levinson, Barry. *See* Baltimore Pictures

Levitt, Helen. Filmmaker, cinematographer, producer, screenwriter. *b.* 1913, New York, New York. Photographer Helen Levitt created *In the Street* (1952) with **James Agee** and Janice Loeb. She was a cinematographer on the docudrama *The Savage Eye* (1960), directed by **Joseph Strick, Ben Maddow**, and Sidney Meyers. Levitt was also a screenwriter, along with James Agee, Janice Loeb, and Sidney Meyer, for the **documentary** *The Quiet One* (1949). In 1963 Levitt produced Ben Maddow's *An Affair of the Skin.*

Lewis, Herschell Gordon. Director, screenwriter, producer, director of photography, composer. *b.* June 15, 1926, Pittsburgh, Pennsylvania. Herschell Gordon Lewis is a respectable English professor who taught graduate courses in mass communications for over twenty years, a professional lecturer who is in demand worldwide and the owner of an advertising and consulting firm, Communicomp. Lewis is also the director of *Blood Feast* (1963), *2000 Maniacs* (1964), *She-Devils on Wheels* (1968), and *The Gore-Gore Girls* (1972). Lewis started his movie career directing **soft-core films**, then began his ascent to king of the gore films that feature bloody, flesh-ripping, bone-breaking effects. Bad acting married *Blood Feast*, Lewis's early work in the field, but its cheesy, bloody gore effects, which relied on pounds of animal entrails, remain the standard for the genre. Lewis instilled a pure camp sense of humor in his films, which was lost by his many imitators. *Blood Feast* was shot in 35mm color for $24,000.

All of Lewis's films made money because of his rigorous formula of a 2:1 **shooting ratio**, a seventy-minute running time, and a budget cap of $60,000 to $70,000. Lewis often worked in Florida, settling for bad takes to keep on schedule and budget. His unconventional cinematic technique included covering the sound recorder with Reynolds Wrap to quiet the machine's hum. Dissolves were created with an old mechanism on his

A graphic example that Herschell Gordon Lewis delivers in *Blood Feast* (1963). Courtesy of The Del Valle Archive

BNC Mitchell camera that was thirty years out of date. Wipes, historically created optically so one image could push the other offscreen, were done with a shirtboard over the lens. In the early 1970s Lewis retired from the film business, worn down by the financial treachery of industry practices. He became a direct-mail consultant. Lewis's infamous career also includes *Boin-n-ng* (1963), *Scum of the Earth* (1963) and *Stick It in Your Ear* (1970). In 2001 Herschell Gordon Lewis was the executive producer of *Blood Feast 2: All U Can Eat*. In 2002 he executive produced *2001 Maniacs*.

BIBLIOGRAPHY

Curry, Christopher Wayne. *The Films of Herschell Gordon Lewis.* London: Creation Books, 1999.

Lewis, Joseph H. Director, editor. *b.* April 6, 1907, Brooklyn, New York. *d.* August 30, 2000, Santa Monica, California. After attending DeWitt Clinton High School in the Bronx, Lewis followed his brother Ben, a film editor, to Hollywood. Aspirations to be the next Rudolph Valentino quickly shifted when Ben got him a job as a camera assistant. A professional and inventive journeyman during his entire career, Lewis talked his way into an editor-in-chief position at Republic Studios after apprenticing as an assistant for his brother and others. Only giving his last name, they assumed he was Ben, and he easily got the position. At Republic he created many title sequences that included graphics and images, a trend other studios often imitated.

Lewis began directing low-budget B Westerns at Universal, shooting six films in six months. He was nicknamed Wagon Wheel Joe for his visual experimentation, shooting through a wagon wheel to create pictorial interest. Lewis experimented with camera angles and cinematic staging. He shot very little coverage and had an intuitive sense about how a film should look. He made them fast and cheap. *Bombs over Burma* (1942) was made for only $25,000, but his optimistic enthusiasm and passion drove him beyond convention. The 1955 film *The Big Combo* was the first American film to imply the act of oral sex. From 1937 to 1958 Lewis directed over forty films with little fanfare. He suffered a major heart attack when he was forty-six and eventually retired.

In the late 1960s Lewis was rediscovered by auteurist **critics** in France and the United States who proclaimed him a visionary filmmaker who boldly created his own film language and applied it to the genre film. His reputation was topped by reaction to *Gun Crazy*, a 1949 film noir that featured an uninterrupted ten-minute take shot from the back seat of a car during a bank robbery. The shot made the audience a participant in the crime and was a brave aesthetic choice as well as a cost-cutting measure for filming an elaborate sequence. The film was shot in thirty days for $400,000. Traveling internationally, Lewis was a motivating force and enjoyed the respect of filmmakers and students who clamored to hear him speak.

The films of Lewis were considered **B-movie** fare, but Lewis was a professional artist who tirelessly experimented with cinematic tools. He found depth in the scripts he was given, expressing meaning he discovered through the art of his craft. Just some of his films include *The Spy Ring* (1938), *Blazing Six Shooters* (1940), *Pride of the Bowery* (1941), *The Mad Doctor of Market Street* (1942), *The Undercover Man* (1949), *Retreat, Hell!* (1952), *A Lawless Street* (1955), *Man on a Bus* (1955), and *Terror in a Texas Town* (1958). In 1997 the Los Angeles Film Critics Association gave Lewis their lifetime achievement award.

BIBLIOGRAPHY

Bogdanovich, Peter. *Who the Devil Made It.* New York: Knopf, 1997.

McCarthy, Todd, with Charles Flynn, eds. *Kings of the Bs: Working within the Hollywood System: An Anthology of Film History and Criticism.* New York: E.P. Dutton, 1975.

Lievsay, Skip. Sound designer, supervising sound editor. After working in set design and construction for the theater, Skip Lievsay worked on a low-budget film multitasking as a gaffer, location scout, slate marker, and an apprentice picture and sound editor—his introduction to his life's career in postproduction sound. He gained additional film experience working on short films that aired on NBC's nascent *Saturday Night Live*. The New York film community began offering him sound editing jobs. One of Lievsay's first credits as a sound editor was *Polyester* (1981), directed by **John Waters**. He worked with **Spike Lee** on *Do the Right Thing* (1989), *Jungle Fever* (1991), *Crooklyn* (1994), and *Clockers* (1995); with **Jonathan Demme** on *The Silence of the Lambs* (1991); and on the **Coen** brothers' *Barton Fink* (1991). Lievsay has established long relationships collaborating with independent filmmakers. They include **Martin Scorsese**, *After Hours* (1985), *The Color of Money* (1986), *Cape Fear* (1991), and *The Age of Innocence* (1993); the **Coen** brothers, *Blood Simple* (1984), *Raising Arizona* (1987), *Miller's Crossing* (1990), *The Hudsucker Proxy* (1994), *Fargo* (1996), *The Big Lebowski* (1998), and *O Brother, Where Art Thou?* (2000); **John Sayles**, *Matewan* (1987), *City of Hope* (1991) and *Passion Fish* (1992); and Barry Sonnenfeld, *Get Shorty* (1995), *Men in Black* (1997), and *Wild, Wild West* (1999). Lievsay also created sound environments for *Zebrahead* (1992, directed by Anthony Drazan; *Fast, Cheap & Out of Control* (1997), directed by **Errol Morris**; *Beloved* (1998), directed by Jonathan Demme; and *Shaft* (2000), directed by John Singleton. Recent credits for Skip Lievsay's work in film sound include: *O Brother Where Art Thou?*, directed by the **Coen brothers**, *Shaft*, directed by John Singleton (both 2000), *The Center of the World* (2001), directed by **Wayne Wang**, and *Death to Smoochy* (2002), directed by Danny DeVito.

Lievsay is a shy, articulate man with complex abstract ideas like using the sound of a slowed-down Staten Island ferryboat horn and bat wings fluttering in the crack den sequence in *Jungle Fever* (1991). For the conclusion of *The Silence of the Lambs*, Lievsay played oil rig squealing sounds when Buffalo Bill stalks Clarice in the dark. As a sound designer, Lievsay layers, augments, and synthesizes sounds into what he calls "scenarios" that enrich the narratives. Independent filmmakers were once discouraged from experimenting with sound—told it was too expensive or not part of the **guerrilla filmmaking** aesthetic. Lievsay's work in the field motivates the indie to create an emotional impact with a microphone, a tape recorder, and sound equipment, recognizing that imagination has no limits.

Liman, Doug. Director, producer. *ed.* Brown University, University of Southern California. Before Doug Liman captured the 1990s zeitgeist with *Swingers*, he directed *Getting In*, aka *Student Body* (1994), a satire about a medical student who becomes a murder suspect when applicants ahead of him start to die. The film got little attention, but *Swingers* (1996) tapped into Rat Pack, retro-cool that stimulated the twenty-something crowd. The screenplay by Jon Fareau, who also stars, is about a group of self-styled hipsters who make the LA and Las Vegas scene drinking drinks, spouting lingo, and trying to live like Frank and Dino. Mike, played by Fareau, is lovesick for his girl back home, and the comedy centers around the politics of the phone answering machine. Liman directed and photographed the stylish film that was made for $250,000 and sold to **Miramax** for $5 million. *Swingers* was a critical success and audience pleaser. *Go* (1999) follows the lives of hedonistic LA teens during a twenty-four-hour period seen through multiple points of view. Again Liman was speaking to the youth crowd consumed with a lifestyle of partying, networking, and the relationship game. In a surprising career turn, Liman signed on to direct *The Bourne Identity* (2002), starring Matt Damon in an adaptation of the bestselling thriller by Robert Ludlum. In 2000 Liman produced *See Jane Run* and was the associate producer of *Kissing Jessica Stein* (2002).

limited partnership. State-regulated, limited partnerships concern a fiscal arrangement created by two or more parties with general, limited, or silent partners to finance a motion picture project. The general partners manage the partnership, while others only contribute capital, property, or services for a percentage. Limited partners do not participate and have no liability toward the project beyond their investment. Compliance with federal and state securities laws is required when limited partnerships are employed to finance a film. State partnership acts vary from state to state; some allow the deal to be structured so the general and limited partners have more liability than corporate statutes allow.

Linklater, Richard. Director, writer. *b.* 1961, Austin, Texas. *ed.* Sam Houston State University. Ingenious Generation X director and founder of the Austin Film Society, his 1991 feature *Slacker* is a clever slice of social dropout life in Austin, Texas, and a superb model of **guerrilla filmmaking.** His follow-up film *Dazed and Confused* (1993), produced by Linklater's Detour Production Company, is an engaging autobiographical snapshot of the last day of high school circa 1976 in suburban Texas. In 1995 Linklater wrote and directed *Before Sunrise*, a forthright romance of a young man's (Ethan Hawke) loving brief encounter on his last night in Europe. Linklater collaborated with Eric Bogosian to adapt Bogosian's play *SubUrbia* (1996), a caustic examination of postteen disaffection. In 1998 Linklater departed from contemporary subject matter and indie status with a $27 million studio production of *The Newton Boys*, a 1920s period saga of four bank-robber brothers featuring young turks Matthew McConaughey, Skeet Ulrich, Ethan Hawke, and Vincent D'Onofrio. The feature was not commercially successful and quickly exited to video.

Waking Life (2001) is a surreal animated film billed as a companion piece to *Slacker*. In 2001 Richard Linklater also directed *Tape*.

BIBLIOGRAPHY

Linklater, Richard, and Denise Montgomery. *Dazed and Confused: Inspired by the Screenplay by Richard Linklater*. New York: St. Martin's Griffin, 1993.

Lipton, Lenny. Filmmaker, author. *b.* 1940, Brooklyn, New York. *ed.* Cornell University. In 1965, in addition to receiving royalties for a hit record *Puff, the Magic Dragon* based on his Ogden Nash–inspired poem and performed by Peter, Paul and Mary, Lenny Lipton was bitten by the film bug and immersed himself in learning the art and craft of the medium. Lipton began making **16mm** and **Super 8mm** shorts in the mid-1960s including *We Shall March Again* (1965), *Memories of an Unborn Baby* (1966), and *Let a Thousand Parks Bloom* (1969). He became the film columnist for *The Berkeley Barb* and the director of **Canyon Cinema** and taught film at the San Francisco Art Institute.

In 1972 Straight Arrow Press, owned by Rolling Stone publisher Jann Wenner, published Lenny Lipton's book *Independent Filmmaking*, a how-to, step-by-step guide to making films outside Hollywood. The book was an immediate success and was revised in October 1973. In the early 1970s young filmmakers were turning anywhere they could to learn more about the cinematic process. Film literature was in its infancy, and the Lipton book became a bible for aspirants. The number of independent filmmakers Lipton's book has educated and inspired is incalculable. In 1979 *Lipton on Filmmaking* was published to educate the person he called a basement filmmaker. The book went into advanced areas of study including Polavision, 3D, adding sound to Super 8mm, print making, and the professional application of Super 8mm filmmaking. Lipton also wrote *The Crystal Eyes Handbook* (1991), *Foundations of the Stereoscopic Cinema* (1982), and *The Super 8 Book* (1975).

In the 1970s Lenny Lipton continued to make independent films including *Far Out, Star Route* (1971), *Dogs of the Forest* (1972), and *Children of the Golden West* (1975).

BIBLIOGRAPHY

Lipton, Lenny. *Independent Filmmaking*. San Francisco: Straight Arrow Books, 1972.
———. *Lipton on Filmmaking*. Ed. Chet Roaman. New York: Simon and Schuster, 1979.

Liquid Sky. Independent **midnight movie** with a distinct cult following, directed, cowritten, and produced by Slava Tsukerman, a Russian émigré who arrived in New York in 1976. Tsukerman was ready to explore every exotic pleasure and antisocial attitude banned in his country. He became attracted to the burgeoning punk, bisexual, and performance art scene in Lower Manhattan. The 1983 film stars a gender-bending Anne Carlisle who cowrote the screenplay with Tsukerman and Nina V. Kerova and plays the dual role of Margaret and Jimmy. *Liquid Sky* was very low budget, produced by a largely unknown cast and crew. It defies genre classification. It is a psychedelic, social commentary about a narcissistic segment of American youth culture that looks like a cross between a 1960s **Roger Corman** drug movie and an **experimental film** by Jordan Belson, the Whitney brothers, or **Kenneth Anger**. The narrative concerns invisible aliens who crave heroin and come to Earth in a mini flying saucer. As their luck would have it, the creatures land on top of a New York apartment building inhabited by a drug dealer and his female, androgynous, bisexual, nymphomaniac lover who works as a fashion model. The aliens discover that human pheromones, which are created in the brain during an orgasm, are preferable to a heroin rush. A lonely female German scientist living across the street and tracking the aliens and an androgynous male model (Carlisle plays both models) observe the female model's sex partners disappearing. *Liquid Sky* features imagery of the Empire State Building glowing against turquoise and lavender skies photographed by Yuri Neyman, who also created the special effects that appear to be developed in lysergic acid. Marina Levikova's costumes combine punk, Kabuki, and ragtag fashion for the spacey models, junkies, and emerging performance artists as Tsukerman investigates every exotic, nihilistic, and self-destructive behavior imaginable. What makes *Liquid Sky* original, daring, and unique is the underground strata as observed by a Russian visionary and the POV of heroin-addled aliens. No other film can claim those coordinates.

Little Fugitive. Landmark independent film (1953) directed by Ray Ashley, **Morris Engel,** and Ruth Orkin, who also wrote the original story and screenplay, with a cast of unknowns. It concerns a young boy who runs off to Brooklyn's Coney Island after he is tricked into believing he has killed his older brother. The seventy-five-minute low-low budget film is a lyrical, poetic, comedy/drama that follows little Joey Norton, played by Richie Andrusco, as he collects pop bottles and returns them for pocket money so he can wander around the world-famous beach and amusement park. Morris Engel was director of photography, and the editors were Ruth Orkin and Lester Troob, who was also sound and music supervisor. *Little Fugitive* captured the imagination and respect of the **New American Cinema Group** and filmmakers over the decades. *Little Fugitive* was difficult for cineastes to screen until it was finally distributed on video by Kino Video. *See also* Engel, Morris

Living in Oblivion. See DiCillo, Tom

Lloyd, Harold. Actor, producer. *b.* April 20, 1893, Burchard, Nebraska. *d.* March 8, 1971, Beverly Hills, California. Harold Lloyd became one of the most successful and wealthy comedians of the silent film era, in contrast to many of his contemporaries who made the studios rich while their careers ended with little to show for their hard-earned popularity. Lloyd made his film debut as an extra for the **Edison Company** in 1912. In 1913, he appeared in Keystone comedies, again doing extra work. In 1914, Hal Roach formed a film company and hired Lloyd to play Willie Work in one-reel comedies. Roach couldn't sell Lloyd to his audience so the comedian moved to Mack Sennett's Keystone Company until the two men became mutually dissatisfied with their arrangement. Roach reorganized his company and was sponsored by Pathé, and Lloyd came back to Roach.

The two men created the Lonesome Luke character patterned after **Charlie Chaplin.** Neither man was happy with the result, but Luke was popular with the public. Between 1916 and 1917 Lloyd appeared in 100 short comedies. In 1917 Roach gave Lloyd the oversized horn-rimmed glasses that became his trademark. Lloyd's image began to develop as he dropped slapstick and visual gags for characterization and dangerous and hilarious stunts that found Lloyd dangling from buildings.

In 1923, Lloyd and Roach parted amicably, and Lloyd began producing his own films with Paramount. Lloyd owned his later films outright and made an enormous income from the release and rereleases of *The Freshman* (1925), *Speedy* (1928), and *Movie Crazy* (1932). Lloyd's popularity waned during the sound era, but his fortune continued to grow because of his independent ownership of his films.

Lorentz, Pare. Documentary filmmaker, journalist, film critic. *b.* December 11, 1905, Clarksburg, West Virginia. *d.* March 4, 1992. *ed.* Wesleyan College. In the early 1930s President Franklin Delano Roosevelt appointed Pare Lorentz to his resettlement program. Lorentz made two important **documentaries,** *The Plow That Broke the Plains* (1936) and *The River* (1937), which explored and revealed the destruction of the American landscape. Lorentz scripted the treatment for **Willard Van Dyke**'s landmark documentary *The City* (1939). He organized and led the U.S. Film Service, but *Fight for Life* (1940), an examination of the dangers of childbirth in the underprivileged, was too controversial for governmental morality. In an uproar over the film, Congress voted to dissolve the U.S. Film Service and cut off all funding for the vital project. In the early 1940s, Lorentz made shorts for RKO. In 1946 he was appointed chief of the film section of the War Department's Civil Affairs Division. With his commitment to pressing social issues, a search for the truth, and the development of new nonfiction forms, Lorentz influenced generations of documentary filmmakers.

Lumet, Sidney. Director. *b.* June 25, 1924, Philadelphia, Pennsylvania. *ed.* Professional Children's School, Columbia University, studied acting with Sanford Meisner. Sidney Lumet was trained as a director during the Golden Age of Television. In 1957, Lumet directed his first feature, *12 Angry Men*, an adaptation of the Reginald Rose teleplay. The producer and star Henry Fonda chose Lumet to direct the all-male ensemble cast in a searing courtroom drama of a man who has to convince eleven jurors of the innocence of a young minority man. The independent production was shot in New York in nineteen days for $343,000. Director of photography **Boris Kaufman** received an Oscar nomination, as did Lumet, who also won the DGA award.

With his first film, Lumet established the qualities that would define his work as a director for over forty years. Moral and ethical issues, right and wrong, political corruption, and our judicial system are his thematic obsessions. Lumet is an actor's director, cultivating performances and developing characters to tell the story. He is a fierce cinematic stylist. Because of his live television and theater training each film is planned to the smallest detail. Lumet often shoots very little film, no more than three takes on a shot. Painstaking rehearsal supports his need to shoot fast. Early on, Lumet decided he wanted to get a film out approximately every year and a half, and he set up home base in New York City. Lumet shoots with little or no coverage—before production he sees the finished film in his mind and only shoots what he needs—a significant frustration to the wonderful New York film editors he's worked with. Dede Allen, who cut *Dog Day Afternoon* (1975) and *Serpico* (1973), is an exception; as a result, these are two of his finest films. Allen's editing philosophy is that editing is story and character. She solved logistical problems caused by limited coverage and cherished the actors and narratives. Lumet is a man of unlimited energy, hard to keep up with in mind and body; he is constantly planning or shooting or in postproduction on a film project. He has been fascinated with the immorality of police corruption, a theme featured in *Serpico* (1973), *Prince of the City* (1981), and *Q & A* (1990).

As a New Yorker attuned to the Broadway theater, Lumet adapted many stage productions including *The Fugitive Kind* (1960), *A View from the Bridge* (1961), *Long Day's Journey into Night* (1962), *The Sea Gull* (1968), *Equus* (1977), *The Wiz* (1978), and *Deathtrap* (1982). Lumet also was attracted to literary works: Mary McCarthy's *The Group* (1966), Agatha Christie's *Murder on the Orient Express* (1974), and E.L. Doctorow's *Daniel* (1983), a fictionalized account of the Rosenberg case. Lumet is a political liberal, far to the left of **Stanley Kramer** with the moral conscience of a rabbi. *Fail-Safe* (1964) examined the moral and political quagmire facing an American president after a nuclear accident annihilates Moscow. *The Pawnbroker* (1965) portrays the mental and spiritual pain of a Holocaust survivor. *Network* (1976), from a screenplay by Paddy Chayefsky, is a devastating indictment of abuse of power administered by television networks and the extent to which the powers-that-be will go for big ratings. *The Verdict* (1982) features Paul Newman as a down-and-out ambulance-chasing lawyer who is forced into a life-altering decision to take settlement money or fight for justice. *Running on Empty* (1988) probes the underground life of 1960s radicals on the run, and in *A Stranger among Us* (1992), a policewoman poses as a religious Jew to solve a murder inside a Brooklyn Hasidic community so Lumet can examine the conflict of religious and secular morality and law.

In over forty films, Sidney Lumet has produced a body of work that documents the complexity and personal conflicts of his beloved New York City and other worlds that attract his ever-curious and morally responsible character. Sidney Lumet has remained stubbornly independent. He makes his films quickly and cheaply with other people's money and studio distribution—a small price to pay for total artistic control and for being the social conscience of the New York film community and beyond. Recent credits for Sidney Lumet include the cable television series *100 Centre Street* (2001), and *Whistle* (2003). *See also* Kaufman, Boris

BIBLIOGRAPHY

Boyer, Jay. *Sidney Lumet*. New York: Twayne Publishers, 1993.
Cunningham, Frank R. *Sidney Lumet: Film and Literary Vision*. 2nd ed. Lexington: University Press of Kentucky, 2001.
Lumet, Sidney. *Making Movies*. New York: Knopf, 1995.

Lunch, Lydia. Actress. *b.* 1959, Rochester, New York. **Punk, No-Wave** actress, performer, composer who had an impact on the underground during the late 1970s and throughout the 1980s. Lunch was the prototype for the punk woman with dead black hair, spiky short bangs, and thick shaggy strands framing her face, snaking down her back and shoulders. Her face is in a permanent sneer but is as elusive as the Mona Lisa's smile, her brows and eyes dark with pencil and mascara, and lips perpetually in a punk pout. Lunch was the superstar of No-Wave films, appearing in *Black Box* (1979) and *Vortex* (1983) from filmmakers **Scott and Beth B** and **Nick Zedd**'s *The Wild World of Lydia Lunch* (1983). Zedd and Lunch had a brief relationship during which they considered dangerous and forbidden transgressional ideas for projects concerning infanticide and **snuff films.**

Lunch selected Richard Kern to direct *The Right Side of My Brain* (1984), a sexual, emotional drama of a poor girl who has been physically and sexually abused. The film explores the psychology behind the victim's desire to be abused and the woman's involvement in a dominant lesbian sadistic/masochistic relationship. The Lower East Side diva explored the dark side of sexuality in many of her films. Lunch probed the connection between sex, violence and power in sexual relationships in *Fingered* (1986), a black-and-white **Super 8mm** film noir epic directed by Kern and written by Lunch. The film portrays disgusting and demeaning behavior like firing a pistol she has just had sex with.

In 1996 Lydia Lunch performed in *Power of the Word* and *Visiting Desire*. Lunch is an independent **underground film** actress. Her training was not from Actor's Studio, Julliard, or the Yale Drama School. She prepared for her role in the **cinema of transgression** by living the life of a punk rocker and sexual astronaut in the Lower East Side sadomasochism scene. She is a performer who blurs and perhaps erases the line between movie reality and a life outside tradition.

Lupino, Ida. Actress, director, producer, screenwriter. *b.* February 4, 1918, London, England. *d.* 1995. *ed.* Royal Academy of Dramatic Arts. Gutsy, unsentimental contract player for Paramount and Warner Bros. in the heyday of the studio system, Ida Lupino carved a niche in the 1930s, 1940s, and 1950s in such features as *The Adventures of Sherlock Holmes* (1939), *The Light That Failed* (1939), *They Drive by Night* (1940), and *Beware, My Lovely* (1952). Lupino is notable as a pioneering female feature film director. Beginning with *Not Wanted* (1949), she functioned behind the camera as coproducer of Filmmakers, a production company with her then-husband Collier Young and as a co-screenwriter. She directed *Not Wanted* uncredited when the director became ill at the start of production. Between 1950 and 1953 Lupino coproduced, cowrote, and directed *Never Fear* (1950), *Outrage* (1950), *Hard, Fast and Beautiful* (1951), *The Hitch-Hiker* (1953) and *The Bigamist* (1953), in which she also acted.

Lupino's independent achievements during this concentrated period placed her in a nearly unique position among women filmmakers of the time. Her directorial contributions are recognized for their realistic subject matter, technical expertise, finesse with actors, and spare budgets. Lupino spent the remainder of her career acting and directing steadily in television. As a principal of Four Star Productions, her efforts helped influence TV fare throughout the next several decades.

BIBLIOGRAPHY

Donati, William. *Ida Lupino: A Biography*. Lexington: University Press of Kentucky, 1996.

Lurie, John. Actor, musician. *b.* 1952, Worcester, Massachusetts. A denizen of the downtown New York music scene, John Lurie developed a cult following and a career as an actor and composer in independent films.

The cool, deadpan, saxophone-playing Lurie appeared in *Permanent Vacation* (1982), *Stranger Than Paradise* (1984), and *Down by Law* (1986) for director **Jim Jarmusch**; *Paris, Texas* (1984), for Wim Wenders; *Desperately Seeking Susan* (1985), for **Susan Seidelman**; **Martin Scorsese**'s *The Last Temptation of Christ* (1988); **David Lynch**'s *Wild at Heart* (1990); and *Smoke* and *Blue in the Face* (both 1995), for **Wayne Wang**. As a film composer, Lurie has scored *Permanent Vacation, Stranger Than Paradise, Down by Law, Mystery Train* (1989), *Blue in the Face, Manny & Lo* (1996), *Excess Baggage* (1997), *Clay Pigeons* (1998), and *Animal Factory* (2000), **Steve Buscemi**'s sophomore film as a director. In 1998 John Lurie composed the score to *Lulu on the Bridge* directed by Paul Auster. Lurie worked as in actor in **Abel Ferrara**'s *New Rose Hotel* (1998) and *Sleepwalk* (2000).

Lynch, David. Director, screenwriter, producer, sound designer. *b.* January 20, 1946, Missoula, Montana. *ed.* AFI. David Lynch is an American artist with little regard for commercial concerns except when his weird vision connects with the general public. It all began with short films. *Six Men Getting Sick* (1967) is a one-minute animated film in which abstract figures fill up with a colored substance that causes them to vomit. *The Alphabet* (1968) is an animated film in which a girl lies on a bed listening to the sound of children reciting their ABCs. She sees the letters in the sun. A life form materializes and a plant drops letters, turning it into a bloody form that sprays the girl and her white bed with red dots. Letters appear; the girl is told she's learned her ABCs and is engulfed in plant tentacles, causing her to vomit blood on the white sheets. *The Grandmother* (1970) is an animated story of a lonely unhappy boy in a home. A plant produces an old woman that is kind to him. His parents laugh when she dies and the boy is transformed into a plant.

The Amputee (1974) is Lynch's first live-action film. A woman with two severed legs mentally composes a letter about troubled relationships while a doctor attends to the stumps of her legs without her acknowledgment. Lynch was working from an aesthetic closer to Surrealism, Dada, and Conceptual Art rather than traditional cinematic narrative.

A good-natured Boy Scout type who says "Golly" and does little to explain the demented dream world of his imagination, Lynch exploded onto the independent film scene with *Eraserhead* (1977), a black-and-white film about a lonely man with a cosmic, rising hairstyle and a part animal/part human baby. The film is scored with a creepy, atmospheric, and psychologically dense sound design and music that gives audiences the willies. Lynch developed and produced the film over several years while at the AFI. *Eraserhead* was released into the **midnight movie** circuit and gathered a huge audience, mainly through word of mouth. Lynch's next project (1980), an adaptation of the play *The Elephant Man* for **Mel Brooks**'s production company, could have been seen as a sellout, except

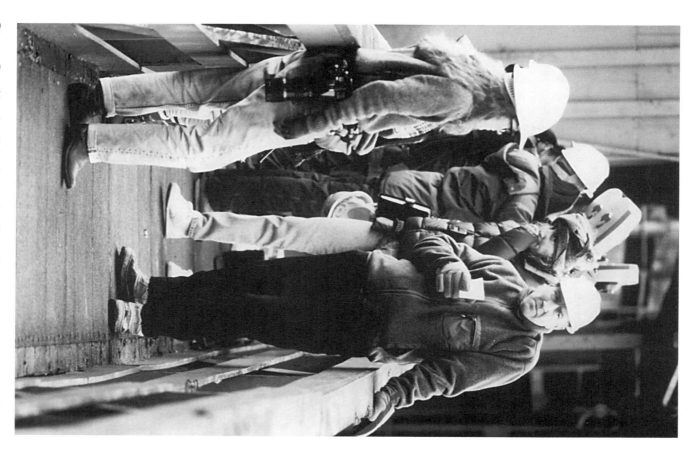

Director David Lynch with hardhat and coffee as he ponders his next vision on the set of *Twin Peaks*. Courtesy of The Del Valle Archive

Lynch used the spine of John Merrick's story as a vehicle for his obsession with disenfranchised characters perceived as freaks by society. Lynch's gift is finding the organic strangeness and humanity within them.

Dino and Raffaella De Laurentiis chose Lynch to film (1984) an adaptation of the popular science fiction novel Frank Herbert's *Dune*. Again, Lynch did not sell out but interpreted the material through his strange visual sensibility and narrative rendering, not necessarily what the fans of the novel had in mind. Lynch was roundly criticized; few considered it part of the director's oeuvre and ridiculed his interpretation, which was to him another David Lynch film. Two years after the failure of *Dune*, Lynch directed *Blue Velvet* (1986), hailed as one of the ten best films of the decade. *Blue Velvet* established and popularized Lynch's twisted vision of Americana. The nontraditional story of a young man's plunge into a criminal netherworld appeared to be a neo-noir, but Lynch managed to connect the private, inaccessible world of *Eraserhead* to commercial success.

Weird was in—Lynch became so fashionable the ABC network actually invited him create *Twin Peaks*, an episodic television series, that quickly captured the nation's imagination. The show was surrealistic yet rooted in traditional American values.

Wild at Heart (1990) took the American nightmare on the road with a convoluted story filled with symbols and hallucinatory imagery. The film was critically acclaimed, but audiences were perplexed. The television series ended with more questions than answers, and Lynch directed a feature *Twin Peaks: Fire Walk With Me* that took the series beyond the audience's comprehension and was a complete failure, sending Lynch back to his cult audience.

Commercial acceptance was over—weird was out. But Lynch lives in the world of his films. He didn't make another feature for five years during which he tried unsuccessfully to regain a television audience with *On the Air* (1992) and *Hotel Room* (1993). In 1997 Lynch returned with his least accessible but most brilliant work of cinematic art, *Lost Highway*, a neo-noir, **road movie** that was dark (both visually and narratively) and for connoisseurs of American art films. Surprisingly in 1999, Lynch came back with *The Straight Story*, the endearing tale of a man who travels to his sick brother on a lawnmower. This mature work was deftly directed and surprised Lynch cultists with its classical approach. Again Lynch wasn't denying his weird vision but brought his command of quirky midwestern America, treating the old man's story with dignity and insight into the unconventionality that is uniquely American. No backward voices, midgets, or druggy illusions here but a straight story with Lynch's compassion for eccentricity. With *Mullholland Drive* (2001) Lynch returns to weirdsville with a thriller about Hollywood.

BIBLIOGRAPHY

Lynch, David. *Lynch on Lynch*. Ed. Chris Rodley. London: Faber and Faber, 1997.

Woods, Paul A. *Weirdsville USA: The Obsessive Universe of David Lynch*. London: Plexus, 2000.

M

Maddow, Ben. Screenwriter, director. *b.* August 7, 1909. *d.* October 9, 1992. *ed.* Columbia University. Highly effective blacklisted screenwriter, in 1936 Ben Maddow, Sidney Meyers, **Willard Van Dyke, Irving Lerner, Ralph Steiner, Paul Strand** and **Leo Hurwitz** formed The World Today. This newsreel service embraced a politically left perspective to counter what the filmmakers perceived as the conservative propaganda promoted by the popular *The March of Time*, the monthly screen magazine series that had dominated America's movie screens since 1935. Maddow was blacklisted for his political activities in the 1940s. Under the pseudonym David Wolff, he collaborated on the screenplay for *Native Land* (1942) along with Leo Hurwitz and Paul Strand. During the 1940s and 1950s Maddow wrote Hollywood features, mainly **B-movies** either uncredited or fronted by fellow screenwriter Philip Yordan. Maddow wrote or cowrote *The Asphalt Jungle* (1950), *The Wild One* (1954), *God's Little Acre* (1958), and *Murder by Contract* (1958), directed by **Irving Lerner.** In 1960 Maddow cowrote, directed, and produced *The Savage Eye* with Sidney Meyers and **Joseph Strick,** and in 1963 he wrote and directed *An Affair of the Skin* and produced *The Balcony*, an adaptation of the Jean Genet play directed by Joseph Strick.

Mailer, Norman. Author, director, screenwriter, actor. *b.* January 31, 1923, Long Branch, New Jersey. *ed.* Harvard University. Norman Mailer may have come close to writing the Great American Novel his first time out with *The Naked and the Dead*. As one of the creators of the nonfiction novel, Mailer won the Pulitzer Prize for *The Executioner's Song*, but to the serious wordsmith, the cinema was a lark. Mailer's first three films were self-financed star vehicles with more experimental than traditional narratives. In *Wild 90* (1967) three thugs led by a Mafia chieftain portrayed by Mailer talk shop in a bar for two hours. Mailer was inspired by **Andy Warhol** and began improvising the situation with his pals Mickey Knox and Buzz Farber. The film cost Mailer around $50,000 and was a victim of the indie nemesis, bad sound, that caused problems for audiences trying to decipher the dialogue of three nonactors fueled by arrogance and alcohol as they made up their lines and role-played. Farber had worked at CBS, where he ran into documentarian **D.A. Pennebaker**, who photographed the film in the **cinéma vérité** style of the time. Pennebaker also gave Mailer access to editing equipment. *Wild 90* was shot in single-system with the sound recorded onto the film like a television news shoot of the period. There was no script to follow. Mailer, who knew nothing about making a film, would shoot twenty different scenes, then select one and discard nineteen, instead of shooting multiple takes of one scene. Mailer maintained the theory that everyone was an actor. He relied on the power of the editing process to present metaphysical, ethical, and moral issues. His method was unconventional, at best, and *Wild 90* became an oddity in the New York **underground** film community.

Beyond the Law (1968), financed with royalties from Mailer's novel *An American Dream*, is the writer's favorite of his cinematic oeuvre. He plays L.T. Francis Xavier Pope, an Irish homicide detective. Mailer again cast friends for the roles, and they all improvised a night between cops and criminals in a police station. Mailer told interviewer Joseph Gelmis that in *Beyond the Law* he was creating the reality below the reality, beneath the reality of one night in a police station. *Beyond the Law* was shown at the New York Film Festival. Members of the film community ran for the exits. The experience did not discourage Mailer, who was having too much fun as a carouser and hell-raiser. His entourage deluded him into thinking he was onto something cinematically.

Mailer's next film *Maidstone* (1969) was more of a be-in than a movie. The project was even more chaotic than the usual Mailer set. In *Maidstone* he plays Norman Kingsley, a presidential candidate in the middle of a campaign. The film takes place mainly on an estate peopled with droves of the author's friends cavorting, making up the story and wildly improvising. Again, Pennebaker was the cinematographer, but this time there were four to five cameras out in the Hamptons shooting the raucous goings-on for four days straight. Actor Rip Torn was also in the cast. Mailer had given the adventurous and dangerous actor a specific direction. Torn's character was to attempt to assassinate the character of Kingsley. In the finished film completed by Pennebaker, *Maidstone* is an uncontrolled happening with handheld cameras jiggling, shaking, falling in and out of focus, following the improvisational rants and raves of Mailer and his friends. *Maidstone* ends with Mailer, now himself, thanking the cast and crew for participating in his **experimental** movie. After his wrap speech, Mailer begins to walk away when a crazed Rip Torn wielding a hammer winks maniacally into the camera and takes off to "assassinate" Kingsley. Pennebaker runs after Torn and documents the real event of the actor smashing Mailer with a hammer. Mailer, who also fancied himself a semiprofessional boxer, puts up a good struggle against Torn even though he is bleeding profusely. *Maidstone* may not be a good film, but the conclusion is a real cinéma vérité moment.

The debacle retired Mailer from film directing until 1987 when he convinced **Cannon** Films to finance his adaptation of his novel *Tough Guys Don't Dance*. Mailer directed the film in a conventional contemporary independent film style with acceptable production values and a professional cast including Ryan O'Neal, Isabella Rosselini, **Wings Hauser,** Clarence Williams III, Frances Fisher, Penn Jillette, and Laurence Tierney. The neo-noir/black comedy about a man who may have committed murder but can't remember received a limited commercial release. The story's quirky characters all speak in purple prose, a style that worked effectively in the novel but relegates Mailer's fourth, and most likely last, directorial effort to no more than a cinematic oddity.

BIBLIOGRAPHY

Dearborn, Mary V. *Mailer: A Biography.* New York: Houghton Mifflin, 1999.
Gelmis, Joseph. *The Film Director as Superstar.* Garden City, NY: Doubleday, 1970.
Manso, Peter. *Mailer: His Life and Times.* New York: Simon and Schuster, 1985.

Malpaso Productions. *See* Eastwood, Clint

Mamet, David. Playwright, screenwriter, producer, director. *b.* November 30, 1947, Chicago, Illinois. *ed.* Goddard College, Neighborhood Playhouse School of Theatre. David Mamet is a man of the theater, recognized as one of America's most significant contemporary playwrights with a body of work that includes *American Buffalo, Glengarry Glen Ross,* and *Speed the Plow.* Mamet's ear for dialogue is legendary—terse and deadly accurate with every dropped syllable, halt, and word repetition controlled by the author's hand. Mamet's themes are set in a man's world of scams, deals, and moral choices.

Starting in the 1980s Mamet brought his distinctive voice, long compared to Harold Pinter, to writing screenplays just like the British master playwright. They include the sexually charged adaptation of *The Postman Always Rings Twice* (1981), *The Verdict* (1982), *Vanya on 42nd Street* (1994), and *Wag the Dog* (1997). In 1987 Mamet made his film directing debut with *House of Games,* a tightly plotted, labyrinthine scam presented with an assured hand but cinematically constipated visual style. *Things Change* (1988) is a comic fable about a shoemaker who takes the rap for a Chicago mob murder for the money. Mamet brings precision to the character and plot but is unable to enliven the film cinematically by use of camera, design, and editing. *Homicide* (1991), which deals with a detective's Jewish identity, is Mamet's best effort as a filmmaker. *Oleanna* (1994), Mamet's adaptation of his own play about sexual harassment, is a fine record of the theater piece that doesn't transcend its original source. *The Spanish Prisoner* (1997), like *House of Games*, is a fascinating elaborate scam within the restrictive confines imposed by the director. *The Winslow Boy* (1999) is Mamet's version of the Terrence Rattigan play, directed in the **Merchant-Ivory** style. *State and Main* (2000) is an out-of-touch and overly controlled comedy about a movie company in Vermont. In 2001 David Mamet wrote the screenplay for *Hannibal*, directed by Ridley Scott, and *Heist* which he directed from his script. In 2002 he was the writer and director of *The Diary of a Young London Physician*. He has also written the screenplay *Whistle* (2003) for **Sidney Lumet**. Although Mamet is an independent artist in any medium, he is more adept in theater than as a film director.

BIBLIOGRAPHY

Mamet, David. *On Directing Film*. New York: Viking Press, 1991.

David Mamet directing Alec Baldwin in *State and Main* (2000). Kobol Collection/Bridges, James/El Dorado/UGC Films

Margaret Mead Film & Video Festival. Founded in 1997 by the American Museum of Natural History to honor pioneer anthropologist Margaret Mead on her seventy-fifth birthday and fiftieth year of association with the museum. Mead was one of the first anthropologists to acknowledge the importance of utilizing film for fieldwork. From 1936 to 1938 Mead worked with Gregory Bateson and cinematographer Jane Bilo to produce films about the Balinese people, including *Trance and Dance in Bali* (1952), *Learning to Dance in Bali* (1978), and *Karba's First Years: A Study of Balinese Childhood* (1952). Mead also produced films that examined child rearing from a cross-cultural point of view.

As many as 700 films are submitted a year from film and videomakers worldwide for selection at the festival held every fall. Preprogrammed themes and discussion topics that come from the submissions are considered and analyzed. Independent filmmakers create the majority of the films, but about 20 percent have direct **anthropological** input. The mission of the festival is to balance work by social scientists, indie filmmakers, videographers, and indigenous media creators.

Mariposa Group, The. In 1975 producer Peter Adair began a two-year search for funding. He wanted to create a short film about gay life that could be used as a positive message in schools. When he failed to raise a cent from foundations, Adair went to the private sector. The producer joined forces with his sister Nancy, assistant cameraman Andrew Brown, sound editor Veronica Selver, and filmmakers Lucy Massie Phoenix and **Rob Epstein**, who called themselves The Mariposa Film Group. The collective chose 26 gay men and women of 200 they interviewed. Each of the 26 were interviewed and filmed in their daily lives. The group worked for over a year producing a two-hour-and-fifteen-minute cut out of fifty hours of footage. The final form was released as *Word Is Out* (1978), a landmark independent documentary intended to give gays and lesbians a voice. *Word Is Out* helped shatter the damaging stereotypes purported by decades of Hollywood demonization and ridicule. *See also* Epstein, Rob; gay cinema; lesbian cinema

Maysles, Albert and David. Documentary filmmakers. David Maysles, *b.* January 10, 1931, Brookline, Massachusetts. *d.* January 3, 1987, New York City. *ed.* Boston University. Albert Maysles, *b.* November 26, 1933, Brookline, Massachusetts. *ed.* Syracuse University, Boston University. David was an assistant to the producer on two Marilyn Monroe vehicles, *Bus Stop* (1956) and *The Prince and the Showgirl* (1957). Albert taught at his alma mater Boston University for several years. In 1955 during a visit to the Soviet Union, Albert worked on his first **documentary**, a film that examined psychiatry in Russia. In 1957 the brothers began collaborating on documentary films and experimenting with the form. Traditionally, documentaries relied heavily on narration because the cumbersome camera and sound equipment made on-location sync-sound impossible, but as the 1960s began, lightweight equipment was developed. Albert, a talented cinematographer, began shooting documentaries for other filmmakers. In 1960 he photographed *Primary*, a film about the 1960 Democratic primary race between Hubert Humphrey and John F. Kennedy. He shot *Yanki No!* (1961) for the Time Inc. *Living Camera* series, and he shot the Jean-Luc Godard episode of the 1965 compilation film *Six in Paris*. Later Albert was part of the documentary team on two rock music films, *Monterey Pop* (1969) and *The Grateful Dead* (1977).

In 1962, the Maysles formed their own documentary filmmaking production company, bankrolled by commissions, television commercials, and **industrial films** they produced at their fully equipped facility. In 1963, the Maysles made *Showman*, a revealing portrait of movie mogul Joseph E. Levine. Throughout the 1960s the Maysles created a series of film biographies that expanded the growing form of **direct cinema**. Albert and David codirected their films on location. Albert photographed and David recorded sound on *What's Happening! The Beatles in the U.S.A.* (1964), *A Visit with Truman Capote*, and *Meet Marlon Brando* (both 1966). The films are remarkably candid, a departure from the controlled, staged publicity-driven promo film. The Maysles intended to go beyond the contrived image of celebrity and retained fierce artistic control over the final cut to guarantee their vision would not be altered.

In 1969 the Maysles made the landmark feature-length documentary *Salesman*. The film, which followed a Bible salesman on the road, received a theatrical release and a wave of critical and audience attention. The salesmen told their own stories as the Maysles followed them into their cars and into American homes, filming them with unobtrusive ease. *Salesman* was edited by **Charlotte Zwerin** who became the Maysles's constant collaborator. The film came to life during the postproduction process by structuring the footage into a distinct point of view that examined the relationship between religion and commerce in America.

In 1970, the Maysles released *Gimmie Shelter* that started out as a concert film following the Rolling Stones on their American tour. The Maysles filmed the Stones' concerts at Madison Square Garden, and the documentary would have remained a series of musical performances, but history intervened. It was 1969, and the Woodstock Festival signaled a new era of mega rock concerts where America's youth could celebrate their counterculture lifestyle of sex, drugs, rock 'n' roll, peace, and love. Woodstock was in August; by December the Stones decided they would hold a free concert. The Maysles captured all the business machinations mediated by the pompous and self-righteous lawyer Melvin Belli. The original venue fell through, and a deal was struck with the Altamont Speedway—it was not Max Yasgar's farm. The fatal mistake came when the Stones' management contracted the Hell's Angels for the security detail. The Maysles and their massive camera crew, including a young George Lucas, captured the evil in the air as soon as the disastrous and fatal event began. The dream of the Aquarian era died a quick and bloody death as a man in the audience is stabbed to death after a Hell's Angel sees him with a gun. The murder is captured on film, and the masterful editing of Charlotte Zwerin puts the viewer at the vortex. *Gimme Shelter* had a successful theatrical run and has become a cultural document of the end of the optimistic 1960s.

In 1973 the Maysles began a relationship with the environmental artist Christo, documenting his controversial and visually provocative projects with *Christo's Valley Curtain* (1972), followed by *Running Fence* (1978), *Christo in Paris* (1991), and *Umbrellas* (1994). In 1975 the Maysles released *Grey Gardens*, a disturbing and poignant portrait of the quirky and squalid life of two female relatives of Jacqueline Bouvier Kennedy. The film was relentless in revealing the strange behavior and odd charm and humor of the two women in a declining situation.

In 1987, David Maysles died suddenly. Albert continued to run their successful production company and eventually found a new codirector, Susan Froemke. Albert began to focus on classical music with *Horowitz Plays Mozart* (1987) and *Jessye Norman Sings Carmen* (1992). In 1998 Albert Maysles was the writer, director of photography and director of the documentary, *Concert of Wills: Making the Getty Center*. In 2001 he was director of photography on *The Paris Review: Early Chapters* and *LaLee's Kin: The Legacy of Cotton*. The Maysles brothers made landmark films that were part of a contemporary documentary movement that positioned independent filmmakers in the real world to find the stories that define our times. *See also* cinéma vérité; direct cinema; Zwerin, Charlotte

McBride, Jim. Director. *b.* September 16, 1941, New York City. *ed.* Kenyon College, New York University. Jim McBride found the independent movie scene rough going from the start. He began studying English at NYU, then switched to the film department. Frustrated he wasn't learning how to make films, McBride went to Brazil on an exchange program, saw a lot of movies, and came back to finish up at NYU. After graduation McBride couldn't get a job in New York or Hollywood and felt the industry didn't value student filmmakers. A series of jobs gave him experience but still didn't prepare him for his goal to make personal films. McBride worked as a gofer for a casting agent, then as an apprentice film editor for **industrial** filmmakers. He and **Chuck Hirsch** ran a film society at The Gate, an Off-Broadway theater where they programmed short works, historically a training ground for filmmakers.

McBride became a full editor for a real estate company in Florida that made in-house productions. On weekends he borrowed their **Bolex** camera and zoom lens and began shooting people passing by his window. McBride was using out-of-date film stock, and his boss allowed Jim to process the footage on the company tab. Not pleased with the results, McBride rented an Auricon **16mm** camera, Nagra tape recorder, and accessories for a one-day rental on a Saturday so he could have the equipment for the entire weekend for $60. He learned by shooting and reading everything in sight about technical matters.

Eventually he met Michael Wadley who as Michael Wadleigh directed *Woodstock* (1970). Wadley encouraged him to make *David Holzman's Diary* (1967). After completing the film McBride had difficulty getting a distributor, but prints got around. This sub rosa distribution established his reputation as a hot young filmmaker. His second feature, *My Girlfriend's Wedding*, was completed in 1969. McBride continued to work in the **cinéma vérité, documentary,** and **diary** traditions, basing the film on what was happening in his life at the time. The girlfriend was Clarissa, a woman from England who was living with McBride. In order to stay with McBride in the United States, she married a yippie who was pleased to participate in getting back at the system. Paradigm Films distributed *My Girlfriend's Wedding*. It is structured in four parts: an interview with Clarissa shot on the day of the wedding; the ceremony at a municipal building plus lunch with Clarissa; McBride and the yippie husband; an evening wedding party where a few friends show up to celebrate and a concluding segment with McBride and Clarissa driving cross country en route to the San Francisco Film Festival.

In 1971, McBride directed Steve Curry and Shelly Plimpton in *Glen and Randa*, the story of teenage lovers after a nuclear holocaust who search for the city of Metropolis using clues they've discovered in a comic book. The independent production was shot in 16mm color for $240,000 and blown up to 35mm for theatrical distribution by UMC Pictures. After *Glen and Randa* McBride's career fizzled. He began driving a cab and taught film at NYU to make ends meet. He had a bad experience with **BBS**, who he perceived as rich guys playing hippies. His project with the company, *Gone Beaver*, was shut down one day before principal photography. In the 1980s, McBride resurfaced, directing acceptable box office fare in what he would consider a conventional New Hollywood style. He directed *Breathless* (1983), *The Big Easy* (1987), and *Great Balls of Fire* (1989). Recent credits for Jim McBride include: *The Informant* (1997), and many television movies. Among them are *Meat Loaf: To Hell and Back* (2000) for VH1, and the Golden Globe winning HBO cable series, *Six Feet Under*. *See also* Carson, L.M., Kit; *David Holzman's Diary*; Hirsch, Charles

BIBLIOGRAPHY

Gelmis, Joseph. *The Film Director as Superstar.* Garden City, NY: Doubleday, 1970.

McDonough, Tom. Cinematographer, author. Brooklyn-born Tom McDonough was educated by Jesuits and later developed a passion for filmmaking and writing. McDonough's most accomplished work is *Best Boy* (1979), the Oscar-winning **documentary** directed by **Ira Wohl**. McDonough not only shot the transition of Wohl's cousin Philly, a mentally challenged man, from his home to independence in an adult residence, but was by Wohl's side through the entire conception, planning, production, and postproduction. In 1997 Wohl and McDonough collaborated again for *Best Man: 'Best Boy' and All of Us Twenty Years Later.* McDonough is also a talented prose writer who often writes about the film industry in a personal, novelistic style. His book *Light Years: Confessions of a Cinematographer* (1987) is an insightful insider's look at the life of the freelance, independent filmmaker and the challenge of photographing low-budget films.

McElwee, Ross. Filmmaker. *b.* 1947, North Carolina. *ed.* Stanford Summer Institute, Rhode Island School of Design, Massachusetts Institute of Technology. McElwee is a documentarian greatly influenced by **Richard Leacock** and **Ed Pincus**, who were his teachers at Massachusetts Institute of Technology. McElwee's films combine the aesthetics, philosophy, and technique of **cinéma vérité** and the **diary film**. His best-known work is *Sherman's March* (1986), a portrait of the South that touches on the racial divide as well as a myriad issues that captivated the filmmaker's free-associating mind. The film was shot without collaboration, and McElwee utilizes the process to discover relationships and to find out more about himself. The viewer gets to go behind the camera and into the mind and perceptions of McElwee. McElwee is both a documentarian and a diarist. He is a documentary filmmaker because he films real-life events and uses a direct cinéma vérité approach and not the carefully staged recreations of early documentarians. He is a diarist in that his films are most often subjective and only at times pull back to objectify what he is recording. McElwee's other films include *Charleen* (1980), *Backyard* (1984), *Something to Do with the Wall* (1991), *Time Indefinite* (1993), and *Six O'clock News* (1997).

Meade, Taylor. Actor, filmmaker. *b.* Chicago, Illinois. Taylor Mead is a quirky, childlike, funny, poetic performer who has been an indispensable and legendary figure in **underground cinema.** In 1962, Mead played a convict in Adolphas Mekas's *Hallelujah the Hills.* Mead was a member in good standing at **Andy Warhol's** The Factory and appeared in many of his films including *The Nude Restaurant* (1967) and *Lonesome Cowboys* (1968) in which he played nurse to Viva, another Warhol superstar, in a panting and delirious performance many feel is his best role. Mead played the title role in Ron Rice's *The Flower Thief* (1969) and *The Queen of Sheba Meets the Atom Man* (1963). Mead has created his own underground films. Most are held in the Andy Warhol archives, made during the halcyon days of The Factory, when Warhol produced as many as five films a week. As a performer Mead worked with film students and legendary experimentalists. He has been called original, charming, and the king of camp and has been compared to the great silent comedians **Chaplin, Keaton,** and Harry Langdon.

Mekas, Jonas. Filmmaker, archivist, publisher, theoretician. *b.* December 24, 1922, Semeniskiai, Lithuania. *ed.* Johannes Guttenberg University at Mainz, University of Tübingen, City College. Jonas and his brother Adolfas fled their native Lithuania in 1914. They spent eight years in a forced labor camp in Germany, then four years in a displaced persons camp where Mekas first saw films when they screened neorealist and German cinema.

In 1949, the Mekas brothers arrived in Brooklyn, New York, and bought a **16mm** camera. Filmmaking became an avenue of expression for Jonas Mekas to cope with his status as a refugee. The first films Mekas saw in New York were *The Cabinet of Dr. Caligari* (1920) and *The Fall of the House of Usher* (1928) at the New York Film Society run by theorist Rudolf Arnheim. Mekas worked in a factory and spent all his money on film stock. He read about the cinema including Pudovkin and Eisenstein and began writing scripts. Mekas attended regular screenings at Cinema 16 and The Theodore Huff Society run by William K. Everson.

Mekas and Gideon Bachmann founded The Film Group in 1951. They held screenings once a month and rented **experimental** and **avant-garde** films while Mekas wrote the program notes. In 1953 Mekas ran a short film series at the Gallery Easton on First Street and Avenue B. In 1954 Jonas and Adolfas Mekas started Film Forum. At one of the first shows, Jordan Belson was present to show his films when there was a confrontation with a union projectionist. The electricity was turned off, and Mekas was physically threatened; so the screening was stopped.

During the 1950s, Mekas documented his Brooklyn community of displaced Lithuanians with his movie camera. Eventually Mekas was able to break away and moved to Manhattan where he chronicled the art scene with his 16mm **Bolex camera.** In 1961, Mekas completed *Guns of the Trees,* an experimental narrative film. Mekas had become endeared to the Hollywood film so he began sending scripts to Hollywood producers and directors like **Stanley Kramer** and Fred Zinnemann. Later when he saw the **Little Fugitive,** Mekas understood there were other possibilities for creating, distributing, and exhibiting films.

In 1960 Mekas filmed the Off-Broadway production of *The Brig* performed by Julian Beck's Living Theater. When he approached Beck with the notion, Mekas was told the play, which had been running for a year, was being shut down the next day. Mekas quickly organized the shoot, getting three Auricon sound-on-film cameras, and asked Louis Brigant and Ed Emshwiller to crew as assistants. The cast and crew slid down a coal chute to get into the closed theater. Mekas photographed the play as an experiment and critical analysis of **cinéma vérité**. When film ran out and he switched cameras, Mekas stopped the action and backed up the play, so overlaps were captured on film. Mekas built an intense soundtrack utilizing the production sound and a separate tape recorder he ran as backup. Distortion from a too-close microphone led to amplifying the cruelty of the play. Eventually the overlaps and dead spots were edited, as were twenty minutes from the original play.

In 1968 Mekas filmed *Walden*, the first in a series, *Diaries, Notes and Sketches*, of personal experiences, daily life, and the seasonal changes of New York City, the 1964 to 1968 cultural scene, portraits of Tony Conrad, **P. Adams Sitney, Stan Brakhage,** Carl Dreyer, Timothy Leary, Marie Menken, Gregory Markopolous, Allen Ginsberg, The Velvet Underground, **Ken Jacobs, John Lennon,** and **Yoko Ono,** and home movies, dedicated to Lumière and a return to the cinema's origins. Throughout the 1960s Mekas experimented with 16mm technique, shaky handheld camera, single-frame shooting, and bursts of quick imagery. By the end of the decade, the new cinematic language Mekas helped create became accepted.

In 1976 Mekas completed *Lost, Lost, Lost*. The 178-minute film contains images of a family reunion; scenes photographed when he first arrived in the United States; Jonas and Adolfas visiting the Hamburg camp where they were interred; and Jonas's art world family, Peter Kubelka, Annette Michelson, and Ken and Florence Jacobs. The project helped Mekas find an aesthetic homeland so he could begin to live creatively again. *Lost, Lost, Lost* was completed with one of four $20,000 grants given out by the New York State Council on the Arts.

In Lithuania, Mekas had been a celebrated poet. He became a film poet, his camera style similar to the way he connected images and ideas in an erratic, conjoined writing style. Mekas merged the two mediums by putting intertitles to structure his films. The text became part of the cinematic style. The influence of documentary filmmakers John Grierson and Paul Rotha took Mekas away from his poetic/Lithuanian inclinations; but later he returned to them using transcribed written diaries as his film text. Mekas's writing style created disconnected, collagelike impressions interpreted cinematically by Mekas's gestural camera, flickering frames, and the controlled, orchestrated shake and roll of the lens that developed a new set of conventions in reaction to traditional cinema.

In 1978, Mekas made *Notes for Jerome*, a visit with filmmaker Jerome Hill who created *Schweitzer* (1951) and *Film Portrait* (1970). Mekas's friendship with Hill turned into an inheritance from the wealthy man when he passed away. The money became the major support for **An-thology Film Archives**, founded by Mekas. *Paradise Not Yet Lost*, aka *Oona's Third Year* (1979), is a film portrait of the third year of Mekas's first child. In 1983 Mekas finished editing several performance films he shot in 1966. *He Stands in a Desert Counting the Seconds of His Life—1969-1984* (1985) contain 124 brief sketches and portraits of Hans Richter, Roberto Rossellini, Marchel Hanoun, Henri Langlois, Alberto Cavacanti, **Kenneth Anger**, Mike and George **Kuchar**, Robert Breer, Hollis Frampton, **John Lennon**, and Jackie Onassis Kennedy.

Mekas's most significant contribution was in organizing the avant-garde community and providing forums for films to be exhibited and archived and for filmmakers to be acknowledged, understood, and funded. He was the force behind the **New American Cinema Group.** Mekas set out to change the film society model of noncommercial exhibition and distribution established in the United States by **Amos Vogel** and Cinema 16. He opposed the eclectic potpourri approach pioneered by Vogel. Mekas established the single artist show at The New American Cinema Group, The New York Cinematheque, and Anthology Film Archives. He promoted a cooperative distribution system where filmmakers decided which films to distribute. All the rental fees went back to the filmmaker, minus expenses to keep the **co-op** running.

In 1957 Mekas helped found *Film Culture* magazine. From 1959 to 1971 Mekas wrote the "Movie Journal" column for *The Village Voice.* Mekas was not a film critic but a cheerleader, promoter, and polemicist for independent filmmaking. After the death of JFK, Jacqueline Kennedy shared with Jonas that her children were struggling with the assassination and asked if he could involve them in filmmaking. The pope of independent filmmaking gave Caroline and John Jr. **8mm** cameras and tutoring in the art of film. Both children produced creative work, especially John who made four-screen films that Mekas likened to artist Harry Smith. For Mekas, every new filmmaker is a member of the community of artists. "I make home movies, therefore I live," Mekas once said, defining his lifelong commitment to independent filmmaking. In 2000 Mekas released *As I Was Moving Ahead Occasionally I Saw Brief Glimpses of Beauty.*

BIBLIOGRAPHY

James, David E. editor. *To Free the Cinema: Jonas Mekas and the New York Underground.* Princeton, NJ: Princeton University Press, 1992.

Mekas, Jonas. *Movie Journal: The Rise of a New American Cinema 1959-1971.* New York: Collier Books, 1972.

Menendez, Ramon. *See Stand and Deliver*

Merchant-Ivory Productions. Independent production company internationally famous for civilized literary adaptations of Henry James and E.M. Forster as well as films about social/political/cultural events in India. Refined and sophisticated director/screenwriter James Ivory (b. June 7, 1928, Berkeley, California. *ed.* University of Oregon, University of Southern California) does not convey the typical image of a New York independent filmmaker. The critical establishment has dismissed Ivory's work as PBS/*Masterpiece Theater* on the big screen. Few recognize Ivory as a legitimate New York indie who worked outside of Hollywood in the 1960s and 1970s, along with **John Cassavetes, Jonas Mekas,** and **Andy Warhol.** Ivory was raised in Kamath Falls, Oregon, and entered college with intentions to become a set designer but was attracted to film direction. He enrolled in the USC film department for graduate work, where he directed a ten-minute short. On a trip to Europe, Ivory directed a half-hour documentary, *Venice: Themes and Variations* (1957), with financial aid from USC. After a hitch in the service Ivory resumed filmmaking with the **documentary** *The Sword and the Flute* (1959) concerning Indian art objects.

In 1960 Ivory was commissioned to make a documentary on location in India financed by the Asia Society. He remained in India for several years, attracted by the culture and beauty of the spiritual land. The dichotomy of wealth and poverty and the strict caste system attracted his curiosity. As an American, Ivory possessed objectivity; as an intellectual drawn to tradition and history of civilization, rich narrative themes began to influence him. Ivory met local producer Ishmail Merchant, who later introduced him to writer Ruth Prawer Jhabvala, and Merchant-Ivory was formed. Ivory chooses the material, Merchant produces and Jhabvala writes the screenplays. Ivory explained the organization of Merchant-Ivory succinctly to *DGA* magazine: "I have always thought that the three of us are a bit like the United States Government....I'm the president, Ishmail is the Congress, and Ruth is the Supreme Court." All three live in the same New York apartment building where their offices are maintained.

In *The Householder* (1963) and *Bombay Talkie* (1970) Merchant-Ivory explored the cultural landscape of India, its customs, rigidity, and mystery. *Roseland* (1977) is a New York story following the lives of inhabitants of the famed dance palace. The company has had a loyal audience, older viewers seeking civilized entertainment, a haven from the exploitative sex and violence trend that Merchant-Ivory transcended with adaptations of Henry James's *The Europeans* (1979) and *The Bostonians* (1984). *Quartet* (1981) is based on the work of Jean Rhys. Their 1986 production of E.M. Forster's *Room with a View* was a huge success.

Jhabvala's work as a writer is layered in literary construction and character nuance. Merchant-Ivory has achieved stardom and recognition with independent, low-budget (for period dramas) productions that the studios couldn't do as well for triple the amount. Ivory's interpretation of character and theme is masterful; the physical and behavioral detail is immaculate. *Howard's End* (1992), again based on Forster, featured fine performances and impeccable, tasteful direction. *Remains of the Day* (1993) is a period drama based on Yashiro Ishiru's novel about the service staff of an Englishman who embraces the Nazi regime.

The film was the nadir of Merchant-Ivory's long career. Since the resounding box office success of *Remains of the Day*, Merchant-Ivory has not connected with a general audience. The core audience for a Merchant-Ivory film is aging and not visiting the movie house. *Jefferson in Paris* (1995), based on the true story of the statesman and his romantic relationship with a black slave, left audiences cold; they were unable to accept Nick Nolte as the former president, even though research shows the casting is accurate. *Surviving Picasso* (1996) didn't capture the old magic; neither did *A Soldier's Daughter Never Cries* (1998), the true story of novelist James Jones and his daughter. In 2000 Merchant-Ivory released an adaptation of the Henry James novel *The Golden Bowl*. Their latest project is *Le Divorce* (2003), an adaptation of the novel by Diane Johnson. Merchant-Ivory continues to ignore market research, pursuing their innate sense of taste and style, making intelligent films produced on a frugal budget that refuse to follow trends and fads.

BIBLIOGRAPHY

Long, Robert Emmet. *The Films of Merchant Ivory*. New York: Harry N. Abrams, 1991.

Metzger, Radley. Director, producer. *b.* January 21, 1929, New York. *ed.* City College of New York, Columbia University. Radley Metzger screened the entire Museum of Modern Art collection while still in high school. After serving in the Air Force Motion Picture Unit during the Korean War, Metzger worked as a gaffer and film editor and later was an assistant editor at RKO Studios in New York. Metzger and Bill Kyriakis made *Dark Odyssey* (1961), a very low-budget production utilizing family and friends that took nine months to shoot. At one point they ran out of money. Metzger landed a job preparing the English-language version of Renoir's *French Can-Can* (1955). He was hired by Ava Leighton at Janus Films to edit American versions of *L'Avventura* (1960), *Jules and Jim* (1961), and many Ingmar Bergman films including *Through a Glass Darkly* (1961). The experience developed Metzger's European sensibilities and determination to bring elegance and art to his own films. While at Janus, Metzger heard of *Mademoiselle* (1966), a French film that contained about one minute of bare breasts. He bought it, borrowed money to complete the deal, made a trailer, and dubbed the film into English.

Metzger remained with Janus for twelve years. He and Leighton became partners—a thirty-year relationship ending when she died in 1987. They created Audubon films, named after the Audubon Theater in Washington Heights where Metzger saw his first films.

The Dirty Girls (1964) was written, directed, produced, and edited in a cutting room in Metzger's office for $35,000 to $40,000. The erotic story of two prostitutes, *The Dirty Girls* had artful production values. It made $100,000 in profit. *Carmen Baby* (1967) was a color adaptation of Bizet's *Carmen*, shot on location in Slovenia, Yugoslavia, and posted in New York. Metzger shot scenes silent and post-synced all the dialogue in the Italian tradition. Even without nudity, the erotic film grossed more money than *The Wizard of Oz* (1939). *Therese and Isabelle* (1968), based on Violette Leduc's book, featured an erotic relationship between two women. Metzger shot it in Paris and created French- and English-language versions. American audiences were attracted to the artistic allure generated by Metzger's art house and tasteful European aesthetics. Little sex was actually shown, but erotic passions intrigued the audience accustomed to overt innuendoes, crass and vulgar American films, and the stigma of **hard-core** porn. Metzger is a sophisticate whose domain is sexual eroticism and the emotional, psychological aspects of physical life.

The Lickerish Quartet (1970) was photographed in a castle, restaurant, and hotel. The four-character film was shot in three days in the famed Cinecitta Studios where Fellini made his masterpieces. In *The Lickerish Quartet* Metzger moved into more explicit terrain with nudity, simulated sex, and a cornucopia of sexual preferences among a father, mother, son, and a beautiful female who appeared in a porn film they had been watching. The **self-referential** film shifts forward and back in time and experiments with cinematic reality. Lavishly designed and photographed, *The Lickerish Quartet* borders on going over the top with pretentious dialogue and philosophical goals well beyond the scope of the **soft-core film** genre. Metzger reinvented the **adult film**, believing in his art, casting attractive performers with good, if mannered, elocution, style, and a sense of elegant intrigue.

Little Mother (1973), based on the life of Eva Peron, was shot on location in Yugoslavia. Several sex scenes were added to the plot to connect the social/political aspects of the narrative to the exploitation values of glamorizing kinky sex. *Score* (1972), based on the play by Jerry Douglas, is one of Metzger's most daring films, as a married and newlywed couple swing to indulge their every fantasy. For two years Metzger turned to hard-core adult films, directing *The Opening of Misty Beethoven* (1975), which ran in Washington, D.C., for seven years, and other explicit films under the pseudonym Henry Paris. The decision was purely economic.

Metzger's visual style is baroque, sophisticated, rich, and decadent. The films are simultaneously seriously erotic and outrageously campy.

The dialogue sounds like a soap opera we are supposed to take in earnest, the plots are labyrinthine, and the sex is out of the literary world of Colette, Anaïs Nin, D.H. Lawrence, and Laurence Durrell.

Meyer, Russ. Director, producer, screenwriter, cinematographer. *b.* March 21, 1922, Oakland, California. Russ Meyer writes, directs, produces, shoots, and edits all of his films, each financed with the gross profits from the previous movie. Meyer directed over twenty feature films in twenty years. His releases consistently earn profits, he has a loyal cult following, and many of the films have enjoyed popular success with a wider audience. Meyer has been the subject of retrospectives at many prestigious cultural institutions, including one at the New York Cultural Center in the 1970s when the artistic, cinematic, aesthetic, and thematic importance of his work was acknowledged by curators and historians, despite having been known as "King Leer" and the "King of the Nudies."

A Meyer film contains copious amounts of female nudity, simulated sex acts, and the American-as-apple-pie combination of sex and violence. But Meyer is not to be confused or critically evaluated with the denizens of **sexploitation**, who are simply involved in responding to supply and demand. Meyer is an American film artist influenced by and working in the stylistic tradition of **Don Siegel** and Sam Peckinpah and the social/political satiric legacy of Jonathan Swift and Henry Fielding. He is a twentieth-century cinematic satirist whose subject is the American male's obsession with female breasts and sexual aggression. It is predicated on the psychiatric observation that an average man fantasizes about sex no less than every ten seconds.

Meyer is an absurdist whose films cannot be taken purely as male gratification pornography. They feature Amazonian women with breasts larger than the average man can fantasize, most engineered by plastic surgery. Like **Andy Warhol**, Meyer has created his own superstar system. His mega-buxom beauties include Edy Willams, Erica Gavin, Tura Satana, Uschi Digard, and the incomparable Kitten Natividad.

Meyer began making **8mm** amateur movies when he was twelve years old. At fifteen he won second prize in a nationwide Eastman Kodak contest. During World War II Meyer was a newsreel combat cameraman. After the war, he became a freelance still photographer specializing in the growing market of men's nudie magazines. Meyer rose to the top of the profession shooting six *Playboy* centerfold layouts in the 1950s. He made the transition to filmmaking with **nudie cuties.** His first effort, *The Immoral Mr. Teas* (1959), starring Eve, his wife at the time, a former Playboy Playmate, was followed by *Eve and the Handyman* (1961). *The Immoral Mr. Teas*, made with a $24,000 investment, became the first **soft-core film**

An enthusiastic Russ Meyer directs two unclad actresses in *Beyond the Valley of the Dolls* (1970), written by Roger Ebert. *Courtesy of The Del Valle Archive*

to turn a large profit. The film grossed more than $1 million, breaking open the sexploitation market.

Meyer's films became less innocent with the changing times. In the 1960s, he directed the classic *Faster, Pussycat! Kill! Kill!* (1965) that combined sex, violence and a rock 'n' roll, **juvenile delinquent** consciousness. In the late 1960s Meyer's *Vixen!* (1968), produced for $76,000, grossed over $6 million. The studios took notice. In the 1970s Meyer made two studio-financed films, the legendary *Beyond the Valley of the Dolls* (1970), written by Roger Ebert and having nothing to do with the Jacqueline Susann novel, and *The Seven Minutes* (1971), which had little to do with the Irving Wallace novel.

Meyer didn't like the restrictions of going legit, and his last three films were the independent *Supervixens* (1975), *Up!* (1976), and *Beneath the Valley of the Ultra-Vixens* (1979). They are his raunchiest and most sophisticated films. Meyer worked in a cartoonlike photographic and design style, a cross between *Li'l Abner* (1959). Playboy's long-running *Little Annie Fanny* cartoon, and a **hard-core film** without explicit details. The later Meyer films are fueled by a rapid, repetitive montage editing style, hilarious narration full of social commentary, and a flood of exaggerated satirical sex scenes. Meyer is an independent filmmaker with a thematic vision of an oversexed, overviolent America and a cinematic style as pure as filmmakers with loftier goals. High art or low art, Meyer has completed a body of work as rigorous and worthy of attention as the most politically correct filmmakers.

Micheaux, Oscar. Director, producer, screenwriter. *b.* January 2, 1884, Metropolis, Illinois. *d.* March 25, 1951, Charlotte, North Carolina. Pioneer African American filmmaker, the son of freed slaves, Oscar Micheaux was raised in poverty and left home at seventeen with no formal education. After working as a shoeshine boy, laborer, Pullman porter, and homesteader on a South Dakota farm, Micheaux published three novels. A black film company was interested in the screen rights to the third book, *The Homesteader*, written in 1917, but negotiations failed. Micheaux was determined to make the film himself. He formed the Micheaux Films and Book Company and sold shares in his project at churches, schools, and social gatherings. In 1919 Micheaux's directorial debut *The Homesteader*, an eight-reel silent film, was released and returned $5,000 on a $15,000 investment.

Over the following thirty years Micheaux produced, directed, and edited over forty feature films. Regrettably, most are lost, thus limiting the attention given to this important black filmmaker. Historians are slowly becoming more aware, but Micheaux's enormous contribution to black cinematic heritage has for too long been confined to black studies in academic circles, leaving a misleading gap in the accurate history of the **African American cinema** in the twentieth century.

Early on in his career Micheaux fabricated still photographs that he showed to theaters for cash advances in order to finance his productions. Micheaux created many **exploitation films**, often inserting erotic sequences not part of the narrative construction. He avoided stories that took place in the ghettos and presented life among the black middle class. Micheaux did put aspects of black life on film that others ignored. *Within Our Gates* (1920) contains a vivid lynching sequence that reveals the horrors of hatred from the black perspective, and *Birthright* (1939) examined the social obstacles facing a black Harvard graduate. The 1925 silent film *Body and Soul*, featuring Paul Robeson in his first film role, addressed a recurring Micheaux theme—crooked preachers.

Working totally on his own and with limited resources, Micheaux's films were understandably primitive in technical aspects and often disjointed in their presentation of story and theme. But he was a prolific, audacious, and consummate showman who managed to survive and even thrive independent of the Hollywood Studio System. The tall, handsome, sharply coutured Micheaux toured from city to city with a print of one of his new productions, armed with advertising material to sell his work directly to theaters. Micheaux averaged three pictures a year, produced either in Chicago, New Jersey, or New York. His budgets were often less than $15,000, and the majority of scenes were filmed in one take.

Where other **race film** producers put out a black version of Hollywood hits, Micheaux took on controversial black themes such as intermarriage, prostitution, the numbers racket, racially motivated injustice, and the KKK for the urban black audience he wanted to inform and educate to the ways of the world. During the Great Depression and talkies era many race movie producers went bust, but Micheaux made the transition. In 1931 he made *The Exile*, the first race feature with sound. The white owner of Harlem's Apollo Theater financed the film.

Although the quality of Micheaux's output decreased with the sound film, he continued to produce a feature-length motion picture in about a week for $15,000 or less, usually shot in one location with a **shooting ratio** running between 2:1 and 1:1. A working strategy to achieve this was to have his actors read long passages of the script from cue cards—blown-line readings, mistakes, warts, and all made it into the final cut to maintain the low, low budget. In the 1932 *The Girl from Chicago*, Micheaux can be heard on the soundtrack talking the actors through their paces, even shushing for quiet. Micheaux took advantage of the fascination white audiences had with Harlem's famed Cotton Club by booking midnight screenings for *Darktown Revue* (1931) and *Harlem after Midnight* (1934), which attracted Caucasian viewers looking for exotic entertainment.

Unfortunately, economics forced Micheaux to reject the socially oriented content of his silent work. By the mid-1930s Micheaux was resigned to making the films his white financial backers approved of—such as *God's Step Children* (1938), which proclaimed black Americans should return to the farm and featured the light-skinned actors they favored over actors with darker pigmentation. Micheaux was damned by the black upper-class press, protests condemned him, and some of the films were withdrawn from exhibition. The trailblazer became a victim of his acumen as a showman and businessman. From 1930 to 1940 Micheaux directed sixteen more feature films. In 1948 he directed his last film, *The Betrayal*. The film was over three hours long and returned to socially relevant topics. Distributed by Astor Pictures, a **poverty row** studio, *The Betrayal* opened in white theaters and was panned by *Variety* and the mainstream press. It flopped around the country.

Micheaux died in 1951 while on one of his high-spirited promotional tours. In recent years some of Micheaux's lost films have been discovered. In 1987 Micheaux, the self-taught trailblazer, received a star on the Hollywood Walk of Fame.

BIBLIOGRAPHY

Bowser, Pearl, and Louise Spence. *Writing Himself into History: Oscar Micheaux, His Silent Films, and His Audiences.* Piscataway, NJ: Rutgers University Press, 2000.

Green, J. Ronald. *Straight Lick: CHECK the Cinema of Oscar Micheaux.* Bloomington: Indiana University Press, 2000.

midnight movies. Film concept started in the 1970s that introduced public screenings at the midnight hour. *El Topo* (1970), *Eraserhead* (1978), and *The Rocky Horror Picture Show* (1975) are among the most prominent examples. The Elgin and 8th Street Theaters in New York City were established locales for these events. Later the specialty idea spread to selected theaters in other cities. Midnight movies had subject matter and an approach that did not fit into mainstream distribution methods. The screenings became enormously popular through word of mouth. Attendance at a midnight movie was as cool as going to the right after-hours club, twenty-four-hour eatery, or private party. The films had an inherent nocturnal atmosphere, a dreamlike excursion into imagination, fantasy, alternate universes, and the verboten.

BIBLIOGRAPHY

Hoberman, J., and Jonathan Rosenbaum. *Midnight Movies.* New York: Da Capo Press, 1983.

Mikels, Ted V. Director, producer, writer, editor, cinematographer, actor, composer. *b.* Theodore Vincent Mikcacevich. Ted V. Mikels may be the only independent filmmaker who employed a harem to run a production company. Mikels, a magician turned film producer, director, and distributor, originally lived in a castle on the outskirts of Hollywood that was a featured location in many of his **exploitation films.** The barrel-chested Mikels, with a Dalíesque mustache, goatee, and long white sideburns, looks like a cross between a 1950 stage magician and a body builder in the mold of Jack La Lanne. Mikels lived in a communal setting with seven women he called his castle ladies. He trained each woman as a filmmaker, and they assisted in day-to-day operations. Over the course of his career Mikels was responsible for training 400 to 600 people, mostly women, about the film industry. Later Mikels relocated his "family" to Las Vegas when financiers promised to provide funding and build him a studio.

At ten, Mikels developed film in his bathtub. As a teenager he began shooting features as a cinematographer, filming magic shows, educa-

TRANSYLVANIAN

Tim Curry as the transvestite Doctor Frank-N-Furter holding court with cast members of *The Rocky Horror Picture Show* (1975), the longest-running midnight movie. Courtesy of The Del Valle Archive

tional, sales, and training films, TV spots, commercials, rock music videos, and half-hour melodramas. At seventeen, Mikels toured with Mandrake the Magician. With his massive physique and expert skills as a fencer and horseman, Mikels entered the film industry in the 1950s working as a stuntman and bit player. He was a newsreel cameraman in Oregon. Mikels quickly learned the methods of the low-budget indie. He purchased outdated **short ends** and enlisted up to fifty people for a weekend shoot. Mikels worked 24/7 before it was trendy.

The Corpse Grinders (1972) is a horror/comedy about a cat food company that grinds up boys to make its product. (The corpse-grinding machine was built for $38, utilizing lawn mower blades, odd junk, red light bulbs, and discarded plywood.) The food causes felines to attack their owners. It was a fun shoot for Mikels using Cecil B. DeMille's home as the location. The cinematographer had shot some **16mm** film but needed Mikels to tutor him in camera operation. The no-budget film became Mikels's highest grosser, landing a number eleven spot of the top fifty films during its first week of release.

Mikels, with well over 100 credits, never hustled for funding. His projects were put together with small loans, bank money, lab credit, and a crew who worked in exchange for Mikels's filmmaking instruction. Mikels believed anyone could make a film and turned students without practical knowledge into production assistants. In the early 1960s, the castle was strewn with sleeping bags and people eager to become filmmakers.

Mikels founded Geneni Film Distributors to release his films. *The Girl in Gold Boots* (1968) was the tale of a draft dodger and his girl surrounded by crime and sin in Hollywood. *The Astro-Zombies* (1968) starred John Carradine as a mad zombie, Wendell Corey as a CIA chief, and Tura Satana of **Russ Meyer**'s *Faster, Pussycat! Kill! Kill!* (1965) fame as a foreign agent. Mikels claims he made the first **blaxploitation** film, *The Black Klansman* (1966), and that his 1974 film *The Doll Squad* was ripped off by the producers of the hit television series *Charlie's Angels*.

Mikels has developed as many as six projects at once, often without the ability to complete postproduction on his slate of pictures. He complains he's lost hundreds of thousands of dollars from pirated prints and disreputable industry types. Mikels gripes about producing—all he really loves is making film after film; the rest is a nuisance. Mikels's catalog includes *Blood Orgy of the She Devils* (1972), *10 Violent Women* (1982), and *Operation Overkill* (1984). Recent credits for Ted V. Mikels include: *Dimensions in Fear* (1998), which he photographed and directed, and *Mark of the Astro-Zombies* (2002) as screenwriter, producer and director. With Mikels it is the man and his methods that fascinates more than the movies. Even connoisseurs of **psychotronic films** have pronounced Mikels's films as just plain bad—so bad, that one day a theoretician will write a position paper on the bad aesthetics of Ted V. Mikels.

Millennium, The. Founded in 1966 and incorporated as an independent nonprofit New York organization in May 1967, along with **Film/Video Arts**, it is one of the oldest media arts centers in the United States. Filmmaker **Ken Jacobs** was the first director of The Millennium. The Millennium has always offered editing, production, and screening capabilities and a continuous Personal Cinema series with film and video artists who present their work and dialogue with the audience. In 1968, Jacobs left The Millennium, and it has long been in the capable hands of filmmaker **Howard Guttenplan.** In 1975 The Millennium moved to a larger space in a city-owned building on East 4th Street. In 1978 the first issue of *The Millennium Film Journal* was published and has produced issues covering surrealism in the cinema, autobiography, animation, and new technologies. Dedicated to film as art, The Millennium and its journal have been a home for **avant-garde** and **experimental film** and video and have embraced the work of almost every important artist including **Stan Brakhage,** Warren Sonbert, George Landow, Michael Snow, Su Friedrich, and Carolee Schneemann and **critics** and theorists **P. Adams Sitney,** Noel Carroll, Amy Taubin, and Scott MacDonald. Among the workshops and classes held at The Millennium are basic filmmaking, **16mm** film editing, animation, and a class on the **optical printer**—the photographic tool utilized to create magical, poetic images for countless personal films. *See also* Guttenplan, Howard; Jacobs, Ken

Miramax. Independent production and distribution company created by Harvey and Bob Weinstein in 1979 in New York City. The most profitable, powerful, and successful indie company of the last twenty years, Miramax is named after the parents of the brothers who built their power base by distributing foreign and domestic art films that brought substantial financial rewards. The Weinsteins' golden touch resulted in four Oscars in a row for foreign films they released: *Pelle the Conqueror* (1987), *Cinema Paradiso* (1988), *Journey of Hope* (1990) and *Mediterrano* (1991). In 1989, Miramax claimed the independent film mantle by releasing **Steven Soderbergh**'s *sex, lies and videotape* (1989). They began coproducing films: *Scandal* (1989), *Enchanted April* (1992), *Map of the Human Heart* (1992), *Into the West* (1992). Other acquisitions such as *The Thin Blue Line* (1988), *Like Water for Chocolate* (1992), *My Left Foot* (1989), and *Farewell My Concubine* (1993) grew Miramax into an indie power player. In 1993 the Walt Disney Company acquired Miramax as an autonomous subsidiary—contractually under the complete artistic and financial control of Harvey and Bob Weinstein until 2005. After a bloody marketing duel, Miramax beat the other indie giant DreamWorks to win the best picture Oscar for *Shakespeare in Love* over Spielberg's *Saving Private Ryan* (both 1998). In recent years the Weinsteins and their company have come under intense fire, especially from **critic** Jonathan Rosenbaum whose investigation into Miramax's methods has alleged disturbing practices of reediting a director's work and getting behind fashionable projects (like those starring Gwyneth Paltrow) and letting others die quickly with little support. The old adage power corrupts and absolute power corrupts absolutely may apply here, but if an indie company can't survive in the mainstream market, it folds.

BIBLIOGRAPHY

Rosenbaum, Jonathan. *Movie Wars: How Hollywood and the Media Conspire to Limit What Films We Can See*. New York: A Cappella Books, 2000.

Mitchell, Eric. Filmmaker. Eric Mitchell was at the epicenter of the 1980s punk, **No-Wave** scene in New York City's East Village. He is the screenwriter, director and coproducer of the legendary cult film *Underground U.S.A.* (1980), a No-Wave retelling of the *Sunset Blvd.* story. Mitchell plays a bisexual hustler who hooks onto an over-the-hill movie queen played by Patti Astor. No-Wave actor and saxophonist **John Lurie** contributed to the soundtrack. Indie ace cinematographer **Tom DiCillo** photographed *Underground U.S.A.*, and **Jim Jarmusch** recorded the production sound. In 1984 Mitchell directed *The Way It Is*, starring **Steve Buscemi** and Vincent Gallo, who cowrote the original music. Mitchell performed in *Dreamland* in 1994 and *À Vendre (For Sale)* in 1998.

Mitchell, Jim and Artie. Jim Mitchell, *b.* November 30, 1943, Stockton, California. Artie Mitchell, *b.* December 17, 1945, Lodi, California. *d.* February 27, 1991, shot to death by his brother Jim. The Mitchell brothers were pioneering **hard-core** filmmakers who built a sex empire in San Francisco in the 1970s. They moved to San Francisco during the 1960s and opened a chain of **adult film** theaters amidst the hotbed of peace, drugs, and free love. The brothers were inseparable and as close as identical twins. On July 4, 1969, Jim and Artie opened the O'Farrell Theater that featured what is known in the trade as "beaver films," films that flaunt female genitalia. The brothers were a self-contained porn corporation. They began making their own adult films and screening them in their theaters, thus bypassing the greedy **distributors** of the subindustry. Although Jim was famous for saying, "The only art in this business is my brother," they constructed elaborate quasi-artistic, quasi-pretentious narratives. The Mitchells discovered Marilyn Briggs, a topless model who became the Ivory Snow girl. They made Marilyn Chambers, her biz name, into an adult film superstar with **Behind the Green Door** (1972) and *Inside Marilyn Chambers* (1975). The Mitchell brothers also directed and produced *Resurrection of Eve* (1973), *C.B. Mamas* (1976), *The Grafenberg Spot* (1985), *The Grafenberg Girls Go Fishing* (1987), and *Behind the Green Door, the Sequel* in 1986. Eventually the bubble burst. In 1991, Jim became frustrated by Artie's erratic drug-induced behavior. On February 27, 1991, Jim shot Artie to death. Looking at their films today they appear tame in the light of the **direct-to-video** all-sex-of-all-kinds industry product. See also *Behind the Green Door*

BIBLIOGRAPHY

McCumber, David. *X-Rated: A True Story of Sex, Money, and Death.* New York: Simon and Schuster, 1992.

Mondo Cane. Italian **documentary** made in 1963 that highlighted strange human behaviors, bizarre customs, rituals, and pastimes around the globe. The shocking film directed by Paolo Cavara, Gualtiero Jacopetti and Franco E. Prosperi took the world by storm, racking up enough box office to produce sequels in 1964, 1986, and 1988. *Mondo Cane* was narrated by Jacopetti, who edited and also produced and cowrote the film with Cavara. In living color, *Mondo Cane* presents such oddities as religious fanatics washing a stairway with their tongues, a chicken smoking cigarettes, a town populated by distorted look-a-like descendants of Rudolph Valentino, a yearly celebration where men smash a garage door with their bare hands, living insect jewelry, and meals concocted out of cooked insects. The Italian creators offset the squeamish sights in their film by contracting Nino Olivero and Riz Ortolani to write a love song for the picture's theme. Not in any way inspired by the ghoulish and offbeat subject matter, they came back with "More," which won the Oscar for Best Song. The popular tune has been covered by countless crooners and played at more weddings than can be calculated.

Mondo Cane was a documentary that captured real events, but for *Mondo Cane 2* (1964) some scenes were created and staged for comic effect, ignoring the adage that truth is stranger than fiction. In addition to the sequels, *Mondo* imitators flooded the market, hoping to cash in on the public's desire to witness taboo happenings. As many as twenty *Mondo* features were released in the 1960s. *Mondo Bizzaro* (1966) was almost completely faked by the filmmakers. *Mondo Teeno* and *Mondo Mod* (1967) uncovered the rites of teenagers. *Mondo Hollywood* (1967), aka *Hippie Hollywood: The Acid Blasting Freaks,* featured Bobby Beausoleil of the notorious Charles Manson family. Many Mondo films dealt with sex: *Hollywood Blue* (1970), *Mondo Erotico* (1973), *Mondo Keyhole* (1966), *Mondo Topless* (1966) and *Mondo Depravados.*

None of the imitators had anything to do with *Mondo Cane,* a precursor to the craze that eventually inspired television's present mania with tabloid and reality television. In the 1970s the *Mondo* films faded from the big screen with the exception of an occasional foray like the mid-1970s *Mondo America.* In 1978 the gruesome *Faces of Death* began showing up in local video stores and has been a successful, if deranged, **franchise** that continued into the 1980s and 1990s.

Monitor, The. Newspaper of New York independent film scene. A monthly publication that contains practical news for indie filmmakers:

profiles, crew calls, casting notices, production and history articles, production guide, classifieds, service ads, festival news, and useful inside information. Low-budget price—two bucks an issue.

Moore, Michael. Documentary filmmaker. *b.* April 23, 1954, Flint, Michigan. *ed.* University of Michigan. Moore grew up as a political activist writing for the alternate press, *Mother Jones*, then founded the *Michigan Voice*, which he edited for ten years. Moore's politics were anti-big business and pro worker. His parents had both worked for General Motors in Flint, Michigan. The downsizing of America in the 1980s under the leadership of Ronald Reagan left the workers in Flint in economic strife. As a journalistic mission to save Flint, Moore decided to make *Roger & Me* (1989), a **documentary** targeting GM CEO Roger Smith. The supersized Moore with his out-of-date shag haircut, unfashionable glasses, and a baseball hat adorned with the slogan "I'm Out for Trout" is a hysterically funny yet politically potent presence as he tries relentlessly to secure an audience with Smith. Along with facts about layoffs and lines of workers waiting to receive government surplus cheese and butter, Moore takes the film in bizarre and hilarious directions by intercutting subplots: a deputy sheriff who evicts Flint residents who can't pay their rent during the Christmas season; Pat Boone, Anita Bryant, Robert Schuller, Bob Eubanks, and the presence of Ronald Reagan, all brought in to save Flint and steer the unemployed toward other jobs at Amway and Taco Bell. Flintites make ends meet in extraordinary ways like the woman who sells rabbits for "pets or meat" and a man who donates blood every day but Saturday and Sunday when the clinic is closed. Moore and his editors were not experienced in documentary film construction, but their naïveté freed them from conformity and allowed a new kind of documentary to emerge. *Roger & Me* is not **cinéma vérité.** Moore's constant presence dominates and orchestrates the proceedings of the film that took three years to make. His commanding comedic sense softens the delivery of the political rhetoric, so the audience enjoys the lesson and absorbs Moore's POV without question.

After prolonged negotiations, filmmaker's rep **John Pierson** made his first-ever studio sale, selling *Roger & Me* to Warner Bros. for an astounding $3 million, nearly twenty times Moore's budget. Warner's was impressed by the film's performance on the festival circuit and committed an additional $6 million to promotion. *Roger & Me* got great reviews and landed on more than 100 ten-best lists. It won Best Film awards at the Toronto, Vancouver, and Chicago film festivals; Best Documentary honors from The New York Society of Film Critics and The National Board of Review; and the Audience Award at the Berlin Film Festival. The film became a national phenomenon, grossing $7 million, the most money

Michael Moore directing Roger and Me *(1989). Kobol Collection/Warner Brothers*

ever for a nonmusical documentary, but Warner's was still disappointed because of the $9 million they had expended.

Moore is credited with reinventing the nonfiction form along with **Errol Morris** and **Ross McElwee.** Moore was interviewed and appeared everywhere in the media. He became the hero of the under class, but the bubble burst. Journalists from *Film Comment, The New Yorker,* and *Time* uncovered that Moore had compressed and reordered many of the facts concerning the Reagan administration. Ultimately, he was accused of patronizing and exploiting the poor and unemployed of Flint for film profits. Moore countered that as a committed leftist he would use any means necessary to fight big corporations who prey on workers and taxpayers.

Three years later Moore followed up with a twenty-five-minute sequel, *Pets or Meat: The Return of Flint* (1992) made for television. It revisited Flint's economic situation and revealed that Roger Smith, no longer GM CEO, claimed never to have seen the film that made him and General Motors a disgraceful nationwide joke.

In 1995, Moore shifted from nonfiction to the theatrical feature *Canadian Bacon* (1995), starring John Candy, Alan Alda, Rhea Pearlman, Kevin Pollak, Rip Torn, Steven Wright, and James Belushi. The political satire concerns an incumbent president of the United States who declares war on Canada to gain support for his reelection. The film failed to go beyond a one-joke premise and was a box office dud.

In 1996 while on tour for his bestselling book *Downsize This*, Moore directed *The Big One* (1997), a **guerrilla**-style documentary in which he tries to meet with many CEOs laying off employees. All but one was smart enough to say no. Phil Knight, the Nike CEO, did meet with Moore, to his chagrin. Later he dispatched a public relations man to offer a bribe in hopes that Moore would cut out two scenes where the man behind "Just Do It!" sounded a bit racist and uncaring about Indonesian workers at a Nike plant. Knight stepped into the trap that Roger Smith avoided, but both films are activist documentaries that use ridicule and Moore's ability to whip up the masses with humor and the truth about corporate America as he sees it. In 1998 Michael Moore directed the documentary *And Justice For All*. In 1999 he wrote, hosted and was the executive producer of the television series *The Awful Truth* for the Bravo cable network. Moore also wrote and directed the non-fiction film *Bowling for Columbine* (2003).

Morris, Erol. Filmmaker. *b.* February 5, 1948, Hewlett, Long Island, New York. *ed.* University of Wisconsin at Madison, Princeton University, University of California at Berkeley. Early on, Errol Morris had studied cello, but he gave up on music when he became a history major at the University of Wisconsin. After graduating in 1969, Morris drifted for several years and earned a meager living from odd jobs such as a television salesman and term paper writer. Morris returned to academic study, briefly attending Princeton graduate school, then went to Berkeley in 1972 as a Ph.D. candidate, eventually attaining a master's degree in philosophy.

Morris turned in another direction and became involved in the Pacific Film Archives, determined to become a filmmaker. He raised $120,000 from his family and a financially connected classmate and in the spring and summer of 1977 shot *Gates of Heaven* at two disparate pet cemeteries, one successful and one in decline. For Morris the nonfiction film was a metaphor for America's misguided priorities. Morris was interested in content and aesthetics from the outset. *Gates of Heaven* was photographed with an immobile fixed-lens camera instead of the probing handheld camera or investigating eye of the zoom lens. His technique was designed to allow subjects to reveal themselves without cinematic devices. Morris employed this approach again on his second film *Vernon, Florida* (1981), the nonfiction profile of the eccentricity of people in a small southern town.

Morris became interested in the real-life story of Randall Adams, a convicted killer the filmmaker believed was wrongly accused of the murder of a Dallas police officer. Morris spent years rigorously researching the case and interviewing everyone involved. Slowly, he raised the money to finance the project and eventually made a vanguard nonfiction film that was instrumental in freeing Adams. *The Thin Blue Line* (1988) was enormously successful, and many of its structural elements redefined the aesthetics and rules of nonfiction filmmaking. *The Thin Blue Line* is fact based and contains talking head interviews, but that's where the comparison with the traditional **documentary** ends. Morris recreates the crime with imagery that pushes the docudrama and tabloid television visual style into a postmodern realm. By stylizing and constantly repeating and restructuring the staged version of the crime, the words of Randall Adams and his adversaries and defenders take on a clarity and communicate what really may have happened in a manner the conventional documentary could not achieve. Morris utilizes old film clips and archival footage to illustrate the speakers, often mocking their disingenuous remarks and loyalty to the Texas tradition of hang 'em high justice.

Many documentaries have employed a musical score that functions as a dramatic, narrative device and imparts emotion and atmosphere as it would in a fictional film. Morris asked Philip Glass to compose music for *The Thin Blue Line*, and his choice gave the work a transcendent quality. The hypnotic, repetitive score reinforces the editing structure and communicates Adams's Kafkaesque situation.

Next Morris tackled the Stephen Hawkings book *A Brief History of Time* (1992). The challenge was to translate the complex ideas inside Hawkings's genius mind trapped in a wheelchair-confined body wracked with a disease that requires him to use a computer communication device to vocalize his thoughts. Again Morris was innovative. To photograph the film Morris departed from traditional documentary cameramen and selected New Hollywood cinematographer John Bailey (*Mishima* [1985], *The Big Chill* [1983]) to give the film a distinctive look. Imagery to illustrate the complex ideas was conceived, but it was the talking head interviews that Morris aimed to revolutionize. He shot the interview subjects on sets built on a soundstage. The sets were detailed recreations of their own offices. Using a feature film approach, *A Brief History of Time* is imbued with a replicated reality that was meant to put the subject at ease but functions as a strategy to give the nonfiction film a fictionally created aura. Morris revealed a personal eccentricity that attracted him to his offbeat subjects and his radical approach to nonfiction filmmaking.

In 1991 Morris adapted Tony Hillerman's novel *The Dark Wind*, about a Navajo police officer, with backing from executive producer Robert Redford, who has a lifelong commitment to Native American life. The film disappointed in every respect. It failed at the box office and was uncharacteristically uncinematic and ponderous in its narrative. None of Morris's visual acuity or eccentric vision was evident, and the fictional debut was a dead end.

Fast, Cheap & Out of Control (1997) brought Morris back to his brand of off-center reality and teamed him with director of photography Robert

Richardson, the cutting-edge cinematographer who expanded visual horizons with Oliver Stone. The film explored the lives of a topiary gardener, a lion tamer, a robot scientist, and a naked mole-rat expert. Morris embraced these odd individuals and created a film about passion for work as a driving life force.

His next major project was *Mr. Death: The Rise and Fall of Fred A. Leuchter, Jr.* (1999). Leuchter, an expert on execution devices, was duped by Ernst Zundel, a historian spreading propaganda that the systematic extermination of 6 million Jews was a lie. He had Leuchter examine Auschwitz for evidence that no gas chambers existed at the notorious death factory. Amazingly, Leuchter makes videos documenting his tests that conclude there was no sign of poisonous gas in the walls and environs of the death camp. Zundel is a hater, but Leuchter is a victim of his own stubbornness and lack of a social conscience. Unaware of the consequences, Leuchter's high standing in the national law enforcement community is destroyed by his collaboration with the neo-Nazi. *Mr. Death* is more than just another Morris trip into oddball land; it reveals the evils of science without morality.

Morrissey, Paul. Director, producer, screenwriter, actor. *b.* February 23, 1938, New York City. *ed.* Fordham University. After serving in the army, Paul Morrissey worked as a social worker and insurance clerk before making **underground** short films in the early 1960s. Morrissey met **Andy Warhol** and worked as a production assistant and cameraman at The Factory. Eventually, Morrissey produced and directed Warhol's films. Prior to Morrissey, Warhol's films were highly conceptual and structural, many created in one take with no cinematic aesthetic. Morrissey brought order and filmmaking ability to Warhol films. *Flesh* (1968), *Trash* (1970), and *Heat* (1972) took Warhol out of the underground to the fringe of the mainstream. Morrissey made the films bare bones and low budget with a semblance of production values and a series of outrageous performances by Warhol superstars. He gave the films a stark, overlit, and barely composed look. The Morrissey films owe as much to the emotional excesses of **John Cassavetes** as the minimalism of Andy Warhol. Sex and celebrity with plenty of squalor were the common denominators. *Andy Warhol's Frankenstein* (1974) and *Andy Warhol's Dracula* (1974) had a trash film aesthetic applied to the Gothic horror classics. In the mid-1970s, Morrissey left Warhol and tried to make a transition from underground art films to commercial vehicles, but *The Hound of the Baskervilles* (1977), with Peter Cooke and Dudley Moore, and *Spike of Bensonhurst* (1988) didn't quite get him there. *See also* Warhol, Andy

movie brat generation. *See* American New Wave

Museum of Modern Art. *See* Cineprobe

Nair, Mira. Director, producer. *b.* October 15, 1957, Bhubaneshwar, Orissa, India. *ed.* Delhi University, Harvard University. Mira Nair studied sociology in India and enjoyed acting in amateur productions, but a course on **documentary** filmmaking at Harvard motivated her to direct film. Nair made the United States her base of operations and directed four documentaries about the changing culture in India: *Jama Masjid Street Journal* (1979), *So Far from India* (1983), *India Cabaret* (1985) and *Children of Desired Sex* (1987).

Nair's first feature *Salaam Bombay* (1987) was celebrated with the Camera d'or at Cannes and an Oscar nomination for best foreign film. Sooni Taraporeva developed the script for *Salaam Bombay!* (1988), and the two women researched the project as if it were a documentary—they hung out with street gangs to understand their world. Nair started a workshop in a rented church in downtown Bombay. One hundred and thirty street children showed up, and 24 were selected. Nair rehearsed and ran acting exercises for seven weeks, nine to six each day. She used real streets and a brothel for locations. The children were shown movies, and Nair videotaped them performing scenes from the *Salaam Bombay!* screenplay. Scenes were refined, and realism, not acting for the camera, was encouraged. Capital for the bare bones production was raised daily, with the total budget at $900,000. Channel Four in Britain had given Nair $10,000 to develop the screenplay. They gave her half the budget, and Nair raised the rest from nonprofit foundations in America. Nair tried to presell the television rights to venues with a known interest in documentaries, even though the film was fictional, but no one was interested. Nair and her director of photography, Sandi Sissel, had to shoot by the first week in September to capture the massive festivals for the film's finale. The National Film Development Corporation in India gave

Nair $150,000. She presented a $6 million budget to Channel Four and told them she had $150,000 before she actually did. They gave the production $300,000 so shooting could commence. Sissel, who captured the exquisite light and the filth of poverty, beautifully rendered the duality of Bombay on film.

Mississippi Masala (1991), with Denzel Washington, was financed by Channel Four and other independent sources. The film called for seventy-nine speaking roles and locations in several countries with a budget of $7 million. Nair's theme was the hierarchy of skin color about which she had personal experience as a brown-skinned person who moved between black and white worlds. An article about Asians expelled from Uganda, Indians who only know Africa as their homeland, and African Americans who have not experienced Africa, the land of their ancestors, sparked the idea. Again collaborating with Sooni Taraporeva, they researched for six months before writing the screenplay and traveled to Uganda and Kenya to interview displaced people.

In 1995, Nair directed *The Perez Family*, employing star power with Marisa Tomei, Anjelica Huston, and Chazz Palminteri to tell the story of a Cuban plantation owner and twenty-year political prisoner who migrates to Florida in the 1980 *Mariel* boat lift. The dramedy failed to find an audience. In 1996 Nair directed *Kama Sutra: A Tale of Love*, an erotic feminist story of sexual politics in sixteenth-century feudal India. The film was released with an NC-17 rating, and an R-rated version was edited to give video renters a choice. Recent credits for Mira Nair include: *The Laughing Club of India* (1999), a short documentary for television, *Monsoon Wedding* (2001), and *Hysterical Blindness* (2002).

BIBLIOGRAPHY

Cole, Janis, and Holly Dale. *Calling The Shots: Profiles of Women Filmmakers*. Kingston, Ontario: Quarry Press, 1993.

National Endowment for the Arts (NEA). Created by Congress in 1965 as an independent agency of the federal government to award grants to the arts. Their mission was to nurture creativity and excellence through grants in partnership with state art agencies, regional arts organizations, other federal agencies and the private sector. The NEA set out to enhance Americans' access to the arts in dance, design, folk arts, literature, film, television, radio, audio, music, musical theater, opera, theater, and multidisciplinary arts. The grants were open to nonprofit tax-exempt U.S. organizations. As the NEA grew, the endowment was substantial and able to support many independent film productions. Disaster struck in the 1980s and 1990s when fundamentalists and right-wing politicians, notably Donald Wildmon, Jerry Falwell, and Senator Jesse Helms, attacked the organization. The focus of their vitriol was Robert Mapplethorpe's sadomasochistic photographs and performance artist Karen Finley. As the NEA came under fire the budget was slashed, and support to the arts was demonized by propaganda to convince the public that federal monies were being spent on pornography. The battle was hard fought, but the big picture of the NEA was severely damaged, and considerably less grant money was made available. An expensive medium like motion pictures took a severe hit. The NEA is still supplying grants to filmmakers, but the endowment continues to shrink, and each decision is watched closely by the cultural arbiters who want to control what we see and hear.

Nava, Gregory. Director, screenwriter. *b.* April 10, 1949, San Diego, California. *ed.* University College of Los Angeles. In 1973, Gregory Nava, born and raised in southern California with a Mexican-Basque heritage, wrote a feature screenplay, *The Confessions of Amans*. The tragic medieval love story is a love affair between a young philosophy tutor and a lord's wife. The narrative presented the moral choice the couple faces with a Bressonian sense of detachment. Nava mounted the period production in Spain for only $20,000, utilizing costumes from *El Cid* (1961). He wrote, produced, directed, photographed, and edited it. *The Confessions of Amans* (1976) won the first feature prize at the Chicago Film Festival but was barely distributed, so it did little to launch his career as a writer/director. In 1980 Nava produced and photographed a horror film, *The Haunting of M*, directed by his wife Anna Thomas, that took place in an old Scottish dwelling. It is the story of a family haunted by the spirit of one of their ancestors.

Nava's breakthrough came with the 1983 release of *El Norte*. Getting the film made was a two-year struggle for Nava and Thomas, his producer and cowriter. The project was financed for $850,000 by PBS's ***American Playhouse*** and several private sources, shot in 150 separate locations in Mexico with a cast of more than sixty speaking roles. Hostilities threatened the cast and crew shooting in the Mayan highlands. The production manager was kidnapped, and some of the original negative was stolen. Thomas had to pay $17,000 in ransom for their release. To insure the safety of the company, the Mexican scenes were switched to Los Angeles with an unanticipated additional budgetary expense. *El Norte* translates to "The North" and refers to the narrative plight of a brother and sister as they flee from a terror-driven village in Guatemala. The harrowing journey takes them through a corrupt migrant industry in Mexico to an uncertain future in southern California. The story is told in Spanish, Mayan, and English by unknown Latin American actors. *El Norte* is fabled in the magical realism style of Latin American authors Gabriel García Márquez, Jorge Amado, Julio Cortázar, and Isabel Allende and is a compelling emotional cinematic experience. *El Norte* premiered at the Telluride Film Festival and was well received by critics and audiences. The domestic grosses alone were over $5 million, earning *El Norte* the distinction of being the most successful American-made foreign-language film in history at the time. Nava and the screenplay received an Oscar nomination.

Nava's next film, *A Time of Destiny* (1988), again cowritten and produced by Anna Thomas, with the assistance of Columbia Pictures, did not fulfill the promise of *El Norte.* The sudsy World War II melodrama reworks the tired theme of revenge between friends. The hyperdramatic plot doomed the fine cast including William Hurt, Timothy Hutton, and Stockard Channing.

After this failed flirtation with Hollywood, Nava continued to try for a wide appeal and commercial acceptance. *My Family/Mi Familia* (1995), financed through *American Playhouse* and independent sources and godfathered by **Francis Ford Coppola**'s **American Zoetrope,** was a Latino epic designed to be a box office smash, but it didn't receive the reception to accomplish this lofty goal. The story, written by Nava and Thomas, is the history of a Mexican American writer's family who immigrated to Los Angeles during the 1920s. The story traces three generations. The huge cast features many fine Hispanic performers including Edward James Olmos, Jimmy Smits, Esai Morales, and Jennifer Lopez. Nava and his cinematographer **Ed Lachman** give each period a color palette that sets the atmosphere for the time in this encompassing cultural history. It premiered at **Sundance,** then opened wide on 400 screens, grossing $11 million, just enough to get Warner Brothers to distribute his next film, *Selena* (1997), a biopic of the slain superstar known as the Hispanic Madonna. In 1998, Nava directed *Why Do Fools Fall in Love,* the complicated love life of 1950s teen pop star Frankie Lyman, financed and distributed by Warner Bros. The film failed to find an audience. In 2002 Gregory Nava was the producer and director of *Killing Pablo,* and the creator, writer, executive producer and director of the television series *American Family* for the Public Broadcasting network.

negative pickup. A financial arrangement common to independent films where a contractual commitment is made to the producer from a **distributor** to buy or license their feature film for an agreed-upon price after delivery of the completed project.

Nevins, Sheila. Executive. One of the most powerful forces behind independent **documentary** and nonfiction filmmakers, HBO executive Sheila Nevins is responsible for commissioning and buying hundreds of films and original programming created by independent filmmakers. Projects under her direct, hands-on supervision have won numerous awards including several Oscars for documentary filmmaking. Films she has produced include *One Survivor Remembers* (1995), *The Celluloid Closet* (1995), *Paradise Lost: The Child Murders at Robin Hood Hills* (1996), *4 Little Girls* (1997) and *Lenny Bruce: Swear to Tell the Truth* (1998). Recent documentaries shepherded by Sheila Nevins include: *Fashion Victim: The Killing of Gianni Versace*, *Dwarfs: Not a Fair Tale* (both 2001), *Devil's Playground*, *American Standoff*, *The Execution of Wanda Jean* (all 2002), and *He's Having a Baby* (2003).

New American Cinema Group. Formed in 1960, the New American Cinema Group sought to form a closer relationship between the production and distribution of independent films. Organized by independent icons like **Jonas Mekas**, **Shirley Clarke**, and **Robert Frank**, the Group's argument against the polish of Hollywood films and encouragement of directors coincided with the French New Wave's unofficial "manifesto," François Truffaut's "A Certain Tendency in French Cinema," which stated similar goals. Though not as influential as Truffaut's declaration, the Group's "First Statement of the New American Cinema Group" certainly resonates with today's independent filmmakers in its argument that the slickness of Hollywood films "has become a perversion covering the falsity of their themes, their lack of sensitivity, their lack of style." *See also* Mekas, Jonas

BIBLIOGRAPHY

Battock, Gregory, ed. *The New American Cinema: A Critical Anthology*. New York: E.P. Dutton, 1967.

Newfield, Sam. Director. *b.* December 6, 1899, New York City. *d.* November 10, 1964. In thirty years as a director of low-budget action movies for **poverty row** studios, Sam Newfield made 223 films—an average of more than 7 films a year not including the comedy shorts he directed when he entered the industry in 1919. Some of his programmers are *Code of the Mounted* (1935), *Border Caballero* (1936), *The Texas Marshal* (1941), *The Mad Monster* (1942), *His Brother's Ghost* (1945), *Gas House Kids* (1946), *Jungle Flight* (1947), *Radar Secret Service* (1950), *Scotland Yard Inspector* (1952), *The Gambler and the Lady* (1952), and *Wolf Dog* (1958). Newfield's best-known film is *The Terror of Tiny Town* (1938). The sixty-three-minute black-and-white western features an all-midget cast—a novelty film frequently programmed at World's Worst Films Festivals. Newfield was a professional, not an auteur. He was good at what he did best, which was to competently direct films that were neither good nor bad but served their purpose to support the A-picture on a double bill.

Newsreel. A 1960s radical militant filmmaking **co-op** founded by **Robert Kramer** and others with offices in Chicago and New York. Newsreel was originally located in the garment district; after relocation the name changed to Third World Newsreel. By 1974, it was serving an audience of 20,000 with 2,000 bookings for films they distributed primarily to college groups. Newsreel's catalog grew with films brought to them from many sources. Popular rentals included *Salt of the Earth* (1954), *El Pueblo se Levanta* (*The People Are Rising*), *Rompiendo Puertas* (*Break and Enter*), *La Luta Continua*, *We Are the Palestinian People*, and *Vivas Frelimo*. Newsreel focused on specific political topics and collected films to support these themes and causes. Subjects included prisons, the military, due process, laws, civil rights, trials, police, women's liberation, ecology, working-class struggles, national liberation struggles, views of socialist societies, North Vietnam, and liberated sectors of South Vietnam. *See also* Kramer, Robert

BIBLIOGRAPHY

Nichols, Bill. *Newsreel: Documentary Filmmaking on the American Left*. New York: Arno Press, 1980.

New York Foundation for the Arts (NYFA). Established in 1971 by the New York State Council on the Arts as a separate organization to encourage and facilitate arts activities throughout the state. The NYFA provides grants, regrants, loans, and financial services to the diverse New York arts community. The NYFA supports education, artist-in-residence programs, and artists fellowships. In 1984, they created *FYI*, a quarterly newsletter for artists and in 1995 The Visual Artists Information Hotline that gives one-to-one assistance to artists. Independent filmmakers have reaped many benefits, assistance, and support from the NYFA's good works.

New York Underground Film Festival. Started in 1993, held at **Anthology Film Archives** with the mission to showcase film and video from the fringes of independent filmmaking, the one-week festival presents work from many countries.

Night of the Living Dead. *See* Romero, George A.

No-Dance Film Festival. Founded by Jim Boyd and a handful of other filmmakers who felt shut out of the **Sundance** and **Slamdance** festivals. In 1998 the No-Dance Film Festival provided walk-on screenings to anyone who wanted to show their film. The next year projects were submitted on VHS and couldn't be more than thirty minutes. The current incarnation of No-Dance is digital and has gone into cyberspace on its Web site. *See also* Slamdance Film Festival; Slamdunk Film Festival; Sundance Institute.

No-Nothing Cinema. A landmark San Francisco experimental film venue forced to give up its space as a victim of urban renewal in the late 1990s. The home of an iconoclastic cadre of filmmakers who create short works that cannot be codified by current political and aesthetic trends, it relocated and reincarnated as the New-Nothing Cinema. In 1998, they curated "New **16mm** Beatniks," a show featuring 16mm shorts from New York, Milwaukee, Denver, Los Angeles, and local cinema rebels from the San Francisco area, proving that not every filmmaker wants to conform to commercial or independent trends.

nontheatrical film rental. Venues that include schools, universities, private industry, film societies, community groups, airplanes, hotels, libraries, ships, governmental agencies, and prisons.

Noonan, Tom. Actor, director, screenwriter, composer. *b.* April 12, 1941, Greenwich, Connecticut. *ed.* Yale University. Tom Noonan has composed music for the stage and has performed in over thirty feature films. In the 1980s he began writing and directing television. In 1982 Noonan founded the Paradise Theater in Lower Manhattan. In 1992 Noonan wrote the play *What Happened Was . . .* that he also directed and performed in at the theater. Noonan's film adaptation (1994) won the Grand Jury Prize and the Waldo Salt Award for the screenplay at **Sundance.** The film also garnered two Spirit Nominations. *What Happened Was . . .* starred Noonan and Karen Sillas as a lonely odd couple who are also coworkers. Noonan made his first theatrical feature with $50,000 he had earned as an actor. The production cost $47,000; the crew worked on **deferments.** Noonan got a free camera package through Sundance and the Panavision Corporation. When filming wrapped, the project was granted $17,000 from the **National Endowment for the Arts.** Postproduction costs of $75,000 were paid for with Noonan's earnings on *Last Action Hero* (1993), starring Arnold Schwarzenegger. The 35mm feature came in at a $122,000 cash budget, and when deferments were paid, the total came to just over $300,000. *What Happened Was . . .*, distributed by the Samuel Goldwyn Company, was shot in eleven and a half days, mostly in sequence and on one set to capture the real-time claustrophobic atmosphere of the play.

In 1994 Noonan's play *Wifey* was mounted at the Paradise. It starred Wallace Shawn, Karen Young, Julie Haggerty, and Noonan, who won an Obie for playwriting. *The Wife* (1996) was Noonan's second independent film adapted from his stage production. The four-character story structured in real time was shot on location in upstate New York. When the play closed after a successful sold-out run, the crew took two weeks to make final preparations for production. The cast was on location for ten days to rehearse before the March 4, 1994, start date. Noonan edited on location and received funds to complete postproduction. CIBY 2000 committed to distributing the dark comedy about New Age therapists played by Noonan and Julie Haggerty who are visited by a patient and his mentally unbalanced wife.

In 1999 *Wang Dang* was released. Noonan wrote and starred in the film with LeAnne Croom and Megan Edwards. In 1998 Tom Noonan received a Guggenheim Grant for filmmaking. Genre Pictures is Noonan's production company. He is also a film educator who teaches screenwriting at his headquarters in the Paradise Theater. Recent acting credits for Tom Noonan include: *The Photographer*, *The Opportunist* (both 2000), *The Pledge*, directed by Sean Penn and *Knockaround Guys* (both 2001).

Nothing But a Man. *See* Roemer, Michael; Young, Robert M.

No-Wave Cinema. Downtown New York movement in existence from 1978 to 1987. Part of the No-Wave, East Village scene of artists and filmmakers that grew out of small galleries and clubs that sprung up during this period. Named by composer and musician Brian Eno, the No-Wave movement wanted to distinguish itself from the more commercial New Wave packaging. No-Wavers synthesized performance art, acting, new media, and art films into an art/music/film scene that even **critics** and cultural arbiters couldn't codify. The story goes that the No-Wave Cinema movement began when a fence sold a dozen $600 stolen **Super 8mm** cameras for $60 each, thus empowering a new wave of **underground** filmmakers. Notable films and filmmakers of No-Wave Cinema include *Rome '78* by James Nares, *The Offenders* (1980) by **Scott and Beth B,** *Space Party* by Wolfgang Staehle and Steve Pollack, *Wild Style* (1982) and *The New York Hip Hop Convention* by **Charles Ahearn,** and **Eric Mitchell's** legendary *Underground U.S.A.* (1980). Other No-Wave figures include Vivienne Dick and **Lydia Lunch**. The Super 8mm and **16mm** films crossed over from punk to performance art films and are documents of a segment of East Village culture. The films were independently made and shown in the scene's clubs and galleries.

nudie cuties. Films that feature topless women in innocent and innocuous situations for exploitation purposes. **Russ Meyer's** *The Immoral Mr. Teas* (1959) was one of the first popular examples. In 1961, **Francis Ford Coppola** made his directorial debut with a nudie *Tonight for Sure*. Nudie cuties represented the still-innocent time before **soft-core** and **hard-core films** deflowered America.

Nunez, Victor. Director, writer, producer, cinematographer, editor. *b.* 1945, Deland, Florida. *ed.* Antioch College, UCLA Film School. A diligent, steadfastly independent filmmaker, Victor Nunez works at a noncommercial pace, completing one or two films a decade. His first feature was *Gal Young 'Un* (1979), a poignant portrait of a middle-aged widow betrayed by a manipulative grifter. The film is set in the 1920s in rural Florida where Nunez was raised. Nunez wrote, directed, shot, edited, and produced *Gal Young 'Un* for under $100,000. The film was well received critically and won the Grand Jury Prize at the 1981 **Sundance Film Festival**. Nunez directed, wrote, shot, and edited his next film, *A Flash of Green* (1984). Based on a John D. MacDonald novel, it starred indie film mainstays Ed Harris, Blair Brown, John Glover, and Richard Jordan, who also produced. In 1993 Victor Nunez wrote, directed, and edited *Ruby in Paradise*, which showcased newcomer Ashley Judd in a gentle coming-of-age story. Nunez, who could not raise funding for the project, financed the film with a $400,000 inheritance. In 1997 Nunez produced his most commercially successful film, *Ulee's Gold*, set again in the Florida panhandle and starring **Peter Fonda** in a heartfelt tour-de-force as a reticent beekeeper. Fonda was nominated for an Academy Award, and Nunez became the only director to receive a second Grand Jury Prize at the Sundance Film Festival. In 2002 Victor Nunez wrote, produced, directed and edited *Coastlines*.

Ono, Yoko. Artist, musician, filmmaker. *b.* February 18, 1933, Tokyo, Japan. *ed.* Gakushuin (Peer's School) in Tokyo, Gakushin University, Sarah Lawrence College. From 1966 to 1971 Yoko Ono made a substantial contribution to the **avant-garde cinema**. With few exceptions her cinematic works are not currently in circulation. In the 1960s Ono was an established and accomplished artist as a singer, performance artist, and avant-garde painter. She was part of the New York art circle that included John Cage, Merce Cunningham, and La MonteYoung. An active filmgoer, Ono began writing mini film scripts and contributed to three films in the Fluxfilm program presented by the **Fluxus** group of **structural** filmmakers. Ono created one of the first contemporary single-shot films (a reference to early cinema before narrative montage was developed).

In 1966 Ono made her first long film work, *No. 4 Bottoms*. The eighty-minute black-and-white film is structured of close-ups of naked human buttocks. The images fill the screen and are composed so the frame is divided in half. The average duration of a shot is fifteen seconds, but some are less than ten seconds. The soundtrack consists of the subjects talking about the film and the boredom it will produce; the result becomes part of the viewer's experience. In 1963 Ono created the soundtrack for Taka Iimura's *Love* by hanging a microphone out a window.

Ono collaborated on a number of film projects with her third husband, **John Lennon.** They were identified either as a Lennon or Ono film depending on who initiated the idea. *Film No. 5 Smile* (1968) is a fifty-one-minute two-shot film photographed in color with a high-speed camera shooting 333 frames per second to produce extreme slow motion. Shot one is Lennon's face as he forms an O with his lips (perhaps it is a kiss). In the second shot Lennon's face is more active; he blinks, sticks his

Artist and filmmaker Yoko Ono with her husband former Beatle and filmmaker John Lennon. Courtesy of The Del Valle Archive

tongue out, and smiles broadly two times. *Film No. 5* is a minimalist work even by avant-garde standards.

Rape (1969) is a seventy-seven-minute work in which the camera stalks a woman who was not a willing participant in the filming. *Fly* (1970) consists of an extreme close-up of a fly on a woman's naked body. The soundtrack is composed of a vocal performance and John Lennon's music. *Apotheosis* (1970) is a single-shot film that starts on Lennon's and Ono's cloaked bodies, then the camera floats upward to the sky above a village, snowfields, into the clouds, and rises into a sunny skyscape above the clouds. *Imagine* (1971) was their final filmic collaboration, featuring sketches and their music. Ono has also made music videos about recovering from the murder of John Lennon and uses the medium to record art objects. In 1989 the **Whitney Museum** held a retrospective of Ono's art objects and films. *See also* Fluxus; Lennon, John; structural film-making

BIBLIOGRAPHY

MacDonald, Scott. *A Critical Cinema 2: Interviews with Independent Filmmakers.* Berkeley: University of California Press, 1992.

———. "Yoko Ono: Ideas on Film (Interview/Scripts)." *Film Quarterly* 43. 1 (Fall 1989): 2–23.

optical printer. Photographic device used by many **experimental** film-makers and animators to create optical effects such as multiple frame printing, skip-frame printing, and superimposition.

Orkin, Ruth. *See* Engel, Morris; *Little Fugitive*

P

padding. A technique employed by **exploitation** filmmakers to expand a film to feature length. A majority of exploitation films were devoid of story and came up short after running out of material. Padding was often accomplished by filming acrobats, stunt cyclists, Latin dance teams, jugglers, singers, and dancers, then intercutting them into a scene where the protagonists visit a nightclub, thus creating the illusion the show was part of the scene. The film *Test Tube Babies* (1953) inserted a striptease into a party scene. *Racket Girls* (1951) has wrestling matches and women working out in a gym. *The Flesh Merchant* (1955) has a prostitute dancing for clients. Padding was an inexpensive method to insure the finished product was long enough for theatrical release.

Page, Bettie. Actress, model. *b.* April 22, 1923, Nashville, Tennessee. Bettie Page, who appeared in dozens of bondage and domination films in the 1940s and 1950s, was almost born in a Tennessee movie theater and became a devout Hollywood movie fan when she was nine. The dark-haired beauty was a legendary pinup model photographed by Bunny Yeager and *Playboy* magazine, but it was **Irving Klaw**, the camera store operator who ran a booming, sub rosa girlie-photo business, who exploited the dark fantasies Bettie's sleek figure and appealing girl-next-door personality evoked in men. Klaw's main income came from the pinup photos he sold by the yard, but he quickly realized the potential for Page in less than socially acceptable erotic motion picture genres. The Klaw films, which were never longer than fifteen minutes, featured Bettie Page in sadomasochistic situations with other female models. These films had no artistic or cinematic value and depicted whip and leather bondage scenarios. During the seven years she modeled, Page always appeared spontaneous and enthusiastic on camera. Although she made

The girl next door as dominatrix, Bettie Page, in one of the snapshots that made her the principal fantasy woman to thousands of men during the 1940s and 1950s. Courtesy of The Del Valle Archive

more money posing for two hours than a secretary took home in a week, Page never received royalties for her work and was paid a $10-an-hour modeling fee. In the 1950s Page went into seclusion and was out of public view for four decades until she resurfaced in the 1990s to tell her story. *See also* Klaw, Irving

BIBLIOGRAPHY

Foster, Richard. *The Real Bettie Page: The Truth about the Queen of the Pinups.* Secaucus, NJ: Birch Lane Press, 1997.

Pearce, Richard. Cinematographer, director. *b.* January 25, 1943, San Diego, California. *ed.* Yale University, The New School for Social Research. Richard Pearce is a socially and politically conscious independent filmmaker. As a **documentary** cameraman he photographed *America Is Hard to See* (1969), *Woodstock* (1970), *Marjoe* (1972), and the controversial Vietnam War film *Hearts and Minds* (1974).

In 1980, Pearce directed the fictional film *Heartland* based on the true story of Elinor Stewart. The project was developed as part of *The Wilderness* series. In 1977 Annick Smith and Beth Ferris received an $82,000 grant to develop the series with the *Heartland* script by Ferris intended as a pilot. They brought in Pearce and other directors to develop the individual projects. Michael Hausman was called to coproduce, and Fred Murphy was director of photography. In October 1978 *Heartland* received a $600,000 grant to shoot the ninety-minute film in **16mm**—it was the largest grant of its kind at the time. The decision was made to switch to 35mm for an eventual theatrical release after it aired on PBS. Conchita Ferrell and Rip Torn were cast in the lead roles. Pearce was paid $25,000 with another $25,000 in **deferrals.** The producers did not make an agreement with the Director's Guild of America, who hit the production with punitive damages. Pearce and the crew had to be paid union minimums before *Heartland* could be released. The five-week production schedule from March to May 1979 was made difficult by inclement weather. *Heartland* premiered at the first American Independent Film sidebar at the 1979 New York Film Festival. Even with a rave review from Vincent Canby of the *New York Times*, *Heartland* took a year and a half to obtain a **distributor.** After many rejections, a deal was struck with Jerome Pickman of Levitt-Pickman. *Heartland* was sold to three cable outlets, Showtime, Warner Amex, and Channel Z. PBS waited to air the film until the theatrical and cable runs were completed. *Heartland* opened at New York's Paris Theater in 1981 to good box office, a long play off, and a repertory life renting to college film societies. The film portrayed the life of a young pioneer woman in 1910 who survives by working for a serious-minded rancher in the wilderness of Wyoming. *Heartland* hit historical and emotional chords with American audiences and was praised for its positive portrayal of a Western woman as a complex, capable and strong figure.

In 1984, Pearce directed *Country*, starring Sam Shepard and Jessica Lange, inspired by the economic misery imposed on midwestern farmers by the policies of the Carter administration. Pearce continued working steadily, but the purity of his thematic vision as an indie began to change. In 1986 Pearce directed the mainstream Richard Gere–Kim Basinger mismatch, *No Mercy*, a Bayou murder mystery, and *Leap of Faith* (1992), another commercial venture about a tent-show evangelist with a failed performance by Steve Martin. Both films fared poorly at the box office. Like many indies, Pearce turned to television to continue working rather than spend his days shopping around for features, funding, and distributors. In 1990 Pearce returned to a socially conscious cinema venture with *The Long Walk Home* about the segregated American South and the consciousness raising of a privileged woman played by Sissy Spacek and her relationship with a struggling, hardworking housekeeper portrayed by Whoopi Goldberg. Richard Pearce's recent credits as a director in television include: *Thicker Than Blood* (1998), *Witness Protection* (1999), and *South Pacific* (2001).

Pennebaker, D.A. Documentary filmmaker. *b.* Donn Alan Pennebaker, July 15, 1925, Evanston, Illinois. *ed.* Yale University, Massachusetts Institute of Technology. Pennebaker quit engineering after five years and changed the direction of his life. He wrote advertising copy, was a fine arts painter, and began to make experimental films and documentaries. In 1959 Pennebaker joined Filmmakers, a cooperative venture with **Richard Leacock, Shirley Clarke, Willard Van Dyke,** and the **Maysles** brothers. The **co-op** shared a workspace and film equipment and worked on joint projects. Pennebaker helped Francis Thompson finish *N.Y., N.Y.* (1957), produced documentaries for the YMCA and the Girl Scouts, and assisted Gypsy Rose Lee in putting together the legendary ecdysiast's home movies in preparation for a film of her life. Pennebaker spent three months in Moscow with Albert Maysles, who was making a film about the Soviet Union. They ran into Ricky Leacock, who was making a film about Leonard Bernstein and the New York Philharmonic. Maysles and Pennebaker helped Leacock with his project and in return received twelve rolls of film stock. Leacock had a portable sync-sound rig that offered new possibilities for the documentary form, which was labored with heavy cameras and sound equipment, hampering mobile sync-sound filming on location. Documentaries had relied on narration and visual storytelling for so long; now live recording directly in sync-sound liberated filmmakers and inspired a new era in nonfiction filmmaking.

Robert Drew of the *Life* organization interested Time Inc. in the development of a film journal for prime-time television. Pennebaker became involved in the project but left Drew Associates in the middle of production to set up his own fully equipped company for independent film production. Pennebaker made the landmark film *Don't Look Back* (1967), a portrait of the enigmatic Bob Dylan. Leacock and Pennebaker became partners in production and distribution of documentaries and commercials. Later Pennebaker formed a partnership with his wife, Chris Hedeus, which produced *The War Room* (1993), a highly praised documentary about the 1992 Clinton presidential campaign that probed the contrasting characters of campaign managers George Stephanopoulos and James Carville.

Pennebaker has been there for many documentary landmarks, notably *Primary* (1960) and the concert film *Monterey Pop* (1968). Pennebaker was cameraman on **Norman Mailer**'s *Wild 90, Beyond the Law* (both 1968), and *Maidstone* (1969) and directed *One P.M.* (*One Parallel Movie*, 1972), about the making of Godard's unfinished *One A.M.* (*One American Movie*), and *Ziggy Stardust and the Spiders from Mars* (1983), documenting David Bowie's 1973 tour. Recent documentary credits for D.A. Pennebaker include: director, cinematographer and editor of *Down from the Mountain* (2000) featuring the music from the **Coen brothers'** *O Brother Where Art Thou?*, producer and additional video on *Startup.com* (2001), and director, cinematographer and editor on *Only the Strong Survive* (2002).

The camera of Pennebaker probed, shook, searched, shifted focus, and moved through space in search of cinema truth. He created a raw and vital aesthetic that continues to influence nonfiction and fictional filmmakers alike. He continues his legacy by making films and teaching a documentary film workshop at Yale. A highly intelligent, articulate man both verbally and through the eye of a camera, Pennebaker is always searching for the relationship of content and form to communicate the real world through the reel one. *See also* Drew, Robert; Leacock, Richard

Pennell, Eagle. Director. *ed.* University of Texas. Pennell is a notorious, self-destructive boozer and brawler who made successful low-budget indie features that gained him critical and popular acceptance and a moniker as a Texas desperado filmmaker. Despite his achievements, he has been down and out and homeless. He grew up in College Station, Texas, and as a teen filmed his younger sister improvising skits with his dad's **Super 8mm** camera. At the University of Texas in Austin, Pennell couldn't decide on a major and then came upon the Radio-Television-Film department. He was attracted to the films of Sam Peckinpah, John Ford, and **John Cassavetes** but dropped out of college before the end of junior year.

Pennell worked at a company that produced highlight films of the Southwest Conference football games. In his off time, Pennell borrowed

company equipment and filmed a **documentary** about a rodeo school just outside of Austin. Confident in his filmmaking abilities, Pennell shot *Hell of a Note*, an independent handheld, **16mm**, thirty-minute short loosely based on a *Texas Monthly* article by Larry L. King about two good old boys, Floyd and Jimmy Lee. The project was funded mainly out of Pennell's pocket for $1,200. *Hell of a Note* premiered at Austin's Dobie Theater and starred Sonny Carl Davis and Louis Perryman, a team Pennell calls "a sort of Mutt and Jeff of Texas." Perryman worked on the crew of *The Texas Chainsaw Massacre* (1974) and met Pennell at the time of its release. Pennell moved into his house uninvited. Davis was a member of the satirical bar band Sons of the Uranium Savages who sang "Idi Amin Is My Yard Man."

The Whole Shootin' Match (1978), a film about two hapless Texas buddies, again featured Pennell's alter egos, Davis and Perryman. The film was shot for $30,000 in and around Austin with improved production values and better acting. Pennell's peers found him stupid, drunk, inconsiderate, unreliable, and also singled-minded, self-confident, and with the necessary resources to make a film. After *The Whole Shootin' Match*, Pennell won a small development deal with Universal Pictures and headed to Hollywood with Davis and Perryman.

Last Night at the Alamo (1983), Pennell's best-known film, is about an alcoholic, hen-pecked modern-day cowboy who tries to save the Alamo Bar from its fiscal woes. Pennell found The Old Barn Bar in East Houston, which resembled the actual Alamo Bar in San Antonio. The film was shot in less than a month without air-conditioning, the hot Texas air made even more stifling by the burning movie lights. The $50,000 budget came from the **National Endowment for the Arts**, with the other half from SWAMP, The Southwest Alternative Media Project, which also gave Pennell equipment and office space. **Kim Henkel**, screenwriter of *The Texas Chainsaw Massacre*, wrote the earthy and salty script. The profane, down-to-earth dialogue gave a regional, homey honesty to well-intentioned redneck characters. *Last Night at the Alamo* played the New York Film Festival and received high praise from Vincent Canby of the *New York Times*, Stanley Kauffmann of the *New Republic*, and Roger Ebert. Pennell, who destroyed many relationships with his hard-drinking/hard-living ways, was considered sweet when sober, but his drinking took a toll on the final night of shooting on *Last Night at the Alamo*. He was too inebriated to work; Henkel wrapped the film by directing the last shoot.

Next Henkel and Pennell wrote *The King of Texas*. Michael Shamberg, Warner Bros., and Jersey Films were interested, but Pennell lost the project when he made unwanted sexual advances to a female producer. On another occasion, Pennell threatened to shoot Tom Sims, the special project director for SWAMP, over a dispute. In 1989, Pennell directed a

Melissa Gilbert vehicle, *Ice House*, for Upfront films. Pennell's hired-hand gig was poorly received, and he returned to the indie world with *Doc's Full Service* (1994) and then *Heartful of Soul*, sponsored by SWAMP and NEA grants. Pennell, again featuring Davis and Perryman, shot the film from the hip, but the results were dismissed as amateurish. Pennell's drinking had him in and out of rehab. Katie Cokinos at SWAMP tried to get Pennell to direct a western she budgeted at $500,000. Pennell was stunned at the amount and unable to proceed after making $20,000 to $30,000 movies. Perryman went back to driving a cab, occasionally playing a role in a Texas film production. Davis appeared in the television miniseries *Lonesome Dove* and Ridley Scott's *Thelma and Louise* (1991). Pennell is a consultant for Cactus Films. *See also* Henkel, Kim

Perry, Eleanor. Screenwriter. *b.* 1916. *d.* March 14, 1981. After a long partnership with her husband, director **Frank Perry**, that produced *David and Lisa* (1962), *Ladybug, Ladybug* (1963), *The Swimmer* (1968), *Trilogy* (1969), *Last Summer* (1969), and *Diary of a Mad Housewife* (1970), the couple divorced. Throughout the 1960s Eleanor Perry was celebrated and respected as a female screenwriter in a male-dominated field who delved deep into the psyche of her characters. Frank and Eleanor Perry had an equal collaboration as director and screenwriter. They were partners in creating low-budget films that broke ground exploring mental illness, sexuality, and the changing role of women in American society. *Diary of a Mad Housewife* was an early **feminist** film. After the divorce, Perry was part of a consciousness-raising group led by feminist Susan Brownmiller. At the 1971 New York Film Festival, she participated in the panel discussion "Women as Prostitutes and Love Objects." At the 1972 Cannes Film Festival, Perry led a group of female protesters who sprayed red paint on posters for *Fellini's Roma* that pictured a woman with three breasts. They picketed screenings of the film holding placards that read, "Women are people, not dirty jokes," "Writers are the women of the film industry." Her dream was to direct, but it was not to be. Perry worked hard supporting young women who wanted to become film directors. She formed workshops for women at the American Film Institute and spoke passionately at a Senate educational committee in Washington, D.C. The woman who wrote the first feminist western, *The Man Who Loved Cat Dancing* (1973), was part of a force responsible for eventually changing industry attitudes toward women and for bringing a female perspective to movies.

Perry, Frank. Director, producer. *b.* August 21, 1930, New York City. *d.* August 29, 1995, New York City. Frank Perry was a New York film director who turned his back on Hollywood and made low-budget films that explored the spectrum of human relationships without tinseltown glamorization. After serving in the Korean War, Perry began in films as a production assistant. Like many New York film directors, Perry received his early training in television, where he was a coproducer and moderator of *The Playwrights at Work* series. His wife **Eleanor Perry** was a gifted screenwriter who provided thought-provoking stories about contemporary male/female relationships and pressing social issues in a rapidly changing American society. *David and Lisa* (1962) was a groundbreaking independent film about mentally disturbed teenagers, played by Keir Dullea and Janet Margolin. Perry's debut established him as a director who probed the emotional depths of his characters, and Eleanor was lauded for her honest and compassionate screenplay.

Ladybug, Ladybug (1963) concerns the effect of a civil defense warning of an impending nuclear attack on a group of rural schoolchildren. Eleanor Perry based her screenplay on a real-life incident. *The Swimmer* (1968) starred **Burt Lancaster**, adapted by Eleanor from a John Cheever short story of a middle-aged man who swims from pool to pool in his suburban upscale community on a hot summer's day. Each encounter evokes his past in the psychologically unsettling drama. *Trilogy* (1969) was adapted from three Truman Capote stories. *Last Summer* (1969) was an adaptation of the Evan Hunter novel of teenagers who become sexually aware at a summer resort and discover the darker secrets that motivate them. The provocative film starred Richard Thomas, Barbra Hershey, Bruce Davison, Cathy Burns, Ralph Waite, and Conrad Bain. The film originally received an X-rating and was cut to get an R so it could have a mainstream release.

Diary of a Mad Housewife (1970) was Eleanor Perry's adaptation of Sue Kaufman's novel about a housewife trapped by a needy and rigid husband who seeks self-discovery in an affair with another man. The film became a flashpoint for the women's movement at the dawn of the 1970s. *Diary of a Mad Housewife* also ended the collaboration between director and screenwriter, who separated in 1970 and divorced in 1971. *Doc* (1971) was a revisionist western about Wyatt Earp and Doc Holiday scripted by New York reporter Pete Hamill. *Play It as It Lays* (1972) is the film version of Joan Didion's novel about the shunned wife of a self-consumed film director. *Man on a Swing* (1974) is based on a true-life story of a clairvoyant who tries to help a cop solve a sex killing but discovers more questions than answers. *Rancho Deluxe* (1975) is the tale of present-day cattle rustlers based on the cult novel *92 in the Shade* by Thomas McGuane. *Monsignor* (1982) was a moral investigation of an ambitious and sinful priest portrayed by Christopher Reeve who becomes the Vatican's business manager. *Compromising Positions* (1985) is a black comedy about a Long Island housewife who becomes obsessed with the murder of a local dentist with a womanizing past. Susan Issacs wrote *Hello Again* (1987), about a Long Island housewife brought back to life by her witchy sister.

Perry didn't make another film for five years as he fought prostate cancer. *On the Bridge* (1992) is an autobiographical documentary of his personal odyssey. Critics have not always been kind to Perry, labeling him as an arty, pretentious filmmaker who, at times, took serious drama into unintentional comedy and camp. Perry was an independent filmmaker with a conscience who never sold out. His self-imposed isolation from the industry did create rigidity in style and theme. He was a filmmaker who did not grow and expand beyond his limitations. Nevertheless, he stubbornly clung to his brand of exploration into subjects that were ignored or sugarcoated by Hollywood.

pickup. When a major studio or **distributor** buys a low-budget, independently made film that is partially completed or finished, for additional funding or distribution. Not to be confused with a negative pickup when a contractual financial arrangement is made prior to the completion of a film.

Pierson, John. Filmmaker representative, author, television host. *b.* 1954. *ed.* New York University. John Pierson, the self-styled guru of independent filmmaking, has launched the careers of many groundbreaking indies by acquiring funding and/or placing the film with a distributor. Just a fraction of the filmmakers Pierson has represented include **Spike Lee, Kevin Smith, Michael Moore** and **Richard Linklater.** Pierson was a repertory exhibitor for the Bleecker Street Cinema, the director for the American Mavericks Festival, programmer of **Film Forum 2,** and manager of the Film Forum complex for Karen Cooper. From the mid-1980s to the mid-1990s, a fertile time for the American independent film, Pierson ran John Pierson Associates, a company that supported his work representing independent filmmakers trying to get their films made and exhibited. He was also the founder of Islet, the first completion funding company, currently known as Grainy Pictures.

In 1995, Pierson changed directions and became the unauthorized historian of indie films of the 1980s and 1990s with his informative, lively, and highly subjective book *Spike, Mike, Slackers & Dykes: A Guided Tour Across a Decade of American Independent Cinema.* From 1992 to 1996 **Miramax** (who also published the book, primarily out of self-interest) sponsored workshops for filmmakers that Pierson ran in Cold Springs, New York. From 1997 to 2000 Pierson was the host of *Split Screen* on the **Independent Film Channel,** a magazine format show that was an inside look at U.S. independent filmmaking.

BIBLIOGRAPHY

Pierson, John. *Spike, Mike, Slackers & Dykes: A Guided Tour across a Decade of American Independent Cinema.* New York: Miramax Books/Hyperion, 1995.

Pincus, Edward. Filmmaker, educator, author. *b.* July 6, 1939, Brooklyn, New York. *ed.* Brown University. Edward Pincus wrote *Guide to Filmmaking,* published in 1969 as a Signet Paperback priced at $1.50. The 256-page handbook and production manual became the bible for practically every film student, teacher, and independent filmmaker. *Guide to Filmmaking* covers **8mm** and **16mm** gauges, the camera, lenses, exposure, raw stock, production, lighting, the laboratory, preparing the original negative for printing, sound production, and editing. *Guide to Filmmaking* was the first book of its kind, accessible to brigades of young filmmakers with a rabid passion to express themselves in a medium long inaccessible to everyone outside of Hollywood professionals. The red book, with the photograph of a three-lens turret camera and projector, was in the hands, backpacks, on the set, and at the editing bench of the legion of film generation baby-boomers that wanted to become filmmakers. Pincus was their teacher, adviser, and technical guru. Pincus and his book helped to start a revolution.

As an independent filmmaker, Pincus was also part of the American **avant-garde/experimental** community. At Harvard, Pincus studied philosophy, still photography, and politics. In 1963 his friends joined the freedom rides of the civil rights movement. Pincus began to see his multiple interests could be channeled into filmmaking. He saw the **Maysles'** documentary *Showman* (1962), a complex portrait of Joseph E. Levine, and was inspired to make a cinematic adaptation of Camus's short story "The Adultering Woman," shot with a borrowed camera he taught himself to use. Pincus joined friends in Mississippi who were making a film about the civil rights movement called *Black Natchez* (1967). He helped to shoot forty hours of **cinéma vérité** footage. They had raised $10,000 but ran out of money and went into debt. Pincus taught himself how to operate a Moviola and edited the film for fourteen months. The project embodied the Students for a Democratic Society (SDS) philosophy of "Let the people decide," so they argued over the social/political implication of each edit. The filmmakers received a Rockefeller grant and sold the black-and-white film to *NET Journal* for $10,000, one of the largest amounts paid for a **documentary** up to that time.

Pincus was also involved in a project for the Public Broadcasting Lab (PBL) in 1967. The PBL was given a $10 million grant from the Ford Foundation. PBL was composed of CBS staffers Fred Friendly and McGeorge Bundy. Av Westin, the executive producer of *ABC News,* was asked to be PBL's director. Pincus was commissioned to make their inaugural effort, a film about the burgeoning West Coast hippie youth culture. The one-hour color project was budgeted at $80,000. PBL first gave Pincus $10,000 to decide which of two ideas to film. Pincus decided to make a documentary on a rural commune rather than a film on the rock band Country Joe and the Fish. The PBL administration changed while Pincus was filming. He went back to New York headquarters with some of the commune footage. Knowing the material was controversial, Pincus was not convinced PBL would air the completed film, so he bought back the television rights and the nonbroadcast rights for six months for $13,000.

The commune broke up at the beginning of the documentary, causing conflict and profanity among the commune members. The network wanted to bleep out the offending words; Pincus was angered at the suggestion and cut two versions of the film. For the broadcast version, whole scenes were deleted. Av Westin was still not satisfied and ordered additional changes. Fifty-six felonies were captured by Pincus's camera, and PBL had sixty-eight objections to the completed film. Educational television Channel 2 in Boston found the film obscene and in bad taste, deeming it too strong for public and home consumption. After a few years the team still wasn't willing to put money into it, so Pincus bought back the option from them.

Next PBL asked five filmmakers including **Richard Leacock, Jonas Mekas** and Pincus to each do a fifteen- to twenty-five-minute-long film on the state of the country. The filmmakers represented many philosophies from **self-referential** to Marcusian thought. Westin okayed the project and told the filmmakers PBL would censor later as needed. Pincus's film was a portrait of a McCarthy supporter and covered Senator Eugene McCarthy's presidential campaign. Pincus's segment was aired, but he didn't own any of the rights to his work. Pincus's *Panola* (1970), about a black wino, was edited from footage shot in 1965 during the making of *Black Natchez* (1967). The final cut was reedited. *Harry's Trip* (1969) was an eleven-minute uninterrupted take of a hippie during an LSD trip—the film was shown once. Eventually Pincus became cynical of the so-called political revolution the SDS and other radical groups had predicted.

Pincus was an active voice in the endless debate over the ethics and methods of cinéma vérité. He argued the position of hippie radicals who had their own take on the truth in film and saw it as valid and as subjective as all documentarians who search for and promote their own version of truth in cinema. In 1982 Pincus made *Diaries*, working in the experimental **diary film** genre that recorded observations, memories, and feelings in the same way a writer would document words in a private volume.

The *Filmmaker's Handbook* was updated in 1999, subtitled *A Comprehensive Guide for the Digital Age.*

BIBLIOGRAPHY

Pincus, Ed. *Guide to Filmmaking.* New York: Signet, 1969. Expanded, *The Filmmaker's Handbook: A Comprehensive Guide for the Digital Age,* by Ed Pincus and Steven Ascher. New York: Plume, 1999.

Pixelvision. The PXL-2000 video camera manufactured by Fisher-Price in the late 1980s. The children's toy did poorly in the marketplace, and the popular toy company soon canceled production. After a few years Pixelvision works were screened at film festivals, and **underground** filmmakers developed interest in the format. The camera records audio and video on standard audiocassette tapes, fitting about five minutes of material per side of a ninety-minute tape. The image quality of Pixelvision is grainy, black and white, and has a slow-motion-effect look with many signal dropouts. **Richard Linklater** used Pixelvision in *Slacker* (1992) in a bar scene, and in Michael Almereyda's *Naja* (1996), he utilized Pixelvision to present the point of view of Dracula's daughter. The Pixel This Festival in Venice, California, has been in existence since 1990.

Poe, Amos. Director, writer, producer, actor, editor. Influenced by the films of Godard and **Warhol**, Amos Poe was in the vanguard of the New York City downtown punk movement in the mid-1970s. Punk was a consciousness that had its own music, fashion, language, behavior, and plenty of attitude. The music and fashion captured the attention of popular culture first, but a wave of filmmakers including **Scott and Beth B** and **Eric Mitchell** emerged. In 1976 Poe was at the flashpoint with *The Blank Generation,* a New Wave/punk concert **documentary** shot at CBGBs, the small Bowery club that gave birth to the punk music scene. Poe's camera captured early performances by The Ramones, Blondie, Television, Patti Smith, Wayne County, The New York Dolls, The Heartbreakers, and The Miamis. The film was produced by Poe Productions and self-distributed by Poe Vision, Inc.

In 1980, Poe directed *Unmade Beds,* which featured Debbie Harry of Blondie fame and Eric Mitchell. The punk aesthetic embraced crime fiction and film noir. In 1981 Poe wrote, directed, and coproduced *Subway Rider* about a psychotic sax player played by real-life horn player **John Lurie,** who lured his prey to desolate areas with his music and shot them dead. The cast also included Robbie Coltrane, Lance Loud (of *An American Family* notoriety), **Lydia Lunch,** Poe, and Susan Tyrell. The film triumphed at the Berlin Film Festival.

Alphabet City (1984) took place in New York's downtown East Side where Avenues A and B were the home of many punksters, a drug-infested area known as Alphabet City. The film is about a drug dealer who has to escape from the mob when he decides to get out of the life. This step up from **underground** films to a commercially viable indie was distributed by Atlantic Releasing Corp. and featured Vincent Spano, Kate Vernon, Jami Gertz, and Zohra Lampert. Poe went back to self-distribution for his next film *Triple Bogey on a Par Five Hole* (1991), featuring Eric Mitchell, Robbie Coltrane, and Philip Seymour Hoffman. In 1995, Poe wrote the story, directed, and coproduced *Dead Weekend* for IRS Media and Showtime, starring Stephen Baldwin and David Rasche in a near-future story with a city under martial law so the True World forces can capture an alien who changes appearances. *Frogs for Snakes* (1998) was financed by Rain Film and The Shooting Gallery, also the **distributor** of the film, about unemployed theater actors who make ends meet collecting money for a loan shark who owns an Off-Broadway theater.

In 1988, Poe wrote *Rocket Gibraltar*, the story of a seventy-seven-year-old family patriarch, played by **Burt Lancaster**, whose grandchildren vow to carry out his unusual final wish. It was made into a mainstream film first directed by Poe, who was fired. Daniel Petrie replaced him. Poe produced *Joey Breaker* in 1993, a comedy about a workaholic agent who represents actors, screenwriters, and comedians. He falls in love, mellows, and become tolerant of others until his girlfriend gets on a career path. Richard Edson played Joey with Gina Gershon, Philip Seymour Hoffman, Michael Imperoli, and Parker Posey also in the cast.

Back in the 1970s, Poe had a dream to create a "Film Generation," a New York movement of filmmakers like the French New Wave. Poe's plans were for a wave of cheap **16mm** black-and-white features that would change the consciousness of moviegoers. It didn't quite unfold in the historic proportion Godard, Truffaut, and other Francophiles achieved, but Poe was a man with a vision and a true affinity for his times. Punk lives in many submovements of the current underground film including the work of **Nick Zedd** and the **Cinema of Transgression,** Jeri Cain Rossi, Casandra Stark Mele and Todd Phillips.

porno chic. Movement in the 1970s encouraged by the success of *Deep Throat* (1972) that made it respectable and the in-thing for couples to go to an adult theater and watch an X-rated film containing **hard-core** sexual activity. The films were produced and distributed on film. In the late 1970s when the VCR revolution began, the films were transferred to tape and available at local video stores. In the 1980s the industry made the transition to shooting and distributing on tape. The theaters closed, and the home market took their place. In the digital age the pornsters, always on the lookout for new venues, moved to the Internet and the growing

DVD format. *See also* adult film industry; Damiano, Gerard; *Deep Throat*; hard-core films; Jim and Artie Mitchell

BIBLIOGRAPHY

Flint, David. *Babylon Blue: An Illustrated History of Adult Cinema.* London: Creation Books, 1999.

Ford, Luke. *A History of X: 100 Years of Sex in Film.* Amherst, NY: Prometheus Books, 1999.

Posey, Parker. Actress. *b.* November 8, 1968, Baltimore, Maryland. *ed.* State University of New York at Purchase. Comedic actress who built a successful career in independent films. The prolific Posey has already appeared in almost forty movies including a long collaboration with **Hal Hartley.** Samplings of Posey's performances that earned her the title of indie film queen include *Dazed and Confused* (1993), *Amateur* (1994), *Party Girl* (1995), *Flirt* (1995), *The Doom Generation* (1995), *Basquiat* (1996), *Waiting for Guffman* (1996), *SubUrbia* (1996), *Henry Fool* (1997), and *Scream 3* (2000). Recent acting credits for Parker Posey include: *Best in Show* (2000), *The Sweetest Thing* and *Personal Velocity: Three Portraits,* directed by Rebecca Miller (both 2002).

P.O.V. Public television series that features independent, personal, and nonfiction films exploring life in all its humanity. The award-winning series was created by Marc N. Weiss and is funded by the John D. and Catherine T. MacArthur Foundation, The Florence and John Schuman Foundation, the **National Endowment for the Arts,** and public television viewers. *P.O.V.* is committed to diversity and to independent producers. *P.O.V.* receives more than 600 submissions a year for consideration.

poverty row. Name coined for films made through minor studios by fly-by-night producers for very low budgets during the Classical Hollywood Studio System era. The companies were housed in shabby buildings with a maze of offices with exposed wires and pipes. They were run by producers looking for a fast buck and did business in the Sunset Boulevard and Gower Street section of Hollywood. But the term *poverty row* didn't refer to the geographical location—rather to any production by a minor company and not a major studio. Poverty row studios were independent of the majors and included Grand National, Mascot, Producer's Releasing Corporation (PRC), Monogram, Allied Artists, Tower Ambassador, Puritan, and Grand National. Columbia Pictures began on poverty row and grew into a major through its success with Frank Capra. **William Beaudine** and **Sam Newfield** also started their directing careers on poverty row.

Prelinger, Richard. Archivist. President of Prelinger Associates Inc., home of the Prelinger Archive that houses 33,000 **industrial,** advertising, education, **documentary,** and amateur films. The archive also stores 30,000 cans of unedited footage. Prelinger has critically codified films like *Oxydol Goes into High* (1939), and *Heavy Petting, About Fallout, Our Mister Sun* (1956), directed by Frank Capra, *Citrus on Parade,* and *Portrait of a Businessman,* defined as ephemeral films that reveal what he calls "our secret century." The 600,000 ephemeral films produced between 1920 and 1990 uncover more about twentieth-century American culture and society than independent and commercial feature films. Prelinger is a consultant, lecturer, cinematic philosopher, and businessman. The archives have provided footage for Oliver Stone's *Natural Born Killers* (1994), *Heaven* (1987), directed by Diane Keaton, and David Byrne's *True Stories* (1986), as well as many traditional documentaries. *See also* classroom films; industrial films

Preminger, Otto. Director, producer, actor. *b.* December 5, 1906, Vienna, Austria. *d.* April 23, 1986, New York City. *ed.* University of Vienna. As a director Otto Preminger was demanding, cruel, egotistical, confident, and a terror on the set. As a producer he was fearless in taking on taboo subjects, challenging the Hollywood censorship machine. Preminger was assigned to direct **B-movies** for Twentieth-Century Fox. After his third project, studio chief Daryl Zanuck fired Preminger.

Finding himself blacklisted in Hollywood by the powerful mogul, Preminger returned to the theater where he began, now playing a Nazi in Clare Booth Luce's play *Margin for Error.* Preminger was Jewish but made a convincing Prussian on stage and in the movies. Fox wanted Preminger to reprise his role in the film version of *Margin for Error* (1943), but he would agree only if he could direct the picture. Zanuck was overseas fighting in World War II, so Fox brass gave Preminger his way. Zanuck returned from the front and was outraged to find Preminger on the lot. When he cooled down, Zanuck allowed Preminger to produce, not direct, *Laura* (1944). Rouben Mamoulian was assigned to direct, but Zanuck was disappointed with the rushes and handed the film over to Preminger. The result was a big box office hit and Preminger's first Oscar nomination. The opportunity launched Preminger's studio career as an A-list director.

In 1953 Preminger made the courageous decision to break free from studio control. He became an independent producer/director with *The Moon Is Blue,* the first commercial feature to use the words "virgin" and "pregnant." Preminger boldly embraced adult subjects and explored them with candid intelligence. His independence allowed him to avoid the prison of the rigid standards that remained in the Hollywood Studio System. *Carmen Jones* (1954) was an all-black adaptation of Bizet's opera

Carmen, The Man with the Golden Arm (1955) was one of the first commercial films to deal directly with the horrors of heroin addiction. Casting a star of Frank Sinatra's magnitude heightened the dramatic impact, especially in the cold turkey sequence that forces the viewer to experience the physical assault caused by the dangerous drug. *Advise and Consent* (1962) and *The Cardinal* (1963) presented moral dilemmas in government and religion, and *Hurry Sundown* (1967) broke ground with sexual undercurrents and expression, vividly illustrated in a notorious scene where Jane Fonda on her knees plays saxophone between the open legs of Michael Caine.

Preminger was an outspoken liberal, openly discussing his experimentation with LSD. Along with Kirk Douglas, he ended the ugly Hollywood blacklist by crediting Dalton Trumbo with the screenplay for *Exodus* (1960), as Douglas did for Trumbo on *Spartacus* released in the same year. As a director, Preminger was not in the same league as contemporaries Alfred Hitchcock, John Ford, and Howard Hawks, but he was a fearless producer and consummate showman who paved the way for commercial films to reflect the complexities of society.

BIBLIOGRAPHY

Bogdanovich, Peter. *Who the Devil Made It.* New York: Knopf, 1997.
Pratley, Gerald. *The Cinema of Otto Preminger.* New York: Castle Books, 1971.

Projectionist, The. *See* Hurwitz, Harry

psychotronic film. Critical term to codify cult movies such as *Attack of the Killer Tomatoes* (1978) and *Let Me Die a Woman* (1979). The theoretical observations of **Michael Weldon**, first publisher of a Xeroxed weekly guide to Z-movie television programming concerning films featuring has-beens in sports, music, politics, entertainment and beauty queens of all sorts, he called psychotronic films. In 1983 Weldon published *The Psychotronic Encyclopedia of Film,* a detailed reference volume demonstrating his thesis. Psychotronic films are the step-child of the independent film, celebrating exploitation as they cheerfully outrage and delight the viewer. The study of psychotronic films has analyzed and documented the aesthetic of the "bad movie," an art into itself. Psychotronic films include *Cuban Rebel Girls* (1960), starring Errol Flynn in his last motion picture, *Girl Hunters* featuring Mickey Spillane as his own creation, hard-boiled detective Mike Hammer and *Billy the Kid vs. Dracula* (1966), starring John Carradine. *See also* Weldon, Michael

BIBLIOGRAPHY

Weldon, Michael, with Charles Beesley, Bob Martin, and Akira Fitton. *The Psychotronic Encyclopedia of Film.* New York: Ballantine Books, 1983.
———. *The Psychotronic Video Guide.* New York: St. Martin's Press, 1996.

public domain. A story, novel, or play that is no longer covered by copyright ownership. Independent filmmakers are constantly on the lookout for material in public domain so that they don't have to pay for story costs or create an original narrative.

Pull My Daisy. Beat Generation 1959 film directed by **Robert Frank** and Alfred Leslie, written and narrated by **Jack Kerouac.** The autobiographical text created by Kerouac is based on a fall 1955 visit to the Los Gatos, California, home of Neal and Carolyn Cassidy. The three were drawn to spiritual experiences and regularly met with Bishop Romano, a Swiss man of God ordained by the liberal Catholic Church. The bishop believed in reincarnation and was opened to the doctrines of all religions. The bishop professed that his sermons were delivered by a higher being and channeled through his instrument. The Cassidys arranged for the bishop to come to their home for a meeting with Kerouac, Allen Ginsberg, the bishop's mother and aunt, Peter Orlovsky, and Pat Donovan. Kerouac was on the floor, drunk, leaning against the bishop's leg, proclaiming his love, while Neal Cassidy asked the holy man numerous questions about Eastern and Western religions. Ginsberg kept asking about sexual matters.

After the 1957 publication of *On the Road,* Off-Broadway producer Leo Garin approached Kerouac to write a play. Legend has it that the stream-of-consciousness author wrote *The Beat Generation or the New American Church,* a three-act play concerning the events of the meeting with the bishop. The theatrical work was never produced on the stage, but when Leslie, Frank, and Kerouac discussed doing a film together, they decided to make the third act, which would feature an ad-libbed narration by Kerouac. Shooting began on January 2, 1959, in Alfred Leslie's loft on 12th Street and Fourth Avenue in New York City. The cast included Ginsberg, Peter Orlovsky, Larry Rivers, Gregory Corso, and Richard Bellamy (an employee of the Green Gallery who played the bishop), David Amram (who also composed the score), Alice Neal, Sally Gross, Denise Parker, and the young Pablo Frank (son of the codirector). The only professional actor was Delphine Seyrig, credited as Beltiane. The landmark film, the first true **Beat** cinematic work, takes place in a New York City apartment. Kerouac improvises the narration like a jazz poet riffing from beginning to end as the minimalist action slowly unfolds. People enter, talk, and go about their bohemian ways as Kerouac comments in prehistoric rap, explaining the goings-on and putting ideas and phrases in our consciousness.

Pull My Daisy premiered at Cinema 16 on November 11, 1959. Along with **John Cassavetes's** *Shadows,* it won the second *Film Culture* Independent Film Award. *Pull My Daisy* was a radical extension of the **cinéma vérité** movement that sparked an endless debate as to whether the film was staged or captured by the filmmakers. *See also* Frank, Robert; Kerouac, Jack

Pulp Fiction. *See* Bender, Lawrence; Tarantino, Quentin

punk cinema. Film movement that grew out of punk music and lifestyle that arrived in New York in the mid-1970s. Punk filmmakers include **Beth and Scott B, Amos Poe,** and **Eric Mitchell.** The films were independently produced mainly on **Super 8mm** and were screened at rock and punk clubs in the downtown scene. The films featured musical performances, film noir narratives, and plenty of nihilism. Seminal punk films include *The Blank Generation* (1976), *Underground U.S.A.* (1980), and *G Men* (1978). *See also* B, Beth and Scott; Kowalski, Lech; Mitchell, Eric; Poe, Amos

BIBLIOGRAPHY

McNeil, Legs, and Gillian McCain. *Please Kill Me: The Uncensored Oral History of Punk.* New York: Grove Press, 1996.

Putney Swope. *See* Downey, Robert

queer cinema. A term and concept introduced at the Toronto Festival of Festivals in 1991 to codify films of the late 1980s that reexamined the image of gays. Derek Jarman's *Edward II* (1991), **Tom Kalin's** *Swoon* (1992), and the early films of **Gus Van Sant, Todd Haynes,** Jennie Livingston, and Gregg Araki are examples of this political and social gay movement. Rose Troche's 1994 debut film *Go Fish* eschewed gay film conventions by focusing on everyday lives rather than sexuality. In 1999's *Bedrooms & Hallways*, Troche focused more attention on sexual identities and followed a more conventional style but maintained her acumen for gender and queer identities. Queer theory began to be applied to Hollywood films from **Nicholas Ray's** *Johnny Guitar* (1954) to George Roy Hill's *Butch Cassidy and the Sundance Kid* (1969), to define, identify, and make gay behavior better understood as a positive, acceptable social lifestyle.

BIBLIOGRAPHY

Creekmur, Corey K., and Alexander Doty, eds. *Out in Culture: Gay, Lesbian and Queer Essays on Popular Culture.* Durham, NC: Duke University Press, 1995.

Doty, Alexander. *Flaming Classics: Queering of the Film Canon.* New York: Routledge, 2000.

Hanson, Ellis, ed. *Out Takes: Essays on Queer Theory and Film.* Durham, NC: Duke University Press, 1999.

Waugh, Thomas. *The Fruit Machine: Twenty Years of Writings on Queer Cinema.* Durham, NC: Duke University Press, 2000.

R

race films. Films with all-black casts that began appearing during the silent era. Independent black filmmakers Emmett J. Scott, George and Noble Johnson, and **Oscar Micheaux** produced films for all-black audiences who watched in segregated theaters. The films imitated Hollywood genres—westerns, musicals, and melodramas—and portrayed black characters as heroes and professionals, offering positive images to oppose Hollywood representations primarily limited to butlers and maids. Eventually, white-owned companies jumped on the low-budget, race film bandwagon. Financial and distribution problems brought the era to a close at the conclusion of the 1940s and led to a reassessment of the role of black Americans in mainstream movies. Slow progress was made until the 1980s when black filmmakers became empowered by making their own films. *See also* African American cinema; Micheaux, Oscar

BIBLIOGRAPHY

Bernardi, Daniel, ed. *The Birth of Whiteness: Race and the Emergence of U.S. Cinema.* New York: Rutgers University Press, 1996.

Bogle, Donald. *Toms, Coons, Mulattos, Mammies & Bucks: An Interpretive History of Blacks in American Films.* New York: Continuum, 1989.

Rafic. Film supply company created by Raffe Azzouny, aka Rafic *b.* 1942. *d.* February 27, 1999. Rafic operated out of a large walk-up loft on 11th Street and Broadway in New York. It sold inexpensive raw stock, film equipment, supplies, and video-transfer services that benefited the independent film community. Rafic was the founder of U-P Film Group Cinema, which supported many of **Jack Smith's** projects and the O.P. Cinema that became a showcase for **Super 8mm, punk** features. After his death, a memorial was held at **The Millennium,** a fitting tribute to a man who believed film was an art and contributed directly to the survival of independent filmmaking. The company in his name continues to supply moviemakers with the tools of their trade.

Raimi, Sam. Director, producer, screenwriter. *b.* October 23, 1959, Royal Oak, Michigan. *ed.* Michigan State University. Recognized for his dynamic, energetic and inventive directorial style, Sam Raimi burst onto the indie scene with *The Evil Dead* (1982), which dominated the year's Cannes Film Festival. Raimi obsessed about filmmaking from age eight when he began making **8mm** films. As a college English major he devoted his attention to a half-hour horror film that was the genesis of *The Evil Dead* and parlayed it into $500,000 from local investors. Along with friend and longtime producer Robert Tapert and actor Bruce Campbell, who appears in virtually every early Raimi film, they founded Renaissance Motion Pictures. Raimi directed the offbeat but unsuccessful *Crimewave* (1985), a collaboration with **Joel and Ethan Coen,** who wrote the script. He developed two *Evil Dead* sequels, *Evil Dead II* (1987) and *Army of Darkness* (1993), replete with Raimi's frenetic shaky-cam camerawork, black comedy, horror, and gore. Raimi's first studio assignment was *Darkman* (1990), a comic book adventure starring Liam Neeson. Raimi stamps it with a hyperdirectorial style, a kinetic camera, in-jokes, and visual horror. In 1995 he directed *The Quick and the Dead*, a parody of spaghetti westerns with Sharon Stone as the **Clint Eastwood** persona. Several studio films have followed: *A Simple Plan* (1998), a dark melodrama; the baseball movie *For the Love of the Game* (1999); and *The Gift* (2000), scripted by and starring Billy Bob Thornton who had worked with Raimi in *A Simple Plan.* In 2002 *Spiderman* was released, Sam Raimi's entry into the blockbuster and **franchise** sweepstakes.

Rainer, Yvonne. Director, choreographer. *b.* 1934, San Francisco, California. A significant **experimental** filmmaker who created cinematic works characterized by patterning, tasks, and games, Yvonne Rainer moved to New York in 1957 to study theater and became drawn to filmmaking and dance. After studying with Martha Graham and Merce Cunningham and becoming one of the cofounders of Judson Dance Theater, she directed the short films *Volleyball* (1967), *Hand Movie, Rhode Island Red,* and *Trio Film* (all 1968). Rainer's philosophy was to treat the body as an instrument capable of an infinite variety of movements—more than an expression of emotional drama traditionally presented. Rainer often included filmed segments in her dance performances and by the mid-1970s switched her focus to independent filmmaking.

Rainer's early films were experimental narratives addressing social and political issues that combined reality with fiction, sound, and images. In 1972, Rainer created her first feature-length film, *Lives of Per-*

Rainer, Yvonne

Army of Darkness (1993), directed by Sam Raimi. *Courtesy of The Del Valle Archive*

formers, a ninety-minute work about a man who can't choose between two women and makes them both suffer, expressed solely in choreographed and performance art terms. Subtitled *A Melodrama*, the backstage romance was presented in thirteen long segments. The characters in this love triangle play themselves, real-life performers in a group working with Rainer who as a filmmaker blurs and erases the borders between fiction and nonfiction, **documentary** and dramatic forms. The personal, political, concrete, and abstract are interconnected, producing an unpredictable cinematic atmosphere. The result is a bold, direct, feminist sensibility often demonstrating a quirky deadpan humor that has been compared to **Buster Keaton**.

Film about a Woman Who . . . (1974) vacillates between the roles of fool, heroine, and victim. The film is shaped and structured to mirror the complexities of communication. *Film about a Woman Who . . .* does not create a narrative continuity—it presents stylized action, moving still images and text to import ideas, feelings, and emotion. *Kristina's Talking Pictures* (1976) is set in the circus world. Kristina is a lion tamer from Budapest who immigrates to New York to become a choreographer. *Journeys from Berlin/1971* (1980) features film theorist Annette Michelson in session with a psychiatrist. The viewer both observes and participates vicariously in Michelson's mind trips, which flow in a stream of consciousness illustrated with surrealistic images from modern Berlin, revolutionary Russia, Leon Trotsky, and an obscene phone caller.

The Man Who Envied Women (1985) deals with issues of sexuality, aging, power in relationships, and political activism. *Privilege* (1990) is a subversive film about menopause and sexual identity. *MURDER and Murder* (1996) is a soap opera/black comedy, political meditation about two women who fall in love. It reflects the work of **Stan Brakhage** and Jean-Luc Godard, but the relationships are more like those in a **Woody Allen** film. Space and time are layered in a nonnaturalistic fashion. Rainer taps into emotion and volatility, analyzing her characters in psychological motion picture collages of language and cinematic space.

The films of Rainer have been shown extensively in the United States and around the world in alternate film exhibition showcases. In 1988, Rainer received the American Film Institute **Maya Deren** Award. In 1969 and 1989 she received Guggenheim Fellowships, and from 1990 to 1995 Rainer was given a MacArthur Fellowship. In 1996 Yvonne Rainer wrote, produced, directed and edited *MURDER and Murder*. A feminist, slapstick modernist who embraces Keaton and Brecht, Rainer is a meta-cinematic deconstructionist who formulates films out of her mind, body, and feminine soul. *See also* dance films

BIBLIOGRAPHY

Green, Shelly. *Radical Juxtaposition: The Films of Yvonne Rainer*. Metuchen, NJ: Scarecrow Press, 1994.

Rainer, Yvonne. *A Woman Who . . .: Essays, Interviews, Scripts*. Baltimore, MD: Johns Hopkins University Press, 1999.

Rappaport, Mark. Filmmaker. *b.* 1942, New York. *ed.* Brooklyn College, New York University. Mark Rappaport could be a character in the nineteenth-century Victorian novels he adores and studied in college. Rappaport defies classification; his films float between the **avant-garde** and narrative forms and are not fully accepted by either community. Rappaport makes literate films that refer to Hollywood's studio past but are more like European melodramas embracing the themes of love, jealousy, and revenge. Rappaport began working as a film editor and self-financed **16mm** shorts including *MUR 19* (1966), *Friends, Blue Frieze* (both 1967), *The Stairs, Bay of Angels* (both 1968), *Persepolis, Chronicle* (both 1970), *Blue Streak,* and *Fluorescent* (both 1971).

In 1973, Rappaport wrote, directed, and photographed his first feature, *Casual Relations*. The low-budget indie distributed by Planet Pictures employs narration to tie together a series of episodes—a separated couple with communications problems, a woman molested by a man shown from each character's point of view, a gay man obsessed with newsreels of catastrophes who meets another man in a movie theater to share the experience, a man who feels a gallery photograph is looking back at him, a woman who has a bad dream, a man on a bad LSD trip who thinks he's dying, and a secretary who remembers with dismay a dream with men who don't touch her.

Mozart in Love (1975), again distributed by Planet Pictures, is an impudent look at the composer's relationship with the sisters Weber—Constanza, whom he married, and the unrequited love of Louisa and Sophie. Rappaport utilized rear-screen projection as his characters mime to various Mozart arias, commenting on reality through the musician's art. In 1977, *Local Color* was produced by Rappaport Productions. *The Scenic Route* (1978), produced and distributed by New Line Cinema, is one of Rappaport's most celebrated productions, the story of a woman, her sister, and a man told as a Victorian melodramatic, grand opera and as if a classical painting had come to cinematic life. *Impostors* (1980), produced by First Run Features, follows the emotional ups and downs of a romantic hero and murderous magician passing as twins. *Chain Letters* (1985) is an absurdist comedy about nine characters linked by a chain letter created by an officeworker killer. Rappaport muses about conspiracy, Agent Orange, secret government experiments, paranoia, sibling rivalry, and gay and straight relationships.

Rock Hudson's Home Movies (1992) is a **documentary** of the iconic actor who died of AIDS. A narrator who sounds like he is reading from a diary explores Hudson's sexual orientation on- and offscreen. Rappaport uses clips from more than thirty of the superstar's films. The sixty-three-minute film examines the macho and the homosexual Rock Hudson, distributed by Couch Potato Productions. *Exterior Night* (1993) was shot in high-definition video as a young man searches for his past, visualized with rear-screen, film noir images from *The Big Sleep* (1946), *Mildred Pierce* (1945), and *Strangers on a Train* (1951). *From the Journals of Jean Seberg* (1995) is a cinematically inspired biopic of the actress told in a first-person narrative with Mary Beth Hurt portraying Seberg. Rappaport used the opportunity to meditate on the cinema, society, culture, and film theory.

Rappaport takes on the larger subject of **women in film** by penetrating the careers of Jane Fonda and Vanessa Redgrave. *The Silver Screen: Color Me Lavender* (1998) is a narrated study of homosexuality in the Hollywood cinema. Our guide is visually apparent in the clips as he comments on the obvious and hidden examples of male love embedded in the films.

BIBLIOGRAPHY

Rosenbaum, Jonathan. *Film: The Front Line.* Denver, CO: Arden Press, 1983.

Ray, Nicholas. Director, screenwriter, educator. *b.* Nicholas Kienzle, August 7, 1911, Galesville, Wisconsin. *d.* June 16, 1979, New York City. *ed.* University of Chicago, University of Wisconsin. After studying architecture with Frank Lloyd Wright and becoming involved in left-wing theater in New York City, Nicholas Ray was an assistant director on several films including **Elia Kazan**'s *A Tree Grows in Brooklyn* (1945). Ray's theatrical feature debut was *They Live by Night* (1949), a John Houseman production for RKO. From the outset, Ray was fascinated by doomed love and emotionally damaged fugitives from society. *In a Lonely Place* (1950) featured Humphrey Bogart and Gloria Grahame in a turbulent story of a self-destructive screenwriter having an affair while trying to clear his name from a murder rap. In 1954 Ray directed *Johnny Guitar*, a Freudian western infused with a hyperbolic frenzy that brought it to the apex of cult status among auteurists and **American New Wavers** of the 1970s. Ray was a role model for filmmakers who probed alienation and emotional undercurrents that belied the American dream. His dark vision of postwar America damaged by broken promises and unleashed passions fueled a generation of filmmakers.

In 1955 Ray directed *Rebel without a Cause*, his signature film, which immortalized James Dean as the timeless misunderstood and angst-ridden young man. This seminal film launched hundreds of **B-movies, juvenile delinquent films,** and **exploitation** movies. For subsequent decades, these films, many of them indies, investigated the subterranean life of young people struggling with their identities and rebelling against the Greatest Generation's America. Ray's social rebel became the antihero and restless outsider taking centerstage away from the boy-next-door hero that dominated the first half of the American film century.

Ray's submersion into alcoholism and drug abuse eventually destroyed his Hollywood career. In 1971 he became a cinema professor at Harpur College in New York. At sixty he became intensely involved with radical politics and made a film about the murder of Black Panther Fred Hampton with his film class, which he turned into a student filmmaking collective. From 1973 to 1976 Ray and his students filmed *We Can't Go Home Again*. The rambling experimental, psychodramatic narrative was jeered at the 1973 Cannes Film Festival. Ray's last film was *Lightning over Water* (1980), cowritten and directed by Wim Wenders while Ray was dying of lung cancer. The personal portrait/documentary explores Wenders's fascination with the cult leader of an American film generation of baby-boomers and celebrates Ray's life and death. Ray lived hard, raw, and open. His films were a festering sore for his pain and a source of identification for the independent filmmakers who idolized him.

BIBLIOGRAPHY

Eisenschitz, Bernard. *Nicholas Ray: An American Journey.* Trans. Tom Milne. London: Faber and Faber, 1993.
Ray, Nicholas. *I Was Interrupted: Nicholas Ray on Making Movies.* Ed. Susan Ray. Berkeley: University of California Press, 1993.

Redford, Robert. *See* Sundance Institute

Reggio, Godfrey. Director. *b.* 1940, New Orleans, Louisiana. *ed.* College of Santa Fe, New Mexico. Director of the visually stunning *Koyaanisqatsi*, Reggio was a monk for fourteen years when the Catholic Brothers Teaching Order disrobed him in 1968 for ideological insubordination and his stance on social issues. Reggio had worked with street gangs in the barrios of northern New Mexico. When he saw Luis Buñuel's *Los Olvidados* (1950), a devastating film about the lives of street youths, it was a cinematic religious experience. Merging his spiritual training with his newly found form of expression, Reggio formed a media collective with three colleagues in the early 1970s. The Institute for Regional Education created public interest spots about the invasion of privacy and the negative impact of Ritalin on school-aged children, sponsored by the American Civil Liberties Union and funding from traditional left-wing sources.

Many of these images seeded Reggio's imagination for his first feature film, *Koyaanisqatsi* (1983), the Hopi Indian word translating to "life out of balance," a film that took from 1975 to 1982 to produce. The nonnarrative **experimental film** was created from a dramaturgy in five movements that presents the organic world of the Northern Hemisphere and how the human race transforms it into a synthetic world by altering nature and forging it into a frenetic, crowded series of hyperindustrial, technological grids. The film finds vibrant beauty in the synthetic world with patterns of lights, fast-moving cars, and hordes of people, but the danger of destroying or tampering with natural environments is clear and constant to almost everyone who experiences the visually demanding juxtapositions of images.

Koyaanisqatsi was produced at a **shooting ratio** of 35:1, thirty-five minutes for each minute of completed film. Three hundred and fifty thousand feet of film were exposed for the ambitious independently financed and produced undertaking. Financial angels backed the project, but money was acquired periodically over the seven years of production. *Koyaanisqatsi* was designed without sync-sound dialogue or narration—purely a fusion of images and music. The seventeen pieces of music are exhilarating, repetitive but evolving, mathematical yet emotional. Philip Glass composed the score. Reggio believed Glass's music was a metamorphic force that expanded the physical and transcendental qualities inherent in the imagery.

Production on *Koyaanisqatsi* began in **16mm** with $40,000 from a financial angel who believed in Reggio's vision. When Reggio saw the power and complexity of the images being captured by his small but substantial crew, he decided to proceed in 35mm. He blew up the 16mm to the larger commercial standard gauge so the film could be released theatrically in more widely screened venues. Over seventy individuals poured money into the daring project. A single angel gave $2 million. Cinematographer Ron Fricke, who later directed the stunning *Baraka* (1992), had never before shot in 35mm but ably captured dynamic and expressive footage. The high-speed and time-lapse sequences that give *Koyaanisqatsi* its signature style were later imitated in television commercials and in Madonna's *Ray of Light* music video. As the editors refined the massive footage into a controlled flow of images during the postproduction process, Reggio learned about the Hillary Harris film *Organism* (1975), which contained hyperkinetic patterned shots of people and traffic. Harris was willing to sell footage to Reggio, and it was structured with the New York material shot by Fricke.

Francis Ford Coppola was the first to screen the completed film and enthusiastically lent his name to *Koyaanisqatsi*; then George Lucas offered his endorsement. *Koyaanisqatsi* premiered at the New York Film Festival with a special screening at the famed Radio City Music Hall. The film enjoyed a commercial run and the largest audience ever for an experimental film. *Koyaanisqatsi* grew a loyal, if not fanatical, following and was frequently rented on the U.S. college circuit, especially on Earth Day.

Critics and scholars intimate with **avant-garde**/experimental film history accused Reggio of exploiting and commercializing the aesthetic and visual strategies of **underground** filmmakers without sincere commitment or philosophical weight. Others codified *Koyaanisqatsi* with the City Symphony genre, which includes Alberto Cavalcanti's *Rien que les heures* (1926), Walter Ruttman's *Berlin, Symphony of a Great City* (1927), Dziga Vertov's *The Man with a Movie Camera* (1929), and Francis Thompson's *NY, NY* (1957).

Reggio's second in the trilogy, *Powaqqatsi* (1988), representing life in transformation, was a transcendent work compared to its predecessor and concentrates on the Third World changed by technology. The Southern Hemisphere is seen living a hand-made life as the seduction of progress alters tradition and the souls of the people. Reggio trained his cameras on children and never identified the countries he filmed, creating a portrait of a hemisphere living closer to the natural world than its Western counterpart. *Powaqqatsi* had a $4.2 million budget. Reggio and his backers put in $2 million, and **Cannon Group**, through an introduction by Coppola, matched that amount. Cannon made a **negative pickup** agreement and retained all rights to the film, leaving the angels with a bad deal. Reggio remained in full artistic control of his vision—his primary concern.

Reggio had two production crews working in the same city or region and divided his directorial time. This time 500,000 feet of 35mm negative was exposed—a shooting ratio of 50:1. Coppola and Lucas presented *Powaqqatsi*, and Lucas gave Reggio free access to Sprockets, his postproduction facility. The reception for *Powaqqatsi* was not up to the filmmaker's expectations. The contemplative images and the reflective environmentally accurate music disappointed the masses expecting a more frenetic visual and aural trip—a repeat of the hyperhypnotic *Koyaanisqatsi*.

Lack of box office and audience reaction did not give Reggio the momentum he needed for *Naqoyqatsi*, the still uncompleted final work in the trilogy about the effects of war on planet earth. The dramaturgy was coauthored by Reggio and Glass and employs archival footage of epic battles and destruction by armed conflicts. The projected budget was $6 million, with Coppola and Lucas credited as presenters and Lucas as coexecutive producer. Reggio continues to raise money to complete the project.

In 1991, Reggio directed *Anima Mundi*, a short film supported by the World Wildlife Fund. The cinematic love letter to the beauty of animals in their natural habitat is scored by Glass and thrilled animal lovers with its reverence. *Evidence* (1995) is a short film about the effects of television on children.

Reggio is an independent filmmaker with a big vision requiring massive resources and capital to make personal films that reach out spiritually across the globe.

Reiner, Rob. *See* Castle Rock Entertainment

Reject Film Festival. No longer in existence due to lack of funding and sponsorship that plagued the year 2000 operating budget of this alternative film festival. The Philadelphia-based festival accepted any filmmaker who presented a rejection letter from another festival. Mason Bendewald and Don Argoit founded it in 1997 when the Philadelphia Festival of World Cinema rejected their film *Clayfeet*. In 1998 they featured more than thirty films and an appearance by **John Waters**. The mission of the Reject Film Festival was to "showcase filmmakers who created art on their own terms."

René, Norman. Director. *b.* 1951. *d.* May 24, 1996, of AIDS. In 1990 Norman René achieved critical acclaim and respect for *Longtime Companion*, the first theatrical film to deal directly and fully with the AIDS epidemic and its emotional impact on the gay community. Written by playwright Craig Lucas, and produced by the PBS *American Playhouse*, the film begins in the early 1980s and covers the decade when the illness became a plague. There are inspired performances by Patrick Cassidy, Brian Cousins, Dermot Mulroney, Mary-Louise Parker, and the laudatory Bruce Davidson, who received an Oscar nomination. **Lindsay Law** of *American Playhouse* undertook a long struggle to find a **distributor** brave enough to take a risk with the controversial subject. The Goldwyn Company made the commitment, and the low-budget film grossed $4.6 million, touching a wide, mainstream audience.

In 1992, René directed the film adaptation of Craig Lucas's play *Prelude to a Kiss*, starring Alec Baldwin, Meg Ryan, Kathy Bates, Ned Beatty, Patty Duke, Annie Golden, Stanley Tucci, and Sydney Walker, a romantic comedy with a strange twist. René's last film, *Reckless* (1995), featured Mia Farrow, Scott Glenn, Mary-Louise Parker, Tony Goldwyn, Stephen Dorff, Eileen Brennan, and Giancarlo Esposito in an absurdist take on Frank Capra's *It's a Wonderful Life* (1946) and Christmas movies. The dark, satiric comedy didn't find an audience. René's short career as an independent filmmaker with a conscience and a quirky, gentle sense of humor was an inspiration to the independent tradition.

Rinzler, Lisa. Cinematographer. *ed.* Pratt Institute, New York University. Rinzler first studied painting, then at NYU began to shoot student films and decided to pursue cinematography as a profession. Rinzler shot two short films for the controversial still photographer Robert Mapplethorpe and *Reverse Angle* (1982), an art journal film for Wim Wenders. After working assistant camera in the 1980s, Rinzler was director of photography on the **documentaries** *World's End, Kitty, No Sense of Crime, Hookers, Hustlers, Pimps and Their Johns* (1993), plus a film on the making of John Huston's final film *The Dead* (1987). Rinzler photographed *True Love* (1989), **Nancy Savoca**'s directorial debut. She also shot a series of music videos for Tamara Davis and Davis's feature debut *Guncrazy* (1992), a color, neo-noir starring Drew Barrymore. Davis led wunderkind twin filmmakers **Albert and Allen Hughes** to Rinzler who screened *The Drive-By*, their **Super 8mm** film that led to an audacious collaboration on *Menace II Society* (1993) and *Dead Presidents* (1995).

Rinzler shot **Steve Buscemi**'s directorial debut *Trees Lounge* (1996) and won the cinematography prize at **Sundance** for *Three Seasons* (1999), the first American feature film to be filmed on location in Vietnam, directed by **Tony Bui**. Rinzler was director of photography on *Pollock* (2000), the directorial debut of actor Ed Harris who portrayed the tortured and innovative painter Jackson Pollock. Rinzler always returns to small, experimental projects such as Jo Andres's *Black Kites* (1996), based on the wartime journal of a Sarajevan woman. Recent credits for Lisa Rinzler's work as a cinematographer include: the documentary *The Buena Vista Social Club* (1999) for Wim Wenders, *Love Liza*, and *Welcome to Collingwood* (both 2000).

Rinzler is versatile, fearless, and centered between fiction and nonfiction projects that appeal to her artistic and social conscience. As she has said, "I want to feel that whatever the story I am part of telling—I stand behind the material and am proud to have my name on it."

BIBLIOGRAPHY

LoBrutto, Vincent. *Principal Photography: Interviews with Feature Film Cinematographers*. Westport, CT: Praeger, 1999.

A moment of future action and violence in *Death Race 2000* (1975), directed by Paul Bartel and distributed by Roger Corman's New World Pictures. Courtesy of The Del Valle Archive

road movies. A popular low-budget indie genre that grew out of westerns, film noir, **exploitation**, and **biker films** that came of age during the 1970s after the youth revolution caused by the sleeper success of *Easy Rider* in 1969. The genre became a metaphor for the search for a changing America, a journey to find soul and purpose, often ending in self-discovery, disappointment, tragedy, and despair. Significant road movies include *Two-Lane Blacktop* (1971), directed by **Monte Hellman**; *Vanishing Point*, Richard Sarafian (1971); *Duel*, Steven Spielberg (1971); *Near Dark*, **Kathryn Bigelow** (1987); *Thelma & Louise*, Ridley Scott (1991); *Lost Highway*, **David Lynch** (1997); and *Death Race 2000*, **Paul Bartel** (1975). Road movies embrace the mythic quest, the eternal search for identity and home that traces back to Homer's *The Odyssey* and **Jack Kerouac**'s contemporary *On the Road*.

BIBLIOGRAPHY

Sargeant, Jack, and Stephanie Watson. *Lost Highways: An Illustrated History of Road Movies*. London: Creation Books, 1999.

Robert Flaherty Film Seminar, The. In 1954, Frances H. Flaherty, wife of the pioneer documentary filmmaker **Robert Flaherty**, founded this annual event. It began as an informal weeklong gathering of filmmakers and students at the Flaherty farm in Vermont to encourage exploration, discussion, and analysis of the moving image. The purpose of the seminars is to develop the potential of independent filmmakers to investigate the human spirit. Over the years, the most significant documentary filmmakers and scholars have attended. It is an immersion into the media in an intense, intimate retreat setting. The Robert Flaherty Film Seminar presents screenings and discussions of the aesthetics, history, and technology of the nonfiction motion picture form. Over the decades the seminar has hosted "Flaherty on the Road," a series of miniseminars at various universities and art center venues.

Robinson, Amy. Producer, actress. *b.* April 13, 1948, Trenton, New Jersey. Amy Robinson played **Harvey Keitel**'s epileptic girlfriend in **Martin Scorsese**'s *Mean Streets* (1973), then segued into a career as a producer. She worked with **Joan Micklin Silver** on *Head Over Heels* (1979), aka *Chilly Scenes of Winter*, which she coproduced with actor/producer **Griffin Dunne** through their company Double Play Productions. They worked on **John Sayles**'s *Baby It's You* (1983), starring Rosanna Arquette with an original story written by Robinson. Robinson reunited with Scorsese to produce the black comedy *After Hours* (1985), along with Dunne who costarred. Double Play produced **Sidney Lumet**'s *Running on Empty* (1988), then Luis Mandoki's *White Palace* (1990) and in 1991 Lasse Hallström's *Once Around.* Robinson produced *With Honors* (1994) and the Kevin Costner melodrama *For Love of the Game* (1999), directed by **Sam Raimi.** *Drive Me Crazy* (1999) was produced by Amy Robinson Productions. She collaborated on the romance *Autumn in New York* (2000), directed by actress Joan Chen. *See also* Dunne, Griffin

Rodriguez, Robert. Director, producer, screenwriter, cinematographer, editor. *b.* June 20, 1968, San Antonio, Texas. In 1992 Robert Rodriguez made indie history when *El Mariachi* was released by Columbia Pictures. Word was out that the film cost only $7,000. Film production teachers across the country shared a communal migraine as film students everywhere announced they were making features, rather than learning the craft by creating a short film. When the voices of reason explained it was impossible at the time to complete a **16mm** feature film for anywhere near $7,000, the mantra was *"El Mariachi* cost $7,000," and the name Robert Rodriguez was spoken as the new **guerrilla filmmaking** messiah. Just when the legend grew to Johnny Appleseed proportions, Rodriguez published a book that revealed the $7,000 had gotten the film in the can and edited on video. Based on the video cut, Columbia committed to *El Mariachi* and footed the postproduction bill, including film editing, creation

Rodriguez, Robert

George Clooney ready to do battle with the unearthly in From Dusk Till Dawn (1996), directed by Robert Rodriguez, story by Quentin Tarantino. Courtesy of The Del Valle Archive

of a soundtrack, and release prints to the tune of nearly $100,000, a fact that sent indies and students back to the short film drawing board. That stunt and the Peckinpahesque bravado of *El Mariachi* got Rodriguez a studio deal to remake the film in 35mm with a professional cast and crew. The result, *Desperado* (1995), starring Antonio Banderas, lacked the vitality of the original and sunk quickly.

"The Misbehaviors," Rodriguez's segment in the compilation film *Four Rooms* (1995), was generally trashed in the critical and public bashing of the whole ego-loaded enterprise that included segments by **Quentin Tarantino, Allison Anders,** and Alexandre Rockwell. In 1996 Rodriguez directed *From Dusk Till Dawn* from a Tarantino script, an action film turned into a grossout horror spectacular aimed at a youth market. It has an impressive visual style, but the excessive, contrived, and derivative spectacle adds up to little. *The Faculty* (1998) is another Rodriguez excursion into horror with students battling their otherworldly monstrous teacher and school staff. The film is a standard "one weekend for all the box office marbles" horror flick with a flair for gore, grossout, and eye-candy visuals.

In 2001 Rodriguez broke into the mainstream with the popular, hi-tech, and wholesome *Spy Kids*, with sequel to follow. In 2002 Robert Rodriguez released two sequels *Desperado II: Once Upon a Time in Mexico* which he wrote, produced, directed and edited, and *Spy Kids 2: The Island of Lost Dreams* where he again wore the same creative hats. Rodriguez is an extremely talented cinematographer and editor but is less successful as a storyteller and director of actors. Nevertheless, he is a courageous indie who pulled himself out of an early struggling existence to the status of no-low-budget role model and Hollywood player.

BIBLIOGRAPHY

Rodriguez, Robert. *Rebel without A Crew; Or How a 23-Year-Old Filmmaker with $7,000 Became a Hollywood Player.* New York: E.P. Dutton, 1995.

Roemer, Michael. Director, producer, screenwriter. *b.* January 1, 1928, Berlin, Germany. *ed.* Harvard University. Michael Roemer has lived in the United States since 1945. While attending Harvard he directed *A Touch of the Times* (1947–1949), a comedy/fantasy film about kite flying, which may be the first college-made feature film. Roemer worked in production with **Louis de Rochemont** as the New York producer's assistant director and editor. Later Roemer became partners with **Robert M. Young,** producing educational shorts. Roemer's first feature as a director, *Cortile Cascino* (1962), is a **documentary** about a Sicilian slum. The project was deemed too realistic, and it was never released. In 1964 *Nothing But a Man* was released. This seminal low-budget independent movie dealt with levels of prejudice in black life in a candid and honest fashion. The film won two awards at the Venice Film Festival and was admired by the French New Wave critics. After such recognition Roemer hit bad luck again with *The Plot against Harry,* a New York City story about an aging gangster whose life comes apart. The film was shelved in 1969 and released to critical favor twenty years later when film festival screenings and a **distributor** resurrected it from the black hole of the film vault.

In 1993 Young's son Andrew and his wife Susan Todd returned to Sicily to pick up the story of Angela Capra and her husband from the unreleased *Cortile Cascino.* Color footage of new material was intercut with original black-and-white documentary material. It became *Children of Fate: Life and Death in a Sicilian Family* and is credited as directed by Michael Roemer, Susan Todd, Andrew Young, and Robert M. Young. Roemer became a teacher at Yale University. He was the executive producer of the short film *Short Change* (1996) and played a reporter in *My Next Funeral* (2000). *See also* de Rochemont, Louis; Young, Robert M.

Roger & Me. *See* Moore, Michael

Rogosin, Lionel. Documentary filmmaker. *b.* January 22, 1924. *d.* December 8, 2000. Lionel Rogosin stepped into independent film history with his first film, *On the Bowery* (1956), a study of New York's Skid Row. The film was nominated for an Oscar, won the Venice Film Festival's **documentary** grand prize, and was championed by **Jonas Mekas** and the community of experimental filmmakers. In 1959, Rogosin made *Come Back, Africa*. He persuaded South African authorities he was making a musical so he could secretly record the black African struggle under apartheid.

The son of a wealthy immigrant industrialist who studied chemistry and was later in charge of the textile division of his father's business, Rogosin was propelled into documentary filmmaking by his sense of social responsibility. Rogosin lived in New York's Greenwich Village and discovered firsthand the Skid Row misery of the Bowery district where homeless men and women drank themselves into illness and slow death. With his own money Rogosin produced and directed *On the Bowery* (1956), a sixty-minute documentary. Rogosin employed hidden cameras to directly document the daily human despair and suffering in hopes of social compassion and political change. Rogosin also contributed to the exhibition of independent film by leasing and renovating the Greenwich Village Theater and opening The Bleecker Street Cinema, a venue for independent films in 1962 that he sold in 1974.

Romero, George A. Director, screenwriter, editor. *b.* February 4, 1940, Bronx, New York. *ed.* Ivy League Suffield Academy, Carnegie Institute of Technology (now Carnegie-Mellon University). George Romero, a film enthusiast from childhood, watched every movie he could. Bright, but fearful and lonely, Romero took solace reading E.C. horror comics deemed verboten because of their explicit violent images. E.C. Comics was the brainchild of *Mad Magazine* creator, William M. Gaines. Published from 1950 until 1955, E.C. delighted teenage boys and infuriated parent groups and censors with gory and graphic horror tales. Some of the titles under the E.C. banner include: *Tales from the Crypt of Terror, Haunt of Fear, Vault of Horror* and *Weird Fantasy*. Romero's Uncle Monroe (Monnie) Yudell, a wealthy doctor, owned an **8mm** Revere camera that fascinated his movie-mad nephew. When his parents got him an 8mm projector for Christmas, George began working on Uncle Monnie to borrow the prized Revere. Romero began making movies, creating soundtracks on a reel-to-reel tape recorder that never stayed in sync with the picture (the bane of all aspiring filmmakers who couldn't gain access to sync-sound equipment).

Romero organized Herald Pictures, an 8mm production group. Their first feature, *The Man from the Meteor* (1954), borrowed unabashedly from **Edgar G. Ulmer**'s *The Man from Planet X* (1951). When an extraterrestrial is zapped by a ray gun, Romero created the special effect by scraping lines onto the celluloid so they appeared to be electronic pulses emitting

Zombies walk the earth in George Romero's *Night of the Living Dead* (1968). Courtesy of The Del Valle Archive

from the weapon. To create the illusion the creature was on fire and fell off a roof, Romero set a dummy on fire and tossed it from atop a building. Security guards arrested the nascent director. Romero's second feature, *Gorilla* (1955), was a jungle adventure filmed on location in Scarsdale, an upscale community in Westchester, New York. Premieres were held in Uncle Monnie's basement. Romero created illustrated programs, charged ten cents a ticket, and even sold hot buttered popcorn and candy. Romero created an 8mm **documentary** on geology for a science fair that won a Future Scientists of America award. During his summers at the Suffield Academy, Romero worked as a gaffer on Hitchcock's *North by Northwest* (1959) and on *It Happened to Jane* (1959), directed by Richard Quine.

Romero was accepted at the Carnegie Institute of Technology (CIT) where he aspired to study commercial art. At CIT, Romero met the collaborators who would contribute to his success as an indie giant: Rudy Ricci, Ray Lane, John Russo, and Russell Streiner. Romero progressed to 16mm when Ricci's cousin, known as The Rev, gave him access to the University of Pittsburgh's audiovisual department. Romero began *Curly*, but left it unfinished. It was a film that combined the artful atmosphere of a 1960s foreign film and the angst of *Rebel without a Cause* (1955). In his third year at college, Romero played a lead role in the Pittsburgh Theater's production of the Jack Gelbert landmark play about junkies, *The Connection*. Impressed with Romero's theater potential, the dean of drama convinced him to switch majors, but he later quit.

Out of school, Romero and his filmmaking companions set to work on a compilation of short films. Their thematic goals were lofty—drama, life, death, comic, artistic, and poetic. The collaborators flew to New York with Romero to see Uncle Monnie who was concerned about his out-of-work nephew. They returned with a $5,000 loan and called their company Ram Pictures. Ricci and The Rev wrote the screenplays; Romero handled cinematography and editing. *Expostulations* was a compilation film that included *A Door against the Rain*, a story of a boy living in an industrial wasteland who escapes reality by going through a doorframe built by his grandfather. When the boy passes through the frame, life turns sunny. *The Trilogy* is a philosophical drama of a black boy in a ghetto who witnesses his father's murder. *The Rocketship* was a science fiction farce about aliens crashing into a mountain. Thirty-five hundred dollars was spent on a 16mm **Bolex camera**, a tripod, and lighting package; after editing there was no money left to complete postproduction. Romero met John Szwergle at the only film lab in Pittsburgh, who processed the film and taught the director how to prepare for completion.

In 1963, the team formed Latent Image and worked out of a $65 a month storefront in South Philly. To stay in business they did baby and communion photography. Latent Image met Vince Survinski, the owner of a local roller-skating rink who collaborated with Ricci on a story about a German defector. *The Flower Girl* (1963) was financed with $10,000 from Survinski. Latent Image spent the money on other expenses and the project fell through. Survinski agreed to another $10,000 as an investment in Latent Image—he then became the company's manager. Eventually, they began working in commercials. They received a Pennsylvania Regional Industrial Development loan of $30,000. This allowed them to move to downtown Pittsburgh. From 1965 to 1967 Latent Image was commissioned for scores of commercials, **industrials**, and political spots.

Latent Image purchased a 35mm Arriflex camera and lenses, which enabled them to regroup and make a low-budget horror film that would make independent film history. *Night of the Living Dead* (1968) turned the zombie movie into an apocalyptic horror that transformed all members of society into graphically deformed creatures, relentless in their pursuit to conquer. The graphic violence and explicit special effects body makeup by **Tom Savini** were landmark precedents for the new subfield of **splatter** and gore films. Romero also invigorated horror films by making an intelligent, literate African American the hero, shattering decades of stereotyping. Audiences found the film truly frightening and word of mouth was intense.

Latent Image followed up their defining hit with *There's Always Vanilla* (1972), a film that caused consternation among the filmmakers about what direction they should take. Shot in 16mm, later blown up to 35mm with a budget of $100,000, the film directed, photographed, and edited by Romero is the story of a rock guitarist tired of life on the road and of playing other performers' tunes. He goes home to rediscover his roots and learns he is the father of an ex-girlfriend's child, but he has an affair, and the plot meanders until he leaves town without learning any life lessons. The film was a disappointment and a big letdown to fans that wanted more zombie gore.

Jack's Wife (1973), another failure, was written, directed, photographed, and edited by Romero with Latent Image. The film, which suffered from poor production values and acting, is about a woman who can't communicate with her husband and her daughter and is disassociated from her Catholic beginnings and sexual experience. Alienation and a search of identity take her into witchcraft and a renewed interest in her sexuality.

The Crazies (1973) was a Pittsburgh film production through Latent Image and distributed by Cambist Films, shot in 35mm and concerns an accidental release of a biological weapon into a town's water supply as the military attempts to contain the deadly situation. The horror film demonstrated Romero's skill in shooting and editing rapid-action sequences. Filled with violence and chaos it was a moderate success among fans but did not make money.

Romero's fortunes reversed when he met Richard P. Rubinstein, who became president of their new company, Laurel Productions. Like Romero, Rubinstein was not formally educated in filmmaking except for a few elective film history courses at Columbia. Rubinstein bought a video camera and wrote a column for *Filmmaker's Newsletter*, becoming involved with the New York alternative television movement. Rubinstein was a video consultant to a Wall Street brokerage firm that invested in feature films and nonbroadcast video services for corporate communications. He also was a video consultant to CBS stations. To get Laurel in fiscal health Rubinstein used tax shelter strategies to make a series of sports documentaries before they could proceed with the fictional features they really wanted to produce. The series, called *The Winners*, was produced from 1973 to 1976. The fifteen-hour-long films include portraits of Karem Abdul-Jabar, Mario Andretti, Terry Bradshaw, Reggie Jackson, and *Juice on the Loose*, a sports bio of O.J. Simpson.

In 1978 Laurel and Libra Films released *Martin*, about a teenager who believes he's a vampire but without fangs; he relies on razor blades to draw blood and the signature Romero/Savini gore. Romero continued to use the splatter genre for social and satirical purposes. In 1979, a sequel to *Night of the Living Dead*, *Dawn of the Dead*, was released in which four people set up camp in a mall to fight off the ever-growing zombie population. *Knightriders* (1981) was a change in direction for Romero. The film features an unknown Ed Harris as a modern-day King Arthur in the offbeat and original story of a traveling troupe of medieval performers who joust on motorcycles and attempt to live by a code of honor in a morally deteriorating society. *Creepshow* (1982) is E.C. horror comics brought to the screen. Five segments written by **Stephen King** feature many grossouts including the spectacle of hordes of cockroaches exploding out of a man's stomach.

In 1985 Romero directed the third zombie installment with *Day of the Dead*. This time a female scientist is trapped by the living dead in a bunker with military sexists who reject her mission to study the creatures. Much talk, little action until the third act when Tom Savini is let loose with his blood and gore steamer trunk of horrific magic. *Monkey Shines: An Experiment in Fear* (1988) is the tale of a monkey injected with human brain cells who assists a quadriplegic that is only of interest to the Romero diehards. *Two Evil Eyes* (1990) was codirected by Romero and his Italian counterpart Dario Agento who presents two Poe stories that were not up to the standards of **Roger Corman**'s beloved Poe Cycle. *The Dark Half* (1993) was a handsomely mounted production of the Stephen King bestseller about a two-sided author. *Bruiser* (2000), Romero's first film after a seven-year absence, was about a man who wakes up without a face and ready for revenge on a world who made him conform. Romero then adapted Stephen King's *The Girl Who Loved Tom Gordon*.

BIBLIOGRAPHY

Gagne, Paul. *The Zombies That Ate Pittsburgh: The Films of George A. Romero*. New York: Dodd, Mead, 1987.

Rooks, Conrad. Director, producer, screenwriter, actor. *b.* December 15, 1934, Kansas City, Missouri. After serving in the marines, Conrad Rooks traveled to New York where he studied film and television production. After his studies, Rooks was unable to find a job in the industry so he and a friend founded Exploit Films, a production company created to service the popular **nudie cutie** film market. They produced three films including *White Slaves* (1974) and *Girls Incorporated* until his partner ran off with the receipts and the talent. Rooks began hanging out in Greenwich Village where he met underground artists who inhabited the hotbed of counterculture activities. Rooks met the **experimental** filmmaker Harry Smith, known for his magical animation experiments in film. Legend has it Rooks taught **Andy Warhol** how to load film.

Rooks became imbued in the culture including alcoholism and drug abuse. Eventually he became heavily addicted to heroin and a cornucopia of hallucinogens. When his father died suddenly in 1962, Rooks grew contemplative and took a rest cure in Zurich to rid himself of the addictions that plagued him. When he returned home he decided to make a film and bought the rights to William Burroughs's *Naked Lunch* but gave up the project as impossible (a feat cleverly pulled off by **David Cronenberg** in 1991).

Rooks then embarked on a project that would serve as therapy and stave off temptations. The result was *Chappaqua* (1966), which Rooks financed with his inheritance. The film's psychedelic celebration of spirituality and visions has become legend. Although not completely accepted by the **underground** or commercial film communities, Rooks was catapulted into film history with *Chappaqua*, a film more talked about than actually seen. *Chappaqua* wiped out Rooks financially.

It wasn't until 1973 that he directed again. Rooks had become spiritually involved in Eastern and American Indian religions. The transformation led him to a cinematic adaptation of Herman Hesse's masterpiece, *Siddhartha* (1972). The theme of a young man in India on a journey to find the meaning of existence occupied Rooks since his recovery and own search for inner peace. Rooks, who also wrote the screenplay, independently produced the project. He employed an all-Indian cast and asked the great Swedish cameraman Sven Nyvkist to photograph the film. Rooks did a respectable job realizing the metaphysical story, but admirers of the beloved book (especially hippies and counterculture types) couldn't accept any interpretation of Hesse's vision but the one they experienced reading the book repeatedly. The film fared poorly at the box office. After *Siddhartha*, Rooks's career waned, and he followed a spiritual path. *See also Chappaqua;* trip movies

BIBLIOGRAPHY

Sargeant, Jack. *The Naked Lens: Beat Cinema.* London: Creation Books, 1997.

Rosenthal, Jane. *See* De Niro, Robert; Tribeca Film Center

Rouch, Jean. *See Chronicle of a Summer*

Rubinstein, Richard. *See* Romero, George A.

roughies. Low-budget independent **exploitation films** made in the 1960s that combined sex with violence. *Scum of the Earth* (1963) by **Hershell Gordon Lewis** is one of the first examples of the genre.

Rudolph, Alan. Director, screenwriter. *b.* December 18, 1943, Los Angeles, California. Alan Rudolph was a 1960s college dropout who studied accounting and then entered the film industry, working in different studio departments. In 1969 he was accepted in the DGA's training program for assistant directors. Rudolph directed a few shorts to hone his filmmaking skills. His feature debut as a director was *Premonition* (1972), a horror film where red flowers cause three college students to experience deadly premonitions. The counterculture horror film featured Barry Brown, folk music, and dreamy, trippy hallucination scenes. Rudolph remained in obscurity with another low-budget horror film, *Nightmare Circus* (1973), about three showgirls kidnapped on their way to Las Vegas by a maniacal young man. He trains them as circus performers in a house next to a nuclear test site that has turned his father into a homicidal mutant.

Rudolph's career was transformed when he became a protégé of **Robert Altman** as the maverick filmmaker's assistant on *The Long Goodbye* (1973), *California Split* (1974), and *Nashville* (1975). He cowrote *Buffalo Bill and the Indians, or Sitting Bull's History Lesson* (1976). Altman had a permanent influence on Rudolph's compressed-perspective visual style and his philosophy toward a quirky, peopled cinema.

Altman produced Rudolph's directorial debut, *Welcome to L.A.* (1977), which featured an ensemble cast: Sally Kellerman, Geraldine Chaplin, **Harvey Keitel**, Lauren Hutton, Viveca Lindfors, Sissy Spacek, Denver Pyle, John Considine, and Richard Baskin, who created the repetitive, droning song score. The project was an examination of southern Californians emotionally lost and seeking human connections through quickie sex rather than real love. Because of Altman's power, Rudolph got a strong art house sendoff.

Remember My Name (1978) was a fractured and disorienting narrative about a woman who returns from prison to disrupt her ex-husband's new life. Alberta Hunter's distinctive blues score was the film's greatest asset. *Roadie* (1980) was a backstage look at rock 'n' roll starring Meat Loaf, Art Carney, Alice Cooper, Roy Orbison, Hank Williams Jr., Ramblin' Jack Elliot, Blondie, and Soul Train's Don Cornelius. Meat Loaf plays a roadie who searches the film's clunky narrative for horror/rock star Alice Cooper. The project failed with **critics**, general audiences, and the art house crowd who had endorsed Rudolph's previous two films. *Endangered Species* (1982) was the true story of a New York cop who discovered cattle mutations in the West. Rudolph's moral and political message is heavy-handed and saddled with his usual LA pretensions toward serious subjects. *Return Engagement* (1983) is a nonfiction film about the college circuit debates of LSD guru Dr. Timothy Leary and Watergate thug G. Gordon Liddy. Rudolph's study of opposite factions finds them equally flaky and self-feeding in an attempt to define a dis-oriented, damaged America.

Choose Me (1984), one of Rudolph's biggest indie hits, features Geneviève Bujold, Keith Carradine, Lesley Ann Warren, Rae Dawn Chong, John Larroquette, and John Considine. The film offers a song score by Teddy Pendergrass and focuses on the relationship between a sex talk show host and a bar owner. *Songwriter* (1984) was a troubled production about two country singers that team up to battle an unscrupulous businessman. The laid-back meandering narrative stars Willie Nelson, Kris Kristofferson, Melinda Dillon, Rip Torn, Lesley Ann Warren, and Richard Sarafian and plenty of music with little story substance. *Trouble in Mind* (1985) was a near-future neo-noir attempt to comment on the morality of law enforcement and the optimism of youth unaware of the corruption of cynicism. Rudolph goes through great pains to obscure time, place, and meaning in the name of West Coast film art.

Made in Heaven (1987) is a ponderous fantasy/romance about a young man who dies and in heaven meets a yet unborn beauty and falls in love. *The Moderns* (1988) is a period film of artistes in Paris circa 1926. Rudolph tries to identify himself as worthy of Ernest Hemingway and Gertrude Stein in this mishmash of real and undigested characters in a central period in cultural history. *Love at Large* (1990) casts Neil Young and Tom Berenger in the same movie as rival detectives. *Mortal Thoughts* (1991) is Rudolph's most defined dramatic film, produced by Demi Moore, who is joined in the cast by Glenne Headley, Bruce Willis, John Pankow, and Harvey Keitel. Well-acted, coherent characters and a clever flashback structure present the story of a woman questioned about the murder of her best friend's husband. The actors create an electricity often missing in Rudolph's work. *Equinox* (1993) is a trip back to Rudolph's paceless attempt at mystery and endless musings on contemporary morality. *Mrs. Parker and the Vicious Circle* (1994) was a limited critical and box office success in its re-creation of the famed Algonquin Round Table of the 1920s. The film is too long and is flawed by a catalog of mannered and overshot performances evoking Dorothy Parker, Robert Benchly, and their erudite, bitter-tongued colleagues. A particular standout in this heavy-handed approach is Jennifer Jason Leigh playing the formidable Dorothy Parker, sounding more like Katharine Hepburn.

Afterglow (1997), produced by Altman, was a triumph for Julie Christie playing a movie actress who can't climb out of her self-pity. *Breakfast of Champions* (1999) was a dream project of Altman's from the 1970s. Rudolph took one of Kurt Vonnegut's best novels and trivialized its potent satire. The director is unable to find the visual and narrative style of the material and relies on his recycling bin of stuck in the seventies, LA depressive mullings. *Trixie* (2000) is a noir screwball comedy about corruption kibashed by Rudolph's obsession with cinematic effect over substance and story. *Investigating Sex* (2001) is about a group of men and two female stenographers who study sex through a scientific prism. In 2002 Rudolph wrote the screenplay for *Voltage*, directed by Robert Altman.

Rudolph has created a consistent body of work protected by his fierce independence and fueled by his devotion to Robert Altman's artistic principles. With Altman the results are original; with Rudolph it's more than once removed. Altman is an artist; Rudolph keeps trying to prove it and has a coterie of fans to back him up.

Rush, Richard. Director, producer, screenwriter. *b.* 1930, New York City. Richard Rush directed nine low-budget movies from 1960 to 1969, accomplished **biker movies** like *Hell's Angels on Wheels* (1967) and *The Savage Seven* (1968) and the psychedelic classic *Psych-Out* (1968). Rush was in the right place at the right time to be a major player in the **American New Wave** of the 1970s, but as with **Monte Hellman**, it never happened. Rush got off two films that became cult items but was lost in the plethora of counterculture movies churned out by the studios in the first years of the decade.

Getting Straight (1970) starred Elliot Gould and Candice Bergen in the timely story of a graduate student choosing between academia-speak and his core beliefs. *Freebie and the Bean* (1974) starred James Caan, Alan Arkin, Loretta Swit, Jack Kruschen, Mike Kellin, and Alex Rocco in an action/comedy as San Francisco cops tear apart the city to get a numbers man. Rush was not heard from for the remainder of the historic cinema decade.

In 1980, Rush made a triumphant return with *The Stunt Man*, a reality-bending **self-referential** black comedy starring Peter O'Toole and Steven Railsback, about a Christlike film director who replaces his ace stuntman with a fugitive who has accidentally murdered him. Ironically, the film took nine years to accomplish. It was finished in 1978 but sat on the shelf. The film was critically acclaimed, and Rush was nominated for an Oscar, but the resurrection didn't last. It was fourteen more years until Rush's next film *Color of Night* (1994), a thriller with Bruce Willis, Leslie Anne Warren, and Jane March, with hyped-up sex scenes that didn't bring money to the till. Rush was forced to trim Willis's frontal nudity and other sex shots to get an R rating (of course, a director's cut is available on video, but it is still rated R).

Russell, David O. Director, screenwriter. *b.* David Owen Russell, August 20, 1958, New York City. *ed.* Amherst College. As a teenager Russell was absorbed with 1970s movies like *Taxi Driver* (1976) and *Chinatown* (1974). After graduation in 1981 Russell became a left-wing activist and taught at a Sandinista literacy program in Nicaragua. At twenty-eight, Russell changed direction and became a caterer. He also began to write screen-plays. Russell's first feature was released when he was thirty-six and had more life experience than many first-time directors right out of film school. His debut, *Spanking the Monkey* (1994), is a dark comic family saga that includes incest and masturbation interruptus due to a barking dog. It is a twisted coming-of-age tale. *Flirting with Disaster* (1996), star-ring Ben Stiller, Patricia Arquette, Mary Tyler Moore, and George Segal, is about a neurotic man seeking his biological parents. *Three Kings* (1999) starred George Clooney, Mark Wahlberg, Ice Cube, Spike Jonze, and Nora Dunn in an action film about renegade U.S. soldiers who attempt to pull off a gold heist at the end of the Persian Gulf War. Russell's most accomplished film, *Three Kings* is inventive, funny and violent and brings a new dimension to the war televised on CNN. Russell produced *The Slaughter Rule*, and played himself in *Adaptation* (both 2002), directed by Spike Jonze.

Russo, John. *See* Romero, George A.

S

Sarno, Joe. Director, screenwriter. *b.* 1921. *ed.* New York University. The most prolific and narratively daring of all the 1960s **sexploitation** sleaze-meisters, Joe Sarno was infamous for his suburban taboo sex scenes, unusual characters, and compelling story lines. Sarno made over 200 features in thirty years, most shot in no more than a week or two. Sarno began his career working in all areas of filmmaking in Manhattan and Sweden: **industrials,** shorts, **educational** films, **documentaries,** music videos, films for children, and news programs. He even worked as a film doctor. While he was studying psychology at NYU, Sarno wrote numerous articles on behavioral science.

Sarno's 1962 film *Sin in the Suburbs,* independently released by Jovin and denounced by the Catholic Bishop's Association, was a sexploitation flick based on a story he read in *Coronet* magazine about suburban swingers who wore masks during their sex sessions. Sarno conducted interviews before each movie to understand the changing sexual mores and practices as American society evolved during the swinging sixties. *Moonlighting Wives* (1966) was developed from a true story, and *Young Playthings* (1972) was adapted from a Swedish fairytale in the **public domain** so Sarno avoided paying for story rights. The film featured Sarno's wife Peggy, who was also his assistant, and was shot in just ten days.

From 1967 to 1971 Sarno made many films in Europe. *Daddy, Darling!* (1968) was produced in Denmark, a country with more liberal attitudes toward nudity and sexuality than America. Sarno was interested in the unconscious desires of his characters and the power of human sexuality. He examined social, sexual behavior with the cool detachment of a psychiatrist and the voyeuristic obsession of a sexploitation filmmaker. *The*

Beach House (1967) was shot on location on Fire Island, a place long known for sexual adventure.

Sarno was a rare sexploitation filmmaker who investigated the female point of view. He intuited that women had a richer sexual imagination layered with fun, costumes, and dress-up. Sarno portrayed women who had bisexual, underground lives and then returned to their families and the role of housewife. A sophisticated intellectual man, Sarno lived a cosmopolitan life in an apartment near the Museum of Modern Art with Peggy and their son. In 1983 Joe Sarno directed *Wolf Clubs* starring Harry Reems of *Deep Throat* infamy.

Savage Eye, The. Released in 1960, this unusual black-and-white film about a divorced woman looking for love in Los Angeles is a conglomeration of many cinema styles: neorealism, **exploitation**, art house, **documentary** and fiction. *The Savage Eye* was written, directed, and edited by filmmakers representing diverse strata of the community. **Joseph Strick** came from a documentary background, **Ben Maddow** was a Hollywood screenwriter, and Sidney Meyers was a film editor who cut Martin Ritt's *Edge of the City* (1957). *The Savage Eye* was independently produced over four years of shooting on weekends for $65,000. Cinematographers **Haskell Wexler**, Jack Couffer, and **Helen Levitt** worked on the project. Leonard Rosenman, who scored *East of Eden* and *Rebel without a Cause* (1955), composed the music. Verna Fields, who edited *Jaws* (1975), was the sound editor, and **B-movie** director **Irving Lerner** was a technical adviser (some say codirector). The film starred Barbara Baxley, Gary Merrill, and Herschel Bernardi.

Baxley's character is exposed to the seamy side of mid-twentieth-century urban America. As she seeks love, she experiences the violence and grandeur of the modern city and is given a lesson in low culture, exposed to boxing and wrestling matches, saloons, strip joints, and faith-healing ceremonies. Unfriendly faces and despair are everywhere, often caught by hidden camera. The nontraditional cinema narrative has no dialogue and a hard-boiled, stream-of-consciousness voiceover spoken by "The Poet," voiced by Gary Merrill. The woman has an affair and later suffers a psychiatric break. Eventually she begins to reconnect with people.

The Savage Eye was hailed as a labor of love and a forceful display of cinematic pyrotechnics. The film that said no to nothingness made an impression throughout Hollywood, but *The Savage Eye* never found its audience in theatrical release. It has become a rarely seen gem of independent filmmaking.

Savini, Tom. Makeup artist, special effects creator, actor, director. *b.* November 3, 1946, Pittsburgh, Pennsylvania. The man known as "The Gore

Savini, Tom

Special effects master Tom Savini, working on a monster for *Friday the 13th* (1980), directed by *Sean S. Cunningham. Courtesy of The Del Valle Archive*

King" and "The King of **Splatter**" for his gruesome but innovative work as a makeup creator in horror films heard the call to his profession when, as a twelve-year-old, he saw *Man of a Thousand Faces* (1957), a Hollywood biopic of legendary actor and makeup pioneer Lon Chaney. As a teenager Tom Savini put together his own makeup kit and copied monsters from the pages of **Forrest J. Ackerman**'s *Famous Monsters of Filmland*. His first professional makeup job was playing Dracula at a movie house as a promotional stunt; he was paid in chocolate milkshakes. Savini's early background was in classical monster makeup as seen in Universal's *Dracula* (1931), *Frankenstein* (1931), and *The Wolfman* (1941).

Savini served as a combat photographer during the Vietnam War where he witnessed and photographed the real gore of men slaughtered in battle. As a human experience it was traumatic, but he worked out his emotions through the ghoulish, violently deformed creatures and effects he created for the graphic, bloody mutilated images in the horror movies of the 1970s and 1980s. Savini is responsible for the special makeup effects in *Dawn of the Dead* (1978), *Martin* (1978), *Maniac* (1980), *Creepshow* (1982), *Friday the 13th: The Final Chapter* (1984), *Day of the Dead*

(1985), *The Texas Chainsaw Massacre 2* (1986), and *Killing Zoe* (1994), Savini is directly associated with the director's malevolent vision of zombies and dismembered flesh.

In 1990 Savini made his directorial debut with *Night of the Living Dead*, virtually a scene-by-scene color remake with a Romero script that added more violence, an empowered heroine, and a new ending. *Vampirates* (2001) stars Apollonia Kotero, of *Purple Rain* fame, and Philip Michael Thomas. In 2001 Tom Savini was the special effects supervisor for *Web of Darkness*. Savini is also a charismatic actor. Some of his many on-screen appearances include Arthur in *Martin*, Blades in *Dawn of the Dead*, Disco Boy in *Maniac*, a garbage man in *Creepshow*, The Creep in *Creepshow 2* (1987), Morgan in *Knightriders* (1981), and Sex Machine in **Robert Rodriguez**'s *From Dusk Till Dawn* (1996). *See also* Romero, George A.

BIBLIOGRAPHY

Savini, Tom. *Bizarro!: A Learn-by-Example Guide to the Art & Technique of Special Make-Up Effects*. New York: Harmony Books, 1983.

Savoca, Nancy. Director, screenwriter. *b.* 1960, Bronx, New York. *ed.* New York University. The daughter of Sicilian and Argentine immigrants, Nancy Savoca has alternately explored the Italian experience and cultural relationships in a way that male directors have yet to attempt. Upon graduating from New York University's film school, Savoca spent several years raising funds for her first feature, *True Love*. Written in 1982 with her husband and producer Richard Guay, the film was released in 1989. Drawing from her own parents' experiences as a culture-clash couple, the film stars Annabella Sciorra as the Italian American fiancée of commitment-phobic Ron Eldard. He prefers hanging out with his old high school friends; she'd rather spend time with him. The comedic film is set in the days leading up to their wedding. *True Love* surprised many critics and won the Grand Jury Prize at the 1989 U.S. Film Festival (later to become the **Sundance** Film Festival).

Savoca's next project, the bittersweet 1991 film *Dogfight*, starred Lili Taylor and River Phoenix. The film detailed the last night of freedom for a soon-to-be-shipped-out Marine and the sexism rampant in military culture. Although the film as released by Warner Bros. did not enjoy the same attention as *True Love*, it provided an early showcase for the film's talented leads.

Taylor joined Savoca again for the magical-realist *Household Saints* (1993), which film curator David Schwartz claims "may well be the first American movie about three generations of an Italian-American family that doesn't have a criminal as a main character." Savoca tells the story of a teenage girl (Taylor), possibly a saint, and her mother (Tracy Ullman, in a change of pace), whose husband (Vincent D'Onofrio) won her hand in a pinochle game. Many filmgoers didn't know what to make of this leisurely paced odd film, but it further advanced the careers of Taylor, Ullman, and D'Onofrio and confirmed Savoca as a major director in the independent film community.

Savoca made *The 24 Hour Woman* in 1999, a frenetic film about a pregnant television producer and the new baby's effect on her career. It made a brief appearance in theaters, and while it garnered some critical accolades, it disappeared quickly.

Sayles, John. Director, writer, editor, actor. *b.* September 28, 1950, Schenectady, New York. *ed.* Williams College. As one of the most fiercely independent filmmakers in the country, John Sayles defies the career path taken by most. Whereas many directors use independent cinema as a launching pad to Hollywood, Sayles remains in independent film to tell his complex, often political stories that do not necessarily have mass audience appeal. Beginning his career as a short-story writer and novelist after graduating from Williams College, Sayles supported himself as a nursing home attendant and meat packer while he continued to write.

Recognizing his talent, **Roger Corman** hired Sayles and assigned him the scripts for *Piranha* (1978), *The Lady in Red* (1979), *Alligator* (1980), and *Battle beyond the Stars* (1980). Although the films were little more than schlock, Sayles's work stood out for its good humor. The Corman screenplays gave Sayles money for his first feature, *The Return of the Secaucus 7* (1980), which he self-financed for $60,000. The film follows seven former 1960s radicals who reunite for a weekend in the country and garnered the Los Angeles Critics Award for best screenplay of the year. Sayles's attempts at cost cutting included using his friends as actors and setting most of the action in a single location that doubled as boarding for the cast and crew.

Sayles was given a MacArthur "genius" grant in 1983 that gave him $30,000 a year, tax free, for five years and allowed him to dedicate all of his time to filmmaking. That same year, Sayles made *Lianna*, a challenging film about a woman's realization that she is a lesbian. Made for $30,000, most of which was raised in a public offering of the film's profits, *Lianna* could easily have been patronizing and inaccurate, but as Leonard Maltin noted in his 2002 movie and video guide, "It had not one false note." The most mainstream film of Sayles's career came in 1983 with *Baby, It's You.* The film follows a young greaser's courtship of a whitebread teenage girl in the 1960s, with rock 'n' roll classics peppering the soundtrack. The film was generally well received but did not increase Sayles's stature in the film community.

Sayles planned to make *Matewan* next, but when a large part of the funding fell through, Sayles found himself with $300,000 and a crew ready to make a movie. He wrote the screenplay for *The Brother from*

Another Planet (1984) in one week. The film stars Joe Morton as an alien who crash-lands in New York City and ends up in Harlem, delighting residents with his "intelligence" without ever speaking a word. It was Sayles's most accessible film to date. For the first, but certainly not the last, time in his career, Sayles did not cash in on his success. Instead, he made *Matewan* (1987), a period piece based on the true story of a tragic coal miner's strike. In addition to his usual chores of writing, directing, and editing the film, Sayles also wrote the labor songs that are featured prominently. Photographed by **Haskell Wexler**, it is Sayles's most visually striking film. The next year, Sayles made another period drama, also based on a true story. *Eight Men Out* (1988) tracks the 1919 Chicago Black Sox scandal in which members of the baseball team were accused of fixing their own games. These films were well received by critics and Sayles's small devoted following, but both lost money.

Inspired by political developments in the Soviet Union and Yugoslavia, Sayles wrote and directed *City of Hope* in 1991. Set in an unnamed metropolitan city, the film is a tapestry of stories revolving around the tribalism Sayles saw on a global scale. *City of Hope* includes black, Italian, and police "tribes" trying to coexist. Shot over a five-week period, the film managed a small profit once it was released on home video. In 1992, Sayles was nominated for a screenplay Oscar for *Passion Fish*. The film stars Mary McDonnell (also nominated) as a soap opera star recovering from a paralyzing accident, helped by a nurse played by Alfre Woodard. Once again critical acclaim did not translate into box office revenue, as the film barely broke even.

The year 1994 brought Sayles his biggest hit, *The Secret of Roan Inish*. Based on a 1959 Irish novella, the film appealed to children and adults with its fairy tale–like story of a mermaid (known as a Selkie in Ireland) who longs to return to the ocean. The steady box office success gave Sayles the freedom (and a $4 million budget) to begin his most complex film. *Lone Star* (1996), which tackled racism, immigration, and Mexican border wars in a richly detailed film, won Sayles more attention and financial success than he had yet experienced. Focusing on a young sheriff's investigation into his father's past, Sayles received his third Academy Award nomination for its screenplay.

In his most prominent refusal to piggyback on success, Sayles released the Spanish-language *Men with Guns/Los Hombres Armados* in 1998. Shot entirely in Mexico and featuring a cast of Mexican actors unknown to American audiences, Sayles challenged audiences once again with his story of an elderly man confronting his own past and lifestyle. While the film did not turn a profit, it confirmed Sayles's stature as one of the most serious, politically minded filmmakers in the business. *Limbo* (1999), with Mary Elizabeth Mastrantonio, David Strathairn, and Kris Kristofferson, takes place in Alaska with characters at emotional crossroads. The highly literate and emotionally probing narrative did not get the audience it deserved. In 2001 John Sayles was the writer, director and editor of *Sunshine State*. In 2002 he wrote and directed *Casa de Los Babys*.

Like Orson Welles and **John Cassavetes**, Sayles has built a career by subsidizing his work with money earned as an actor. In films like *Something Wild* (1986), *Straight Talk* (1992), *Malcolm X* (1992), *Matinee* (1993), and *Gridlock'd* (1997), Sayles has shown himself as a naturalistic actor in small roles. He has also earned money as an uncredited script doctor, revising screenplays for Hollywood films like *Apollo 13* (1995) and *The Quick and the Dead* (1995). While his films differ in their thematic and visual content, Sayles strives for one thing, as he told Gavin Smith in *Film Comment*: "When people leave the theater, I want them to be thinking about their own lives and the lives of other people they knew."

BIBLIOGRAPHY

Molyneaux, Gerry. *John Sayles: An Unauthorized Biography of the Pioneering Indie Filmmaker*. Los Angeles, CA: Renaissance Books, 2000.
Sayles, John. *Sayles on Sayles*. Ed. Gavin Smith. London: Faber and Faber, 1998.
———. *Thinking in Pictures: The Making of the Movie Matewan*. Boston: Houghton Mifflin, 1987.

Schmidt, Rick. Filmmaker, author, educator. Rick Schmidt's *Feature Filmmaking at Used-Car Prices: How to Write, Produce, Direct, Film, Edit and Promote a Feature-Length Film for Less Than $10,000* hit the bookstores one year before the low-budget sensation *sex, lies, and videotape* (1989) shook up the Hollywood mega-buck system. Schmidt was already there to supply the details and secrets and smash all the myths about making films for the cost of the Aroma Therapist line item on a Julia Roberts project. Schmidt started making low-budget films in 1973. In his no-budget debut *A Man, a Woman, and a Killer* (1975), a gangster waits for a hit man coming to kill him during shifting realities of the narrative. The film was codirected with his then-roommate **Wayne Wang.** Their first feature premiered at The Bleecker Street Cinema and won Director's Choice at the Ann Arbor Film Festival. *1988—The Remake* (1978) is about an audition for a remake of *Showboat*, while an actor brings his bad childhood to the musical form, and was funded by the **National Endowment for the Arts** and AFI. *Emerald Cities* (1983), in which a young woman goes off to seek her fortune and steps into the new dark ages of 1984 was made with an NEA production grant and completed Schmidt's American Dream trilogy.

Morgan's Café (1988), played the **Sundance,** Berlin, San Francisco International, and the New Directors/New Films festivals and followed his book's advice (at least the third edition), coming in for $15,000. *American Orpheus* (1992) premiered at the Rotterdam and Seattle film festivals and won a Gold Award at the Houston International for best low-budget feature. *Blues for the Avatar* (1995) played **Slamdance**, after which Schmidt started coproducing **16mm** and digital videotape features with his son Morgan Schmidt-Fend as part of feature workshops he organized. *Chetzemoka's Curse* was a digital video collaborative feature made by six members of Schmidt's workshop in 1993, shot in ten days in Port Townsend, Washington. The no-budget film was the second American film officially certified by **Dogme 95** after **Harmony Korine's** *Julien Donkey-Boy* (1999). In 1998 Rick Schmidt was the writer, executive producer and director of *Welcome to Serendipity*. In 1999 he wrote and directed *Sun and Moon*, and directed *Maisy's Garden*.

The workshops Schmidt runs in Berkeley, California, and Las Vegas accept applicants from all backgrounds. Former participants include a house painter, security guard, a high school drama teacher, and a psychologist. Schmidt's philosophy purports that everyone understands how movies work from watching, and it encourages students to express personal ideas. Schmidt is an independent filmmaker responsible for inspiring throngs of people to make movies. In the digital age you don't have to go to Hollywood. You just have to go to the bookstore and then to your nearest Sony dealer.

BIBLIOGRAPHY

Schmidt, Rick. *Feature Filmmaking at Used-Car Prices: How to Write, Produce, Direct, Shoot, Edit and Promote a Feature-Length Movie for Less Than $15,000.* 3rd ed. New York: Penguin Books, 2000.

Schneider, Alan. *See* Film

Schneider, Bert. *See* BBS

Scorsese, Martin. Director, producer. *b.* November 17, 1942, Flushing, Queens, New York. *ed.* New York Union. As a boy in New York's Little Italy, Martin Scorsese drew elaborate storyboards and later made amateur films with his friends. *Vesuvius VI* (1959) was modeled after television's *77 Sunset Strip*. Italian American culture, a fascination with Little Italy "wiseguys," and a devotion to the Catholic Church were all forces that shaped Scorsese. First dedicated to joining the priesthood, he discovered girls and rock 'n' roll and then surrendered to life as a film director. At NYU Scorsese made a series of independent short films including *The Big Shave* (1967), *It's Not Just You, Murray* (1964), and *What's a Nice Girl Like You Doing in a Place Like This?* (1963) that were award-winning experiments.

Scorsese's first feature, *Who's That Knocking at My Door?* (1969), was a crude, highly personal, and original film about Italian American youth

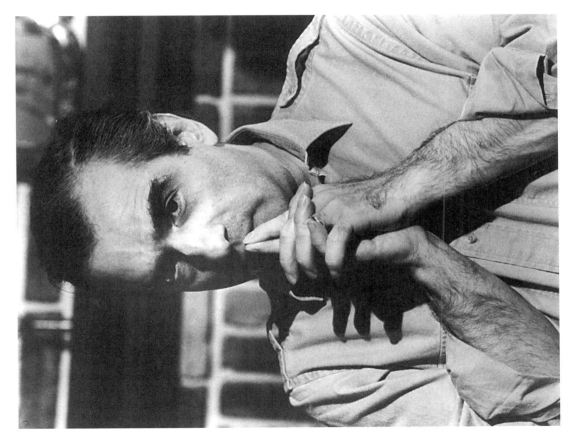

Director Martin Scorsese in 1991 on the set of his reinterpretation of *Cape Fear* (1962). Courtesy of The Del Valle Archive

and a young man's struggle with the shackles of his religion and the unwritten laws that prevent him from having a loving relationship. The film was directed with unabashed emotion for his characters and their ritualized life. Scorsese, a New Yorker raised on Forty-Second Street movies, was compelled to move to Hollywood, where he struggled to establish himself for ten years before returning to his actual and spiritual home. *Boxcar Bertha* (1972), an **exploitation film** made for **Roger Corman**, was a dead end to Scorsese's dream of being a personal filmmaker. He edited films to survive and was known as "The Butcher" for his fearless reediting of films that couldn't be released without surgery. **John Cassavetes** was a cinematic father figure who implored Scorsese to stop making projector fodder for **drive-ins** and make movies about what mattered to him.

This drove Scorsese back to an old screenplay, *Season of the Witch*, that became the independently produced, studio-distributed *Mean Streets* (1973). The film about Little Italy wannabe wiseguys was brimming with energy, humanity, and universal inner conflicts. It launched Scorsese's career. In 1974, Scorsese directed the independent **documentary** *Italianamerican*, which explored the Italian American experience through interviews with his parents, historical stills, and plenty of lively, honest, and hilarious anecdotes about life in the old country and Little Italy. The film is an important social document and part of the oral history of the New York City melting pot.

Scorsese directed two studio films: *Alice Doesn't Live Here Anymore* (1974), as a hired hand for its star Ellen Burstyn, and *New York, New York* (1977), an excessive, obsessive homage to movie musicals, especially by director Vincente Minnelli. *Taxi Driver* (1976), starring **Robert De Niro** and Jodie Foster, released by Columbia Pictures, was a deeply personal expression of white male rage and violence in the early 1970s fueled by disillusionment with Vietnam, economic recession, the end of the Aquarian 1960s, drugs, and sexual repression. In 1978 Scorsese directed two documentaries, *The Last Waltz*, a music and interview film celebrating The Band's last concert, and *American Boy: A Profile of Steven Prince*, shown at the New York Film Festival. *American Boy* is a brutally candid and funny portrait of a drug-addicted music business road warrior associated with Neil Diamond and other rock acts who had played the gunrunner in *Taxi Driver*.

Scorsese was perilously close to death from a combination of severe asthma, an illness that plagued him from childhood, and cocaine abuse. He found redemption in *Raging Bull* (1980), a film as much about Scorsese's personal demons as about boxing and Jake LaMotta. *The King of Comedy* (1983) explored the absurdity of celebrity and the maniacal danger of stalkers. It was a box office flop that critics predicted would be understood one day (in the 1990s David Letterman and Teresa Saldana, who appeared in *Raging Bull*, were involved in celebrity-stalking incidents). Scorsese plunged deeper into his well of emotion and tried to mount a production of *The Last Temptation of Christ*. De Niro dropped out, studios were skittish, and the Religious Right attacked as blasphemous a project Scorsese envisioned as an expression of faith. Scorsese then directed the black comedy *After Hours* (1985) with a small New York crew and an independent budget and resources. The film was a modest hit, and New York street filmmaking reenergized Scorsese. *The Color of Money* (1986) was a hired-hand assignment to direct the sequel to *The Hustler*. The film made money and earned an Oscar for star Paul Newman. Scorsese realized his dream of bringing Nikos Kazantzakis's novel to the screen, but the release of *The Last Temptation of Christ* in 1988 brought death threats, character assassination, and ugly protests from religious fanatics culminating in a theater firebombing in France. The American Academy of Motion Pictures Arts and Sciences honored him with an Oscar nomination for best director.

In 1990 Scorsese directed a documentary of his friend designer Giorgio Armani, again to express the culture of his family's ancestry. *GoodFellas* (1990) was the second in Scorsese's crime trilogy. *Mean Streets* was about the wannabes; *GoodFellas*, the lower-tier street guys; and *Casino* (1995), about the capos and lieutenants who ran Las Vegas before it became a Disneyesque playground. *Cape Fear* (1991) was a postmodern remake and genre experiment. *The Age of Innocence* (1993) was a lush period film about old New York aristocracy and the emotional pain of relationships. *Kundun* (1997) was the epic story of the Dalai Lama and another affirmation of faith.

Bringing Out the Dead (1999) was a New York street movie to get his **guerrilla filmmaking** juices going. The film, about the harrowing life of an emergency medical service (EMS) worker, is more like *Taxi Driver* lite and seems out of touch. Scorsese reached back to a project about turn-of-the-century New York, based on Herbert Ashbury's nonfiction study *The Gangs of New York*, a prehistory to his gangster trilogy. New York is totally recreated on lavish period sets, and the gangsters are of Irish descent, arriving in New York before the Italian immigration. Scorsese is a personal filmmaker who makes films to understand his physical and spiritual worlds. He is an inspiration as a film director and with an abiding commitment to cinema history and preservation. *See also* De Niro, Robert; Keitel, Harvey

Seidelman, Susan. Director, producer. *b.* December 11, 1952, Philadelphia, Pennsylvania. *ed.* Drexel Institute of Technology, New York University. After studying fashion art and design, Susan Seidelman was accepted to the NYU film school, where she directed three short films that garnered awards: *And You Act Like One Too* (1979), *Deficit* (1980), and *Yours Truly, Andrea G. Stern* (1980).

Seidelman began her first feature *Smithereens* (1982) in 1980 when she inherited $10,000 from her grandfather. Seidelman knew that if she took the project to Hollywood, they would never let a woman direct it, so she turned to the New York crew that worked on her shorts. Seidelman raised $25,000 to $30,000, confident it would be enough to complete a feature. By the end of the second week of the five-week schedule, $20,000 was already spent; then the lead actress fell off a fire escape and broke her leg. On the tenth day eating pizza for meal break, the crew mutinied, so time off benefited the troubled production. Seidelman regrouped and took the opportunity to revise the screenplay and raise more money. *Smithereens* was shown in official competition at Cannes where a **distributor** immediately committed to its release. *Smithereens* dramatically explores the new downtown punk scene; it is the story of Wren, a tough streetwise young woman who will do anything to become a successful punk rock 'n' roll band manager. The film received considerable praise for Seidelman's confident and hard-edged direction, but subsequently the director was only offered dumb teen comedies.

For her next project Seidelman turned to a screenplay she had written in 1974 and revised it for 1982. The original Susan in *Desperately Seeking Susan* was a hippie now updated for the 1980s. The 1985 film, starring Rosanna Arquette and Madonna in coup de grace casting, is the story of a bored housewife fascinated by a wacky character she locates in the personal ads and later becomes mistaken for. The postmodern film was done in upscale production values and crashed through the **underground** film ghetto to become a popular success.

Making Mr. Right (1987) was a feminist comedy about a scientist who has created a human android in his own image and a public relations woman who sells the concept to the public. The risky retro attempt at a science fiction romp with a message failed to find an audience. *Cookie* (1989) is the story of a teenage girl who meets her gangster father for the first time after his long stay in the big house. The whimsical comedy didn't connect with moviegoers and critics. *She-Devil* (1989) starred Meryl Streep and Roseanne Barr and is about an unliberated housewife who plots to destroy the life of her husband who walks out on her and forge a new beginning for herself. Streep gives a bravado comedic performance, but another box office failure hurt Seidelman's reputation.

Confessions of a Suburban Girl (1992) is a fifty-minute **documentary** commissioned by BBC Scotland that explores evolving sexual attitudes in Seidelman's hometown outside Philadelphia. Seidelman intercuts clips from her films with interviews of childhood friends discovering that her interest in bad girls comes from her suburban roots, hanging out with tough Italian hipsters. *The Dutch Master* (1995) featured Mira Sorvino and Aida Turturro and was produced by the German production companies Regina Ziegler Filmproduktion and West Deutscher Rundaunk. The story centers on Teresa, a young woman who is obsessed with a museum painting of a young Dutch man. The fantasy becomes an alternate reality when the scenery in the painting comes alive. *A Cooler Climate* (1999) stars Sally Field as a divorced woman who takes a job in coastal Maine for a well-to-do but sour woman. The film advocates acceptance of what life offers and focuses on mutual respect as the women come together. *Gaudi Afternoon* (2001) is the story of a woman alone in a foreign city that delves into the family skeleton closet to resolve her own past. In television Susan Seidelman has directed the movie *Beauty and Power*, and episodes of *Now and Again*, and *Sex in the City*.

With her work in the 1980s Seidelman opened doors for the 1990s wave of female directors **Nancy Savoca**, **Allison Anders**, **Mira Nair** and Stacy Cochran.

self-referential filmmaking. A film that refers to itself. The narrative makes the audience aware they are watching a film. Aesthetic, narrative, and technical elements of the self-referential film include revealing cameras, lighting or sound equipment, crew members, narration or dialogue that addresses the filmmaking process directly, scratches, badly exposed footage, leader, flash frames, and other physical properties of the raw materials of film. Independent filmmakers like Dziga Vertov and *Man with a Movie Camera* (1929) have long been fascinated with exploring the nature of their medium and destroying the illusion created by the narrative and aesthetic rules of the Hollywood Studio System. *The Projectionist* (1971) uses silent filmmaking as a motivation for the character's daydreams and fantasy life. *David Holzman's Diary* (1967), *Coming Apart* (1969), and *The Blair Witch Project* (1999) are pure self-referential films in which we are witnessing the making of the film we are watching. **Radley Metzger's** *The Lickerish Quartet* (1970) moves in and out of the reality of the film we are watching and the film the characters are watching that features them. *The Last Movie* (1971) is about the making of a film, but as it progresses, **Dennis Hopper** inserts "Scene Missing" titles that give the impression the film we are watching is the one the characters are filming. *Two-Lane Blacktop* (1971) ends with a self-referential moment when the frame that pictures the two main characters slowly freezes and burns up as a metaphor for their aimless lives driving on an existential mission. **Experimental** filmmakers often work in the self-referential mode. In Morgan Fisher's *Standard Gauge* (1984) the filmmaker shows and explains the industry standards by presenting examples of film stock tools available to filmmakers. Self-referential films are not to be confused with films that quote or reference scenes in other films. Self-reflective films utilize the text of other films for their own cinematic strategies.

Selznick, David O. Producer. *b.* David Oliver Selznick, May 10, 1902, Pittsburgh, Pennsylvania. *d.* June 22, 1965, Hollywood, California. David O. Selznick was an independent Hollywood producer whose contribution goes far beyond financing and administration. Selznick was a total filmmaker who meticulously planned every detail of production—he was the producer as auteur. David assisted his father Lewis, a film magnate, in film promotion and distribution. In 1923 Lewis declared bankruptcy. David made two **exploitation documentaries,** a boxing film and one featuring Rudolph Valentino judging a beauty contest in New York's Madison Square Garden. Selznick lost his profits in publishing ventures. In 1926 he was reluctantly hired by his father's former partner Louis B. Mayer as assistant story editor and the associate producer of MGM's **B-movies.** In 1927 Selznick moved over to Paramount, where he was an associate director. He was vice president in charge of production for the slumping RKO in 1931.

In 1933 Irving Thalberg became ill, so Mayer brought Selznick back to MGM as vice president and producer. In 1936, Selznick produced a string of highly successful films. He decided it was time to strike out as an independent so he could control his productions without studio interference. For years Selznick planned and wrote hundreds of his famous memos obsessing about and controlling the production that would propel him into history, an epic adaptation of the Margaret Mitchell novel *Gone With the Wind* (1939). The project went through fifteen screenwriters, with Selznick writing much of the final script, and three directors, with Selznick directing some scenes himself. In 1940 Selznick brought director Alfred Hitchcock from England to direct *Rebecca,* his first Hollywood film. The relationship, which included *Spellbound* (1945), *Notorious* (1946), and *The Paradine Case* (1947), was always an at-odds collaboration, with Selznick trying to make each film in his own vision, while Hitchcock had his own directorial plans.

In 1946 Selznick tried to top *Gone With the Wind* with the overheated *Duel in the Sun,* a sex-soaked western known in the industry as "Lust in the Dust," featuring Jennifer Jones, a young actress who became Selznick's latest obsession and then wife. In 1949 Selznick produced the Carol Reed classic *The Third Man* and featured Jones and Montgomery Clift in *Terminal Station* (1953), a coproduction directed by Vittorio De Sica.

Selznick died an unfulfilled man in spite of his tremendous accomplishments and the distinction of being an independent force in a company town. He never topped *Gone With the Wind,* a notion that became an impossible obsession for a man who defined what a producer could bring to a film. His name was not only above the title; it identified a movie as synonymous with excellence at any cost, fiscally and personally—it was always a David O. Selznick production.

BIBLIOGRAPHY

Behlmer, Rudy, ed. *Memo from David O. Selznick.* New York. Viking Press, 1972.

Thompson, David. *Showman: The Life of David O. Selznick.* New York: Knopf, 1992.

Robert Englund as the evil Freddy Krueger in *A Nightmare on Elm Street Part 2: Freddy's Revenge* (1985), one of independent filmmaking's most successful franchises. Courtesy of The Del Valle Archive

sequel. A film that picks up or continues the narrative and character development of the original film. Sequels are generated by box office interest. They are a financial benefit to the independent producer as there is a built-in audience for the sequel and support from financiers and **distributors**. The indie's dream is for a sequel to turn into another sequel and eventually a **franchise**. Sequels are rarely a satisfying viewing experience but offer the audience something familiar and an aura of anticipation as they wait for the next installment. By the late 1990s and into the twenty-first century, the industry has played it so safe that even modest hits (and some bombs) have been sequelized. *See also* franchises

sex, lies, and videotape. See Soderbergh, Steven

sexploitation films. At the beginning of the 1960s **exploitation films** took a turn from exploiting drugs, vice, troubled youth, and tame peekaboo

An example of 1930s poster art for sexploitation films. Courtesy of The Del Valle Archive

sex to a new, more daring film genre with copious nudity and a direct discussion of the intimacy, reality, and fantasy of sexual life. The new genre was dubbed sexploitation. The new films like *The Twilight Girls* (1961), *The Fourth Sex* (1962), and *Sexus* (1964), along with liberated European films, put the old exploiters in the backseat. The public, now in the Age of Aquarius, wanted more hedonistic films. **Radley Metzger** and **Russ Meyer** were the auteurs of sexploitation. *Carmen Baby* (1967) and *Lorna* (1964) gave the public what they were looking for—movies with plenty of nudity and sex. A new breed of producer came on the scene. David Friedman from Chicago became a sexploitation king. *The Adventures of Lucky Pierre* (1961), directed by The Wizard of Gore **Herschell Gordon Lewis**, was a high-stakes production costing $45,000. Bob Crese unleashed sadomasochism into the market with *Once Upon a Knight* (1961). Jack Harris made the first **adult film** in 3D. Sexploitation became violent and depraved: *Love Camp Seven* (1968), *The Touch of Her Flesh* (1967), *The Curse of Her Flesh* (1967), *The Kiss of Her Flesh* (1968), *Olga's Girls* (1964), *Olga's Massage Parlor* (1965), and *White Slaves of Chinatown* (1964). By the 1970s sexploitation made the next step into **hard-core.**

Shooting Gallery, The. Filmmaking collective formed in the early 1990s by Nick Gomez, producer Bob Gosse from the SUNY/Purchase film program, and Larry Meistrich, headquartered just blocks from the **Tribeca Film Center.** They produced Gomez's *Laws of Gravity* for $38,000 in cash in 1991. The Shooting Gallery grew into a media conglomerate, expanding into Los Angeles, Vancouver, Toronto, and Miami and into television music and digital production managed by Meistrich and Joseph J. Di Martino. The mission of The Shooting Gallery is to produce films with a singular voice, to maintain a creative community, and to enjoy the process of making motion pictures. Acquisitions and distribution products include *Sling Blade, Croupier, Henry Fool,* and *Niagara, Niagara.* In 1988 The Shooting Gallery proposed building the region's biggest sound stage complex in New Jersey. That deal fell through, and they opened an office and postproduction facility for local filmmakers in New York's West Village. In 2000 Itemus, an Internet company, offered to buy 80 percent of The Shooting Gallery, but by March 2001 they were over $60 million in debt and struggling to survive.

shooting ratio. The total amount of footage exposed for a project compared to the total footage of the completed film. The shooting ratio of 10:1 means ten feet of film were exposed for each foot of film in the final cut. Shooting ratios in **documentaries** run as high as 40:1 to 100:1 or better. Big-budget films consistently run up high ratios, especially when multiple cameras are utilized. Independent filmmakers shoot at low shooting ratios, 5:1, 3:1, or less depending, on budgetary restrictions.

short ends. On big-budget production if there is not enough negative left in the camera to complete a take, the roll is removed and the remainder, called short ends, is often given or sold to indie filmmakers who save money by not paying premium prices for raw stock. On high-budget films raw stock and developing costs are minimal compared to actor salaries, union crew wages, location, and production costs. For the independent filmmaker, raw stock and lab costs are a prime and daunting budget item. Utilizing short ends and **dated film stock** are just some of the strategies employed by the indie who must be resourceful to solve problems the big leagues just throw money at.

Siegel, Don. Director. *b.* October 26, 1912, Chicago, Illinois. *d.* April 20, 1991, Nipoma, California. *ed.* Cambridge University in England. Siegel's work as a low-budget **B-movie** director had an enormous influence on the themes, visual style, production methods, and aesthetics of the contemporary independent film. In 1933 Siegel established himself in the editorial department, first as a film librarian, then editor, then head of the insert department, which led Siegel to organize the first montage department at Warner Bros. In the 1940s he directed the Oscar-winning shorts *Star in the Night* (1945) and *Hitler Lives?* (1945) Siegel made his feature debut with *The Verdict* in 1946, and in 1956 directed the classic *Invasion of the Body Snatchers.* Siegel made an effective sci-fi thriller about aliens turning humans into pods as a metaphor for a society deadened to human emotion and compassion. Thematically Siegel was attracted to social outcasts and loners, characters who would develop into the antiheroes of 1970s cinema.

He became a crime specialist with *Crime in the Streets* (1956), *Baby Face Nelson* (1957), *The Lineup* (1958), and *The Killers* (1964). Siegel's extensive editing background taught him to work in a professional and economical manner, shooting just what he needed without unnecessary coverage, knowing how scenes would go together in the cutting room. His camera style was direct and unpretentious and told the story without artifice.

Siegel was a mentor to two important filmmakers: Sam Peckinpah was Siegel's assistant and learned the craft of directing from watching his padrone. In 1968 Siegel directed **Clint Eastwood** in *Coogan's Bluff,* and the pair began a long association. Siegel was directly responsible for preparing and launching Eastwood's long and illustrious career as a low-budget independent filmmaker. Their most accomplished collaboration was the landmark *Dirty Harry* (1971), a right-wing political statement encouraging the police to take the law into their own hands.

Siegel directed almost forty features in as many years. Among them are *Riot in Cell Block 11* (1954), *Madigan* (1968), *Two Mules for Sister Sara* (1969), *The Beguiled* (1971), *Charley Varrick* (1973), *The Shootist* (1976), and *Escape from Alcatraz* (1979). Throughout his career Siegel entertained au-

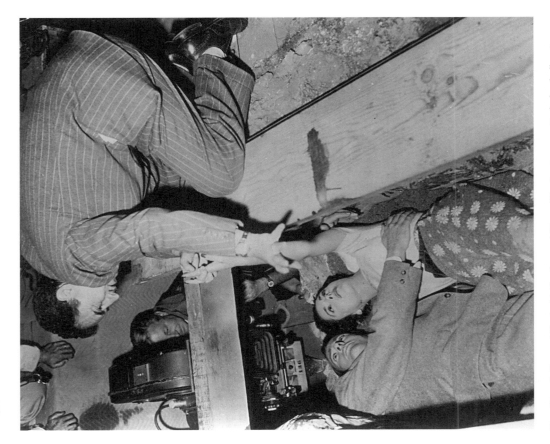

Don Siegel directed Kevin McCarthy and Dana Wynter in a particularly challenging camera set-up from *Invasion of the Body Snatchers* (1956). Courtesy of *The Del Valle Archive*

diences and was ignored by the American press and revered by the French. Siegel's tough-minded explorations into crime and the underworld have impacted on every filmmaker who followed the outer edges of society, an area independent filmmaking continues to explore. *See also* Eastwood, Clint

Silver, Joan Micklin. Director, screenwriter. *b.* May 24, 1935, Omaha, Nebraska. *ed.* Sarah Lawrence. Joan Micklin Silver is best known for her debut feature *Hester Street* (1975). Silver wrote and directed this ethnic story of Old World Jewish traditionalism at odds with the new mores of Manhattan's Lower East Side at the turn of the century. She and her real estate developer husband **Raphael D. Silver** founded Midwest Films, which produced and distributed the film on a $320,000 budget. Silver was considered one of several New York–based independent feminist directors to emerge at an active point in the woman's movement.

Her follow-up project, *Between the Lines* (1977), a film about an underground newspaper (Silver worked for the *Village Voice* for a time), is notable for an ensemble cast with such impressive up and comers as John Heard, Lindsay Crouse, Jeff Goldblum, Jill Eikenberry, Bruno Kirby, Stephen Collins, Michael J. Pollard, Lane Smith, Joe Morton, and Marilu Henner. In 1979 Silver turned to Hollywood in an ill-fated collaboration with **United Artists** to direct Ann Beattie's novel *Chilly Scenes of Winter* with John Heard and Mary Beth Hurt. Silver lost control of the project that underwent a title change (released as *Head Over Heels*) and reworked ending. Silver's output was minimal for most of the 1980s, but in 1988 she returned to her roots with *Crossing Delancey*, a whimsical comedy about Jewish matchmaking that starred Amy Irving. In 1999 Joan Micklin Silver directed *A Fish in the Bathtub* starring Jerry Stiller and Anne Meara and the television movie *Invisible Child Dirt. Charms for the Easy Life* (2001) was another television film directed by Silver. *See also* Silver, Marisa; Silver, Raphael D.

Kaminksy, Stuart M. *Don Siegel: Director*. New York: Curtis Books, 1974.

Siegel, Don. *A Siegel Film: An Autobiography*. London: Faber and Faber, 1993.

Silver, Marisa. Director. *b.* April 23, 1960, Cleveland, Ohio. *ed.* Harvard University. The daughter of **Raphael D. Silver** and **Joan Micklin Silver** may be the most talented director in the family. In 1982 Marisa Silver codirected a short documentary with nonfiction veteran **Richard Leacock**. *Old Enough* (1984), her directorial debut, was an insightful and sensitive story of two adolescent girls from diverse social classes who are committed to growing their friendship despite the travails and pressures against them. She returned with a strong sophomore effort *Permanent Record* (1988), in which high school students struggle with the suicide of one of their classmates. There are fine performances by Keanu Reeves, Alan Boyce, Michelle Meyrink, and an ensemble of talented young actors. *Vital Signs* (1990) starred Adrian Pasdar, Diane Lane, Jimmy Smits, Laura San Giacomo, and William Devane. The film followed third-year medical students through their rites of passage. *He Said, She Said* (1991) was codirected with Ken Kwapis and featured Kevin Bacon, Elizabeth Perkins, Sharon Stone, Nathan Lane, and Anthony LaPaglia. The comedy gimmick here is two journalists who are dissolving their relationship and turn their rival point/counterpoint columns into a popular TV attraction. Kwapis directed from Bacon's point of view and Silver from Perkins's POV. In 1992 Marisa Silver directed the television movie *Indecency*.

Silver, Raphael D. Producer, director, screenwriter. The husband of **Joan Micklin Silver** and father of **Marisa Silver**, both film directors. Before Silver made his own directorial debut he personally raised $370,000 for Joan's *Hester Street* (1975), which played the Cannes Film Festival, was critically lauded, and grossed $5 million. Silver produced his wife's second feature *Between the Lines* (1977), which they self-distributed. In 1978 Silver directed *On the Yard*, and Joan returned the favor and produced his prison drama. The film starred John Heard, Thomas G. Waites, Mike Kellin, Richard Bright, Joe Grifasi, and Lane Smith. Unfortunately the narrative reworked a shopworn prison genre, and the film didn't find an audience. Silver's second feature *A Walk on the Moon* (1987) did no better. The independent film starred Kevin Anderson, Terry Kinney, and Laila Robins. In 1999 Silver coproduced and cowrote Joan's *A Fish in the Bathtub*, a comedy about long-term relationships, with Anne Meara and Jerry Stiller.

Simens, Dov S-S. Filmmaker, educator. *ed.* Muhlenbey College. Founder of the Hollywood Film Institute (HFI), Dov S-S Simens created the two-day film school touted by **Quentin Tarantino** and **Spike Lee** and a multitude of aspiring filmmakers who have attended his brusque but highly practical seminars. Simens, the self-appointed guru of **guerrilla filmmaking**, presents a patented philosophy he calls "the 38 steps of filmmaking," which tracks the process from production to distribution, identifying the thirty-eight bank checks necessary to write when making a feature film. Simens, who is impatient with disruptions about style and aesthetics, teaches that the cost involved in making a feature film reveals the process. USC and NYU have little to worry about. This radical approach to film production works, but it is not for the faint-hearted.

Simens, who personally conducts the two-day film school across the country, is tough on hecklers or anyone with a question that falls outside his step-by-step instructions. Many enjoy his tough military approach to tearing down the paying participants, only to rebuild them in his own image by the end of the second day. It should come as little surprise that Simens is a former Green Beret who served in Vietnam in 1968.

After his tour, Simens opened a successful bookstore in Carmel, California. After twelve years Simens sold the store in 1981 and headed to Los Angeles for a career in movies. With no formal training or experience Simens made his own opportunities to produce music videos and talk shows by making a 35mm featurette, *The Final Hour*, for only $12,500. His inspiration to teach others how to survive the Hollywood system arrived when one of his unsold screenplays appeared on a major cable network. Simens took on the giant, sued, and won. Shortly after, the HFI was hatched.

Over the years Simens has expanded his operation by creating an audio version of the school; additional specialized courses in screenwriting, directing, and digital filmmaking; a Web site; and his $5.5. million "The Biz"—a "Home Depot" complete resource for filmmakers. Simens has created an indie empire by constantly growling at students, "Shut Up and Shoot," but he is a likable curmudgeon who's made himself rich by selling the dream that he can build anyone into an indie filmmaker within forty-eight hours. Few complain and many have prospered, realizing the Dov S-S Simens method isn't an end-all to film education, but it's a helluva kick-start.

Sinofsky, Bruce. *See* Berlinger, Joe

Sitney, P. Adams. Theorist, historian. Princeton University. Sitney is a pioneer academic authority on **avant-garde** and **experimental films**. He was the director of library and publications at **Anthology Film Archives**, closely associated with **Jonas Mekas** and the growth of the **underground** film documented in his watershed study *Visionary Film: The American Avant-Garde 1943–1978*. In writing the history of the avant-garde movement, Sitney developed the critical terms the *trance film*, the *mythopoetic film*, and the *participatory film* and wrote extensively on **structural** film to chart the development of almost forty years of work. Sitney is widely recognized as a scholar in the field. He is the editor of *Film Culture Reader* and *Modernist Montage: The Obscurity of Vision in Cinema and Literature*. Sitney performed in Adolfas Mekas's *The Double-Barrelled Detective Story* (1965) and has had both a professional and personal involvement with many experimental filmmakers. *See also* Mekas, Jonas

BIBLIOGRAPHY

Sitney, P. Adams. *Visionary Film: The American Avant-Garde 1943–1978*. Oxford: Oxford University Press, 1979.

Sitney, P. Adams, ed. *Film Culture Reader*. New York: Cooper Square Press, reprint, 2000 (first published in 1970).

———. *Modernist Montage: The Obscurity of Vision in Cinema and Literature*. New York: Columbia University Press. Reprint edition, 1992.

16mm filmmaking. The 35mm film gauge has been associated with the theatrical distribution of motion pictures since the Classical Hollywood Studio System. The cost and limited access to equipment put 35mm filmmaking out of reach to industry outsiders. The 16mm gauge is narrower, has half the sprockets, is less expensive, and is within the grasp of independent filmmakers. This gauge made an independent cinema possible. Cameras, projectors, and postproduction equipment used with 16mm gauge were created and manufactured for amateur, semiprofessional, and nontheatrical use. Sixteen millimeter became the format of choice for **avant-garde** and **experimental** filmmakers, film students, independent filmmakers, and home users. When the new gauge arrived it was the first opportunity for artists, still photographers, writers, musicians, and other cinematic dreamers to make their own movies, generally using a **Bolex** or a Bell and Howell camera.

16mm to 35mm blow-up. A 16mm or Super 16mm negative can be blown up, enlarged to 35mm. Some independent filmmakers shoot in **16mm** for budgetary reasons, and when the project is complete, they have the 16mm negative blown up to 35mm for theatrical release. The cost of a blow-up is often part of a distribution deal, with the **distributor** paying for the optical laboratory work. In terms of quality, the blow-up will be increased in grain and decreased in sharpness and detail. Composition and framing are also an issue. Filmmakers intending to shoot 16mm for an eventual 35mm blow-up should consult their lab before shooting to get the technical specifications. Super 16mm is recommended as a format for best results in converting to 35mm because its larger frame size is closer in composition elements to the 35mm aspect ratio.

Slacker. *See* Linklater, Richard

Slamdance Film Festival. Founded in 1994 when filmmakers Shane Kuhn, Dan Mirvish, and Jon Fitzgerald all had films declined by **Sundance.** They joined with other indies they met at the Independent Feature Film Market and held Slamdance '95: Anarchy in Utah—the first annual Guerrilla International Film Festival held in Park City, Utah. In 1996 they received 450 submissions and held the alternative festival at the Yarrow Hotel, which was hosted by Matthew Modine and held tributes to **Robert Altman** and **Roger Corman.** In 1997 there were 1,000 submissions, and Slamdance was relocated to the Treasure Mountain Inn on Main Street in Park City. **Steven Soderbergh's** *Schizopolis* (1996) was screened, and **John Pierson's Independent Film Channel** cable program *Split Screen* was premiered. Slamdance 1998 received 1,300 submissions for forty-one slots, and Sparky, the happy dog statuette was unveiled and awarded to Slamdance winners. Slamdance continues on as a viable alternative to Sundance. In 2000, *Dolphins* won the audience Award for Best Feature and *The Target Shoots First* won both the Best Documentary and Best Editing Awards. In 2002, **Penelope Spheeris** was one of the jurors in a year that witnessed its largest number of submissions from women filmmakers. The Special Grand Jury Honor went to *Stone Reader*, a 153 minute documentary about the author of an acclaimed first novel who disappeared from public view. The Jury Prize for Best Feature was given to *The Holy Land* a film that concerns a rabbinical student who travels to Israel for a spiritual experience but falls in love with a prostitute. *See also* No-Dance Film Festival; Slamdunk Film Festival; Sundance Institute

Slamdunk Film Festival. Founded alongside Robert Redford's Park City, Utah, Festival as an alternate independent film venue. Slamdunk's original venue in 1998 was at the Park City Elks Lodge, a block away from **Sundance**'s Egyptian Theater. Appropriately they opened with **Nick Broomfield**'s *Kurt & Courtney* (1998), which was dropped by Sundance after Courtney Love threatened legal action. In May 1998 Slamdunk hosted screenings at the College International de Cannes as an alternative for American indies overlooked by the established Cannes Film Festival. In 1999, Slamdunk relocated to the Harry O's nightclub on Park City's main street. Speakers included Doug Liman and **Allison Anders.** In September 1999, Slamdunk held screenings alongside the Toronto Film Festival. In 2000 they appeared below Harry O's in Utah and returned to Cannes, this time atop the Noga Hilton. The ever-changing venues and commitment to outlaw films like *Zachariah Farted* (1998) and the short *Dog Dance 2000* (2000) make Slamdunk a film festival independent in all phases of the definition. *See also* No-Dance Film Festival; Slumdance Film Festival; Sundance Institute

slasher film. Bloody horror film subgenre often involving the mutilation and killing of women. Slasher films include *Friday the 13th* (1980), *Halloween* (1978), *A Nightmare on Elm Street* (1984) and *I Know What You Did Last Summer* (1997). Slasher films became such a popular genre that the above all inspired **sequels.** All with the exception of *I Know What You Did Last Summer* (give it time), became successful **franchises.**

Sling Blade. A 1996 independent film partly responsible for general audience acceptance of indies. Billy Bob Thornton was an actor looking to get out of stereotypical roles in small films. He wrote a short film, *Some Call It a Sling Blade*, directed by **George Hickenlooper,** in which he played Karl Childers, a man who was in a mental institution for killing his mother with a machete. Thornton expanded the story into a feature, raised the money, and cast the project with actor friends and pals from his native Arkansas, where he directed the film for $1.2 million. **Miramax** bought *Sling Blade* for the sum of $10 million. The film earned respectable reviews and a large audience base, and Thornton received two Oscar nominations for Best Actor and Best Adapted screenplay, winning the latter. *Sling Blade* also won the Independent Spirit Award for best first feature.

The long form developed the character of Karl, who had spent twenty-five of his thirty-seven years in an institution for his mother's murder. He is released and makes a living repairing lawnmowers. He befriends a boy, his mom, and her gay coworker, played by John Ritter. Country performer Dwight Yoakam plays the mother's violent boyfriend to the hilt. The volatile combination of personalities leads to consequences. Robert Duvall puts in a cameo, and J.T. Walsh is chilling as he reprises his role as a sexually obsessed inmate. As a director Thornton is strong on story, acting, and depth of character. Visually, the film is shot in long takes, often in medium shot, and is undramatically paced. *Sling Blade* captured audiences with its honesty. *Sling Blade's* success resides in its real story told without Hollywooden conventions—just the drama of humanity.

Slumdance Film Festival. Slumdance was created in 1997 as an alternative to the other Park City, Utah, Film Festival, Robert Redford's **Sundance.** The more independent and rebellious filmmakers and festival goers who attended the yearly U.S. film event felt that Sundance was becoming too much like the annual Hollywood Oscar ritual. Redford created the Sundance Institute and film festival as a forum to celebrate low-budget independently made films that didn't feature big stars and embraced content the big boys were afraid of. In time the restless spirit of cutting-edge filmmakers felt Sundance had become too chic, too trendy, where cell-phoned studio execs panted over the next flavor of the month indie and were so big that they rejected films that deserved a venue.

Slumdance was founded in a former Mrs. Fields cookie factory. The filmmakers could squat in a large loft with a fully equipped kitchen, so they could dish their own meals. The walls of Slumdance were painted in outrageous colors, the décor thrift shop au courant; there were hammocks and lawn chairs to hang out on, a dance floor with a DJ spinning, and video monitors running nonstop.

Slumdance programmed films by hard-core indies who weren't interested in being discovered—moviemakers more representative of the grassroot student, amateur, and nontraditional cinema working outside the organized commercial and independent film industry. The awards given at Slumdance include The Gold Rat and The **Miramax** Shelf Award. Celebrities who attend Slumdance include Roger Ebert, who won a "Rat" of his own, and the iconoclast **John Waters.**

After the 1997 event there wasn't another Slamdance for three and a half years. The organizers claimed they were unmotivated vagrants who were too exhausted with all the legwork until June 2000, when they were back, delighting those tired of Armani outfits, bottled water, and those damn wireless communication devices. *See also* No-dance Film Festival; Slamdunk Film Festival; Sundance Institute

Smith, Jack. Filmmaker. *b.* November 14, 1932, Columbus, Ohio. *d.* September 25, 1989, Manhattan, New York, of AIDS. Jack Smith was a performance artist before the term was coined. As an **experimental** filmmaker he explored sexuality considered deviant and celebrated the culture of homosexuality in every facet. Smith was not a politico or a gay activist, but he became a beacon for homosexual freedom. His 1963 film *Flaming Creatures* is a landmark **avant-garde** film that caused a censorship and legal firestorm. Its aesthetic led to the trash cinema movement of **Andy Warhol**, the **Kuchar brothers** and **John Waters**. Smith loved Hollywood studio cinema and incorporated its imagery and icons into his own outrageously decadent state of consciousness. Drugs, magic, and a mannered madness inspired his outlandish dress and deranged behavior.

Nurtured on Forty-second Street double bills, Smith began to make independent films in the 1950s. *Scotch Tape* (1962) was intended as a segment for **Ken Jacobs**'s still unfinished underground opus *Star Spangled to Death*, an epic compilation of found footage intercut with interludes of Smith cavorting, clowning, and creating the prehistory of performance art. Jacobs brought the costumed Smith and two other performers to a demolished apartment building at the site where Lincoln Center now resides. Smith borrowed Jacobs's **16mm** camera and filmed the whacked-out and colorful characters dancing among rusted cables, cracked concrete slabs, and green plastic flowers. Editing in the camera, Smith filmed shots where the decrepit environment was more prominent than the people. When the film returned from the lab, Smith discovered a dirty piece of cellophane tape had been embedded in the camera gate, and its image was printed in the upper right of every frame. Pleased with this aesthetic accident, Smith celebrated it in the title, *Scotch Tape*. Theorists found that the tape's fixed position provided a formal counterbalance to the shot changes and identified *Scotch Tape* as an early example of **structural filmmaking.**

It was *Flaming Creatures* that propelled Smith to independent film superstar status. The genesis of the infamous film was a Scheherazade party on the rooftop of the Windsor, a Lower East Side movie theater. The festivities lasted for seven consecutive weekends. Attired in drag, Smith and his friends staged scenes of an imaginary transvestite Roman orgy replete with limp penises, bare breasts, and a Marilyn Monroe vampire. The soundtrack accompaniment was 78 rpm recordings of German tango bands, Latin American pop songs, a 1930s rumba, mock radio commercials, Bela Bartok, Kitty Wells, a Cuban bolero, the Everly Brothers, "Be-Bop-alula," and the title music to a 1940s Japanese movie.

With *Flaming Creatures* Smith imposed a radical sexual politic on American film otherwise governed by puritanical codes and suppressed by censors. The independent release of *Flaming Creatures* was the **underground** grand scandal of the 1960s. Theaters that screened the film in New York, Austin, Ann Arbor, and Toronto were raided; prints were seized by the New York Police Department and the U.S. Customs Department. The film was presented to the U.S. Congress as an example of deviant culture.

The forty-five-minute black-and-white 16mm film was photographed by a handheld camera on various stolen and expired film stocks and was enhanced by overexposure that gave it a dreamlike faded quality. Smith never established a physical grounding for his fantasy—there is no sense of perspective or place. *Flaming Creatures* has no traditional narrative thread; scenes are so long they seem never to end. The Flaming Creatures all appear as bored androgynous variations of social icons: a sailor, a classically draped nude, a señorita, and a dowager. These characters were dubbed as superstars by Smith—the phrase and concept first applied to underground film actors and then to mainstream movie stars.

Flaming Creatures played every hour at the Gramercy Arts Theater in New York from 1963 to 1964. Harassment and legal action eventually wore Smith down, and he pulled the film from circulation. There was an obscenity trial held at New York Criminal Court. **Jonas Mekas** was a devout defender of Smith's film. Witnesses included documentarian **Willard Van Dyke**, film historian Herman G. Weinberg, **critic** Susan Sontag, filmmaker **Shirley Clarke,** and beat poet Allen Ginsberg. The defense of the film became a debate on the definition, importance, and function of art. *Flaming Creatures* was found to be legally obscene and remains in that status. It is the only American avant-garde film to be described in the *Congressional Record.*

Flaming Creatures was followed by *Normal Love* (1963), photographed in full living color. The film stars Mario Montez dressed in mermaid drag, a tribute to Smith's obsession with actress Maria Montez, an exotic Hollywood actress who was known as the queen of Technicolor for her many roles in Arabian Nights adventures. *Normal Love* is set in a Turkish environ. A black muscular man in hot pink tights pushes a white woman wearing a taffeta flower on a swing. Copulation abounds as the film quotes both Botticelli's *The Birth of Venus* and Universal horror films. Anonymous and androgynous limbs are piled together in a bargain basement poetic fantasy generated by the unreality of Hollywood yarns.

By 1970 Smith grew frustrated with filmmaking, censorship, and constant attack from community watchdogs. He stopped making films and reinvented himself as an outrageous performance artist. Smith was angry, funny, irreverent, disreputable, and a true American original. His work in performance and film grew out of his love of Hollywood culture filtered through his sexual proclivities and the theater of the absurd.

BIBLIOGRAPHY

Leffingwell, Edward, and Carole Kismaric, eds. *Jack Smith: Flaming Creatures: His Amazing Life and Times*. London: Serpent's Tail, 1997.

Sontag, Susan. "Jack Smith's *Flaming Creatures*." In *Against Interpretation*. New York: Dell, 1964. Essay originally appeared in 1964 in *The Nation*.

Smith, Kevin. Director, producer, writer, actor. *b.* August 2, 1970, Red Bank, New Jersey. When Kevin Smith's 1994 debut film *Clerks* was released, a younger teenaged audience not yet exposed to independent film experienced a freewheeling, no-holds-barred production style they embraced as their own. In this respect, Smith did more than any director before him to lure young people into the indie world. Smith dropped out of The New School for Social Research's creative writing program when school administrators called his parents because he was dropping water balloons from his dorm window. Smith saw an ad for the Vancouver Film School and immediately enrolled, dropping out four months later to move to Leonardo, New Jersey, where he took a job at a local convenience store.

Smith saw **Richard Linklater**'s seminal independent film *Slacker* (1991) and was motivated to make his own movie. He called his former Vancouver classmate Scott Mosier, and they agreed to make a film. The story behind *Clerks* is now legendary. Money for the film came from Smith's unused college fund and from the sale of his prized comic book collection; Mosier's parents also contributed. Using the convenience store where he was working as the principal location, *Clerks* was shot after hours in twenty-one nights. All told, the film's budget came to $27,575. Following a sometimes exciting, mostly boring day in the life of a convenience store clerk, what the film lacks in plot it makes up for in clever, pop culture–influenced dialogue.

Smith debuted *Clerks* at the **Independent Feature Project** in New York City, where it created enough buzz to secure entry into **Sundance.** *Clerks* became the hit of the festival, earning Smith a contract with Creative Artists Agency (CAA) and a distribution deal with **Miramax.** The MPAA slapped the film with the dreaded NC-17 for a raunchy bit of dialogue, but the rating was changed to R when attorney Allen Dershowitz intervened. The film eventually grossed more than $1 million and became the most successful film of 1994 relative to its cost. Lines from the film became catchphrases, and two of the film's characters, Jay and Silent Bob (the latter played by Smith), became cult heroes.

Following *Clerks'* immense success, Smith was hit with one of the more obvious cases of the sophomore jinx. His second film, *Mallrats* (1995), featured many of the same actors (some in their roles from *Clerks*) as well as then-unknown Ben Affleck and a similar lack of emphasis on plot; but the film bombed. Funded by Gramercy Pictures for $5.8 million, *Mallrats* struggled at the box office as fans and **critics** turned against Smith. The film's reception was so vicious that Smith offered a mock apology at the 1995 Independent Spirit Awards.

After the big-budget failure of *Mallrats*, Smith scaled back his next film, *Chasing Amy* (1997), to just $250,000. The film completed his "New Jersey trilogy" and featured then-girlfriend Joey Lauren Adams, Ben Lee, and Ben Affleck in a dramedy that examines sex and relationships in the late 1990s. It was a critical success and reestablished Smith. As with *Clerks*, *Chasing Amy* was praised for its dialogue and characterizations.

Dogma was released in 1999 and starred Matt Damon, Ben Affleck, Linda Fiorentino, Alan Rickman, Salma Hayek, Chris Rock, Alanis Morissette, Bud Cort, and George Carlin in a comic allegory about a battle between outcast angels, God and the Devil in contemporary America. *Dogma's* approach to its religious theme caused controversy among conservative groups, and the uproar harmed the perceptive film's chance to deliver its wise message about Catholic spirituality.

Jay and Silent Bob Strike Back (2001) is a new adventure for the boys in which they take on Hollywood. In 2002 Kevin Smith wrote and was the voice of Silent Bob for the animated film *Clerks: Sell Out*. He is the writer, producer, and director of *Fletch Won*, and the writer and director of *Jersey Girl* (both 2003). Smith's unique film sensibility sets him apart from most other independent directors of his age, and while some have questioned his ability as a director, praise for his writing is universal.

Smithereens. *See* Seidelman, Susan

Smoke Signals. Billed as the first film produced, written, and directed by a Native American, *Smoke Signals* opened with a splash at **Sundance** in 1998, where it won both the Filmmaker's Trophy and the Audience Award. Developed at the 1995 Sundance Lab, it is based on a short story in *The Lone Ranger and Tonto Fistfight in Heaven* by Native American author Sherman Alexie and was directed by Chris Eyre. *Smoke Signals* is a **road movie** that follows the journey of a stoic young Native American traveling cross-country with his nerdy pal to retrieve his father's ashes. *Smoke Signals* is notable for eschewing Native American stereotypes and instead dealing with modern Native American problems without the usual baggage. It was a crowd-pleasing hit, eventually grossing nearly $7 million.

snuff films. Aka death films. When the horrors of the Tate/La Bianca murders were revealed in the late 1960s, a dark, unhealthy curiosity developed about the Charles Manson family. Rumors surfaced that the devilish cult had made actual death films—films depicting an actual murder. In 1976 *Snuff* was released, a film that specifically claimed to have captured an actual murder on film. *Snuff* was rated X for violence and sparked protests, wild speculation, investigation, yards of publicity, and cries for a ban. The violence engineered by *Snuff* delighted the Times Square street crowd and had decent folk claiming it was pornography, not of a sexual nature but in pure murderous violence.

Whether *Snuff* was real or not, another Pandora's box of popular culture had been opened. Many of the ***Mondo*** films proclaimed to include real death and murder as well as the infamous Faces of Death home video series. *The Killing of America* (1981) is a **documentary** exploiting the murders of JFK and Martin Luther King and presents archival footage of Charles Whitman, who killed sixteen people from a Texas clock tower. *True Gore* (1987) includes suicides, tortures, and faked cruelty rit-

Evan Adams and Adam Beach in *Smoke Signals* (1998), directed by Chris Eyre. Kobol Collection/Duchin, Courtnay/Miramax

uals. *Death Scenes* (1989) presents images of death from a Los Angeles police officer's collection of early-twentieth-century mayhem. *Executions* (1995) is what it says it is. *Family Movies*, aka *Manson Family Movies* (1984), is an **8mm** film that recreates the events that led to the murders that may have started the cycle described as the devil's documentary, Satan's **sexploitation**, and film noir from hell.

BIBLIOGRAPHY

Kerekes, David, and David Slater. *Killing for Culture: An Illustrated History of Death Films from Mondo to Snuff.* London: Creation Books, 1994.

Society of Independent Motion Picture Producers, The. A secretly formed organization founded by **Charles Chaplin, Walt Disney, Samuel Goldwyn,** Alexander Korda, Mary Pickford, **David O. Selznick,** Walter Wanger, and Orson Welles in the early 1940s to bring down the power of the Hollywood Studio System. It had victories in antitrust action against the powerful moguls, but in 1958 the group, lacking funds, came under the control of the Walt Disney Studio.

BIBLIOGRAPHY

Aberdeen, J.A. *Hollywood Renegades: The Society of Independent Motion Picture Producers.* Los Angeles, CA: Cobblestone Entertainment, 2000.

Soderbergh, Steven. Director, producer, screenwriter, cinematographer, editor. *b.* January 14, 1963, Atlanta, Georgia. At fifteen, Steven Soderbergh took an animation course at the College of Education at Louisiana State University where his father was a professor and dean and made **16mm** shorts including *Janitor.* After high school Soderbergh worked as a film editor in Hollywood. In 1986 the rock band Yes hired Soderbergh to create a feature-length concert film, which won a Grammy nomination for the *9012 Live* video.

Next Soderbergh made the short *Winston,* later expanded into his first feature, *sex, lies, and videotape* (1989), a benchmark film that is generally accepted as the genesis of the contemporary independent film movement. The lauded film won the Palme d'Or at Cannes, the Independent Spirit Award for best director, and an Oscar nomination for best original screenplay. James Spader, Andie MacDowell, Peter Gallagher, and Laura San Giacomo star in the story of a lawyer visited by a college friend who has an impact on the personal life of everyone he meets. The low-budget project enticed audiences who were tired of formulaic movies and slick production methods that manipulated their emotions. They related to the subtle presentation of real life achieved by Soderbergh. *Sex, lies, and videotape* started a revolution. It inspired indie filmmakers, and the money barons took notice of the box office receipts for the low-budget film.

Soderbergh's *Kafka* (1991) created great expectations. The Lem Dobbs screenplay had bounced around Hollywood for years, and some insiders considered it one of the most inventive screenplays in years. The fictional story features insurance clerk Franz Kafka, played by Jeremy Irons, and was shot on location in Prague. The period film takes place in 1919 and weaves several Kafka stories into a strange Kafkaesque narrative. The visual design is impressive, but Soderbergh fell into the same trap as Orson Welles with his adaptation of *The Trial* (1963). Dutch angles and a surreal atmosphere did not translate to Kafka's paranoia and strangeness—it was the ordinariness that filled the environment with dread. The film failed to find an audience.

King of the Hill (1993) was Soderbergh's adaptation of the A.E. Hotchner memoir that was critically acclaimed for its vivid recreation of the depression era. *Underneath* (1994) is a remake of the film noir classic *Criss Cross* (1949) that did little to recapture Soderbergh's initial fame as the independent film messiah. *Gray's Anatomy* (1996) is a cinematic record of Spaulding Gray's fiftieth birthday monologue. *Schizopolis* (1996) is a satire of society done up in classic **underground** film style. Soderbergh wrote, directed, and starred in the film that reclaimed his independence but was not widely seen.

Then everything changed for Steven Soderbergh. *Out of Sight* (1998) was a box office smash, *The Limey* (1999) performed respectably, and the year 2000 brought mainstream success. *Erin Brockovich* was a blockbuster for which Julia Roberts won her first Oscar and Soderbergh won the statuette for best director of *Traffic*. In 2001 Soderbergh prepared to remake the Rat Pack classic *Ocean's Eleven*.

In 2001 Steven Soderberg was the executive producer of the documentary *Who Is Bernie Tapie*. In 2002 Soderberg was the executive producer of *Confessions of a Dangerous Mind* directed by George Clooney, screenwriter director and director of photography on *Insomnia*, director and director of photography on *Full Frontal* and writer, director of *Solaris* based on the Stanislaw Lem novel originally adapted for the screen by Andrei Tarkovsky in 1971. Soderberg is the executive producer for *Tishmingo Blues* directed by Don Cheedle, the director of *The Informant* (both 2003).

Soderbergh has become a formidable mainstream director with a cutting-edge, hands-on approach. He often shoots and edits on his films. Independent film owes Soderbergh a debt for rekindling the indie flame. *Sex, lies, and videotape* made independent film fashionable, profitable, and acceptable.

soft-core films. Motion pictures that contain nudity, often more female than male, and simulated sex but no explicit acts. Soft-core films were popularized in the 1950s and 1960s with **nudie cuties,** films that featured topless females in naughty but innocent situations. During the 1980s and 1990s cable television became a venue for soft-core product as well as the Playboy Channel and other adult services. Often **hard-core films** are reedited to soft-core status to meet community standards and a double market. **Zalman King** has made a personal industry out of marketing soft-core films, a tamer form of **adult films** that reach a wider audience. Nudity and simulated sex scenes in narrative fiction films do not qualify as soft-core films, which, like their more explicit hard-core relation, have codified narrative structures and predictable and required sex scenes at predetermined intervals. *See also* adult film industry; hard-core films; nudie cuties; porno chic; sexploitation

Solondz, Todd. Director, screenwriter. *b.* October 15, 1959, Newark, New Jersey. *ed.* New York University. Solondz made award-winning short films while a student at NYU that gave him the opportunity to star and direct in his first feature *Fear, Anxiety & Depression* (1989), a neurotic New York comedy also featuring Stanley Tucci. The film released by **Samuel Goldwyn** was written six years earlier and was inspired by the television series *The Wonder Years* more than real experience. The film bombed at the box office and went largely unseen. The failure drove Solondz away from the movies for six years—a period when he taught English to Russian immigrants.

In 1989, Solondz wrote a screenplay first named *Faggots and Retards*, then *The Middle Child*, then retitled *Welcome to the Dollhouse* (1996). Producers Ted Skillman and Dan Partland raised $800,000 to put the project into production. The film won at **Sundance** and became an art house hit. It is a dead-on portrayal of the pain of puberty and features a remarkably nuanced performance by Heather Matarazzo as a seventh grader tortured by her classmates and treated with indifference by her suburban family. Solondz directed with vision, style, and a brutally honest voice.

His next film, *Happiness* (1998), caused a stir with its nonjudgmental point of view toward one of society's darkest subjects—pedophilia. The story centers on an unhappy family and others who have a range of personal demons. Solondz uses humor to see the truth behind the characters. The narrative is realistic, so it makes the viewer feel simultaneously revolted, compassionate, and uncomfortable. *Happiness* was self-released by **Good Machine** when October films was pressured into not distributing the controversial film by their parent Universal.

Storytelling (2001) is structured in two parts: In "Fiction," a college student submits to sexual advances from her African American writing teacher in the name of political correctness. "Non Fiction" attacks **exploitative** independent films with the story of a hack **documentary** filmmaker who is making a film about an insipid New Jersey teenager.

Solondz has the capacity to create uneasiness with his warts-and-all understanding of life, a wicked sense of humor, and his willingness to present human portraits without flinching.

Spheeris, Penelope. Director, screenwriter. *b.* December 2, 1945, New Orleans, Louisiana. *ed.* UCLA. After producing short films for Albert Brooks in the early seasons of *Saturday Night Live* (SNL), Penelope Spheeris moved on with the comedian to produce his first theatrical feature *Real Life* (1979). Spheeris directed early music videos for Fleetwood Mac, Ry Cooder, The Funkadelics, and other acts for her own independent film company Rock & Reel. Spheeris made her career-defining directorial feature debut with *The Decline of Western Civilization* (1981), a **documentary** about the L.A. Punk music scene. More than a concert film, Spheeris uses the punk lifestyle as a metaphor clearly stated in the title. In 1983 Spheeris continued to explore the punk phenomenon, this time in a fictional film, *Suburbia*, which entered the lives of the alienated, angry punk kids who sported spiked hair and torn clothes not for a fashion statement but to express their nihilistic philosophy. *Suburbia* was an honest attempt to reveal the subterranean youth culture that was shadowing America's suburban bliss.

Hollywood Vice Squad (1986) ran down three narrative lines concerning prostitution, child pornography, and organized crime as members of the Hollywood Vice Squad investigated. The screenplay, which confused drama with parody, was poorly written by a real-life Hollywood vice squad chief. In *The Boys Next Door* (1985) Spheeris again focused on alienated youth, crime, hopelessness, and the bleak prospects of late-twentieth-century life. *Dudes* (1987) continued Spheeris's obsession with the punk movement, now transplanting it to the West for a contrast of a subculture meeting the dark side of America's heartland. *Dudes* was considered little more than a cult oddity. In 1988 Spheeris returned to the documentary with *The Decline of Western Civilization Part II: The Metal Years*, which that goes underground into the heavy metal subculture. The combination of concert footage and personal interviews explore the music and the decadent no-future lifestyle.

Spheeris's career changed dramatically when she was hired to direct *Wayne's World* (1992), a feature film based on the popular *Saturday Night Live* sketch developed by Mike Myers and Dana Carvey. The film was a blockbuster, taking Spheeris from the edges of film culture to mainstream Hollywood. Now considered to be an A-list adapter of television fare to the big screen, Spheeris directed feature versions of *The Beverly Hillbillies* (1993) and *The Little Rascals* (1994), *Black Sheep* (1996) is a virtual reworking of *Tommy Boy* (1995), featuring SNL stars Chris Farley and David Spade. *Senseless* (1998) is a college meets big business comedy with Marlon Wayans, David Spade, Rip Torn, and Brad Dourif.

In 1998 Spheeris returned to the punk life after ten years of working in the above-ground Hollywood world of big-budget mainstream comedy with the third installment of her documentary. In *The Decline of Western Civilization Part III*, like a cinematic Dante, Spheeris continues to document the punk legacy with the latest generation still living a doomed life of nihilistic behavior that leads to death and loss.

In 1999 Spheeris directed the documentary *Hollyverid*. In 2001 she was the director of *Posers* and *Closers*.

With future productions planned to return to comedy, Spheeris continues to live in two worlds, the subterranean independent documentary world of a true youth movement, now more fashion than lifestyle, and the allure of commercial comedies. One is for the few; the other, the masses. A woman who rejects the stereotype of a "woman" director, Spheeris is an obsessed filmmaker, some say exploiter, who no longer can be accused of cashing in on a trend. She is a filmmaker determined to follow her career-long theme and cinematic purpose, only taking time out to pay the bills and renew her sense of humor as she slides down the decline of Western civilization with camera and microphone in tow.

splatter films. Critical classification of horror films that feature blood, gore, and extreme violent acts filmed in explicit detail. **George Romero** is a filmmaker who often works in the genre, especially with his zombie series. Writer John McCarty is considered the historian of splatter and gore, author of *Splatter Movies: Breaking the Last Taboo of the Screen* and two film guides to the field. Examples of splatter movies include *Blood Feast* (1963), *Two Thousand Maniacs* (1964), *Night of the Living Dead* (1968), *Mark of the Devil* (1970), *The Texas Chainsaw Massacre* (1974), *Pumpkinhead* (1988), *Friday the 13th* (1980), *The Evil Dead* (1983), *Rawhead Rex* (1986), *Two Evil Eyes* (1990), *Tremors* (1990), and *Popcorn* (1991). The most important and prolific directors in splatter and gore are **Tobe Hooper,** George Romero, **Herschell Gordon Lewis,** Andy Milligan, **David Cronenberg, John Carpenter,** Dario Argento, and Al Adamson.

BIBLIOGRAPHY

McCarty, John. *Splatter Movies: Breaking the Last Taboo of the Screen.* New York: St. Martin's Press, 1984.
Whitehead, Mark. *Slasher Movies.* North Pomfret, VT: Trafalgar Square, 2000.

square-up. An opening statement delivered by text or an on-screen spokesman before an **exploitation film,** articulating the serious social or moral problem the film purports to address. This approach was designed to legitimize the exploitative material to follow that in truth had no redeeming social or cultural value. It also warned, titillated, and apologized for what audiences were about to see. The square-up can be traced

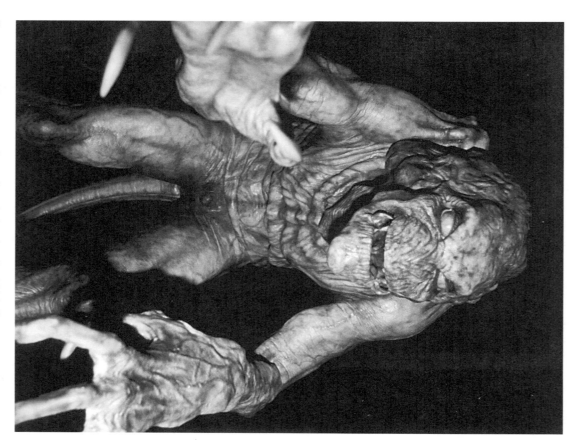

The unstoppable, gory, murderous Pumpkinhead in the 1988 film named after the creature written and directed by special effects wizard Stan Winston. Courtesy of The Del Valle Archive

back to 1912 but was a standard device throughout the 1950s when exploitation films were flourishing.

Stand and Deliver. In 1983, recent film school graduate Ramón Menéndez read a newspaper article in the *LA Times* about Jaime Escalante, a Garfield High School math teacher in East Los Angeles whose students passed a second advanced placement test in calculus after they were accused of cheating the first time around. Menéndez and his film school buddy Tom Musca met with Escalante for months, trying to convince him to sell them the rights to his remarkable story. The initial option was $1 against a $10,000 purchase price. Ultimately Escalante even got a bonus of $185,000 and profit participation. Menéndez and Musca wrote a twelve-page story treatment, and for eight months they pitched their idea for a TV movie to Hollywood with no real offers. The two men collaborated with Carol Sobieski and proceeded to write the screenplay based on Escalante's life. In October 1984 *American Playhouse* granted $12,000 to develop the screenplay. During November and December Menéndez and Musca sat in on Escalante's math class. They interviewed twelve of the fourteen students who had been accused of cheating. In five months of 1985 they wrote the first draft of the script, then called *Walking on Water*. In the summer of 1985 the project was submitted to *American Playhouse*. Menéndez and Mosca revised the script, and the second draft was approved in October. *American Playhouse* gave the filmmakers a proposed grant of $500,000 if they could raise another $500,000. They raised $4.5 million from various corporations and foundations including Atlantic-Richfield Corporation, The National Science Foundation, the Ford Foundation, and the Corporation for Public Broadcasting. The Pepsi Foundation and Anheuser-Busch made product placement deals.

Actor Edward James Olmos was cast as Escalante and entered into a deep study of the remarkable teacher. He even gained forty-one pounds and pruned out his hairline to capture Escalante physically. Shooting began in the spring of 1987. The film, now called *Stand and Deliver*, premiered in 1988 at a small film festival, then the **Independent Feature Project** Independent Feature Film Market. The buzz grew white hot; every indie **distributor** wanted it. The film was screened on studio lots. Warner Bros. won the competition, buying the rights with a $3 million advance. *Stand and Deliver* was given a wide international release, earning $18 million worldwide. At Oscar time Edward James Olmos earned a nomination for his remarkable performance, inhabiting the inspiring teacher. The cast also included Lou Diamond Phillips, Rosana De Soto, and Andy Garcia.

The story of a Hispanic math teacher empowering his inner-city students with the self-esteem and tools to succeed in the corporate world was inspirational to audiences. The success of a "little" indie made out of passion and commitment motivated aspiring and struggling filmmakers to persevere with their dream projects. *See also American Playhouse*

Steckler, Ray Dennis. Director, producer, actor, screenwriter, cinematographer. *b.* 1939. A man of many pseudonyms including Sven Christian, Harry Nixon and Cindy Lou Sutters. An **exploitation film** master, Steckler directed his best-known film *The Incredibly Strange Creatures Who Stopped Living and Became Mixed-up Zombies* (1963) before he was twenty-four. The first monster musical, *Incredibly Strange Creatures* was shot in eleven days for $38,000. Steckler, a born promoter and showman, followed the premiere of the film across the country. At critical moments in the plot, Steckler would jump out into the theater in monster garb and attack the audience, who howled with fear and laughter. Steckler shot **8mm** movies as a teen in Reading, Pennsylvania, rounding up the neighborhood kids as his cast. Steckler studied photography and served as a cameraman during the Korean conflict. When a pal asked him to shoot *The World's Greatest Sinner* (1962), staring Timothy Carey, Steckler began his Hollywood career.

Steckler was not in the union, so he had to shoot *Secret File: Hollywood* (1962) without screen credit. Steckler worked out of Las Vegas for ten years. As an independent he had his own equipment, fifteen motion picture cameras and fifteen Moviolas for postproduction. Well prepared, Steckler always had 20,000 to 30,000 feet of raw stock in his refrigerator ready for a new project at a moment's notice. Steckler was always fast, but *Blood Shack* (1971), for which he took the directorial credit as Wolfgang Schmidt, was made in only three days, tying the **Roger Corman** U. record. In 1962 Steckler directed *Wild Guitar*, starring **Arch Hall** Jr. and Sr. photographed in black-and-white film by **Vilmos Zsigmond**.

Steckler's oeuvre includes the psychotronic classics *The Thrill Killers* (1964), *Rat Pfink a Boo Boo* (1965), *The Lemon Grove Kids Meet the Monsters* (1965), *The Sexorcit Devil* (1974), *Perverted Passion* (1974), *Teenage Hustler* (1975), *Hollywood Strangler Meets the Skid Row Slasher* (1979), *Plato's Retreat West* (1983), and *Las Vegas Serial Killer* (1986).

Steckler has enjoyed a long marriage with **B-movie** actress Carolyn Brandt, his muse and star of many of his films. In 1987 Steckler directed *War Cat* but the film was credited to **Ted V. Mikels.** He was also the producer of the documentary *Carolyn Brandt: Queen of Cult* (1994).

Steiner, Ralph. Director, cinematographer. *b.* February 8, 1899, Cleveland, Ohio. *d.* July 13, 1986, Thetford, Vermont. Ralph Steiner was an established still photographer before he turned to filmmaking with *H2O* (1929), an examination of light and shadow on water. The silent movie was an early **experimental film** that abstracted the patterns created by the sun and a body of water in a variation of reflections. *Surf and Seaweed* (1930) pursues imagery found in and surrounding ocean surf. *Mechanical Principles* (1930) is a seventy-two-shot film of pistons, arms, and wheels that create circular movement, then the meshing of gear teeth, and a conclusion of images that create optical illusions. Steiner became a member of The Workers Film and Photo League, where he documented the political response to the Great Depression, starting with the 1931 May Day demonstrations in New York City. *Pie in the Sky* (1935) was a silent film featuring **Elia Kazan** and Elman Koolish in a series of humorous sketches satirizing the American economic predicament and the failure of capitalism in the 1930s. *Hands* (1934) was sponsored by the Work Projects Administration (WPA). The short silent film was a study of workers' hands, a piece of government propaganda to raise morale. Between 1934 and 1942 Steiner contributed as a cinematographer to many **documentaries** including *The Plow That Broke the Plains* (1936), *People of the Cumberland* (1938), *The City* (1939), *New Hampshire Heritage* (1940), *Youth Gets a Break* (1941), and *Troop Train* (1942). From 1960 to 1975 Steiner created a series called *The Joy of Seeing* that included the films *Seaweed*, a *Seduction* (1960), *One Man's Island* (1969), *Glory, Glory* (1971), *A Look at Laundry* (1971), *Beyond Niagara* (1973), *Look Park* (1974), *Hooray for Light!* (1975), and *Slowdown* (1975). The **avant-garde** films are a celebration of sight and the act of seeing.

Stern, Bert. *See Jazz on a Summer's Day*

Stillman, Whit. Director, producer, screenwriter. *b.* John Whitney Stillman, 1952. *ed.* Harvard University. Raised in Cornwall, New York, by his mother, a former debutante, and a father who was a member of President John Kennedy's administration, Whit Stillman was a journalist after graduating Harvard in the early 1970s, then entered the publishing training program at Doubleday. While on assignment in Barcelona, Spain, he married a Spanish woman. In Madrid Stillman convinced producers that he could sell Spanish-language films to American television. This resulted in Stillman working as a sales agent for directors Fernando Trueba and Fernando Colomo. After ten years in Spain, Stillman returned to the United States in 1984 and ran an illustration agency.

Stillman wrote the screenplay for *Metropolitan* (1990) from 1984 to 1988 and financed his first film with $50,000 from the sale of his apartment and contributions from friends and family to complete the $175,000 to $200,000 budget. *Metropolitan*, which premiered at the IFFM, played **Sundance** and was nominated for a best original screenplay Oscar. *Metropolitan* introduced a unique voice that explored the rarified world of New York's upper crust, the debutantes, and their escorts about to enter the social scene. *Metropolitan* featured an ensemble cast of unknown young actors. The literate film was character and dialogue driven in the tradition of a drawing room comedy.

Barcelona (1994) is the story of two American yuppie cousins living in Spain, played by Taylor Nichols and Christopher Eigeman, who both appeared in *Metropolitan*. The talky comedy examines anti-American attitudes in a changing Old World country during the concluding months of the Cold War. Stillman based the film on his experiences living in Spain.

The Last Days of Disco (1998) is the completion of Stillman's yuppie trilogy. Chloë Sevigny and Kate Beckinsale portray two friends who are publishing trainees by day who hang out in a trendy disco at night in the early 1980s. Characters from the earlier Stillman films make an appearance here to tie the films together.

Strain, Julie. Actress, director, screenwriter, producer. *b.* February 18, 1962, Concord, California. The Amazonian six-feet-one-inch beauty known as the current Queen of the **B-movies**, Julie Strain has appeared in over sixty **exploitation** feature films in the last ten years. The legend of Strain begins in Concord, California, where the thirteen-year-old outstanding athlete, already her full height, was known as a wild hellraising child. After high school Strain's first boyfriend, a body builder, led her to the gym where she developed the physicality that would be her greatest commercial commodity. She graduated college with honors and then experienced a life-altering event: While riding her beloved horse, Strain was thrown and suffered head injuries that virtually wiped out memories of her past. As she was recovering, Strain attended a championship-boxing match in Las Vegas. She was courted by several entertainment industry suits and decided to head for LA. At twenty-eight when many actresses in Hollywood are considered heading over the hill, Strain reinvented herself into a one-woman promoter—her product: Julie Strain. At first Strain had to sleep in her truck, but after becoming the *Penthouse* Pet of the Year she had the capital to start Julie Strain Inc. She auditioned tirelessly and accepted every role she was offered. Her early films include *Carnal Crimes* (1990), *Sunset Heat* (1991), *Kuffs* (1992), *Ambitious Desires* (1992), *Psycho Cop Returns* (1993), and *Bikini Squad* (1993).

Strain became a marketing master, merchandising herself in photos, Zippo lighters, CD-ROMS, calendars, posters, greeting cards, coffee mugs, dolls, and trading cards. An accomplished still photographer working in the tradition of the 1940s and 1950s pinup movement, Strain has shaped the careers of budding starlets and has been photographed by renowned photographers like Helmut Newton. Her powerful, strong, sexy persona and pretty girl-next-door face have been imitated and sought after by the glamour scene. The animators working on *Heavy Metal 2000* (2000) meticulously recreated Strain for the film's main character, Julie. Strain has been largely associated with exploitation kensei Andy Sidaris. Just a few of the films that made her an independent star self-owned and -represented without studio shackles include *Blonde Heaven* (1995), *Sorceress II: The Temptress* (1996), *Busted* (1996), *Bimbo Movie Bash* (1997), *Lingerie Kickboxer* (1998), *L.E.T.H.A.L. Ladies: Return to Savage Beach* (1998), *Armageddon Boulevard* (1998), *The Bare Wench Project* (1999), and *Millennium Queen* (2000). In 2000 Julie Strain appeared in *Millennium Queen* and *Centerfold Coeds: Girlfriends*. In 2001 she was in *.com for Murder* and *The Bare Wench Project 2: Scared Topless*. In *Sex Court the Movie* (2002), Strain played Jude Julie.

Through all her fame, the endless personal appearances, the Web site, and the constant whirling of the still, movie, and video cameras, Strain has retained her charming sense of humor, loyalty to her fans, and the female empowerment of the new feminism. Kick butt, show butt, keep what you make: It's yours.

Strand, Paul. Documentary filmmaker. *b.* October 16, 1890, New York City. *d.* March 31, 1976. Strand was a noted still photographer and the standard-bearer of a political and socially committed cadre of filmmakers including Fred Zinnemann, **Elia Kazan, Ralph Steiner, Willard Van Dyke, Pare Lorentz,** Sidney Myers, **Leo Hurwitz** and John Howard Lawson. In 1937, Strand founded Frontier Films, a company dedicated to production of politically progressive **documentaries** along with writers John Dos Passos, Lillian Hellman, Archibald MacLeish, and Clifford Odets and the film director Lewis Milestone. World War II interrupted the group's efforts, and in 1948 Strand returned to still photography but remained a socially conscious artist. Strand's documentary credits include *Redes* (1936), a documentary about Mexican fishermen that he produced and photographed, while Fred Zinnemann (*High Noon* [1952], *The Nun's Story* [1959]) directed. Strand was one of the cinematographers on Pare Lorentz's *The Plow That Broke the Plains* (1936) and was the codirector, cowriter, cinematographer, and coproducer of *Native Land* (1942), narrated by Paul Robeson.

Strick, Joseph. Director, producer, screenwriter. *b.* July 6, 1923, Braddock, Pennsylvania. *ed.* University College of Los Angeles. Strick was a cameraman in the air force during World War II. In 1948 he codirected a black-and-white short film, *Muscle Beach*, with **Irving Lerner.** Strick worked as a weekend copyboy for the *Los Angeles Times* and later was employed in television. For five years Strick developed an independent production *The Savage Eye* (1960), a drama about a divorcee starting a new life in Los Angeles, shot and staged to look like a **documentary,**

codirected by Strick, **Ben Maddow**, and Sidney Myers. Next Strick directed an adaptation of three challenging literary works, *The Balcony* (1963), a low-budget screen version of the Jean Genet play with Shelley Winters, Peter Falk, Lee Grant, Ruby Dee, Jeff Corey, and Leonard Nimoy. In 1967, Strick took on the impossible and thankless job of putting James Joyce's *Ulysses*, one of the most daring of twentieth-century novels, on film. *Ulysses* was shot on location in Ireland and transferred much of the complex prose to the screen but without visual context to support the allusions of Joyce's experimental use of language. The film failed miserably. In 1970, Strick took on Henry Miller's *Tropic of Cancer* with Rip Torn and Ellen Burstyn in an X-rated film version of the sexual adventures of the author in 1920s Paris. In 1970 Strick won an Oscar for best short subject with *Interviews with My Lai Veterans*.

In 1974 Strick attempted to work in the **American New Wave** style with *Road Movie*, a gritty story of two independent truckers who pick up an emotionally damaged prostitute and go on an ambiguous trip through a darkly changing America. The film tried, not too successfully, to attract the youth market who were fascinated with the **road movie** genre, but Strick was heavy-handed enough to actually name the film *Road Movie* in an overanxious attempt to stay modern. In 1979 Strick adapted another Joyce masterwork, *A Portrait of the Artist as a Young Man*, also on location in Ireland. Again, Strick was too literal, missing the visuals inherent in the rich poetry of Joyce's prose. In 1996 Strick returned to the documentary form with *Criminals*, an independent production. *See also The Savage Eye*.

structural filmmaking. A form of **experimental** filmmaking where the shape of a film is predetermined often utilizing a particular camera grammar such as a pan or zoom. The cinematic structure is the content and point of the work. Structural filmmaking came of age in the mid-1960s and finds its prehistory in **Andy Warhol's** *Sleep* (1963), *Empire* (1964), and other early films made at his Factory. *Wavelength* (1967), a film with what appears to be a continuous forty-five-minute zoom shot, is a celebrated example of structural filmmaking, as is much of Michael Snow's work in the mid-1960s and 1970s. Other structural filmmakers include George Landow, Ernie Gehr, Joyce Weiland, Paul Shartis, and Tony Conrad. Structural filmmaking had its admirers in the critical, view, and filmmaking community. It also alienated many who found the films strident and cinematically limited. Theorist **P. Adams Sitney**, who called the movement one of the most significant to enter the development of the **avant-garde** film, championed structural filmmaking.

studio boutique. A production company that finances and distributes independent films but is a subsidiary of a major studio such as Fox Classics and Sony Pictures Classics.

Sundance Institute. Created in 1981 when Robert Redford gathered colleagues and friends in Utah to discuss how to vitalize and preserve the creativity of American film. Out of that meeting the nonprofit corporation Sundance Institute was created, dedicated to the support and development of screenwriters and directors and to the exhibition of new independent fiction and nonfiction films. Sundance is composed of many programs and the annual Sundance Film Festival, which has become the most important and respected independent film event of the year. The Writers Fellowship Program includes working retreats at labs held in Utah, internationally, and during the film festival. The program gives emerging screenwriters an opportunity to work on writing projects mentored by creative advisers and professional writers. The Fellowship Program gives members opportunities to observe and talk with filmmakers, theater, composers, and creative artists working at the Institute. After completing the yearlong program, the participants can apply for funding from the James Irvine Foundation through the Institute.

The Feature Film Program began in 1981 to support next-generation filmmakers. Directors develop new work in labs under the guidance of industry professionals. Sundance's mission is to support diverse and daring material. Sundance also runs a Composer's Lab that brings composers and filmmakers together and exposes them to professional and new vistas to explore new ways of storytelling with music and images. The Native American Program provides support, visibility, and assistance to Native American filmmakers. The Documentary Program, launched at the 2000 Sundance Festival with "House of Docs," takes on the networking and financial challenges presented to the nonfiction filmmaker.

Each year the Sundance Film Festival exhibits around 100 independent films selected from over 3,000 submissions. The Feature Film Competition includes nonfiction and dramatic films. The Grand Jury Prize is the most prestigious award of the festival. The Waldo Salt Screenwriting Award celebrates writers, and The Freedom of Expression Award recognizes excellence in nonfiction work. Cinematography, directing, and an Audience Award are given. The American Spectrum Program offers diverse and eclectic documentary and dramatic films. Frontier features experimental works. The World Cinema Program screens innovative international films. The public votes on The World Cinema and Audience Award winners, and a Jury Award honors an outstanding Latin American filmmaker. The Native Forum presents films that explore Native culture, history, politics, spirituality, and contemporary life. Short films are selected and screened during the festival.

Park City at Midnight is an after-hours offering of the main festival's more cutting-edge works. Historic independent films from the Sundance Collection at UCLA are shown during the festival. The Piper-Heidsieck Tribute to Independent Vision honors an actor's contribution to independent cinema. The festival offers important premieres of indie films, which have included *Central Station* (1998), *Ulee's Gold* (1997), *Go* (1999), *American Psycho* (2000), *The Virgin Suicides* (1999), and *Love and Basketball* (2000). Panel discussions with industry representatives, **critics**, journalists, and scholars are held to discuss issues pertinent to independent film. The Gen-Y Studio is a recent addition to the festival, bringing national and international high school students together to explore filmmaking and share their views with peers, filmmakers, and the media. Sundance also offers live theater, a digital center, and an online film festival.

Once considered a radical alternative to commercial moviemaking, over the years many have complained that Sundance has become too conservative, conventional, and chic-chic to represent the full spectrum of independent film. Cell phones, Armani, bottled water and trendy parties give Sundance the image of being part of the establishment. The festival has become a haven for studio suits over the film as art seekers. In reaction many festivals have sprung up in the Park City area such as **Slamdance** and others, each created when the other rejected films looked for another venue. The Academy of Motion Picture Arts and Sciences represents the commercial industry, AFI trains filmmakers, and Sundance still offers an alternative. But with new filmmakers developing every day, it is far from the end-all in embracing the independent film that lies outside of commercial standards.

BIBLIOGRAPHY

Anderson, John. *Sundancing: Hanging Out and Listening in at America's Most Important Film Festival*. New York: Avon Books, 2000.

Smith, Lory. *Party in a Box: The Story of the Sundance Film Festival*. Salt Lake City, UT: Gibbs-Smith Publishing, 1999.

Super 8mm filmmaking. Format with smaller sprocket holes and a larger picture area than regular **8mm**. Super 8mm was introduced as an upgrade to the earlier format and was popular for home use in the 1960s and 1970s. Many independent filmmakers worked in the format, and there were forecasts in the late 1960s that Super 8mm would soon be accepted in theatrical venues, but like Coppola's Oscar rabble about making moves with your brainwaves, it was thrown aside as a counterculture fantasy. Super 8mm camera and projectors were an improvement and offered the viability of recording sound on film that freed 8mm filmmakers from auxiliary tape recorders and painstaking problems with synchronization. **Experimental** filmmakers embrace Super 8mm as did **punk** filmmakers in the late 1970s into the 1980s. The format had little professional application other than some work in television news and in features to create a home movie effect. The camcorder put both 8mm formats to bed as a home format, but Super 8mm still exists in indie filmmaking, with practitioners buying used equipment and seeking out the few labs that still develop Super 8mm film. Regular 8mm was sold on an open reel; Super 8mm was packaged in a plastic cassette. Filmmaker and author **Lenny Lipton** is the scholar on the subject. Editing Super 8mm is tedious, relying on small hand-cranked viewers. Video killed the Super 8mm star just when hopes, dreams and technical advances were leading to an affordable film medium. *See also* 8mm filmmaking

Susskind, David. Producer, talk show host. *b.* December 19, 1920, New York City. *d.* February 22, 1987. *ed.* University of Wisconsin, Harvard University. Susskind is best rememberd as the moderator of the long-running late-night talk show *Open End* that had the distinction of having no specific running length. Susskind was a press agent for Warner Brothers and a talent agent for Music Corporation of America. In 1948 Susskind opened his own agency, Talent Associates. In the 1950s Susskind began producing Broadway plays, television, and movies. Susskind produced low-budget movies that often had serious social or political content. His credits include *Edge of the City* (1957), *Requiem for a Heavyweight* (1962), *All the Way Home* (1963), *Lovers and Other Strangers* (1970), *Alice Doesn't Live Here Anymore* (1974), *Buffalo Bill and the Indians, or Sitting Bull's History Lesson* (1976), and *Fort Apache, the Bronx* (1981).

T

Tarantino, Quentin. Director, screenwriter, producer, actor. *b.* March 27, 1963, Knoxville, Tennessee. A high school dropout notable as the first successful graduate of the **video store film school**. While working at a Los Angeles video emporium, Tarantino taught himself film history, screenwriting, and film direction by watching everything from official classics to fringe cult items. Customer contacts gave Tarantino entry to the industry. He made his professional debut as a screenwriter with *True Romance* (1993), directed by Tony Scott, and *Natural Born Killers* (1994), directed by Oliver Stone. Tarantino's directorial debut was *Reservoir Dogs* (1992), and his sophomore effort *Pulp Fiction* (1994) won a screenwriting Oscar and made him the flavor-of-the-month phenom.

Tarantino demonstrated a near-perfect ear for dialogue and the ability to create inventive nonlinear story lines. He took film referencing to a new level, drawing on his encyclopedic knowledge of Kung Fu, **blaxploitation**, Jean-Luc Godard and everything else he devoured as a cineaste. Tarantino did not draw on life experience, instead relying on his fascination with cinema crime and violence cultivated from Hong Kong flicks and Sam Peckinpah.

After astounding **critics**, audiences, and the industry with a prestigious talent that opened the floodgates for a new approach to narrative filmmaking, Tarantino took one of the biggest falls from grace since Orson Welles and his onscreen persona George Miniver in *The Magnificent Ambersons* (1942). Tarantino was everywhere with his wise-guy smirk and know-it-all comments. Then cineastes and scholars equally schooled in cinema cultism uncovered and disclosed with point-by-point evidence that Tarantino had lifted the premise and plot for *Reservoir Dogs* from the 1987 Ringo Lam film *City on Fire*—a revelation that blew a large hole in the kudos he received for originality.

Director/writer Quentin Tarantino in one of his many screen roles, seen here with George Clooney in *From Dusk Till Dawn* (1996), directed by Robert Rodriguez based on an original story by Tarantino. Courtesy of The Del Valle Archive

Tarantino and Oliver Stone had a public fight over *Natural Born Killers*. Tarantino was critical of Stone's treatment of his script. As an actor, Tarantino further damaged his image. His performances were largely amateurish and lacked craft, especially in contrast to the first-class ensemble casts assembled in both of his first films. The bragging, bad mouthing, and taunting wore thin quickly, as did his performances in *From Dusk Till Dawn* (1996) and *Desperado* (1995), plus his participation in *Four Rooms* (1995), the vehicle that brought on his comeuppance. The compilation film with segments directed by Tarantino, **Allison Anders,** Alexandre Rockwell, and **Robert Rodriguez** was not only a box office and critical disaster; it literally tore Tarantino's page off the flavor-of-the-month calendar.

In 1997 Tarantino began resurrecting his career with *Jackie Brown*, a revisionist blaxploitation film accepted by critics, filmmakers and enthusiasts, if not general audiences, for its performances by Pam Grier, Robert Forster, and **Robert De Niro** and its attention to craft and not flash. Tarantino was growing up. Tarantino's producing credits include Robert Avary's *Killing Zoe* (1994) and Robert Rodriguez's *From Dusk Till Dawn* (1996), which he also scripted. In his role as film historian, Tarantino is no **Martin Scorsese,** but he has appeared in documentaries on Pam Grier and Jackie Chan and has a home video line where he introduces and gives afterthoughts on his favorite films including *Switchblade Sisters* (1975) and *Chungking Express* (1994). Tarantino's fourth feature film in ten years as a director, *Kill Bill* (2003), is a film noir about a prostitute shot by her pimp who sets out for revenge when she awakens from a coma nine years later. Recent credits for Tarantino include: executive producer of *From Dusk Till Dawn 2: Texas Blood Money* (1999) and *From Dusk Till Dawn 3: The Hangman's Daughter* (2000). He put on his actor's hat for *Little Nicky* (2000).

BIBLIOGRAPHY

Bernard, Jami. *Quentin Tarantino: The Man and His Movies.* New York: Harper-Collins, 1995.

tax shelters. Investors interested in sheltering income have financed many low-budget independent films. The investors buy a share in the production as a tax deduction. The Internal Revenue Service has guidelines concerning such investments and concomitant deductions. Individual states also have regulatory laws. The heyday of this fund-raising technique is past, as recent laws have limited the practice that saw local dentists, doctors, lawyers, and businesspeople in the 1980s happily financing independent films.

Texas Chainsaw Massacre, The. *See* Henkel, Kim; Hooper, Tobe

Thomas, Wynn. Production designer. *ed.* Boston University. In the 1990s Wynn Thomas designed big-budget studio films such as **Tim Burton's** *Mars Attacks!* (1996), Barry Levinson's *Wag the Dog* (1997), and Harold Ramis's hit comedy *Analyze This* (1999). Obtaining work on commercially viable mainstream projects as well as exciting independent films like *To Wong Foo, Thanks for Everything, Julie Newmar* (1995) and *A Bronx Tale* (1993) was a challenge for Thomas, who began as one of the first African American production designers. Thomas studied stage design at Boston University and for ten years designed for the stage, spending several seasons with the Negro Ensemble Company. After becoming a member of the design union, he designed many ABC *After School Specials* with a goal to make the difficult transition to feature films.

Thomas got his break through the good graces of veteran production designer Richard Sylbert, who brought Thomas into the **Francis Ford Coppola** production of *The Cotton Club* (1984) as a model builder. While working as the art director on *Beat Street* (1984), Thomas met **Spike Lee** and formed an enduring collaborative relationship that includes *She's Gotta Have It* (1986), *School Daze* (1988), *Do the Right Thing* (1989), *Mo' Better Blues* (1990), *Jungle Fever* (1991), *Malcolm X* (1992), *Crooklyn* (1994), and *He Got Game* (1998), Wynn Thomas has also designed *The Original Kings of Comedy* (2000) and *A Huey P. Newton Story* (2001) for **Spike Lee.** Thomas designed *Keeping the Faith* (2000), directed by Edward Norton, *A Beautiful Mind* (2001), directed by Ron Howard and winner of the Oscar for Best Picture, and the sequel to *Analyze This, Analyze That* (2002). From low-budget independent films exploring the urban experience to high-profile studio projects, Thomas is a committed artist who has contributed substantially to the independent film community.

BIBLIOGRAPHY

LoBrutto, Vincent. *By Design: Interviews with Film Production Designers.* Westport, CT: Praeger, 1992.

titles. Many low-budget, **exploitation,** and genre films are sold on the title alone. Deals can be made with only a title and no script—a business method brought to an art form by **Roger Corman** and **American International Pictures.** If the title promises sex, drugs, rock 'n' roll and violence, it will guarantee a particular core audience. The movie is secondary. Getting them into the seats with a provocative title and a titillating poster is the marketing secret for exploitation, genre, and action films. Titles are often changed for rereleases without changing the movie, so the film can be given a new life absent negative name recognition.

Tolkin, Michael. Director, screenwriter. *b.* October 17, 1950, New York City. *ed.* Middlebury College. A novelist and widely published journalist who arrived on the national film scene when **Robert Altman** made one of his numerous comebacks directing Tolkin's adaptation of his book *The Player,* a dead-on satire of contemporary Hollywood. Buzz on the 1992 film had been so intense during production that it made Tolkin hot, and he took advantage by parlaying the interest into his directorial debut, *The Rapture* (1991). This disturbing film starred Mimi Rogers as an immoral woman who undergoes an evangelical Christian transformation and is swept into a religious apocalypse. To research the project Tolkin watched hours and hours of evangelical Christian television, a process that made him sympathetic to fundamentalism and a conflict toward their philosophy concerning solutions for the ethical and moral disintegration of society. Tolkin preferred older movies that inspired the audience with identity and insight. His motivation was to create a film that was a critical reaction against 1980s movies that manipulated the audience into a lynch mob frenzy united against a common scapegoat. *The Rapture* caused a major controversy at its Telluride Film Festival premiere. The film was distributed by Fine Line, who marketed *The Rapture* as an intellectual, religious horror movie. The devout either loved or hated the film, but it never generated the controversy necessary to make it the event film Fine Line planned for. Ticket sales were slim, and after a brief run this original and morally challenging film faded fast. **Critics** and cinephiles took notice of Tolkin's individualistic voice and bold vision.

In 1994 Tolkin returned with *The New Age*, a deadpan satire about a couple who lose their high-powered jobs when they go into business with a boutique. Tolkin again was making a bitter critique of American money and status culture associated with the Reagan years. The film was barely released by Warner Bros. Tolkin's next project *20 Billion* (2001) continues his black comic assault on the "players" of our time with a parody of Bill Gates and his omnipotent Microsoft empire. In 2002 Michael Tolkin wrote the screenplay for *Changing Lanes*.

Townsend, Robert. Director, actor, screenwriter, producer. *b.* February 6, 1957, Chicago, Illinois. *ed.* Illinois State University, Hunter College. Entrepreneurial Robert Townsend studied acting with Stella Adler, performed with the Negro Ensemble Company, and paid the bills as a stand-up comic at The Improv. After roles in *Cooley High* (1975), *Willie and Phil* (1980), *Streets of Fire* (1984), *American Flyers* (1985), and *Ratboy* (1986), Townsend transitioned to directing.

From 1984 to 1986 Townsend developed vignettes in preparation for his first feature. Initially, they were self-contained short films created for a reel to demonstrate his acting skills, but in the process, his first film, *Hollywood Shuffle* (1987), was conceived. There was no completed shooting script prior to production. Keenan Ivory Wayans cowrote the project with Townsend and performed on screen. It cost $100,000 to get to the rough-cut stage. Townsend put up his own money from a three-picture acting deal with Richard Pryor's Indigo Productions. He still needed $40,000 to complete the project, so he used several credit cards as capital. Five thousand dollars in credit on a Visa card purchased 10,000 feet of raw stock; a Saks Fifth Avenue card purchased wardrobe later given to the cast instead of salary. Townsend's Montgomery Ward card paid for the catering bill, and other lines of credit were eaten up for various budget-line items. At one point production was halted when a new credit card was lost by the post office.

Townsend began shooting in Los Angeles in October 1984 with a crew of friends and students and spent $20,000 in just four days. In 1985 he shot for four days, and for six days in 1986 when the individual segments were structured into a feature format. Townsend used every **guerrilla filmmaking** technique in the book; he shot exteriors in front of his apartment building and outside Wayans's house. He shot on locations without a permit; he had his crew wear UCLA tee shirts so onlookers thought the production was a student film; and he appealed to filmmakers to donate **short ends** and shot the film in fourteen long days over three years.

Once completed, Townsend had one month to sell *Hollywood Shuffle* before the credit payments bankrupted him. A workprint was assembled in December 1985 and shown at the Writer's Guild of America screening room. To create a buzz, Townsend invited everyone he knew in the business. Many **distributors** turned him down, labeling the film amateurish, but Samuel Goldwyn Jr. took the risk, and Townsend used the cash advance to pay the actors. The film was running seventy to seventy-five minutes at the time, so Goldwyn gave Townsend completion funds to shoot additional scenes and wrap up postproduction. The company did attain the valuable world rights but put $1 million into promotion and publicity to give the film a chance. *Hollywood Shuffle* grossed more than $5 million nationwide. Townsend's directorial career unfortunately didn't grow according to his spectacular send-off.

In 1987 he returned to his stand-up roots directing *Eddie Murphy Raw* (1987), a performance film. *The Five Heartbeats* (1991) was an endearing story of a Motown-like band struggling to make it in the music business. The film never found an audience. *The Meteor Man* (1993) is a silly story of a timid urban schoolteacher hit by a meteor that turns him into a superhero. Critics and audiences found many social messages but little humor, so the film quickly failed. In *B*A*P*S* (1997), two black American princesses go west to LA and wind up living in the mansion of a wealthy man. The too-often-told fairytale sweetened by cameos of sports and music personalities had a quick demise. Townsend's directing career has shifted from low-budget theatrical features to television movies: *Little Richard* and *Livin' for Love: The Natalie Cole Story* (both 2000). In 2001 Townsend performed in *I Was a Teenage Faust* and directed *Carmen: A Hip Hopera* for MTV. In 2002 he directed the television movie *10,000 Black Men Named George* and appeared in *Book of Love*.

Tribeca Film Center. State-of-the-art office building located in downtown Manhattan created for the film and entertainment industry. It is equipped with a screening room, production suites, a banquet hall, a restaurant, kitchen facilities, and conference rooms. Home of Tribeca Productions founded in 1988 by **Robert De Niro** and Jane Rosenthal to capitalize on and encourage the creative resources in New York. The company develops projects on which De Niro is producer, director, and/or actor. Rosenthal produces, along with De Niro, and oversees all aspects of project development. Tribeca Productions produced De Niro's directorial debut *A Bronx Tale* (1993), *15 Minutes* (2001), and *About a Boy* (2002). In 1992, the Tribeca Film Center and the Eastman Kodak Company in conjunction with the **New York Foundation for the Arts** created the First Look Series, a showcase for emerging filmmakers. The invitation-only screenings are for distribution companies, agents, casting directors, producers, reps, film festival programmers, and Web and print journalists but not reviewers.

Dennis Hopper looks on while Peter Fonda kisses a hippie love child in the defining LSD movie, *The Trip* (1967), directed by Roger Corman from a screenplay by Jack Nicholson. Courtesy of The Del Valle Archive

trip movies. A subgenre of the 1960s **exploitation films** influenced by the psychedelic counterculture of LSD, peyote, and other hallucinogenic drug use celebrated by underground figures such as Timothy Leary, Ken Kesey, and members of The Grateful Dead. Historians of the movement credit **Conrad Rooks**'s *Chappaqua* (1966) as the initial trip film, followed by *The Trip* (1967), *The Love-Ins* (1967), *Blonde on a Bum Trip* (1968), *Psych-Out* (1968), *Easy Rider* (1969), and *Blue Sunshine* (1976). Other LSD films include *Hallucination Generation*, *The Evil Pleasure* (both 1966), *The Acid Eaters*, *Turn On, Tune In, Drop Out*, *The Weird World of LSD* (all 1967), *Acid Mantra: Or Rebirth of a Nation*, *Alice in Acidland*, *Wild in the Streets*, *Skidoo*, *Mantis in Lace* (all 1968), and *Wanda, The Dean's Wife*, *The Big Cube*, *The Sadistic Hypnotist*, and *Satan's Sadists* (all 1969). Andy Milligan made *Depraved!* (1967), and **John Waters** directed *The Diane Linkletter Story* (1969). **Roger Corman**'s *The Trip* and **Richard Rush**'s *Psych-Out* are among the best of the run. Eventually the trip film moved on to cocaine, crack, and heroin, but LSD, with its psychedelic colors, psychotic and sexual behavior, and trippy images, was the cinematic drug of choice. *See also Easy Rider;* Rooks, Conrad

BIBLIOGRAPHY

Stevenson, Jack. *Addicted: The Myth and Menace of Drugs in Film*. London: Creation Books, 2000.

Troche, Rose. *See* queer cinema

Troma Studios. Totally independent, New York–based film production and distribution company known for extremely low-budget **B-movies** with no production or moral values. Troma films delight their cult legion of fans who can't get enough blood, gore, slime, topless starlets, cheapo special effects, and monsters, making Troma cofounders Lloyd Kaufman and Michael Herz kings of a cheesy empire that defies all Hollywood conventions.

Kaufman, born Samuel Weil, the more vocal, visible, and extraverted of the team, graduated Yale with honors and bows to **Roger Corman** and Samuel Z. Arkoff as his mentors. He learned the film business by working on **John Avildsen**'s *Joe* (1970), *Rocky* (1976), and *Slow Dancing in the Big City* (1978) and John Badham's *Saturday Night Fever* (1977).

Troma films are known for their vulgar humor, Tromettes, the women who bare all, bargain basement gross-out effects, and minuscule budgets averaging $350,000 a title. In the finest tradition of the B-movie, a Troma title tells you all you need to know: *Surf Nazis Must Die* (1987), *Chopper Chicks in Zombietown* (1989), *Tromeo & Juliet* (1966), and *Killer Condom* (1997).

Kaufman and Herz codirected *The Toxic Avenger* (1985), which put Troma on the **psychotronic** map. The popular spoof tells the story of a ninety-pound weakling who is transformed into a monster when he falls into a barrel of toxic waste and sets out to do good and (of course) get revenge. The creature, a lumbering, bloodthirsty, mass of sludge and mire, falls for a blind babe billed as Toxie "the first super-hero from New Jersey." The film spawned two sequels.

Like Corman, Troma has given many aspiring filmmakers their first break, but unlike Corman's illustrious roll call of graduates, no Troma film director has amounted to as much. Troma's genius is in attracting hungry filmmakers and technicians who want to make a movie at any cost. Many don't feel exploited because of their fanatical devotion to the cult. Kaufman and Herz have directed many of their inventory. Kaufman directed *Squeeze Play* (1980), *Waitress* (1981), and *Sgt. Kabukiman N.Y.P.D.* (1990). Together the Troma team codirected *Stuck on You* (1981), *The First Turn-On!!* (1983), *Troma's War* (1988), *The Toxic Avenger Part II* (1988), and *The Toxic Avenger III: The Last Temptation of Toxie* (1989).

A collection of Troma characters and Tromettes, part of the wacky world of Troma Studios. Courtesy of The Del Valle Archive

BIBLIOGRAPHY

Kaufman, Lloyd, and James Gunn. *All I Need to Know About Filmmaking I Learned from The Toxic Avenger: The Shocking True Story of Troma Studios.* New York: Berkley Boulevard Books, 1998.

Tsukerman, Slava. *See Liquid Sky*

Tyler, Parker. Film critic. *b.* Harrison Parker Tyler, March 6, 1904, New Orleans. *d.* 1974. After moving to New York City, Parker Tyler explored acting, dancing, and drawing before making the decision to write. Tyler first wrote film criticism in 1940. Although he continued to write poetry, biography, art, and literary criticism, he is best known for his serious examination of films from the Hollywood Studio System, foreign films, and **underground cinema.** Parker wrote groundbreaking works on **experimental film** defining the aesthetics and psychological, political, and sexual images he interpreted from the films. Tyler was a regular contributor to *Partisan Review, Sight and Sound,* and **Film Culture.** He was a central figure in the **avant-garde** and experimental film communities. His books on the cinema include *Magic and Myth of the Movies* (1947), *The Three Faces of the Film* (1960), *Classics of the Foreign Film* (1962), *Sex, Psyche, Etcetera in the Film* (1962), *Underground Film: A Critical History* (1970), *Screening the Sexes: Homosexuality in the Movies* (1972), *The Shadow of an Airplane Climbs the Empire State Building: A World Theory of Film* (1972).

U

Ulmer, Edgar G. Director, screenwriter, art director. *b.* September 17, 1904, Vienna. *d.* September 30, 1972. *ed.* Vienna Academy of Arts and Sciences. Edgar G. Ulmer had an early résumé with all the trappings of an A-list director and an unlikely one for a **poverty row**, low-budget, obscure cultist who became the darling of the auteurists. Ulmer studied architecture and philosophy and was an actor and set designer for theater legend Max Reinhart. He designed sets for Martin Beck's Broadway productions and on films for Universal Studios. In 1925 Ulmer assisted F.W. Murnau on *The Last Laugh* and *Faust* and came back to Hollywood with Murnau, where he worked on *Sunrise* (1927) and *Tabu* (1931). Back in Berlin in 1929 Ulmer collaborated with director Robert Siodmak and a year later settled in Hollywood as an art director. In 1933 Ulmer made the transition to directing but did not gravitate to the mainstream. Instead he turned to poverty row, studios like Allied Artists and PRC, the world of low-budget films where he created distinctive films in various genres: horror, Yiddish cinema, film noir, venereal disease **educational** films, women-in-prison dramas, musicals, mysteries, melodrama, sci-fi genre, and all-black films for distribution to segregated theaters. His films include *Mr. Broadway* (1933), *The Black Cat* (1934), *Moon over Harlem* (1939), *The Light Ahead* (1939), *Girls in Chains* (1943), *Bluebeard* (1944), *Ruthless* (1948), *The Man from Planet X* (1951), *Babes in Bagdad* (1952), *Murder Is My Beat* (1955), *Daughter of Dr. Jeckyll* (1957), and the classic film noir *Detour* (1945) that runs only sixty-seven minutes.

underground cinema. Term created to identify personal, independent, nontraditional, and noncommercial films developed and exhibited outside mainstream cinema. The phrase *underground cinema* was coined by **experimental** filmmaker Stan Van der Beek. The movement grew out of the Beat Generation of the 1950s and had its roots in New York and San Francisco. Filmmakers associated with the movement include **Andy Warhol, Kenneth Anger, Jack Smith, Shirley Clarke,** and **Lionel Rogosin.** The term continues to be used as general reference to particular personal, experimental, and independent films.

BIBLIOGRAPHY

Tyler, Parker. *Underground Film: A Critical History.* New York: Grove Press, 1969.

United Artists Corporation. Independent production and distribution company created in 1919 by **Charles Chaplin, D.W. Griffith,** Mary Pickford, and **Douglas Fairbanks** to empower actors and directors by giving them greater artistic and financial control. In 1957 UA went public; in 1967 it became a subsidiary of TransAmerica Corporation. In 1981, UA was sold to MGM, and in 1983 it merged as MGM/UA. MGM/UA was acquired by the French bank Credit Lyonnais in 1992. Credit Lyonnais restored the name MGM. This reformulated entity no longer reflects the independent philosophy of its founders. *See also* Chaplin, Charles; Griffith, D.W.; Fairbanks, Douglas

BIBLIOGRAPHY

Balio, Tino. *United Artists: The Company That Changed the Film Industry.* Madison: University of Wisconsin Press, 1987.

Universal Studios Young Filmmaker's Program. Created after the success of *Easy Rider* (1969) and headed by Ned Tanen. The program's mission was to comb the country for young filmmakers the studio thought would bring them a similar pot of gold by tapping into the youth market. Tanen hired **Charles Hirsch,** who later met his partner **Brian De Palma** at the program. The grand scheme never really materialized, as the studio didn't put its trust or money behind discovering and developing new talent. Universal made a few youth films including **Dennis Hopper's** *The Last Movie* and **Peter Fonda's** *The Hired Hand* (both 1971), but lighting didn't strike twice for the Captain and Billy. Eventually Universal dropped the official program and went back to business as usual.

V

Vachon, Christine. Producer. *b.* 1962, New York City. *ed.* Brown University. Daring and courageous independent producer who has fostered honest films about gay and lesbian life and has supported directors like **Tom Kalin** and **Todd Haynes** whose unpopular visions are polar opposites to the Hollywood establishment. The openly gay Vachon who has been crowned the Queen of the New **queer cinema** (a title that makes her cringe) and once was called "godmother to the politically committed film" by the *New York Times*, began her career as a gofer in 1984. Vachon advanced from assistant on the landmark gay film *Parting Glances* (1986), one of the earliest films to address the AIDS crisis, to third assistant director, production coordinator, and second unit director on *Magic Sticks* (1987) and *My Demon Lover* (1987) and formed Apparatus, a production company, with Haynes. Then in 1989, Vachon coproduced her first feature *He Once Was* with Todd Haynes.

The 1990s belonged to Vachon as the premier cutting-edge producer, first as a founder of Kalin Films Production Inc. and later with her own production company Killer Films with partner Pamela Koffler. Vachon produced a body of work that established her as a producer with the vision of an auteur. A politically and socially committed independent producer, Vachon remains an indie and is not interested in "moving up" to the so-called big leagues. Vachon supports gay-themed films with characters proud of their sexual orientation and lifestyle though often troubled and disconnected from a judgmental society whose hatred impacts on their psyches.

In ten years Vachon produced films others turned their backs on: *Poison* (1991), *Swoon* (1992), *Dottie Gets Spanked* (1993), *Postcards from America*, *Go Fish* (both 1994), *Stonewall*, *Safe*, *Kids* (all 1995), *Plain Pleasures*, *I Shot Andy Warhol* (both 1996), *Office Killer*, *Kiss Me Guido* (both 1997),

Velvet Goldmine, Happiness (both 1998), *Wildflowers, I'm Losing You, Boys Don't Cry* (all 1999). From 2000 to 2002 Christine Vachon has many projects in various stages of development, production and release. They include: *Crime and Punishment in Suburbia*, directed by Bruce Wagner, Rose Troche's *The Safety of Objects, Hedwig and the Angry Inch*, directed by John Cameron Mitchell, *Women in Film* directed by **Rick Schmidt**, *Series 7: The Contenders* directed by Daniel Minahan (both 2001), **Todd Solondz's** *Storytelling, The Grey Zone*, directed by Tim Blake Nelson, *Chelsea Walls*, directed by Ethan Hawke, *Fine and Mellow*, directed by Hilton Als, *One Hour Photo*, directed by Mark Romanek, and **Todd Haynes'** *Far from Heaven*.

In 1994 Vachon received the Frameline Award for Outstanding Achievement in Lesbian and Gay Media. In 1996, New York Women in Film and Television gave Vachon their MUSE Award for Outstanding Vision and Achievement. Vachon is an activist producer both in her commitment to incendiary content and for working side by side with her directors. As producer, she nurtures each project so it reflects the creator's vision, thereby restoring respect and importance to a job title too often worn only for show.

BIBLIOGRAPHY

Vachon, Christine, with David Edelstein. *Shooting to Kill: How an Independent Producer Blasts Through the Barriers to Make Movies That Matter.* New York: Avon Books, 1998.

Vajna, Andy. *See* Carolco Pictures

Van Dyke, Willard. Documentary filmmaker. *b.* December 5, 1906, Denver, Colorado. *d.* January 23, 1986. *ed.* University of California. After working as a bank clerk, insurance salesman, x-ray technician, and still photographer, Willard Van Dyke found his life's passion in **documentaries** as one of three cameramen on **Pare Lorentz's** *The River* (1937). In 1939, Van Dyke made his documentary directing debut *The City* in collaboration with **Ralph Steiner**, a film about urban planning. In 1945, Van Dyke created the official film about the founding of the United Nations and made documentaries for television, the U.S. Information Agency, **industrials**, and films for various foundations. From 1965 to 1973 Van Dyke was director of the Film Department of the Museum of Modern Art. He was also the vice president of the International Federation of Film Archives. Van Dyke made documentaries for a prestigious group of sponsors including The Rockefeller and Ford Foundations, television's *Omnibus, The Twentieth Century*, CBS, and *The Twenty-First Century*, Van Dyke was president of **The Robert Flaherty Film Seminar** and member of the advisory board for the Learning Corporation of America, a division of Columbia Pictures.

Van Dyke's many documentaries include *Valley Town* (1940), *The Bridge* (1942), *Steel Town* (1943), *Journey into Medicine* (1946), *New York University* (1952), *Skyscraper* (1958), with Shirley Clarke, and *So That Men Are Free* (1962). His two sons, Robert and Murray, both followed their father into filmmaking.

vanity production. Film where one person wears many cinematic hats. Some independent filmmakers who direct, produce, photograph, edit, act, and do other functions on their films have no problem taking all the credit. Others invent pseudonyms for credits so the film doesn't appear to be a one-man-show.

Van Peebles, Melvin. Director, screenwriter, actor, producer, composer, editor. *b.* Melvin Peebles, August 21, 1932, Chicago, Illinois. *ed.* Wesleyan University. This pioneering African American filmmaker wrote several novels in Paris. *Le Permission* was the tale of a black American soldier that Van Peebles later adapted into his first feature film, *The Story of a Three-Day Pass* (1968). The film secured a deal with Columbia Pictures, making him one of the first black directors, along with Gordon Parks, to direct a studio production. Throughout his life, Van Peebles has been an entrepreneur, an actor, and stock trader. He learned his craft as a filmmaker with three short films, *Three Pickup Men for Herrick* (1957), *Sunlight* (1957) and *Cinq cent balles* (1963).

The Story of a Three-Day Pass is about a black soldier stationed in France who gets a three-day pass because of his "he knows his place" behavior. He meets a Caucasian Parisian; they begin a romance and are forced to deal with racial prejudice. Van Peebles didn't play it safe with his Columbia contract. *Watermelon Man* (1970) is an outrageous satire of a white bigot who turns black and is forced to experience prejudice directly. The style and content are far removed from a commercial product and led Van Peebles to work as an indie to further develop his voice as a black filmmaker.

Sweet Sweetback's Baad Asssss Song (1971) was a vanguard independent film, written, directed, produced, edited, composed, and starring Van Peebles. The film is a bold indictment of America's treatment of African Americans. When a dead black man is discovered, Sweetback (Van Peebles) helps two white police officers by allowing them to bring him in as a suspect. When the officers turn on him, arrest him, and then beat a young black man senseless, Sweetback goes on the run, now radicalized. This audacious film is not only daring in its point of view but is shot and edited in a highly nontraditional style with rapid cutting and an aggressive montage-driven structure. The film was rated X for sex and violence. Van Peebles capitalized on the restrictive rating by flaunting the slogan "Rated X by an All White Jury." Van Peebles self-promoted the movie and his image as a badass maverick black filmmaker.

In 1973 he wrote and directed *Don't Play Us Cheap*, a comedy starring Avon Long, Theresa Merritt, and Esther Rolle. *Identity Crisis* (1989) was written and starred Melvin's son Mario, a comedy about a white fashion designer and a black rapper who are switched into each other's bodies. Van Peebles has written many screenplays including *Panther* (1995), the story of the Black Panthers in Oakland, California, directed by his progeny Mario. In 1998 Melvin Van Peebles acted in *Love Kills*, directed by his son Mario. *Classified X* (1998) is a documentary directed by Melvin. In 1999 he acted in the film *Smut*. In 2000 Melvin Van Peebles was the screenwriter, director and composer on *Bellyful*, and an actor in *Antilles sur Seine*. Before **Spike Lee** there was Melvin Van Peebles—godfather of the black filmmaking movement in the 1980s and 1990s who continues on because of his courage, vision, business acumen, and badass attitude.

Van Sant, Gus. Director, producer, screenwriter. *b.* July 24, 1952, Louisville, Kentucky. *ed.* Rhode Island School of Design. Growing up Gus Van Sant painted and made **Super 8mm** autobiographical shorts for $30 to $50 with titles that included *Blood Root* (1967), *The Happy Organ* (1971), *Little Johnny* (1972), and *½ of a Telephone Conversation* (1973). After exposure to the films of **Stan Brakhage, Jonas Mekas,** and **Andy Warhol,** Van Sant changed his academic major from painting to cinema. He lived in Europe and then moved to Los Angeles where he worked as a production assistant for writer/director Ken Shapiro. Van Sant made *Alice in Hollywood* (1981), about a young actress who gives up her ideals after experiencing the Hollywood way. The film was never released.

Van Sant became interested in the subculture of down-and-outers populating Hollywood Boulevard. Artistically, he began to shape his vision, investigating the fringes of society. *Mala Noche* (1985) was financed with $25,000 he earned at a New York advertising agency. The film was adapted from Walt Curtis's semiautobiographical novel about the doomed relationship between a gay liquor store clerk and a Mexican immigrant. The openly gay director made the black-and-white film without judgment or political agenda. *Mala Noche* gained instant recognition at film festivals and was named best independent film of the year by the *LA Times*.

Hollywood took notice, but the studios rejected Van Sant's story pitches for *Drugstore Cowboy* (1989) and *My Own Private Idaho* (1991). Van Sant left Hollywood for Portland, Oregon. He made *Drugstore Cowboy* with Avenue, an independent production company, a film about four junkies who rob drugstores to keep the goods flowing for their habits. Van Sant received great critical recognition for his realistic and insightful portrayals of *Cowboy's* fringe characters. Audiences and reviewers no-

River Phoenix and William Richert in Gus Van Sant's *My Own Private Idaho* (1991). Courtesy of The Del Valle Archive

ticed Matt Dillon who had been typed in troubled teen movies. *My Own Private Idaho* was a bold examination of two male hustlers portrayed by Keanu Reeves and River Phoenix, whose character is a narcoleptic. The theme of a family unit among the disenfranchised became a recurrent concept in Van Sant's films along with alienation and unrequited love. Both films won Independent Spirit Awards for their screenplays.

Next Van Sant misstepped by taking on the challenge of adapting the cinematically unadaptable Tom Robbins's seminal novel *Even Cowgirls Get the Blues* (1993). The $8.5 million film was a major flop. In 1995 Van Sant made a significant comeback with *To Die For*, a black comedy featuring Nicole Kidman as an ambitious weather forecaster with murderous ways. The film marked Van Sant's first association with a major studio, Columbia Pictures. At the same time Van Sant produced the notorious *Kids* (1995), directed by **Larry Clark** whose photographs of junkies had inspired Van Sant's *Drugstore Cowboy.*

In 1997 Van Sant broke through with a mainstream success, *Good Will Hunting*, written and starring Matt Damon and Ben Affleck. The film, about a troubled blue-collar genius, grossed over $220 million worldwide. Van Sant was Oscar-nominated for best director, Damon and Affleck won for best original screenplay, and an Oscar statue went to Robin Williams for best supporting actor. Although the film still had Van Sant's vision of marginalized youth, the story and cinematic approach were the most traditional of his career.

In 1998 Van Sant made a disastrous decision for an indie with opportunity—a frame-by-frame recreation (not a traditional remake, update, or sequel) of *Psycho* (1960). Few could understand Van Sant's rationale for this futile exercise. He claimed by recreating the film it would give him the opportunity to see through Alfred Hitchcock's eyes. As the obsession proceeded, changes were made; the most unpopular was trying to motivate Norman's vicious knife attack on Marion Crane by adding a shot of him masturbating while he peeps at her undressing. Film students, many filmmakers, and Hitchcockians were outraged, and general audiences were not impressed.

Van Sant followed up with *Finding Forrester* (2000), a feel-good youth movie about a reclusive author, modeled on J.D. Salinger and played by Sean Connery, and his mentorship of a brilliant black street kid. The film had its heart in the right place, and Van Sant created a realistic atmosphere, an evocative visual style, and a sound but safe narrative. However, the story is just another underdog defeats the evil empire cliché, leaving Van Santians puzzled about why their indie hero would continue to water down his commitment to the outer rim of society. In 2001 Gus Van Sant produced *Standing Room Only* and in 2002, wrote and directed *Gerry*.

video store film school. Since the advent of VHS technology in the later 1970s and the recent DVD technology, filmmakers have had personal access to films as a school of self-teaching. **Quentin Tarantino** is the most famous graduate. By obsessively studying a wide range of films on tape, he taught himself how to make movies. The access to films for home study has had a major impact on the training of independent filmmakers, and the results are evident in their work. The trend has increased the use of visual quotes, references, and hybrids with creators drawing on other films rather than direct experience.

Vincent, Chuck. Director, producer, screenwriter, cinematographer, editor. *b.* Charles Vincent Dingley, 1940. *d.* September 23, 1991, Key West, Florida, of AIDS. Chuck Vincent was an **adult film** director who used various pseudonyms including Felix Miguel Arroyo, Larry Revene, Marc Ubell, and Martha Ubell so he could wear many hats as a hands-on **hard-core** filmmaker. His films include *Dirty Little* (1977), *This Lady Is a Tramp* (1980), *Games Women Play* (1981), *Puss 'n' Boots* (1983), and *Sex Crimes 2084* (1985). Vincent was by no means a typical porn director. He worked in regional theater as a stage manager and director and was associated with the prestigious Yale Repertory and Negro Ensemble companies. Those experiences gave him a respect for the crafts of acting and storytelling.

In the 1970s Vincent made the transition to filmmaking and founded

Platinum Pictures, a fully equipped production facility in New York City. Vincent learned all aspects of the craft and became a competent cinematographer and film editor so he could make films by himself. He chose to enter the growing hard-core market. Vincent saw an opportunity to cross over the genre with a more artistic story and character-driven approach. In 1981 he released *Roommates*, a breakthrough film about genuine people created to appeal to audiences that wouldn't normally go to an adult film. The film received critical praise, but the central adult film audiences wanted strict exploitation and were put off by the three-dimensional characters and complex narratives. *Roommates* did poorly at the box office where it played in art houses. However, it did have an impact on the explosion of **soft-core films** programmed for cable television stations. Vincent identified with his female characters and tried to reverse the strict male perspective of the genre. When a woman is raped in *Roommates* she doesn't learn to enjoy the brutal act, a dangerous myth perpetuated in so many porn films. The character expresses anger and humiliation over the violation of her body and free will.

In 1983 Vincent released *In Love*, widely considered to be the most artistic adult film of its time. The story follows a couple who meet in Florida and spend a passionate weekend. They part and twenty years pass before they meet again. Critics were confused by Vincent's intentions. Was *In Love* an elegant erotic film or just a bad romantic soap opera?

Vincent developed a stable of well-trained actors including Jerry Butler, Veronica Hart, Kelly Nichols, and Samantha Fox, who were willing to play nontraditional roles that required intimate sex acts. But these actors were a large cut above the typical porn performer chosen for physical attributes, often with no legitimate acting experience. Vincent discovered trained actors gave the characters in his films believability and heightened the erotic over the explicit.

By 1986 Vincent accepted that there was little support or financial interest in serious adult sex entertainment. He experimented with bringing in action and violence to his films that still contained action and sex acts. Vincent's change in direction produced some hard R rated films as well as the standard X of the genre he helped expand and elevate. Just some of the almost seventy films Chuck Vincent created under many pseudonyms include: *Luscious, Wildest Diamond* (both 1980), *RSVP* (1982), *New York's Finest* (1987), *Student Bodies, Thrilled to Death* (both 1988), and *Young Nurses in Love* (1989). Chuck Vincent was a maverick innovator who was ahead of his time in the 1990s, by which time audiences were more willing to cross over between dramas and adult films.

Vinterberg, Thomas. *See* Dogme 95

Vogel, Amos. Film programmer, historian, theorist, educator, author. *b.* 1921, Vienna. *ed.* Haversham College, University of Georgia, New School for Social Research. Amos Vogel fell in love with cinema when at age ten or eleven his father gave him a 9.5mm hand-cranked projector on which he screened Krazy Kat, Mickey Mouse, Charlie Chase, and **Charlie Chaplin** by running the films forth and back endlessly. An avid moviegoer, Vogel joined a film society in Vienna and immigrated to the United States in 1939.

Vogel attended the New School from 1943 to 1944. His love for film continued to grow. As Vogel investigated the cinema venues in New York at the time, he felt strongly that **16mm** films were not exhibited properly and set out to change the situation by creating Cinema 16, a film club dedicated to **avant-garde**, nonfiction, and independent cinema. The first program at Cinema 16 included *Lamentation* (1943), featuring Martha Graham, the **documentary** *Monkey into Man* (1938), James Broughton and Sidney Peterson's *The Potted Palm* (1946), and *Glens Fall Sequence* (1946), an animated film created on glass. **Maya Deren** rented the Provincetown Playhouse, and Vogel, his wife Marcia, and friends raised money to put on film programs. The early shows were big successes, but the New York State censorship office complained they had not approved the films for screening. The group had to submit the films in advance and needed to hire a stenotypist to create a script for a French animated film. After consulting a lawyer they decided to create a private membership film society, which eliminated precensorship, although the police could still intervene if a film was considered obscene by community standards. They sold one-year memberships for $10 in advance; membership was good for sixteen performances and two free guest tickets. No individual tickets were sold.

Six months after Cinema 16 started the organization, it became nonprofit and tax exempt and employed union projectionists. After a brief stint in Provincetown, Cinema 16 moved to the New York art house—Fifth Avenue Playhouse. The first show at this venue featured the premiere of Hans Richter's *Dreams That Money Can Buy* (1947). Cinema 16 next moved to a bigger space at the Central Needle Trades Auditorium. Later, additional screenings at various art theaters took place as members, and members of the cultural scene. The mission of Cinema 16 was to exhibit films that would disturb, contribute to personal knowledge, and incite change. Vogel gave little attention to the box office and put the money back into keeping Cinema 16 vital, building it into the most successful film society in American history and the first to specialize in the distribution of avant-garde films.

Program notes were written and distributed, and speakers included **Parker Tyler.** Each year Vogel, assisted by his wife and Jack Goelman, previewed hundreds of avant-garde, documentary, **animation**, foreign, independent feature, and scientific films. The chosen films were structured into feature-length programs with an effort to create a cultural collision by contrasting very different films. The audience became divided into two factions, nonfiction and avant-garde. They did not get along, creating a combustible but invigorating atmosphere. Bosley Crowther, film critic of the *New York Times*, was openly hostile to independent films and got his revenge by not reviewing them. The tensions between the two factions of the film community led to a falling out with **Jonas Mekas**, who helped form the **New American Cinema Group,** which dedicated programs to the work of one filmmaker and had regular screenings of **experimental films** in opposition to the Cinema 16 format. Some felt Vogel had too much power. Producer Ely Landau tried but failed to bring Mekas and Vogel together. Cinema 16 set up at another location at 175 Lexington, and it finally failed in May 1963. Vogel has lamented that the avant-garde movement could have flourished if he and Mekas had collaborated. Mekas attacked Vogel from his bully pulpit in the *Village Voice* column, and Vogel moved on to cofound the New York Film Festival with Richard Roud.

BIBLIOGRAPHY

McDonald, Scott. *A Critical Cinema 3: Interviews with Independent Filmmakers.* Berkeley: University of California Press, 1998.

von Trier, Lars. Director, screenwriter, cinematographer. *b.* April 30, 1956, Copenhagen, Denmark. *ed.* Danish Film Academy. The man most associated with **Dogme 95,** which was cofounded with Thomas Vinterberg, Lars von Trier has become *the* hero to indie filmmakers worldwide for his defiance of the tradition of American narrative filmmaking that he finds overmanipulated and dishonest. Von Trier, the darling of Cannes (*Europa* [1991] and *Breaking the Waves* [1996] both won a special Grand Jury prize, and *Dancer in the Dark* [2000] won the Palme D'Or), made **8mm** movies as a child, then began directing **16mm** shorts in 1971.

In 1994 after directing forty television commercials to hone his craft, von Trier made *The Kingdom,* a surrealistic hospital soap opera/ghost story that has been described as *E.R.* meets *The Shining* (1980). *The Kingdom* propelled him into the international spotlight as a stunning visualist and outrageous storyteller. Von Trier's roots were in film noir and German Expressionism. His first feature, *The Element of Crime* (1984), won prizes at the Cannes, Chicago, and Mannheim festivals. Von Trier created a doom-laden, haunted atmosphere by painting the film with a yellow tint and shafts of blue light.

The Kingdom put the word out about the coming filmmaking messiah who would lead the cinema into the next millenium, and *Breaking the*

Waves delivered it. The story of a woman who pledges to her severely injured husband she will have sex with men and report her experiences back to him was photographed by Robby Muller and von Trier in an onslaught of roller-coaster camera moves structured with jump cuts. The visual style didn't appear to directly illustrate the content, but von Trier went beyond that construct, creating a separate psychological inner narrative expressed through use of camera and an editing structure beyond Godard's *Breathless* (1959) that was truly a radical departure from Hollywood filmmaking. Von Trier even went beyond **John Cassavetes** into a cosmic home movie style combining the controlled closed-eye vision of **Stan Brakhage** with a mind-set filled with anxiety, pain, confusion, and constant disturbance.

Dancer in the Dark (2000) captured a harrowing performance and original song score from Bjork and an even more turbulent visualization. The first long section of the film featured von Trier's camera movements that invoke stomach-churning, then musical sequences shot with more digital video cameras than any indie could dream of acquiring to capture the inner life of a disturbed young woman thrown into a whirlpool of murder and death. The film represents a new cinema liberated from convention that makes the viewer work as hard as the actors and crew to take in the full visual and traumatic emotional experience. In 2002 von Trier was the writer, director and camera operator on *Dogville* and *D-day-Den fædige film.*

A new motion picture language is being written, and von Trier is at the forefront. New stories need new aesthetic treatment. A new madman of the cinema has arrived. *See also* Dogme 95

Vorisek, Richard (Dick). Rerecording mixer *b.* February 21, 1918. *d.* November 7, 1989. The pioneer of New York sound for film, Dick Vorisek began his career at Reeves sound studios. By the late 1940s directors who disliked life in Hollywood set up their production companies in New York, and Vorisek began mixing feature films directed by **Elia Kazan, Otto Preminger,** Robert Rossen, and Robert Wise.

Until the late 1960s film sound could only be rerecorded in one direction, requiring technicians to perform all of the sound cues on a ten-minute reel in real time, moving forward. If a mistake occurred the entire reel had to be done over. In the Hollywood system it was decided three mixers would sit at three separate stations, one for dialogue, a second for sound effects, and a third for music to minimize the possibilities for mistakes. There were few qualified mixers in New York. Vorisek was the man, so he worked all alone. Vorisek would study and rehearse with the cue sheet and then perform the ten-minute feat by himself, rarely making a mistake.

Vorisek's amazing résumé includes an enormous catalog of independent films and the work of maverick filmmakers including *The Hustler* (1961), *Lilith* (1964), *Salesman* (1969), *Alice's Restaurant* (1969), *Wanda* (1970), *End of the Road* (1970), *Little Murders* (1971), *Slaughterhouse-Five* (1972), *Dog Day Afternoon* (1975), *Network* (1976), *Carrie* (1976), *Pretty Baby* (1978), *All That Jazz* (1979), *Arthur* (1981), *Reds* (1981), *Come Back to the Five and Dime, Jimmy Dean, Jimmy Dean* (1982), *The World According to Garp* (1982), *Tender Mercies* (1983), *After Hours* (1985), *House of Games* (1987), and *The Untouchables* (1987). Vorisek was the sound of New York filmmaking. His legacy inspired every mixer who followed.

Vorkapich, Slavko. Editor, director, producer, screenwriter, art director, special effects creator, cinematographer, theorist, educator. *b.* March 17, 1892, Yugoslavia. *d.* October 20, 1976. Educated in Belgrade and Budapest, Slavko Vorkapich was a commerical artist in Paris and New York before arriving in Hollywood in 1922, where he became a studio special effects director and a producer of short subjects. Vorkapich became a noted expert in montage and created specific montage sequences for features produced by MGM, Columbia, RKO, and Paramount studios, including *The Good Earth* (1937), *Maytime* (1937), *Boys Town* (1938), *Mr. Smith Goes to Washington* (1939), *Meet John Doe* (1941), and *Viva Villa!* (1934), for which he created a montage depicting the outbreak of the Mexican Revolution. For *Maytime* he created a sequence showing Jeanette MacDonald's character's rise to fame. In 1932 Vorkapich created a sequence showing the boom and bust of the 1920s and the memorable Furies sequence in the Ben Hecht/Charles MacArthur film *Crime without Passion* (1934), which was reminiscent of Sergei Eisenstein's *Strike* (1925).

In 1928, while under the employment of the studio system, Vorkapich made *The Life and Death of 9413: A Hollywood Extra* with **Robert Florey.** The tragic-comic cinematic examination of the conceptual and political roles of a Hollywood extra and a movie star was produced for $96, shot in Vorkapich's home. Vorkapich was the principal cinematographer, and Gregg Toland shot close-ups thirteen years before *Citizen Kane* (1941). Florey and Vorkapich worked out of an aesthetic practice closer to the **avant-garde cinema** of the time, as opposed to the narrative rules followed by the studio system that supported Vorkapich. The characters are dramatically side-lit and isolated against a dark background to contrast their social/political class in the Hollywood universe. Exterior and interior environments are represented by cut-out silhouettes and miniature scaffolding constructions. The film was lit with a single-moving light source. Vorkapich created montages professionally and helped to define the narrative and editorial aesthetics of the Hollywood montage sequence, but the experimental short was shot and cut without employing Vorkapich's editorial philosophy, with the exception of an occasional rapid subjective camera movement. *The Life and Death of 9413: A Holly-*

wood Extra went through editorial evolution. It was originally synchronized to Gershwin's *Rhapsody in Blue*. The film received an audience through Florey's connections. **Charlie Chaplin** arranged screenings for the Hollywood community. Another associate led to a distribution deal, a Broadway opening, and a circuit release.

Vorkapich persuaded MGM to support two short films, a pictorial interpretation of Wagner's *Forest Murmurs* and Mendelssohn's *Fingal's Cave*. MGM financed the Mendelssohn film, but they shelved it as too artistic, and it was never screened publicly. In 1955 Vorkapich directed *Hanka*, which demonstrated principles of filmmaking. He later headed the film department at the University of Southern California (USC) where he mentored many notable filmmakers including cinematographer Conrad Hall.

As a theorist Vorkapich had articles published on film language, kinesthetics, which he called our sixth sense—the inner response and impulses that precede action. Vorkapich wrote extensively on the craft of montage in a manifesto entitled *Rules of Visual Presentation*. Influenced by Eisenstein, Pudovkin, and the early Russian filmmakers, Vorkapich transformed American film with his compressed mininarrative film inventions. Vorkapich was a significant educator who empowered USC film students with his kinetic visual ideas. Many of his students carried the Vorkapich philosophy into contemporary film that in the 1960s and 1970s became montage driven. The films of mavericks Sam Peckinpah, **Martin Scorsese** and Oliver Stone bear Vorkapich's imprint. *See also* Florey, Robert

BIBLIOGRAPHY

Kevles, Barbara L. "Slavko Vorkapich on Film as a Visual Language and a Form of Art." *Film Culture*, no. 38. (Fall 1965): 1–46.

Walking Tall. Based on true events surrounding Tennessee sheriff Bufford Pusser. With courage and single-handedly, Pusser rid his county of corruption, wielding a four-foot wooden club. *Walking Tall* was released in 1973 and struck an immediate emotional chord with a vigilante-loving, revenge-hungry national audience. **B-movie** veteran **Phil Karlson,** who was sixty-five at the time and had a formidable financial stake, directed the powerful film labeled by **critics** as a Hixploitation drama. Joe Don Baker gives a forceful performance as Pusser and is supported by Elizabeth Hartman as his wife, Leif Garrett as his son, and Noah Beery Jr. as Grandpa Carl Pusser. The reactionary political viewpoint is clear: Individuals should take the law in their own hands. When criminals attack the Pusser family, the sheriff shoots the manager of a local brothel and runs over redneck bad guys with his car. *Walking Tall* spawned two sequels, *Walking Tall Part II* (1975), directed by Earl Bellamy with Bo Svenson as Pusser, and *Final Chapter* (1977), again with Svenson, directed by Jack Starrett. In 1974 Charles Bronson and director Michael Winner cashed in on the popular revenge genre with *Death Wish,* which was also sequelized and adored by closet vigilantes everywhere. *See also* Karlson, Phil

Wang, Wayne. Director, screenwriter, producer. *b.* January 12, 1949, Hong Kong. *ed.* College of Art and Crafts. After studying art and film in Oakland, California, Wayne Wang returned to Hong Kong to work on a television comedy show. Wang's first directorial experience came on *Golden Needles* (1974), a thriller directed by Robert Clouse for which Wang directed the Chinese sequences—the producers were looking for authenticity. In 1975, Wang was in America rooming with filmmaker

Rick Schmidt of *How to Make a Film at Used Car Prices* fame. They co-directed *A Man, a Woman, and a Killer*, a no-budget sci-fi comedy/drama.

Wang had returned to Hong Kong in 1972 and found he didn't fit in. Working in San Francisco's Chinatown, Wang came to the realization he was neither Chinese nor American but a mix of the two cultures. His father Americanized him as a boy in Hong Kong. In fact, he was named for actor John Wayne after his parents saw *Red River* (1948). Wang made a prominent entry into independent filmmaking with a **16mm** black-and-white film shot in Frisco's Chinatown. *Chan Is Missing* (1982) was co-written, produced, directed, and edited by Wang. The majority of cast and crew were of Chinese descent, making it the first indie crafted almost entirely by Asians. It helped herald the multicultural cinema of the 1980s and 1990s. *Chan Is Missing* is a quirky comedy/mystery that explores Chinese culture in America. It was made for $22,000 with grants from the American Film Institute and the **National Endowment for the Arts.** Everyone worked for back-end deferrals, and Wang received many donations of services, props, and locations. Wise in the ways of **guerrilla filmmaking** from his experience with Schmidt, Wang shot the Asian film noir on 16mm blown up to 35mm for distribution. Critics and audiences responded warmly, and Wang received a lot of personal attention.

Dim Sum: A Little Bit of Heart (1984) chronicles a Chinese American family living in San Francisco. In 1987 Wang directed *Slamdance*, a thriller about an underground cartoonist, played by Tom Hulce, framed for murder. Audiences rejected Wang's attempt to stretch past Asian subject matter into mainstream filmmaking. Wang returned to Asian culture with *Life Is Cheap . . . But Toilet Paper Is Expensive* (1990), a disturbing film about a courier who is sent to Hong Kong to deliver a mysterious case but is unable to and instead explores the city. Graphic violence threatened assignment of an X-rating from the MPAA, so Wang released the film uncut and unrated.

The Joy Luck Club (1993) was a big-budget studio production of Amy Tam's bestselling novel dealing with several generations of Asian women. Wang proved he could work with a large cast, expansive narrative, and in-depth characters. In 1995, Wang returned to indie filmmaking, shooting two films back to back, *Smoke* and *Blue in the Face*, both situated in a Brooklyn smoke shop. The second film grew out of improvisations with the actors and in collaboration with novelist Paul Auster. The films established Wang as a hip postmodern filmmaker after the staid traditionalism of *The Joy Luck Club*. *Chinese Box* (1997) was a Japanese, French, U.S. production about the final six months of British rule in Hong Kong prior to China's takeover.

In 1999, Wang surprised **critics** who tried to type him as an Asian filmmaker by turning in a workmanlike directing assignment on Mona Simpson's novel *Anywhere But Here* (1999), about a quirky single mother and her daughter seeking a new life in Beverly Hills. *The Center of the World* (2001) is a drama concerning a Silicon Valley venture capitalist and a stripper who spend three days together in Las Vegas. Wayne Wang is also the writer and director of *The Beautiful Country* (2001), and director of *The Chambermaid* (2003). *See also* Asian American cinema

Warhol, Andy. Artist, filmmaker. *b.* Andrew Warhola, August 8, 1927, Cleveland, Ohio. *d.* February 22, 1987. *ed.* Carnegie Institute of Technology. Andy Warhol, the pop artist who brought the Campbell Soup can into the gallery, made an extraordinary impact on cinema in the second half of the twentieth century. Warhol was a totally independent filmmaker who made movies he financed and shot in his studio known as "The Factory." Warhol made films that were anticinematic, redefining the medium's tendency to capture time and space. *Sleep* (1963) was an eight-hour film of a man sleeping. *Empire* (1964) was a multihour single-shot study of the Empire State Building. The early Warhol films, which include *Kiss* (1963), *Haircut* (1963), and the notorious *Blow Job* (1963; a close-up of a man's face while fellatio is performed below the camera frame) were shown at The Factory, private screenings, and eventually art theaters and museums; they were not theatrically released.

The films were an extension of Warhol's art and reflected his lifelong love of the Hollywood Studio System. Warhol redefined the notion of celebrity by his prophetic fifteen-minutes-of-fame quote, and by the end of the century, his prediction had become reality. The troupe of Warhol superstars, including Viva, Ultra Violet, Mario Montez, Candy Darling, and Ingrid Superstar, were Warhol's recreation of the star system, replacing Marilyn Monroe, Cary Grant, and Bette Davis with transvestites, homosexuals, and others groomed for Warhol's stock company.

In the late 1960s and 1970s Warhol handed over the director's role to **Paul Morrissey** and set out for commercial distribution with *Flesh* (1968), *Trash* (1970), *Heat* (1972) and Warhol's versions of the Frankenstein and Dracula legends. The Morrissey films were more cinematically conventional than Warhol's but were scant on production values and abundant in outrageous behavior and ennui.

Warhol made a major contribution to trash cinema and had a substantial influence on **Amos Poe** and **John Waters** and the evolution of reality television in America. The hit TV series *Survivor* reminds us that Warhol's notion of celebrity is with us. When he spoke his prophetic quote, Warhol couldn't have known that Monica Lewinsky, Linda Tripp, Elian Gonzales, and the O.J. saga were not far off. When his short life was ended by a botched routine operation, a twentieth-century visionary and true independent artist was lost. *See also* Morrissey, Paul

Jane Forth and Joe Dellesandro, two superstars in Andy Warhol's Trash (1970), directed by Paul Morrissey. Courtesy of The Del Valle Archive

BIBLIOGRAPHY

Hackett, Pat, ed. *The Andy Warhol Diaries*. New York: Warner Books, 1989.

Koch, Stephen. *Stargazer: Andy Warhol's World and His Films*. New York: Praeger, 1973.

Waters, John. Director, screenwriter, producer, actor, editor, cinematographer. *b*. April 29, 1946, Baltimore, Maryland. An early movie fan, Baltimore's Prince of Puke and Pope of Trash was given an **8mm** movie camera by his grandmother for his seventeenth birthday. His dad became his first producer and financier, providing the budget for his early films, *Hag in a Black Leather Jacket* (1964), *Eat Your Makeup* (1967), *Mondo Trasho* (1969), *The Diane Linkletter Story* (1969), and *Multiple Maniacs* (1970). Waters hung out with his counterculture friends, many of whom were gay, like him. Waters was obsessed with violence, gore, and depravity and combined a gay, drug-oriented, anarchistic, nihilistic, depraved, and disgustingly lurid consciousness to create a filmmaker with an unusual, sick point of view who delighted in destroying any sense of taste or socially redeeming values.

The early 8mm and **16mm** films were screened in Baltimore church halls that Waters rented. They were publicized by word of mouth and leafleting the neighborhood. The crowds grew larger as Waters became a more accomplished and shocking filmmaker. Waters received a lot of

Danny Mills and Divine in *Pink Flamingos* (1972), directed by John Waters. Kobol Collection/Dreamland Productions

ink in the Baltimore papers. In the early 1970s he persevered until he got his films screened in movie theaters. After much schmoozing, a Waters film went legit—but at **midnight** screenings appropriate for the director's sicko worldview and for an audience brave and crazy enough to watch them with glee.

In 1972, Waters went past the Baltimore boundaries with *Pink Flamingos*, one of the most infamous of all independent films. It ended with the star, Waters's friend Harris Glenn Milstead, known in transvestite transformation as Divine, actually eating dog poop. *Pink Flamingos* was a scandale flouting all ethical, moral standards. The production values were as shameful as the content, falling well below the standards of a bad **B-movie**. Along with **Andy Warhol**, John Waters created the aesthetic for trash cinema. Like Warhol, Waters created his own superstars: the incomparable Divine, Edith (Edie the Egg Lady) Massey, Davie Lochary, Cookie Mueller, Mink Stole, and Mary Vivian Pearce.

In 1975 Waters returned with *Female Trouble*, which starred Divine as a renegade criminal who is ultimately executed by the state. Divine's character, Dawn Davenport, connects with a husband and wife beautician team who turn her into a beauty scarred with acid by the insanely jealous Edith Massey. Waters had been obsessed with the Manson family and their horrific crimes. The notion of a dysfunctional family to the nth degree inspired Waters to mythologize this counterculture nightmare into films that were revolting, but perversely hilarious at the same time. Waters's sweet personal nature, his ghoulish preoccupation with murder, mayhem, and aberrant behavior, and his genuine good-mannered persona, complete with conservative suit, thin tie, and pencil mustache, were a contrast that attracted the bad boy/bad girl in many of us.

Desperate Living (1977) starred Mink Stole as a bipolar housewife who goes on a crime and deviant spree with her 400-pound former maid, Grizelda. A psychotic transsexual wrestler, a gang rape, and a rabies poisoning are par for the rambling deliciously devious contrived plot. *Polyester* (1981), notorious for its "Filmed in Odorama" gimmick that gave viewers a scratch-and-sniff card coordinated by on-screen cues, was sick enough to include the smell of Divine passing gas. Classically Watersian, it features a dysfunctional band of perverts and degenerates and a dog who commits suicide by leaving a note announcing, "Goodbye, cruel world."

Seven years later in 1988, a kinder, gentler, more commercial (if that's possible) John Waters reappeared with *Hairspray* (1988), followed by *Cry-Baby* (1990), *Serial Mom* (1994), *Pecker* (1998), and *Cecil B. DeMented* (2000). The new John Waters now works with professional craftspeople producing a clean, slick visual style and employing real Hollywood actors like Johnny Depp, Kathleen Turner, Edward Furlong, and Melanie Griffith. The films remain funny and in bad taste but have achieved a more acceptable form.

Waters is incapable of selling out—he's far too twisted for that. He continues to attend every horrendous, high-profile murder trial he can. Waters has aged gracefully but hasn't lost his sick, tasteless humor. Always the master showman, his time off between phases afforded him the insight to retool his vision from the anything-goes 1970s to the retro 1980s and 1990s where camp and vulgarity are in. Waters is now an elder statesman of independent and **underground** film. He has given the keynote address at the Independent Spirit Awards and is a popular speaker and author. Waters is a nice guy, witty, never mean-spirited, terribly civil, and satisfied to be the "P.T. Barnum of Scatology" and all other such honors.

Watson, James Sibley. Director, cinematographer. *b.* August 10, 1894, Rochester, New York. *d.* March 31, 1982. Watson and his collaborator **Melville Webber** created the early **avant-garde** surrealist films *The Fall of the House of Usher* (1928) and *Lot in Sodom* (1933). Watson was a medical student and intern in physiology until 1923 when he put medicine aside for twenty years to pursue literary and arts criticism and to make films as a hobby. In 1931 Watson merged his interest in filmmaking with medicine when he created an **industrial** *Eyes of Science* for Bausch and Lomb.

In 1937 Watson made *Highlights and Shadows* for Eastman Kodak research laboratories. Watson was an American who was an avid consumer of European art and films and spent considerable time abroad. From 1920 to 1929, Watson, the heir to the Western Union fortune, bought stock in *The Dial*, an arts journal he published, that included drawings, film, art, theater, and literary criticism. Watson's positions were formal, not political. His tastes were parochial and conservative and featured respectable avant-garde art. Both *Lot in Sodom* and *The Fall of the House of Usher* were influenced by European cinema, expressionism, surrealism, futurism, cubism, and Soviet constructivism. Watson rejected Hollywood style and considered film an art. In 1928 he founded the Cinema Club in Rochester, New York, and became its chairman.

As an amateur independent production, *The Fall of the House of Usher* was highly regarded by the avant-garde community. The film reduced Poe's story to narrative essentials and communicated visually through an artful use of silhouette, multiple exposures, and rhythmic editing. The settings are suggested by light and patterns made by folded paper, not painted backdrops or three-dimensional objects. The chairman of *Films in Review* called it the most outstanding contribution to motion pictures as an art form since *The Cabinet of Dr. Caligari* (1920). The film and the unfinished *The Dinner Party*, which Watson began by himself, were based on a shooting script by e.e. cummings. *Lot in Sodom* was loosely based on the nineteenth chapter of Genesis. The film deals with gay male desire and heteronormative prohibition. *Lot in Sodom* is composed of symbolic erotic tableaus. While sexual references are obscure, it still wasn't permitted commercial distribution. Because it was filmed in 35mm the film was not available to **16mm** markets such as film societies. Watson created *Highlights and Shadows* and *Experiments in X-Ray Motion* by himself. A man dedicated to art, Watson supported many in the literary community. Although he respected the limited use of Hollywood cinematic grammar, he was aesthetically, if not socially or politically, committed to the avant-garde.

BIBLIOGRAPHY

Horak, Jan-Christopher, ed. *Lovers of Cinema: The First American Film Avant-Garde 1919–1945*. Madison: University of Wisconsin Press, 1995.

Webber, Melville. *See* Watson, James Sibley

Weinstein, Bob. *See* Miramax

Weinstein, Harvey. *See* Miramax

Weldon, Michael. Publisher of *Psychotronic*, a Xeroxed weekly guide to television programming of Z-movies like *Attack of the Killer Tomatoes!* (1978) and films that celebrate ghouls, science fiction, mad scientists, crazed farmers, axe murderers, gorillas, and of course sex, drugs, and rock 'n' roll. In 1983, Weldon published *The Psychotronic Encyclopedia of Film*, a reference volume that cataloged, analyzed, and offered critical insights into films that historians and reference books have ignored. Weldon introduced valuable scholarship to the world of low- and no-budget films and the underground empire of exploitation, the outrageous and the aesthetics of the just plain bad movie. In 1996 Weldon followed up his classic book with *The Psychotronic Video Guide* to make it easier for fans who scanned late night television, old video stores and other haunts to locate their psychotronic faves. *See also* psychotronic film

BIBLIOGRAPHY

Weldon, Michael, with Charles Beesley, Bob Martin, and Akira Fitton. *The Psychotronic Encyclopedia of Film.* New York: Ballantine Books, 1983.

———. *The Psychotronic Video Guide.* New York: St. Martin's Press, 1996.

Wexler, Haskell. Cinematographer, director, documentary filmmaker, producer. *b.* February 6, 1926, Chicago, Illinois. Haskell Wexler is a complex film figure. In addition to his many accomplishments photographing commercials and Hollywood feature films, he has also photographed *Matewan* (1987) and *The Secret of Roan Irish* (1994) for indie giant John Sayles. Wexler is a politically radical documentarian associated with *Brazil: A Report on Torture* (1971), the controversial Vietnam War film *Introduction to the Enemy* (1974), and *Underground* (1976), an unprecedented view into the Weather Underground. In 1969 Wexler directed the fictional feature *Medium Cool*, a watershed film, the first to challenge the ethics, morality, and agenda of the media. Recent credits for Haskell Wexler include: director of photography on *Limbo*, directed by John Sayles, codirector producer and director of photography on the documentary *Bus Rider's Union* (both 1999), director of photography on the documentaries *Good Kurds, Bad Kurds* and *The Man On Lincoln's Nose* (both 2000), and director of photography on the cable television film *61**, directed by Billy Crystal. A maverick, indie, and Hollywood professional with integrity and conviction, Wexler remains a vital force in all walks of cinematic life.

white coater. A **sexploitation film** that uses a medical figure or medical **documentary** footage to introduce and rationalize the film's real purpose: to show down-and-dirty sex.

Whitney Museum of American Art. The Whitney has a long commitment to independent **experimental film** and video with regular screenings and installations. Since the 1970s the Whitney has featured work by **Stan Brakhage, Bruce Baillie,** Ernie Gehr, and many in the pantheon of film art. The Whitney also partnered with Museum of Modern Art to catalog nearly 650 films by **Andy Warhol,** called The Andy Warhol Film Project, the largest archival research project in the history of American **avant-garde** filmmaking.

Wild Style. See Ahearn, Charles

Williamson, Kevin. Screenwriter, director. *b.* March 14, 1965, New Bern, North Carolina. Just when everyone thought every conceivable low-budget horror narrative had been done and redone, Kevin Williamson revitalized the genre with his inventive original screenplay for *Scream* (1996), shaped into a blockbuster sleeper by a veteran of the form, **Wes Craven.** Williamson made the conventions of the 1970s and 1980s horror films part of the narrative, giving the story a clever **self-referential** context. He wrote the 1997 sequel and the last installment of what became a trilogy (not a **franchise,** to the integrity of everyone involved) based on the original characters he created.

In 1997 *I Know What You Did Last Summer* was released. The film was another blockbuster. The story of four friends who accidentally run over a pedestrian, dispose of the body, and then begin receiving notes (hence the title) was shrewd but more formulaic than his groundbreaking debut script. In 1998 Williamson executive produced and made an uncredited contribution to the screenplay for *Halloween H2O: Twenty Years Later,* directed by Steve Miner, and wrote *The Faculty,* another self-referential narrative, for director **Robert Rodriguez.** Williamson made his directorial debut with *Teaching Mrs. Tingle* in 1999, the tale of three high school students who tie their hardhearted teacher to her bed when they learn she threatens their college careers. Recent credits for Kevin Williamson include: creator of characters for *Scream 3* (2000), writer, producer and director on *Her Leading Man* and writer and producer on *Cursed Writer* (2001). *See also* Craven, Wes

Wiseman, Frederick. Documentary filmmaker. *b.* January 1, 1930. *ed.* Williams College, Yale Law School, Princeton University, John Jay College of Criminal Justice, Lake Forrest College, Williams College, University of Cincinnati. Frederick Wiseman is a nonfiction auteur who has directed over thirty feature **documentaries,** most supported by a long-term arrangement with PBS and Wiseman's Zipporah Films, Inc. After the initial air dates, Zipporah distributes the films to schools, organizations, and film societies. Wiseman has total control over every aspect of the content, style, and form of his work. With few exceptions, his career-long subject has been the institutions that reveal and define life in American democracy. Many of the titles are self-explanatory: *High School* (1968), *Hospital* (1970), *Basic Training* (1971), *Juvenile Court* (1973), *Welfare* (1975), *Racetrack* (1985), *Central Park* (1989), *Zoo* (1993), and *Public Housing* (1997). This body of work, which stands as a social, political, and anthropological history of the latter twentieth century, began with *Titicut Follies* (1967), a documentary inside a prison for the criminally insane.

The films are produced with Wiseman recording sound and a cinematographer photographing in a direct but unobtrusive manner. Wiseman and his cinematographer discuss his approach before and after each shooting session. Signals are worked out to communicate silently during shooting. Often Wiseman inhabits his subjects by just observing. Wiseman decides what to shoot and when to pass. Shooting proceeds over a long period, with ratios as high as 400:1 for a project. As editor, he makes choices based on a subjective but open point of view of what he experienced during his time in the environment. Scenes are often long, playing out in perceived real time without editorial compression. Wiseman's subjects appear unaware and unaffected by his presence. He rarely editorializes or presents a proscribed thesis; life unfolds slowly with human drama, realism, warts, and moments of enlightenment. Wiseman doesn't make grandiose claims for social change with his films, but they incite action by bearing witness to the cruel stupidity of many bureaucracies. Not a propagandist but a civil libertarian, Wiseman's instincts for the petty injustice and repressive bureaucracies inflame audiences patient with his painstaking efforts to dedramatize situations, which intensifies the viewers' emotions as the results reveal themselves during the slow and methodical tour Wiseman takes on each outing. Wiseman disdains the term **cinéma vérité**. His law training has taught him that the truth is always subjective, but lawyers must remain objective and open to the facts and circumstances before them. Wiseman coined the phrase "reality fictions" to describe his filmmaking philosophy.

Independence and industry support have given Wiseman freedom and unprecedented longevity but at a price. His early films displayed great passion for the ills present in the justice and social institutions he documented. Eventually, Wiseman began to run out of subjects worthy of his in-depth exploration, so the approach style and methods remained the same, but the life of models (*Model*, 1980), the day-to-day operation of Neiman Marcus (*The Store*, 1983), and the environment of a public park (*Central Park*, 1989) do not present the human drama of life and death evident in *Hospital* (1970), the injustice of the welfare system (*Welfare*, 1975), or the fate of youthful offenders in *Juvenile Court* (1973). It has been said Wiseman's work is a time capsule of our shared experience. It is also the record of the obsessions and artistic rigor of an independent filmmaker with unimpeachable integrity and commitment to the way he observes the society we live in. Recent documentaries by

Frederick Wiseman are *Public Housing* (1997), *Belfast, Maine* (1999), and *Domestic Violence* (2001).

BIBLIOGRAPHY

Atkins, Thomas R. *Frederick Wiseman.* New York: Monarch Press, 1976.
Benson, Thomas W., and Carolyn Anderson. *Reality Fictions: The Films of Frederick Wiseman.* Carbondale: Southern Illinois University Press, 1989.

Wohl, Ira. Documentary director, producer. Ira Wohl, the Oscar-winning director of *Best Boy* (1979), a **documentary** about his mentally challenged cousin Philly, was an editing room assistant to Orson Welles on his legendary and never-completed film adaptation of Cervantes's *Don Quixote*. Wohl then established himself in the New York working-filmmaker community editing commercials and **industrials** and creating his own short documentaries. *Co-Co Puffs*, a nonfiction portrait of a jazz drummer giving lessons to a female student, took first prize at the 1973 Ann Arbor Film Festival. In 1974 with four shorts under his belt, Wohl joined the Peabody Award–winning children's series *Big Blue Marble*, where he researched, produced, directed, and edited documentary segments.

Wohl began to develop the idea for *Best Boy* that started a four-year odyssey about his family and the universal struggle for independence. The project began when Wohl, concerned that Philly's parents were elderly and couldn't take care of their son for much longer, decided to prepare him to live alone and find his place in the world as an individual. In embarking on this personal issue out of compassion for his family, the filmmaker in Wohl sensed it should be documented on film. *Best Boy* is a humane and life-affirming film about responsibility, compassion, family struggles, and the importance of an individual's right to happiness and the pride of independence. The film won first prize at the Houston, Miami, Chicago, San Francisco, and London film festivals. The New York Film Critic's Circle created a documentary award especially for *Best Boy*, and the honors culminated in the Oscar for best documentary in 1980. The film had a long theatrical and television run worldwide as well as an active nontheatrical, educational, institutional, and home entertainment distribution life.

In 1990 Wohl returned to the University of Southern California for three years and graduated with honors, receiving a master's in clinical social work. He produced, directed, and edited a three-hour series on psychological diagnosis for distribution to mental health professionals and students nationwide. In 1997 he directed *Best Man: "Best Boy" and All of Us Twenty Years Later*. Wohl now practices as a psychotherapist.

women in film. A short but succinct history: During the Classical Hollywood Studio System women were prominent on screen as actors. Behind the camera the male-dominated industry made few exceptions. Dorothy Arzner and later **Ida Lupino** directed. Francis Marion, Anita Loos, and others wrote screenplays. There were female editors and costume designers, but women were excluded from the crafts of cinematography, production design, sound, and music. In the executive branch, males retained studio power. The social and political liberation movements of the 1960s did little to change the situation, although there was some improvement.

The 1970s women's movement and affirmative action laws opened doors. Independent film portals offered new opportunities especially in **documentaries**, which was also a training ground for directors, cinematographers, and editors. Elaine May and **Joan Micklin Silver** broke through as directors. The 1980s were a time of change. Women began to enter the industry in bigger numbers and fought against the dominant male gaze point of view that had dominated movies since their inception. The long male-dominated areas of producing cinematography, production design, sound, music, and the executive suites began to change with the presence of women in these jobs. A female point of view and the beginning of some semblance of equality began to gain strength. Clearly, independent filmmaking has offered many more opportunities for women as well as television and nonfiction filmmaking to express their cinematic voices and to make a living as a filmmaker. From the 1980s into the twenty-first century just a sampling of the women who have made important contributions to filmmaking include: **Lizzie Borden, Ayoka Chenzira,** Joyce Chopra, **Martha Coolidge, Julie Dash,** Jodie Foster, Su Friedrich, **Jill Godmilow,** Randa Haines, **Faith Hubley, Barbara Kopple,** Penny Marshall, **Mira Nair, Yoko Ono, Yvonne Rainer, Susan Seidleman, Penelope Spheeris,** Barbara Streisand, **Christine Vachon,** Claudia Weill and Joyce Wieland.

BIBLIOGRAPHY

Cole, Janis, with Holly Dale. *Calling the Shots: Profiles of Women Filmmakers.* Kingston, Ontario: Quarry Press, 1993.

Kaplan, E. Ann. *Women & Film: Both Sides of the Camera.* New York: Methuen, 1983.

Seger, Linda. *When Women Call the Shots: The Developing Power of Women in Television and Film.* New York: Henry Holt, 1996.

Women in Film. Organization founded in 1973 after Sue Cameron wrote a column for *The Hollywood Reporter* exposing a secret Writers Guild of America study that stated only 2 percent of episodic television scripts were written by women. The *Reporter's* publisher, Tichi Wikerson-Kassel, called a meeting in her office with Marcia Borie, Norma Zeph-Bogert, Nancy Malone, Portia Nelson, Georgeanne Heller, and Francoise Ruddy and formed Women in Film (WIF). They dedicated themselves to ending the degradation of women in movies and to being educators and mentors to women entering the industry. The WIF Foundation distributes finishing funds for films dealing with social issues. They sponsor screenings and maintain an oral and video history of significant women in the industry. The WIF has committees for ageism, women in film international, performers, directors, and screenwriter workshops, and committees supporting stuntwomen and empowerment. WIF produces public service announcements for local charities to provide members the opportunity to gather experience and professional credits. Each year the WIF presents its Crystal Awards for outstanding achievements in entertainment and the global communications industry. The WIF has chapters in Los Angeles and New York.

women in prison films. This provocative and exploitive genre was first contrived in Hollywood in the late 1920s. In 1929 Cecil B. DeMille directed a silent and later a sound version of *The Godless Girl*. Paramount produced *Ladies of the Big House* (1931/1932), with Sylvia Sidney, and *Prison Farm* (1938). Warner Bros. put out *Ladies They Talk About* (1933) and *Girls on Probation* (1938). RKO had *Condemned Women* (1938), and Columbia released *Women in Prison* (1938). The Producers Releasing Corporation released *Prison Girl* (1942) and *Girl in Chains* (1943). Republic had *Girls of the Big House* (1945). These **B-movies** borrowed conventions from the male prison picture, but incarcerated women presented filmmakers with a natural narrative viaduct for sordid sex, sadism, abuse, and the dark side of femininity, all captured through the male gaze. The films featured catfights, lesbianism, and fetishes provided by women in uniform. Popular B-movie actresses played women-gone-wrong roles to the hilt, showcasing moral degradation, nudity, and graphic depiction of violence and sex acts. Voyeurism was heightened by all-female casts and confined settings. Women in prison films featured blatant stereotypes and melodramatic narratives and performances.

These films reemerged in the 1950s with John Cromwell's *Caged* (1950) and *Girls Town* (1959), starring blond bombshell Mamie Van Doren. **American International Pictures** embraced the genre with its own brand of youth market exploitation including: *So Young, So Bad* (1950), *Running Wild* (1955), *Girls in Prison* (1956), *Reform School Girl*, *Sorority Girl* (both 1957), *Girls on the Loose*, *High School Hellcats* (both 1958), and *Teenage Gang Debs* (1966). Other films include *Why I Must Die* (1960), *House of Women* (1962), *99 Women* (1969), *Women in Cages*, starring Pam Grier (1971), *Women in Cell Block 9*, *Sweet Sugar* (both 1972), *The Big Bust Out* (1973), *Caged Heat* (1974), produced by New World Pictures, *Barbed Wire Doll* (1975), *Ilsa the Wicked Warden* (1977), *Sadomania* (1981), *Caged Women* (1982), *Women's Prison Massacre* (1983), Demme's directorial debut, *Re-*

form *School Girls* (1986), *Prison Heat* (1992), and *Girls in Prison* (1994). **Hardcore** producers couldn't resist the possibilities the genre invited: *Caged Desires* (1970), *Prison Babes* (1976), and *Bare Behind Bars* (1987). Many women in prison films evolved into **soft-core** adult product. *The Big Doll House* (1971), *The Big Bird Cage*, produced by **Roger Corman**, *The Hot Box* cowritten by **Jonathan Demme** (both 1972), and *Terminal Island* (1973) are just a few examples. Roger Corman exploited the formula as did pornographers often working out of Germany. In 1976, Pamela Anderson made *Barb Wire*. In 1983, a grown-up exorcised Linda Blair appeared topless in *Chained Heat* and Sly Stallone's ex, Bridjette Nielson, was in 1993's *Chained Heat II*.

Women Make Movies. Established in 1972 to address representation and misrepresentation, this organization became the largest North American **distributor** of women's media. The national, New York–based feminist, multicultural organization retains a catalog of almost 500 films and videotapes. Their Production Assistance program offers women producers financial sponsorship services, workshops, and seminars. In a five-year period Women Make Movies returned over a million dollars in royalty payments to women producers.

Wood, Edward. Director, producer, screenwriter, actor. *b.* October 10, 1924, Poughkeepsie, New York. *d.* December 10, 1978, North Hollywood, California. Before he was immortalized in **Tim Burton**'s black-and-white biopic *Ed Wood* (1994), before *Plan 9 from Outer Space* (1959) received the Golden Turkey Award, and long before he became a retro cosmic joke as the universal choice for the worst film director of all time, Ed Wood was an unusual **B-movie** director who loved movies and was unaware of his future fate. Everyone has had fun with Wood, but historical and critical perspective must prevail. Two facts sit side by side. On a technical and narrative level, it is likely a fair statement that Wood may well be the most incompetent filmmaker, independent or otherwise, of the Hollywood era. Unlike many B- or no-budget filmmakers working subterranean during the Hollywood era, each time Wood set out to make a *Citizen Kane* and was often ecstatic with his results, oblivious to how he was judged. This may be hard to fathom when encountering an Ed Wood film for the first time.

This writer first saw *Plan 9 from Outer Space* on television in the early 1960s. After learning from the television guide that *Chiller Theater* was showing a film with our favorite horror thespian, Bela Lugosi, my dad and I stoked up the popcorn popper, poured beverages, and settled in front of the tube to have Bela work his magic. I was years from my film consciousness in education and experience. I don't remember which of us howled with laughter and disbelief first, but I remember convulsing

Director Ed Wood in his white dinner jacket next to his favorite actress, Vampira, at the premiere of the Woodian classic, *Bride of the Atom* (1956). Courtesy of The Del Valle Archive

with laughter and rolling onto the rug in hysterics many times. Bela seemed to be in another movie (now well documented elsewhere—he was). The actors playing police officers looked like they were pulled off the street, and I don't mean Hollywood and Vine. Their high-pitched voices and ridiculous dialogue caused many great heckle lines between dad and me. The special effects were grade double Z. The plot made little sense, and the production values were subbasement variety. This couldn't be for real, but no one back then could be so satirically brilliant to deliberately create a bad or trash film aesthetic—which would come later. *Plan 9 from Outer Space* was so bad it took on its own rules and created its own cinematic universe.

Wood displayed an interest in film when he was just four or five years old. His mother dressed him as a girl, and Wood wore woman's clothes throughout his life. He is remembered for his Angora sweaters, and as a Marine during World War II, reportedly he wore a bra and panties under his uniform during combat. Wood married Norma McCarthy, but the sight of him in her nightgown quickly ended the marriage.

Wood developed many film projects and in 1953 independently raised the money to make his directorial debut, *Glen or Glenda/ I Changed My Sex*. The film featured Bela Lugosi who had fallen on hard times. Wood, under the stage name Daniel Davis, plays Glen who struggles with his compulsion to wear his fiancée's clothes. The film is a narrative confusion of stock footage, twisted dream sequences, and Wood's pitch for tolerance and acceptance. Lugosi narrates the film from a haunted house. In 1953 Wood also directed his first western, *Crossover Avenger: The Adventures of the Tucson Kid*. A sequel and two unsold television pilots released as a fifty-minute film, *The Adventures of the Tucson Kid*, followed.

Jail Bait, aka *The Hidden Face* (1954), concerns a young man drawn to a life of crime and forced to have a plastic surgeon change his face when the law is about to catch up with him. *Bride of the Monster*, aka *Bride of the Atom* (1955), with Lugosi and Tor Johnson features a giant rubber octopus that terrorizes. In 1957 Wood wrote, directed, and produced *The Night the Banshee Cried* and *Final Curtain* in which the vampire star of a horror play lurks about the empty theater, motivated by an unknown source forcing him to seek out an unknown object. Lugosi was reading the script when he passed away.

The year 1958 saw *The Bride and the Beast* in which a woman learns on her wedding night she was Queen of the gorillas in a former life, a screenplay that only could come out of the mind of Ed Wood. That year he also wrote, directed, and produced *Night of the Ghouls*, aka *Revenge of the Dead*, a sequel to *Bride of the Monster* with a little *Plan 9 from Outer Space* thrown in. Two cops investigate reports that ghosts were sighted in Los Angeles, which leads them to a mystic. In *The Sinister Urge* (1960) recurring cops played by Keene Ducan and Duke Moore hear their assignment is to shut down a smut picture racket headed by a brassy blonde with a four-foot quill pen. The film takes the position that photos of plump women in lingerie cause juvenile delinquency.

From 1961 to 1970 Wood wrote but didn't direct *Married Too Young* (1962), *Shotgun Wedding* (1963), *Orgy of the Dead* (1965), *One Million AC/DC* (1969), *Operation Redlight* (1969), *Gun Runners* (1969), and *The Photographer* (1969), a **nudie cutie**. In 1970 Wood was back writing and directing *Take It Out in Trade* (1971), a nudie with the Woodian touch. *Necromania* (1971) is a **soft-core** film in the Wood style. The thin plot concerns a sorceress in a haunted house who has a love potion that ignites sexual passion. Wood directed the film in a weekend for $7,000, dressed in a pink babydoll number. *The Only House* (1971) is a film with the same plot as *Necromania* without the supernatural acts. In 1975 Wood and Charles Anderson directed a series of twelve, twenty-minute **Super 8mm** films under the title *Sex Education Correspondence School*.

Before there was **Jack Smith, Andy Warhol**, and **John Waters**, Ed Wood was out there making independent movies and perplexed by their poor reception. Now, more than twenty years after his death, Wood fans are delighted by how bad the movies are.

BIBLIOGRAPHY

Grey, Rudolph. *Nightmare of Ecstasy: The Life and Art of Edward D. Wood, Jr.* Portland, OR: Feral House, 1994.

X—The Man with the X-Ray Eyes. Low-budget sci-fi, horror **exploitation** film produced and directed by **Roger Corman** for **American International Pictures** in 1963. This cult favorite stars Ray Milland in one of his best remembered roles as Dr. Xavier who develops X-Ray vision from experimental eyedrops. The doctor can see through everything, which opens up a world of possibilities for him (all nudity is cleverly hidden by plants and furniture). He accidentally commits a murder and takes cover as a carnival mind-reader where his boss is played by Don Rickles. X's sight becomes so strong he is driven mad by the time the film concludes. A remake has been scheduled.

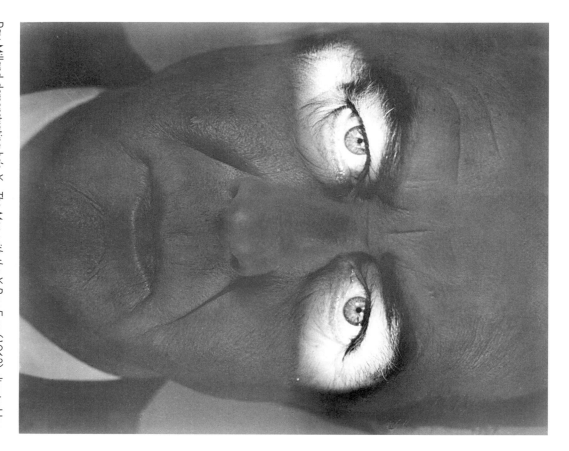

Ray Milland demonstrating he's *X—The Man with the X-Ray Eyes* (1963), directed by Roger Corman and distributed by American International Pictures. Courtesy of The Del Valle Archive

Y

Young, Irwin. Film laboratory executive. The head of New York's DuArt Film and Video, founded by his father in 1922 and the oldest film lab in the country, is a pioneer supporter of independent filmmaking. Young's fervor and commitment to filmmakers working outside the system has been consistent over decades. To get a first indie film completed, the filmmaker needs a laboratory willing to extend credit, defer fees, or even invest in the project. Young has been unconditionally generous to filmmakers who appeal to him, desperately needing to get their dailies developed or final cut printed. He has assisted a strong list of aspiring talents now established members of the indie film community: **Edward Burns, Abel Ferrara, Terry Zwigoff, Spike Lee, Whit Stillman, Richard Linklater, Hal Hartley, Jim Jarmusch,** and many others. Young extended credit to Lee to complete his career-launching *She's Gotta Have It* (1986). He gave Linklater a 35mm blow-up of his **16mm** negative for his breakthrough film *Slacker* (1991). There is a caveat in working with Young: After the nascent filmmakers leave the friendly and embracing office of Young, they have to deal with the labyrinthine bureaucracy of DuArt itself, encountering Young's bad cop, Howard Funsch, in the credit office and the hard-nosed shipping and receiving staff. In the end, embattled filmmakers, especially film students, exhausted and frustrated by rejection, misinformation, unreturned phone calls, and incomprehensible and unreasonable procedures, manage to deal with the harsh pitfalls of indie filmmaking, and Young's tough-love assistance is invaluable.

Young, Robert M. Director, screenwriter. *b.* November 22, 1924, New York City. Considered a father figure of the indie movement, Robert M. Young has dedicated much of his respected career to honest and realistic portrayals of Latinos on screen. Young began in **documentaries**: *Secrets of* *the Reep* (1957) and the prize-winning *White Paper* documentaries for the NBC network. He was fired when he codirected *Cortile Cascino* (1962) for the series. The documentary revealed extreme poverty in a Sicilian slum. Network executives decided Young's result was too real for the public to handle, and the show was not aired. In 1964 Young was the cowriter, coproducer, and director of photography on the landmark *Nothing But a Man*, one of the first films directed by a white director (**Michael Roemer**) to honestly portray African American life.

In 1977 Young made his directorial debut with *Alambrista!*—a fictional feature film about illegal farm laborers starring Edward James Olmos, Ned Beatty, Linda Gillen, Domingo Ambriz, and Trinidad Silva. *Short Eyes* (1977), based on Miguel Pinero's play, was a harrowing prison drama of pedophiles behind bars. *Rich Kids* (1979) is a New York City film about the effects of divorce on upper-class youths. *One-Trick Pony* (1980) was a showcase for singer/songwriter Paul Simon about an aging rock star trying to keep his marriage together while dealing with the mercurial tastes of his diminishing audience. *The Ballad of Gregorio Cortez* (1982) was the true story of a Mexican in 1901 who murdered a sheriff, then eluded a 600-strong posse for two weeks. The **American Playhouse** production starred Edward James Olmos as Cortez in a historically accurate period production.

Saving Grace (1986) featured Tom Conti as a young pope who, after experiencing the uselessness of his ceremonial role, sneaks out of the Vatican into a small Italian village that has lost its identity. In *Extremities* (1986), William Mastrosimone adapted his play about a woman victimized by a rapist who turns the table on her tormentor. *Dominick and Eugene* (1988) starred Tom Hulce and Ray Liotta as twin brothers, one a young medical intern (Liotta), the other a childlike underdeveloped man (Hulce) who needs and gets constant care and unconditional love from his morally responsible sibling. *Triumph of the Spirit* (1989) with Willem Dafoe and Edward James Olmos is the true story of a Greek/Jewish boxer sent to Auschwitz. The grim production was filmed on location. *Talent for the Game* (1991) continued Young's long and fruitful relationship with Olmos, who plays a California Angels baseball scout who discovers a pitching prodigy on an Idaho farm. The film had a minor theatrical release, left quickly, and went **direct-to-video.** In *Roosters* (1993) Olmos is an ex-con overpowered by his machismo when he returns home to the rural South; it was coproduced by *American Playhouse.*

In 1993 *Children of Fate: Life and Death in a Sicilian Family*, the documentary made for NBC but never aired, was released with additional material from Young's son and daughter-in-law who pick up the story. The original black-and-white 1961 footage is intercut with the 1990s color material. The Capra family has divorced, and the documentary reveals the wife's newfound self-identity as the family continues to struggle in the Palermo slum. *Caught* (1996) is a variation of *The Postman Always Rings Twice* (1946). The neo-noir featured Olmos and Maria Conchita Alonso in the story of a relationship disrupted by a mysterious drifter. Throughout his career, Young has remained loyal to his roots in independent low-budget filmmaking and to making films that not only entertain but enlighten. *See also* Roemer, Michael

Youngblood, Gene. Film and video theorist, author, lecturer, educator. *b.* May 30, 1942. An internationally recognized scholar on the history and theory of **experimental film** and video arts, Gene Youngblood has taught and lectured globally for more than thirty years on the art and politics of electronic and digital media and telecommunications. Youngblood made an enduring contribution to independent filmmaking with his 1970 milestone book *Expanded Cinema*. Youngblood was a seer who predicted the video and digital applications and influences that have transformed filmmaking over the last three decades of the twentieth century. He posited philosophical, aesthetic, and technological concepts of what he called the global/media network long before home video, computers, and digital imaging came into the public sector. The book investigated and explained the advanced image-making technologies of experimental video, computer graphics, multiprojection environments, and laser imagery. *Expanded Cinema* sat on the shelf of every postwar and baby-boomer generation filmmaker curious about the future of moving images.

Over the years, Youngblood has received prestigious grants for his work, including from the Rockefeller Foundation and the **National Endowment for the Arts.** He has been a consultant to the Library of Congress and has taught video at the California Institute of the Arts for over seventeen years. His prestigious teaching curriculum vitae includes the California Institute of Technology, The School of the Art Institute of Chicago, Columbia University, and the film departments of USC and UCLA. *See also* expanded cinema

BIBLIOGRAPHY

Youngblood, Gene. *Expanded Cinema*. New York: E.P. Dutton, 1970.

Z

Zaentz, Saul. Producer. *b.* February 28, 1921, Passaic, New Jersey. Saul Zaentz, one of the most powerful independent producers in Hollywood, began in the music business as an owner of Fantasy Records, a jazz and blues company. Zaentz's mogul status was achieved in 1972 when Fantasy expanded to features and produced *Payday*, a portrait of a country singer coming apart, with a powerhouse performance by Rip Torn. *One Flew Over the Cuckoo's Nest* (1975), a box office bonanza that dominated the Oscars, was next. That success funded The Saul Zaentz Film Center in the San Francisco Bay area—a state-of-the-art film and audio facility. In 1984 Zaentz again hit box office and Academy gold with *Amadeus*, followed by *The Mosquito Coast* (1986), *The Unbearable Lightness of Being* (1988), and *At Play in the Fields of the Lord* (1991). In 1996 Zaentz won the Triple Crown with *The English Patient*, another financial and Oscar blockbuster. Zaentz received a lifetime achievement award from the Academy in 1997. Zaentz has parlayed independent filmmaking into big business and gained broad acceptance and commercial success in the process.

Zedd, Nick. No-budget **underground** filmmaker who founded and named the **cinema of transgression** movement in 1979 after making *They Eat Scum*. Zedd edited *The Underground Film Bulletin* under the pseudonym Orion Jeriko and wrote the movement's manifesto in 1985, proclaiming an all-out cultural war against academia, film schools, media centers, and film **critics** he saw as responsible for boring films. Working out of New York's Lower East Side and influenced by the downtown punk and no-wave music scenes, Zedd explored blood, shame, pain, and ecstasy in such films as *The Bogus Man* (1980), *Geek Maggot Bingo* (1983), *Thrust in Me* (1984), *School of Shame* (1984), *Go to Hell* (1986), *Whoregasm* (1988), *War*

Daniel Day Lewis and Juliette Binoche in *The Unbearable Lightness of Being* (1988), produced by Saul Zaentz and directed by Philip Kauffman. Courtesy of The Del Valle Archive

Is Menstrual Envy (1990–1992), *Why Do You Exist?* (1998), *Ecstasy in Entropy* (1999), and *Thus spake zarathustra* (2001). *See also* cinema of transgression

BIBLIOGRAPHY

Sargeant, Jack. *Deathtripping: The Cinema of Transgression.* London: Creation Books, 1995. Updated 2000.

Zedd, Nick. *Bleed: The Autobiography of Nick Zedd.* New York: Hanuman Books, 1992.

Zipporah Films Inc. *See* Wiseman, Frederick

Zsigmond, Vilmos. Cinematographer. *b.* June 16, 1930, Szeged, Hungary. *ed.* The Budapest Film School. Zsigmond fled Hungary during the 1956 uprising with fellow student and colleague **László Kovács.** In the United States, after working in still photography and as a cinematographer on **educational** shorts, he began in low-budget, nonunion feature films in 1963. In four years he shot fourteen features for little or no salary, developing his craft on **exploitation films** such as *The Sadist* (1963), *The Incredibly Strange Creatures Who Stopped Living and Became Crazy Mixed-up Zombies* (1964), *Psycho a Go-Go!* (1965), *Rat Fink* (1965), and *Mondo Mod* (1967).

In 1971, Zsigmond gained industry-wide attention for his collaboration with **Robert Altman** on *McCabe & Mrs. Miller* and continued with *Images* (1972) and *The Long Goodbye* (1973). He then worked with **American New Wave** directors **Steven Spielberg** on *The Sugarland Express* (1974), **Brian De Palma** on *Obsession* (1976), **Martin Scorsese** on *The Last Waltz* (1978), and Michael Cimino on *The Deer Hunter* (1978).

Zsigmond helped revolutionize the look of American film in the 1970s and 1980s by flashing film stock by hand to create a soft color look and by liberating the camera with his deft handheld operation. Zsigmond won an Oscar for *Close Encounters of the Third Kind* (1977) and has been honored by the American Society of Cinematographers. Recent credits for Vilmos Zsigmond as director of photography include: *The Ghost and the Darkness* (1996), *Playing by Heart*, *Illegal Music* (both 1998), the short film *The Argument* (1999), *The Body* (2000), and *Life as a House* (2001).

BIBLIOGRAPHY

Schaefer, Dennis, and Larry Salvato. *Masters of Light: Conversations with Contemporary Cinematographers.* Berkeley: University of California Press, 1984.

Zugsmith, Albert. Producer, director, screenwriter. *b.* April 24, 1910, Atlantic City, New Jersey. *d.* October 26, 1993, Woodland Hills, California. *ed.* University of Virginia. Before Albert Zugsmith directed *Sex Kittens Go to College* (1960) and *Psychedelic Sexualis* (1966) and produced *Confessions of an Opium Eater* (1962) and *Sappho Darling* (1969), he was the publisher and editor of the *Atlantic City Daily News*, a broadcasting executive, and a drama producer for Universal Studios. During his remarkably paradoxical career, the same man who directed cheap, sleazy **sexploitation** like *College Confidential* (1960) and *The Incredible Sex Revolution* (1965) also produced the science fiction classic *The Incredible Shrinking Man* (1957), directed by **Jack Arnold**, Douglas Sirk's *Written on the Wind* (1956), and even Orson Welles's *Touch of Evil* (1958). In 1961, he actually directed the family film *Dondi*, based on the popular comic strip of the lovable war orphan finding his way in the United States.

Zwerin, Charlotte. Editor, director, producer. *b.* August 15, 1931, Detroit, Michigan. Major figure in the **direct cinema documentary** movement of the 1960s, Charlotte Zwerin collaborated with the **Maysles** brothers, editing and codirecting their watershed documentaries: *Showman* (1962), *Meet Marlon Brando* (1966), *A Visit with Truman Capote* (1966), *Salesman* (1969), *Gimme Shelter* (1970), and *Running Fence* (1977). Zwerin's editorial skills helped to structure and shape these documentaries, contributing to the final narrative form. She is a highly respected member of the New York nonfiction community.

In 1989 Zwerin produced and directed *Thelonious Monk: Straight, No

Guy Williams as *The Incredible Shrinking Man* (1957), produced by Albert Zugsmith and directed by Jack Arnold. Courtesy of The Del Valle Archive

Chaser, a documentary on the legendary musician, executive produced by **Clint Eastwood**. The film weaves footage of Monk made for German television and shot by filmmaker Christian Blackwood in 1967 and 1968, along with new interview material. Zwerin creates a disturbing and compelling portrait of the musician who slowly went mad from a mental illness that plagued him throughout his life. The film informs Monk's musical experimentations with historical and personal facts. It premiered at the New York Film Festival and received critical and audience acclaim.

Zwerin also directed two other music documentaries, *Horowitz Plays Mozart* (1987), with Susan Fromke and Albert Maysles, and *Music for the Movies: Toru Takemitsu* (1994), the Japanese composer who scored *Woman of the Dunes* (1964), *Does'kaden* (1970), and Kurosawa's *Ran* (1985). In 1999 Zwerin directed the documentary *Ella Fitzgerald: Something to Live For*. *See also* Eastwood, Clint; Maysles, Albert and David

Zwigoff, Terry. Director, producer, screenwriter. *b.* 1948. An intense interest in comic art, music, and a perception of the creative dysfunctional merged to create the **documentaries** of filmmaker Terry Zwigoff. *Louie Bluie* (1985) is a documentary search for the 1930s African American bluesman Howard "Louie Bluie" Armstrong who was seventy-five when Zwigoff and his camera found him. The mandolin and violin blues master who paints, writes poetry, and rabble-rouses comes alive in interviews with him and eyewitnesses to his life and music. Zwigoff bonds with his subject and reveals the world of African American string blues. The documentary also examines the racism that faced black bluesmen in the 1930s.

Zwigoff developed his next documentary, *Crumb* (1994) for six years. The filmmaker had a longtime relationship with R. Crumb, creator of *Fritz the Cat* and *The Keep on Truckin' Man* and a pioneer of underground comics. Crumb's comics explored the boundaries of good taste, peppering the funny papers with sex, drugs, and rock 'n' roll. The comics were funny, outrageous, and insulting to just about everyone over thirty during the 1960s. Zwigoff gained Crumb's confidence and managed to capture a startlingly personal portrait that analyzed the impetus behind Crumb's dark and, at times, racist and misogynistic images and traced them to his pathologically dysfunctional family. Crumb survived by constantly drawing his fantasies and demons. Zwigoff received funding from *The Simpsons'* creator Matt Groenig. **David Lynch** allowed his name in a presentation credit to give both credibility and the stamp of genuine weirdness to the project. The distinguished film editor and sound designer Walter Murch (*American Graffiti* [1973], *Apocalypse Now* [1979], *The English Patient* [1996]) lent his creativity to postproduction. *Crumb* played the New York and Toronto film festivals. *Crumb* received critical praise for its honesty and psychological depth. With his quiet and unobtrusive nature, Zwigoff managed to peel back layers that Crumb had hidden in his funny, exaggerated drawings. Without judgment, Zwigoff presents the uncensored, dark thoughts that motivated Crumb's work. *Crumb* is funny, disturbing, human, and honest beyond the viewer's expectations.

Zwigoff's next project was to be a documentary portrait of **Woody Allen,** but when Zwigoff insisted on total artistic control, Allen backed out and later cooperated with **Barbara Kopple** for *Wild Man Blues* (1998), the documentary of his jazz band's European tour. In 2001 Zwigoff directed a fictional feature *Ghost World,* featuring **Steve Buscemi,** Brad Renfro, and Illeana Douglas, based on a comic by Daniel Clowes who cowrote the screenplay with the director. In 2000 Terry Zwigoff directed *Bad Santa.*

Appendix A: 100 Significant Independent Films

Bad Lieutenant (1992)

Best Boy (1979)

Beyond the Valley of the Dolls (1970)

Billy Jack (1971)

Birth of a Nation, The (1915)

Blood Simple (1984)

Brother's Keeper (1992)

Buffalo '66 (1998)

Carnival of Souls (1962)

Chan Is Missing (1982)

Chappaqua (1966)

Chelsea Girls, The (1966)

City of Hope (1991)

Clerks (1994)

Coming Apart (1969)

Connection, The (1961)

Crazy-Quilt, The (1966)

Crumb (1994)

Decline of Western Civilization, The (1981)

Detour (1945)

Dog Star Man (1961–1964)

Drugstore Cowboy (1989)

Easy Rider (1969)

El Norte (1983)

Eraserhead (1978)
Evil Dead, The (1982)
Faces (1968)
Flaming Creatures (1963)
General, The (1927)
Gimmie Shelter (1970)
Gold Rush, The (1925)
Greetings! (1968)
Gun Crazy (1949)
Halloween (1978)
Harlan County, U.S.A. (1976)
Heartland (1979)
Heathers (1989)
High Art (1998)
High School (1968)
Hills Have Eyes, The (1977)
Homesteader, The (1919)
Honeymoon Killers, The (1970)
In the Company of Men (1997)
Kids (1995)
Killing, The (1956)
Laws of Gravity (1992)
Lickerish Quartet, The (1970)
Little Fugitive (1953)
Little Shop of Horrors, The (1960)
Longtime Companion (1990)
Marty (1955)
Mean Streets (1973)
Menace II Society (1993)
Meshes of the Afternoon (1943)
Music of Chance, The (1993)
Nanook of the North (1922)
Near Dark (1987)
Nothing But a Man (1964)
One False Move (1992)
On the Bowery (1956)
Our Daily Bread (1934)
Paris Is Burning (1990)

Parting Glances (1986)

Pi (1998)

Pink Flamingos (1972)

Pinocchio (1940)

Point of Order (1964)

Pulp Fiction (1994)

Putney Swope (1969)

Return of the Secaucus Seven, The (1980)

Ride in the Whirlwind (1965)

River's Edge (1986)

Roger & Me (1989)

Safe Place, A (1971)

Salesman (1969)

Savage Eye, The (1960)

sex, lies, and videotape (1989)

Shadows (1959)

Sherman's March (1986)

She's Gotta Have It (1986)

Shock Corridor (1963)

Shooting, The (1967)

Slacker (1991)

Smithereens (1982)

Spanking the Monkey (1994)

Stranger Than Paradise (1984)

Sweet Sweetback's Baadasssss Song (1971)

Swoon (1992)

Texas Chainsaw Massacre, The (1974)

Thin Blue Line, The (1988)

True Love (1989)

Trust (1991)

Walking Tall (1973)

Welcome to the Dollhouse (1996)

Wild Style (1982)

Woman under the Influence, A (1974)

Word Is Out (1977)

Working Girls (1986)

Zebrahead (1992)

Appendix B: Winners of the Sundance Film Festival and Independent Spirit Awards

Key:

SF	=	Sundance Film Festival Best Feature Award
SD	=	Sundance Film Festival Best Documentary Award
IF	=	Independent Spirit Best Feature Award
ID	=	Independent Spirit Best Director Award
IFF	=	Independent Spirit Best First Feature Award

1984	SF	*Blood Simple*, Joel Coen
	SD	*Seventeen*, Joel DeMott, Jeff Kreines
1985	SF	*Smooth Talk*, Joyce Chopra
	SD	*Private Conversations*, Christian Blackwood
	IF	*After Hours*
	ID	Tie: Joel Coen, *Blood Simple*; Martin Scorsese, *After Hours*
1986	SF	*Waiting for the Moon*, Jill Godmilow
	SD	*Sherman's March*, Ross McElwee
	IF	*Platoon*
	IFF	*She's Gotta Have It*
	ID	Oliver Stone, *Platoon*
1987	SF	*Heat and Sunlight*, Rob Nilsson
	SD	*Beirut: The Last Home Movie*, Jennifer Fox
	IF	*River's Edge*
	IFF	*Dirty Dancing*
	ID	John Huston, *The Dead*
1988	SF	*True Love*, Nancy Savoca
	SD	*For All Mankind*, Al Reinert
	IF	*Stand and Deliver*

IFF Mystic Pizza

ID Ramón Menéndez, Stand and Deliver

1989

SF Chameleon Street

SD H-2 Worker; Water and Power

IF sex, lies, and videotape

IFF Heathers

ID Steven Soderbergh, sex, lies, and videotape

1990

SF Poison, Todd Haynes

SD American Dream, Barbara Kopple; Paris Is Burning, Jennie Livingston

IF The Grifters

IFF Metropolitan

1991

ID Charles Burnett, To Sleep with Anger

SF In the Soup, Alexandre Rockwell

IF Ramblin' Rose

SD Finding Christa, Camille Billops, James Hatch

IFF Straight Out of Brooklyn

ID Martha Coolidge, Ramblin' Rose

1992

SF Ruby in Paradise, Victor Nunez; Public Access, Bryan Singer

SD Silverlake Life: The View from Here, Peter Friedman, Tom Joslin

IF The Player

IFF The Waterdance

ID Carl Franklin, One False Move

1993

SF What Happened Was . . . , Tom Noonan

SD Freedom on My Mind, Connie Field, Marilyn Mulford

IF Short Cuts

IFF El Mariachi

ID Robert Altman, Short Cuts

1994

SF The Brothers McMullen, Edward Burns

SD Crumb, Terry Zwigoff

IF Pulp Fiction

IFF Spanking the Monkey

ID Quentin Tarantino, Pulp Fiction

1995

SF Welcome to the Dollhouse, Todd Solondz

SD Troublesome Creek, Jeanne Jordan, Steven Ascher

IF Leaving Las Vegas

IFF The Brothers McMullen

IF Mike Figgis, Leaving Las Vegas

1996	SF	*Sunday*, Jonathan Nossiter
	SD	*Girls Like Us*, Jane C. Wagner
	IF	*Fargo*
	IFF	*Sling Blade*
	ID	Joel Coen, *Fargo*
1997	SF	*Slam*, Marc Levin
	SD	*The Farm: Angola USA*, Jonathan Stack; *Frat House*, Todd Phillips, Andrew Gurland
	IF	*The Apostle*
	IFF	*Eve's Bayou*
	ID	Robert Duvall, *The Apostle*
1998	SF	*Three Seasons*
	SD	*American Movie*, Chris Smith
	IF	*Gods and Monsters*
	IFF	*The Opposite of Sex*
	ID	Wes Anderson, *Rushmore*
1999	SF	*Girlfight*, Karyn Kusama; *You Can Count on Me*, Kenneth Lonergan
	SD	*Long Night's Journey into Day*, Frances Reid, Deborah Hoffman
	IF	*Being John Malkovich*
	IFF	*The Blair Witch Project*
	ID	Alexander Payne, *Election*
2000	SF	*The Believer*
	SD	*Southern Comfort*, Kate Davis
	IF	*Crouching Tiger, Hidden Dragon*
	IFF	*You Can Count on Me*
	ID	Ang Lee, *Crouching Tiger, Hidden Dragon*
2001	SF	*Personal Velocity*
	SD	*Daughters from Danang*, Gail Dolgin and Vicente Franco
	IF	*Memento*
	IFF	*In the Bedroom*
	ID	Christopher Noland, *Memento*

Appendix C: Distributors of Independent Films

Aires
Alive
Angelika
Arrow
Avenue
Castle Rock
Cinecom
Cineplex
Cinevista
Circle
Concorde
Film Dallas
First Look
First Run Features
Fox Classics
Frameline
Goldwyn
Good Machine
Grey Cat
Hemdale
Horizon
IRS
Island

Mad Dog
Miramax
Mystic Fire Video
New Century
New Line
New World
New Yorker Films
Northern Arts
October
Orion Classics
Rainbow
Red Carnelian Films
Roxie Releasing
Skouras
Sony Pictures Classics
Spectrafilm
Spotlight
Strand
Trimark Pictures
Triton
Triumph
Vestron
Zeitgeist

Bibliography

Aberdeen, J.A. Hollywood Renegades: The Society of Independent Motion Picture Producers. Los Angeles, CA: Cobblestone Entertainment, 2000.

Abramowitz, Rachel. Is That a Gun in Your Pocket? : Women's Experience of Power in Hollywood. New York: Random House, 2000.

Agee, James. On Film Volume 1: Essay and Reviews by James Agee. New York: Grosset and Dunlap, 1969.

———. On Film Volume 2: Five Film Plays by James Agee. New York: Perigee Books, 1983.

Andre, Geoff. Stranger Than Paradise: Maverick Film-makers in Recent American Cinema. New York: Limelight Edition, 1999.

Asher, Steven, and Edward Pincus. The Filmmaker's Handbook: A Comprehensive Guide for the Digital Age. New York: Plume, 1999.

Atkins, Thomas R. Frederick Wiseman. New York: Monarch Press, 1976.

Bach, Steven. Final Cut: Dreams and Disaster in the Making of Heaven's Gate. New York: William Morrow, 1985.

Barsam, Richard Meran, ed. Nonfiction Film Theory and Criticism. New York: E.P. Dutton, 1976.

Battcock, Gregory, ed. The New American Cinema: A Critical Anthology. New York: E.P. Dutton, 1967.

Behlmer, Rudy, ed. Memo from David O. Selznick. New York: Viking Press, 1972.

Benson, Thomas W., and Carolyn Anderson. Reality Fictions: The Films of Frederick Wiseman. Carbondale: Southern Illinois University Press, 1989.

Bernard, Jami. Quentin Tarantino: The Man and His Movies. New York: Harper-Collins, 1995.

Biskind, Peter. Easy Riders, Raging Bulls: How the Sex-Drugs-and-Rock 'n' Roll Generation Saved Hollywood. New York: Simon and Schuster, 1998.

Black, Andy. Necronomicon: Book 2. London: Creation Books, 1996.

Bogle, Donald. Blacks in American Films and Television: An Illustrated Encyclopedia. New York: A Fireside Book, Simon and Schuster, 1989.

Bouzereau, Laurent. *The De Palma Cut: The Films of America's Most Controversial Director*. New York: Dembner Books, 1988.

Boyer, Jay. *Bob Rafelson*. New York: Twayne, 1996.

Brakhage, Stan. *Film at Wit's End: Eight Avant-Garde Filmmakers: Broughton, Conner, Deren, Hill, Jacobs, MacLaine, Menken, Peterson*. New York: Documentext, McPherson and Company, 1989.

Breskin, David. *Inner Views: Filmmakers in Conversation*. Boston: Faber and Faber, 1992.

Carson, L.M. Kit. *David Holzman's Diary: A Screenplay by L.M. Kit Carson from a Film by Jim McBride*. New York: Farrar, Straus and Giroux, 1970.

Channess, Danford. *The Hollywood Guide to Film Budgeting and Script Breakdown for Low Budget Features*. Rev. ed. Los Angeles, CA: Stanley J. Brooks, 1988.

Christopher, Nicholas. *Somewhere in the Night: Film Noir and the American City*. New York: Henry Holt, 1997.

Coen, Joel, and Ethan Coen. *Blood Simple: The Screenplay*. New York: St. Martin's Press, 1988.

———. *Raising Arizona: The Screenplay*. New York: St. Martin's Press, 1988.

Cole, Janis, with Holly Dale. *Calling the Shots: Profiles of Women Filmmakers*. Kingston, Ontario: Quarry Press, 1993.

Cones, John W. *Film Finance & Distribution: A Dictionary of Terms*. Los Angeles, CA: Silman-James Press, 1992.

———. *43 Ways to Finance Your Feature Film: A Comprehensive Analysis of Film Finance*. Carbondale: Southern Illinois University Press, 1995.

Corman, Roger, with Jim Jerome. *How I Made a Hundred Movies in Hollywood and Never Lost a Dime*. New York: Random House, 1990.

Curran, Trisha. *Financing Your Film: A Guide for Independent Filmmakers and Producers*. New York: Praeger, 1986.

Curtis, David. *Experimental Cinema: A Fifty-Year Evolution*. New York: Universe Books, 1971.

De Grazia, Edward, and Roger K. Newman. *Banned Films: Movies, Censors & the First Amendment*. New York: R.R. Bowker, 1982.

De Navacelle, Thierry. *Woody Allen on Location: A Day-to-Day Account of the Making of Radio Days*. New York: William Morrow, 1987.

Dika, Vera. *Games of Terror: Halloween, Friday the 13th, and the Films of the Stalker Cycle*. Rutherford, NJ: Fairleigh Dickinson University Press, 1990.

Dixon, Wheeler Winston. *The Exploding Eye: A Re-visionary History of 1960s American Experimental Cinema*. New York: State University of New York Press, 1997.

Dworkin, Susan. *Double De Palma*. New York: New Market Press, 1984.

Ehrenstein, David. *Film: The Front Line 1984*. Denver, CO: Arden Press, 1984.

Eliot, Mark. *Walt Disney: Hollywood's Dark Prince*. New York: HarperCollins, 1993.

Falsetto, Mario. *Personal Visions: Conversations with Contemporary Film Directors*. Los Angeles, CA: Silman-James Press, 2000.

Fielding, Raymond. *The American Newsreel 1911–1967*. Norman: University of Oklahoma Press, 1972.

Flint, David. *Babylon Blue: An Illustrated History of Adult Cinema*. London: Creation Books, 1999.

Ford, Luke. *A History of X: 100 Years of Sex in Film.* Amherst, NY: Prometheus Books, 1999.

Fraigneau, Andre. *Cocteau on the Film.* New York: Dover, 1972.

Frolich, Billy. *What I Really Want to Do Is Direct: Seven Film School Graduates Go to Hollywood.* New York: E.P. Dutton, 1996.

Gabler, Neal. *An Empire of Their Own: How the Jews Invented Hollywood.* New York: Crown Publishers, 1988.

Gagne, Paul R. *The Zombies That Ate Pittsburgh: The Films of George A. Romero.* New York: Dodd, Mead, 1987.

Gallagher, John Andrew. *Film Directors on Directing.* New York: Praeger, 1989.

Gardner, Gerald. *The Censorship Papers: Movie Censorship Letters from the Hays Office 1934 to 1968.* New York: Dodd, Mead, 1987.

Gelder, Ken, ed. *The Horror Reader.* London: Routledge, 2000.

Gelmis, Joseph. *The Film Director as Superstar.* Garden City, NY: Doubleday, 1970.

Goodell, Gregory. *Independent Feature Film Production: A Complete Guide from Concept through Distribution.* Rev. and updated ed. New York: St. Martin's Press, 1998.

Goodwin, Michael, and Naomi Wise. *On the Edge: The Life and Times of Francis Coppola.* New York: William Morrow, 1989.

Gray, Beverly. *Roger Corman: An Unauthorized Biography of the Godfather of Indie Filmmaking.* Los Angeles, CA: Renaissance Books, 2000.

Green, Shelly. *Radical Juxtaposition: The Films of Yvonne Rainer.* Metuchen, NJ: Scarecrow Press, 1994.

Gregory, Mollie. *Making Films Your Business: Covering: Proposals, Grants, Distribution, Financing, Budgets, Copyrights, Video, Contracts and the Future.* New York: Schocken Books, 1979.

Grey, Rudolph. *Ed Wood: Nightmare of Ecstasy: The Life and Art of Edward D. Wood, Jr.* Portland, OR: Feral House, 1994.

Haller, Robert A., ed. *Brakhage Scrapbook: Collected Writings 1964-1980.* New York: Documentext, 1982.

Handling, Piers, ed. *The Shape of Rage: The Films of David Cronenberg.* New York: New York Zoetrope, 1983.

Hanke, Ken. *Tim Burton: An Unauthorized Biography of the Filmmaker.* Los Angeles, CA: Renaissance Books, 1999.

Hickenlooper, George. *Reel Conversations: Candid Interviews with Film's Foremost Directors and Critics.* New York: Citadel Press Book, Carol Publishing, 1991.

Hill, Lee. *Easy Rider.* London: BFI Publishing, 1996.

Hoberman, J. *Bridge of Light: Yiddish Film between Two Worlds.* New York: Museum of Modern Art/Schocken Books, 1991.

Hoberman, J., and Edward Leffingwell, eds. *Wait for Me at the Bottom of the Pool: The Writings of Jack Smith.* New York: High Risk Books, 1997.

Horak, Jan-Christopher, ed. *Lovers of Cinema: The First American Film Avant-Garde 1919-1945.* Madison: University of Wisconsin Press, 1995.

James, David E., ed. *To Free the Cinema: Jonas Mekas and the New York Underground.* Princeton, NJ: Princeton University Press, 1992.

Johnstone, Nick. *Abel Ferrara: The King of New York.* London: Omnibus Press, 1999.

Jones, G. William. *Black Cinema Treasures Lost and Found.* Denton: University of North Texas Press, 1991.

Kaminsky, Stuart M. *Clint Eastwood.* New York: Signet, 1974.

Kass, Judith M. *Robert Altman: American Innovator.* New York: Popular Library, 1978.

Kaufman, Lloyd, and James Gunn. *All I Need to Know About Filmmaking I Learned from The Toxic Avenger: The Shocking True Story of Troma Studios.* New York: Berkley Boulevard Books, 1998.

Koszarski, Richard. *An Evening's Entertainment: The Age of the Silent Feature Picture, 1915–1928.* New York: Charles Scribner's Sons, 1990.

Kramer, Stanley, with Thomas M. Coffey. *A Mad, Mad, Mad, Mad World: A Life in Hollywood.* New York: Harcourt Brace, 1997.

Kuenzli, Rudolf E., ed. *Dada and Surrealist Film.* New York: Willis Locker & Owens, 1987.

Landis, Bill. *Anger: The Unauthorized Biographer of Kenneth Anger.* New York: HarperCollins, 1995.

Larson, Rodger, with Ellen Meade. *Young Filmmakers.* New York: E.P. Dutton, 1969.

Lax, Eric. *Woody Allen: A Biography.* New York: Knopf, 1991.

Lee, Spike. *Spike Lee's Gotta Have It: Inside Guerrilla Filmmaking.* New York: Fireside, 1987.

Lee, Spike, with Lisa Jones. *Do the Right Thing.* New York: Fireside, 1989.

———. *Mo' Better Blues.* New York: Fireside, 1990.

Leff, Leonard J., and Jerold L. Simmons. *The Dame in the Kimono: Hollywood Censorship, & the Production Code from the 1920s to the 1960s.* New York: Grove Weidenfeld, 1990.

Le Grice, Malcolm. *Abstract Film and Beyond.* Cambridge: MIT Press, 1977.

Levin, G. Roy. *Documentary Explorations: 15 Interviews with Film-Makers.* Garden City, NY: Anchor Press, 1971.

Levy, Emanuel. *Cinema of Outsiders: The Rise of American Independent Film.* New York: New York University Press, 1999.

Lewis, Jon. *Whom God Wishes to Destroy: Francis Coppola and the New Hollywood.* Durham, NC: Duke University Press, 1995.

Lippy, Tod. *Projections 11: New York Film-makers on New York Film-making.* London: Faber and Faber, 2000.

Lipton, Lenny. *Independent Filmmaking.* San Francisco: Straight Arrow Books, 1972.

———. *Lipton on Filmmaking.* Ed. Chet Roaman. New York: Simon and Schuster, 1979.

LoBrutto, Vincent. *By Design: Interviews with Film Production Designers.* Westport, CT: Praeger, 1992.

———. *Principal Photography: Interviews with Feature Film Cinematographers.* Westport, CT: Praeger, 1999.

———. *Sound-on-Film: Interviews with Creators of Film Sound.* Westport, CT: Praeger, 1994.

———. *Stanley Kubrick: A Biography.* New York: Donald I. Fine, 1997.

Lowenstein, Stephen, ed. *My First Movie: Twenty Celebrated Directors Talk About Their First Film.* New York: Pantheon Books, 2000.

Lumet, Sidney. *Making Movies.* New York: Knopf, 1995.

Lyons, Donald. *Independent Visions: A Critical Introduction to Recent Independent American Film.* New York: Ballantine Books, 1994.

MacDonald, Scott. *A Critical Cinema: Interviews with Independent Filmmakers.* Berkeley: University of California Press, 1998.

———. *A Critical Cinema 2: Interviews with Independent Filmmakers.* Berkeley: University of California Press, 1992.

———. *A Critical Cinema 3: Interviews with Independent Filmmakers.* Berkeley: University of California Press, 1998.

———. *Avant-Garde Film Motion Studies.* Cambridge: Cambridge University Press, 1993.

Maltin, Leonard, ed. *The Whole Film Sourcebook.* New York: New American Library, 1983.

Mamet, David. *House of Games: The Complete Screenplay.* New York: Grove Press, 1985.

Mason, Paul, and Don Gold. *Producing for Hollywood: A Guide for the Independent Producer.* New York: All North Press, 2000.

McCarthy, Todd, with Charles Flynn, eds. *Kings of the Bs: Working within the Hollywood System: An Anthology of Film History and Criticism.* New York: E.P. Dutton, 1975.

McCarty, John. *Splatter Movies: Breaking the Last Taboo of the Screen.* New York: St. Martin's Press, 1984.

———. *The Official Splatter Movie Guide.* New York: St. Martin's Press, 1989.

———. *The Official Splatter Movie Guide Vol. II.* New York: St. Martin's Press, 1992.

McClelland, C. Kirk. *On Making a Movie: Brewster McCloud.* New York: Signet, 1971.

McDonagh, Maitland. *Filmmaking on the Fringe: The Good, the Bad, and the Deviant Directors.* New York: Citadel Press, 1995.

McGee, Mark Thomas, and R.J. Robertson. *The J.D. Films: Juvenile Delinquency in the Movies.* Jefferson, NC: McFarland, 1982.

McGilligan, Patrick. *Robert Altman: Jumping Off the Cliff: A Biography of the Great American Director.* New York: St. Martin's Press, 1989.

McNeil, Legs, and Gillian McCain. *Please Kill Me: The Uncensored Oral History of Punk.* New York: Grove Press, 1996.

Meade, Marion. *The Unruly Life of Woody Allen: A Biography.* New York: Scribner, 2000.

Mekas, Jonas. *Movie Journal: The Rise of a New American Cinema 1959–1971.* New York: Collier Books, 1972.

Merritt, Greg. *Celluloid Mavericks: A History of American Independent Film.* New York: Thunder's Mouth Press, 2000.

Miller, Don. *B Movies.* New York: Ballantine Books, 1988.

Monaco, James. *American Film Now: The People, the Power, the Money, the Movies.* New York: Oxford University Press, 1979.

———. *The New Wave: Truffaut, Godard, Chabrol, Rohmer, Rivette.* New York: Oxford University Press, 1976.

Mordden, Ethan. *Medium Cook: The Movies of the 1960s.* New York: Knopf, 1990.

Morris, Gary. *Roger Corman.* Boston: Twayne Publishers, 1985.

Musser, Charles. *The Emergence of Cinema: The American Screen to 1907*. New York: Charles Scribner's Sons, 1990.

Oumano, Ellen. *Film Forum: Thirty-five Top Filmmakers Discuss Their Craft*. New York: St. Martin's Press, 1985.

Pierson, John. *Spike, Mike, Slackers & Dykes: A Guided Tour across a Decade of American Independent Cinema*. New York: Miramax Books/Hyperion, 1995.

Pye, Michael, and Lynda Miles. *The Movie Brats: How the Film Generation Took Over Hollywood*. New York: Holt, Rinehart and Winston, 1979.

Queenan, Joe. *The Unkindest Cut: How a Hatchet-Man Critic Made His Own $7,000 Movie and Put It All on His Credit Card*. New York: Hyperion, 1995.

Ravetch, Irving, and Harriet Frank, Jr. *Hud, Norma Rae, and The Long, Hot Summer*. New York: Plume, 1988.

Ray, Nicholas. *I Was Interrupted: Nicolas Ray on Making Movies*. Ed. Susan Ray. Berkeley: University of California Press, 1993.

Rees, A.L. *A History of Experimental Film and Video*. London: BFI, 1999.

Rich, B. Ruby. *Chick Flicks: Theories and Memories of the Feminist Film Movement*. Durham, NC: Duke University Press, 1998.

Robinson, David. *From Peep Show to Palace: The Birth of American Film*. New York: Columbia University Press, 1990.

Rodley, Chris, ed. *Cronenberg on Cronenberg*. London: Faber and Faber, 1993.

———. *Lynch on Lynch*. London: Faber and Faber, 1997.

Rodriguez, Elena. *Dennis Hopper: A Madness to His Method*. New York: St. Martin's Press, 1988.

Rodriguez, Robert. *Rebel without a Crew: Or How a 23-Year-Old Filmmaker with $7,000 Became a Hollywood Player*. New York: E.P. Dutton, 1995.

Rosen, David, with Peter Hamilton in association with The Sundance Institute and The Independent Feature Project. *Off-Hollywood: The Making & Marketing of Independent Films*. New York: Grove Weidenfeld, 1990.

Rosenbaum, Jonathan. *Film: The Front Line*. Denver, CO: Arden Press, 1983.

———. *Movie Wars: How Hollywood and the Media Conspire to Limit What Films We Can See*. Chicago: A Cappella Books, 2000.

Rosenthal, Alan. *The Documentary Conscience: A Casebook in Film Making*. Berkeley: University of California Press, 1980.

———, ed. *New Challenges for Documentary*. Berkeley: University of California Press, 1988.

Rotha, Paul. *Robert J. Flaherty: A Biography*. Ed. Jay Ruby. Philadelphia: University of Pennsylvania Press, 1983.

Russo, John. *Making Movies: The Inside Guide to Independent Movie Production*. New York: Dell, 1989.

Salamon, Julie. *The Devil's Candy: The Bonfire of the Vanities Goes to Hollywood*. Boston: Houghton Mifflin, 1991.

Salisbury, Mark, ed. *Burton on Burton*. London: Faber and Faber, 1995.

Sargeant, Jack. *Beat Cinema*. London: Creation Books, 1997.

———. *Deathtripping: The Cinema of Transgression*. London: Creation Books, 1995.

Sargeant, Jack, and Stephanie Watson. *Lost Highways: An Illustrated History of Road Movies*. London: Creation Books, 1999.

Sayles, John. *Thinking in Picture: The Making of the Movie Matewan*. Boston: Houghton Mifflin, 1987.

Schaefer, Eric. "Bold! Daring! Shocking! True!": A History of Exploitation Films, 1919–1959. Durham, NC: Duke University Press, 1999.

Schatz, Thomas. The Genius of the System: Hollywood Filmmaking in the Studio Era. New York: Pantheon Books, 1988.

Schickel, Richard. Clint Eastwood: A Biography. New York: Knopf, 1996.

Schmidt, Rick. Feature Filmmaking at Used-Car Prices: How to Write, Produce, Direct, Shoot, Edit and Promote a Feature-Length Movie for Less Than $15,000. 3rd ed. New York: Penguin Books, 2000.

Schumacher, Michael. Francis Ford Coppola: A Filmmaker's Life. New York: Crown Publishers, 1999.

Sherman, Eric, for the American Film Institute. Directing the Film: Film Directors on Their Art. Los Angeles, CA: Acrobat Books, 1976.

Silver, Alain, and Elizabeth Ward. Film Noir: An Encylopedic Reference to the American Style. Woodstock, NY: Overlook Press, 1979.

Singh, Rani, ed. Thinking of the Self-Speaking: Harry Smith—Selected Interviews. Seattle, WA: Elbow/Cityful Press, 1999.

Sitney, P. Adams, ed. Film Culture Reader. New York: Praeger, 1970.

——. Visionary Film: The American Avant-Garde 1943–1978. Oxford: Oxford University Press, 1979.

Skal, David J. The Monster Show: A Cultural History of Horror. New York: W.W. Norton, 1993.

Smith, Gavin, ed. Sayles on Sayles. London: Faber and Faber, 1998.

Smith, Ken. Mental Hygiene: Classroom Films 1945–1970. New York: Blast Books, 1999.

Steinbeck, John. Zapata. New York: Penguin Books, 1993.

Sullivan, Monica. VideoHounds's Independent Film Guide. Detroit, MI: Visible Ink, 1999.

Timpone, Anthony. Men, Makeup, and Monsters: Hollywood's Masters of Illusion and FX. New York: St. Martin's Griffin, 1996.

Tyler, Parker. Underground Film: A Critical History. New York: Grove Press, 1969.

Vachon, Christine, with David Edelstein. Shooting to Kill: How an Independent Producer Blasts Through the Barriers to Make Movies That Matter. New York: Avon Books, 1998.

Vale, V., and Andrea Juno, eds. Incredibly Strange Films. San Francisco, CA: Re/Search #10, 1986.

Waters, John. Shock Value. New York: Dell, 1981.

——. Trash Trio: Pink Flamingos, Desperate Living and Flamingos Forever. New York: Vintage Books, 1988.

Weldon, Michael, with Charles Beesley, Bob Martin, and Akina Fitton. The Psychotronic Encyclopedia of Film. New York: Ballantine Books, 1983.

Whitehead, Mark. Slasher Movies. North Pomfret, VT: Trafalgar Square, 2000.

Wiese, Michael. Film and Video Budgets. Westport, CT: Michael Wiese Film Productions, 1984.

——. The Independent Film and Videomakers Guide. 2nd ed. Studio City, CA: Michael Wiese Productions, 1998.

Williams, Linda. Hard Core: Power, Pleasure, and the "Frenzy of the Visible." Berkeley: University of California Press, 1999.

Wurlitzer, Rudolph. *Pat Garrett and Billy the Kid*. New York: Signet, 1973.

———. *Two-Lane Blacktop*. New York: Award Books, 1971.

Youngblood, Gene. *Expanded Cinema*. New York: E.P. Dutton, 1970.

Zalcock, Bev. *Renegade Sisters: Girl Gangs on Film*. London: Creation Books, 1998.

Index

Page numbers in **bold** indicate location of main entries.